REMODEL!

REMODEL!

An Architect's Advice on Home Renovation

GREG GIBSON, AIA

JOHN WILEY & SONS, INC.

New York / Chichester / Brisbane / Toronto / Singapore

Library of Congress Cataloging-in-Publication Data:

Gibson, Greg, 1948-
    Remodel! : an architect's advice on home renovation / Greg Gibson.
      p. cm.
    Includes index.
    ISBN 0-471-12260-2 (pbk. : alk. paper)
    1. Dwellings—Remodeling—Management. 2. Construction contracts.
  I. Title.
TH4816.G53   1996   95-46221
643' .7–dc20

Printed in the United States of America

10 9 8 7 6 5 4 3 2 1

DEDICATION

I was talking to a colleague recently who was surprised to learn that I had written this book. There may have been just a hint of envy in his voice, for many of us believe we have something valuable to add to the bookshelves. But I must warn all closet authors: Your literary effort will require more outside assistance than you might imagine. In the chaos of work and family, others must help clear a bubble for you to write within. For me, it is my wife Celeste who has given this unselfish and often taxing gift. And maybe a little more indirectly, my sons, parents, and brothers have winked and forgiven me when I was not there. I do see the love in it, guys. Thank you.

PREFACE

If I tried really hard, I suppose I could convince myself that this text is the Christmas card that I have been meaning to send my past clients. You see, I sort of elbow my way into their lives for the better part of a year, and then move on when the redo is complete. During that time we become trusted friends, and afterwards I must let the relationship wane. It is for you and folks like you that I undertook this effort. Please accept this as atonement for those overtures that I could not properly reciprocate.

The impetus for this book came from a good friend, Jim Wentling, who is an accomplished residential architect and author. I was in Jim's office one day when he opened a file, laid out its contents on the desk, and, in so many words, said: "Here's how I wrote my first book. You are welcome to give it a whirl." Which I did. Now I need to say thanks, Jim. That was truly "gnarly" of you. When I make it to the big time, I will be sure to whisper your name in Geraldo's ear!

To my publishing team at John Wiley & Sons I owe a sincere "thank you." The supreme commander for me in New York is my acquiring editor, Amanda Miller. But I cannot forget the editorial program assistant Mary Alice Yates, and assistant managing editor Ira Brodsky.

I worry, perhaps more than I should, about the quality of the advice being tendered herein. This is because in my practice, I never seem to have enough time to ask other pros what they think about the business of remodeling. To keep me from suggesting something stupid, I knew that this book needed dart-throwing sessions from contiguous professionals. The question was, could I find experienced people who would wade through the manuscript merely for the love of learning? I am happy to report that the good guys like to burrow for new information as much as they relish having someone interested in their point of view. I should have known that this is how they "get good" in the first place. So thanks to the following gentlemen; although I guess I could have done it without you, I am glad I didn't have to try. Your help made the book much better.

- Robert Levy, Edifice Rex Construction, Philadelphia, PA
- Michael J. Donnelly AIA, Herman Hassinger Architects, Moorestown, NJ
- Alan C. Kessler, an attorney with the law firm of Buchanan Ingersoll, P.C., Philadelphia, PA
- F. F. and G. B., two nearly nameless but extremely helpful pros, Rosemont, PA

The attorneys acknowledged in this book specifically disclaim that they have offered legal advice, representations, or opinions to be relied upon in any way. In addition, although the book contains approved AIA and other forms, neither the author nor those acknowledged warrant those forms nor that the forms will address every issue or contingency that could or may arise. Actual contractual terms, as well as any legal advice or opinions, will depend upon the facts and circumstances of each situation. The forms are simply provided as examples for the reader's consideration. To the extent the reader has any questions or concerns of a legal or contractual nature, the author and those acknowledged suggest that the readers consult their architect and legal counsel.

I wish I had a dollar for every time I thought about penning "he/she" into this manuscript. When deciding against it, I felt safe in the knowledge that my publisher would have the politically correct, gender-neutral, and yet efficient solution at the ready. As it turns out, there is no such animal. Please understand that the use of "he" and "him" and so on in this book should not imply that women cannot fare well in the world of architecture and remodeling.

Unless noted otherwise, and with regard to the architecture, photography, artwork, and opinions expressed herein, I take full responsibility.

CONTENTS

CONTENTS

REMODEL!

CHAPTER 1

SOME PERSPECTIVE ON REMODELING

HELTER-SKELTER VIGNETTES

Recently some friends asked me to help them with their remodeling project. Their builder had been unable to secure a building permit. I was dismayed to find that the builder was submitting a drawing prepared by a moonlighting "designer" who was in fact a clerk in a retail store, based on input from her brother who was "thought to be" a builder. The drawing was not a construction drawing but a crude sketch, made by a totally inexperienced person. My friends had spent many long hours agonizing over decisions they should not have had to make. The results would have created a resale-cancer on their $400,000 home. They could not seek competitive proposals from any other builder because they were emotionally committed to their easygoing general contractor. They had given their word. The builder did not have the courage to tell them the "designer" was not a pro. He turned out to be so easy-going that his subcontractors told him when they would show up and how much things would cost. They spent just short of $100,000 for a project that cost $20,000 more than it should have.

Other neighbors down the block have been trying to kick off an addition to their home. They have taken refinance money out of their equity and can't wait to spend it. Four general contractors have been invited over to talk about what they want, and can afford. The neighbors like two of them, but fortunately, they can't just close their eyes and say "do it." The builders all have different ideas about what is appropriate. The wife thinks the solution is to make the upper addition a new master bedroom; her husband would rather expand the existing one. There is a hint of marital subterfuge: each is afraid of not getting their individual idea explored or used. They don't think they can afford an architect. The contractors have reinforced this notion with their horror stories of drawings made worthless by being over budget. It is, of course, prudent to be afraid of cost over-runs. The builders' estimates have differed by over $25,000. My neighbors have no way of knowing what kind of architecture each of the estimates would yield. They talk about the stress of "not being in control." This should be an exciting time for them, not a stressful one, as their dream teeters on the threshold of reality.

Too Much Turmoil

And so goes the helter-skelter world of remodeling. Not a week goes by that I don't encounter another unfortunate story—of intelligent, honest, owners,

A

ADDITION PLUS A FACELIFT

When project size passes $25,000–$30,000, owners should consider performing other major maintenance or repair work at the same time. Reroofing, residing, repainting, and air conditioning upgrades are typical add-on tasks. At some imperceptible point, the poor condition of the rest of the residence begins to penalize the resale value of dollars spent on the addition. For example, it is inadvisable to put a top-of-the-line kitchen in a tract home with serious marketing warts. Some of this money should be held out of the kitchen effort and used to improve other critical areas. Many times, correction of such resale "negatives" becomes part of a redo design program. If the budget can stand it, owners will get more "bang for their buck" by rolling these jobs into the larger building project. Photographs A and B offer a "before" and "after" look at a project that expanded its scope to include upgrading the curb appeal of the entire front elevation. In an upscale area, and with a large modern floor plan, this house's original builder-developer had gutted the stucco architecture to get a cheap "leader" unit up and sold quickly. The owners were in search of an additional bedroom for their children and an upstairs study and library. The roof of the second-floor expansion was designed to lay under the main roof to balance the massing of the house, and to allow the new shingles a logical stopping plane. Although matched as carefully as possible, after installation the owners were not happy with the distinction between the old roof and new. They elected to roof over the rest of the house, front plane only to the ridge, a rather common practice for roofers. New fiberglass shutters and some carefully color-matched trim paint completed the facelift, a $3,000 add-on to a $50,000 redo.

B

designers, and contractors teaming up to do dumb things, the consequences of which come in $5,000 and $10,000 increments. I see registered architects who arc unable to provide adequate redo services but haven't the sense to pass on the commission. I see do-it-yourself owners leaving projects unfinished to the point of deterioration and devalue. I see contractors lying to owners about everything from what is "code" to how much they pay for products. I see wonderful old houses with ugly, inappropriate additions protruding like warts. I encounter educated doctors and lawyers in financial trouble because they hired nonprofessional people to alter their largest single investment, their house. I see much fodder for litigation.

The fact is, most home-owners are not able to orchestrate such projects very well. This is not surprising, of course—they have never done it before. They either take the "hands-off" route and place their faith in a single professional, or they micro-manage seasoned tradesmen into producing amateurish results. While unprepared to make good project decisions, somehow they all do seem to be well prepared for the mental anguish that looms ahead.

Reasons for Chaos

But for all the craziness I have witnessed in my years in this market, I have to say that I have seen only one truly unscrupulous professional. Rather, most designers and contractors genuinely attempt to do a good job for a fair price. So why all the turmoil? First, major remodeling is an extremely complex, expensive, and under-rated undertaking. Having done a lot of both, I know it is much easier to design and build a residence from scratch than to radically remodel one. Second, although our culture seems to preach otherwise, honest, hardworking, experienced people will make mistakes. And due diligence should be built into the process. Attentions lapse, and gaffs occur. I have laid my share of eggs on clients, and have seen respected contractors do the same (of course, the "good guys" step up and make it as right as possible).

Homeowners often find themselves following advice that has a hidden proprietary taint. And many times the pros do not realize how much their perspective is colored. It is a rare occasion when a contractor stands in the owner's shoes and recommends a harder, dirtier, less-profitable course of action for himself to carry out. I find that because the work takes place in the home, a personal relationship normally develops between the owner and the workers. This places the owner at a disadvantage when disagreements occur or difficult decisions need to be made. Bringing morning coffee amid friendly chatter, and then making the builder tear out yesterday's work, is a "hat-change" most home owners fail to accomplish.

Most problems occur because the scale of the project is misidentified. At the outset, the owner wants to believe that his redo is no big deal. He tries to "undersell" its scope because he knows construction costs are high. His preference is to deal with it the same way in which he had his roof replaced. It is rather common to find homeowners on their way to a $100,000 remodeling project, committed to several inappropriate contractors whom they previously used for maintenance work.

But at some point, say above $30,000 or $40,000, the nature of the beast changes. The project surpasses the abilities of "jobbing" contractors and owners to do a quality remodeling job at a competitive price. And it moves into a zone where designer-specialists can afford to operate, and their service makes economic sense to the owner. This larger, more complex project requires a different, consciously managed process.

This is a picture of "redo reality." It shows some own-ers making the best of the chaos that reigns when work is done in your bedroom. Note the three large "wardrobe" boxes to the left of the bureau, temporarily holding the con-tents of the closet now under con-struction. It looks like the cosmetics underneath could quickly fill the vanity in the new master bath that is taking shape.

BEDROOM CHAOS

A BALANCED TEAM

Unfortunately, the typical designer and builder will provide only short-hand services for projects of this size. Because they are concerned with viability, they develop an abbreviated version that protects their own

interests first, partly because owners do not know the difference. You see, owners are in the game only once. The homeowner always brings two things to the remodeling table—the need, and the money to pay for its satisfaction. But he is usually unable to contribute the requisite third element—the management exper-

A

B

MASTER SUITE OVER FAMILY ROOM

This is probably the most common redo. Even when owners only want to expand their second-floor bedroom, an addition will normally need to fill in the first floor underneath, and considering the large upper area needed, this means "family room" whether required or not. Luckily both of these spaces are marketable assets at resale. A master suite normally involves larger closets (his and her walk-in's if possible), a bath/shower, a vanity/dressing area, and a casual sitting space for reading or watching TV (budget permitting). Family rooms may encompass a large sitting area focused on a media center and/or fireplace. Sometimes game tables, libraries, computer stations, and outdoor spaces augment

the core function. In this case the owners wanted a new master suite upstairs. A prior owner had built an ill-planned and shoddily constructed family room in the logical spot. After considering several options, the owners elected to demolish the existing first floor, reuse the footings, and get an all-new family room in the project. Photograph A shows workmen preparing new sill plates after the old structure has been demolished. Plywood covers a doorway and pass-through to the kitchen/dining area. In Photograph B the second-floor frame waits for roof, protected by the familiar blue tarp. The roof is up and shingled in Photograph C, and the redo nears completion in Photograph D. Note that the existing house has been re-sided in conjunction with the addition work.

A

APPROPRIATE DESIGN CONCEPTS

Preparing "plans" is different than conceptualizing a design scheme; they are important but separate tasks. Through formal study and experience, professional designers learn how to make functional solutions feel wonderful. This project uses a two-story space and selectively placed openings to connect an unused basement room to the upper public areas of the home. The design concept was to draw guests downstairs by providing a dining room "overlook" and removing partitions around the basement stairwell. A greenhouse unit bathes both floors in natural light, and is held up high in the space to keep the lower family room thermally comfortable and private, particularly at night. These renderings were prepared for promotional use, and are more finished than typical redo design drawings.

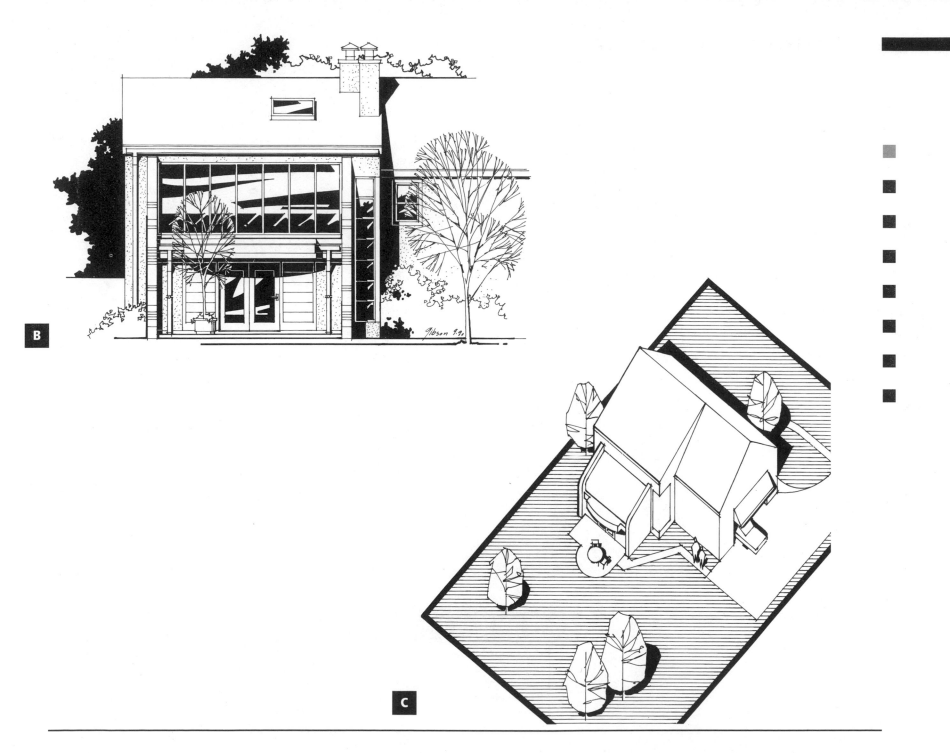

B

C

A

COMPLEX ROOF LINES About the only reason a remodeling builder will recommend that the owner go find an architect is if the "roof lines" of the residence are complicated. This should not be the only reason to hire a designer, of course, but it is first on the general contractor's list. It is not easy to take all the owner's spatial requirements, use contemporary materials and techniques, and create a mass that will mesh sympathetically with the old home. Just like building the redo, designing one takes experience and effort as well.

B

A

B

MAXIMIZING SPACE

This redo does a great job in a small footprint. Although only adding 5'-8" of depth to the original one-story bumpout (Photograph A), it has transformed a dark, inaccessible kitchen and opened up the back yard to daily living. Notice in Photograph B how the deck allows just enough room for a small table group in the back, and redirects traffic to a lower patio area where the prior functional steps have become bleachers for sitting. Not only does the trellis structure define a comfortable exterior space and encourage the owner's green thumb, it also provides the framework for a sophisticated low-voltage lighting scheme. This lighting, recessed into the beams and rails, lets the outdoor area become a useful night room when weather permits (Photograph C), perfect for those afternoon barbecues that taper into evening coffee-and-dessert. Viewed from inside, the trellis fretwork, plants, and hanging objects are seen through the corner window-group, creating the perception of a much larger eat-in kitchen (Photograph D). The fast-food type booth in Photograph E tucks tightly into the room, allowing four people to enjoy breakfast while watching squirrels play in the yard. The raised floor allows sliding into the booth to be more comfortable.

C

D

E

tise to assure success. To ensure a successful project, the owner must engage a team whose members have an inherent balance of power, and a penchant for cross-checking each other. The players must be matched to the task at hand. Like a medical operation, a redo requires divergent expertise and needs the equivalent of a surgeon and an anesthesiologist.

For many remodeling scenarios, including an architect in his traditional role assures just such a team. This provides the expertise of two construction professionals, wedded independently to the owner, and a long list of services intermingled between all three actors: owner, designer, and contractor. Based on a methodology periodically refined by joint contractor-architect committees, and spelled out in AIA (American Institute of Architects) contract forms, Remodel! relies heavily on lessons learned in my architectural practice. It gives the homeowner a process to solve most remodeling problems before they can occur.

You Are the Owner-Manager

I am frequently amused at people's idea of what architects do. Many have confided that they fantasize about starting over and becoming a "neo-Frank Lloyd Wright"; it seems to be mostly lawyers and doctors who don't normally rub shoulders with construction pros. Within the following chapters, I do not suggest that homeowners mimic architects, although most are eager to get out their paper and pencil and sketch out their dream home. Businesspeople know that having several worthy ideas is an important, but really a rather small part, of completing a complex, quality project. A tremendous amount of unglamorous, tedious work is mandatory; it even seems that the simpler and more elegant the solution, the more grunt work is required to pull it off. Also, I do not recom-

mend that owners build their own projects. They have no business negotiating with the excavator, or any other of the numerous jobs that will come up for builders. I have prepared this book to keep you, the remodeling owner, focused on your best role, that is, as planner and manager of the entire process. As the owner-manager, you will need to find the optimum team and ensure its completion of an array of tasks, focused on the project objective. When this is your goal (and Remodel! is on the night table) a work environment will evolve that yields pleasant surprises . . . and ultimately, excellent architecture.

Do I Need a Designer?

Remodeling builders frequently recommend that owners avoid independent designers. This is advice borne of their own unfortunate history and poorly managed projects. Although Chapter 3 outlines several other reasonable scenarios, most homeowners should carefully select an experienced residential designer, who should then help select a builder. I have a bad-builder story for every one of their crazy designer ones. Remember, the contractor has a strong proprietary interest in not having a designer around, and the reverse is not true. His job is much easier that way. And although a builder may say it is not worth the money, if the job is properly drawn, put out to bid, and the designer remains engaged throughout the project, he will be proven dead wrong. The money he is worried about is padding that he may have to give up, in the competitive environment facilitated by the designer's work. There are many very good reasons why the remodeling projects you like in the magazines have architects associated with them. The high-end ambiance that "designer" projects are associated with is really the cream on top of sound financial justification. But, just to protect against those "crazy design-ers," this text teaches owners how to find a good one and negotiate for those services he needs.

FRANK LLOYD PARIAH?

I have to admit to a little trepidation as I forwarded this manuscript to my publisher. Maybe my construction colleagues will not appreciate the exposé. Is it sedition to treat the architect and builder equally in a precise business methodology? Is it too bold for me to take my prior experience with residential developers, combine it with a specialization in remodeling, and apply it on behalf of neophyte homeowners? Why does it give me intestinal butterflies, when I go to book-stores and fail to find anything resembling this book?

I hope most of my discomfort is the result of a unique and valuable perspective on the marketplace. Some, I am sure, is because I expect my advice to step on many industry toes. And to those folks, I ask you to get beyond your own turf and consider that "pro-fessionalism" is serving the needs of your clients first. Maybe you should dwell on the top-down discussion in Chapter 3 which suggests that when one actor opti-mizes his own business in a vacuum, he surely hinders the team's delivery of good architecture to a satisfied customer. I do know that if you are a homeowner intending to remodel your home in a substantial way, this is my absolute best cut at how you should go about it. Regardless of where the chips may fall. In writing this book I have tried to fine tune a process from your perspective. Not mine, not the builders, but yours. I have tried to create a voice that would answer my best friend who came to me and said "Greg, I know you are unable to come to town and take care of this for me, but what do you recommend I do?" For me, the methodology in this book is a living thing, always ready for improvement. So by all means drop me a note and let me know how your job works out.

CHAPTER 2

PROJECT VIABILITY

WHAT IS POSSIBLE

Do you think it is possible to add a new third floor to my house for an open playroom? Will my plumbing allow for a new master bedroom suite on this side of the house? From a technical standpoint, the answer to these types of questions is normally "yes." That is, structurally and mechanically, even aesthetically, residential designers and contractors have enough options in their toolboxes to accomplish almost anything. As long as pros are involved, and your local zoning code is not unusually constraining, it will be possible. The more appropriate question is, "How much will it cost me . . . and is it worth it?"

LET'S TALK MONEY

When people call to talk about redoing their home, I try to ease them into a cost discussion as soon as possible. Like walking onto a new car lot, after you see the first few "stickers," you know whether you can afford to be shopping for a new automobile at all. And actually, a car is one of those value indicators that I frequently point to. When you build an average-sized new room, it will cost you about the same as an average automobile, say $15,000. A large family room is roughly equal to two cars, or $30,000. But you must

beware: These costs are as deceiving as dealer base prices—they presume that there are no options included. The rooms are simple finished shells, with plain drywall, carpet, and a minimal amount of windows and doors. Unlike automobiles, remodeling options can be more expensive than the base price itself. Including a "kitchen package" in the room, for such things as cabinets, appliances, and finishes, can add $20,000 to the shell number. Adding in a "plumbing package" can be anywhere from $2000 to $10,000 extra, depending on whether it is for a powder room or a master bathroom.

Particularly for remodeling, estimating variations occur in the work that is to be performed on the existing structure, and in the general complexity or quality of the job. An average-sized room that undergoes major partition changes and some new finishes can cost $3000 or more. Replacing the old roof can add from $2000 to $15,000 to the job. Most builders will add degree-of-difficulty adjustments to their quotes for such things as temporary kitchen setups and dust walls, masonary penetrations, long structural spans, or equipment access problems. Thus, mitigating factors can easily add $10,000–$20,000 price swings to the project. Then there are the things that get tacked onto the "showroom" price just before you write the check, like taxes-tags-&-title, the cost of the designer, a property survey, or financing costs, that are not normally

A

B

Relatively speaking, houses are lightweights. And using engineered members when major openings are needed is commonplace. As with many other issues, cost determines what is possible. This house (Photograph A) will have roughly 16 lineal feet of first-floor wall removed (basement/family room) plus 10 lineal feet on the second floor near the pair of double-hung windows (dining room). Here a porch roof has been removed and forms are in place for addition footings. Photograph E shows the new structure being built beside and over the existing home. As with the typical redo, this new work will be "closed in" to the weather before penetrations are made. In Photograph B the major first-floor opening is being made. A temporary shoring wall of 2 x 4 studs holds the floor above until new members can carry the load. Photograph C exposes the existing structure, concrete block on the first floor and wood frame above. To the right is a new two-story frame wall. A new 3-1/2" steel column will sit close to the block on the right and support an inverted steel "T" beam which will span the large opening. Plastic sheeting on the shoring wall will be kept in place until the addition is weather-tight. In Photograph D, a high-performance wood member is used to span the 18' opening for the greenhouse system. Two 11 3/4" deep microlams will carry the new shed roof for the addition.

C

D

E

A

B

FRENCH DOOR

This is a Marvin, single-glazed, true-divided-lite door set. Photograph A shows it delivered and waiting for installation; it is a pre-hung package, complete with frame and threshold, as most patio-type doors are. This unit is primed for painting inside and out. In Photograph B, notice that the door has been specified as a center-hinged, fixed-right-side unit. This allows the operating door to nest in front of its fixed sister when open. The single screen slides into position from the left (viewed from outside in Photograph C). This contemporary product offers many improvements over its previous counterpart (Photograph D).

In Northeastern America, finding that you have a skip-sheathed roof can spell extra expense in remodeling projects. Most building departments prevent the application of a third lamination in reroofing a home. If you presently have two in place, the contractor will need to rip off the old material before applying new shingles. If your attic has 1 x 3 purlins running across the top of your rafters, it should be investigated further. You will probably find cedar shingles on the skip sheathing, which indicates that a past owner has switched to the cheaper asphalt shingle at some point in your home's history. This means that the reroofing of your house must be preceded by completely ripping up all layers of shingles and resheathing it in plywood, which closes the skips between purlins and allows for a different shingle nailing pattern. Although a redo will not normally require the replacement of an entire roof, these are the kinds of "discoveries" that swing the meter in that direction.

expressed as part of the project, although they most assuredly are. If you follow the methodology in this book, and have a $50,000 or more project in mind, the architect's fee will normally be covered by these kinds of rough cost estimates. But to make sure you keep these add-on costs in mind, allow an additional 15% for contingencies beyond that calculated for the "sticks and bricks" alone.

Estimating the Cost of Your Redo

Use the chart in Example 1 to estimate the cost of your dream project. Please be sure to read the adjacent captions, to understand the nuances therein. Based on a finished, building-shell concept, this esti-

mating method should be used to weigh competing options. It should not be used to quote (and then build) a construction project. The table recognizes the cost implications of new one-story and two-story floor areas, of existing space requiring alteration, and of one-time costs for finish/fixture packages unique to specific rooms, and combines these values with realistic room sizes.

So, to figure a project's cost, you should first find the floor area required for each room, using the table. Then decide whether it's a one-story or two-story structure or a combination of the two, and whether it is Alter-Existing or New space. If in doubt, use the big number. Last, go through and put in the one-time charges. As an example, for fixtures and finish changes

This is an area often overlooked by everyone except the builder. Access and clearances for equipment will determine the tools that can be brought to bear on the job. This redo had the luxury of a direct access through the back fence and an amicable adjacent-property owner. The front yard and street trauma that normally is associated with a large remodel, will be totally absent here. Note the backhoe excavating the foundation, while the general contractor's step-van parks close but off-site. The builder will bend over backward to keep this neighbor happy.

SITE ACCESS

in the master bath, add $10,600 to the New Shell cost. When you total the figures, bear in mind that this is a working estimate with numbers generated in 1994, for the Philadelphia area. The values in the table should be updated periodically. Because detailed bids by pros may differ by 30% or more, an educated guess is all your estimate can be up front.

POTENTIAL ZONING CONSTRAINTS

For a redo that may expand the structure, the home-owner should first identify potential zoning constraints. Even builders and architects overlook this

check early in a project. Busy owners may let their architect handle this, but he will expect to get paid even if the project is abandoned. A zoning glitch will most likely be uncovered, but if left until the building department reviews construction drawings for a building permit, it can cause a lot of lost time and money. I therefore suggest that owners use this as an opportunity to see how their municipal government works.

The presence of a zoning problem is easily determined. You should call your municipal building department and ask to speak to a zoning official. Tell him you are considering alterations to your house, that you would like to get a summary of zoning criteria for your address, and see if there is anything of use in your

SPATIAL REQUIREMENTS AND CONSTRUCTION COSTS FOR RESIDENTIAL REMODELING

Category	Description	Size [feet]	gross Area [SF]	New 1 story $86.00	New 2 story FL 1 or 2 $66.00	Alter Exist. $29.00	add'l one time costs [$]
Master BR	King size bedroom with his/her WIC's, dressing area	14x18	252	21672	16632	7308	
MSTR Bath	MBath w/custom tile shower, sink/5' vanity/mirror, WC, finished shell	6x12	72	6192	4752	2088	
	other costs incl fixtures/cabinets/tops, tile floor/wainscot						10600
Family RM	family/recreation room, finished shell	16x20	320	27520	21120	9280	
	other costs, masonry fireplace, patio dr, extra windows, built-in media/library wall						9500
Kitchen	Kitchen U-shape, finished shell	12x14	168	14448	11088	4872	
	new appliances: refrig, sink/faucet, hood, range/oven, disposer, DW, microwave						5500
	new stock hardwood cabinets and 21LF solid surface countertops						11500
	install cabinets, set/level appliances, tile floor/splash, plumbing						4050
Eat-in Nook	Kitchen space for 6 seat table-group, finished shell	10x12	120	10320	7920	3480	
	other costs incl tile floor						1700
Bedroom	secondary bedroom with closet	12x14	168	14448	11088	4872	
Bathroom	secondary bathroom, finished shell	6x9	54	4644	3564	1566	
	other costs incl tub/shower, sink, WC, tile floor						5500
Powder RM	Powder room finished shell	5x6	30	2580	1980	870	
	other costs incl sink, WC, base cabinet/top, mirror, tile floor						2550
Laundry	laundry finished shell	9x7	63	5418	4158	1827	
	other costs incl new washer/dryer, utility sink, vinyl floor						2300
Vestibule	vestibule with 5LF coat closet, finished shell	6x8	48	4128	3168	1392	
	other costs incl exterior glass/wood door, tile floor						2070
Garage	one-car attached garage, concrete floor, fire wall	12x22	264				9150
Fin Bsmt	exist. basement finished incl heat, new partitions, acoustic clg, carpet/paint	16x40	640				11200
Patio	brick patio set in sand, herringbone bond	12x16	192				3460
Deck	exterior grade level deck, treated framing and cedar, stained	12x16	192				2480

QUICK COST ESTIMATE

EXAMPLE 1. *Based on a finished, building-shell concept, this estimating method should be used to weigh options. It should not be used to quote (and then build) a construction project. The table recognizes the cost implications of new one- and two-story floor areas, of existing space requiring alteration, of one-time costs for finish/fixture packages unique to specific rooms, and combines these values with realistic room sizes.*

*The **New Shell** value includes the cost of permits and refuse removal, wood frame floor over excavated crawl space with rat slab, 2 x 4 stud walls with housewrap, unfinished wood frame attic over 8' ceiling, gable shed or hip roof, 20-year fiberglass shingle roof, fiberglass insulation to code, factory-painted double-glazed wood windows, bevel-cedar siding unstained, aluminum K-gutters and downspouts to splash blocks, solid core wood-paneled interior and exterior doors, taped and finished gypsum interior walls and ceiling, carpeted floor, all wood trim including closet fitouts, prime plus two coats painting throughout: oil-base trim and latex walls/ceilings, typical electric controls and fixtures, heating by electric baseboard or extended supply from existing furnace, new 3' wide penetrations through existing frame walls, broom-cleaned at punch out.*

*The **Alter-Existing** value includes tear-out of existing walls and new partition framing, new drywall feathered to existing drywall or plaster, new electric heat or supply extended from existing furnace, new electric, new carpeting and interior wood trim throughout, new paint throughout, broom-cleaned at punch-out.*

***Add-ons.** Rough estimates for the following items should be added to the values in the table: significant roof overframing, large window groups or french/patio doors, penetrations through existing masonry walls, any finish changes, major appliance/fixture changes, major lighting upgrades, built-in cabinets not in the table, plumbing drainage or heating/air conditioning not in the table, landscaping, temporary walls or other major segregation techniques, long structural spans, painting/siding/roofing of adjacent planes or spaces, maid-quality cleaning.*

MUSICAL WINDOWS

Having looked through a window for several years, you begin to consider it a substantial and immobile object. But builders are quite adept at taking out old ones and putting in new ones. Remodeling projects almost always require changes to old windows to make way for new structure. This is because the cost is small in relation to the overall job, but its presence may largely shape the new architecture. This photo is taken inside a redo, before the openings are made into the existing building on the right. The window on the right is original equipment, but it's sister has been removed and relocated into the new structure on the left. After the addition is closed in against the weather, the stucco wall to the right will come down and its window will follow it into the dumpster.

file. Although most of this can be handled by telephone and mail, I recommend making an appointment and meeting with the official. He will look up your address on a zoning map, refer to the latest zoning code, and describe how your structure needs to conform.

Bear two things in mind: First, zoning ordinances are instruments of our democracy that have trickled down to you. Although they seem overblown and idiotic at times, they protect you from a potential inconsiderate neighbor and attempt to steer your community in directions set by the political process. So keep your humor. And second, the technicians and officials in our building departments don't always have the perspective to grasp the negative impact that these codes might have on your project. And they cannot set aside any code requirement without a lengthy and expensive variance process, so don't ask them to. Although many pros claim they have "influence down at zoning," don't risk money on it. Requesting variances should be a last resort when your architect can't satisfy your space requirements within the parameters of the code.

Your Property File

Building departments keep separate files containing any paperwork generated for your address. The file for

A

B

AGAINST THE ZONING ENVELOPE

Because of an odd-shaped lot, this remodel was severely constrained on both sides and rear by zoning setback lines. Accordingly, an engineered survey was done upon which to base the design work. The architect "greased the wheels" for the ultimate building permit by familiarizing himself with the borough building code (all their own) and their zoning ordinances, and then called the building official for a "seat-of-the-pants" assessment before design began. With preliminary design drawings in hand, he then met with the official and secured a verbal approval. This was followed by a "this is our understanding following our recent meeting" letter. The builder had no problem securing the permit. After construction began, the elderly neighbor became livid at the prospect of the redo expanding in her direction. She caused much noise and worry for everyone, going as far as taping-off dimensions as

C

D

construction progressed. But because the municipal authorities had been consulted, these officials showed up personally to defend the remodeling homeowner. The design program called for a new child's bedroom upstairs, a small master bath, a small family room, an entry vestibule, a new powder room, a new air conditioning system, new roofing, and minor alterations to the kitchen. After construction the owners learned that they had beaten the odds and had made money on their redo! Why? Great location, plus lots of simple but marketable amenities within a very small new-construction envelope. Photograph A is the "before" view on the contested side. The entry door opens directly into the living room. Photograph B catches the builder on a break in rough framing. The roof sheathing is on and the porch is temporarily supported in Photograph C. In the finished redo (Photograph D) note the compatibility of white siding with existing white stucco.

your property is public record and you have the right to have it copied, although you may have to pay and wait to get it. Look into the file for several things. First look for a plot plan. This is a document that graphically depicts your property as described in your deed. There may be a survey, which looks similar to the plot but is an engineer's documentation and certification of measured conditions. Sometimes there are other site documents that synthesize plots and surveys with other information. Secure two copies of the most current drawing showing the building on the site with property lines and lengths (one is for your designer, who may trace portions of this drawing for his new Site Plan). If your file is found lacking, the technician may need to direct you to tax maps to see a graphic of your property. I always take tracing paper on visits to building departments. This lets me quickly overlay and trace simple drawings that are difficult or expensive to copy. If you do this, remember to record the north arrow and drawing scale.

If there are architectural drawings in the file, make notes about their contents. Are building elevations included? Sections and details? When is it dated? Does it show your current structure or some previous version? If legible, inquire about the cost for copying the set. The information in this drawing set is probably of value to your architect, and you should try to get a credit for it during upcoming negotiations.

A Preliminary Zoning Evaluation

Ask the zoning official to examine the plot plan with you. Have him call-out building setback lines or yards to determine how close your home may be to the property line or public street. You need to get the official's "seat of the pants" assessment of whether something might preclude your project. Ask him about any height limitations, easements, or buried utilities that might be present. If you are in a highly developed urban or suburban area, the code may require conformance to such things as maximum building coverage, minimum open space, maximum site hard-surface, tree protection, etc. Don't worry about these details—your architect will review at all this information later. Ask the official if your neighbors have had problems meeting site-coverage criteria, or if there is any other history to your property that you should know about.

Again, your primary concern at this point is whether there are there zoning constraints to increasing your home's envelope. With your plot plan in hand, walk around your home. Roughly check and ensure that the drawing conforms to what you can see. "Is the building really 14 feet from where I think my property line is?" On those sides where additions are likely or where setback lines may be close to the structure, you may want to measure off the property line and place a stake where the setback would limit construction. If there isn't room on the logical side of the house, relax! It is rare to find a home where an addition is constrained to the point of "no-way-out." Take note of any setback lines which will be close to new or existing structures and which property lines are without clear monuments. For close calls, your architect, builder, or building official may require a new engineered survey. This is a cost that should be accounted for in upcoming cost projections.

Other Constraining Covenants

It is possible that your property is bound by agreements to be found other than in the local building department. The most likely place will be your most recent title report (probably the one produced when you acquired the home). Here, you might find such encumbrances as a common driveway or utility easement, or a building setback deal made with an adjacent owner. Frequently the criteria generated by homeowner associations, historic districts, or architectural review committees will constrain improvements to residences. If you suspect that your home falls under any one of these jurisdictions, you should investigate it further, and be sure to mention it to your architect. These kind of hidden glitches can be expensive if not uncovered early on.

REQUIREMENTS FOR A BUILDING PERMIT

While at the building department, ask to talk to the person who issues building permits. This may or may not be the zoning official, depending on how large the municipality is. After explaining that you are considering remodeling your home, ask the following question: "Is an architect or engineer's seal required on construction drawings submitted by the builder for permit, if they are not prepared by the homeowner?" For many communities, the answer is "yes." A "no" answer will allow you to lengthen the list of potential designers.

Construction pros have been known to promise that they can get drawings "sealed" for a fee. (Sealing or stamping is the formal mark or signature of the licensee. It contains his state license identification number.) In most states the law requires that sealed drawings be prepared under the architect or engineer's "direct and responsible supervision." This precludes an architect from sealing a drawing prepared by the builder, for example. Professionals who do otherwise can lose their license, and expose themselves to the all-too-common construction lawsuit. Because of their frivolous consideration of these facts, they are "marginal pros" whose advice is to be avoided. In Pennsylvania, design-build firms must have a registered architect own at least 50% of the business. And it is illegal for builders even to "offer" the services of an architect (and then treat him as a subcontractor, for example). These requirements are put in place to protect the neophyte's "health, safety, and welfare" and should not be circumvented.

EXAMINING COST VERSUS VALUE

Once your are sure that zoning problems will not prevent the project, a "go" or "no-go" decision will hinge on how you feel about the costs and benefits of the redo. Your house is an extremely valuable asset and construction costs are shockingly high. Unless you are a financially secure "empty nester" and not concerned with recouping equity when sold, It is important to think about your project in a business like way. Real estate agents tell me it is not uncommon for families to price themselves out of their neighborhood with remodeling projects.

Money spent on remodeling your home will never compete with other forms of capital investment. It is similar to buying an expensive car. You purchase it to solve a transportation problem or because you expect to enjoy owning and driving it. Most people find something that is affordable and will hold as much resale value as possible. But in fact they take a financial "bath" as soon as they drive it off the lot. You won't make money buying a car or remodeling your home. A 1993 Cost Versus Value Report by *Remodeling Magazine*[1] finds that for the most common remodeling jobs, costs recouped (national average) varied

SKIRTING THE GROUND

A quality project always pays attention to how the building meets the ground. One way to do it is to create an architectural "reveal" to transition from grade to building skin. This reveal strip should be dark and heavily textured to mask the discoloration to be expected from rain-splashed soil. Where the building will receive horizontal siding, a wide skirt-board will balance the other trim. In Photograph A, the existing stone skirt has been reinterpreted as grey split-faced block. This show-block has been carefully planned into the foundation wall; it does not continue under the deck where its expense could not be justified. Using this technique requires that the wood skirt above be detailed to sit well below the addition floor line. Note in Photograph B how high the bottom of the door is in relation to the skirt board. Probably the most common way to position the trim is to set the top of the skirt flush with the floor level as in Photograph C. But if a significant deck area is to abut the new wall, the designer may choose to raise the skirt board so that it sits above the adjacent floor line (Photograph E). This provides a consistent trim to the wall area where it is needed most; the place where deck money is spent, and where people will come in close contact (Photograph F). With a high skirt, the rim-joist zone can be finished with a material similar to the lathe and stucco in Photograph D. The wood-skirt and stucco-reveal treatment also makes a lot of sense when grade changes radically, and exposes large expanses of the raw foundation wall.

A

B

C

D

E

F

A

B

HARVESTING SPACE OVER THE GARAGE

If you can get a second-floor plan to function well, the space over the existing garage will be the cheapest redo option. This is because the cost of the foundation and stair access is prepaid, that is, provided that the old work passes current standards. Photograph A shows how simple it is to beef up an over-spanned ceiling, to allow it to carry a new second-floor structure. Notice that a new girder of two 2 x 12's has been set into position. It will be supported by a reinforced header over the garage door at one end, and new jack-studs in the wall. A new 4" steel column will be installed at midspan, replacing the temporary post shown here. Photograph B has been taken from inside the garage attic, and shows an access door into a bedroom closet. The fact that the second floor in the residence and the garage ceiling sit flush at the top indicates that this add-on was anticipated in the design of the original home. With the new second-floor frame up, carpenters begin to break away the old exterior stucco in Photograph C. The access door is still visible at the bottom right.

C

A

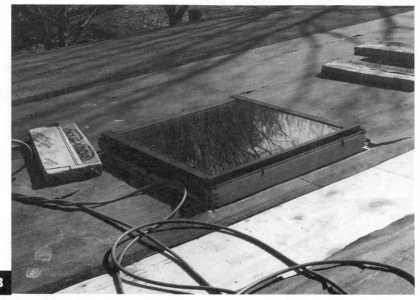

B

HOLES IN THE KITCHEN

For simple kitchens, sometimes "freshening up" should not involve new cabinets and tops. For about the same money, you may get more impact by carefully adding more natural light and spatial connections. Photograph A shows a carpenter as he begins to cut a pass-through into a kitchen. A later view shows the completed opening (Photograph C). This new little surround will nest bifold shutters on each side, have task lighting to brighten a new laminate counter, and will contain a new base-cabinet underneath, for linen. In the kitchen beyond, the ceiling is being opened up into a new light-well that will culminate with the large, operable Velux skylight in Photograph B. Barely visible is the opening into a new addition where the over-the-sink window has been replaced with a wider-cased opening. Thus, three major openings have been made, creating a light and spacious-feeling kitchen, and the existing appliances, counters, and cabinets have remained intact.

C

COST/VALUE WORKSHEET   Owner: Address: Date:

Existing Characteristics [1]   Fair Market Values [2]   Existing Value [3]

_____   _____
_____   _____
_____   _____   Redo Value [7]
_____   _____
_____   _____

Exist. Plus Redo Features [4]   After Redo Values [5]   Future Value [6]

_____   _____
_____   _____   Cost Recouped [13]
_____   _____
_____   _____
_____   _____

Redo Amenities [7]   Construction Costs [8]   Construction Cost [9]

_____   _____
_____   _____
_____   _____
_____   _____   Project Cost [12]
_____   _____
_____   _____

                                 Other Redo Costs [10]   Other Costs Tot.[11]
Architect
Other (survey, financing, etc)   _____
                                 _____

                                                                     Mortgage Pmt Increase [14]

COST/VALUE WORKSHEET

EXAMPLE 2. *Completing this form will help you decide where your financial thresholds are. It requires you to investigate real estate "comparables," and to consider the cost of the project in relation to present property value. Start with the Existing Characteristics (item 1) of your home. Refer to Example 1 to help enter new Redo Amenities (item 7) and their corresponding Construction Costs (item 8). Item 4 should combine Existing Characteristics (1) and Redo Amenities (7). To get an estimate of market value (items 2 and 5) you need to secure the advice of at least two professional real estate agents, synthesizing them into single values (items 3 and 6). Subtract Existing Value from Future Value (item 6 minus 3) to find the Redo Value (7). The designer's fee, any finance charges, and surveys, if required, should be listed (item 10) and included in the overall Project Cost (item 12). Redo Value (7) divided by Project Cost (12) will yield the percentage of Cost Recouped (item 13).*

from a high of 101% (minor kitchen remodel) to a low of 71% (sunspace addition). These results are from "paper" projects with pros estimating construction costs and resale value. The surveys make several important market assumptions, such as that the remodeling projects are done to midpriced homes in established neighborhoods. Changing these assumptions will skew the numbers radically. Therefore, each redo should be examined for its future cost-recouped value in its own real estate market.

A Cost/Value Worksheet

Completing the worksheet in Example 2 will help you decide where your financial thresholds are. Start with the Existing Characteristics (item 1) of your home; this should be a synopsis of your property as if you were placing a "for-sale" ad in the real estate section of your newspaper. Include the bedroom/bathroom counts, etc. Refer to Example 1 to help enter new Redo Amenities (item 7) and their corresponding Construction Costs (item 8). Item 4 should combine Existing Characteristics (1) and Redo Amenities (7).

To get an estimate of Fair Market Value (items 2 and 5), you need to secure the advice of at least two professional real estate agents. They should not be your friends, and they should work for brokers whose sale signs are frequently seen in your neighborhood. You should not have to pay them for this advice. Most consider it another way to meet future clients and to keep their "ear to the ground" in their market area. Give them a partially completed copy of the worksheet and tell them to assume the hypothetical resale with improvements will be within one year of remodeling. Don't color their responses by letting them see other agents' estimates, and don't even hint that you might consider moving

(that comes later). It is important that each agent respond to common criteria, not to what you may say (or not say), which is always unequal. When your responses come back, synthesize them into single values (items 3 and 6); use either "worse-case" numbers or average the results (after throwing out unusually high or low ones).

Subtract Existing Value from Future Value (item 6 minus 3) to find the Redo Value (7). Remember that the construction cost in Example 1 assumes average-sized rooms and mid-priced construction techniques, adequate for determining items 8 and 9. The designer's fee, any finance charges and surveys if required, should be listed (item 10) and included in the overall Project Cost (item 12). Redo Value (7) divided by Project Cost (12) will yield the percentage of Cost Recouped (item 13).

Finding Your Comfort Level

When the cost-recouped value falls below 75%, you should ask one of the real estate agents to show you a property-for-sale of the same characteristics (item 4). Add moving costs to the asking price, and compare it to the potential Redo Value (item 7). Should you move instead of improve? Only you know where your comfort levels are. If you find out that you will spend, say, $90,000 for your redo and can expect to get less than 25% of that back if sold within a year, I think I would explore alternate routes to your dream home! Of course, after having done all your practical homework (the worksheet), it is okay to remodel your home simply because "it's something that I've always wanted to do." Or because "I don't want to move, period." The longer you intend to live in and get enjoyment from your home, the less important resale numbers become.

CHAPTER 3

THE OWNER-MANAGER

THE UNIQUE ROLE OF THE OWNER

Most remodeling problems are not caused by incompetence or dishonesty, but by unshared expectations between team members. And the owner sits in the best position to alleviate this dilemma; he is the one with the whole view and the clout to affect change. He can establish a cut-throat, compartmentalized workplace or an open, problem-solving one. Unless the owner has the luxury of living elsewhere during construction, he will be intimately engaged in project decision making. He has no choice. When building a new home, a separate site ensures that the owner will not micromanage all the intra-trade problems that arise. But in remodeling, it is not possible to "turn your head" and let the builder or architect catch and resolve all the issues that come up. Each night when the dust settles, the owner sees something new to worry about. A passive tack will yield undue emotional stress. This chapter is written in the spirit of very familiar axioms. "The best defense is a good offense." And "be prepared." The owner is the most important team member. Most of his pivotal tasks take place in the front end.

It is absolutely essential for owners to assess their own objectives before professionals are engaged. Important commitments are made during the hiring dance, whether conscious or not. "What am I looking for? How do I want my job to run? What should the project look like when finished? How do I want to feel when I am using the space? Am I after a Mercedes or a Subaru, or something in between?" I once had clients tell me they wanted to have their new kitchen featured in the local newspaper "design" section. This was great, because I understood what they were after. They had done their assessment homework and were communicating it with specifics. Knowing what you want will largely determine who you hire to make it happen. I recommend writing a sentence or two (no more than a paragraph) that outlines the project goals. This will be most important to married folks. Although each co-owner will have different views, they must begin rendering consensus-type decisions for others to act upon. Usually one partner jots down a first draft, the other marks it up, and then final language is agreed upon. Chapter 4 will show you how to use this objectives-statement to hire your architect.

SELECTING THE RIGHT TEAM SCENARIO

With some degree of self-assessment complete, owners should choose from a short list of potential methodologies. Only with a discreet process in mind can you then hire the right players, set an appropriate "tone" for a working environment, and guide the project down the road to success. Here are four redo scenarios that should be considered. Each has appealing facets, as well as some pitfalls.

Builder With Designer Scenario

Many remodeling projects happen this way. This is essentially a builder-driven path. Typically the owner asks the builder to provide a price to do the project and he provides drawings of the design and its projected construction cost. The builder may do the drafting himself, direct its preparation by an employee or subcontractor, or simply introduce an independent designer to provide parallel work for the owner. But make no mistake—in all these scenarios, the builder calls the shots. Although the owner may pay the designer directly, when push comes to shove even registered architects will be in the builder's corner when disagreements occur. The builder's referral represents a future income stream that the designer will not readily dissolve.

This scenario is a good choice when style or sophistication takes a back seat to the accuracy of cost projections. It is most appropriate for small or uncomplicated add-on jobs. Many folks remodel this way because they can't get comfortable with an architect-driven scenario. Either they can't find one they like, or they are advised to the contrary. For those prepared to spend $30,000 or more and intending to use the Builder with Designer Scenario, I have several recommendations.

1. Ask that a professional designer be hired by the builder (not the builder himself) to provide the drawings for his proposal. Experience has shown me that most builders want to design their own

jobs but they are not very good at it. Although this sits in the gray zone of Pennsylvania's prohibition against a builder offering architectural services, it is a common occurrence even here. Insist on having "sit-down" sessions with the designer directly, rather than letting the builder be the middle man for a hidden draftsman. Pay the designer's fee in a way that does not further obligate you to the builder (call it "phase one" of his service). Let it be known from the start that you will shop the drawings around for competitive proposals, and then do just that.

2. Identify another experienced builder or architect to act as a consultant. He should quickly review and revise the construction documents to be used by your favorite contractor, before the deal is cast. Particular attention should be paid to itemized product allowances or specifications, maximum labor rates and markups for "extra" work, and the lump-sum contract form itself. This consultant should be on the sidelines for quick (and paid) second opinions as the project moves forward. I have never met a lawyer whom I think could do this and relatively few architects. Don't let your consultant throw out your builder's work (his drawings for instance) or overinflate his own role. He should "fill in and around" to clarify areas needed to protect your interests. By all means loan him your copy of this book.

3. Do your "private-eye" homework before selecting the builder. Be sure you read Chapter 7, for tips on how to go about it. You will need to trust him. But you also must be prepared to satisfy your curiosity elsewhere and disagree in a respectful way. I would bet that simply your "preparedness" will preclude your actual use of any cross-checking activities.

Kitchen/Bath Dealer Scenario

A large number of projects are orchestrated by product retailers. Operating out of a showroom, these companies offer homeowners direct access to product samples, and an intimate knowledge of what they sell. They have a strong loyalty to a mix of suppliers that they recommend. Dealers may have several installers on payroll, but most of their kitchen and bath work is subcontracted out to specialty trades. They will provide plumbing, electric, flooring, painting etc., as required. They might be considered a specialty general contractor, except for one important distinction: they make most of their money selling material, not labor. This will color their advice accordingly. Their design services and business policies vary greatly from company to company. The best dealers have professional designers who concern themselves with all aspects of interior design. Their expertise should be solicited in kitchen work regardless of the scenario chosen (particularly in the builder-driven path). You should expect to pay a design fee to take a drawing away with you, some or all of which is credited back if you elect to place a major order with them. At their worst, kitchen and bath showrooms can seem like used-car lots with their designers functioning as high-pressure salesmen. With these dealers, the design drawing is quickly prepared free of charge to quote a price and sell the job, but is withheld later to prevent customers from getting competitive quotes. In general, however, their "people-handling" skills and business acumen are better than the average builder. They, like the other redo players, have a vested interest in delivering pleasant, functional places and satisfied customers.

The dealer scenario is appropriate when the work is clearly limited to either kitchens or baths, and when you are comfortable with their design credentials. If the construction perimeter will encompass other major rooms in the home (such as a new family room), another path is better. In any other scenario the expertise of the dealer can still be utilized as designer, product supplier, or installer, but subordinated to the builder. In this case, the dealer's design drawing is used as a "shop drawing," providing more detail to the builder's construction drawings and iterating back to the other players for approval of any proposed changes.

In my architectural practice I rarely find owners who want a kitchen or bath remodeled "in a vacuum." Most clients' want to spatially connect kitchens to large breakfast areas, patios, decks, and family/media rooms. Many new bathrooms get molded into suites encompassing sleeping, sitting, dressing, closet, and bathing functions. I have done several "ten-year plans" that start with a kitchen redo to be followed by a new family room with expanded master suite above. For such complicated or long-term objectives, owners should avoid contracting solely with a kitchen/bath dealer. They have a penchant for avoiding architectural changes and emphasizing high-priced cabinets, fixtures, and finishes. Design work for future phasing does not put bread on their table. I prefer to design kitchen/bath spaces in context to adjoining functions, specifying all products, but using items that owners can substitute out, given the recommendations of the builder's kitchen/bath dealer. This gives a framework for other designers to work around (something to throw darts at) and they rarely fail to improve on my humble work.

Architect/Builder Cost-Plus Scenario

This scenario is useful where style, quality, or timeliness is extremely important and the cost is not. These projects tend to be extensive remodels of upscale properties, roughly $200,000 and up (new work). In a cost-plus arrangement the builder "opens the books" to the owner. He discloses all his costs and then adds on his fee, either a fixed sum or a percentage. The architect is either paid hourly or at a percentage of construction cost, and his service normally includes administration of the builder's contract which serves to define team roles. This scenario is much like a time-and-materials arrangement with a single contractor but on a larger scale and supported by AIA[1] contract forms. Here, the order in which the builder and architect are retained is not important. The architect and builder are invited to do the job because they are known to have high credentials. The pair may come pre-joined. Competitive pricing for both their service and the cost of construction is secondary.

The best cost-plus method has the builder and architect separately contracted to the owner to form a team that communicates even in preliminary phases of the project. A cost-plus service package can be a good choice when initial information is scarce or when quick completion is mandatory. For example, when an existing structure requires destructive investigation (frequently, test holes to find framing directions and bearing walls) and the owner wants a quick start, a cost-plus scenario allows portions of the design work to be deferred until the builder has labor on the job to open up the building.

The cost-plus process choice may happen imperceptibly. The owner may see a project in a magazine and jot down the architect's name. He may call and say "I want you to redo my home. When can you start?" Then the architect might say "who do you want to build it?" and the owner responds with "you pick him." For homeowners that can afford such a casually formed cost-plus arrangement, I recommend hiring an experienced real estate/construction lawyer to tailor these service agreements to protect their interests. Taking the onus of cost control off the project may free up creative juices, but it also raises the risk of unpleasant surprises. Bear in mind that hiring two firms that are familiar with each other but unknown to the owner practically eliminates the counterbalance present in other scenarios. This added risk needs to be compensated for with more thoughtful preparation of the contracts, by an advocate in the owner's corner. An upscale cost-plus arrangement also infuses more custom detail into the architecture, and therefore hiring the designer for "construction administration services" is imperative. This forces the builder to work with the architect to resolve the inevitable glitches associated with custom styling.

Architect Then Builder Scenario

This book details the advantages of the Architect Then Builder Team because I consider it the optimum path for most middle-income projects. It is also where I see the most confusion. In a nutshell, this method pays for the services of the architect by the competitive selection of the builder, and by removing much of his risk from the construction process. It provides the level of planning required for the complexities encountered in $30,000 plus projects. An Architect Then Builder Scenario requires the identification of a local designer who is experienced in remodeling, which may be a tall order to fill in some communities. In this methodology, the architect and builder are equal players, providing the owner with an ongoing pair of specialists. They are given specific tasks and responsibilities through the use of standard AIA documents. The architect secures the owner's approval and determines "what it is" and the builder establishes "how to put it in place."

The owner gets a pre-scripted, semi-competitive environment and a built-in second opinion. Finding this experienced team and correctly managing them through the process is the owner's role, and is the crux of this book.

So which scenario should you choose? If there is comfort in numbers, a recent *Kitchen & Bath Business Magazine* survey[2] reported that American kitchens are being designed by architects, builders, and dealers in roughly equal increments (independent designers a distant fourth). That is, one third of owners needing a kitchen redo are opting to use a builder-designed scheme, etc. I was surprised to see that most kitchens are designed by architects. For owners who have completed successful projects using variant scenarios, I consider them fortunate. They were at considerable risk during their redo. If you are an owner on the threshold of such a project, you should not be overly influenced by any single example, no matter how successful it appears on its face. A pattern of success is, of course, another matter. The important point is that the homeowner must be proactive. He must "decide" on his own appropriate process to follow and not be "sold" by one of the actors.

Avoid the Designer Owner Builder Scenario

Many horror stories come from this methodology, and I do not recommend it for residential remodeling. From this process comes most builders' disdain for designers. It is common to find owners who employ a professional architect or designer and then use the drawings to hire and direct a builder. They want the quality feeling of an architect-designed solution and they want to keep absolute control over the redo as well. They do not keep the designer engaged through the construction process, thinking that they are saving money.

This is similar to the way speculative developers do new housing. The architect provides a "builder's set" of construction drawings signed-and-sealed for permitting, and may never see the project again. There is a strong likelihood that anything that goes awry will get blamed on him because he is "the last guy out the door." The drawings are as minimal as will allow the developer to gain municipal approvals. They specify mostly generic products, and exclude custom detailing. Sexy design renderings and then simplistic working drawings give the merchant builder maximum front-end sizzle to "set the hook" and back-end room to wiggle. It is a tough business, and the process is not appropriate for remodeling. Warning: Many architects known for their residential work are really "developer's architects," delivering generic front-end design work only, and have little construction experience.

Homeowners are not seasoned real estate developers, and remodeling is not new, repetitive housing. You can't buy a plan book for your redo. For those homeowners who want the "good stuff" they see in the magazines, you have to hire a professional designer. He is the one who can mold "what you want" and "what you have to work with" into an exciting complimentary package. But you have to hire him to stick around so that when bids come in, he can help get the costs in line if necessary. He needs to debug construction problems with the builder on short notice. His drawings have to have a certain level of custom detailing because he has to match new-to-existing, and because "freshness" or "flair" is expected. It is said that the designer is worth 90% of his fee in the first and the last 10% of a project. But this is true only if the last portion is, in fact, provided. He is the one who worries

THE SCIENCE OF SKIN

Trying to match existing material is rarely the best way to integrate new with old. I have only seen this accomplished with white rough-textured stucco on converging planes. Rather than rely on the craftsmanship of the contractor for this limited situation (white stucco), and to avoid redoing the skin of the entire house, the designer has to come up with a color-material combination that is different but compatible. Photograph A shows some of the riffs used in this redo. The existing home and garage were grey stucco, impossible to match successfully. Further, the owners were interested in facelifting the entire front elevation even though treating the whole residence was not in the budget. To keep the garage "connected" to the main house, the first-floor stucco was used as the basis for the new scheme (and protected during construction). Breaking up the two-story mass and covering the new-old seam, small roof pents were used between floors. The wall plates on the second floor were set out so the final corner trim would pass over the existing stucco below. This wide corner trim and broken-pent combination (Photograph B) was selected because it allowed opaque paint on the trim to be exactly matched to the stucco grey and used on the second floor to "stitch together" the various colors. Note how the downspouts have been planned to integrate into corner trim, miss the roof pents, and avoid crossing the siding field. A half-round molding has been added to the bottom of the dormer window trim to underscore the change from white to grey trim. Cedar bevel-siding with semi-transparent grey stain was used because it offered the textural change needed to be "better than" but "respectful of" the rest of the elevation.

A

B

about how spaces will furnish, how lighting works, and the feel of the front door hardware. If you don't care about these details, if your project is rather small and straightforward, or if the Architect Then Builder path doesn't feel right, use one of the other scenarios, not this one.

THE DO-IT-YOURSELF OWNER

In researching this book I was dumbstruck to find how many do-it-yourself remodeling books were on the shelves. So I know there are a lot of us out there (yeah, that's right, me too). We are the guys who are handy with tools and enjoy figuring out how to make things. But in my professional life I see redo-reality up close. And I say this: If you are single, or newly married with lots of spit-n-vinegar, and loads of free time for the next year or two, go for it! Yes, you will probably save some money, if you do a close-to-professional job. Just do what you can and subcontract the rest. Much can be done by quick learners if you are prepared to go slowly . I suggest you not secure your guidebooks from the library though, for they will be dog-eared and dusty when returned.

But most folks find it hard enough to handle the craziness even when pros come in and make a "surgical strike"! When my clients begin talking about contracting out the job themselves, I recommend that they proceed with the project assuming they will let a general contract for the entire job. As the bidding documents are prepared we target several tasks that are candidates for the do-it-yourselfer. These become bid alternates for which quotes are set out by bidders. When the builder is selected, his contract is written specifying unit prices for the jobs that the owner may perform when the go/no-go point arrives. Owner involvement in the work is not a good idea while construction is open to the weather, while the mess factor is high, or while many subcontractors are on the job. This is when time is precious and trade choreography critical.

The best jobs for weekend warriors tend to be painting, final grading, landscaping, and cleanup. Something like half of the intended do-it-yourself work that I see is actually completed by the owner. By the time the finish work rolls around, most owners want the project to be over quickly and the money seems less important. As I write this chapter, I am finishing up an $85,000 remodeling job where we took the interior painting out of the construction contract for the owner to complete. As the owner wrote a final $10,000 check to the builder, her mood was unusually sour. She was grasping at straws to keep items on the punch list. My wife put it into perspective for me. "She has just spent enough money to buy three BMW's and now she is going to be left with a messy house, plus a month of nonstop painting to do. I would be depressed, too!"

Moonlighters, Neighbors, New Graduates, and Wanna-bes

You would be amazed at the convoluted scenarios that arise when a homeowner says the equivalent of "I have set out $50,000 to remodel my home." Human beings love to spend other people's money! Make sure you treat the project as an investment, not a shopping spree. Politely turn down volunteers because their help will probably hurt. Majoring in architecture or working for several years as a carpenter does not qualify someone to spend your redo money. Stay with professionals if at all possible. You get what you pay for.

What About These Guys?

People frequently ask me what I think about other professionals handling their remodeling project—building designers (nonregistered architects), engineers, interior designers, decorators, kitchen designers, carpenters, sales consultants, etc. The list is extensive. Theoretically, these pros could have the kind of experience and personality to effectively manage a major redo. Personal experience and drive are more important than paper credentials (note that your building department may require an architect's or engineer's seal on permit drawings). But a word of caution: You must see a long line of successful projects wherein they contractually managed other trades before hiring them. The only person I ever met from this group who could "deliver the goods" was an interior designer. She was very construction-savvy, which is important. My opinion? Unless there are mitigating circumstances, don't do it. Stay in the mainstream with your primary hires.

Prewired Builders and Referrals

Most clients come to me after having "toyed" with the redo idea for years. Sometimes they bring with them an emotional commitment to a particular contractor who has been helpful and has stayed in contact to keep his "foot in the door" for the work. Occasionally the owners have verbally promised the job to him. This can pose a problem for me. I feel that I have an obligation to speak up if I see an extremely poor choice. If the client cannot afford such a casual attitude toward money (as one would find in the upscale Cost-plus Scenario), I am compelled to suggest that the owner use only a "general" contractor for his job and not force-fit any major prewired sub on him (see Chapter 7 for some exceptions to this). And further, I recommend that the builder be required to compete for the job. I am privy to the wide array of bidprices that can be expected; neither the owner nor the builder has this perspective. It is not uncommon for bids to spread by 20% to 30%. This means that the choice of builders is at least a $10,000 decision in most remodeling jobs. And my experience is based on very tightly specified jobs where there is very little "grey," other than labor, and the bidders are known professionals. This number can easily be $30,000 or more. Therefore, except for situations where there is special personal chemistry between owner and prewired problem builder, I usually ask the owner to consider the following options. (1) He can honor his commitment to the builder and we will tailor a scenario whereby his shortcomings (in my opinion) are shored up somehow; (2) he can (or I will) explain to the builder that he has changed his mind and will solicit competitive proposals for the work, for which he is enthusiastically invited; or (3) he can "stretch the truth" about the project going into limbo, wait for some time and proceed without him. When the builder finds out, he will be disappointed of course, but if he is a businessperson, he will understand. But this won't happen if the owners are referred to me by the problem builder. In such case, I will invent an excuse to pass on the job.

This is because business referrals are a pro's dirty little secret. "Referral" is code for "special handling." Owners need to bear in mind that even good guys will not bite the hand that feeds them. When a job is brought to me by a competent builder, I will avoid jeopardizing his position in the job. This is because he could send me many future projects and the owner is most likely good for just one. Accordingly, I will not suggest that the owners bid their job out, although I know it will normally save big money. It just ain't kosher! This is the primary reason why most owners should seek out the designer first.

CONTRACTS

Your redo will require you to make many financial agreements, whether you want to or not. You will need to control the way your money is spent, by giving marching orders to other people. These directions and understandings must be acknowledged in writing, and cast in your interest. A sure sign of business sophistication is when the monied party passes down his contract form. Although the experienced contracting firm may pass it upstairs, the agreement will be in the format preordained by the client. He is simply doing legwork for the heavyweight. Money makes the rules and largely determines the contract form. Most of the "lawyering" for your redo is boilerplated into the forms that I recommend in subsequent chapters. I am not aware of any others that do the job as well.

This is not to say that you should avoid hiring an attorney to help with your redo contracts. To the contrary, I highly recommend it. But I also suggest three things. First, you should make sure he is an experienced, local construction or real estate lawyer. Second, retain him only after consultation with your selected designer. And third, provide the attorney with both the architect and builder contract forms suggested herein, agreeing to a flat fee for his review and alteration. You should be very skeptical if he wants to diverge from the AIA form family, for he should know how to quickly tailor them to bring his experience to bear in your interest.

Unlike the forms offered by many remodeling builders, these contracts have been developed by construction lawyers to protect the interests of all three parties. Even if you elect to use a nonarchitect scenario, make sure you use the AIA form to hire your builder (and strike all references to architects). These forms are instantly recognized by experienced lawyers, architects, and builders. This universal recognition is part of their power. Only changes need to be discussed. You should not sign any customized letter-type agreement, because you can be sure that every word is intended to protect the offerer's interests, not yours. When I was inside large architectural firms, there was always an effort to make customized agreements appear "set in stone" so owners wouldn't scrutinize all the fine print. They always did, of course. Or rather, their lawyers did it for them.

Do not let the idea of a contract intimidate you. It is simply an understanding between parties. It does not have to be typed, for legible handwritten ink is just as binding. If you have not retained an attorney, and even though your designer will normally prepare these contracts as part of his service, redo owners should exert absolute control of the undertaking. The architect's role should be seen as a clerical function for recording language that will bind you up. Photocopying of the original instruments (available at your local AIA chapter in major cities) is to be avoided because it can mask the recognition of changes. The value of the AIA forms is that they try to fairly assign rights, roles, and responsibilities of the parties to the agreement. Within the boilerplate are contingencies for the nightmare scenarios that might go wrong with your project. They bring forward an amazing amount of construction experience, to facilitate good architecture. Having used them for years, I still reread sections periodically to check what I am doing for a given client. "Am I doing what I said I would do? Am I doing what the industry expects me to do?" The answers are there in my contract with the owner.

In preparing this manuscript, I considered writing sections on "how to fire your architect or builder." I have been engaged in two jobs where the builder was let go. In both cases, the AIA contract was used by myself, the owner, and the problem builder himself for guidance when the contention was taking place. And later it was used by the arbitrators to measure everyone's performance. On the "firing" issue, rather than paraphrasing for you, I have decided to let the contracts speak for themselves. Both primary agreements have very clear guidelines to follow for advising the pro of his nonperformance, and dissolution of the agreement.

Many such issues are covered in the contracts. As you read them, remember that both the Owner-Architect and Owner-Builder forms are interrelated. If you don't understand or agree with the language, speak up. There is a good chance the builder or architect will feel the same way. If you want, call your lawyer. Strike out the language, or rewrite a new clause. It is more important that you and the other party understand what is meant than for the wording to appear "lawyerly." If you are worried about an issue, propose text that places the concern in the agreement, somehow, somewhere. When changes are made to boilerplate, line through the text (no white-out) so it is clear what was removed, and have all parties initial each revision. Use the contract as a common receptacle for understandings. Because it asks the right questions, it is your management checklist; it is your instrument for directing your team.

DECISION MAKING

We have all heard that "knowledge is power." As an owner-manager you do not have to know everything. You do have to know, however, just what it is that you do not know. You must identify knowledge gaps. It is not helpful to shield your ignorance, because ultimately it will become known. You are a generalist, not a specialist, a clock-driven decision maker. Your role is to identify a potential problem, gather information, render the decision, and move on to the next logical one. And this needs doing without encroaching into the responsibility of your hired help. You are a path-clearer. You never want to supplant the builder's or architect's personalization of "your" project. Your pros should make it their own.

If an issue arises that will have a major dollar or perceptual impact on the redo, then it is probably worth your time to investigate. For some issues you will want to seek the advice of an expert. Do not get bogged down in small detailed issues. Pass these kinds of "hot potatoes" down to your pros. Be sure not to ask for expert opinion indiscriminately. If you ask advice of people with inappropriate experience, you will certainly receive a wrong answer. Increasing the number of queries to unqualified sources will not increase the likelihood of an adequate response. Yes, you should seek professional counsel as often as you can afford, but the question should be succinctly posed and the source of the advice should be carefully targeted. Ask the question only of people engaged in the particular "expertise area" as a full-time pro. Human nature ensures that you will get many earnest and lengthy responses. Make sure they are not from moonlighters or wanna-be's. If someone is going to guess, it should be you. At least this way, you understand the basis upon which the decision was made and therefore its reliability.

Do not ask advice of anyone with a major negative proprietary interest in the answer. Translation: If he stands to make substantially more profit at your expense, don't ask him the question. Period. For example, if you ask your builder's roofing sub "which is a better roof, fiberglass or cedar?", can you rely on the answer? If he is contracted to do your upcoming fiberglass roof, probably not. His contract could double in value if he answers in a "marketing" mode. That is what he is trained to do. He has mouths to feed, too. The question is better posed to another roofer who installs both types of roofs and who understands that you have already hired someone else for the job.

Don't be surprised if expert opinions diverge; there are usually several "right" answers. If there is no consensus, go back to your "obligated" source. That is, act on the opinion of the expert who is fully prepared to take on the work from you and stand behind his recommendation. You have isolated the proprietary slant by seeking untainted outside opinion; now you can use the proprietary pull to seek some performance guarantee.

Beware of the "adjacent-trade-syndrome" and seek out the core expertise of workmen before asking advice. Many pros "absorb" experience by working next to other trades. After awhile they begin to offer the services of the adjacent tradesmen because they are perceived to be the same, and they have become familiar with the work. They should not be considered experts in these peripheral areas. For example, I frequently hear owners ask painters what color they should paint their house. Do I ever hear the painter suggest consulting the designer who is trained in the use of color on buildings? Never. Usually they are flattered that their advice is being sought, they are worried that a designer will suggest a solution they haven't covered in their quote, and they typically offer poor direction.

This doesn't mean that there aren't examples of pros who break the rules. They do exist. And although the owner has the right to object to and

have a subcontractor replaced, this rarely happens. The general contractor should be trusted to bring the appropriate expertise to his team even if they fit into a "beware" category below. But when "expert" advice is needed, you as the owner-manager should not turn to these people:

- Engineers designing residential HVAC systems or buildings
- Electricians doing lighting design and fixture selection
- Plumbers doing heating and air-conditioning systems
- Painters doing color selections, special faux finishes, or complex plastering
- Carpenters doing hardwood floors
- Carpenters doing complex or wet-bed ceramic tile
- Carpenters doing extensive prepaint prepping on old trim
- Carpenters fabricating on-site cabinetry other than open shelving
- Architects doing general contracting work
- Architects doing specification or purchasing of furnishings
- Builders or kitchen/bath dealers doing architectural design work
- Nonlocal and non-real estate lawyers doing zoning hearing board work
- Architectural illustrators or draftsmen doing architectural design work

Known by Action

It is very difficult to evaluate a person's credentials. Experienced marketing people can walk into a conference room and make participants believe they can do

This is a neat way to protect furnishings in rooms that will not be altered. Inside this library, tarps were draped over furnishings and the door was temporarily plugged. The plug was made with a wooden frame, covered with poly sheeting, and circumscribed with a 1″ felt strip. This created a friction-fit that protected the cherry casing, was practically dustproof, and allowed the panel to be easily removed.

DOOR PLUG

it all. I suspect that they read so much about how to do it, and talk about it so often, that they actually begin to believe that they have done it. You and I can be duped by attractive people and confident body language. We know what can be done with the written word, suggesting things that are not really so. Further, statistics can be tailored in many different ways to support even conflicting positions. Much of your job as owner-manager has to do with sizing up genuine experience. Although I will talk about how to check out particular redo players later on, here are several suggestions to help cut through the baloney.

You should form your opinions about people upon directly observed action, not on what is said or promised—"by your actions you are known." When you can identify exactly what was produced by this person before they met you, you will know a lot about them. The produced work does not necessarily have to be redo efforts, to offer clues. When it's all you have, small personal habits can be markers for the way larger jobs are done. I would never hire an architect, for example, whose studio is not a fresh and fun place to work. If he can't do it for himself, how can he make it happen for others? A general contractor who is late, forgetful, and disorganized is a bad sign, for the essence of his job is juggling many trades in a changing calendar.

Verifying past experience by talking with others is less than reliable. The well-worn references list is not enough. You don't have to be very expert to find three people who will attest to your "good citizenship," especially via telephone. One of my worst nightmares was caused by a builder who (I later found out) sandbagged his references. He was lucky enough to have a relative who had recently completed a redo, and he talked them into assuring his potential client that he had built the addition. I suppose the family members

did it because they wanted to help him get work and felt that they didn't owe the unknown homeowner the truth. It turned out that I referred these relatives their genuine builder, and was privy to the scenario from several different perspectives. To this day, these upstanding folks have no idea the trouble they caused other people by misrepresenting the related builder's role. I understand what trial attorneys mean when they talk about the unreliable nature of eye witnesses. People who are disconnected from direct consequences are liable to say and do anything, particularly when pushed by a pro in pursuit of his livelihood. And now that I think of it, I have to confess that I have let a relative of mine use me as a reference in a rather deceitful way. The point is that you should trust your own observations as much as possible. And you should avoid relying solely on second-hand testimony, particularly from sources offered by your candidate.

The Pro Probe

On top of observable action, you can test a candidate's credibility in a quick one-question quiz. This has happened to me a number of times, in initial meetings with astute businesspeople. It was awhile after the first occurrence that I realized that my professional experience had been probed by an expert, something like a Vulcan scanner-beam.

I can remember that the query came at me a little out of context in the conversation, but I recognized it immediately as a worthy, interesting question. There were several associates on their side watching my body language and listening to my response as the car we were riding in got deathly silent. "So, Greg, what do you think would be a fair price for these units?" It was one of those scenes that I played out over and over in the shower at home as I critiqued my own answer.

What did they think about my response? How could I have better answered the question? In hindsight I recognize that we had detoured past a new residential development for the sole purpose of implementing this probe. They wanted to see what I knew.

In later chapters we will use such well-posed questions to help hire your designer and builder. The common thread to these kinds of queries is that it takes a pro of considerable experience to ask a sophisticated question. As a general rule, you must turn to others to help pose the question in advance. But they are an important arrow in the owner-manager's quiver.

Simmering Major Decisions

Most owners will know when they are facing a major decision. Their stress level will be accelerated and sleep will be fitful. The typical remodel will require that you make somewhere between two and ten tough calls. Almost all will involve money. If you ever get to the point where you seem overwhelmed by too many hard decisions, then you are micro-managing the project to fault. You need to be more selective in the problems you take on. Treat the smaller decisions with some humor and take more of the advice offered by your builder or designer. For those few crucial ones, however, I advise my clients to never make such a major decision upon one hearing, regardless of who is framing it for them. If required, "buy" some extra think time by shifting attention to the issues that force the difficult decision to the front burner. Seek several recommendations immediately, ensure that you pose the dilemma fairly, and attempt to understand the advice from the expert's perspective. Set an absolute deadline for yourself and let your pros know when to expect the decision. Then put the issue on "simmer," making sure it is not forgotten. Post a reminder in a spot that you frequently pass during the day. This will force you to consider the issue many times and in many different moods. When I do this, as I pass my simmering decision, unique ideas and considerations surface with amazing clarity, and sometimes I jot down another revelation for the note wall. It is not long before the problem has been replaced by a "this is what I have decided to do" note. And then I "wear" the decision up until the deadline, reflecting on it momentarily as I glance to the wall. For homeowners this may take two or three days, but this is rarely a problem for redo projects. If your pro needs direction sooner than this, he probably has made a mistake by omitting your requisite "heads-up" notice; do not compound his gaff with one of your own. Take the time to get comfortable with your big decision.

TEAM PSYCHOLOGY

A redo owner usually has a difficult time directing his pros. They know what they are doing, and the owner does not. The essence of this book is to level the playing field some. I prefer to think of the owner's role as that of the head coach of a sports team, and his major hires as assistant coaches. First, it is not possible for the head coach's key people to recommend how they themselves should be managed. The honcho-homeowner must do as much homework as he can, and come in with his demeanor set. He should avoid highlighting the fact that he is learning the role in the team's presence, although we know that this is exactly what will happen. Once players are onboard the team, much of the manager's job is psychological. With his assistants he plans and practices until he knows exactly what he wants to do, and the team knows what is expected. Construction is (you guessed it) game time!

A

B

TOP-DOWN TRANSOM

Some problems will arise whenever products are mixed. In photograph A, the transom window is by Anderson Corporation, which does not make a true-divided lite insulated french door. The builder shopped and found a pre-finished oak door package that satisfied the spec and that the owner loved. He got the interior trim right, but on the exterior he couldn't bring himself to throw away the luxurious oak casing, although shown otherwise in the drawings. Flagged by the architect, the co-operative and capable builder is required to correct the trim problem. Photograph B shows that even with aluminum capping butted to vinyl siding (an inexpensive technique), a much better solution can be found. This time the overall look of combined products is more important than preserving an optimized component.

The quarterback is the builder's lead carpenter. The builder and architect: offensive and defensive co-ordinators. Most field decisions are theirs. They send major issues upstairs to the head coach. Of course, the head coach can always take the reins directly, but he only does this in emergencies. He wants to give his assistant coaches and their players room to maneuver. They need to be allowed to fail slightly, just to the point of self-realization, but still within recovery distance. The game plan is meticulous, but everyone is heads-up for those turning points where improvisation is necessary.

As the owner you are a leader, not a "commander." If you want pleasant surprises from your team, you must not operate by fear or intimidation. Even corporate managers who "command" their subordinates know much more about their production process than you do yours. Ex-CEO Harold Geneen of ITT fame[3] says these loud-mouth generals are off-base anyway. Your own personal quest for excellence should pull them willingly into the process. Intimidation only works in the short run; genuine love of the game, mutual respect, goal setting, healthy competition, hard work, and leadership win in the long haul. It is great fun to do things well!

The redo head coach should hire driven people. Not yes-people who can be easily lead. They should be leaders themselves. Assume that they will make or break the job, not you. They should be people prone to adding a little touch here and there to make themselves proud of the job regardless of where the money falls. They should have a strong enough personality to talk down an obstinate worker if necessary. They should be optimists with enough experience to know the downside. They must be flexible. They must consider other viewpoints and enthusiastically pick up and carry a new torch simply for the challenge of it.

Your primary mission is to keep your key players motivated. Their attitude will catch fire and spread to the entire crew. You always want them to see the overall goal as their own first, and yours second. So you never want to blow the wind out of their sails, particularly in someone else's presence. You want them bringing future clients around boasting about "their" this and "their" that. Critiquing their work must be done with wisdom and a little forethought. The pro's pride in his work is your secret weapon. I recommend sugaring things with positive, then negative, then positive like I do to my son's soccer team. It could go something like this. "Bob, you were right. The bathroom tile is looking great. I am worried, however, about the oak threshold in the family room. I think we are all going to be sorry when this gets further along. I think it will look raggedy alongside the other new stuff. What do you think?" (discussion follows, and then) "I don't think I will be happy with what I see. What do we have to do to come up with a better solution?" (Then the exchange should end with another positive, where your pleasure with some other aspect is expressed.) If the pro is any good, he will explore the better solution and make a recommendation you will like. But most importantly, he will not resent the change in direction. You described the need to do something different and he put his name on the answer. And later when he sees you were right, he will begin to trust your judgment and bring you directly into his own decision-making process.

Don't expect the work to progress in a strictly linear way, one task building upon the other. Many builders encourage this because they have to mentally construct and price the job in this in-line fashion. This is their target. But it is not possible even with an architect providing reams of drawings to predict all aspects of the work. You and the builder should expect to go backwards occasionally to get something right. Changing work does not necessarily mean "extra" costs above his contract price. Bear in mind that it is a real pain to undo something you have just completed, so choose these critical issues carefully. In fact, this should be one of the primary goals in the construction phase: to catch these inevitable changes before the builder has to undo major portions of the work. This is a terribly demoralizing task. Therefore, intend not to plow straight ahead regardless, but to reduce these back-steps to relatively painless and inexpensive diversions. It seems to contradict the obvious, but by their research, *In Search of Excellence*[4] authors Peters and Waterman have shown that excellence comes from spirited teams that operate in rather chaotic and redundant ways.

To ensure that your pros will work with your best interest at heart, you must first show them your commitment to reciprocate the sentiment. The best professional managers have different "riffs" to use for this, and each subject has a different personality and a different set of concerns. My research for this book unearthed a plant manager who had many facilities to oversee with little time to spend in each. Prior to each visit he would study seating charts of the plant floor so he would know key people's names, faces, and something about their family. As the inspection entourage of executives passed through the facility he would pause periodically, interrupt the local bosses and talk for a minute with a worker. He would express sorrow at a recent death or touch on other details in their lives. By the end of the day, everyone in the plant knew of these inconspicuous conversations. The result: a warm fuzzy spot in the minds of its workers, and a grass-roots renewal of the company's goals. This did not happen in an impromptu way. It was secretly rehearsed.

The smart homeowner therefore should put such a demonstration on his to-do list very early in the redo. For each key person, probably your architect, builder, and lead carpenter, identify a different "riff" to use. What are they worried about? What family event is coming up? Then take some small but considerate action on their behalf with no fanfare. It can be something special for their daughter's birthday or it can be cleaning up the job site on a particularly grueling day. A pot of hot coffee and muffins at the right time. I had a client give me a coffee-table book on the work of Frank Furness, who had designed her original townhome. From this point on, I protected her interests like she was "family." These "riffs" should not be too frequent for they will lose their sparkle, but they will come back to you many times multiplied. Isn't it encouraging to know that being nice also means smart business?

MYTHS ABOUT PROCESSES WITH ARCHITECTS

Of the many remodeling-builders that I know, most are ill-informed about designer roles in general. When they have worked in teams they were unclear about what the architect was contracted by the owner to do, and many were hazy even as to what their own responsibilities were. This is not all the builder's fault, of course, but it is the primary reason for half-truths about such team processes.

So even the group perceived as most-knowledgeable has their share of architect myths. Small remodeling builders are a breed unto themselves. Few have played on the healthy teams typical in larger construction work. Out of necessity, they have evolved their own way of doing things. They may like one or two architects because their service "fits" the way they personally like to work. And they can move to extremes as they get more experienced, "loving" their fellow pro and "kicking dirt" on all others. Many perpetuate a negative stereotype of architects in general, based in part on their own ignorance and self-interest.

Probably the biggest myth of all is that architects "supervise" construction work. Even in full-service scenarios, the architect's role is carefully threaded among the other players so that he "observes" the progress of the builder's work as "agent" for the owner. The architect has set out (in drawings and specs) what the owner wants the redo to be, and the builder is responsible for the "means and methods" employed to make it happen. The roles of the triad (owner, builder, designer) are sewn together by cash flow. The builder does not work for the architect; he is paid by the owner. But he must pass potential changes and normal payment requests through the architect to the owner. The wisdom of this choreography escapes most people; it is a sophisticated management tool to force independent players to resolve their differences and operate in the owner's interest. But the designer should never tell the general contractor how to build.

Another myth causes much trepidation among architects. Owners, contractors, and unfortunately many designers themselves believe that architects must have all the answers. You know, the Renaissance man nonsense. Rarely does a project go by where a tradesman fails to confront me with a knowledge-challenge of some sort. I think it also comes from a general disdain for pencil-pushers. I take great delight in answering "how the hell should I know?" Architects do not possess the sum of experience of all the potential trades on a job. They are simply higher up on the deci-sion-making ladder. They don't know how to sweat copper pipe or balance circuits. But you should beware of those who pretend they do.

Cost Control

The rap about architects and cost overruns is not a myth, as much as I would like to be able to report the contrary. Even "us guys" who are in a position to know have a penchant for underestimating project costs. And for most redos this poses a genuine threat. Accordingly, the owner must ensure that many cost-control measures are built into the entire process. A lot of the designer bad press is exaggerated by builders. These are the same guys who might well fall out of the bid-cluster by $20,000 to $30,000! But this does not excuse missing the mark. Rather, it means that it is very difficult to estimate remodeling costs, particularly for designers. Unfortunately, there is no single, magic bullet. This entire book is laced with many interconnected ways to control project costs. As the process moves along, you must protect several important, imbedded, cost concepts.

First, you as owner should set the project budget several notches below your threshold for pain. And then you must maintain its sanctity with your best pokerface. Cost-creep happens at every turn, from the first sketch until the last window is cleaned. If you let your diligence wane, the disease will spread more rapidly. I will forgive you for lying to your team when you say "I don't have a nickel more to spend" although you know you have a cushion set aside. You should not "discover" this extra money until construction is well underway. The optimum point would be after all major surprises have been resolved but before final flooring, lighting, and hardware selections have to be made. Just as a skeet shooter must "lead" the pigeon,

A

B

CONTROL AND IMPROVISATION

Most builders will try to resist the concept of a Retainage, particularly if it is a "line-item" Retainage. This is where the owner withholds a percentage of the builder's progress payment for each cost category, until the entire redo is judged acceptable, and the Retainage released. This means that subcontractors whose task is completed early on have to wait for final payment. This is not what the subs want, of course. They want to get in, get paid, and get out, like the installers of the chimney for the zero-clearance fireplace in Photograph A. In this case, there was no Retainage, and when the architect tried to get a storm-collar placed over the flashing at the chimney (a standard component), the result was blank stares. Although the builder represented that he called the fireplace crew back, they never materialized. Because the owners had originally been concerned about the appearance of the prefab fireplace and chimney, the architect fabricated the component from a trash-can lid (Photograph B). With a little paint (flashing color-matched to the roof), the raggedy installation is corrected (Photograph C. Notice that the master bathroom window on the second floor has not been sacrificed for a masonry or frame chimney.) Improvisation such as this is the mark of a balanced team. In this case, the extra effort put forth by the designer overcame the lack of control of the work.

C

A

B

DECK LOW-DOWN

In most cases, rear decks should attempt to embrace the backyard. They should be designed to create a surface for specific outdoor activities, and to minimize railings as much as possible. Lighting should be integrated if it is affordable. Photograph A shows how a very inexpensive 2 x 6 pressure-treated deck can be well planned. Here 2 x 8 framing is used to keep the profile shallow, and the 20" deep steps are designed to float on final grade with only a gravel base. Note how the continuous 2 x 4 edge trim has been softened by a deep 45-degree bevel (Photograph B), and creates an identical profile on the side of the deck and step. The resulting two-riser deck satisfies its function with simple planes (Photograph C), and the steps can be repositioned in the future if the owners wish. In this redo, outdoor lighting was trimmed out of the budget. But a switch, a box for a low-voltage transformer, a wire-sleeve through the foundation, and a trim-plate on the exterior wall (right of the casement window) with wire coiled behind it, have been provided for a future do-it-yourself deck lighting project.

A

C

B

APPROPRIATE HIGH-END PRODUCTS

Doors are one of those places where every extra dollar you spend directly translates into quality ambiance. And of course, everyone seems to want those "french" or "patio" doors. This particular set by Pella (Photograph A) is for a lower-level family room that was to be private. Here the internal mini-blind option has been specified (between the double-glazing), which precludes the wear and tear external "window-treatments" would normally receive. The door is aluminum-clad on the exterior (in a special-order color) for low maintenance, and will be primed and painted on the inside (Photograph B) to match the interior color scheme. It has been fitted-out with stainless steel hardware, rather than the standard brass. Besides letting people pass, it can let light inside (Photograph D) or button-up for privacy as in Photograph E. This door cost almost twice what another french door might have. Part of the extra cost is spent on product support. Photograph C shows where the edge of the cladding has received a dent during construction. A call from the general contractor to the supplier produced a service call within two days, complete with a friendly technician who had the parts to fix the door on site. As the saying goes, you get what you pay for.

D

E

you must aim at a point short of the target and anticipate costs to fly into your comfort zone. But please, don't tell anyone about the secret budget.

Second, your major hires (the designer, builder, and maybe an expensive subcontractor) should be competitively solicited in both a businesslike and lineal fashion: First hire the architect using the expertise in this book, then the builder using the architect's skills, and then potentially a primary subcontractor using the builder's experience.

Third, as each team member is brought onboard, you should kick off a separate cost-cutting initiative. Each player should be asked for a recommendation similar to "what do we have to do to take $5,000 and then $10,000 out of this job?" The number goals will vary in relation to the job. These cost initiatives will force some heated discussions, but the project will benefit. In most cases the architect will need to revise the Contract Documents to record the changes made. Critical points for these initiatives are in the architect's sketch stage where several schemes are still under consideration; after the preliminary design is fixed and before construction drawings begin; and immediately after the builder is tagged as the selected-bidder and before his contract is drafted.

Finally, both builder and architect should be contractually obligated to control costs, but in different ways. The builder is familiar with signing the recommended fixed-sum type agreements. But the contract form should also include specific detail to minimize cost-creep as much as possible. A prime target is the builder's profit margin when the inevitable Change Order happens. For architects, it will be harder to bind-up their cost responsibilities because of the volatility of both construction cost estimates and the decision-making patterns of unknown, neophyte owners. When the architect is hired, the project usually exists only in the owner's mind. When the builder is

hired, the project should be well documented. But like any other profession, designers will agree to help you control your costs, if you know how to ask them, and if you are prepared to help them control theirs. The following chapter will show you how to hire an architect who is cost-conscious.

THE RUM LINE AND WORK TRIANGLE

Here are two important business concepts that owner-managers should keep in mind when negotiating for what you want. The Rum Line (Example 3) is a way to think about proposals containing a large amount of labor, which includes just about all groups you will likely do business with in a redo. You need to understand that when a pro prepares a quote for any job, he has a number range that he uses to figure his costs and therefore what he will charge for the job. The rum line is where he thinks most of his jobs should fall, say 75% of them, or really his bread-and-butter. But on each side of this Rum Line number are two other numbers that represent extreme prices that he is prepared to go to. To the right might be his expensive unit price for situations where he will risk losing the job. It may be "dirty" work that he'd just rather not do, he may sense that you will not check his number, or he may be busy and not sure how he will get it done (but at this price, he'll move something around). So he quotes a high number and moves on. If he hears from you, "great!" and if he doesn't, "no big deal."

On the other side of the Rum Line is his competitive number. This may be at or below a breakeven point where he pays his bills without making any profit. He will go to this number for jobs that he really

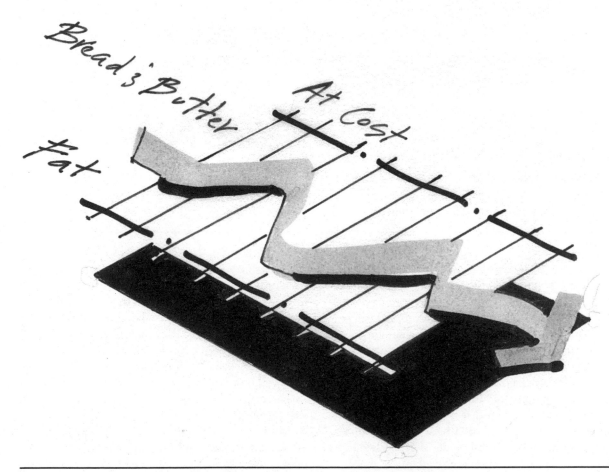

Bread & Butter

At Cost

Fat

EXAMPLE 3. *This is a way to visualize prices in professional proposals. To one side is his "take it or leave it" price, and to the other is his "I want to make sure I get this one" fee. Down the middle is the bread-and-butter of his business. Around 75% of his quotes will be centered along the Rum Line.*

THE RUM LINE

wants. Most commonly, he justifies this number for marketing reasons. This could be a major redo on a corner lot in an affluent neighborhood that he hasn't been able to work in. If he can see the "after" project photo augmenting his "brag book," he will set his proposed price short of the Rum Line. Maybe he wants to work with the other players in the project for future referrals. Or maybe he has just lost another job and

will use yours to bridge his crew to the next profitable one. Bear in mind that an account executive or a lead carpenter will not have the authority to vary from the Rum Line. It has to be the boss.

For redo owners, most number-noodling should be taken care of in the process of bidding the builder's contract. Hopefully the builder will shake out his sub prices. But there will be times when portions of the work must

Fast

Cheap

good

THE WORK TRIANGLE

EXAMPLE 4. *The rule for labor-intensive tasks: you can have any two facets, but not three.*

change, and a straight apples-to-apples competition is not practical. Holding the Rum Line concept in mind during these negotiations can be very rewarding. First, ask yourself "does this guy not want the job, and will he price it on the fat side?" If this is the case, find someone else. Most often your objective will be to try to move the price below the Rum Line. I suggest you first take his fast quote as a reference point, describe all the reasons he should want the job, ask him to think about a better price point, and have him defer his answer so he can "simmer" the idea. Notice that I have not called these Rum Liners unethical or dishonest. They are neither; they are businesspeople. And now, so are you.

Good managers know that all tasks cannot become the "Taj Mahal." Much of the art in management is intertwining both coarse and craftsmanly execution into an appropriate whole. And to a certain extent each trade has the potential to give it to you either way, and still in a professional manner. The Work Triangle is a good way to keep this nuance in mind. Example 4 shows a triangle whose corners are labeled Good, Fast, and Cheap. The triangle represents Work of any kind. The

rule says that you can have only two aspects of the triangle, and in any combination. If you ask in a respectful way, you should be able to get the same group to do the work in different ways. They can probably do it Good and Cheap if you don't need it Fast. Painters, for instance, like to keep a backlog of indoor work that they can turn to when other outdoor work gets rained out. They will buy-down some jobs to keep in this hopper. And according to the Work Triangle, if you need a Good and Fast job, do not waste time trying to get it Cheap. There are many variations. Take a minute to spin the Work Triangle and test how you want your hardwood floors done! You have more choices than most people realize; you just have to ask for them.

THE POWER OF TWO

Recently a client and I met with an attorney to discuss a Zoning Appeal for her redo. The zoning officer had disapproved my preliminary site plan because of his interpretation of a 100-year-old corner lot building setback. The meeting was to solicit the lawyer's thumbnail opinion of the situation, and to later retain him if the meeting "vibrations" were good. The attorney had come highly recommended by various local sources. He brought a young person from his office to the meeting, introduced him as his code research specialist, and by omission of the term "attorney," I assumed that he was either a paralegal or a law-degreed intern working at passing his bar exam. Several times during the meeting, the attorney asked his counterpart for specific code readings and opinion. After the meeting, my client expressed reservations about the attorney's command of the facts and his reliance on the younger technician. My response surprised her a bit.

I took reassurance in their two-man team. You see, professional service firms have a propensity to be poorly managed groups of underlings intent on making the marketing partner look his best. They are organized along ego lines. It is rather common to find architectural, engineering, law, and construction firms who try to hide the fact that most of the critical project work is performed by the second echelon. In too many complex professional settings, the "mouthpiece" is extensively briefed on details before he goes into the pressure cooker. And rather frequently he makes impromptu decisions that, when later examined by the project team, turn out to be both contraindicated and irreversible because of the negative light to be cast on the firm. I learned from savvy real estate development groups to look for functioning Guy-1 Guy-2 teams. They are careful to look at the "project manager" who will work exclusively on their project as well as how the principal is engaged in the delivery process. The two-guy is frequently written into the contract because they know that it is his enthusiasm and attention to detail that will bring pleasant surprises. The pro with his name on the shingle will be distracted by juggling other projects and problems. Although they will press for maximum involvement by the principal, they are secretly more concerned about the next rung down. So bear in mind that in firms larger than three or four employees, Guy-1 sets goals, manages money, and keeps the path clear for Guy-2 to keep you happy.

This axiom extends to every aspect of remodeling work. As owner you should look for two-man teams that compliment each other. You have seen the good-cop, bad-cop routine work on TV! In an architect-builder scenario the builder is the detail person who must deal with practical solutions, while the architect must keep the vision of a quality end-product on the table. In hiring builders, for example, I consider it a negative if the principal swings a hammer full time on the job. There is too much coordination and communication to be done elsewhere. A construction company employing the lead carpenter concept is preferred, all other things being equal.

COMMUNICATING BY DRAWING REDLINES

In construction, much discourse happens about and through architectural drawings. Every builder, lead carpenter, architect, drafter, project manager, and redo owner should learn the technique for communicating via drawing redlines. Redlining is a time-saving way to assure thorough coverage of any issue occurring in drawings. Just as its label suggests, the process involves marking up blueprints with a red pen or pencil. To redline a drawing set means to review every line or image on the prints, and leave a red mark for any comments that come to mind. Because architectural drawings are frequently very complex, small but important elements are easily lost. When red marks are made,

A

B

LEAD CARPENTER

The builder who has a strong "lead carpenter" has a distinct advantage. This allows him to let this long-time employee have one-job tunnel vision, which is what many carpenters really want. Then he can work in his high-value zone, making things for one client (Photograph C), without having to worry about the larger problems associated with running a business. He is frequently a jack-of-all-trades, but particularly good at trim carpentry, inside and out (Photograph A). Although he will not normally make money-deals with subs, he is the one who directs them. In Photograph B, a Lead Carpenter shoots elevations with a transit to guide the excavator. He will know every nuance of the construction drawings, but will probably not be privy to the Contract For Construction between the owner and builder.

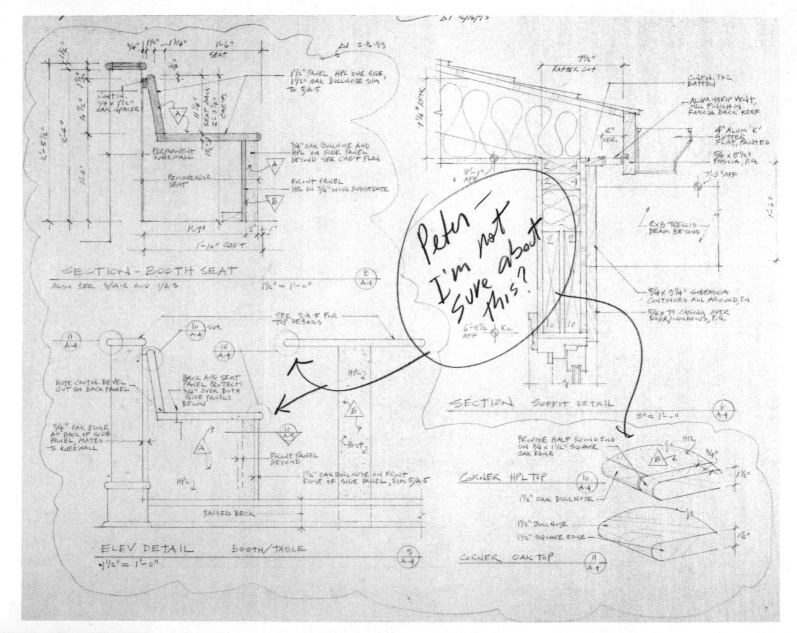

EXAMPLE 5. *Architectural drawings should be treated as communication tools. Reviewing and "redlining" prints is an important, time-saving technique for asking questions or giving direction. When the architect is in the design or construction document phase of his service, you should ask for progress prints, review them closely, mark them up, and return them promptly.*

they should be considered instructions for the person who will next receive the drawings to work from. The redlines should preclude having to talk directly to the person; ideally, they should be self-explanatory.

For example, as I prepare working drawings for a redo and approach completion, I make it a habit to run a set of blueline prints for internal review. Then in a different workspace I go through the documents, redlining the entire set, top to bottom. Both the new prints and new location help me take a fresh look. Either myself or a draftsman will then execute the redlines by isolating each red mark, resolving the issue, illustrating the change in the drawing, and then checking off the image on the redline set. Marking over the redlined issue with yellow pencil is an architectural convention that indicates resolution of the problem. This allows me (or anyone else) to walk up to a drafting station, glance at the redline drawings, and immediately know the status of the work. It also facilitates retracing the production process when trying to find the cause of an error. I frequently ask new builders to redline a drawing set, along with my version, as a precursor to a cost-cutting or shakedown meeting. Also, I try to get owners to redline drawings at several different project stages, both in design and construction documents.

The redlining technique is an important management tool to learn, even if you think you will not understand everything in the drawings. There is no reason why a redline mark can't be a big circle with a note saying "I don't get it!" This tells the designer to explain it to you. Your returning a set of drawings well-bloodied, as we say, is an important signal to send to your designer, particularly if he knows you have a copy. The message he gets is that you expect a response to each redlined item, and will probably start the next meeting by going over your version. Or restated: you will hold him to the details, and are creating a paper trail to retrace if necessary. You should buy yourself several red pens at the outset of your redo, and ask that you be given at least two copies of all drawings provided by your architect, for your review. When given the set, let the designer know when he will receive a redlined response. Ask for a briefing on his drawing notations to speed up your learning the way different graphics refer back-and-forth. When you review the drawings, find a large flat table, and go through them slowly. Work right-to-left, and top-to-bottom, which is the way they are prepared. When finished marking your redlines, date the set, and then make a copy to keep. Whether you mail or deliver them to the recipient, you can be sure he will be impressed, and subsequently, on his toes. You will have systematically and completely expressed your wishes, while saving everyone's time in the process.

DIGITAL DANGER

I wonder if my machine knows when I talk negatively about its digital brethren? Should I back-up my files before I do? Like any other sophisticated tool, a computer will perform miracles in a given task, and be a total waste of time in others. And just like a cement mixer, if you put dirty aggregate in it, you will get weak concrete, regardless of how many new buzzers and whistles are on the machine. But computers have a unique and astounding ability to make the uninitiated see "competency" and "precision" where the exact opposite may exist. When an architect, a builder, or a kitchen dealer talks about his-computer-this, and his-computer-that, your BS-radar should begin its audible alarm.

Architects and engineers are the worst culprits at overselling digital services. I was at a land planner's office awhile back, talking about color printers for no

COMPUTER CRAZIES

If you are a computer buff, don't waste your time trying to draw your plans with the software that implies it can make you an overnight designer. A better use you would be to put the machine to work managing your redo, starting with the forms provided herein. Be sure to place the project bid results in a spreadsheet before selecting a builder, so you can see if any bargains are hidden in the numbers. Another appropriate use would be the maintenance of product schedules, to give to the designer. This would combine shopping for things you would like to use in the project, and record-keeping. A database maybe. Also be sure to try to work a new computer area into your plans. How about in the kitchen? If you want to draw something with a CAD application, refer to Chapter 5 and make a library of Planning Objects to help the architect sophisticate the design.

particular reason. To illustrate a point, he went into his flat files and pulled out a 30" x 42" staking plan for a subdivision that was absolutely beautiful. A civil engineering firm had plotted it, multicolored, with their state-of-the-art CAD system. He said, "Don't be too impressed, Greg, because it is totally bogus. Full of glitches. The owners are suing the engineers for the $20,000 it cost, because it is not even close to being accurate." I, who should have known better, would have sworn that it had come from NASA itself.

In fact, problems with computers go beyond just creating a false impression of precision; the operators themselves frequently lack the hands-on experience to shape the product for use in the real world. It is as if their mastery is of the software, at the expense of the widget that squirts out the other end. In architecture, this translates into CAD specialists that trade-off construction field-expertise for drawing production capability. Now in some specialties, like spec office buildings, single-family spec homes, or complicated, long-

lived projects like hospitals and airports, this may be a smart trade. But not in remodeling, where the lifespan of the project on the boards is short, the detailing is custom, and personnel must be more adept at construction administration and building costs than at their layering logic in AutoCad. Please don't misunderstand. Computers are solid-gold in the right place. In my practice I use them for many things. But I believe that it is a serious mistake for a designer to force his documentation to be 100% computer generated, although I have met a handful who espouse this philosophy. They are computer advocates. And like other zealots, they are prone to laying bad eggs with other people's money.

If Stephen Spielberg combined film, hand art, and computer choreography to create Star Wars, then surely a mixed bag is appropriate for your redo as well. As I was reading a computer magazine the other day, I noticed that even computer animation specialists use hand-drawn artwork to "storyboard" projects before final production begins. So even the guys who make their living off them know that computers must be used judiciously. Before I set a computer to a production-line task, I make sure that the operator has very precise and limited marching orders, much as I would do to kick off some complicated structural engineering work. A mistake or unlucky break in managing such high-priced, specialized efforts can seriously damage the production budget, and therefore the quality of the overall project that I have to deliver.

Example 6 shows a typical CAD drawing by a highly respected kitchen dealer. This 3-D view would normally be accompanied by a cabinet plan and elevations. While such software is marketed heavily, some offering rudimentary color rendering capability, the advantages for the owner are limited. The fact is that another dealer's drawing would be effectively indistinguishable from this one, given the same layout. Although the translation from 2-D to solid is surely fast and elegant, particularly if viewed on the monitor, the design "touches" that make all the difference are absent. Your assurances as to what can be expected are sketchy, certainly no better than a hand-drafted one would have been. Kitchen design is a lot more than placing and counting cabinets. A better design job could have been done with quick marker sketches, combined with a sample/swatch board and selected details. This is what interior designers do. Ultimately, the quality of the kitchen that is fabricated in your home is in the minds of the sales staff and in the hands of its crew, outside the PC software. On the other hand, there are many genuine advantages that accrue to the dealer when he uses the computer system, not the least of which is a product-specific database linked to his plan. This, of course, places your order like greased lightning, as soon as you write the check.

Many builders try to attract design-build work by touting inhouse CAD systems, but the documents they produce are as simplistic as their buildings are ugly. Computers cannot substitute for design training and experience. And when bidding, general contractors will talk profusely about their computer estimating systems. But as we will see in later chapters, sometimes this makes them reluctant to show you numbers the way you need to view them. They may have invested in a system that hampers their ability to be flexible, which is one of the primary things to look for in your team. You should presume that they know how to generate their quotes with some accuracy, the same way you presume the architect will design a building that will stand up.

So, you should take all the computer talk with a large grain of salt, and not be too concerned with how your pros produce their service. And you should beware of the machine's ability to mask inexperience and place inappropriate detail in the wrong spot. Results are what is important. You need only require that these results arrive as substantial and well-crafted instruments, in a timely manner, according to contract, and end up in the hands of field people who know what to do with them. Don't buy anything because it is said to be computer-designed. For the remodeling owner, computers are primarily marketing devices, by which they can be just as misleading as they are effective.

POSITIVE REDUNDANCY

Where did we get the idea that it is a mistake to do things twice? It may have sprung from our natural tendency toward optimism. Builders particularly perpetuate one-time tasking because it is one of their primary objectives; it directly affects their profit margin. But

A KITCHEN CAD DRAWING

EXAMPLE 6. *The printed output from kitchen-design software can be a double-edged sword. A perspective drawing such as this is exclusively a communicating tool, not a contractual instrument. While it is great for representing how your cabinets and appliances will mass together, don't expect its every nuance to appear in your home. These kinds of illustrations will all carry the disclaimer that reads something like: "This is an artistic representation . . . We do not warrant that the actual kitchen will not vary somewhat . . . etc." Unless the kitchen is designed independently and documented better, the quality of your kitchen will depend largely on the minute details that exist in the intentions of the dealer and his installers, most of which they are not capable of documenting, and attaching to your purchase agreement. This detail-documentation zone is traditionally the domain of interior designers. To get comfortable with what you are buying directly from a kitchen dealer, you must visit successful installations and pay attention to small details, such as toe-kicks, appliance fits, counter edges and their terminations, and lighting, just to mention a few. (Kitchen design and illustration by Petersen Kitchens, Inc., Bryn Mawr, PA.)*

in complex and expensive undertakings like remodeling, preparing for the "downside" is wise, not wasteful. You can imagine the relief of white-knuckled passengers when hearing of the number of redundant systems built into airplanes. As owner-manager, you must remember that the gaps between trades, such as from carpenters to electricians, and builders to designers, are always prone to problems. Cross-checking is one way to strengthen the weak zone.

The following chapters describe several areas where I recommend that a backing-up task be performed. Probably the best example is in the specification and purchasing of owner-sensitive products. Here the builder is required to have suppliers prepare complete "catalog cut" packages to verify purchases, even though the designer has performed his own version earlier. This is one of those areas in which experience has taught me to expect problems that can hold up the job or create unnecessary Change Orders. It is where the owner is always intimately engaged, and where job quality can die quickly. If product purchases were baseball, the architect would be third base and the builder, shortstop. The designer plays out front and catches anything he can touch, while the shortstop overlaps his field of play behind. He must assume that the third baseman will drop the ball, and he will have to make the catch. And we all know that the third baseman will bobble a few. The smart manager will make sure his team works on back-up responsibilities in the seam, between positions, before game day.

White Lies and Shooting High

I spent many years taking pride in being bluntly honest. Then as my hair silvered, I began to see that from a management standpoint, honesty is not always the best policy. Strangely enough, I think the realization began in some long-lost conversation about the Vatican and birth control. And then the opinion took its final form when I struggled with a reasonable scenario, whereby President Clinton would earnestly confess that he had tried but never inhaled marijuana! Now as I tick back through the shortlist of managers I consider special, I see that excellent leaders must tell a few well-placed white lies. And further, being fallible, we human beings usually fall short of our lofty goals. We will, however, shift from slovenly to brilliant if the mark is set well beyond our slip-back point by an experienced manager. I can still remember a project engineer telling me that he had set his internal delivery deadline a week ahead of my requirement. I watched him lovingly direct his team, but he never flinched when he handed off "my" drop-dead time, making me the bad guy. He was setting the goal high, and verbally expressing his absolute expectation of its achievement, while at the same time expecting them to miss the target. At the last minute I knew he would forgive their shortcoming. This he could afford, because he had the downside covered with plenty of overrun time.

One might say that a perfect project is "shooting high" and that the architect's documents illuminate this goal. I confess that I have never completed a redo to my total satisfaction. My drawings and specs are never completely bug-free. When I return to sites I see the things that I tried to get "right" but didn't quite succeed. Other people don't see the blemishes because they aren't privy to the original target. And yes, owners too usually have a mental list of decisions that they would love to have back. Maybe it is a question of scale. That is, a leader must hold up a worthy challenge to the entire group, but stand ready to assist the individual who will surely fall short. But the point for us

HIGH CEILING

Large spaces need more head room than the standard 8-foot ceiling provides. And to get this extra dimension you can either step down several risers, or raise the ceiling height as was done in this redo. Here the new ceiling joists were set on top of the old joists (not flush, as would be expected) on a new bearing plate (Photograph B), totally 12 inches. This is an extremely economical way to convert a typical room into a 9-foot high space, ready to be accentuated by some architectural element such as the large flush-ceiling box window that will be added into the opening in Photograph A. Upstairs in what will become a new master-suite, the level change shown in Photograph C is handled by two curved risers (Photograph D). Because it is well planned, this potential constraint introduces a pleasant level change within the owners' private space, as well as allowing a high ceiling in the family room below.

C

D

folks at the scale of our own humble castle is that the redo-owner must set lofty objectives, feign the total expectation of their fulfillment, and then be prepared to get it "close enough."

LOOSE LIPS

High on the mess-hall wall was a stern looking Marine reminding us that "loose lips sink ships!" And only now, many years after my naval service, do I fully understand how much trouble a few careless words can cause. This is a common problem when construction is taking place, particularly when one of the owners is home during the day. The house may be filled with workmen, many of whom are not privy to the big picture. Most are interested in making their job easier. Their casual conversation with the check-writer may result in inadvertent changes and unhappy owners. Many times the homeowner is not aware of the ramifications of his statements. Or that a change here that seems rather straightforward will cause a big problem over there. Usually the workmen themselves do not understand "why" the work is as specified. As a general rule, owners should be very reluctant to talk about the work with anyone other than the architect and builder. When a workman initiates such a conversation, the owner should answer, "What does Bob think about that?" More than I would like to admit, I see even the builder himself driving wedges into decisions called for in the architect's drawings. He may not agree with a particular product or architectural feature for any number of reasons, which he certainly has a right to do, but the method of airing the problem should be neither underhanded nor inept. He may try for an impromptu okay, and put it quickly in place. The owner rarely gets a credit back (contract price reduced)

for the change, or the builder would not be proposing it in the first place. And if the owner does not like the result, going backward is very expensive. This whole scenario is possible because the owner is not used to playing it close-to-the-vest when managing people. You should talk with the workers about their kids and the weather, but when the work comes up casually, err on the side of quiet. Write yourself a reminder to talk to your architect first and then the builder about the issue. Do not defeat your own system.

TOP DOWN AND BOTTOM UP

Several years ago my older brother sent me some literature on management theory.[5] I was pleased to find therein many nuggets to make remodeling projects go smoother. But you should know that in applying these principles, you will be a smarter manager than most of the pros you will encounter. Most will expect things to go according to outdated thinking. So stick to your guns! Specifically, they will assume that excellent projects follow the assembly of individually optimized parts. For reasons that are mostly economic and technological, today's "perfect systems" need to be built differently. Contemporary "systems" thinking is based on several scientific observations.

> *If given a system whose parts are functioning perfectly, then you can be sure that the whole system will not be.*
>
> *And further, if you have a whole system which is working at maximum efficiency, then none of its parts will be.*

These axioms are at the heart of many remodeling problems. Unfortunately, it is bottom-up thinking that governs most construction trades. Contractors are honest and hard-working, but primarily lineal problem solvers. One particular general contractor I know has bid many of my jobs, but has been awarded very few. His frustration is usually expressed as, "How can these guys do the project for this little money? The owner will get a hack job!" I have recently suggested to him that if he breaks the job down into separate tasks, prices them competitively, and then simply adds them up, he is absent a step. The missing top-down step is to look at the overall project and say "I should be able to do this for X dollars." Where both top and bottom approaches conflict is where a shake-out must occur. Remember: Optimum "parts" will mean a mediocre "whole."

Contemporary managers would work toward four objectives. They should:

- Deal with sets of problems interactively, not in isolation.
- Manage organizations to fulfill the goals of its parts, and in so doing serve its own objectives.
- Guide groups to serve social purposes, and thereby achieve the group's goals.
- Design or use systems which will learn and adapt effectively under conditions of rapid change.

Interactive Problem Solving

From the above list of management objectives, several extremely important ideas emerge. First, consider a rather typical remodeling problem, ripe for an interactive solution. This redo involved a new first-floor family room with master bath above. Because of a tight zoning envelope, the family room was to be unusually small. I had designed it around specific furnishings and it was down to within inches of being nonfunc-

tional. I arrived on the job to find a plumbing chase in a spot that absolutely precluded the owners from placing a sofa facing their eagerly anticipated media center. The plumber was independently contracted by the owner against my advice. The general contractor was engaged to deliver the addition down to primed drywall and final flooring. The plumber's deal was struck upon his hand-written proposal, which failed to attach my construction drawings showing the soil stack within an existing masonry wall. We had a ten-inch-square bump in what should have been a flush wall, for two reasons. First, the plumber felt that cutting his chase out of the block wall was unnecessarily difficult and he intended all along to circumvent the drawings. Second, the lack of communication (and contract) between the builder and plumber prevented the general contractor from raising a red flag, so the architect needed to be the bad guy. In the presence of the owner, builder, and plumber, I explained the importance of this ten inches and placed the hot potato in the builder's and plumber's hands. "What do we have to do to get that chase in the wall?" They came back later with the solution. The builder would rent the plumber his pneumatic hammer-drill and the plumber would split his "extra" with the owner.

The lessons to be learned here in "systems" terminology are numerous. The individual part (plumber) was required to do something he considered ridiculous in order for the whole system (furnished space) to work well. Plus, the owner had almost sabotaged his redo by disconnecting a part (plumbing sub) from the interconnected whole (architect-builder team). He ultimately paid the plumber the money he expected to save by avoiding the general contractor's markup. The owner had made a poor hiring decision. His plumber was really a "jobber" specializing in repair work, which is why he didn't have the appropriate tool. But the real

A

B

C

BONUS READING NOOK

Although not specifically in their design program, these owners have built their children a warm place to store books and browse their library. The architect proposed this space because the program had extra space to fill over the garage, and he wanted to bring light and genuine function into what would otherwise be only a dark, dead-end hallway. To bring natural light deep into the building mass, while up close to the mother-structure, he chose to use a single bay of a greenhouse glazing system. These curved aluminum glazing-bars have integral tracts to accept continuous sun-shades from top to bottom. Photograph A shows the addition taking shape over the existing garage. The existing pair of windows are removed and replaced with a new single unit in Photograph B. Notice how the greenhouse choice defers to the architecture of the adjacent dormer (Photographs C and D). A padded cushion will be added to the window seat in Photograph E, and lighted by the pair of sconces on the high wall. Add a plane of good books and a hanging plant, and the space will practically force the kids to stop and read.

D

E

point here is the interconnected nature of the problem. The answer was not found until owner, plumber, architect, and general contractor were engaged. Notice that the solution required a construction taboo: one trade using another's tools. The system had forced the dismantling of an artificial partition.

Your Goal Is Their Profit

Does "fulfilling the goals of the parts" mean managing your redo to assure that your team makes a profit? Absolutely. This is particularly critical for subcontractors and product suppliers who are too far removed to take pride in your project's successful completion. They are there to make money, as are all your pros. You as the leader should directly address this issue with each contractor, but only after their "deal" is struck. Then individually, or in a group meeting, you and your architect should express this primary goal: to avoid the surprises that hurt anyone financially. This is not at odds with maintaining a cost-competitive environment. Nor is it a mutually exclusive objective. It is possible to get the quality redo you are after, for a fair price, and to protect your team's profitability at the same time. It is your wearing the cloak of their concern that will ensure their extra measure on your behalf.

A recent encounter in a lighting showroom is a prime example. I know that I have more than my share of run-ins with rude salesmen, because when an architect goes to a product showroom (that sells retail as well as to the trade), he normally goes to identify a product for purchase by someone else. He may have seen the item in his catalog but wants to feel its quality. He uses the showroom, and then specifies the product (on behalf of the owner) to a contractor who may or may not choose to buy from that same supplier. Sometimes I accompany the owner on visits to kitchen, flooring, plumbing, and lighting showrooms, and sometimes I venture out on my own. Showroom employees are frequently resentful of the fact that they may have to be more on their toes to assist the pro and then not get the ultimate sale! The showroom owner or sales manager knows, however, that it is the pros who send them big sales, but in rather circuitous ways. So in this recent visit, I introduced myself and my client to the salesman something like this: "We are remodeling a home, and we'd like to look at a list of lighting fixtures for which we have allowances and generic product picks. In the process we'd like to leave with enough information to allow the general contractor or his electrician to call in the order. We want to do everything we can to make sure you get the business; do you have a card?" I was surprised to see his demeanor change and from that point on he was unusually helpful. Why did his manner change? Because we had assured him that our goal was to help him meet his goal, to sell product and feed his family.

Careful with Missionaries

Of the foregoing systems objectives, I would be most cautious with the call to "achieve larger social purposes" through your redo. I have seen a lot of stupid things done with lofty intent. This includes energy conservation, solar utilization, material recycling and reuse, and historic preservation, all of which are certainly worthy individual goals, but only when they are placed in a hierarchy among other important objectives. Too often, these specialists trade off many architectural fundamentals to achieve the exotic objective. Less socially oriented, but just as zealously touted, are timberframing and prefabrication construction techniques, and computer-aided design (CAD) processes. You see, I can warn people about these specialists because I was one.

Early in my career I worked for the AIA Research Corporation in the HUD Residential Solar Demonstration Program. A major part of my job was to scrutinize the process and projects that emerged when federal money was poured into the national solar cause. In hindsight, I understand that although we were trying to "push the envelope" for very good reasons, individual homeowners suffered from what I now consider to be a poor success ratio. From an architectural design standpoint, most of the solar homes were eccentric albatrosses. I was crushed when I toured the much-publicized home of a famous solar architect. There I heard him confess that he was sorry that he had "spit in the eye" of his neighborhood when he built his residence. In a traditional suburban setting he had turned his glass-box to the optimum true-south, contrary to the axis of the confined streetscape. Later research indicated that his degree of off-orientation would have had little impact on solar gain. I am certain that now he recalls those statistics, and winces every time he pulls into his driveway.

I do believe it is important for redo owners to ask themselves how they feel about including social objectives into the project. It is admirable to put your money where your heart is. But bear in mind two things: First, these goals almost always have a higher first-cost. You must be aware that saving and reusing an existing window is always more expensive then throwing the old one in the dumpster. And second, the existing home is usually the millstone that holds down any attempt to break new barriers. As an example, I often recommend that owners insulate their redo only to code minimums and then if they want to spend more money to reduce their utility costs, we will work on the main house which many times is totally inadequate. My recommendation therefore is similar to that required by Health Maintenance Organizations when using doctors. That is, you should hire a general practitioner first and then use him to plan your use of specialists in the social-goal arena. Your generalist architect will weed out the missionaries and make sure that any specialty work is appropriate to the whole. And God bless you for worrying about the big picture.

A Process of Adaptation

Your final objective is really the heart of this text. The ability to learn and adapt will be one of the most important traits to look for when you hire your primary team. In simple terms, when you make out a form for your pro to fill out, he should in fact fill it out even if he considers it silly. He must be able to adapt. After all, the essence of changing a home is adapting old to new. The owner-manager must learn and adapt as well. In subsequent chapters I will continue to lay out a very detailed process. You will follow this path maybe only three quarters of the time. When you get lost or face a problem not addressed, you should come back to the management ideas in this chapter. They will give you a basis upon which to make your own call, and then get back on the prescribed course again. I would be surprised if you find a builder-architect team willing to take the enclosed contracts just as I have written. I expect rather, that some tasks may move from one player to the other (owner included). As long as you learn why these requirements are there, ask them of your pros, and then are prepared to adjust the process a little, you will do just fine.

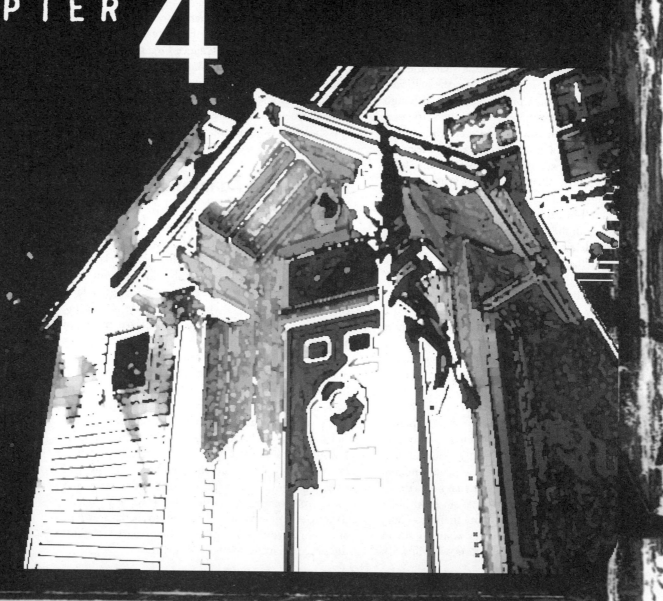

CHAPTER 4

HIRING A DESIGNER

A HIRING METHODOLOGY

I recommend that you hire a designer in four steps. First you need to compile a long list of candidates. Second, you should cull this list to qualified firms only. Then you need to solicit proposals from and meet with the architects on the short list. Finally, you should select your favorite designer and negotiate the terms of his contract. But before we walk through these four steps let's consider a few important issues.

Psychology of the Courtship

As you seek out the first pro for your project, keep in mind that the courtship knife cuts both ways. You want to find a designer who will be easy to work with and will yield your dream home, but it is just as important that you appear to be an attractive "catch" for him. Your new management expertise must make his job easier, not harder. A subtle message in everything you do (at least through signing his contract) should be:

I will be your perfect client. We will do good things together. You will not have to hold my hand because I know what to expect. Aren't we much farther along than your typical client?

I once read that the ideal relationship between an architect and his client is that of the Victorian wife. She operated in the background, getting everything that she wanted, and he thought he did it all! So you want to be able to control your designer's actions, completely undetected. If you follow the management goals in Chapter 3, they tell you to signal to your architect that you want to meet his objectives first. So what is it then, that designers are looking for?

At the top of the list is the prospect of doing excellent work. The designer wants to find clients who care about a quality result and will value his design advice. He wants a zero-hassle, nonconfrontational relationship with the project owner. His favorite client is one who can consider options, render decisions, and then not look back. I discourage my clients from drawing once I have been retained. Owners suffer the same malady as intern architects; they are prejudicial toward any solution that comes from their own hand. Once they have arrived at a design, they have a hard time seeing it any other way. A seasoned designer will take several different approaches, then cut and paste to a synthesis. One of my past mentors had a personal rule that prohibited clients from taking drawings away from sketch-design meetings, which upset some people. His rule was to preclude the owners from trying to debug problems themselves. He did not want the owner drawing parallel to him and then appearing at the

re-rfp.wps
REQUEST FOR PROPOSAL   **Architectural Services**

Date: September 15, 1995   Property: John and Mary Green
                                                                   1492 Columbus Drive
                                                                   Towner, PA 19088

Dear Designer:

You have come to our attention as a designer experienced in local residential work. We would like to entertain your proposal for the design of our remodeling project. I have enclosed some photography of our home. Located at the above address, it is:

A two story brick home with 4 Bedrooms, 2 baths, Dining Room, Living Room, Laundry Room. Without it's single car garage, the home is roughly 2000sf.

Currently, our goals are to:

Reconfigure our home to reflect the absence of all but one of our children. Preserve or downsize the formal LR/DR areas of the home and augment the informal Kitchen-Den areas. The Kitchen-Den area should directly connect to a new outdoor patio space which will be used both day and night. Open up the existing Kitchen into a new Den. The appliances and cabinets in the Kitchen will be replaced. The new Den will include built-in cabinetry for a media center and a fire-place. Also we would like to update the master suite by providing exclusive access to a new bathroom, more closet space, and a dressing/sitting area for TV viewing. We would like to consider the conversion of one of the upper bedrooms to a Work-Studio and Library.

We feel our unique design challenge is to:

Accomplish the functional interior goals and improve the curb-appeal of the home at the same time. The architecture may appear newer (and better) than existing, but it must be respectful of the older structure. We would like to flood more natural light into the house but increase our level of privacy and security. We would also like to create many warm places for indoor plants and art objects.

Please call at your earliest convenience to arrange a meeting at our home. Generally, weekends or weekday evenings are better for us. It is important that you use the attached Proposal Form to facilitate a productive meeting. We also hope you will bring along a portfolio of local remodeling work, a short list of satisfied customers, and sample project instruments. We are eager to see design drawings, construction drawings, and cost estimates for a typical home redo project.

We anticipate conforming our design commission with AIA Document B151, Owner-Architect Abbreviated Form and later contracting a builder with your guidance and AIA Document A107. We hope you will provide Construction Administration for us, as well as the other services noted on the Proposal Form. We have been advised that the indicated service package will ensure a quality project, but of course we will consider advice to the contrary.

It is important that we have your proposal by October 1 so we can be in a position for construction to start sometime next summer. If you need access to the house for preparing the proposal, call Mary at 664-0021 and arrange an appointment. We are excited at the prospect of your help and look forward to meeting you in person.

Respectfully,

A REQUEST FOR PROPOSAL (RFP) COVER LETTER

EXAMPLE 7. *This document should be used in conjunction with Example 8 to solicit design services for your redo.* To prepare your RFP, you will need to substitute your own language into the underlined portions.

---

next meeting with a solution that negated his interim work. I encourage my clients to "think through my pencil" by calling me anytime with ideas. If you have drawings already prepared, you should show them after your architect is hired. And even then, make sure you treat them as exhibits of your "initial intent" and tell him that you expect the design to change.

Any unique promotional aspect to your project will make it attractive. He wants others to hear about the work, so the phone will continue to ring. Your site

re-pform.wps
PROPOSAL FORM   **Architectural Services**

Date: September 15, 1995   Property: John and Mary Green
                                                            1492 Columbus Drive
                                                            Towner, PA 19088

Dear John and Mary Green:

1. For your project as described in the attached RFP, I am pleased to present this proposal. For the following architectural services:

    Design Phase Basic Service:
        kickoff meeting plus one subsequent design-session with owner
        zoning code review, telephone confirmation w/official
        field measurement of the building
        inhouse underlay drawings of existing building's plans/elevations
        design sketches on tracing paper
        final hardline design drawings on diazzo prints, floor plans/elevations, meeting presentation
        written preliminary Estimate of Construction Cost
    Construction Documents Basic Service:
        general specifications
        site plan if required
        structural member design/sizing, assuming standard platform framing/concrete spread footings
        building floor plans and exterior elevations
        interior elevations of bathrooms, built-in cabinet or unique treatment areas
        door and window schedule, product specific
        chases/soffits provided for heating, air-conditioning, and plumbing
        selected details and section drawings
        electric lighting and device plan
        electric lighting schedule, product specific
        room finish schedule and allowances
        generic HVAC spec requiring design-build drawings of builder
        first owner-redline meeting for document revisions at 80% complete
        builder's bid co-ordination, Invitation, Bid Form
        redline meetings and document revisions per builder shakedown
        preparation of builder's Construction Contract
    Construction Basic Service:
        co-ordination of HVAC and plumbing layout
        construction administration including: Change Orders, biweekly Payment Requests, punch lists, Certificate of
                Substantial Completion and Final Payment
        site observation visits, once weekly (not including Job Meetings)
        Job Meetings with owner and builder, weekly
        final one-time color and product finish specification

2. I will require the following compensation:

3. This compensation is exclusive of typical reimbursed expenses. For one such reimbursable item, 24"x36" diazzo blueline prints, I will charge:

4. For preapproved Additional Service labor, I will charge the following hourly rates for myself and other specific individuals:

5. Should the you elect to alter the forgoing mix of architectural services, I will either debit or credit the above compensation as follows:

    Add to the Construction Documents the following services: Credit/Debit
        kitchen/bath plumbing and appliance product schedule $_____
        kitchen/bath cabinet schedule, plan, and elevations $_____

    My recommended changes to the above service mix, as follows: $_____

6. I will be able to begin and complete this work within the following timeframe:

7. This proposal includes the following measures to keep Construction Costs within budget:

Signed:_____   Company:_____   Date:_____

EXAMPLE 8. *This form is for the designer's use in responding to your RFP. It requires him to propose a fee for a standard ser-*

THE PROPOSAL FORM

vice package which can be compared "apples to apples" with other designers, and allows him to propose changes to both services and compensation. The standard service list is repeated in the owner-designer contract (Example 14) which will be used to hire the successful architect.

may have high visibility. Maybe you intend to seek publication in the newspaper, or intend to throw a large house-warming party. Make sure your candidate designer hears these kinds of intentions during the hiring process.

Architects are notorious for acting on behalf of the project at the expense of their own profit. The architect will readily throw-in free services to help the project look as good as possible. Being human, he will be attracted to those who rave about his work. It is a good idea to schmooze him a little as you review his portfolio. "I love how this one is simple and elegant!" His past projects are his children; if you compliment his kids he will like having you around.

Every architect has a backlog of design ideas or "treatments" in his head that he wants to explore—a shift in materials, a detail that he didn't have time to redesign in the last job. Each new project represents an opportunity to refine his work. Because he is a problem-solver, he will be attracted to uniquely posed design challenges. For this reason, a well-worded "challenge statement" is an integral part of your bait. Notice in the example Request for Proposal (Example 7) that these owners ask for perceptual things: warm places, natural light, privacy, security, etc. This is the stuff of good design, making occupants feel targeted emotions. Words like "formal, luxurious, plain, quiet" will get his juices going. You should challenge him to excellence with carefully authored, emotional language.

About Designers

A remodeling designer should be comfortable sitting at your table while the kids play loudly in the next room. You should enjoy having coffee and chatting with him. He will need to meet with you and the builder at your kitchen table many times. This is an important reason to meet your short-listed candidates at your home, not his studio. If he acts pompous or eccentric, he is out of his element. The world of remodeling is one of spousal arguments and barking dogs. He should not come to your home in a three-piece power suit unless that is the way you and your builder will dress during project meetings. He should be brutally honest. If you need to hear bad news, he must be capable of getting the issue on the table. He

must be able to disagree with the builder. You need a guide, not a follower.

Two Types

Construction experts recognize two types of architects—the designers and the technologists. I have heard them described as the Italian Suits and the Brooks Brothers Bunch (although I am not sure where the Flannel Shirt falls into this model). The design architects are the ones with the ability to make quick, exciting sketch presentations to their clients. They are generalists and idea generators. They keep up with market trends and new products. They tend to be good people-managers and are usually moved to marketing positions. They also can suffer from short attention spans, undue optimism, and impracticality.

The technologist-architect is more like an engineer or accountant than an artist. He tends to manage the production of construction documents and write specifications. He frequently becomes a specialist in some field of interest and represents a valuable knowledge base. Technologists are detail oriented and are likely to become the resident number-crunchers. They approach projects in lineal fashion as do the computer stations they frequently occupy. They tend not to be marketing partners because they lack the generalist's overview and resist inevitable project changes. They rarely admit that their talent is other than in design, which is considered to be the professional plum. Most architectural firms try to create Two-Guy teams where a designer and technologist follow the project to fruition. It takes a blend of both to generate good architecture.

When you meet your short-listed designers, this issue should be on your plate: "Is this guy a designer or a technologist?" (Remember, they will both claim to be designers.) A designer will rarely be without drawing materials. In fact, they frequently must sketch or doodle as they describe things. A roll of sketch paper and a drawing-scale in his briefcase is the mark of a marketing design-architect. A technologist-architect is one that must "go back to the office" to respond to "what will it look like?" He is more likely to whip out a calculator and run some cost numbers for you. Taking cues from their personal appearance is not very reliable. Some of the best designers I know have homes and offices that are wonderful, but their clothing is neglected. A "designer look" is a tool that marketing guys frequently nurture and can be misleading. If you can fit your prospective designer into one of the prototypes, you can guard against his potential "bad habits" in contract language. As an example, for a designer-type, I would press for detail in project cost control and construction administration; for a technology guy, I would go for specific scheme counts in the design phase and color/product selection services in the back-end.

What Is a Prima Donna?

This is an architect who is unwilling to view criticism as part of a professional design process. He can't take direction; he is defensive of his design product. This is a "fuzzy" area because clients constantly approach me with their solution already in mind, and we find that the solution rarely holds up under scrutiny. Good designers must first develop functional schemes from both the client's and the builder's perspective, but then they must go further to sophisticate the architecture. This is the critical "last 10%," the top-down design shakeout. Sure it works, but is it excellent? Owners must be carefully led to fresh ground, or they may resent it. However, they do have a right to expect their designer to set off in the direction they choose.

The prima donna is one who shortcuts the process to get quickly to the "sizzle." He goes for style without doing the homework, and many times his buildings are hard to live in. Young designers can be labeled prima donnas because they haven't laid enough "ego eggs" on clients and later regretted it.

Just as often though, seasoned designers get a bad rap because their "charge" does not allow them to revisit design issues. They try to sell the current solution because they can't afford to go backwards and redesign. Resistance to criticism is a way to move the project forward and bill the client. This is the mark of a process out of kilter, but not necessarily that of a prima donna designer. The process can usually be fixed. True prima donnas can be hard to take. But you must remember that there is good "pretzel logic" for their doing eccentric buildings, getting noticed, and keeping commissions coming in the door. Oprah Architecture, I call it. It definitely commands your attention, but I would not want to be the subject of the show! Following a sensible hiring methodology will make sure your redo is not a stepping stone for someone else's design career.

Credentials

In the remodeling marketplace, the acid test for expertise is a string of successfully completed projects. Remember that your local building department will determine who can legally prepare plans for permitting. For regions with well-established infrastructure, and for projects involving load-bearing alterations, this will usually be an architect registered to practice in your state. The titles behind a designer's name (AIA, RA, ASID, IES, CKD, CBD, CGR, CSI, etc.) indicate very little of importance to homeowners. Most of these titles represent paid memberships in professional

A

B

A PLACE FOR GROUPED WINDOWS

If a designer is working with furnishings as he conceives a plan, he will not evolve a building elevation with symmetrically placed windows. Every major space really has several different functions going on inside, and each may have a different requirement for natural light. Even very inexpensive awning windows (Photograph A) can be stripped together, to signal a given interior use. Actually, most any conceivable configuration can be structurally resolved. The trick is to get the trim right inside and out, and find a comfortable spot in the architectural mass. The strip in Photograph B needs to be set unusually high, so a 2 x 6 header is used and one band of the double wall plate is cut. For the group with the roundtop in Photograph D, a double 2 x 4 block is placed between the top and bottom windows, to ensure the cross trim will mimic the vertical casing between units. Notice how nicely these two groups set into both the interior (Photograph C) and the exterior volumes (Photograph E).

C

D

E

A

B

PRIVATE TO PUBLIC SPACE

When you add more second-floor area to your home, if your designer can't work out a scheme that connects at the top of the stairs (Photograph D), then the next option will likely involve transforming an existing bedroom into a public-transit space. The small bedroom in Photograph A has switched its function to a computer den in Photograph C. To do this, a pull-down stair was relocated into the master closet, the clothes closet was converted into a built-in desk/shelf area, new recessed lighting was placed to draw traffic through the room and into the new corridor beyond, and a french door was substituted for the original (Photograph B). This encourages the owners to walk through the den and into a new light-filled library nook, where two new bedrooms are located.

C

D

LOW ROOF RAKE

Remodeling projects always seem to have difficulty in attaching new roofs to the existing structure. And preserving upper windows only complicates the dilemma. Flat roofs are really the option of last resort. They are expensive, prone to leaking, and they aggravate the difficult problem of maintaining watertight integrity at the new-old flashing seam. They are doable, but judiciously so. The first-floor breakfast room being added in Photograph A must occur under two sacrosanct windows. Here, the depth of the desired floor plan has required some special details to allow the fiberglass roof slope to be no flatter than the warrantied 3-in-12 rake. The architect has allowed the room-under to lose almost 10" in height (from the 8-foot standard) at the outside wall, and uses the cathedral ceiling to offset any low "feeling." The minimum height was determined by adding the depth of the window trim to the top of the rough opening set by the adjacent patio door (Photograph D), and then adding several inches to allow the drywall to appear slightly before continuing up the ceiling-slope. This small dimension over the "picture" window opening precipitated the use of an upturned header to support the weight of the roof (Photograph C). All these details of course, break the standard-practice rules that builders operate by. The only way the architect could specify such was for him to provide custom details for the window header and wall, and interior elevations of the rake walls. Photograph B shows roughly 6" clearance where a square passage-opening intersects the cathedral space.

A

B

C

D

associations and should be viewed with a grain of salt. You are looking for a designer with the following:

1. A college degree in an architecture, interiors, or environmental design program.
2. Five plus years internship in a residential architectural or interior design firm.
3. Three-plus years residential construction job-site experience.
4. A portfolio of many local remodeling jobs where he functioned as designer, as well as administrator of the builder's construction contract.
5. Example project "instruments": design drawings, construction cost estimates, and construction drawings.
6. Professional license by the individual entering into the design contract, when required by the building official.

Although these are the things you want, ascertaining whether your candidate designer measures up is quite another matter. Asking for a resume will not be comfortable to either party. Although I will show you ways to ask for some of this information, I wouldn't put too much credence in the answers. It is much more reliable to directly observe the work products that only experienced pros will have available, and to use a selection process which causes the neophytes to politely excuse themselves. Noticeably absent from the above credentials are degrees from curricula without true design training. I have met several individuals with building construction or law degrees who have managed to earn an architect's seal. While they may satisfy a state's requirement to protect public health, safety, and welfare, I do not think they function well in the traditional architect's role. They are without the visual and spatial skills to balance the architect-builder team.

What Will He Do for Me?

The short answer to this question is "whatever you tell him to"! And you tell him what to do via a Request for Proposal (RFP) and later, a contract. Remember, you pay him, therefore he works for you. The contract will define some of his responsibilities in the printed "boilerplate" but to protect your own interests you must add clauses specific to the project scenario you have decided upon (in Chapter 3). A little later, I spell out sample language, which you will give to your selected designer as an entree to negotiating his service agreement. This language tailors a general-purpose AIA agreement to a service-package specific to medium-sized remodeling projects. You should expect him to prepare the final document using your language (or some mutually altered version). But any talk about contract language should be avoided while courting your architects. You must have the contract you want "under your vest" as you begin the hiring dance.

STEP 1—THE LONG-LIST

Initially, you want to find about ten names to scrutinize further. And while you get your designer list together, you may as well ask about builders. Several months into the process you will need builders' names to toss into the hat along with those suggested by the architect you hired. Word-of-mouth referrals are the best way to find your perfect match.

I consider building officials to be one of the best sources. These should not be construction inspectors who rarely have enough overview to judge fairly, but rather senior building or zoning department employees. While they can't recommend a firm, they will be able to answer a factual question such as, "Do any architects come to mind that may specialize in remodeling work in your township?" Or "Were there any well-prepared drawing permit sets submitted for redos in the last several years?" If you were really zealous, you might go look into the file on a property to get the name of the architect and builder off the paperwork. Building officials are a good resource because they are in a day-to-day position to see work by both good and bad designers, and don't have a proprietary interest in answering your question.

Your next category of sources offers a similar perspective: local real estate attorneys, brokers, and sales agents. These folks are information gatherers and will know who is doing what for whom, and if the result is any good. Further down the word-of-mouth resource line are builders. Remember, they may make sure that everything they tell you does not hurt their own chances to construct the project. So you should try to find one who is not interested in the work; maybe he is recently retired or specializes elsewhere. When you ask the builder for names, pose the question something like this: "Ever do any remodeling work? I am looking for an architect to handle my redo. Do you know anyone who is good at remodeling?"

To fill out the long list you may have to turn to the referral files of related organizations. The local AIA chapter will have one, and so will the local home builders association. Remember, however, that this service is one of the benefits of paid membership in the organization, and that the information is prepared by the pros themselves for purposes of self-promotion. You will usually need to visit the association's headquarters to use these files, where project photos and brochures are categorized for flip-throughs. Somewhere near the bottom of the name-barrel is the Yellow Pages. Go to it if you need to, checking to be sure the names are local. Jot down the

ones that say they are "domestic, residential, or rehabilitation" oriented. An architect must prove his in-state registration to be placed in the "architects" category in the phone book.

STEP 2—THE RFP AND THE SHORT LIST

To prepare your RFP package you will need to substitute your own language into the Request for Proposal cover sheet (Example 7) and Proposal Form (Example 8). You can either re-keyboard it entirely, or copy it and then cut-and-paste your own language in place of the underlined text. If you re-keyboard these two forms, do not expand them beyond one page apiece! Including several photos of your home in each package will probably preclude their having to visit your house to fill out the Proposal Form. Designers are not used to filling out forms for homeowners, so photographs are a little honey to sweeten the pill they must take.

In the Request for Proposal under "goals," concentrate on quantitative things that will give the architect a feel for the size of your project. In the "design challenge" blank write about qualitative items, such as how you want it to feel. If you have a promotional carrot to hold out, put it in here. It could take anywhere from four to six months to break ground from the day you hire your architect, so I would spread the start date six months beyond the proposal-due-date. The Proposal Form (Example 8) is for the designer's use, when he responds. You will need to make up about eight RFP envelopes containing the Request for Proposal cover sheet, the Proposal Form, and the photography.

GREENHOUSE SYSTEM

When maximum natural light is the goal, a greenhouse glazing system is the functional choice, but only if the architecture can be worked out stylistically. It is the next logical step beyond large windows and skylights. Their use must be worthy, however, because they are expensive. When specified, they must be meticulously detailed into the structure, their warranty carefully reviewed, and they should only be installed by factory-certified installation contractors, subordinated to the builder. Particular attention should be paid to the product options available. Although shed-type systems are common, the curved-profile greenhouse in Photograph C (by Four Seasons) has been selected because it can be fitted with several different shading or insulating curtain features. The curved profile allows a shade (either manual or motorized) to travel continuously from the top (Photograph B) to the bottom (Photograph D), in slots set into the sides of the aluminum glazing bars. Any number of glass configurations are available; this one will be double-glazed with no high-performance films inside. As the builder roughs out his structural frame to receive a greenhouse unit, close coordination is required with the installer. For this redo, the installer provided a sample glazing bar (Photograph A), so the carpenters could precisely mimic the profile for the side walls. Because the unit arrives as a precut kit and is installed in a day, the sheathed opening must be built to close tolerances all around.

C

D

A

B

STEP DOWN   *Here, as in many remodeling projects, the opening into the existing home has been made at a low stair landing (Photograph A). This height is transitioned down to the new den with three new hardwood treads. In Photograph B, the new curved first riser, available as a stair part, softens the projection into the space. Note how jammed-up the area near the baseboard radiator looks. This would have been better solved by installing a short run of wood baseboard to hold the metal enclosure away from the stair nosing. The windows are unusually tall Anderson casements; they allow just enough room for casing trim to clear the baseboard heater below.*

Now comes the phone work. You want to screen the long-list down to six firms by asking a series of questions. I would make fifteen copies of the questionnaire (Example 9). Then call each firm, making notes on each sheet so you can remember what was said. If the firm is in the residential design business, you will have no trouble getting a response. Talk to the most senior person you can on short notice. Do not arrange any meetings or further obligate yourself. You are cruising for information. Toss out any firm that admits to not having remodeling experience (item 1) or not offering bidding or construction administration services (item 3). Also rule out those with potential conflicts of interests (item 4). Remodeling designers tend to range from one-person operations to firms of less that ten people. Larger firms should be ruled out (item 5). Also cross out a firm that can't suggest a local project for you to visit (item 6). After deleting the groups that have negative attributes, send identical RFPs to the individual you spoke with in each firm on the short list. Send out six packages only.

STEP 3—THE PROPOSAL MEETING

Your candidates should call and arrange a meeting appointment soon after they get the RFP. After a week you may want to call, confirm receipt of the package, and ask if they intend to respond. If you get less than three firms interested, return to several of the culled names from the long list and send them an RFP package. I think you need to meet from three to five architects to get a feel for your options.

The purpose of the meeting is not to hire the particular designer, but to lay the groundwork for hiring one at a later date. So don't get in a hurry. Do not let the meeting degenerate into a lengthy walkthrough of your home or an impromptu design-idea session. You should not hire a designer because he comes up with an idea you like. Your objective should be fourfold. First, the meeting should clarify any grey areas on his completed Proposal Form. When he leaves and you meet with his competition, you need to be able to understand the information in as much of an apples-to-apples comparison as possible. Second, the meeting is a forum to share background information on each other; for you, this is the list of questions to ask. He will be interested to know if you are mentally and financially prepared for redo reality. Third, you need to carefully review his show-and-tell items. And finally, the meeting is the last opportunity to evaluate his basic business acumen. The entire hiring process has given you an excellent preview of many important work habits. It will show how quickly he responds to your calls, how meticulous he is in providing the items you asked for, how punctual he is, and whether or not he, in fact, does what he says he will do. The Agenda and Questionnaire (Example 10) should be copied, taken into the meeting, and marked up with your notes so you can refer to it later. He does not need to have one.

Proposal Review: Services and Compensation

If he does not bring your completed form to the meeting, don't hire him. A prima donna maybe? If he augments or reworks it to make it more useful without losing the requested information, give him brownie points! In microcosm, this is what you want him to do with your remodel. Take the time to go over each item in the form. This form is designed to clarify what he

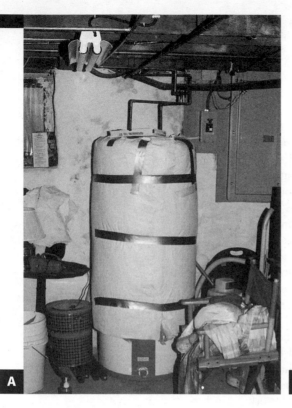

A

B

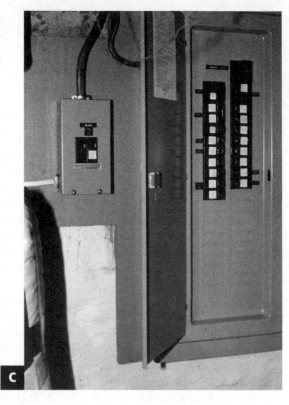

C

MOTHER'S MECHANICALS

The status of the existing mechanical and electrical systems will have a large bearing on new additions. These systems can be very costly to augment, and can determine where new construction can take place. For heating, air conditioning, and electrical systems, the primary issue is adequacy to supply the new load. For plumbing, the critical criterion is location of the sewer exit. Electric and plumbing may need to be renovated to newer code-approved condition. Each redo is unique, and requires experienced pros to consider the ramifications of a remodeling project. You should make it easy for your designer to make realistic design decisions by taking off as much name-plate data as possible, taking several photographs similar to these, and including this in your initial "information package." Photograph A shows an insulated electric hot water heater;

its lack of an exhaust vent (as with the gas-fired unit in Photograph E) makes it easier to relocate if necessary. The heating system in Photograph B is a newly replaced gas-fired boiler, which is smaller and lacks the large tank associated with oil-fired systems. Altering conditioned-air systems such as Photograph E is more difficult because of the size of the supply and return ductwork involved. The electric panel in Photograph D has no room for the new circuits likely to be needed for a major redo, whereas the newly upgraded 200A box in Photograph C has breaker-slots to spare. In Photograph F, notice that the house drain (sewer) exits the basement through the slab. This is a luxury that many homes do not have; this allows drains even for appliances placed in the basement to have long falling runs. If the sewer line passes out high in the basement wall, new bathrooms and kitchens will require careful drain planning.

re-phone.wps

INITIAL TELEPHONE QUESTIONAIRE   **Date:**

For Use In Selecting A Remodeling Designer

Hello, my name is <u>Mary Green</u>. I am considering remodeling my home and am in search of an architect. May I speak to your design or marketing principal? Before you transfer me, who will I speak to? Do I have the name and address right?

Address/Phone Number/Names:

1. Do you do design work for residential remodeling?

2. Can you give me a thumbnail sketch of your firm's expertise?

3. Do your services include bidding and administration of builder's construction contracts?

4. Do you have any proprietary relationships with builders, developers, or product vendors that I should be aware of?

5. How many people are included in your firm?

6. Do you have a Remodeling Project in my vicinity that I might drive by and see?

INITIAL TELEPHONE QUESTIONNAIRE

EXAMPLE 9. *This form is a good way to narrow candidates to a short list of designers who will receive your Request For Proposal via mail.*

will to do and how much he will charge. Between the lines, the list of services contains my own personal quality-assurance philosophy, and I expect other designers to disagree somewhat. For example, I believe the planning and selection of windows/doors, lighting, and final finishes are the Achilles heel of remodeling architecture. They are a real pain to do for most home-owners (which is why many architects omit them) but

they make the difference between o-kay and o-yeah! Do not get uncomfortable and avoid talking about the fee aspect of his service; big dollars are on the table. A great way to break the ice is to slip the "how can I help you make your profit?" question into the conversation. You want him to make money, and you also want to know what you will be paying for. Pay particular atten-tion to his recommended mix of services and be sure

re-agend.wps
MEETING AGENDA AND QUESTIONAIRE   **Date:** _____

For Proposal Meeting with Designers

Attending:

Agenda:

Review Proposal Form
        services, as specified, his recommended mix, why?
        compensation
        cost control measures
Share Background Information, his expertise/credentials
Review Requested Items
        portfolio of Redo projects
        list of satisfied customers
Review Sample Project Instruments
        design drawings
        construction drawings
        cost estimates

Other Questions to Sprinkle into the Above Agenda

Will you be the project designer? What is your role in a project?

Do you have a design philosophy?

Who prepares your construction documents?

Who seals the permit drawing sets?

Who will attend meetings to administer the construction contract?

How many 24"x36" sheets would you expect my working drawing set to be?

What is the most important thing I could do to help you make my job profitable for you?

Miscellaneous notes:

MEETING AGENDA AND QUESTIONNAIRE

EXAMPLE 10. *This form should be used as you meet and entertain proposals from candidate designers in your home. It should be marked up so you can refer to it when making your final decision.*

to ask "why" he prefers it over the prescribed package. Even if he convinces you that his service mix is better, make sure you get what he will charge to perform yours. This is important. You can always elect to make a change after you see all the proposals.

His proposed compensation will normally be a percentage-of-construction cost or, in rare occasions, a fixed price. It will probably fall between 5% and 15%.

Don't let the number scare you; remember that his bidding service alone will most likely return all these dollars back into your pocket. His total fee will be less than the builder's profit. Although some architects will want to go hourly in the design phase and then quote you a fixed price for the balance of the work, I don't recommend it. This hinders your ability to compare firm-to-firm pricing. The only way I can figure that a designer could give a fixed price for the RFP specified services would be to inflate the number radically enough to cover his downside. But this hiring process will flush out the answer to these which-is-cheaper questions. Reimbursed expenses are standard fare in architectural agreements because it is impossible to predict how many drawings will be generated in the entire process. Bidding is especially unpredictable for expenses. Blueprinting is considered a money-maker in most firms; I know of architects who charge twice what I do. For remodeling work, almost all expenses will be for xeroxing and blueprinting and should not run beyond $200, spread over six months. But I have put it on the Proposal Form because it shows your candidate how savvy you are, and it will point up a firm that wants to exploit the "reimbursable expenses" loophole.

The form asks for the billing rates for key people because this is another way to find a little extra profit. That is, if work arises outside his Basic Service, he will seek the owner's approval to do the work and then bill hourly according to his contractual Additional Service rates. This rarely becomes a big deal. Additional Services are seldom called for unless a major zoning or cost problem arises. Think of these rates as markers to check his competitiveness. Do not accept the answer "2.75 times Direct Personnel Expense" as an adequate answer in his proposal. This is the standard knee-jerk answer. You are not asking for a contract number, but a proposal price, something you can relate to other rates. Have him quote specific names and rates even if they may not ultimately do the work.

Cost Responsibility

The last question on the Proposal Form is a dirty trick! Regardless of what he writes in the blank, when you review it ask him "What happens if bids come in way over your cost estimate and my budget?" This is one of those pro-probe questions you learned about in Chapter 3. Part of the answer I know; many drawings will have to be revised to reflect a smaller project scope. But does he feel obligated to absorb this cost, which could be several thousand dollars? Is a major post-bid revision included in his Basic Service and therefore his proposed compensation? The AIA Contract boilerplate says that in the absence of any other contract language, he is not so obligated. He will normally bill the owner for Additional Services when this happens. The services specified in the Proposal Form require him make this post-bid revision as part of his quoted fee. While the initial meeting is not the forum to nail this area down entirely, you want to give him the opportunity to commit himself to as much cost responsibility as he can stand. If he objects to the specific requirements in the Proposal Form, your posture should be that you need some assurances in this area, and view it as important criteria for award of the commission. If he guarantees something, write it down. If he gets the job, you will recast this promise in contract language. If he says nothing to the contrary, he will be obligated to revise the project after the successful builder shakes out the fat.

His Background

You should ask the designer to tell you a little about himself, how he got into the business, etc. Steer him into talking about his education if possible. You want to know if he is schooled in design. I would avoid "conversion designers." A pro who was first a builder, an engineer, a realtor, a developer, or an attorney and then became a designer will probably not have good design skills. This type might be able to produce architectural construction drawings with legal seals on them, but they are likely to document a poorly designed product. These guys are better suited to one of the other scenarios outlined in the previous chapter.

Portfolio and Customer List

As you review his portfolio, you want to look for several things. First you should be aware of the title-blocks or logos on his exhibits. If you see anyone else's name on drawings or photos, discreetly jot the name down, and then later ask about the discrepancy. If his answer makes warning bells go off in your head, then you should try to follow up with the noted firm after he leaves. It is rather common for wanna-be's to misrepresent their role in successful projects. Second, you want to get a feel for his style. Does he only do only colonial-looking stuff, contemporary things, or does he move the solution around to fit the project? This is a good time to slip in the "design philosophy" question. Also don't forget to rave a little about the work, even if slightly disingenuous. The customer list is a leave-behind you will turn to later. For potential go-see's, ask him if any jobs on the list are similar to your project.

Sample Project Instruments

If he is without any one of three RFP-requested items, I would worry about him. Neophyte architects often simply start drawings, take them to a certain point, get them approved by owners, and then put more lines on them until they will be adequate for permitting. This process will yield poor architecture. The lack of a definitive design sketch or hardline design drawing should rule him out as a candidate. You may be meeting with a draftsman, not a designer. Design drawings are characterized by their lack of construction notes

and dimensions. They frequently show furnishings, people, color, texture, trees or plants, and shade and shadow (see Examples 11, 12, and 13).

The candidate's constructions drawings should be scanned in the meeting to get a feel for how far they go toward documenting a project. With adequate time you could bounce the drawing set against the services list in the Proposal Form and get a sense of how far apart they are. Does he have a lighting plan and product schedule in the set? Are the windows precisely specified by manufacturer and model number, or are they called out as a generic 3-0x5-0? Roughly half of the architect's effort should go into his construction drawings. For an average-sized remodeling project, I can do a permit construction drawing in one sheet, but I regularly do five and more sheets. While looking through the drawings, ask how the flooring product was picked by the owners. Was he involved? Is it specified in a Room Finish Schedule? Ask him if you can borrow (hopefully have) the construction drawing set to see how detailed it is.

Many residential architects will have to scramble to bring you a cost estimate of a real remodeling project. As I explained earlier, they do mostly spec-builder work and haven't the faintest idea how much things cost. Their portfolio may even be slick looking, but if cost is important to you, don't hire a cost-ignorant designer to handle your job. And avoid getting bogged down with reviewing the estimate; if he did it for a real redo project and he offers the client's name and number, that is all you need to know.

The other questions to ask (Example 10) should be brought up during your meeting in nonintimidating ways. If he volunteers that other people in his firm will design the work or attend job meetings, you should ask to meet them, and then write them into the contract. You will work more with them than with

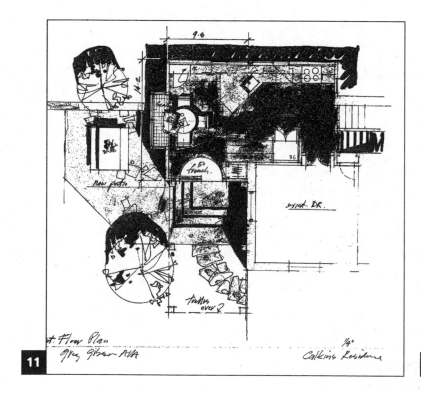

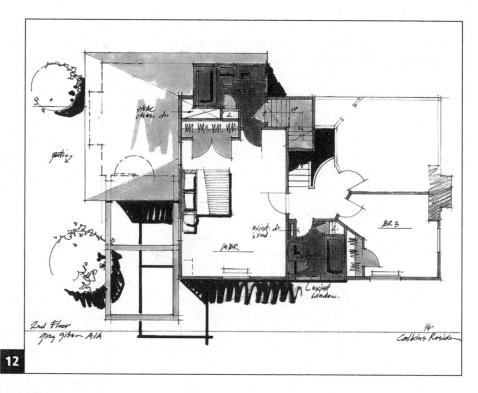

PRELIMINARY DESIGN DRAWINGS **EXAMPLES 11, 12, AND 13.** *This is a series of design drawings for a kitchen redo and a master bathroom addition. When the owner approves the intent shown here, the architect will switch to the production of working drawings. Notice that it shows shade and shadow, in an effort to communicate architectural depth, and includes furnishings to test the functionality of the interiors. This is a color-marker technique on tracing paper, intended to be reproduced by a ledger-sized color copier.*

East. Elev.
greg gibson AIA

North Elev. ¼"
Calkins Residence

13

him. Construction drawings are sometimes produced by other subcontracting architecture firms, but I would not recommend it for remodeling work. If your project will need an architect's seal for permit, don't hire anyone who will have their drawings sealed by someone else. Remember to note your candidate's attributes and any important promises he makes on your agenda sheet as you go. By the time you meet with everyone on your short list, their individual characteristics will have merged.

STEP 4—SELECT YOUR FAVORITE

After you have met your candidates, you will still have a few more things to do before making the decision. You may want to visit some completed projects, in which case I strongly advise against letting the designer show you through. Post-redo owners will be more candid without him there. For your favorite short listers, call enough of their satisfied customers to make sure they exist, and to satisfy your own comfort level. Don't expect him to give you names of customers who think he is a bum. You should not spend much time sniffing out his references because I find post-remodeling homeowners to be fickle with the truth. I think part of it has to do with the fact that, after they expend all the effort and money required, they have to love the result to keep their sanity! After all, who among us admits to bearing ugly children?

Pick your favorite architect (plus a runner-up), then quickly prepare to negotiate with him on the phone. Make a copy of the Owner-Architect Agreement (Example 14) to refer to. Keep the call upbeat and casual. Say that you are excited at having found the perfect fit and "you are it!" Advise him you will be sending along some contract language for him to review and include in the contract. Although there are many more trees in the agreement forest, you should only negotiate around several of the most important ones. Leave the small change alone. I do not recommend that you try to beat his price down while his service stays unchanged, as this may change his enthusiasm toward the job. You should rely on the competitive process thus far to ensure that he has put his best price on the table (this also applies to hiring the builder). If his costs are out of line, you would not have selected him. Tell him you need to talk about the following issues.

A Cost Responsibility Clause

If the architect objected to the part of the proposal service-mix that required a post-bid revision, refresh his memory about your prior budget discussions in the proposal meeting. Tell him you would like to come to agreement on a "fixed limit of Construction Cost" as provided in Article 5.2 (AIA Document B151), and would like him to consider its impact on his proposed Basic Services and Compensation. You propose to include the following subparagraph in Article 12 (altering the cost to fit your own budget):

> 12.3 *The following Fixed Limit of Construction Cost is hereby made a condition of this agreement. The cost of construction in no instance is to exceed: One Hundred Fifty Thousand Dollars ($150,000.00).*

Between you and me (and the other jillions who will buy this book), I have never agreed to such a brick wall myself, but of course no one ever asked either. If they did, and if the project was important to me, I would figure my downside services and costs, tack them onto the proposal, and agree to it. With a little trepidation. I would put more labor into the design phase for another potential scheme iteration, and I would assume that a major redesign after bidding caused all construction drawing sheets to be revised. And I would say "no, you can't have that" a lot to the client even when I was not sure. This might be a $1500 to $3000 number that I would build into compensation for an expanded Basic Service.

When projects have undergone such a redesign in my practice, my Additional Service bills to the owner were less than $1500 to remove between $20,000 to $50,000 out of the construction contract. So with me, it would not be a smart play for the owner. If I were to put the $3000 in the contract and then bring bids in under the Fixed Limit (and the downside does not happen), then I would get a nice bonus, all cream. But maybe your financial advisor demands an absolute hard number in the design contract, or maybe your selected designer is your heads-over favorite but you worry about his cost-consciousness. If so, this is the way to push the guy's button. Who knows what will come out! Maybe you will get what you ask for. If you can agree on some language short of "fixed limit," put whatever it is in a new 12.3 Subparagraph, even if it would make F. Lee Bailey chuckle. If you can't get any further agreement about cost responsibility, don't let it squash the commission. Join the club. Let the contract boilerplate stand as is, and resolve to keep "cost" on the front burner in all meetings.

The Custom Mix of Services

The second issue to talk about over the phone is the services he will provide. You want to get an accurate list to itemize in Article 12, and then a corresponding adjustment in compensation. This is something he should welcome, because it creates mutual expectations. If he is resistive, indicate your need to reconsider your decision, hang up, and call your runner-up designer. You have listed what you think you want in the RFP (Request for Proposal), and he has said that he would prefer to do X on the Proposal Form. So now you need to tell him what the final decisions are. If you have an interior designer whom you want to use for finish selections and furnishings, for example, strike "final color and product finish specification" in the Construction Phase and ask about striking the "room finish schedule" in the Construction Documents. If you have existing architectural drawings of your home or property, try to strike some of the "field measurement" and "underlay drawings" work in the Design Phase.

I have marked those services that I consider absolute necessities in Subparagraph 12.1 (Example 14) with circle bullets. The diamond bullets expand the list; they are my recommendations to get a first-rate job. Subparagraph 12.2 itemizes some Additional Services you may want to consider. A scale model, for example, would be nice to have but it is not necessary for a quality project. I have placed a star bullet beside the task that you want to keep in the Basic Service if it is not too expensive.

I believe a post-bid shakedown is a necessary part of any redo job. It lets the newly hired builder get his expertise into the building and make it smarter and cheaper. It is a great motivator for builders. But most architects treat such a revision as an unforeseen crisis. I would ask about the value of a credit for its deletion and then decide. Start with your RFP service mix, for which you have a price, and then get a credit or debit for each change. How much are these changes worth?

OWNER-ARCHITECT CONTRACT

EXAMPLE 14. *This is a sample agreement between a designer and remodeling couple. Of the eight pages in the form, four require significant input—pages 1, 6, 7, and 8. Here, an additional page is added to accept spillover from the lengthy entry in Article 12. Although the "boilerplate" in Article 1 defines the architect's responsibilities, this needs to be more specifically tailored for redo projects, such as is accomplished by 12.1 and 12.2. Notice the strike-through-and-initial convention in 11.1 that was alluded to in Chapter 3. This allows changes to be made by highlighting both the original language and the altered version. The Designer Agreement Form and the Owner-Builder Contract in Chapter 7 should be used in concert because their language is interrelated, especially regarding project roles and responsibilities.*

THE AMERICAN INSTITUTE OF ARCHITECTS

Sample

AIA Document B151

Abbreviated Form of Agreement Between Owner and Architect

for Construction Projects of Limited Scope

1987 EDITION

THIS DOCUMENT HAS IMPORTANT LEGAL CONSEQUENCES; CONSULTATION WITH AN ATTORNEY IS ENCOURAGED WITH RESPECT TO ITS COMPLETION OR MODIFICATION.

AGREEMENT

made as of the Nineteen Hundred and | Eighteenth Ninety Two. | day of | September | in the year of

BETWEEN the Owner:
(Name and address)

Mary and John Green
1492 Columbus Drive
Towner, PA 19088

and the Architect:
(Name and address)

Peter Wilson
2134 Harrie Road
Wister, PA 19002

For the following Project:
(Include detailed description of Project, location, address and scope.)

Additions and Alterations to the Owner's property at the above address. The existing two story residence (approximately 1400sf) will be modified to provide a larger master-suite with discreet bathroom and dressing area, a new fourth bedroom, a remodeled kitchen and a new adjacent family room, a powder room, a rear patio/deck area, and an enhanced front entry and building elevation. In conjunction with these functions, a greenhouse-type space will be provided where plant-care can be combined with outdoor activities such as table-tennis.

The Owner and Architect agree as set forth below.

Use something like a $400 day ($50/hr) as a baseline and then guess at the effort involved in each task. "Final color and product finish specification," for instance, might involve anywhere from $200 to $800 worth of effort. Then run a quick number:

Assuming a $400 credit, a $100,000 job at a 10% fee

$400/$10,000 = .04 of the fee

or .04 x .10 = .004 off the percentage fee

or .10 - .004 = .096 or a 9.6% fee

TERMS AND CONDITIONS OF AGREEMENT BETWEEN OWNER AND ARCHITECT

ARTICLE 1
ARCHITECT'S RESPONSIBILITIES

1.1 ARCHITECT'S SERVICES

1.1.1 The Architect's services consist of those services performed by the Architect, Architect's employees and Architect's consultants as enumerated in Articles 2 and 3 of this Agreement and any other services included in Article 12.

1.1.2 The Architect's services shall be performed as expeditiously as is consistent with professional skill and care and the orderly progress of the Work.

1.1.3 The services covered by this Agreement are subject to the time limitations contained in Subparagraph 11.5.1.

ARTICLE 2
SCOPE OF ARCHITECT'S BASIC SERVICES

2.1 DEFINITION

2.1.1. The Architect's Basic Services consist of those described under the three phases identified below, any other services identified in Article 12, and include normal structural, mechanical and electrical engineering services.

2.2 DESIGN PHASE

2.2.1 The Architect shall review with the Owner alternative approaches to design and construction of the Project.

2.2.2 Based on the mutually agreed-upon program, schedule and construction budget requirements, the Architect shall prepare, for approval by the Owner, Design Documents consisting of drawings and other documents appropriate for the Project, and shall submit to the Owner a preliminary estimate of Construction Cost.

2.3 CONSTRUCTION DOCUMENTS PHASE

2.3.1 Based on the approved Design Documents, the Architect shall prepare, for approval by the Owner, Construction Documents consisting of Drawings and Specifications setting forth in detail the requirements for the construction of the Project and shall advise the Owner of any adjustments to previous preliminary estimates of Construction Cost.

2.3.2 The Architect shall assist the Owner in connection with the Owner's responsibility for filing documents required for the approval of governmental authorities having jurisdiction over the Project.

2.3.3 Unless provided in Article 12, the Architect, following the Owner's approval of the Construction Documents and of the latest preliminary estimate of Construction Cost, shall assist the Owner in obtaining bids or negotiated proposals and assist in awarding and preparing contracts for construction.

2.4 CONSTRUCTION PHASE—ADMINISTRATION OF THE CONSTRUCTION CONTRACT

2.4.1 The Architect's responsibility to provide Basic Services for the Construction Phase under this Agreement commences with the award of the Contract for Construction and terminates at the earlier of issuance to the Owner of the final Certificate for Payment or 60 days after the date of Substantial Completion of the Work.

2.4.2 The Architect shall provide administration of the Contract for Construction as set forth below and in the edition of AIA Document A201, General Conditions of the Contract for Construction, current as of the date of this Agreement.

2.4.3 Duties, responsibilities and limitations of authority of the Architect shall not be restricted, modified or extended without written agreement of the Owner and Architect with consent of the Contractor, which consent shall not be unreasonably withheld.

2.4.4 The Architect shall be a representative of and shall advise and consult with the Owner (1) during construction until final payment to the Contractor is due and (2) as an Additional Service at the Owner's direction from time to time during the correction period described in the Contract for Construction.

2.4.5 The Architect shall visit the site at intervals appropriate to the stage of construction or as otherwise agreed by the Owner and Architect in writing to become generally familiar with the progress and quality of the Work completed and to determine in general if the Work is being performed in a manner indicating that the Work when completed will be in accordance with the Contract Documents. However, the Architect shall not be required to make exhaustive or continuous on-site inspections to check the quality or quantity of the Work. On the basis of on-site observations as an architect, the Architect shall keep the Owner informed of the progress and quality of the Work, and shall endeavor to guard the Owner against defects and deficiencies in the Work. *(More extensive site representation may be agreed to as an Additional Service, as described in Paragraph 3.2.)*

2.4.6 The Architect shall not have control over or charge of and shall not be responsible for construction means, methods, techniques, sequences or procedures, or for safety precautions and programs in connection with the Work, since these are solely the Contractor's responsibility under the Contract for Construction. The Architect shall not be responsible for the Contractor's schedules or failure to carry out the Work in accordance with the Contract Documents. The Architect shall not have control over or charge of acts or omissions of the Contractor, Subcontractors, or their agents or employees, or of any other persons performing portions of the Work.

2.4.7 The Architect shall at all times have access to the Work wherever it is in preparation or progress.

2.4.8 Based on the Architect's observations and evaluations of the Contractor's Applications for Payment, the Architect shall review and certify the amounts due the Contractor.

2.4.9 The Architect's certification for payment shall constitute a representation to the Owner, based on the Architect's observations at the site as provided in Subparagraph 2.4.5 and on the

AIA DOCUMENT B151 • ABBREVIATED OWNER-ARCHITECT AGREEMENT • THIRD EDITION • AIA® • ©1987
THE AMERICAN INSTITUTE OF ARCHITECTS, 1735 NEW YORK AVENUE, N.W., WASHINGTON, D.C. 20006 **B151-1987 2**

data comprising the Contractor's Application for Payment, that the Work, to the best of the Architect's knowledge, information and belief, has progressed to the point indicated and that quality of the Work is in accordance with the Contract Documents. The issuance of a Certificate for Payment shall not be a representation that the Architect has (1) made exhaustive or continuous on-site inspections to check the quality or quantity of the Work, (2) reviewed construction means, methods, techniques, sequences or procedures, (3) reviewed copies of requisitions received from Subcontractors and material suppliers and other data requested by the Owner to substantiate the Contractor's right to payment or (4) ascertained how or for what purpose the Contractor has used money previously paid on account of the Contract Sum.

2.4.10 The Architect shall have authority to reject Work which does not conform to the Contract Documents and will have authority to require additional inspection or testing of the Work whenever, in the Architect's reasonable opinion, it is necessary or advisable for the implementation of the intent of the Contract Documents.

2.4.11 The Architect shall review and approve or take other appropriate action upon Contractor's submittals such as Shop Drawings, Product Data and Samples, but only for the limited purpose of checking for conformance with information given and the design concept expressed in the Contract Documents. The Architect's action shall be taken with such reasonable promptness as to cause no delay. The Architect's approval of a specific item shall not indicate approval of an assembly of which the item is a component. When professional certification of performance characteristics of materials, systems or equipment is required by the Contract Documents, the Architect shall be entitled to rely upon such certification to establish that the materials, systems or equipment will meet the performance criteria required by the Contract Documents.

2.4.12 The Architect shall prepare Change Orders and Construction Change Directives, with supporting documentation and data if authorized or confirmed in writing by the Owner as provided in Paragraphs 3.1 and 3.3, for the Owner's approval and execution in accordance with the Contract Documents, and may authorize minor changes in the Work not involving an adjustment in the Contract Sum or an extension of the Contract Time which are not inconsistent with the intent of the Contract Documents.

2.4.13 The Architect shall conduct inspections to determine the dates of Substantial Completion and final completion and shall issue a final Certificate for Payment.

2.4.14 The Architect shall interpret and decide matters concerning performance of the Owner and Contractor under the requirements of the Contract Documents on written request of either the Owner or Contractor. The Architect's response to such requests shall be made with reasonable promptness and within any time limits agreed upon. When making such interpretations and initial decisions, the Architect shall endeavor to secure faithful performance by both Owner and Contractor, shall not show partiality to either, and shall not be liable for results of interpretations or decisions so rendered in good faith.

ARTICLE 3
ADDITIONAL SERVICES

3.1 Additional Services shall be provided if authorized or confirmed in writing by the Owner or if included in Article 12, and they shall be paid for by the Owner as provided in this Agreement. Such Additional Services shall include, in addition to those described in Paragraphs 3.2 and 3.3, budget analysis, financial feasibility studies, planning surveys, environmental studies, measured drawings of existing conditions, coordination of separate contractors or independent consultants, coordination of construction or project managers, detailed Construction Cost estimates, quantity surveys, interior design, planning of tenant or rental spaces, inventories of materials or equipment, preparation of record drawings, and any other services not otherwise included in this Agreement under Basic Services or not customarily furnished in accordance with generally accepted architectural practice.

3.2 If more extensive representation at the site than is described in Subparagraph 2.4.5 is required, such additional project representation shall be provided and paid for as set forth in Articles 11 and 12.

3.3 As an Additional Service in connection with Change Orders and Construction Change Directives, the Architect shall prepare Drawings, Specifications and other documentation and data, evaluate Contractor's proposals, and provide any other services made necessary by such Change Orders and Construction Change Directives.

ARTICLE 4
OWNER'S RESPONSIBILITIES

4.1 The Owner shall provide full information, including a program which shall set forth the Owner's objectives, schedule, constraints, budget with reasonable contingencies, and criteria.

4.2 The Owner shall furnish surveys describing physical characteristics, legal limitations and utility locations for the site of the Project, a written legal description of the site and the services of geotechnical engineers or other consultants when such services are requested by the Architect.

4.3 The Owner shall furnish structural, mechanical, chemical, air and water pollution tests, tests for hazardous materials, and other laboratory and environmental tests, inspections and reports required by law or the Contract Documents.

4.4 The Owner shall furnish all legal, accounting and insurance counseling services as may be necessary at any time for the Project, including auditing services the Owner may require to verify the Contractor's Applications for Payment or to ascertain how or for what purposes the Contractor has used the money paid by the Owner.

4.5 The foregoing services, information, surveys and reports shall be furnished at the Owner's expense, and the Architect shall be entitled to rely upon the accuracy and completeness thereof.

4.6 Prompt written notice shall be given by the Owner to the Architect if the Owner becomes aware of any fault or defect in the Project or nonconformance with the Contract Documents.

4.7 The proposed language of certificates or certifications requested of the Architect or Architect's consultants shall be submitted to the Architect for review and approval at least 14 days prior to execution.

3 B151-1987 **AIA DOCUMENT B151** • ABBREVIATED OWNER-ARCHITECT AGREEMENT • THIRD EDITION • AIA® • ©1987
THE AMERICAN INSTITUTE OF ARCHITECTS, 1735 NEW YORK AVENUE, N.W., WASHINGTON, D.C. 20006

This will give you some basis for arriving at a credit for removal of a service from the package. I would not get hung up on the "fair value" of each line item, which as you can see is grey anyway. The important thing is to try to arrive at a separate cost for each item and then sum up. Don't let the tasks get bunched together and then an overall value assigned. If you don't think a fair number is being given as a credit, leave the service in, or trade it for something you would rather have.

ARTICLE 5
CONSTRUCTION COST

5.1 DEFINITION

5.1.1 The Construction Cost shall be the total cost or estimated cost to the Owner of all elements of the Project designed or specified by the Architect.

5.1.2 The Construction Cost shall include the cost at current market rates of labor and materials furnished by the Owner and equipment designed, specified, selected or specially provided for by the Architect, plus a reasonable allowance for the Contractor's overhead and profit. In addition, a reasonable allowance for contingencies shall be included for market conditions at the time of bidding and for changes in the Work during construction.

5.1.3 Construction Cost does not include the compensation of the Architect and Architect's consultants, the costs of the land, rights-of-way, financing or other costs which are the responsibility of the Owner as provided in Article 4.

5.2 RESPONSIBILITY FOR CONSTRUCTION COST

5.2.1 It is recognized that neither the Architect nor the Owner has control over the cost of labor, materials or equipment, over the Contractor's methods of determining bid prices, or over competitive bidding, market or negotiating conditions. Accordingly, the Architect cannot and does not warrant or represent that bids or negotiated prices will not vary from any estimate of Construction Cost or evaluation prepared or agreed to by the Architect.

5.2.2 No fixed limit of Construction Cost shall be established as a condition of this Agreement by the furnishing, proposal or establishment of a Project budget, unless a fixed limit has been agreed upon in writing and signed by the parties hereto. Fixed limits, if any, shall be increased in the amount of an increase in the Contract Sum occurring after execution of the Contract for Construction.

5.2.3 Any Project budget or fixed limit of Construction Cost may be adjusted to reflect changes in the general level of prices in the construction industry between the date of submission of the Construction Documents to the Owner and the date on which proposals are sought.

5.2.4 If a fixed limit of Construction Cost is exceeded by the lowest bona fide bid or negotiated proposal, the Owner shall:

  .1 give written approval of an increase in such fixed limit;

  .2 authorize rebidding or renegotiating of the Project within a reasonable time;

  .3 if the Project is abandoned, terminate in accordance with Paragraph 8.3; or

  .4 cooperate in revising the Project scope and quality as required to reduce the Construction Cost.

5.2.5 If the Owner chooses to proceed under Clause 5.2.4.4, the Architect, without additional charge, shall modify the Contract Documents as necessary to comply with the fixed limit, if established as a condition of this Agreement. The modification of Contract Documents shall be the limit of the Architect's responsibility arising out of the establishment of a fixed limit. The Architect shall be entitled to compensation in accordance with this Agreement for all services performed whether or not the Construction Phase is commenced.

ARTICLE 6
USE OF ARCHITECT'S DRAWINGS, SPECIFICATIONS AND OTHER DOCUMENTS

6.1 The Drawings, Specifications and other documents prepared by the Architect for this Project are instruments of the Architect's service for use solely with respect to this Project, and the Architect shall be deemed the author of these documents and shall retain all common law, statutory and other reserved rights, including the copyright. The Owner shall be permitted to retain copies, including reproducible copies, of the Architect's Drawings, Specifications and other documents for information and reference in connection with the Owner's use and occupancy of the Project. The Architect's Drawings, Specifications or other documents shall not be used by the Owner or others on other projects, for additions to this Project or for completion of this Project by others, unless the Architect is adjudged to be in default under this Agreement, except by agreement in writing and with appropriate compensation to the Architect.

6.2 Submission or distribution of documents to meet official regulatory requirements or for similar purposes in connection with the Project is not to be construed as publication in derogation of the Architect's reserved rights.

ARTICLE 7
ARBITRATION

7.1 Claims, disputes or other matters in question between the parties to this Agreement arising out of or relating to this Agreement or breach thereof shall be subject to and decided by arbitration in accordance with the Construction Industry Arbitration Rules of the American Arbitration Association currently in effect unless the parties mutually agree otherwise. No arbitration arising out of or relating to this Agreement shall include, by consolidation, joinder or in any other manner, an additional person or entity not a party to this Agreement, except by written consent containing a specific reference to this Agreement signed by the Owner, Architect, and any other person or entity sought to be joined. Consent to arbitration involving an additional person or entity shall not constitute consent to arbitration of any claim, dispute or other matter in question not described in the written consent. The foregoing agreement to arbitrate and other agreements to arbitrate with an additional person or entity duly consented to by the parties to this Agreement shall be specifically enforceable in accordance with applicable law in any court having jurisdiction thereof.

7.2 In no event shall the demand for arbitration be made after the date when institution of legal or equitable proceedings based on such claim, dispute or other matter in question would be barred by the applicable statutes of limitations.

7.3 The award rendered by the arbitrator or arbitrators shall be final, and judgment may be entered upon it in accordance with applicable law in any court having jurisdiction thereof.

ARTICLE 8
TERMINATION, SUSPENSION OR ABANDONMENT

8.1 This Agreement may be terminated by either party upon not less than seven days' written notice should the other party

fail substantially to perform in accordance with the terms of this Agreement through no fault of the party initiating the termination.

8.2 If the Project is suspended by the Owner for more than 30 consecutive days, the Architect shall be compensated for services performed prior to notice of such suspension. When the Project is resumed, the Architect's compensation shall be equitably adjusted to provide for expenses incurred in the interruption and resumption of the Architect's services.

8.3 This Agreement may be terminated by the Owner upon not less than seven days' written notice to the Architect in the event that the Project is permanently abandoned. If the Project is abandoned by the Owner for more than 90 consecutive days, the Architect may terminate this Agreement by giving written notice.

8.4 Failure of the Owner to make payments to the Architect in accordance with this Agreement shall be considered substantial nonperformance and cause for termination.

8.5 If the Owner fails to make payment when due the Architect for services and expenses, the Architect may, upon seven days' written notice to the Owner, suspend performance of services under this Agreement. Unless payment in full is received by the Architect within seven days of the date of the notice, the suspension shall take effect without further notice. In the event of a suspension of services, the Architect shall have no liability to the Owner for delay or damage caused the Owner because of such suspension of services.

8.6 In the event of termination not the fault of the Architect, the Architect shall be compensated for services performed prior to termination, together with Reimbursable Expenses then due and all Termination Expenses.

8.7 Termination Expenses are in addition to compensation for Basic and Additional Services, and include expenses which are directly attributable to termination.

ARTICLE 9
MISCELLANEOUS PROVISIONS

9.1 Unless otherwise provided, this Agreement shall be governed by the law of the principal place of business of the Architect.

9.2 Terms in this Agreement shall have the same meaning as those in AIA Document A201, General Conditions of the Contract for Construction, current as of the date of this Agreement.

9.3 Causes of action between the parties to this Agreement pertaining to acts or failures to act shall be deemed to have accrued and the applicable statutes of limitations shall commence to run not later than either the date of Substantial Completion for acts or failures to act occurring prior to Substantial Completion, or the date of issuance of the final Certificate for Payment for acts or failures to act occurring after Substantial Completion.

9.4 The Owner and Architect waive all rights against each other and against the contractors, consultants, agents and employees of the other for damages, but only to the extent covered by property insurance during construction, except such rights as they may have to the proceeds of such insurance as set forth in the edition of AIA Document A201, General Con-

ditions of the Contract for Construction, current as of the date of this Agreement. The Owner and Architect each shall require similar waivers from their contractors, consultants and agents.

9.5 The Owner and Architect, respectively, bind themselves, their partners, successors, assigns and legal representatives to the other party to this Agreement and to the partners, successors, assigns and legal representatives of such other party with respect to all covenants of this Agreement. Neither Owner nor Architect shall assign this Agreement without the written consent of the other.

9.6 This Agreement represents the entire and integrated agreement between the Owner and Architect and supersedes all prior negotiations, representations or agreements, either written or oral. This Agreement may be amended only by written instrument signed by both Owner and Architect.

9.7 Nothing contained in this Agreement shall create a contractual relationship with or a cause of action in favor of a third party against either the Owner or Architect.

9.8 The Architect and Architect's consultants shall have no responsibility for the discovery, presence, handling, removal or disposal of or exposure of persons to hazardous materials in any form at the Project site, including but not limited to asbestos, asbestos products, polychlorinated biphenyl (PCB) or other toxic substances.

ARTICLE 10
PAYMENTS TO THE ARCHITECT

10.1 DIRECT PERSONNEL EXPENSE

10.1.1 Direct Personnel Expense is defined as the direct salaries of the Architect's personnel engaged on the Project and the portion of the cost of their mandatory and customary contributions and benefits related thereto, such as employment taxes and other statutory employee benefits, insurance, sick leave, holidays, vacations, pensions and similar contributions and benefits.

10.2 REIMBURSABLE EXPENSES

10.2.1 Reimbursable Expenses include expenses incurred by the Architect in the interest of the Project for:

  .1 expense of transportation and living expenses in connection with out-of-town travel authorized by the Owner;

  .2 long-distance communications;

  .3 fees paid for securing approval of authorities having jurisdiction over the Project;

  .4 reproductions;

  .5 postage and handling of Drawings and Specifications;

  .6 expense of overtime work requiring higher than regular rates, if authorized by the Owner;

  .7 renderings and models requested by the Owner;

  .8 expense of additional insurance coverage or limits, including professional liability insurance, requested by the Owner in excess of that normally carried by the Architect and Architect's consultants; and

  .9 expense of computer-aided design and drafting equipment time when used in connection with the Project.

The Retainer

If you were really feisty, you might tell your designer that you don't think you need to pay a retainer. But it is rather standard fare for architects to require one before

work begins. The front-end for designers is fraught with dreamers who can't afford a professional construction effort. He has more reason to worry about getting paid for initial work than the builder who knows that the owner has been writing redo checks for

10.3 PAYMENTS ON ACCOUNT OF BASIC SERVICES

10.3.1 An initial payment as set forth in Paragraph 11.1 is the minimum payment under this Agreement.

10.3.2 Subsequent payments for Basic Services shall be made monthly and, where applicable, shall be in proportion to services performed within each phase of service.

10.3.3 If and to the extent that the time initially established in Subparagraph 11.5.1 of this Agreement is exceeded or extended through no fault of the Architect, compensation for any services rendered during the additional period of time shall be computed in the manner set forth in Subparagraph 11.3.2.

10.3.4 When compensation is based on a percentage of Construction Cost and any portions of the Project are deleted or otherwise not constructed, compensation for those portions of the Project shall be payable to the extent services are performed on those portions, in accordance with the schedule set forth in Subparagraph 11.2.2, based on (1) the lowest bona fide bid or negotiated proposal, or (2) if no such bid or proposal is received, the most recent preliminary estimate of Construction Cost or detailed estimate of Construction Cost for such portions of the Project.

10.4 PAYMENTS ON ACCOUNT OF ADDITIONAL SERVICES AND REIMBURSABLE EXPENSES

10.4.1 Payments on account of the Architect's Additional Services and for Reimbursable Expenses shall be made monthly upon presentation of the Architect's statement of services rendered or expenses incurred.

10.5 PAYMENTS WITHHELD

10.5.1 No deductions shall be made from the Architect's compensation on account of sums withheld from payments to contractors.

ARTICLE 11
BASIS OF COMPENSATION

The Owner shall compensate the Architect as follows:

11.1 AN INITIAL PAYMENT OF   Five Hundred   Dollars ($ 500.00) shall be made upon execution of this Agreement and ~~credited to the Owner's account at final payment~~.

11.2 BASIC COMPENSATION

11.2.1 FOR BASIC SERVICES, as described in Article 2, and any other services included in Article 12 as part of Basic Services, Basic Compensation shall be computed as follows:

(Insert basis of compensation, including stipulated sums, multiples or percentages, and identify phases to which particular methods of compensation apply, if necessary.)

Compensation shall be based on the following Percentage of Construction Cost as defined in Article 5: Thirteen Percent (13%)

11.2.2 Where compensation is based on a stipulated sum or percentage of Construction Cost, progress payments for Basic Services in each phase shall total the following percentages of the total Basic Compensation payable:

(Insert additional phases as appropriate.)

Design Phase:	Thirty	percent (30 %)
Construction Documents Phase:	Forty	percent (40 %)
Construction Phase:	Thirty	percent (30 %)
Total Basic Compensation:		one hundred percent (100%)

11.3 COMPENSATION FOR ADDITIONAL SERVICES

11.3.1 FOR PROJECT REPRESENTATION BEYOND BASIC SERVICES, as described in Paragraph 3.2, compensation shall be computed as follows:

Peter Wilson's time at a fixed rate of seventy dollars ($70.00) per hour.

11.3.2 FOR ADDITIONAL SERVICES OF THE ARCHITECT provided under Article 3 or identified in Article 12, compensation shall be computed as follows:

(Insert basis of compensation, including rates and/or multiples of Direct Personnel Expense for Principals and employees, and identify Principals and classify employees, if required. Identify specific services to which particular methods of compensation apply, if necessary.)

Hourly basis for:

Peter Wilson's time at a fixed rate of seventy dollars ($70.00) per hour.
Jane Waterman's time at a fixed rate of forty two dollars ($42.00) per hour.
Any other employee's time at 2.75 times Direct Personnel Expense.

11.3.3 FOR ADDITIONAL SERVICES OF CONSULTANTS, including additional structural, mechanical and electrical engineering services and those provided under Article 3 or identified in Article 12 as part of Additional Services, a multiple of   One Point Two   (1.2) times the amounts billed to the Architect for such services.

(Identify specific types of consultants in Article 12, if required.)

11.4 REIMBURSABLE EXPENSES

11.4.1 FOR REIMBURSABLE EXPENSES, as described in Paragraph 10.2, and any other items included in Article 12 as Reimbursable Expenses, a multiple of   One Point Two   (1.2) times the expenses incurred by the Architect, the Architect's employees and consultants in the interest of the Project.

11.5 ADDITIONAL PROVISIONS

11.5.1 IF THE BASIC SERVICES covered by this Agreement have not been completed within   Twelve Months   (12) months of the date hereof, through no fault of the Architect, extension of the Architect's services beyond that time shall be compensated as provided in Subparagraphs 10.3.3 and 11.3.2.

11.5.2 Payments are due and payable   Thirty   (30) days from the date of the Architect's invoice. Amounts unpaid   Forty Five   (45) days after the invoice date shall bear interest at the rate entered below, or in the absence thereof at the legal rate prevailing from time to time at the principal place of business of the Architect.

(Insert rate of interest agreed upon.)

One Point Five Percent (1.5%) per month.

(Usury laws and requirements under the Federal Truth in Lending Act, similar state and local consumer credit laws and other regulations at the Owner's and Architect's principal places of business, the location of the Project and elsewhere may affect the validity of this provision. Specific legal advice should be obtained with respect to deletions or modifications, and also regarding requirements such as written disclosures or waivers.)

11.5.3 The rates and multiples set forth for Additional Services shall be annually adjusted in accordance with normal salary review practices of the Architect.

---

months before he is engaged. At the very least, I suggest you tell him you want to strike through the following language from contract page 6 Article 11.1:

> *"and credited to the Owner's account at final payment."*

This means that you intend to treat his payments just as he will want to treat the builder's, that is, requiring payment for in-place work. He will operate off the retainer, and then begin billing you as the work progresses. Let him tell you what his retainer amount will

ARTICLE 12
OTHER CONDITIONS OR SERVICES

(Insert descriptions of other services, identify Additional Services included within Basic Compensation and modifications to the payment and compensation terms included in this Agreement.)

12.1 Basic Service includes:
    Design Phase Basic Service:
- kickoff meeting plus one subsequent design-session with owner
- additional design-session with owner
- zoning code review, telephone confirmation w/official
- field measurement of the building
- underlay drawings of existing building's plans/elevations
- design sketches on tracing paper
- final hardline design drawings on diazzo prints, floor plans/elevations, meeting presentation
- written preliminary Estimate of Construction Cost

Construction Documents Phase Basic Service:
- general specifications
- site plan if required
- structural design/sizing, assuming standard platform framing/concrete spread footings
- building floor plans and exterior elevations
- interior elevations of bathrooms, built-in cabinet or unique treatment areas
- door and window schedule, product specific
- chases/soffits provided for heating, air-conditioning, and plumbing
- selected details and section drawings
- electric lighting and device plan
- electric lighting schedule, product specific
- room finish schedule and allowances
- kitchen/bath cabinet schedule, 1/2" scale kitchen plan and elevations
- kitchen/bath plumbing and appliance product schedule
- generic HVAC spec requiring design-build drawings of builder
- first owner-redline meeting for document revisions at 80% complete
- builder's bid co-ordination, Invitation, Bid Form
- redline meetings and document revisions per builder shakedown
- preparation of builder's Construction Contract

12.1 Continues on attached sheet.

This Agreement entered into as of the day and year first written above.

OWNER

Mary Green   *John Green*
_____
(Signature)

Mary Green   John Green
_____
(Printed name and title)

ARCHITECT

Peter Wilson
_____
(Signature)

Peter Wilson
_____
(Printed name and title)

AIA CAUTION: You should sign an original AIA document which has this caution printed in red. An original assures that changes will not be obscured as may occur when documents are reproduced.

AIA DOCUMENT B151 • ABBREVIATED OWNER-ARCHITECT AGREEMENT • THIRD EDITION • AIA® • ©1987
THE AMERICAN INSTITUTE OF ARCHITECTS, 1735 NEW YORK AVENUE, N.W., WASHINGTON, D.C. 20006   **B151-1987 8**

Sample

Attachment To Wilson/Green Agreement, Made on September 18, 1992.

Article 12 (continued from page 8)

  12.1 Basic Service includes (continued from page 8)
    Construction Phase Basic Service:
- co-ordination of HVAC and plumbing layout
- construction administration including: Change Orders, biweekly Payment Requests, punch lists, Certificate of Substantial Completion and Final Payment
- site observation visits, once weekly (not including Job Meetings)
- additional site observation visits, another one per week (NIC Job Meetings)
- Job Meetings with owner and builder, weekly
- final one-time color and product finish specification

  12.2 The Owner may request any of the following Additional Services:
    12.2.1 architectural renderings, models, or photography
    12.2.2 testimony or personal appearances before public authorities
    12.2.3 site plan for preliminary zoning approval
    12.2.4 color enhanced design drawings, markered prints and foamcore/acetate mount
    12.2.5 landscape planting plan
    12.2.6 "as-built" record drawings
    12.2.7 heating or air-conditioning specification and schematic layout plan

be, probably in the $500 to $1500 range. It will be enough to carry his effort to your first sketch design meeting, and will ensure your job gets into his pipeline.

Casting the Agreement

Your call should end with a tentative deal for his services. Specifically, a revised Basic Service task list per

12.1 and 12.2, an adjustment to his proposed fee in 11.2.1, and hopefully a Fixed Limit of Construction Cost clause in 12.3. If you will engage an attorney to review your contracts, he will be better at doing some of the foregoing "mop-up" than you. But if you are going it alone, type up only the language required for these clauses, paste them onto your contract copy, and then make copies to forward to him. He should prepare the true contract originals, filling in the balance of the information. If he acts lost or slightly resistive, you can prepare the contracts yourself.

Call the local AIA Chapter and have them send you four or five forms of the current version of AIA B151. Use the sample contract (Example 14) as a guide, include your newly customized clauses, and prepare two identical documents. Sign and send both to your architect. He will sign both and send you back one original. Be sure to keep a copy to refer to when he gets your mailing. You need to confirm that the information he has entered into the agreement agrees with understandings made in the proposal, such as hourly rates for Additional Services and the like. With the agreement conformed, cut him his retainer check and mark your calendar for the upcoming design kickoff meeting.

CHAPTER 5

DESIGN MANAGEMENT

OVERVIEW

In this chapter you will learn how to get the most from your architect as you move through the design phase of your remodel. Your objective is to lay down a subtle trail of "goodies" that will lead him further than he is used to going. You want to take care of his unpleasant tasks so he can get to the "important stuff" sooner and spend more time there. He is to set out for your approval a detailed vision of what you will ultimately build. In this phase he will not produce drawings that direct the builder; that comes later. I have promised myself that I will not instruct you to tell him how to design. For if you have done a good job in your hiring process, he will be able to teach me a thing or two.

ABOUT DESIGN, TIME, AND ITERATION

Designer jeans, designer sunglasses, graphic designers, design-builders. There are many different perspectives on the term. Is a sculptor really designing when he physically picks up clay and begins to form the idea he has in mind? I think not. He is crafting. Design is primarily done as a predictor of the crafted solution. It is the imaging of the solution before production begins. It's purpose is to try solutions when unpleasant sur-

prises are inexpensive. So iteration is the essence of the design process. A better solution emerges when I work up something quickly three separate times than if I spend the same time and evolve only one refined solution. Particularly in the front end, design quickness is very important so you can sense the whole solution as you scrutinize the details. You must put something on the table so you can make it better. These are visual "what-if's"—What's wrong with this? What if it were like this? Does this work? A good designer starts with a negative presumption about his work; he must be ready to toss it in the trash can. In architecture, because it is complex and lengthy, design iterations are continually spinning off even during the construction process itself. As the building takes shape, design drawings frequently become product mock-ups, whereby physical pieces are combined to predict problems or opportunities.

Design schools teach that each iteration should involve goal setting, research, organizing data, imaging the solution, critique and revision (which is really returning to the beginning of the design loop). I was taught that each solution needed to have a "parti," a single concept to organize design decisions. The building represents a place of "refuge." Or it is really "two separate buildings." There is no doubt that a building which demonstrates clear emotional intent is better. Yes, better for the occupants, and a better cultural artifact as well. But unfortunately, I think to most archi-

A

DECK SPACE

If an exterior deck is on your "wish list" when you begin a redo effort, do not relegate its design to a separate contractor. A successful deck should function as an extension of an interior space, incorporate lighting and specific furnishings or functions, and address the yard in a reasoned way. In Photograph A workmen are setting beams for a deck outside a breakfast room. The new patio door and roof pent have been placed into an existing wall; the three-window group beyond occurs in a new cathedral-ceiling family room add-on. Because most patio doors are notorious for lacking low-maintenance privacy treatments, a trellis has been incorporated into the deck to reduce views from neighboring homes. In Photograph B notice how the deck is set 1" below the breakfast room floor, which helps it function as an extension of interior area. When vining plants take over, and with the doors open at night, two down-lights will wash the trellis, making the deck feel like a part of the home. The tops of lighting standards (cedar 4 x 4's) are designed to hold adjustable low-voltage heads (see photograph C). Notice that the two wall-mounted luminaires on either side of the window group repeat the cedar-top motif; deck lighting and building lighting are totally integrated.

B

C

tects in the trenches, design is more a matter of identifying and solving problems in a descending hierarchy. What are the constraints or opportunities of the site? How must the new structure sit against the existing building? Where are the nonbearing parts of the structure? If we need a media room that seats twenty, how big are we talking? For remodeling work in particular, conceptual design themes are hard to hold onto. One of the first big decisions you need to make may totally subordinate any separate style to that of the mother-house.

Because your intent is design excellence, you must resolve to manage your designer well. And this really means helping him pace decision making according to his contract. If your agreement calls for a kickoff meeting, two sketch sessions, and then a meeting to redline the final design drawing, you will want to have all your information ready to give him in the kickoff meeting. You also must bring to this meeting a consensus as to what conceptual design objectives should be set. You should encourage many schemes, whole-house views, and design partis in the first sketch session. The second session should be somewhat interior-oriented, culminating with a favorite overall concept. The final design meeting is a time for squeaking small things around. In design, as in many other endeavors, timing is everything.

PREPARING FOR THE KICKOFF MEETING

Before your architect puts a line on a piece of paper, a lot of information must be within easy reach. He may prefer to do his first "measure up" visit either before or after the kickoff meeting with you. Several weeks in advance, you should confirm a list of things that you need to give him in the kickoff meeting. It will take that much time for you to find and organize your meeting "package." He may be used to doing some of these things for you, or he may want to check what you have prepared. But the more you can do, the more true design time he can give you.

Revised Objective, Budget, and Design Challenge

This will be the last time you need to jot down the design intent and budget. You have a proposal version and probably a contract version. Now is the last chance to fine tune critical understandings before work begins. You should bring them back into the kickoff meeting in some written form (even if only a markup of the proposal or contract), talk about them profusely, and revise them with the designer. If he needs to reorder or restate them in his own terminology, let him do so. He is trying to personalize the challenge and take up your "hot potato." Take notes so you will remember things. Don't forget to shoot high for design excellence via perceptual goals, to re-emphasize the importance of the construction budget but keep the "real one" secret, and remember to give the designer positive reinforcement.

The Things-I-Like Clip File

Most owners have a manila folder crammed full of magazine pages and newspaper clips, snippets of things that appeal to them in some way. Sift these down to five or ten and bring them to the initial meeting. As you walk through the pictures with the designer, be sure to talk about "why" you like them. If you

A

B

For most of suburban America, vinyl siding is born of necessity. It is quickly installed, lightweight, forgiving, consistent in color, inexpensive, and recycled (Photograph A). But its downfall is trim. Photograph B is what seems to appear in every subdivision when someone says "cheap, low-maintenance siding," that is, vinyl siding in aluminum-capped wood trim. And although high-end vinyl products offer upgraded trim, they never seem to have enough flexibility for remodeling projects. Bottom line: for a quality job use top-grade vinyl only when the architect wants to custom detail the trim. A possible exception is where the existing structure is in terrible shape and the budget allows no alternative.

CHEAP CHIC

feel strongly about a "look" or "treatment," speak up! You are the boss. But don't say that you need this exactly; say, "I would like to have something similar."

Feelings About My House

This turns out to be very important to a designer. As he explores solutions, he will have opportunities to remove things, save things, or add new things that may or may not reinforce old ones. Sometimes he will get lucky and find that hiding a wart is a freebie. You should quickly walk through and around your house asking the question, "What do I like or dislike about my house?" This is particularly true in obvious expansion areas. Sometimes we don't appreciate what we have until it is gone. Write down your thoughts and pass them on to your architect; he will refer to it late one night on the drawing board, stopped at a crossroad. This is how to point him in your direction.

Existing Architectural Drawings

When I begin a new project I consciously reserve design opinions until I am able to look at floor plans of the existing building. In the absence of old prints, I have to prepare new drawings of existing conditions. Many structural and functional relationships are hard to pick up while walking through a home. This of course is more important in large projects where functions may be moved around internally. In my neighborhood, where homes are commonly 50-plus years old, I find spatial surprises all the time, such as closets that were once stairs and concealed fireplaces. Frequently there are thickened walls with plumbing or ductwork in them. Sometimes I find several different structures, built in stages. Usually the structural logic is immediately clear from the plans. Without opening

up messy test holes, you can be 90% certain that a "beam will be here," for example. Having a good floor1-floor2 set of plans makes lower floor load-bearing walls clear. If you are lucky enough to have architectural drawings of your home (see Chapter 2 for looking into municipal files), your designer will be pleased. I hope you have asked for this credit in negotiating his contract (in Chapter 4).The kickoff meeting is the time to hand them over. Make sure he understands that you want them back unmarked. On rare occasions, clients have given me drawings that they have prepared themselves. Although they may save a small step (not enough for a fee credit), I must still check out the house myself. I use their drawings to walk through the home, taking off dimensions, and noting discrepancies. Back at my office I will have to hardline a new underlay.

Survey or Plot Plan

Whatever site plans you have available should be in the kickoff meeting package given to the architect. Your designer must ensure that what he designs will have a good chance of receiving a permit further along in the process. He will use the plot or site survey as an underlay to design with and then he will copy it again as a Construction Drawing. Most townships will require that "permit drawings" include a site plan that shows the entire existing building on the property, makes a distinction between the old and proposed structure, shows the number of stories in the old and proposed structure, and specifically calls out any "critical distances." More bureaucratic towns will have more items on their laundry list. Building permits are normally issued for architectural "construction drawings," which will come later. These are not the design drawings that are about to begin. If a municipal plot plan will suffice, you should secure and forward it to the designer who will trace it into the documents. And so the question constantly reoccurs: "Is the plot plan available at the building department okay, or is a newly engineered survey needed?"

More than half of my remodeling projects require engineered surveys, but this is because my projects are in dense, upscale neighborhoods where every inch seems important. I frequently wrestle with the fine line between the expense to the owner ($500 to $1500 in my area) and the risk involved. The downside is a scenario where a new structure is demolished because it was placed in a location later found to be contrary to the zoning code. My recommendation for surveys is as follows. If your project will run up to the maximum zoning envelope, or if there is reason to question the location or size of your existing house or plot (particularly in the area to be improved), hire yourself a surveyor. But before you do, make sure you ask your architect if he concurs. He should make a note for you about what should be provided in the survey. Spot elevations (for groundfall) or constraining objects (like trees) are the kinds of things that may be important to locate.

Other Project Actors

One of the reasons I enjoy this work is the human comedy I see. Human beings are chock full of surprises and interesting relationships with others. I have learned to ask my clients about other background people who may become involved. If there will be other pros involved later, I want to know about it so their service can dovetail with mine. If there will be trusted friends whose advice may be followed, I want to know about that as well. I once had a client who came back to design meetings with decisions totally different than his previous "leanings." Much to my dismay, I found out that his wife's father was financing the project and executing his veto power in the wings. If I know about these peripheral clients I will try to engage them in the process as directly as possible. Lightning bolt decisions based on second-hand information hurt the quality of the redo and waste money and good will. You should therefore give your designer the courtesy of disclosing these eccentric relationships with people whose advice you value. You will tell him where you want your toilet-paper dispenser, and where you pile your dirty clothes, so tell him this too. If he is smart, he will take their name and phone number and invite them to the sketch-design meetings. If he is not smart, you as check-writer should prepare the invitation for him.

Planning Objects

In an ideal world, your architect would plan all interior space with the furnishings that you would be likely to use. On the other extreme, he could give you generic architecture with no interior design whatsoever, which is rather typical for speculative housing. If you don't push the right buttons, some designers will crank out the latter. Here are two quick clues to determine if you are being short-changed. First, if the architect doesn't ask about furnishings in the kickoff meeting or if his first sketch-design drawings don't show at least some generic furnishings, you have a problem. Second, you may also need to worry if sketch elevations show identical, nongrouped windows, symmetrically placed throughout the new structure. If he is genuinely designing for interior functionality, this will not happen. Within a mile radius of my home there are no less than five new family room additions in the $60,000-plus range with lots of windows, skylights, cedar shingles, and stone veneer. And I know that they

PLANNING OBJECTS

EXAMPLE 15. *This is a visual inventory that has been taken from a home prior to remodeling. Anything large that will remain in the ultimate redo must be planned for. Many designers will try to avoid or delegate this, because it is tedious work. Owners should try to provide as much of this design criteria as possible. The data might include 2-D or 3-D sketches (with dimensions) such as these, or even photographs of furnishings. This will be go a long way toward ensuring a sophisticated, liveable project.*

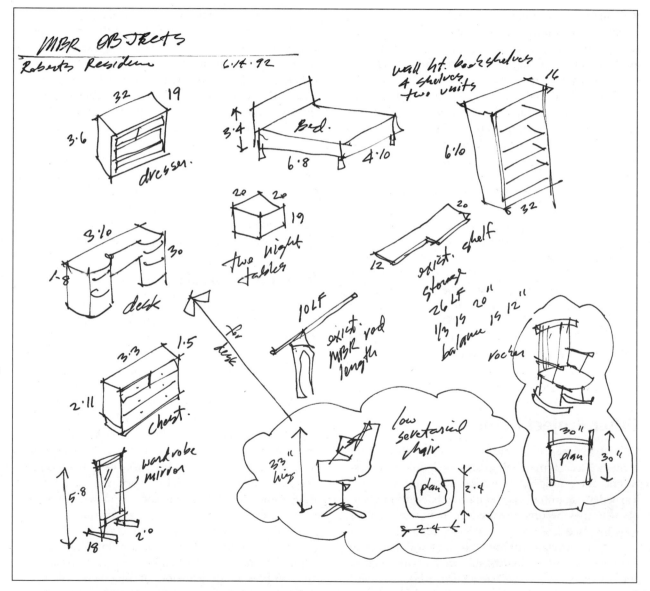

are totally unfurnishable, because I can see right into them from the curb at night! I wish I could have told those homeowners that they have a right to expect their designer to give them a place to put things (and a right to window blinds as well).

A list of planning objects is an absolutely critical item to transfer in the kickoff meeting. Rather than trying to draft plans of your home or sketching a design solution, spend your time here. These objects may be large items that you will definitely place into the altered spaces, such as a valuable painting, a piano, an heirloom china closet, or a master bed with side tables—anything that is important to you or uniquely sized. These planning objects should include exterior items as well—a barbecue grill, an oversized automobile, a golf cart, a picnic table group. If you want your designer to give you sophisticated work, you must make it easy for him to use extra criteria. I recommend that you go further than the simple list and provide him measurements of these items as well. If you can sketch or photograph the objects (Example 15) they will certainly be used; this is the way he thinks, in 3-D.

Thermal Systems

When your home is remodeled, your environmental system will be changed as well. In the very beginning, the architect must decide whether the existing system should be altered, or a second unit provided to supply the added space. This is one of those cost thresholds that needs attention early on. If a new system is required, more mechanical space will be required and another $2000 to $5000 allowed in the budget. The need for a new system is frequently viewed as "bad news" because of the expense, which is roughly equal to a new fireplace. This bitter pill can be made more palatable by using the redo as an opportunity to zone

the house for day-night use. Typically this will be a discreet system per floor, one supplying the sleeping areas at night, and the other supplying the living areas during the day. With clock thermostats, this type of system will save operating costs and increase comfort levels.

You are one of the "experts" who should assess your existing heating or cooling system. Regardless of what load calculations indicate, you are the one who must decide whether the existing system labors to keep up with the thermostat settings. If this is the case, adding more load will mean augmenting the existing unit or providing a completely new one. The other source for system information is your original installer or the subsequent service contractor. If they advise that your system is on its last leg, the decision to replace it with a new, larger capacity unit is easy. If the mechanical contractor is familiar with your system, verbally sketch out what you are planning to do with your home. Then ask about the system's excess capacity and the ramifications of your planned redo. Also ask if he would like to be considered to do the work and ask him for a "ballpark" price to change the system. If you are happy with his firm, you may later elect to have the general contractor solicit a specific quote from him based on the Construction Drawings. As I have said before, separate contracts with the owner, should be made only as a last resort.

You should write a short paragraph about the status of your heating and cooling system for your designer to refer to. It should include the mechanical contractor's phone number if you have it, and whether you want to solicit a proposal from him. Include product literature on your system, if available. For systems on the replacement borderline, I will always assume the worst, that is, a new second system. I will plan in the space and keep the number in the budget. During the bidding process, several different general-sub

A

COOL HOUSE

Having the character of an old home and the benefit of central air conditioning is many people's dream. Most remodeling projects will at least consider the inclusion of this alteration, alongside the need for architectural changes. Although there are infinite variations, most new environmental systems entail extending the existing hot-water heating system to new rooms, and then providing a separate forced-air cooling unit in the attic. Photograph A shows an air-handling unit in the old attic, with round, flexible supply ducts entering the new work at the left. This unit is an electric heat pump, supplying both heated and cooled air to grills distributed throughout the home. Outside, its condenser/compressor must sit on a small slab, and is connected with coolant piping to the attic (Photograph B). Later these conduits will be "dressed" with an aluminum cover matched to the siding color. The location of grilles in old homes is always problematic. Because cool air falls, diffusers should be either in the ceiling or high on a wall; therefore, floors with attics above are rather easy to do. Photograph C shows a three-way diffuser located away from a ceiling fan. This would normally get a four-way grill in the center of the bedroom. For single-unit systems (as apposed to a two-zone, two-unit system) on lower floors, the objective is to find space for a vertical chase for two large ducts (supply and return) in a central location, and then branch ductwork out at the ceiling. Photograph D shows a soffit that has been created in the kitchen to throw air into the dining room beyond. Although the grill on the other side did not require such a long run, the architect required that the soffit extend over the entire doorway to sit more comfortably in the kitchen.

teams will give you their assessment of the system. Ultimately, only the subcontractor who will design the alterations, make the changes, and stick around to ensure that it performs will render the final solution.

Repair or Maintenance History

You should advise the architect about any repairs or improvements that have been made to the house. If you have always intended to replace the old windows, or have avoided repainting the house until the remodel was done, write it down. These exterior maintenance tasks, when combined with the new construction, will go a long way toward integrating old and new (if this is your design intent). A typical bad-news item is the need to rip up and reroof the entire structure as a consequence of the new alterations. This may be a surprise that ranges from $2000 to $15,000. If you have fiberglass or asphalt shingles and know that you presently have two layers, be sure to advise your designer. If the first roof is cedar shingles on skip-sheathing, this can also spell extra expense. This is primarily a budget issue, although I have done a few projects where we tried to keep from replacing the entire roof by interfacing the new roof in a certain way. You will get better unit prices if you can include large maintenance tasks into the new construction work.

Current Problems

Any other problems with the home should be noted. Ask yourself if there are any places that leak or appear to have settled. Cracks in the building should be pointed out. If you worry about them indicating undue settlement, you should try to ascertain the direction of movement of the different planes involved. On a wall,

you can break and glue a glass slide (from a microscope) across the crack to observe slow changes in position. Recording movement through an annual cycle of seasons would be ideal, although several months of observation may show significant change. Some cracking is normal because houses naturally move with temperature and humidity changes. The cycling cracks will move to a stop point and then reverse direction. Their unsightly results can be mitigated by flexible membrane products. But when a component continues to travel in the same direction (or seems to be accelerating!), it could forecast serious failure, and further professional guidance should be sought. You do not want your remodeling project to aggravate existing structural problems.

The Building Department

If your local building department has been involved with your property, you should so advise the architect. This is particularly true where conflicts have occurred. Sometimes properties become informally known as problems-to-watch, spelling potential trouble for new construction. Previous adversarial owners may have left you a legacy of bad will with your municipal officers. If you have had harsh words with building officials, or are in some nonconforming posture as far as they are concerned, your architect and builder need to make sure they dot all their I's and cross their T's. Just like you and me, if someone gives them a hard time and then comes back later for a permit, you can be sure they will not receive expeditious treatment. Municipal employees can make the kinds of rulings that cost you money. Your pros can usually resolve these problems with good people-handling skills, but only if you let them know it is needed ahead of time.

Adjacent Neighbors

Only you know which neighbors will be concerned about your making major changes to your home. You owe them advance notice about the imminent construction, and should do it before the design phase. They may be inconvenienced by worker's trucks and noise. Or dust and debris may be a hazard to their cars and kids. For properties that are close together, you should meet with each neighbor and verbally outline your project for them. You want to hear their opinions about such things as potentially blocked views, increased shade, unclear property lines, and removal of trees. This really is the right thing to do, to alleviate their concern by letting them into your process slightly. Although you frequently cannot satisfy everyone, at least you will have considered their viewpoint.

You should assure your neighbors that you will do a professional job, that you will conform to the neighborhood zoning code, and that you will consider their objections or concerns. As busy as families are today, many neighbors learn of a project on their street when the backhoe arrives to excavate. More than rude, this is not smart. It is rather common for an inflexible neighbor to become upset with a redo and cause problems, particularly when they are responding to rumor. I have attended meetings where we presented projects to an unfriendly neighbor. This can be very stressful for all parties. I know of at least one long-term feud resulting from a remodeling job. It seems to be mostly older residents who have a penchant for resisting change and delving into other peoples' business. If you have senior citizens in close proximity, they deserve special handling. If you have listened to your neighbors early enough, it is rather easy to include some of their concerns into the parameters laid down for your designer. And guess what—the project will be better for it.

Calendar, Occupancy, and Availability

You should come to the kickoff meeting with some notes about your family's schedule for the upcoming year. Things like vacations, camp, hectic periods at the office, and household visitors will all be affected by your project. Design will probably span three to five weeks, wherein you need to arrange roughly one meeting a week (with both spouses present) at your home. For my clients, this tends to be weekend-days or weekday-nights. Preparation of construction documents will take roughly the same amount of time, although your involvement will be much less. Bidding will take three to four weeks. After you hire a builder, it is likely that he will not be able to begin work for several months. Construction will usually take from two to six months to complete and will need to be choreographed with the weather.

In the Philadelphia area, we can dig footings through November; after that the ground is frozen until spring. Having the house open to the elements is not usually a problem because the new structure is built over or beside the old one, closed in, and only then are penetrations made into heated area. If your job is completed while the ground is frozen, the builder will be unable to final-grade and repair your yard until spring. This is not usually a big deal to most folks, although I consider it less than desirable.

As you know, the construction phase has the potential to be rather hectic if you will be living in the home. The ideal arrangement is for the owner to be close enough for consultation on site several times a week, but with no one living in the home. This is rarely possible, although I once did a job where construction took place while the family was on sabbatical. The furniture was moved into several rooms and covered, and

LOOKING FOR TROUBLE

Early in the project, you and your pros should survey the existing structure for signs of trouble. The most likely culprits will be radical settlement or patched wet spots. Photograph A shows an overhanging second floor that has slipped down several inches (one course of brick). This problem (likely to have resulted from water damage) will be stabilized from underneath, before the addition in made. The familiar cracked ceiling in Photograph B is the result of a detachment of wood lathe under the plaster. This is an expensive renovation, particularly when considering that the cracking continues through the integral plaster crown-molding. Photograph E shows a first-floor bearing wall that is deforming the floor. This indicates structural failure in the basement area, which needs shoring up before the home is traumatized with redo activity. Many older homes hold secrets along with their structural surprises. The steel beam in Photograph D (over the left corner of the window) appeared when the small roof-pent was demolished. Removing the ceiling inside (Photograph C) revealed the probable reason for the steel reinforcing: fire damage. Plumbing leaks are prone to weaken a structure as well.

A

A

NEIGHBORHOOD It is important that remodeled homes sit comfortably among their neighbors. This redo (Photograph B) expanded the rear exclusively and therefore could be designed from primarily interior criteria. Although the stucco skin and grey and white trim mimic the older tract house (Photograph A), the contemporary shape is formed by the large greenhouse unit high in the two-story atrium space. In this case resale comparables were of little concern to the retired owners, who were real estate pros as well. Most owners will want to do a cost-value analysis before proceeding with a major redo.

B

then the rooms were sealed. Although the working conditions were ideal and the owners did not have to live with daily noise and dust, their long-distance control of the job was less than perfect. I faxed long status reports to the owners weekly, received decisions via telephone, and occasionally mailed them photographs. Money was wired directly into the builder's and my bank account. They came home to a clean (almost finished) job and missed most of the trauma. It made me a nervous wreck, however, to have the owners come home to a completed job with no budget to make changes. This is what I call a love it or die scenario!

THE KICKOFF MEETING

I have prepared an agenda that you may want to use for your first meeting with the designer (Example 16). It lists the things that you will want to pass to him for later use. Briefly walk through them so he understands what the "package" includes. I also list several issues that you should bring up and discuss. Access for large construction equipment should be considered in the beginning. If it will be a problem, it could skew the design solution. Point out the house-drain location and electric panel to the designer. Location of the sewer exits will determine the better locations for plumbing changes. Electrical service may need to be upgraded, in which case another $1000 should be allocated in the budget.

Function Switching

If you have large underutilized areas in your home, be sure you talk about the possibility of switching functions. Usually it is cheaper to reorganize existing space than to build new area, although reusing space may carry a hassle penalty that new construction doesn't

have. Many times it is desirable to build a new kitchen in a different location while the old one continues to function. This avoids having to clean drywall dust out of the sink before you prepare dinner! Underused rooms can also signal the opportunity to open up spaces vertically or horizontally. High ceilings and glass can make rooms feel great, if professionally done. You want to encourage the architect to design around furnished-space requirements, and maybe even a little smaller than you think you need. Meticulously planned small spaces can be perfectly comfortable when attention is paid to windows and lighting. Remember that the best single way to take money out of a project is to reduce the floor area.

Hopefully your designer will have time in this meeting to isolate the most important functions in your design program, and begin exploring your options and preferences. He may ask questions, do sketches of floor plan vignettes or bubble diagrams (Example 17). Places where the most money will be spent should be explored in detail. These could be kitchens, bathrooms, master bedroom suites, media-seating groups, fireplace, and whirlpool areas, to name just a few. You should ask if there are any large or constraining products you can begin shopping for. Such things as whirlpool-type bathtubs, shower enclosures, large kitchen hoods, and prefabricated fireplaces will need early selection. A little further along you will likely have a long list to consider and approve. Your meeting should end with a list of action items to be done by both parties, and a next-meeting date.

SKETCH-DESIGN MEETINGS

After the architect has measured up your home, you will meet again. Your second design meeting should

re-kicko.wps
KICKOFF MEETING AGENDA   **Date:** ....

For Initial Session With Designer

Review Design Criteria Package:
      Revised Objective, Budget, and Design Challenge.
      The Things I Like Clip-File.
      Feelings About My House.
      Existing Architectural Drawings.
      Survey or Plot Plan.
      Other Project Actors.
      Planning Objects.
      Thermal Systems.
      Repair or Maintainence History.
      Current Problems.
      The Building Department.
      Adjacent Neighbors
      Calendar, Occupancy, and Availability.

Other Issues to Talk About
      Access for Construction Equipment
      House Drain Location and Electric Service Capacity
      Capture Under-used Area First
      Function Switching
      Design To Furnished-Space Requirements Only
      Special Equipment, Furnishings, and Spaces

Action Items:

Next Meeting Date:

KICKOFF MEETING AGENDA

EXAMPLE 16. *This document is a good tool to use in the first working meeting with your newly hired designer.*

include an assessment by the designer that your project will conform to the zoning code. For questionable situations, he should submit a sketch site plan to a zoning official for preliminary approval before any further design work is done. You should also inquire about whether he sees any aspect to the house that is nonconforming to the building code. Depending on the extent and location of changes being made, your construction may have to include unexpected alterations to the life-safety aspects of your home. There are several things to be checked in the design stage:

    stairway proportions and clearances
    garage and mechanical equipment enclosures
    upper bedroom egress
    structural conditions that may not conform to
      current standards

A

B

LANDING BREAK THROUGH

When additions are made, the connection is frequently made at the top or bottom of stairs, because this is what stairs do: they circulate traffic. For the redo in Photograph A, the new work will be accessed by removing the closet at the bottom of the stairs. Photograph D shows break-through work has begun on the outside of the wall in the addition. The solid masonry construction was a surprise, as the architect had incorrectly assumed that the brick was a veneer on wood framing. In Photograph B, the penetration is complete, and shortly thereafter, drywall is finished in-place (Photograph C). New hardwood flooring is being installed on the landing in Photograph E. Note how the old stringer-baseboard (top of photograph) has been reworked to turn down before the new opening. The carpet will be removed and the old hardwood stair will be refinished.

C

D

E

exterior stereo speakers

open counter

foyer bench

kitchen

Breakfast

EXAMPLE 17. *One of the earmarks of a neophyte designer is his over-developing floor plans and then in essence "watering it so the walls grow into a building." Experienced designers bring a three-dimensional concern to a space being sculpted. And remodeling projects always have upper window, room, or roof constraints that mold the solution. Here is a real-time sketch presented by the author at a design meeting with the owners. It is only an idea for discussion. In this redo, the owners elected to proceed with another scheme. Most designers work with markers and sketch paper, expecting the hardlined Preliminary Design Drawings (that will follow) to be a cut-and-paste of these type of idea sketches. The trellis-screen part of this idea did survive and took the final form shown in the photo on page 121.*

Such code-required changes to existing elements of the home are usually limited to floor areas actively being worked on (and a building permit issued for). However, for many municipalities, when the cost of the new construction exceeds 50% of the value of the existing home, the entire structure must be made to conform to current standards.

Hopefully, the designer will not try to "sell" the initial solution. Schemes should be explored, taken apart, and then put back together again. Sketch paper should fly! He should show sketch floor plans, partial building elevations, and 3D vignettes of various spatial ideas. As owner-manager you must be cognizant of where you need to be at the end of meetings and how many iterations you have contracted for. Before the architect goes to a hardline design drawing of the solution, if you aren't happy with what you see coming, you should speak up! Maybe another iteration of meeting-then-drawing board-time will get the extra-something you are after. You can always switch to Additional Services until you get it right.

Spatial Mockups

If you have a hard time translating even the best sketches into reality, you are not alone. Many owners want to say "I know the drawing is of a 10' x 12' dining area, but how big is that really?" One of the advantages to working with home renovating is that parts of the ultimate design scheme already exist. This gives you a frame of reference for understanding scale. As you and your designer go through schemes, don't be afraid to get up and try out how big things feel to you. Aside from drawing materials, I always bring a 24' tape measure and a large roll of white art-tape to design meetings. A quick line of tape on two walls and the floor will let you sense how big another paper-space will be.

In rooms where furnishing dimensions will be critical, I may mock up things like a table and chair group, so the owner can see the clearances I intend to provide. A pass-through, knee wall, or window opening is easily critiqued, when so marked on a wall. Mock-ups are really important ways to understand architecture; you should be alert for any physical object or marking device to help visualize what is to come.

Designing to Budget

The designer should bring to each sketch meeting a rough-cut cost breakout of the current design scheme. You must listen closely to his presentation for "you can't afford it." This is frequently hard for owners to hear. Up until this point, you have been stating what you want. Now the architect should begin to show you what you can have and how much it will cost. If he resists talking about cost, you put the topic on the table. Remember that his estimates are educated guesses for evaluating options, not quotes. True costs will not be known until after builder-bidding is complete.

Trimming costs in design is limited to "scope" issues, because it is not possible to rework detailed cost estimates for each variation. How big is it? How small? Can we include this? We can't afford to work on this. If your designer says the scheme on the table is $10,000 over budget, then you must search for a combination of new floor area, rehab floor area, and fixed cost items to remove from the job. The construction costs shown in Chapter 2 (Example 1) are adequate for trying out different what-if scenarios. If you must have walls of brick or stone veneer, or a slate or cedar roof, the unit prices in this table should be moved upward. You could bring your overrun down to its budget by taking the fireplace, french door, extra windows, and the built-in media wall out of the new

A

B

SLAB VERSUS CRAWL

In the land of basements, frame floors are the first choice for an addition. And owners rarely opt for full basement under the new frame portion, because of the added expense. A crawl space of rough slab under a wood-frame floor is the most common system. It is not the cheapest. A slab-on-grade floor will cost significantly less than a crawl-space floor. But it has its drawbacks. It is cold, hard, and unforgiving for mechanical and electrical systems. Many times the height of adjacent grade will determine what your new floor choices will be. Photograph A shows the new-old juncture of a redo about to happen. The existing doorway is on slab; it is a "walkout basement" that has been converted to a den. Notice that the adjacent grade is slightly above the floor level, and rising. Matching-up new and old floors here requires a concrete slab, and is being provided in Photograph B. Note how close the wood sole plate is to the soil. This is close enough to pose a potential moisture problem, and will be mitigated by special flashing at this seam, and the soil will be regraded to swale water away as much as possible. Notice how high the door threshold is in another redo in Photograph C. This height allows the standard crawl-floor to be constructed in Photograph D. Here, the seam between new block foundation wall and the wood bearing plate will sit high enough out of grade to require no special water-resistant detailing (Photograph E). The addition in Photograph F sits somewhere in between the two preceding examples. Notice the soil level above the top block course in the upper left. Although the grade level suggested a slab, the owners wanted a frame floor. This was accomplished by rather radical final grading away from the building, special flashing techniques at the block-frame seam, and good footing drains. The owner was advised that water could appear in the crawl space, and to cover that eventuality, an opening and gravel pit was put into the crawl slab, for a potential sump pump. At last report, there was no water in the crawl space.

C

E

D

F

A

C

SAVIOR SOFFIT

Those versatile dropped soffits are an important interior design tool. Photograph A shows a bearing wall being replaced by a small steel beam, which is being concealed in the soffit in Photograph B. This lowered ceiling is defining a small furnishing space between two rooms. The soffit in Photograph C occurs high in a two-story space and will conceal a motorized greenhouse shade, while holding recessed lighting. The ceiling architecture in Photographs D and E mimics the shape of a kitchen island below. Notice in Photographs F and G how the media center and library use similar soffits on opposing sides of the cathedral family room space. They bring the grandiose scale down to an intimate level and comfortably house the task lighting.

B

F

D

E

G

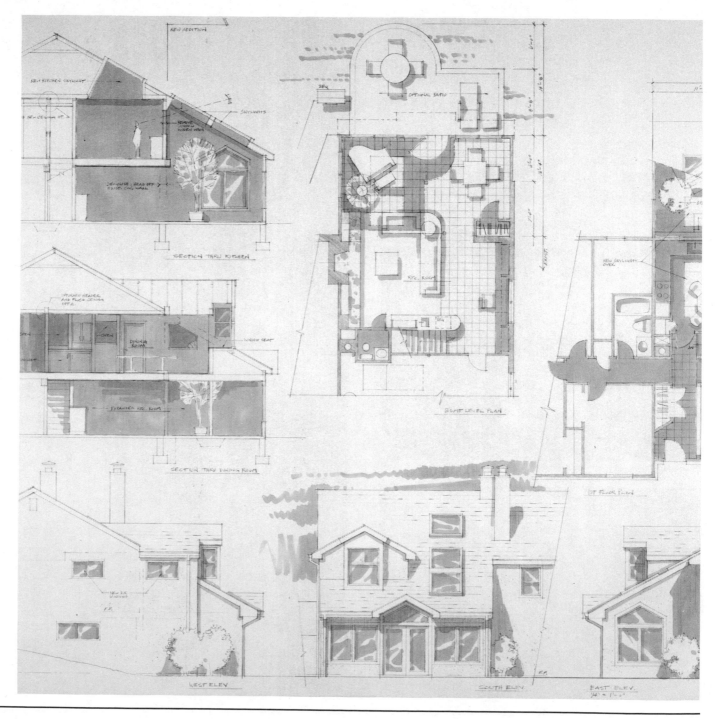

REJECTED SCHEME

EXAMPLE 18. *Many times a designer will bring several different schemes to a design meeting. This is because each one has pros and cons, and it is up to the owner to decide. Often it boils down to cost. It may go like this: "Here is another possibility, but it will cost roughly $8,000 more than the other one." This is a typical hardlined Preliminary Design presentation. It is a diazzo print or blue print that has been enhanced with markers. Architects have a tendency to "marker-up" design drawings to make them look exciting, as well as to communicate the architecture.*

family room. If that sounds a little sparse, maybe putting back the $3000 worth of glass would make it palatable. At $86/sf then you need to lose 35sf of new floor area to stay on budget. Using the 16' x 20' family room in the table, this would mean cutting 2' out of its length. A 16' x 18' family room would be just fine as long as we have those windows and doors in there. Now where can we find $3500 for the lost fireplace, because we want sizzle, not palatable! This is the kind of decision making that is necessary to move construction dollars around in design.

Many times pushing work into a second phase makes a lot of sense. This means that you design now for the space that you want. Then, knowing that you are over budget, you let the architect proceed either through design or bidding. Stopping at design would mean that you use the designer's last cost estimate as the basis for drawing the future-phase line, and only allow construction drawings to begin on the project that will certainly be built. If you truly expect that you will build the next step some day, this is the minimum you must do to avoid blocking off some exciting phase-two possibilities. You would probably get a better value for your architect's services if he went ahead with construction drawings for the total job, rather than piecing the effort up. Establishing the phasing line after bid-verified costs are in hand would mean that the total cost picture would be clearer at demarcation time. I once did a job where the owner expected to move within five years of construction, and he elected to pull-out-the-stops for the phase-two portion of his redo—an extra bedroom, a large pool and exterior deck, and landscaping. We created a very exciting presentation of the overall design, which he ultimately used to sell his property with. I charged him very little for the extra work. He used a designer for what he does best—visualizing and selling architecture. This allowed him to market his home to two separate buyer niches: the improved "what it is now" dwelling, plus the "what it could easily be" version.

Design Drawings and Cost Statement

Your architect will bring hardlined drawings to the final design meeting, and a written statement of Probable Construction Cost. The drawings should synthesize the better ideas into a pleasing whole, the culmination of your prior sketch sessions. Preliminary Design Drawings (Example 18) frequently show generic furnishings, important finishes, and include plans and elevations. It is very important that they depict both the new and old building, so that this relationship is clear. The design drawings are a pretty picture of the architecture to come. Although there is much more designing to do, these drawings fix the larger decisions into place so the focus can shift to smaller details. The optimum final design meeting would produce a few last-minute redlines of the design drawings, the owner's approval to proceed out of the project design phase, and a marked-up questionnaire (covered in chapter 6) for preparation of the Construction Documents.

CHAPTER 6

Construction Documents

BACK TO THE PROCESS

Once you have approved a design scheme for your project, the construction documentation phase can begin. You should now have a three-dimensional picture in your mind of the project to come, and some exciting prints to show your friends. The designer must now develop the design drawings into a package of documents that will facilitate the selection of a general contractor, and later provide him with the information he needs to build the job for you. The builder will use the documents to obligate and supervise his subcontractors and secure a building permit. By now your architect should be a trusted advisor; please remember that he will undoubtedly have unique twists to put on my methodology. In your management role, your job is to make sure the architect delivers on his contractual service list and has a good answer for omitting any of the following recommended instruments. As before, you want to do the kind of homework that keeps him working in his high-value zone. To the degree that you can find the time, you should bring to him the information he needs to know, before he has to ask. The designer should prepare for you the following construction documents:

- Drawings and specifications (AKA working drawings)
- Invitation and guidelines to bid
- Bid form
- Contract for construction

Although the Owner-Architect Contract calls for these in one phase, I will break out bidding steps and instruments separately in Chapter 7. Just remember that all of these documents need to be interconnected to work. Together, they represent the smartest purchase you will make over the life of your project. That's right—a well-prepared description of the project combined with a savvy solicitation for its construction will put tens of thousands of dollars into your budget. Buildings are, after all, similar to new automobiles. If you approach a dealer with a precise specification of the car you want, and ask for his price in the right way, you will save a lot of money.

The most expeditious way to initiate working drawings is to deal with them in the final design meeting. If you need to take more time to "simmer" your prior redo decisions (per Chapter 3) and hold off your proceed order, this is a natural time to do it. If the project still needs cost-cutting, don't let Construction

149

PLANNING AHEAD *Although this electric outlet appearing in a structural steel column may seem insignificant, its presence is not easily achieved. It requires the kind of planning that only a good set of construction drawings can provide. Because a seating group will pass by this column, and because the slab-on-grade floor makes floor receptacles a difficult option, this outlet has been called-out in the documents for a very good functional reason: to provide reading light for a sofa.*

Documents begin until you and the designer concur on some design drawing redlines to make this happen. You will see the architect less now, for he has to go backwards a bit, make many detailed technology-type decisions, and "build the project on paper." If you haven't already done so, this is a great time for you to begin shopping for products for your redo, but only after being pointed in the right direction by your designer.

A DETAILED QUESTIONNAIRE

The partial checklist in Example 19 shows the level of detail that now needs to be addressed. Many of these preferences have been discussed in design. Even so, you and your designer should now review each space again and record the results. The decisions or strong preferences that you have reached thus far should be set out. You do not have to know all these answers. A questionnaire such as this is a way to solidify the activities that each party should undertake within this project phase. This, then, is your homework before the meeting: mark up such a checklist and bring it for review and discussion. In Example 19 I have itemized things to be considered overall and in the two most complex rooms, the kitchen and master bath. I have included the master closet because it seems to be the one most neglected. Your list should be extended to include every space in your design program.

EARLY PRODUCT DECISIONS

The architect should advise you of any product decisions that need to be made before he can go further, and the things he needs to work on before the next meeting. Some spaces should not be detailed and documented until specific appliance or fixture selections have been made. This might mean that you have to hustle out to a showroom and see a specific item to "bless." Although most objects can be either selected by the designer or treated generically for now, there are a few product choices that cannot. These are the decisions that are rather subjective and have to be made by the owner, and that will also radically change adjacent elements. Soaking tubs, for example, are so large and uniquely shaped that a specific product should be picked by the owner as early as possible. Just imagine how a later switch to a corner-type jacuzzi would alter the size and access to the master bathroom! Although I try to present these kinds of product options in the design phase, I find that when owners actually sit down and go through specific product catalogs, they see things they want that I could not have foreseen. For remodeling,

products in this hurry-up-and-decide category are as follows:

- Master tub/shower, size/shape
- Bathroom pedestal sinks, width
- Kitchen range versus separate cooktops, size
- Kitchen wall ovens versus range combination
- Kitchen refrigerator width, 32/36" or wider
- Kitchen sink, width
- Decorative or feature hoods in kitchens, size
- Island or peninsula zero-clearance fireplaces or wood stoves, size
- Large-screen or projection-type television units, size
- Patio or french-type door groups, in-swing, out-swing, sliding
- Circular stair, width
- Greenhouse or other expansive glazing product

SPECIFICATIONS

Working hand-in-hand with graphics, the specifications are an efficient, written way to describe what the builder will be required to provide for your job. Whether the architect places the specs into the large-sheet drawing set, or holds them out in booklet format (also called a project manual) is the designer's decision. I weave my specs into the drawing set because discreet booklets tend to disappear from job sites. This encourages a reoccurring construction glitch. Remodeling plumbers and electricians, for instance, will mark up and use drawing prints profusely, but frequently miss any unique requirements spelled out in written specs. I gave up on commercial spec formats long ago because their voluminous size ensured avoidance by residential workmen. Although I don't always achieve the goal in

re-wd's.wps
OWNER'S QUESTIONAIRE   Date:

For Preparation of Construction Documents

1.0 GENERAL

1.1 Do you know of any hazards, failures, settlements, or leaks present in your home?

1.2 Would you prefer slab-on-grade, crawl-space, or unfinished basement for a foundation?

1.3 Are you aware of the degree of insulation that your present home has? walls, attic.

1.4 To what degree of repair do you want your lawn returned to after construction?

1.5 Any particular measures to be taken to separate construction and living activities?

1.6 Should the builder provide a rental porta-potty or use your bathroom.?

1.7 What are reasonable start/stop times for loud work noises in your neighborhood? Any constraints to a
       Monday through Friday work day?

1.8 Have any arrangements been made with neighbors for construction equipment access or workmen parking?

1.9 Any preferences in heating or air-conditioning systems? Any opinions on extending the existing system
       versus providing a new unit? Cast-iron baseboard radiant hot water/steam, hot water or electric
       baseboard convection, forced air, air-cleaning filtration, electric or hot water radiant panels underfloor or
       in walls/ceilings.

1.10 Describe the capacity and response of your present hot water heater.

1.11 Do you know what your electric-service capacity is (usually 100A or 200A)? How many breaker spots are
       open?

1.12 Do you know the location of any water or soil lines in your floors/walls/attic?

1.13 Are there any plumbing, mechanical, electrical, or lighting changes that you wish to make as part of this
       work beyond the new construction portion? Such as exterior outlets or hose bibs.

1.14 Are there any important privacy measures to be incorporated into construction? Visual, Audible, Security?

1.15 How would you prefer to shop for products for your home? Lighting, Appliances, Cabinets, Plumbing fixtures
       and Accessories, Hardware.

1.16 Do you have any exterior finish preferences? Zero-maintenance versus some? Adjacent surfaces to be
       renovated?

1.17 Do you have any window and door preferences? True divided lite versus snap-in grills? Casement, awning
       or doublehung. Exterior finish options, vinyl or aluminum clad, factory paint, Interior: hollow-core flush or
       embossed, solid paint-grade wood, hardwood, louvers.

1.18 Do you have any interior finish preferences? Paint/paper, carpet, hardwood, vinyl, tile floors. Adjacent
       spaces to be renovated?

1.19 Do you have any interior trim preferences? Match existing wood trim as much as possible from off-the-shelf
       profiles? Mill profiles if required to match exactly? Use new trim profiles that are better but respectful of
       the existing treatments? Painted or stained hardwood?

QUESTIONNAIRE FOR CONSTRUCTION DOCUMENTS

EXAMPLE 19. *This partial checklist shows the level of detail that needs to be addressed prior to the start of Working Drawings. Although this document covers general project issues, plus the kitchen, master bath, and master closet, your list should be extended to include every space in the redo design program.*

this axiom, I do believe it: "If you can't say it in one page, then you haven't worked on it long enough!"

The specifications are the best place to describe the process by which the builder is to construct the job. There must be a balance here between giving him a fair description so that he will know what is expected, and keeping the language succinct enough not to intimidate him into overpricing his quote. Example 20 shows a portion of my spec covering project method-

ology. Of the builders who bid my work, new firms tend to quote high, while experienced ones become extremely below-market competitive. This is because of the wisdom of the builder-architect team set out in the AIA contract roles (Owner-Architect and Owner-Builder). It's rather easy when everyone knows their job. So minimizing the fear of the unknown is an important message that needs to be sent between the lines of the specifications. The specs must not sup-

2.0 KITCHEN

Check the new features or appliances that you prefer. If you know specific brands or model numbers at this point, please so indicate.

oven, fuel source, size/location, wall-mount/under-counter, combination

microwave, location, size, built-in/free-standing, convection, combination

refrigerator, width/depth/height, built-in or standard, finish

freezer, width/depth/height, built-in or standard, finish

sink, type, finish, size, bowls, self-rim/undermount/integral, accessories, separate food prep sink

faucet-set, type, finish, soap dispensers/accessories

cooktop, fuel source, burners, surface type/finish, down/up draft venting

exhaust hood, type, finish

trash compactor, width/size, finish

garbage disposer, right or left location

dishwasher, finish

countertop, materials: solid surface/laminate/granite, edge treatment, special heights or depths, unique food prep surfaces: maple butcher-block/marble/stainless steel

backsplash, materials, height, special profiles

computer, audio source/speakers, phone, TV, or fax, location, type, size

trash and recycling can, location, size, concealment

countertop appliances provided by owner, garaged/exposed, type, location, size

HVAC supply: toekick or radiant wall/ceiling panel heater, heat source, location, AC grilles

unique cabinet requirements: wall heights 84/90/96", open/closed soffit, glass doors, full height utility/pantry cabinets, appliance garages, desk/drawer base unit, drawer bases, roll-out trays, lazy susan base, corner base cabinet type, bookshelves, lighting shroud at wall cabinet bottom, decorative moldings (crown etc) or motifs.

cabinet type, brand, finish preferences, frame/frameless box, concealed/exposed hinge, door style, pull hardware, interior options

cabinet toekick, finish preference

lighting, recessed, task/utility/mood, under wall-cabinet, halogen, incandescent, flourescent, pendant

floor finish, sheet vinyl, vinyl tile, prefinished/custom hardwood, ceramic tile

message center, tackboard, material, size, location

unique planning requirements: display dishes, furniture, art objects

3.0 MASTER BATHROOM

bathing tub/shower preferences, combination or discreet fixtures, color, premolded shower base and/or surround, custom tile or solid surface shower, finish limits, aluminum/glass enclosure type: sliding, frameless, hinged, heavy-duty, obscure or art glass, custom tile accessories: towel bars, shelves, seats, soap shelf

vanity countertop, material: solid surface/granite/laminate/tile/hardwood, width, chair access, mirror size

lavatory and countertop, sink type: self-rim/undermount/pedestal, size, style, material, number of sinks, integral fabrication, solid surface/laminate/granite, edge treatment, backsplash material/profile, mirror size and edge treatment

cabinet, type, brand, finishes, depth 18/21/24", door style, pull hardware, toekick finish

watercloset, type, standard or low rise, water-saving, color

owner provided countertop appliances, hair dryer/dental irrigator/razor, location, size

lighting, utility/task/mood, shower/tub, vanity, sinks, watercloset.

bath accessories, TP holder, towel bars, robe hooks, toothbrush holders, cup shelf, soap shelf, tile/brass/chrome/glass, size, location, brand

finishes, floor: tile/hardwood/carpet, walls/ceilings: paint/paper/tile, finish limits and edge treatment

mechanical: unit heating if preferred, radiant wall/floor, electric wall/ceiling, heat lamp, room exhaust vent

4.0 MASTER CLOSET

privacy configuration, separate storage or combined for his/her use.

long hanging clothes: rod-length required (storage width), rod to bottom dimension, his/hers.

short hanging clothes: rod-length required (storage width), rod to bottom dimension, his/hers.

built in shelves/cubbies: folded clothes or other? capacity, height/width/depth per module

rod and shelf type: ventilated wire system, custom wood, metal utility

built in furniture: seat, valet, dressing counter

factory cabinets, type, brand, finishes, door style, pull hardware, toekick finish

shoe rack or storage shelf, describe

finishes, walls/ceilings: paint/paper, floor: carpet/hardwood

lighting, utility/task

unique planning requirements: furnishings, appliances, exercise equipment, type/location/size

---

plant or confuse language that is "boilerplated" in the upcoming Owner-Builder Contract. It should advise the builder that his commission will require use of the owner's contract form, and advise him of the role the designer (or others) will play. Most specs will go on to provide direction in specific trade categories, allowing the architect's experience to be brought forward from previous jobs. This kind of trade information may be placed into the construction documents in many dif-ferent ways, so the absence of an item in the specs should not necessarily set off warning bells. Product allowances, for example, can be called out in the specs, in the schedules within the drawings, or in the bid form (if attached in the contract). Except to ensure that the designer has them, and that they include a description of the process to come, you should not worry about specifications. These are simply one of the architect's tools by which he delivers his service.

A

B

STOCK CABINETS

For most remodeling projects, cabinet groups will be 95% from stock components. This assures the owners of factory-made quality and predictability. The more expensive lines are generally the ones that offer more factory-supplied options. After the products arrive on site and are fastened into place (Photograph A) a certain amount of custom trimming work will be required. The extra trim components may either be purchased loose from the cabinet supplier, or from the local building supply house, depending on the compatibility of finishes. Photograph C shows a relatively inexpensive cabinet with a pre-finished side. The carpenters have covered the back with oak-veneer plywood from a local supplier, applied outside corner molding, and then stained it to match the pre-finished unit. The absence of a continuous toekick is noticeable, and will mean that the cabinet will show mop and scuff marks before too many years. The base cabinet in Photograph B has used a factory side panel and site-fabricated a returning toekick. This island cabinet group backs up to a gypsum knee wall, eliminating the back-finishing issue. The wall oven cabinet in Photograph D has a pre-finished side. Notice the pulls, which are by a separate hardware supplier. This is a Formica Surell (solid-surface) top with a 3/4" bullnose edge. The top of the stock cabinet (Photograph E) has been corniced with a wood profile trim, painted to match the natural cabinet finish. Because this color is used throughout the kitchen on casing and baseboard, the effect is a unified interior. Lavatory base cabinets may be the only units that rarely require custom trimming. They are easily set into place (Photograph F), and will accept any of the numerous tops currently available, such as this solid-surface product (Photograph G).

C

D

E

F

G

A

B

ECONOMIC CONTRAST IN MATERIALS

Saving money in large expanses of the building's skin allows lavish treatment in strategic spots. In this redo (Photograph A), the designer has elected to contrast the utilitarian vinyl siding (triple 3"), craftsman-style painted wood trim, and the existing stucco. As long as old and new are massed and colored the same, the different textures add interest to the whole. Note how the wood brackets on the new entrance emulate the older version on the bay window in Photograph B. Only wood trim gives the carpenters enough flexibility to fabricate a compacted, vented soffit such as Photograph D, with end-brackets designed to nest aluminum gutters. Photograph E shows that someone is testing clearances for the vinyl siding at the corner-skirt condition (the photographs on page 158 show a less expensive way to combine wood and vinyl). Inside the entry alcove, T&G wood beaded siding is substituted for vinyl. Brickwork on the stoop and a custom door pediment (Photograph C) add special touches to this crucial element of the home.

C

D

E

A

VINYL-IN-WOOD TRIM

The least expensive way to combine vinyl siding and wood trim is to simply butt the j-bead against 5I4" wood trim. Here it will be caulked at the bottom where meeting the skirt board (Photograph A). The 3" holes in the eave (Photograph B) will receive a white aluminum louver to vent the attic. For this job the rafter tail has been exposed to match the rest of the older home. This view (Photograph C) shows a flush rake-fascia and open porch framing being mixed with the vinyl siding. Although not shown here, I recommend a layer of building felt under the corner trim (but over housewrap) and painting the trim (prime plus the first of two coats) before vinyl is installed.

B

C

A

B

UNIT-WIDTH PROBLEMS

Photograph A shows a window that has been trimmed out over a fiberglass entry door. This, of course, is unacceptable interior carpentry, but it is understandable as well. The door and window are from different manufacturers, and their variant widths and jamb profiles have led the builder astray. The solution to most of these unit-width problems can be solved by layering a deeper trim in two steps, first with flat stock, followed by the specified casing set over the perimeter (Photograph B). This extra touch is not a big deal, unless you have to rip out and start over. Photograph C shows the door/transom with reworked casing. Notice how the upper left corner of the trim barely misses the cathedral ceiling. This is a dimension that was planned for by the designer when sizing up the vestibule framing.

A

OUTSIDE ENTRY TRIM

On the outside of the problem transom (see page 160), the width variation was caught in time so ripping out the trim was not necessary. Photograph A shows that the casing will not quite be able to lay over the window nailing-fin and sit 1/4" behind the door jamb below. Because the trim engaged other adjacent casework flush, and gave no perimeter "casing line," this exterior solution was simple. A 1-1/4" half-round molding was run around the group disguising the difference in width (Photograph B). When viewed in its entire entryway (Photograph C) the door and window trim look compatible. Note that the adjacent siding is a triple-three vinyl product, being used without its standard vinyl casing, because only wood is flexible enough to finesse such glitches in the field.

B

re-specs.wps

PARTIAL SPECIFICATION   **Outlining a Process for Remodeling Projects**

For Inclusion in Construction Documents

00700 GENERAL CONDITIONS OF THE CONTRACT: The General Conditions of the Contract for Construction contained in the American Institute of Architects (AIA) Document A107, 1987 Edition are hereby made part of these Construction Documents. The successful Contractor will be required to execute this short-form agreement with the Owner. It specifies the responsibilities of the Contractor, Owner, and Architect for construction of this project. AIA Document A107 is available from the Architect. Note that the Architect will be under separate contract to provide Construction Administration Services for the Owner per Article 10.

00800 MODIFICATIONS TO GENERAL CONDITIONS: The General Conditions portion of AIA A107 is hereby modified as follows:

    Article 8. Owner: following 8.3, add 8.4:
Owner will provide one set of Construction Documents for Bidders. The successful Contractor will be furnished free of charge five (5) copies. Additional sets will be furnished at $2.00 per sheet and $.15 per page plus the cost of postage and handling. If the Contractor so requests he will be furnished one diazzo copy and one reproducible copy of the drawings.
    Article 9. Contractor: following 9.2, add 9.2.1:
All materials delivered to the site, but not incorporated in the building, shall be the property of the Contractor, and the Contractor shall be responsible for its loss or damage except by fire.
    Article 9. Contractor: following 9.12.2, add 9.13:
Contractor shall execute, at the completion of the work, a Release of Liens from the Contractor and all his subcontractors. The General Contractor shall affix to his Release the names of all sub-contractors and prime suppliers. They, in turn, shall submit individual Release of Liens. All coordination of this process shall be by the General Contractor..
    Article 15. Payments and Completion: following 15.1, add 15.1.1:
For retainage, the Owner will pay 90% of each line item (Schedule of Values) until Substantial Completion; final payment will be released upon certification by Architect that the final Punch List has been satisfied.

01005 SUMMARY OF THE WORK: It is the intent of these documents to provide a finished building. The Contractor shall include all necessary accessories, equipment, labor, etc to complete the work when such items may be reasonably assumed to be part of the completed building, even though such items may not be shown herein. The work may be generally described as:

The existing house is four stories plus basement. The kitchen will be replaced, requiring a small expansion of the first floor to a point just short of the second floor above. The master bath will be redone and the master suite will be altered. On the fourth floor one bath is altered and another added. Four floors of finishes will be renovated. The exterior will be repainted.

PARTIAL SPECIFICATION

EXAMPLE 20. *Minimizing the builder's fear of the unknown is an important objective that needs to tailor the language of the specifications. This is a portion of a spec covering redo-project methodology. Most specifications will go on to provide direction in specific trade categories, allowing the architect's experience to be brought forward from previous jobs.*

Retainage

Notice that in the example spec (Example 20) the builder is being advised that the construction process will include a Retainage and a Release of Lien. In the Invitation to Bid we will also advise him that the owner will pay for "work in place," or leveraging, as I call it. These three requirements are very powerful ways to protect your interests and ensure that control of the job remains in your hands. The Retainage is a predetermined amount of money that will be withheld from each payment request. This is a standard convention to ensure that you will always have enough value remaining in the contract to ensure the builder's motivation. This is especially important toward the end of the job, a time infamous for its level of animosity. In practice, the hold-out really is the builder's profit, which he should not be given until total satisfaction of the job. For easygoing general contractors, this is their "out" with their subs. This makes the owner or architect the bad guy, requiring that he hold 10% of each line item until the whole job is judged acceptable. Although some builders complain about Retainages, it should not be a problem for a professional who is intent on delivering a complete and timely job, as long as he is given sufficient lead time to plan his cash flow. For projects with Retainages, the builder will usually need to submit Payment Requests in two-week cycles, which is more frequent than for larger jobs. I advise owners to make the Retainage an absolute requirement of the Bid, and at a later time, to be flexible in arranging the details of payment cycles with the selected builder. Remember, the designer is in the loop to certify the request, so you will receive a form saying, in effect, "the builder is asking for this much, which I judge to be reasonable, and you owe this much." The retainage will have been set aside; you just write the check.

A Retainage requirement is one of those concepts that causes marginal builders with poor credit, or with nonloyal subs, to "pass on the job." I also find some resistance to Retainages from well-established builders who make no claim on cost-competitiveness; they are the equivalent of Prima donna architects. Although they offer genuine assurances (verbal only) that they would never walk away from an unfinished job, the real issue is where risk will reside during construction. Given a little daylight, most builders will ask for one third of the contract up front, which is totally unacceptable of course. This places all the risk at the owner's plate. Should the general contractor cash the check and fall over dead from a heart attack, what happens to the owner and his dream home? The builder has 20 years experience doing this, and the owner, zero. A Retainage combined with managed cash flow levels the playing field.

Release of Liens

The spec also requires the builder to provide you with a Release of Liens before he receives final payment for the job. If you felt uneasy about your designer or any of his subcontracted labor, you could ask him to supply a Lien Release as well (but this is rarely done). The Release of Liens is extra paperwork that the builder needs to do, to ensure that a disgruntled subcontractor or supplier will not come after you for payment outside the contract at some point in the future. Each state has its own mechanic's lien law which allows a workman to lien your property until his complaint has been satisfied in court. There are many examples of disputes that don't involve any claim against the owner for wrongdoing, but that force him to make final payment on the general contract and then fight to clear his property title. Your project specification should

A

B

ANATOMY OF A FLUSH CEILING

This basement den was to expand into a larger two-story space and encourage guests to take the stairs down to the lower level. Because the existing ceiling was extremely low, the designer chose not to use the standard dropped-girder technique to replace the demolished outer wall. Instead a steel "T" member was notched into the existing floor joists (Photograph A), so the new drywall ceiling could be continuous. Unfortunately this upturned-T made air conditioning runs into the new space problematic. The solution was to stop the steel girder short and allow one joist bay at the end, to bear on the old block wall (Photograph C). This allowed a supply duct to run inside the joists, pass around the steel member, and throw conditioned-air from several diffusers along the edge of the second floor deck (Photograph D). Rather than the common practice of breaking the block away, it was cut with a power saw to protect the bearing integrity of the wall to remain (Photograph B). The finished space in Photograph E, with its dead-flat ceiling, looks deceptively simple but successful.

C

D

E

A

C

B

ALUMINUM CAPPING

Driven by the need for flexible low-maintenance exterior trim, builders routinely cover wooden profiles with aluminum sheeting. Although both aluminum and vinyl siding manufacturers have many trim kits to cover the entire exterior skin, the use of their siding butted to aluminum-capped trim is hard to beat. Notice in this job that the fascia board, the subfascia and outside corner trim, and window casing will all be capped (Photograph A). The building inside corners will receive the vinyl-siding bead, as will the butted condition at all capped trim (Photograph F). Capping requires the use of a metal-break (Photograph D) to make long straight bends or cuts in the aluminum stock. The roll-stock comes in 24" wide rolls in colors matched to most siding swatches, and is purchased with nails of the same hue (Photograph C). Carpenters fabricate over-bent profiles so the capping will clasp the wood blocking and require very little nailing. Photograph E shows a piece ready for snapping onto a corner board. The porch trim in Photograph G show the results possible when carefully detailed by the designer. The panel nesting the exterior light and the porch columns are both capped in aluminum. Notice that the hard edge of the aluminum has been softened with a trellis for hanging plants. This flourish is easily accomplished with the old standby: painted wood. Of course, it will have to be repainted in several years; the aluminum will not.

D

E

F

G

A

WORKING DRAWINGS

The construction drawings should be brimming with information that workmen will refer to as the building takes shape. It is common to see the drawings out on the job (Photograph A) when the project first begins and critical dimensions are taken off for the foundation or rough frame. But they have a tendency to disappear as drywall appears on the job. If the documents are as detailed as they should be, they will contain many trim, fixture, and finishing requirements. The builder or lead carpenter should be reminded to keep the set out and visible, encouraging easy referral until final punchout (Photograph B).

B

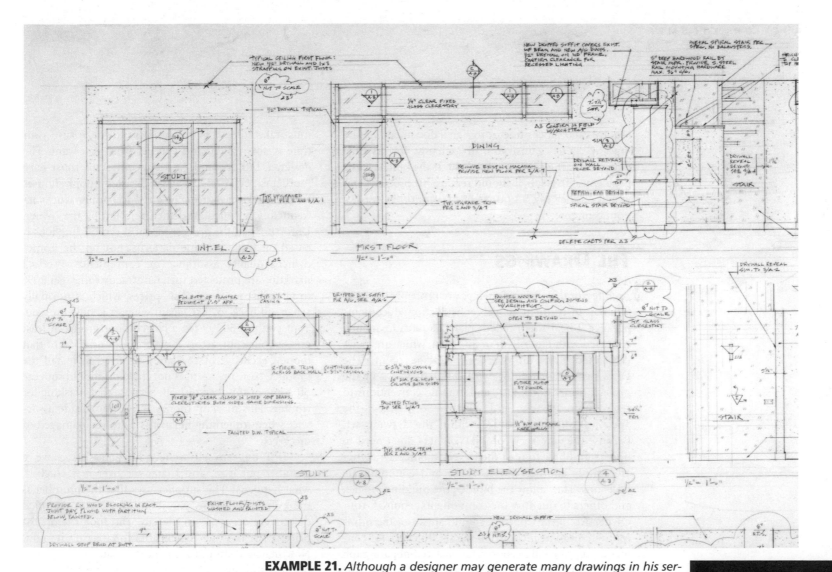

EXAMPLE 21. *Although a designer may generate many drawings in his service, they become "sacred" only when attached to the builder's Contract For Construction. Working Drawings vary widely with respect to level of detail they approach. Your Owner-Architect Agreement should specify the minimum to be included. This is an excerpt from a Working Drawing showing interior elevations. For important spaces like kitchens, media centers, fireplaces, and bathrooms, the set should include such drawings. Interior elevations are an important clearinghouse for where to go for more detail. Following the graphic drawing symbols, you can inspect the specific door 114B required in Elevation 2/A-3, or as shown in Elevation 3/A-3, inspect the detail provided for the planter-pediment on another sheet in Detail 5/A-7 (graphic 5, sheet number A-7).*

WORKING DRAWING

require each subcontractor to sign a document, releasing any claim against you, in exchange for his final payment by the general contractor. If the builder has a problem with a sub, it should remain his problem, not yours. As they say, an ounce of prevention is worth a pound of cure.

THE DRAWINGS

Architectural working drawings are probably the most familiar instrument in the construction documents package. I hear them called "plans," a term frequently confused with Floor Plan or Site Plan, which are views illustrated from an overhead vantage point. The Drawings are brimming with different views of the project, dimensions, lists, and graphic conventions to refer items back and forth. Sometimes the Specifications are included within the drawing set. Because they are very complex, owners don't need to understand how to read their every nuance. Drawings are simply another way to make and communicate decisions. They allow the builder, the building official, and others to quantify the components required. Your Owner-Architect Contract should spell out the minimum items to be included in the set. To check for conformance, you will need to refer back to Subparagraph 12.1, which I hope you discussed in detail with the designer. Other than that, you should rely on the architect to walk you through the Drawings, focusing on appropriate items.

HOW TO SHOP FOR PRODUCTS

Most remodeling projects lack an efficient process to select, approve, purchase, and install products. You must take control of this process to make sure your time is not wasted, and you get what you want. The designer, builder, and each subcontractor must have mutual expectations to avoid disaster. Supply houses have restocking charges for good reason; products are frequently installed, and then rejected by the owner. Unfortunately, the process for most remodeling jobs is based on trade revenue patterns, not on the homeowner's quality assurance or convenience. Product markups are protected turf. Contractors may get 20% to 60% discounts off "list" prices, which is normally remarked back to "list" again when it is billed to you. So if you pay $1500 for a french door group, at least one of your contractors is getting around $500 of that money, exclusive of the labor required to install the product. Now my point is not that you should squeeze off some of this for yourself, because that is asking for trouble. This markup money is your downside assurance when something fails, or is delivered damaged or incorrect.

If I buy myself a new kitchen sink, have a plumber put it in, and I later discover it is cracked, what happens? The supplier says that the plumber is the culprit, and the plumber says it was supplied defective. Because I am the guy who took the off-list price, I am the one responsible for making it right. Now maybe I can put some heat on one of these two, but it is still my problem. And I don't have the leverage with the supplier that the plumber would have, especially if it were "his" supplier. When he buys product from an establishment all year long, and then he brings a sink back and says "this is a bad one," they take his word for it because they value his business. I will have to pay the plumber to disconnect the sink, so I can take it back and try to make my case in nontrade jargon. If I am a good talker and they agree to exchange it, I will still have to get the plumber back for a reinstall. I do not recommend that owners purchase their own products, because things do go wrong. And labor is more expensive than product. You want to be able to call your plumber or general contractor and say, "I don't care whose fault it is, make it right." Call-backs are taken in stride by pros if you haven't broken their chain of responsibility. Just remember that by changing the way purchases are made, you will make money change hands between your general contractor and his subs. Product call-backs are not a problem if these purchase understandings are crystallized up front in the bid.

Conceptually, you want to describe a comprehensive list of products that you want, and then price their provision by as few suppliers as possible. The initial list will never be 100% accurate. And you will not do the initial package shopping, the bidding general contractors will. You and your architect will get the construction document schedules (the Kitchen and Bath Fixture and Appliance Schedule, the Lighting and Electric Device Schedule, etc.) as accurate as possible, but when the builder is selected, you will want to debug them with his suppliers. These suppliers are the ones you want to visit and have show you products.

In practice, this means that you should take the schedules in the drawings at the redline meeting and provide as much additional detail as you have time for. I will leave my clients a Sweet's Kitchen & Bath Source Book[1] for general perusal, plus show specific product "cuts" (pages with pictures on them) for important items I recommend in the schedules. Sometimes I visit showrooms, but this is usually much later, after subcontractors express their preferences. Many times homeowners want to shop early because it gives them a knowledge base for later final selections. Just remember not to promise that you will purchase your products at a particular place, because it is likely that you will not be able to keep the promise. Your should rely on your pros to direct you to the best pricing routes.

It is common that any single supply house is able to supply only about 90% of the specified products. Sometimes they don't carry specific lines for purely competitive or convenience reasons, and sometimes they have a better product to offer. The designer's catalog may not be up to date, or a product may be recently discontinued. At any rate, the expertise of the subcontractor and his supply house should be carefully solicited. This is best done by "catalog cut" packages. The successful builder should instruct his sub to have the supplier refer to the pertinent schedule, and prepare a product "cut" copy for each item, noting any recommended substitutions. This is usually covered by a master quote sheet, which can be correlated to cost corrections if required. This cut package is forwarded back through the builder to the architect for review with the owner. If you, the owner, don't approve of an item, then the general contractor will find another supplier who can provide the product you want. Any differences in price between the contract spec item and the final substitution are adjusted by Change Order.

ALLOWANCES AND FINAL SELECTIONS

An allowance is an amount of money set aside for future purchase of a particular product or service. The smart use of allowances makes the bidding process less risky for builders, and serves to spread out design decisions into the construction phase, rather than

A

B

PLASTIC FANTASTIC STUCCO

There is good reason for those entire communities that are skinned in stucco. It is practical and cheap. It can be shaped into the familiar corner-koines or radiused over wing walls (Photograph B). In Photograph C, a worker lays on the "scratch-coat" over metal lathe. It is priced in the same range as vinyl siding, well below everyone's favorite: bevel cedar siding. Using pressure-treated blocking, and galvanized metal control-joints (Photograph A), the surface can be scored, or fields can vary in color and texture such as in Photograph D. Here a skip-n-drag texture in white will be separated by wood trim (to follow over the wood blocking), from the sand-textured grey stucco.

attempting them all in the front-end. We'll talk about several good ways to make product picks in later chapters. I like to use allowances in the construction documents, as long as I feel confident that the values will be realistic, the contractors will understand and use them consistently, and they are verifiable at the time the actual product prices come in. These cost allocations can be expressed either as a lump sum, or a unit price.

From the owner's standpoint, you should ensure that specified allowances are for material, not labor. This is because your final decision is being withheld primarily because of the product itself, not upon how it is to be installed. The installation aspect of the job will be called out elsewhere in the construction documents, probably in the Drawings or Specs. You want to free up the labor aspect of the job, so that it can be competitively priced by the bidding general contractors. They should all "assume" the same material allowance values. It is also extremely important to make the allowance language as specific as possible. I have seen allowances for ceramic tile, for example, expressed in several different ways; the first allowance below is not acceptable for competitively priced redo projects.

Allowance: $10/sf for ceramic tile

Allowance: $10/sf for the list price of ceramic field tile excluding any installation labor, and excluding any substrate, grouting, or sealing material or labor.

The second unit-price example above tells the contractor to figure all his costs into the specified total contract price, and he is to begin with the "list" cost for the standard field tile (trim shapes are priced differently) as shown. The important thing that most contractors forget is that the allowance should be used by the owner as a budget benchmark as they shop for products. Therefore, the allowance units must be expressed exactly as they will encounter them in showrooms. It should be the homeowner's tool, not simply a way for the contractor to produce a safe quote. When the tile salesman says the price is $12/sf ("list" is implied), and you have a $10/sf allowance for 1000sf of area, then you know you are over your budget by $2000 and must look for a cheaper product. Using a "list" price in the allowance precludes you from having to inquire what the contractor's trade discount is, which is fraught with accuracy problems (not to mention the honesty ones). Lump-sum allowances are easier to use, but any skewed numbers are harder to catch in large quantity products. I frequently use them for things like:

Allowance: $200 list price for pendant light fixture and lamp L9, excluding installation labor

And you thought shopping was going to be so easy! Actually, you just need to quickly check your designer's allowances in the construction documents against what you have learned herein. Remind him to play it safe with the numbers and stay on the fat side. It's better to get credits back when you make your final product picks, not the reverse.

REDLINE REVISIONS MEETING

When construction documents are nearing completion (your Owner-Architect clause 12.1 probably says 80% into this phase), you and the designer should meet again. The architect should bring all the construction documents to your home for discussion and revision. Drawings and Specifications should be complete, except for coordination of notes and dimensions, and possibly a drawing detail or two. Within these instruments you should find the important items called for in his contract. It is important that you go through each sheet or page. Ask if anything has changed, because sometimes this is necessary. If you see something you don't like, try to come to a better solution in the meeting. Remember, however, not to "waffle" on prior design decisions without discussing whether it will cost you extra to go backwards. If the change makes the project better, and doesn't undo too much, I will usually not charge Additional Services.

The result of this meeting should be two sets of documents profusely marked up (red pens are traditional): one is for you and one for him. I recommend having the designer wait until the owner has had several days to peruse the documents at a slower pace. He can get proceed orders via mail, when receiving your marked-up drawings. With your approval to move forward, he will take the redline sets (yours and his), make each revision as noted, and finish up the Drawings and Specifications. You may continue to shop for interesting products to write into your product schedules, or you may want to "shake a few bushes" for your long list of builder candidates.

CHAPTER 7

HIRING A BUILDER

HIRING INSTRUMENTS

In this chapter we will go through a methodology to hire a builder. This process is threaded around three important instruments that round out the architect's Construction Documents Package. The Invitation to Bid and the Bid Form are aids to help the initial solicitation, and The Contract for Construction of course is the document that finalizes the hire. All three of these items attach themselves (via internal language) to the balance of the package, the Drawings and Specifications, which we covered in Chapter 6. Unless you, the homeowner, take the reins, the architect will push the process along. The goal, of course, is to find and hire a builder who is uniquely suited to the project you have planned, and who will do so for a fair price. You are looking for a tandem professional to balance your redo team. Your specific tasks within this objective are to make sure that the solicitation documents are prepared to your liking, that the process moves along as planned, and that you stay involved enough to ensure that the architect is working the methodology in your interest, not his.

Apples-to-Apples Process

It is easy to get lost and worry too soon about unimportant project details. In the same way that you hired the designer, you want to solicit proposals from a qualified group and evaluate them in all the important areas. It is essential that each volunteered bit of information be comparable across all the candidates; in this project phase, an apples-to-apples correlation of bid data is more important than any one construction technique being specified in the documents. You should expect the redo to change slightly when the builder "shakes down" the project after hiring. So for now, the well-managed process is God, for He will bring you a good builder.

FAIRNESS AND RESPECT FOR THE BUILDER'S TIME

Sometimes I get invited into projects to find that the owners have been walking the equivalent of several baseball teams through their house, trying to find someone who will offer them what they seek. Most are builders, who invariably try to produce a drawing of an addition and a price. Usually, the owners have not done their homework and want to rely on the contractors to tell them what they need. They may not really "like" someone, but they will let him "take a run on" the job anyway. They also sense that something isn't adequate (how much can be done for free?), and therefore they can't commit to any

MAKING THINGS

When you remodel your home, you may catch the fever that most builders carry: the love of making things. If you have made your own clothes, built model airplanes, restored an old car, or reworked your garden each year, then you understand the satisfaction derived from seeing direct, physical results from hard work. Altering your home may be the largest lump of clay you will ever sculpt. If you will not be happy simply directing your pros as they lay their hands to the work, you should speak up. Your architect and builder can isolate some portion of the redo for you to personally produce. But make no mistake, your primary role is not swinging a hammer or pushing a broom, and you should not let these chores distract you. Your assignment is people work, that is, actively managing the designer and builder you hired.

BAD TILE WORK *Ceramic tile has a reputation for being hard to get right. This is due in part to the wide variation in product available, and the number of pseudo-professional installers. In general, the larger, thinner, and more expensive the tile, and the larger the area to be covered, the more you should seek out a subcontractor who specializes in this work. This beautiful 12 x 12 travertine marble has been poorly installed. The difference in underlayment has not been corrected at the perimeter, and the unsupported edge can only be expected to continue to break away. In this case, the general contractor will have his subcontractor make it right.*

proposal. So, as the owners proceed with no guide, they waste a lot of time for a lot of people, themselves included.

A bidding process may have a negative connotation to some remodeling contractors, because of the natural cowboy syndrome in the redo marketplace. This is not the case in commercial work, where bidding is the norm. Remodeling builders don't want

anyone telling them how to "herd them homeowners." After having been through it, though, they realize the surgical and respectful nature of such a methodology. It is good business. They are not asked to expend any time until they are genuine contenders for the job, they don't have to play designer-for-free, they don't have to worry as much about missing information or ultimate payment, and they know that all aspects of their proposal will be fairly heard in as succinct a manner as possible. They are not bidding against 15 guys operating out of pickup trucks. And their proposal is heard by owners who are being advised by another pro to value things other than the quoted price.

You should be particularly sensitive to running a process that treats the candidates professionally and fairly. When a builder lays a price on the table, the number itself has been worked and reworked many different ways. It contains subcategories from other contractors and suppliers who themselves have done the legwork to lay their price on the table. Although it may be crudely penciled into the Bid Form, you can be sure that a lot of time has been spent getting it together for you, for free. Enough time should be spent reviewing his numbers so that he understands that you value and understand the estimate. But you want to overemphasize your interest in hearing about the non-money features of his team and their proposal. You and the designer should dress-down for the bid presentation meeting, offer coffee, and sit at your dining table in a nonconfrontational arrangement, to make the builder feel comfortable. Each firm should be treated in exactly the same way. When the architect issues Addenda, he passes on to all bidders any new information that may be generated in the bidding; it is a fairness tool (more about this later). Suggest to your architect that he write the nonsuccessful bidders a "thank you" letter that gives them the bad news, but also spreads out the bidding data from all firms. This way their time will not have been wasted; they can chalk it up to an assessment of their competition. When well managed, a fair, respectful process makes converts of the apprehensive candidates; they never fail to call me back and say "keep me on your list for the next one."

THE LONG AND SHORT LIST

As before with your designer-hire, you need an initial list of candidates, and then you need to cull it to the short list who will receive bid packages. The generation of the long list will most likely be driven by your designer; he should recommend which firms should be solicited directly. It is important that you place several names into the hat, and that at least one or two of your candidates survive the cut. Make sure that the architect gets the message. This will preclude any "secret understandings" between the designer and his favorite builders. The architect should send bid packages to five or six general contracting firms, anticipating that one or two will fade somewhere down the line. You must end up with at least three to four solid proposals to consider in detail. Each proposal will be made in a two-hour meeting format, and because I recommend that you try to funnel the bidding into a single day of presentations, four to five proposals is the absolute maximum you can fairly consider.

You will be looking for four to six names to give to your architect as your contribution to the long list. Talk with your designer about who should do the screening calls to cull the list. I prefer to do the background work for bidders in my practice, but have no problem with owners bringing in information they have gathered on their candidates. If you will do this, a telephone questionnaire similar to Example 22 is a smart way to hit all the important points and record them for discussion with the designer. The most important question, of course, is whether they can show you recent, local projects, in your price range. I would be very skeptical of true design-build firms (with designers on their payroll). My experience with these construction groups is that they are spoiled by

A

B

C

URBAN ECCENTRICITIES

It is not uncommon to meet a builder who chooses not to do work in the big city. Poor access problems are probably only exceeded by the minutia involved in pulling a building permit. And on top of this, the buildings are full of eccentric surprises. This townhouse in Photograph A has all the frontal niceties bestowed by Frank Furness (local architect guru), but just barely has room in the rear for that urban luxury, the car (Photograph B). And while the soaring space and Victorian touches are exquisite in the front room (Photograph E), the kitchen and bathrooms are in terrible shape (Photographs C and D). To redo one of these old homes is a privilege, but it takes a lot of inventiveness to do it well. The niche in the front room, for example, will be accentuated with low-voltage lighting (Photograph F). And the new kitchen will get a large window group over the sink, etched to translucency, that partially ventilates via the integral casement window on the left, and that is protected by a second break-resistant glazing layer outside (Photograph G).

D

E

G

F

INHOUSE FLOORS

Deciding when to require a specialist subcontractor can be a hard call to make. Most of the carpenters on the builder's crew are perfectly capable of applying new hardwood flooring. But the finishing is much more difficult to do well, as is having the elegant solution ready when the notorious "unforeseen problem" rears its head. Think twice when your generalist crew wants to do large hardwood or ceramic tile floor areas. Some can do a great job, but ask to see an example just to be sure.

their own shorthand design process, and can be expected to disrupt any other methodology.

The make-up of the short list should be well thought out. For most middle-income projects, I try to get a mix of genuine pros for the homeowners to look at. A local firm specializing in upscale work should be counterbalanced by a firm working in a more blue-collar community. A young firm operating out of pickups should be offset by a more established organization working with an office staff. A hammer-swinging boss should be countered with a businessman managing a lead carpenter. A group that does everything should be considered alongside a builder that has many subcontracting specialists. This shotgun approach to the short list ensures that the owner and I learn a lot about the different ways to build the job, as

re-phon2.wps
TELEPHONE QUESTIONAIRE   Date:

For Use In Selecting A Remodeling Builder

Hello, my name is <u>Mary Green</u>. I am in the process of remodeling my home and am in search of a builder. May I speak to the owner? Before you transfer me, who will I speak to? Do I have the name and address right?

Address/Phone Number/Names:

1. Do you do residential remodeling work?

2. Can you give me a thumbnail sketch of your firm's expertise?

3. Do you have professional designers on your payroll?

4. Do you have any proprietary relationships with architects, real estate developers, or product vendors that I should be aware of?

5. How many people are on your firm's payroll?

6. Do you have a Remodeling Project in my vicinity that I might drive by and see? (secure directions)

TELEPHONE QUESTIONNAIRE

EXAMPLE 22. *This form can be used by either the owner or designer to qualify builders for the redo long list. It should be marked up for later referral.*

---

a consequence of the bid process. And it allows a look at motivated, fresh faces to keep the stew interesting and costs in line. I usually have early opinions about which type of builder will be best for the job, but I let the process confirm this under the owner's scrutiny. Only after bid presentations are made do you understand what is unique about your particular redo, who is best suited to build it, and how much should it cost.

INVITATION AND GUIDE TO BID

Although this document is a mere one-page cover letter, it is a very important and sophisticated tool. As in your architect-hiring effort, the commitments made during the initial courtship set the stage for everything else that is to come. If the builder will have a

A

CUSTOM CABINETS

You have to be very careful when hiring a contractor to do custom cabinets. To get high-quality work you have to pay a tremendous premium, as if purchasing furniture. Most carpenters advocate the idea of custom cabinetry, because it is enjoyable shop-work for them. But if there will be any significant "operation" to the cabinets, you should only use full-time cabinet fabricators who can show you the "feel" of the drawers in the base unit you want, for instance. Strong and pretty isn't enough; it has to have the kind of "balance" that can only come from years of tweaking. The drawer bases in Photograph E (waiting for a top) were built in the general contractor's shop by his finish carpenter. They are really overbuilt, in that they are too heavy for the slide hardware. On the other hand, finish carpenters can do a great job with stationary work such as bookcases (Photograph C). This unit is made entirely of oak-veneered plywood, routed to accepted the slot-type adjustable shelf hardware (Photograph D), and 1 x 2 oak stock with beaded edges. Its back is simply painted drywall. Laminate counters with hardwood edging, or tops for knee walls, are well within most carpenters' expertise. Note that floor-grills are built into the oak top under the windows in Photograph A, and that mahogany pegs are used as a decorative motif in the edge of the table. The media cabinets in Photograph B are all custom except for the doors, which will be purchased preassembled.

B

D

C

E

A

WOOD COLUMNS

A good way to signal an important spot is to embellish it with wood columns. Photograph A shows two 8" (diameter, measured at the base) members waiting for installation (the unit at the left is a new pull-down attic stair). This particular column is supplied with a wooden base, which the carpenter is preparing for contact with concrete by applying a pressure treated block underneath (Photograph B and C). Photograph D shows the pair, primed for painting, taking their place in front of a new vestibule addition.

B

C

D

problem with the way you intend to run your job, then you want him to object to it at the outset, call the architect, and say, "I think I will pass on this one." Example 23 is a letter that I continue to clone and revise for my work. The due date I set will allow at least three to four weeks for the builders to get their subs through the home and finalize a proposal. The deadline is important, because it is another indication of their business savvy. If they will have a day or two problem meeting the date, I will probably accept their proposal, although it will inconvenience everyone else. But if they have not been working the bid all along, and if they don't give me an "I've got a problem" call in advance, they may as well not bother.

For most owners, weekends are the only time they can set aside enough time to entertain a series of presentations. Several weeks before bids are due, I will call each builder and arrange a meeting time on the pre-set date. I allow two hours per meeting and put thirty minutes padding between appointments so they don't have to run into their competition. I try to get all the meetings in on a Saturday and have the owners hold their Sunday open for runovers if necessary. You and your designer should review the Invitation and Guide to Bid (Example 23) and set up your own rules for bidding. Bidders in your house can be very tiresome if you don't lay down the law. Each builder will have to be inside several different times, and a subcontractor or two may need separate access. Note that item 5 lays down the process that the builder will have to follow, and item 4 will require you to watch your "loose lips" as it proceeds. The architect should retype the Invitation and Bid Guide on his letterhead.

The Bid Form

Example 24 is a typical remodeling project Bid Form. Coupled with the Invitation, this document will save

thousands of dollars. The Invitation tells the builders that you will not accept a proposal unless they use your form; its language is that important. Remember, you have to correlate all this data fairly across all the bidders. The form is the builder's representation to you that after looking at the construction documents and going over your home, he proposes to build the job for a stated lump sum. This lump sum is his price to do the remodel as described in a Base Bid (maybe baseline job is an easier way to think of it). Note that the form asks him to confirm receipt of any Addenda. If any questions have come up in bidding, and the designer changed the documents, he will have issued an Addendum to all builders. This part of the form lets you know that he got the last change (Change Orders only happen after there is a contract) and it is included in his now-quoted Base Bid. Also notice that he is asked to only "estimate" how long it will take to complete the job, because the builder can make only gross predictions about completion dates. Although they are sometimes written into contracts, deadlines and penalties are practically impossible to enforce in the courts. Just as the designer cannot control the variables that determine the project's construction cost, the builder is at the mercy of too many changing parameters to guarantee a completion date and still build the job for a fair lump-sum price. Weather, of course is one of the prime culprits.

Alternate Prices

One of the primary reasons to require the use of your own form in bidding is so the designer can make extensive use of Alternates. This technique is critical in securing the most value for your construction dollar. Alternates are best thought of as what-if schemes. "What if you took this out of the job? What would hap-

re-invit.wps
INVITATION AND GUIDE TO BID   **Construction Services**

Date: August 1, 1995   Property: John and Mary Green
                                                            1492 Columbus Drive
                                                            Towner, PA 19088

Dear Builder:

You are hereby invited to bid the attached work. Please note:

1. Bids will be due on **Friday August 26, 1994** at this office by 5:00PM. The work is expected to begin as soon as possible after contract award. Footings must be poured and the work closed-in before the ground freezes this year.

2. Bids not utilizing the attached **Bid Form** or without **all Alternates completed** will not be accepted.

3. **Bid the work according to the Drawings. It is in your interest not to solicit decisions directly from the Owners at this point.** If you or your subs have questions about something, the G.C should call me. If information is lacking the Architect will issue new guidelines (Addendums) to all Bidders. If you propose Alternates not required in the Bid Form, these should be numbered and added to the Form.

4. **A Personal presentation** of your proposal will be scheduled at the Owner's home on **Saturday, August 27** at a mutually agreeable time. This is the time for you to suggest unique approaches to the work and to **demonstrate your expertise.** You are encouraged to bring a list of references so the Owner may "go-see" your work and talk to satisfied customers.

5. The successful bidder will be expected to execute AIA Document A107, Owner-Contractor, Stipulated Sum, Short Form **Construction Contract** with the Owners. Copies of this agreement are available from the Architect. Note that the Architect will provide Construction Administration for the Owner (Article 10), the Owner will require Certificates of Insurance prior to commencing the Work (Article 17), and payment procedures will require billing for "work-in-place" and a line-item Retainage.

6. The Owners will be absent for a portion of the bid period. You will need to arrange appointments for **access to the house**. Through August 13 call Mary Green at 668-5253; afterwards call Peter Wilson at 664-8259. Generally, weekdays from 9:30 to 4:00 will be most convenient

7. **Selection of the General Contractor** will be based on: (a) demonstrated ability on similar work, (b) enthusiasm and "chemistry" with other team-members, and (c) proposed Contract Sum.

For clarification of these guidelines or any other aspect of the work please don't hesitate to call.

Respectfully,

[signature]

Peter Wilson

INVITATION AND GUIDE TO BID

EXAMPLE 23. *This cover letter is a sophisticated tool for hiring a builder. It should be cloned onto the architect's letterhead and used in conjunction with Example 24. Underlined text should be carefully reviewed and revised to reflect your specific project.*

re-bform.wps
BID FORM   **Construction Services**

Date: August 1, 1995   Property: John and Mary Green
                                                               1492 Columbus Drive
                                                               Towner, PA 19088

Dear Mr. and Mrs. Green:

Having thoroughly examined both the Contract Documents and the site conditions, I hereby propose to furnish all labor and material to accomplish the Addition/Alterations to your home for the following prices.

Base Bid: I agree to perform the Work for the lump sum of:_____

_____($)

Alternate Work: For the work described below and elsewhere in the Contract Documents, you may revise the foregoing Base Bid as follows:

For: Add (+)/Deduct (-)

Alternate 1 - Substitute Downgrade Product for Interior Doors.
Provide a price that reflects the substitution of hollow-core embossed Masonite doors for all new interior doors.   ------------------

Alternate 2 - Install Owner-Supplied Cabinets.
Owner may purchase the stock kitchen and bath cabinets (marked "C" in the Cabinet Schedule) for installation by the General Contractor. Provide an alternate price for installation only; include in the scope of work a line-item to review Owner's pending purchase order and make recommendations. Also include the labor necessary to co-ordinate the supplier's delivery and inventory the contents. This alternate price excludes the General Contractor's provision of all counters marked "T" in the Cabinet Schedule on Drawing Sheet A-2. Provision of custom-fabricated tops remains in the Base Bid.   ------------------

Alternate 3 - Delete Most Interior Painting.
Remove most interior preparation and painting from the Base Bid. Only prime those walls or ceilings that have new plaster or spackling applied. Exterior painting remains in the Base Bid.   ------------------

Alternate 4 - Add New Front Entry Pent.
Add the alterations to the front entry area as noted on Drawing 4/A-1.   ------------------

Alternate 5 - Add New Front Bay Window Pent and Adjacent Finishes
Add the alterations to both floors adjacent to the bay window per Drawing 4/A-1. ------------------

Alternate 6 - Add Relocation of Electric Service
Relocate electric service drop and meter to east side of house per 4/A-1.   ------------------

Alternate 7 - Add Skylight and Hall Lighting.
In the second floor hall add the roof window and drywall attic well per Window Schedule and Drawings. Include painting and changes to lighting as noted.   ------------------

Alternate 8 - Substitute True-divided-lites for Selected Windows/Door.
Upgrade windows and doors by changing to true divided lites in the following fenestration only: windows: E-alt and F-alt, door: #109ALT. These alternate units are specified in the schedules on Sheet A-1.   ------------------

I anticipate that the project will take approximately_____calendar days to complete after securing permits and receiving notice to proceed.

I acknowledge receipt of the following Addenda: Addendum No._____ Addendum No._____
                                                 Addendum No._____ Addendum No._____

Signed:_____ Title:_____ Date:_____
Company:_____ License No.:_____

THE BID FORM   **EXAMPLE 24.** *Just like the Invitation, this form must be prepared by the designer in consultation with the owner. It is to be completed by the builder to make his proposal. A set of real redo Alternates has been left in this document to illustrate their importance; your project Alternates will be different.*

pen to your price?" You see, once the builder is on the team, these what-if scenarios cannot be posed in the same kind of competitive environment. The opportunity for major bargains is unique to bidding. Although sometimes an Alternate or two is included in the Drawings and Specifications, they can quickly confuse bidders. For this reason, I recommend that they become an integral part of the Bid Form. If an Alternate is ultimately accepted by the owner, its language will be brought forward into the Contract for Construction.

Every bidder will want to present you with a detailed breakdown of his costs as a substitute for your form. He has done all this hard work, so he organizes it neatly on his letterhead, and shows it mainly as a way to assure you of its accuracy. If it is software generated, he will likely pitch the perceived computer precision in his presentation. The quote from each builder will be entirely different, grouping the numbers in ways that make them largely unusable for you. His breakout would show electric, plumbing, tile, carpentry, etc., in the same way that he estimates them. But you don't care about these details. After the lump sum shows you how the candidate stacks up against his peers, what you really want to know is stuff like "what happens if I only rough-in my mechanicals for a bathroom, and finish it as a closet for now, so I can do the work in the future?" You want this kind of option (Alternate) priced during bidding.

Alternates are like many other things; overuse of a good thing can be bad. So you and your architect should carefully plan no more than ten major, potential changes, and place them into the Bid Form for credit or deduction against the Base Bid. Their best use is to help you trim dollars out of the project if bids come in high. Keep the form to one page only. The sample Bid Form (Example 24) has eight Alternates, some of which are alluded to in the

Drawings. Alternate 2 has been placed in the form because the owner thinks he can purchase the kitchen cabinets at a below-builder cost, and this will definitively answer the question. Kitchen cabinets, of course, are the kind of high-cost item that should be noodled around a little. Alternate 3 deletes the painting out of the job, which the owner wants to consider doing himself. In this case it is all inside prep and paint work, other than priming of new drywall. Drywall priming is left in, to show finishing blemishes before the builder closes out the job and leaves. Alternates 4, 5, and 6 are typical things that should be done to balance the street appearance of the home, if room can be found in the budget.

Bid Presentation Meetings

Hopefully your designer has been able to orchestrate appointments with your bidders that allow hearing all proposals in a single day. Keeping that objective will require you to control each meeting with an agenda, and to watch the clock. If you have children or other potential interruptions (such as frequent telephone calls or neighbors dropping by) make arrangements ahead of time to ensure they don't happen. The day will be tiring; you will be managing the efforts of four, five, or six professionals and trying to understand a lot of hard work. But of course, it will be extremely rewarding as well.

Example 25 is an agenda that you and your designer will want to review, revise, and copy for use in the bid meetings. After introductions and settling in around your dining table, ask the builder, "So Bill, what do you have in the way of a proposal?" While watching the clock, let him tell you all he has planned to say, then you or your architect should take back control of the meeting and run down the rest of your

A

CORNER WINDOWS

When you need a little something extra for a special spot, consider a corner window group. Just make sure that it does in fact signal an important interior function. To ensure a quality job, the designer must place enough structural strength in the outside corner (Photograph A), and detail both the interior and exterior trim. Photographs B and C show the inside and outside of a stacked corner group, made up of small awning windows by Anderson. The redo in Photographs D and E uses two three-wide groups to give the eat-in kitchen a panorama of the deck and yard. These are true-divided-lite insulated units by Weathershield. The window over the table is fixed; the remainder are operable casements.

B

C

D

E

re-agen2.wps
BID PRESENTATION MEETING   **Agenda and Questionaire**

For Use In Selecting A Remodeling Builder   Date: Attending:

Agenda:

Introductions
Builder Makes Presentation of his Proposal
Review of the Bid Form for Completeness
Qualifying the Bid, marking up the Bid Form
        Any questionable assumptions made in your quote?
        Any misunderstandings about the specified process?
        Any misunderstandings about the distinctions made in the Alternates?
Review Requested Items
        List of satisfied customers, phone numbers & directions for Go-see's
What to Expect, when and how you will decide

Questions to Sprinkle into the Above Agenda

1. What will be your personal role in the process?

2. Who will be your Lead Carpenter or Supervisor? How long has he been with your firm?

3. Can you share some of your background with us? (expertise/credentials)

4. Describe the people who will be on your payroll, and the subcontracted portion of your crew.

5. What provisions have you included in your quote, to segregate construction and living activities?

6. Describe the major equipment you will use, such as dumpsters and excavators (owned or leased)?

7. Any alternative products that you think we should consider using?

8. Will you have any problem supplying a Certificate of Insurance before beginning?

9. How could this job be made better or cheaper? How could we trim out $5,000/$10,000?

10. What is your philosophy on "call-backs" after the job is complete?

11. Have any opinions about how a job is best run with a designer on the team?

12. What is the most important thing I could do, to help you make the job profitable for you and your subs?

13. When could you start?

Non-numeric Quality Indicators (rate 1 to 3-high, attach reasoning notes on separate sheet):

        (   ) Redo Portfolio

        (   ) Depth of Experience

        (   ) Crew/Supervision Mix

        (   ) Hassle-mitigation Techniques

BID PRESENTATION QUESTIONNAIRE AND AGENDA

EXAMPLE 25. *This document should be used by the designer and owner for each meeting with candidate builders. It should be marked up, stapled to the Bid Form, and referred to later, as the successful bidder is selected.*

agenda. The Bid Form should be reviewed for completeness, and the builder should be asked why he omitted any specific item. If he is judged a serious contender, he should be asked to phone in any missing pieces. Next the designer should ask a few questions to make sure the builder, in fact, understands the nuances of the Base Bid, the process, and the Alternates. This is to make sure he hasn't totally missed something, which does happen. If he has missed something, ask him to make the adjustment to his numbers as soon as possible. If he hasn't volunteered it earlier, ask for a list of his satisfied customers and specific information about who to call for a visit to one of his local jobs. As the meeting progresses, you and your architect should take turns asking the questions noted on your agenda sheet. Just before adjourning, you should review the question list and see if anything has remained unasked. Close the meeting by expressing your appreciation of the builder's hard work and promising to advise him of any future decisions.

NON-NUMERIC QUALITY INDICATORS

After the builder leaves, you and the designer should take the time to synthesize your thoughts and record them as Quality Indicators on the questionnaire. Rate his attributes from 1 to 3 (or something similar) and jot down why you have scored him this way. Such notes will unclutter the data at the end of the bidding process and refresh your memory. These are the general characteristics that I look for:

- Redo Portfolio
- Depth of Experience

- Crew/Supervision Mix
- Hassle-mitigation Techniques

His portfolio of projects should be as long as possible; the more they are similar in size to yours, the better. You should get the feeling that the owners of his projects could live next to you. His experience should be deep and wide. More time in the same business is an advantage. His lead carpenter should be a long-time employee. His proposed mix of payroll and subcontract labor should dovetail with the specific needs of the project and owner. For example, if your project has extensive wet-bed tile floors and you want them top-drawer, then this should be done by a specialty subcontractor. Any builder can vary the way he protects the homeowner from construction craziness. These efforts cost money even though they don't change the end product. Consider the mitigation techniques each builder is proposing to do for you and score him accordingly. Here, you are rating level of effort, not good or bad credentials. With the ratings complete, staple the Bid Form and the Meeting Agenda sheet on top of any extraneous notes, and take a break before the next guy shows.

EVALUATING THE PROPOSALS

After bid meetings are complete, you need to consider the pros and cons of each group. For you computer buffs, this is a good place to put a spreadsheet application to work. Example 26 is the real-world result of the Bid Form in Example 24. You will be interested in scrutinizing several things. Start with the Base Bid. If a bid is wildly lower than the others without reason, you should disregard the proposal as a total miss. Extremely high quotes for the Base Bid without a cor-

A

MASTER OF TRANSITIONS

When you "go see" a potential builder's job, look at transition craftsmanship. Floor levels are notoriously difficult to match up. Most builders leave the new floor slightly low and make up the difference by shimming or flash-patching (filler compound) the new underlayment. In Photograph A a builder works on a new oak threshold to mask the scar between new tile and an old oak floor. Interior trim usually involves salvaging as much of the old stuff as possible and mixing in new stock profiles where logical changes can occur. Occasionally, matching profiles have to be custom shaped by millwork shops. In Photograph B a new door frame is trimmed by salvaged casing. Salvaged three-piece baseboard has been installed, except inside the doorway, where new 6" colonial base is used. Note where the new oak stair-tread has been set flush with the floor. Photograph C shows the completed transitions, old living room in the foreground, new vestibule to the left, new powder room at the landing, new opening into a family room addition beyond.

B

c

BID EVALUATION SPREADSHEET

	F & S Builders	Williams Const.	SunShine Const.	Walker, Inc.
Base Bid (dollars)	**$122,300.00**	**$109,300.00**	**$123,470.00**	**$137,470.00**
Alt 1-downgrade interior doors	($725.00)	($1,000.00)	($1,800.00)	($1,350.00)
Alt 2-remove kitchen cabinets	($5,500.00)	($6,800.00)	($4,550.00)	($5,050.00)
Alt 3-remove interior painting	($5,000.00)	($3,750.00)	($8,800.00)	($9,500.00)
Alt 4-add front entry work	$960.00	$1,275.00	no bid	$1,000.00
Alt 5-add bay pent/finishes	$1,850.00	$1,800.00	no bid	$1,550.00
Alt 6-add/relocate electric service	$1,200.00	no charge if 200A	no bid	$1,100.00
Alt 7-add skylight and lighting	$1,700.00	$1,950.00	$1,580.00	$1,580.00
Alt 8-add upgrade windows	$2,600.00	$1,300.00	no charge	$1,700.00
Quality Indicators (1 to 3-high)	**1.75**	**2.25**	**2**	**2.75**
Redo Portfolio	2	3	2	3
Depth of Experience	2	3	2	2
Crew/Supervision Mix	1	2	1	3
Hassle-mitigation Techniques	2	1	3	3

BID EVALUATION SPREADSHEET

EXAMPLE 26. *This spreadsheet allows consideration of several builder's proposals. It is the real-world result of the Bid Form in Example 24. It also includes the non-numeric indicators recorded in Bid Presentation Meetings. Note the variation in both the Base Bid and Alternates. The values in parentheses are debits.*

responding quality increase should also be crossed out. The middle cluster should then be sifted for other desirable features. In the example, Walker Inc. was $28,000 over the low bid and the subjective quality indicators say this should not be a surprise. Unfortunately for him, his kid-glove service, and his proposed temporary walls and cleanup scheme, were judged to be more expensive than the owner was willing to pay for.

Selecting an Alternate scenario is another important way to look at the quotes. I find that the builders will frequently offer very competitive prices for Alternate items because they don't radically change the way they will build the job. Notice the difference to be taken out if the owner opts for a hollow core embossed interior door in Alternate 1, almost a 250% variation for a $1000 spread. Also note that the biggest credit does not come from the highest bid. In fact, Williams

Construction offers the largest credit back for removing kitchen cabinets (Alternate 2) even though they are the low bidder. I have a distinct recollection of discussing Alternate 8 with the builder from SunShine Construction. He convinced me that he could offer the true-divided-lite upgrades for a picture window/casement flanker group and adjacent french doors for the same price as the Base Bid. It had something to do with his supplier's stock and the product switch, although I can no longer recall the details. He was prepared to give away this Alternate, while F&S wanted to charge $2600 for the same change. Strange as it may seem, these kinds of discrepancies in redo bidding are the norm, not an anomaly. Therefore, you should look for bargains in the Alternates, reconstruct the scope of your job to include the cheap ones, and recalculate the adjusted lump quotes. Sometimes the favorite son will change.

Yes, the low bidder, Williams Construction (names have been changed to protect the innocent) was awarded this job. Although I advise owners to be very skeptical of the low bid, in this case I could recommend the firm. His quote was $13,000 off the mid-cluster but still got high marks in all but one of his quality indicators. Because the owner was prepared to live in some chaos, Williams' lack of such things as door-plugs and temporary walls was considered unimportant. In fact, he turned out to be the best configured team for this particular job, which is why he could bring the bid in low. He owned a Bobcat (for backfilling and final grading), and a dump truck (negating the need for the two or three dumpsters his competition were leasing). He had a multi-trade team proposing to do site backfilling and grading, concrete and blockwork, roofing, rough and finish carpentry, drywall hanging and finishing, aluminum trim capping and vinyl siding, hardwood flooring, and ceramic tile work all within his own payroll labor. He would sub only the basics: excavation, electric, plumbing, heating, and a limited amount of painting. His lead carpenter had been with the firm 10 years, and several other workmen were long-standing members as well. His group had done another job for me and was a known quantity. He spent his time planning the job, shopping material, orchestrating his subs, and occasionally pitching in to pick up the pace or fine tune another's work. For another client who was less "value" conscious and more "quality" oriented, I would have preferred that the ceramic tile and hardwood flooring be done by specialists, and that more hassle-limitation measures be included. Because all the costs were higher than expected, the owner elected to delete replacement of his kitchen cabinets, which was an unusual bargain in the Williams bid. The Alternates 4, 5, and 6 were accepted because the $3000 to upgrade the curb appeal of the mother-home, seemed small in relation to the $90,000 that would be invested elsewhere.

REFERENCE CHECKS AND GO-SEES

One or two leading contenders should come out of the bid meetings. These builders should be investigated behind the scenes a little. I don't mind making calls to satisfied customers or visiting a few past jobs, but these tasks are best done by the owner. They mainly serve to shore-up confidence in your pick. Later on in the job, when you wonder if he is telling you the truth, you will reflect on conversations with past clients, and you will be glad you did this homework.

A

B

KITCHEN CHANGES

Completely remodeling a kitchen is an expensive proposition. Many times it is a luxury that owners cannot afford. After all, the existing one does function. But the new powder room, the new family room, or the extra bedroom represent more living space that must come first. So when bids come in high, kitchen dreams usually suffer from budget cuts. The kitchen improvements in Photograph A (before) were scaled back in favor of central air conditioning. The owners got their extra space, including the family room beyond (Photograph B), but kitchen changes were limited to partition and flooring work to facilitate a preplanned, future cabinet/appliance changeover. Notice the widened access into the new space and the new forced-air soffit above.

It takes a builder years to collect the right mix of tools. They help him work faster, better, and therefore more competitively. In fact, you can learn a lot about the kind of work he wants to do simply by reading his tool list. After all, his heart is where he puts his own money, regardless of what comes out of his mouth. This builder has a mix indicative of a suburban remodeling specialist. He owns a large dump truck, a bobcat (small earth-mover), and a large step-van fitted out with tools and frequently needed material. He doesn't need to put several dumpsters on the street; he removes debris with his own labor and according to his calendar. He can get an excavator in and out quickly because he can fine tune grade at his leisure, with the bobcat. And his van gives him the ability to have his "shop" close by, avoiding wasted time. He stores valuable trim stock and other product here, secure from vandalism, out of the weather, and not in the owner's way.

TOOL MIX

On one occasion, I went on a go-see with a client to check up on a selected builder. The general contractor was there to show us through the home, although I don't recommend this. Now, I knew this builder to be a solid citizen in the remodeling business, so the trip was really to give the owner confidence in him. In meetings, the builder had described this fabulous project and had invited us to visit it. At the curb and prior to seeing the "before" photograph, I knew he had made a tactical error. The home that had been a nondescript rancher in a close suburban neighborhood had been transformed into a hugely expensive, garish, neighborhood uglyduckling. The new front elevation with its partial ceramic-tile skin was as ugly as my curiosity had been strong. The homeowner was genuinely proud to show off her new home, which she had designed herself, being a self-described fledgling artist. She confided that most of it had been done impromptu, as they say. Although construction had stopped long ago, I was shocked to see that it was largely unfurnished as well as unfinished in several major places inside. She had run out of money. She looked out at a huge solar-heated swimming pool and deck area, through raggedy openings. The project had been ambitious: radical room changes everywhere. Halfway into the foyer my client whispered to me "can you believe this?" He was as shaken as I was. The design of the home was an unmitigated disaster, with eccentric, unproportioned spaces everywhere. It was a $400,000 add-on to a $200,000 property, for which she would get very little back, if she could, in fact, ever sell it. Although the walls were plumb, the drywall showed no screw-pops, and the tile on the front was meticulously straight and intact; the new client totally lost his confidence. The builder had shot himself in the foot, although I surmised that his part in the disaster was only to have said "sure, we can do that" too many times.

Another time, with another builder and owner, I visited a new home that was built while our young candidate had supervised construction. The owners had employed an architect and an interior designer in the right sequence. The home was well planned down to every color, fabric, and dimmer switch by pros. It was stunning. There were long walls of custom cabinetry, marble and granite work, many different metal fabrications, and custom masonry fireplaces. I could see evidence of specialty subs and subtle design flourishes everywhere. It was a $1.5 million property at least. Although the builder knew every flaw in the home (which means he really was there sweating the details), my guess was that his sub-mix was orchestrated by his boss and given him to coordinate like any other lead carpenter. The visiting owner was ready to hire the young guy there on the spot, until I threw some cold water on the impulse.

The point I am making with these two vignettes is that go-sees are frequently very misleading. If you visit a redo, and it looks super, this is not necessarily a result of the builder's involvement. There are many other factors that yield excellence in such a complex undertaking. In fact, the whole hypothesis of this book is that you, the owner, will do more to influence the success of a project than any other one factor. You can hire an average architect and builder, and manage them into delivering outstanding results. Reference checks and go-sees should be done to your own level of comfort, with the overall picture in mind, and with your designer in tow. Aside from the trust you read in past clients' eyes, you are looking for reoccurring patterns of incompetence, which rarely surface at this stage of the process. But, if you do find something which bothers you, nix him and go on to the next favorite son.

FISHING FOR CONCESSIONS

When you have decided who you want to build your project, this fact needs to be kept secret for awhile. You should now quickly prepare to negotiate a few things, as you move toward conforming an agreement with the builder. Do not under any circumstances say, "you are the one," or advise the other bidders of your choice, until you have the favorite son under contract. For you winning-by-intimidation fans, this is the place to ply your trade, although I prefer a more respectful approach. Your builder is poised in his most motivated posture. He has a tremendous investment in the job by now, and should be given a chance to "throw in" a few things to sweeten the pot.

Within the bidding paperwork, there may still be a few golden nuggets to mine. Carefully bounce your builder's line-item prices against whatever information has been provided by other bidders. Although not asked to do so, general contractors usually volunteer a complete breakout of their quote. If you see, for example, that your builder is paying much more for his air-conditioning subcontractor than any of the other bidders, this is valuable information. There is a good chance that your favorite guy is not even aware of such a radical price discrepancy. If his sub is quoting higher than the others for the same job, he wants to know about it as much as you do.

You (not the designer) should call the builder and express that, although you are still considering the proposals, his and one other firm are the front-runners for the job. Tell him you have called to talk further about his proposal. If it is true that you have cost-sticker shock, advise him that you are very worried about bringing down the project costs. You should have several items jotted down to talk from. At a min-

imum, you should have one price item and one work-scope item on your mini-agenda. At the cost bullet, tell him about your finding the possible cost discrepancy in the bid line item. Ask him to look into the glitch and consider whether a quote by another sub is warranted, or whether there is a misunderstanding about what was specified. Do not let the discussion move to changing the specified work, which will be done later. Move on to a discussion of the work itself, as distinct from pricing. Describe the mix of Alternates that you will likely accept. And then, tell him you were hoping to get the skylight into the job, or any other item that you want, above the Base Bid package. He will be most flexible with labor items versus material ones, such as temporary dust barriers. Ask him to "think about" how much he would charge to throw this task in. Do not push him into quoting prices in this conversation. Expect him to call you back with a response to your requests. At this point, many builders will be heartened by your call, return to their estimating notes, and try to find something to help push you over the decision edge. The savvy ones will know that you are "fishing" in a cordial businesslike way. He will definitely call you back promptly, and he will probably have a concession of some magnitude for you. Even if you aren't comfortable with planning and playing such a negotiating game with the builder, make sure you call him at this crucial point in the process, even if it is just to talk about the weather. If you obey the foregoing rules, he just might offer you a freebie from out of the blue.

SHAKING DOWN THE JOB

When a naval vessel comes out of a shipyard, she gets taken on a "shakedown cruise." Shaking out (the bugs, I presume) is a time for checking the work under realistic conditions, before she is sent to sea with all hands aboard. And so it should be with a redo after the builder is selected. The job should be made better by soliciting the builder's expertise well before construction begins. Your architect should initiate the shakedown after you have advised him of the results of your fishing effort. He should redline the contract documents to include any concession from the builder. This becomes a new mark, around which any changes will be accounted for.

If you have been diligent in hiring your architect, the cost of his service during this phase should be clear (Chapter 4). If not, make sure that you don't give him a blank check, for it makes no sense to pay him all the credits that come out of a leaner redo. Shakedowns for me always put money in the owner's pocket, but I can envision a scenario where it would be costly. If few project changes are anticipated and the architect will be working at an hourly Additional Service rate, you must make him commit to an "upset" price for the revision before authorizing the extra work. Even if the effort only breaks even, you should make sure that it happens. You have gone to a lot of trouble to find your expert builder; now you must listen to him, as well as your architect. The shakedown is worth doing, if only for the way it energizes your relationship with the builder. It lets him take up the torch and make the project his own.

The designer should call your favorite builder and say, "The owner has decided that he wants to contract with you to build the job. But we want you to help us make construction smarter before we revise the construction documents. Are you interested in meeting, redlining the project, and adjusting your proposal? We would like to see the ramifications of taking $10,000 out of the job." The take-out target varies, of course, according to where bids have come in. Even if the bids did not surprise anyone, you want to give the builder such a challenge. This is one of the things he does well—run numbers for construction scenarios. It is not uncommon to make adjustments in techniques that are significantly cheaper, but don't appear to be so. Foundations, roof framing, and detailing methods come to mind as some examples. When these kinds of monies are mined by your builder, they can be reallocated back into the kind of high-profile areas in your home that increase its perceived quality, such as an extra touch in the foyer, special front door hardware, Solid-surface counters instead of laminate, or landscape lighting. If you are to spend this money, you should try to get it out where it can be seen and touched.

HIGH BIDS

Do not be surprised if the bids come in higher than the architect has estimated. Your process is prepared for this eventuality, because it is such a common occurrence, particularly in remodeling. This does not make your designer a bad guy. But if he will not be there to help bring the redo back into the budget zone, then one of the culprits will be in your mirror. But there is more work to be done; the good stuff is harder to do. I do not recommend that the job be redesigned and then re-bid. This borders on "jerking the bidders around" and is not necessary. You need to keep the overall methodology moving forward and rely on your successful bidder to get the prices down, while he is still highly motivated to win the commission. Simply set the cost target where you now want it (with the alternate mix that is better understood) and make sure the designer runs the job shakedown task before the builder signs a contract. You want a clear but unarticulated understanding that if the general contractor takes advantage of the noncompetitive environment and "cushions" his prices, then you will not move to contract with him. The builder and architect will meet, redline the documents further, and then propose to you a revised redo with a new estimate of its cost. When you understand the changes that need to be made to your project, the designer will revise the Drawings and Specifications, and pass them to the builder for his development of the estimate into a new lump-sum bid for the job. Be sure you do not let any member of your team talk you into moving into construction without an updated set of documents. They become an important management tool as saw-dust begins to fly.

THE CONTRACT FOR CONSTRUCTION

I hope you have come away from Chapter 3 with an amicable feeling about contracts. Now, as we talk about the cornerstone of the construction documents, you should also understand the importance of the interrelationship between instruments. They must be well-connected. It is in the interest of all parties to record the many understandings that have been passed around up to this point in the job. It would be much better for you to quickly fill in these recommended AIA forms, hand-written in the presence of the interested parties, and make a few innocent goofs, rather than to sign a well-crafted document provided to you by the builder. I have never seen a redo contractor offer a contract that even marginally protects the owner, not to mention assigning roles in the designer-builder relationship. But you should not have to worry

about crafting documents; either your attorney or your architect should prepare the contract for both you and the builder.

Here is the way I do it. Usually in a phone call, I go over each important clause with the owner, inquiring "do you have any understandings that you want to cast in contract language?" I redline a xerox copy and send it to the builder for his review. He is asked the same question, and frequently wants to "noodle" more things, or add a few understandings of his own. When I receive his revised redline, I will call the owner and go over the builder's changes, trying to find some satisfactory common language. This exercise is important because it divulges a lot about all parties in the process, and their mutual expectations. But of course, this is the value of the contract: it make all parties think about the things they should be worried about, ahead of time. With any misunderstandings resolved, I then prepare three identical documents from original AIA forms. The builder and the owner then sign all agreements, and the originals are distributed. This can either be in a meeting or by mail. I do not sign the Owner-Contractor document, but take a copy because I will need to refer to it during construction.

Because I worry about the adequacy of your designer's or attorney's experience with remodeling, I will go into some detail in the builder's contract. I highly recommend that you copy this chapter and get it to your architect in a way that precludes his admitting to ignorance. If you take my earlier recommendation, and engage a real estate/construction lawyer, do the same for him, and make sure he does not diverge from the AIA forms. He will have a natural tendency to make "a mountain out of a mole-hill." At the very least, when you get your redline, put in some of this language as a starting point for negotiating the agreement.

Sample

AIA Document A107

Abbreviated Form of Agreement
Between Owner and Contractor

For CONSTRUCTION PROJECTS OF LIMITED SCOPE where
the Basis of Payment is a STIPULATED SUM

1987 EDITION

THIS DOCUMENT HAS IMPORTANT LEGAL CONSEQUENCES; CONSULTATION WITH
AN ATTORNEY IS ENCOURAGED WITH RESPECT TO ITS COMPLETION OR MODIFICATION.

This document includes abbreviated General Conditions and should not be used with other general conditions.
It has been approved and endorsed by The Associated General Contractors of America.

AGREEMENT

made as of the   Eighth   day of   January   in the year of
Nineteen Hundred and   Ninety Three.

BETWEEN the Owner:
(Name and address)

     Mary and John Green
     1492 Columbus Drive
     Towner, PA 19088

and the Contractor:
(Name and address)

     J & J Construction, Inc.
     422 Rock Road
     Philadelphia, PA 19003

The Project is:
(Name and location)

     Additions and Alterations to the Owner's residence at the above address.

The Architect is:
(Name and address)

     Peter Wilson
     2134 Harrie Road
     Wister, PA 19002

The Owner and Contractor agree as set forth below.

OWNER-BUILDER CONTRACT

EXAMPLE 27. *This is a sample agreement between a builder and a remodeling couple. Although eleven pages in length, only five require significant input. The "boilerplate" language on pages 6 through 10 sets out the responsibilities of the owner and builder throughout the construction process. These specific forms and the Owner-Architect Contract in Chapter 4 should be used in concert because their language is interrelated. Note the difference between Article 21(Other Conditions) here, and that of another redo in Example 29. As any good contract should, this form brings forward a wealth of experience, asking the right questions to solve problems before they can occur.*

Probably the most important thing to watch for in the contract is how it connects all of the other contract documents together. Example 27 is a remodeling contract for a $76,000 redo. It obligates the contractor to build the project according to the Drawings (in Article 6.1.4) and the accepted Alternates (in Article 3.2.1) for the price agreed to in Clause 3.1. All parties are advised that the Specifications occur within the Drawings themselves (Article 6.1.3) and that the Alternate work as described in the Bid Form itself (Article 6.1.6) is included in the Contract Sum (Article 3.2.1). Changes in the work that have not

ARTICLE 1
THE WORK OF THIS CONTRACT

1.1 The Contractor shall execute the entire Work described in the Contract Documents, except to the extent specifically indicated in the Contract Documents to be the responsibility of others, or as follows:

Where Marvin windows are specified in the drawings, change spec to snap-grilles versus true divided lites.

Change two casement windows (marked D) to double-hung by Marvin with snap-in grilles. Same approximate unit sizes.

ARTICLE 2
DATE OF COMMENCEMENT AND SUBSTANTIAL COMPLETION

2.1 The date of commencement is the date from which the Contract Time of Paragraph 2.2 is measured, and shall be the date of this Agreement, as first written above, unless a different date is stated below or provision is made for the date to be fixed in a notice to proceed issued by the Owner.

(Insert the date of commencement, if it differs from the date of this Agreement or, if applicable, state that the date will be fixed in a notice to proceed.)

Commencement: between February 1 and February 28, 1993 inclusive.
Contractor shall provide the Owner at least seven calendar days prior notice.

2.2 The Contractor shall achieve Substantial Completion of the entire Work not later than

(Insert the calendar date or number of calendar days after the date of commencement. Also insert any requirements for earlier Substantial Completion of certain portions of the Work, if not stated elsewhere in the Contract Documents.)

Sixty calendar days following date of commencement.

, subject to adjustments of this Contract Time as provided in the Contract Documents.

(Insert provisions, if any, for liquidated damages relating to failure to complete on time.)

None

ARTICLE 3
CONTRACT SUM

3.1 The Owner shall pay the Contractor in current funds for the Contractor's performance of the Contract the Contract Sum of
Seventy Six Thousand Nine Hundred Fifty   Dollars
($ $76,950.00   ), subject to additions and deductions as provided in the Contract Documents.

AIA DOCUMENT A107 • ABBREVIATED OWNER-CONTRACTOR AGREEMENT • NINTH EDITION • AIA® • ©1987
THE AMERICAN INSTITUTE OF ARCHITECTS, 1735 NEW YORK AVENUE, N.W., WASHINGTON, D.C. 20006   A107-1987   2

3.2 The Contract Sum is based upon the following alternates, if any, which are described in the Contract Documents and are hereby accepted by the Owner:

(State the numbers or other identification of accepted alternates. If decisions on other alternates are to be made by the Owner subsequent to the execution of this Agreement, attach a schedule of such other alternates showing the amount for each and the date until which that amount is valid.)

3.2.1. Alternate No. 1: remove master bedroom deck.
Alternate No. 2: downgrade counter edge
Alternate No. 3: install new exterior shutters
Alternate No. 5: finish interior garage walls

3.3 Unit prices, if any, are as follows:

3.3.1. Allowance for carpet included the Contract Sum: $20/yd for material only. All required rip-up, padding, and installation is included in the Contract Sum outside this Allowance.
3.3.2. For all HVAC work, included in the Contract Sum: $875.00
3.3.3. For all painting/staining, included in the Contract Sum: $1800.00
3.3.4 Revisions per Article 1.1 as included in the Contract Sum:
Downgrade to snap-in grille windows: credit $550.00
Change two D windows to double hung: credit $40.00

ARTICLE 4
PROGRESS PAYMENTS

4.1 Based upon Applications for Payment submitted to the Architect by the Contractor and Certificates for Payment issued by the Architect, the Owner shall make progress payments on account of the Contract Sum to the Contractor as provided below and elsewhere in the Contract Documents. The period covered by each Application for Payment shall be one calendar month ending on the last day of the month, or as follows:

Fourteen calendar days.

4.2 Payments due and unpaid under the Contract shall bear interest from the date payment is due at the rate stated below, or in the absence thereof, at the legal rate prevailing from time to time at the place where the Project is located.

(Insert rate of interest agreed upon, if any.)

Legal Prevailing Rate

(Usury laws and requirements under the Federal Truth in Lending Act, similar state and local consumer credit laws and other regulations at the Owner's and Contractor's principal places of business, the location of the Project and elsewhere may affect the validity of this provision. Legal advice should be obtained with respect to deletions or modifications, and also regarding requirements such as written disclosures or waivers.)

AIA DOCUMENT A107 • ABBREVIATED OWNER-CONTRACTOR AGREEMENT • NINTH EDITION • AIA® • ©1987
THE AMERICAN INSTITUTE OF ARCHITECTS, 1735 NEW YORK AVENUE, N.W., WASHINGTON, D.C. 20006   A107-1987   3

---

been included in the Drawings or described in an accepted Alternate can be specified in Article 1.1. These two particular cost-saving items resulted from a shakedown session, and monies removed from the Contract Sum are recorded as unit prices along with other things in Article 3.3.4.

SUBSTITUTING A PREFERRED SUBCONTRACTOR

In this redo, the contract page 11 (Example 27, Article 21.1) requires the builder to investigate the potential

ARTICLE 5
FINAL PAYMENT

5.1 Final payment, constituting the entire unpaid balance of the Contract Sum, shall be made by the Owner to the Contractor when the Work has been completed, the Contract fully performed, and a final Certificate for Payment has been issued by the Architect.

ARTICLE 6
ENUMERATION OF CONTRACT DOCUMENTS

6.1 The Contract Documents are listed in Article 7 and, except for Modifications issued after execution of this Agreement, are enumerated as follows:

6.1.1 The Agreement is this executed Abbreviated Form of Agreement Between Owner and Contractor, AIA Document A107, 1987 Edition.

6.1.2 The Supplementary and other Conditions of the Contract are those contained in the Project Manual dated , and are as follows:

Document	Title	Pages

None

6.1.3. The Specifications are those contained in the Project Manual dated as in Subparagraph 6.1.2, and are as follows:
(Either list the Specifications here or refer to an exhibit attached to this Agreement.)

Section	Title	Pages

Any Specifications are located within the Drawings.

6.1.4 The Drawings are as follows, and are dated   11/2/92 revised 11/14/92   unless a different date is shown below:
(Either list the Drawings here or refer to an exhibit attached to this Agreement.)

Number	Title	Date

Sheet A-1 Floor framing, site plan, door and room finish shedule, index, symbol key
Sheet A-2 Elevations, window schedule
Sheet A-3 Section, interior elevations, details, abbreviations, mechanical plan, lighting schedule
Sheet A-4 Selected details

6.1.5 The Addenda, if any, are as follows:

Number	Date	Pages

No Addendum has been issued.

Portions of Addenda relating to bidding requirements are not part of the Contract Documents unless the bidding requirements are also enumerated in this Article 6.

6.1.6 Other documents, if any, forming part of the Contract Documents are as follows:
(List any additional documents which are intended to form part of the Contract Documents.)

The Bid Form dated 12/14/92 describes Alternates set out in Article 3.2 herein and is attached to this agreement.

replacement of his HVAC and painting subs with the owner's workmen. This is a very smart request, in this case. The owners had used some painters that they thought highly of, and preferred to use them again. Because interior painting is frequently a subjective and contentious task, using a known entity could preclude many callbacks. In a similar vein, the heating contractor who had installed the original system, and had serviced it ever since, was an obvious candidate for doing the new work. Because the new addition bordered on

GENERAL CONDITIONS

ARTICLE 7
CONTRACT DOCUMENTS

7.1 The Contract Documents consist of this Agreement with Conditions of the Contract (General, Supplementary and other Conditions), Drawings, Specifications, addenda issued prior to the execution of this Agreement, other documents listed in this Agreement and Modifications issued after execution of this Agreement. The intent of the Contract Documents is to include all items necessary for the proper execution and completion of the Work by the Contractor. The Contract Documents are complementary, and what is required by one shall be as binding as if required by all; performance by the Contractor shall be required only to the extent consistent with the Contract Documents and reasonably inferable from them as being necessary to produce the intended results.

7.2 The Contract Documents shall not be construed to create a contractual relationship of any kind (1) between the Architect and Contractor, (2) between the Owner and a Subcontractor or Sub-subcontractor or (3) between any persons or entities other than the Owner and Contractor.

7.3 Execution of the Contract by the Contractor is a representation that the Contractor has visited the site and become familiar with the local conditions under which the Work is to be performed.

7.4 The term "Work" means the construction and services required by the Contract Documents, whether completed or partially completed, and includes all other labor, materials, equipment and services provided or to be provided by the Contractor to fulfill the Contractor's obligations. The Work may constitute the whole or a part of the Project.

ARTICLE 8
OWNER

8.1 The Owner shall furnish surveys and a legal description of the site.

8.2 Except for permits and fees which are the responsibility of the Contractor under the Contract Documents, the Owner shall secure and pay for necessary approvals, easements, assessments and charges required for the construction, use or occupancy of permanent structures or permanent changes in existing facilities.

8.3 If the Contractor fails to correct Work which is not in accordance with the requirements of the Contract Documents or persistently fails to carry out the Work in accordance with the Contract Documents, the Owner, by a written order, may order the Contractor to stop the Work, or any portion thereof, until the cause for such order has been eliminated; however, the right of the Owner to stop the Work shall not give rise to a duty on the part of the Owner to exercise this right for the benefit of the Contractor or any other person or entity.

ARTICLE 9
CONTRACTOR

9.1 The Contractor shall supervise and direct the Work, using the Contractor's best skill and attention. The Contractor shall be solely responsible for and have control over construction means, methods, techniques, sequences and procedures and for coordinating all portions of the Work under the Contract, unless Contract Documents give other specific instructions concerning these matters.

9.2 Unless otherwise provided in the Contract Documents, the Contractor shall provide and pay for labor, materials, equipment, tools, construction equipment and machinery, water, heat, utilities, transportation, and other facilities and services necessary for the proper execution and completion of the Work, whether temporary or permanent and whether or not incorporated or to be incorporated in the Work.

9.3 The Contractor shall enforce strict discipline and good order among the Contractor's employees and other persons carrying out the Contract. The Contractor shall not permit employment of unfit persons or persons not skilled in tasks assigned to them.

9.4 The Contractor warrants to the Owner and Architect that materials and equipment furnished under the Contract will be of good quality and new unless otherwise required or permitted by the Contract Documents, that the Work will be free from defects not inherent in the quality required or permitted, and that the Work will conform with the requirements of the Contract Documents. Work not conforming to these requirements, including substitutions not properly approved and authorized, may be considered defective. The Contractor's warranty excludes remedy for damage or defect caused by abuse, modifications not executed by the Contractor, improper or insufficient maintenance, improper operation, or normal wear and tear under normal usage. If required by the Architect, the Contractor shall furnish satisfactory evidence as to the kind and quality of materials and equipment.

9.5 Unless otherwise provided in the Contract Documents, the Contractor shall pay sales, consumer, use, and other similar taxes which are legally enacted when bids are received or negotiations concluded, whether or not yet effective or merely scheduled to go into effect, and shall secure and pay for the building permit and other permits and governmental fees, licenses and inspections necessary for proper execution and completion of the Work.

9.6 The Contractor shall comply with and give notices required by laws, ordinances, rules, regulations, and lawful orders of public authorities bearing on performance of the Work. The Contractor shall promptly notify the Architect and Owner if the Drawings and Specifications are observed by the Contractor to be at variance therewith.

9.7 The Contractor shall be responsible to the Owner for the acts and omissions of the Contractor's employees, Subcontractors and their agents and employees, and other persons performing portions of the Work under a contract with the Contractor.

9.8 The Contractor shall review, approve and submit to the Architect Shop Drawings, Product Data, Samples and similar submittals required by the Contract Documents with reasonable promptness. The Work shall be in accordance with approved submittals. When professional certification of performance criteria of materials, systems or equipment is required by the Contract Documents, the Architect shall be entitled to rely upon the accuracy and completeness of such certifications.

9.9 The Contractor shall keep the premises and surrounding area free from accumulation of waste materials or rubbish caused by operations under the Contract. At completion of the Work the Contractor shall remove from and about the Project waste materials, rubbish, the Contractor's tools, construction equipment, machinery and surplus materials.

9.10 The Contractor shall provide the Owner and Architect access to the Work in preparation and progress wherever located.

9.11 The Contractor shall pay all royalties and license fees; shall defend suits or claims for infringement of patent rights and shall hold the Owner harmless from loss on account thereof, but shall not be responsible for such defense or loss when a particular design, process or product of a particular manufacturer or manufacturers is required by the Contract Documents unless the Contractor has reason to believe that there is an infringement of patent.

9.12 To the fullest extent permitted by law, the Contractor shall indemnify and hold harmless the Owner, Architect, Architect's consultants, and agents and employees of any of them from and against claims, damages, losses and expenses, including but not limited to attorneys' fees, arising out of or resulting from performance of the Work, provided that such claim, damage, loss or expense is attributable to bodily injury, sickness, disease or death, or to injury to or destruction of tangible property (other than the Work itself) including loss of use resulting therefrom, but only to the extent caused in whole or in part by negligent acts or omissions of the Contractor, a Subcontractor, anyone directly or indirectly employed by them or anyone for whose acts they may be liable, regardless of whether or not such claim, damage, loss or expense is caused in part by a party indemnified hereunder. Such obligation shall not be construed to negate, abridge, or reduce other rights or obligations of indemnity which would otherwise exist as to a party or person described in this Paragraph 9.12.

9.12.1 In claims against any person or entity indemnified under this Paragraph 9.12 by an employee of the Contractor, a Subcontractor, anyone directly or indirectly employed by them or anyone for whose acts they may be liable, the indemnification obligation under this Paragraph 9.12 shall not be limited by a limitation on amount or type of damages, compensation or benefits payable by or for the Contractor or a Subcontractor under workers' or workmen's compensation acts, disability benefit acts or other employee benefit acts.

9.12.2 The obligations of the Contractor under this Paragraph 9.12 shall not extend to the liability of the Architect, the Architect's consultants, and agents and employees of any of them arising out of (1) the preparation or approval of maps, drawings, opinions, reports, surveys, Change Orders, Construction Change Directives, designs or specifications, or (2) the giving of or the failure to give directions or instructions by the Architect, the Architect's consultants, and agents and employees of any of them provided such giving or failure to give is the primary cause of the injury or damage.

ARTICLE 10
ADMINISTRATION OF THE CONTRACT

10.1 The Architect will provide administration of the Contract and will be the Owner's representative (1) during construction, (2) until final payment is due and (3) with the Owner's concurrence, from time to time during the correction period described in Paragraph 18.1

10.2 The Architect will visit the site at intervals appropriate to the stage of construction to become generally familiar with the progress and quality of the completed Work and to determine in general if the Work is being performed in a manner indicating that the Work, when completed, will be in accordance with the Contract Documents. However, the Architect will not be required to make exhaustive or continuous on-site inspections to check quality or quantity of the Work. On the basis of on-site observations as an architect, the Architect will keep the Owner informed of progress of the Work and will endeavor to guard the Owner against defects and deficiencies in the Work.

10.3 The Architect will not have control over or charge of and will not be responsible for construction means, methods, techniques, sequences or procedures, or for safety precautions and programs in connection with the Work, since these are solely the Contractor's responsibility as provided in Paragraphs 9.1 and 16.1. The Architect will not be responsible for the Contractor's failure to carry out the Work in accordance with the Contract Documents.

10.4 Based on the Architect's observations and evaluations of the Contractor's Applications for Payment, the Architect will review and certify the amounts due the Contractor and will issue Certificates for Payment in such amounts.

10.5 The Architect will interpret and decide matters concerning performance under and requirements of the Contract Documents on written request of either the Owner or Contractor. The Architect will make initial decisions on all claims, disputes or other matters in question between the Owner and Contractor, but will not be liable for results of any interpretations or decisions rendered in good faith. The Architect's decisions in matters relating to aesthetic effect will be final if consistent with the intent expressed in the Contract Documents. All other decisions of the Architect, except those which have been waived by making or acceptance of final payment, shall be subject to arbitration upon the written demand of either party.

10.6 The Architect will have authority to reject Work which does not conform to the Contract Documents.

10.7 The Architect will review and approve or take other appropriate action upon the Contractor's submittals such as Shop Drawings, Product Data and Samples, but only for the limited purpose of checking for conformance with information given and the design concept expressed in the Contract Documents.

10.8 All claims or disputes between the Contractor and the Owner arising out or relating to the Contract, or the breach thereof, shall be decided by arbitration in accordance with the Construction Industry Arbitration Rules of the American Arbitration Association currently in effect unless the parties mutually agree otherwise and subject to an initial presentation of the claim or dispute to the Architect as required under Paragraph 10.5. Notice of the demand for arbitration shall be filed in writing with the other party to this Agreement and with the American Arbitration Association and shall be made within a reasonable time after the dispute has arisen. The award rendered by

AIA DOCUMENT A107 • ABBREVIATED OWNER-CONTRACTOR AGREEMENT • NINTH EDITION • AIA® • ©1987
THE AMERICAN INSTITUTE OF ARCHITECTS, 1735 NEW YORK AVENUE, N.W., WASHINGTON, D.C. 20006

A107-1987 6

7 A107-1987

AIA DOCUMENT A107 • ABBREVIATED OWNER-CONTRACTOR AGREEMENT • NINTH EDITION • AIA® • ©1987
THE AMERICAN INSTITUTE OF ARCHITECTS, 1735 NEW YORK AVENUE, N.W., WASHINGTON, D.C. 20006

Sample

Sample

---

exceeding the capacity of the existing system, and the owner wanted to try to extend its supply ductwork rather than provide a second unit, experience with the mother-system was highly desirable. Notice that the builder is not required to use these other subs, which he cannot be made to do, but he must ask them for a quote for potential substitution in his team. Should he object to the owner's subs, the owner may contract separately with them, although this is inadvisable for both parties. And so this contract is written to cast the

the arbitrator or arbitrators shall be final, and judgment may be entered upon it in accordance with applicable law in any court having jurisdiction thereof. Except by written consent of the person or entity sought to be joined, no arbitration arising out of or relating to the Contract Documents shall include, by consolidation, joinder or in any other manner, any person or entity not a party to the Agreement under which such arbitration arises, unless it is shown at the time the demand for arbitration is filed that (1) such person or entity is substantially involved in a common question of fact or law, (2) the presence of such person or entity is required if complete relief is to be accorded in the arbitration, (3) the interest or responsibility of such person or entity in the matter is not insubstantial, and (4) such person or entity is not the Architect or any of the Architect's employees or consultants. The agreement herein among the parties to the Agreement and any other written agreement to arbitrate referred to herein shall be specifically enforceable under applicable law in any court having jurisdiction thereof.

ARTICLE 11

SUBCONTRACTS

11.1 A Subcontractor is a person or entity who has a direct contract with the Contractor to perform a portion of the Work at the site.

11.2 Unless otherwise stated in the Contract Documents or the bidding requirements, the Contractor, as soon as practicable after award of the Contract, shall furnish in writing to the Owner through the Architect the names of the Subcontractors for each of the principal portions of the Work. The Contractor shall not contract with any Subcontractor to whom the Owner or Architect has made reasonable and timely objection. The Contractor shall not be required to contract with anyone to whom the Contractor has made reasonable objection. Contracts between the Contractor and Subcontractors shall (1) require each Subcontractor, to the extent of the Work to be performed by the Subcontractor, to be bound to the Contractor by the terms of the Contract Documents, and to assume toward the Contractor all the obligations and responsibilities which the Contractor, by the Contract Documents, assumes toward the Owner and Architect, and (2) allow to the Subcontractor the benefit of all rights, remedies and redress afforded to the Contractor by these Contract Documents.

ARTICLE 12

CONSTRUCTION BY OWNER OR BY SEPARATE CONTRACTORS

12.1 The Owner reserves the right to perform construction or operations related to the Project with the Owner's own forces, and to award separate contracts in connection with other portions of the Project or other construction or operations on the site under conditions of the contract identical or substantially similar to these, including those portions related to insurance and waiver of subrogation. If the Contractor claims that delay or additional cost is involved because of such action by the Owner, the Contractor shall make such claim as provided elsewhere in the Contract Documents.

12.2 The Contractor shall afford the Owner and separate contractors reasonable opportunity for the introduction and storage of their materials and equipment and performance of their activities, and shall connect and coordinate the Contractor's construction and operations with theirs as required by the Contract Documents.

12.3 Costs caused by delays, improperly timed activities or defective construction shall be borne by the party responsible therefor.

ARTICLE 13

CHANGES IN THE WORK

13.1 The Owner, without invalidating the Contract, may order changes in the Work consisting of additions, deletions or modifications, the Contract Sum and Contract Time being adjusted accordingly. Such changes in the Work shall be authorized by written Change Order signed by the Owner, Contractor and Architect, or by written Construction Change Directive signed by the Owner and Architect.

13.2 The Contract Sum and Contract Time shall be changed only by Change Order.

13.3 The cost or credit to the Owner from a change in the Work shall be determined by mutual agreement.

ARTICLE 14

TIME

14.1 Time limits stated in the Contract Documents are of the essence of the Contract. By executing the Agreement the Contractor confirms that the Contract Time is a reasonable period for performing the Work.

14.2 The date of Substantial Completion is the date certified by the Architect in accordance with Paragraph 15.3.

14.3 If the Contractor is delayed at any time in progress of the Work by changes ordered in the Work, by labor disputes, fire, unusual delay in deliveries, abnormal adverse weather conditions not reasonably anticipatable, unavoidable casualties or any causes beyond the Contractor's control, or by other causes which the Architect determines may justify delay, then the Contract Time shall be extended by Change Order for such reasonable time as the Architect may determine.

ARTICLE 15

PAYMENTS AND COMPLETION

15.1 Payments shall be made as provided in Articles 4 and 5 of this Agreement.

15.2 Payments may be withheld on account of (1) defective Work not remedied, (2) claims filed by third parties, (3) failure of the Contractor to make payments properly to Subcontractors or for labor, materials or equipment, (4) reasonable evidence that the Work cannot be completed for the unpaid balance of the Contract Sum, (5) damage to the Owner or another contractor, (6) reasonable evidence that the Work will not be completed within the Contract Time and that the unpaid balance would not be adequate to cover actual or liquidated damages for the anticipated delay, or (7) persistent failure to carry out the Work in accordance with the Contract Documents.

15.3 When the Architect agrees that the Work is substantially complete, the Architect will issue a Certificate of Substantial Completion.

15.4 Final payment shall not become due until the Contractor has delivered to the Owner a complete release of all liens arising out of this Contract or receipts in full covering all labor, materials and equipment for which a lien could be filed, or a bond satisfactory to the Owner to indemnify the Owner against such

AIA DOCUMENT A107 • ABBREVIATED OWNER-CONTRACTOR AGREEMENT • NINTH EDITION • AIA® • ©1987
THE AMERICAN INSTITUTE OF ARCHITECTS, 1735 NEW YORK AVENUE, N.W., WASHINGTON, D.C. 20006 **A107-1987 8**

lien. If such lien remains unsatisfied after payments are made, the Contractor shall refund to the Owner all money that the Owner may be compelled to pay in discharging such lien, including all costs and reasonable attorneys' fees.

15.5 The making of final payment shall constitute a waiver of claims by the Owner except those arising from:

- **.1** liens, claims, security interests or encumbrances arising out of the Contract and unsettled;
- **.2** failure of the Work to comply with the requirements of the Contract Documents; or
- **.3** terms of special warranties required by the Contract Documents.

Acceptance of final payment by the Contractor, a Subcontractor or material supplier shall constitute a waiver of claims by that payee except those previously made in writing and identified by that payee as unsettled at the time of final Application for Payment.

ARTICLE 16

PROTECTION OF PERSONS AND PROPERTY

16.1 The Contractor shall be responsible for initiating, maintaining, and supervising all safety precautions and programs in connection with the performance of the Contract. The Contractor shall take reasonable precautions for safety of, and shall provide reasonable protection to prevent damage, injury or loss to:

- **.1** employees on the Work and other persons who may be affected thereby;
- **.2** the Work and materials and equipment to be incorporated therein; and
- **.3** other property at the site or adjacent thereto.

The Contractor shall give notices and comply with applicable laws, ordinances, rules, regulations and lawful orders of public authorities bearing on safety of persons and property and their protection from damage, injury or loss. The Contractor shall promptly remedy damage and loss to property at the site caused in whole or in part by the Contractor, a Subcontractor, a Sub-subcontractor, or anyone directly or indirectly employed by any of them, or by anyone for whose acts they may be liable and for which the Contractor is responsible under Subparagraphs 16.1.2 and 16.1.3, except for damage or loss attributable to acts or omissions of the Owner or Architect or by anyone for whose acts either of them may be liable, and not attributable to the fault or negligence of the Contractor. The foregoing obligations of the Contractor are in addition to the Contractor's obligations under Paragraph 9.12.

16.2 The Contractor shall not be required to perform without consent any Work relating to asbestos or polychlorinated biphenyl (PCB).

ARTICLE 17

INSURANCE

17.1 The Contractor shall purchase from and maintain in a company or companies lawfully authorized to do business in the jurisdiction in which the Project is located insurance for protection from claims under workers' or workmen's compensation acts and other employee benefit acts which are applicable, claims for damages because of bodily injury, including death, and from claims for damages, other than to the Work itself, to property which may arise out of or result from the Contractor's operations under the Contract, whether such operations be by the Contractor or by a Subcontractor or anyone directly or indirectly employed by any of them. This insurance shall be written for not less than limits of liability specified in the Contract Documents or required by law, whichever coverage is greater, and shall include contractual liability insurance applicable to the Contractor's obligations under Paragraph 9.12. Certificates of such insurance shall be filed with the Owner prior to the commencement of the Work.

17.2 The Owner shall be responsible for purchasing and maintaining the Owner's usual liability insurance. Optionally, the Owner may purchase and maintain other insurance for self-protection against claims which may arise from operations under the Contract. The Contractor shall not be responsible for purchasing and maintaining this optional Owner's liability insurance unless specifically required by the Contract Documents.

17.3 Unless otherwise provided, the Owner shall purchase and maintain, in a company or companies lawfully authorized to do business in the jurisdiction in which the Project is located, property insurance upon the entire Work at the site to the full insurable value thereof. This insurance shall be on an all-risk policy form and shall include interests of the Owner, the Contractor, Subcontractors and Sub-subcontractors in the Work and shall insure against the perils of fire and extended coverage and physical loss or damage including, without duplication of coverage, theft, vandalism and malicious mischief.

17.4 A loss insured under Owner's property insurance shall be adjusted with the Owner and made payable to the Owner as fiduciary for the insureds, as their interests may appear, subject to the requirements of any applicable mortgagee clause.

17.5 The Owner shall file a copy of each policy with the Contractor before an exposure to loss may occur. Each policy shall contain a provision that the policy will not be cancelled or allowed to expire until at least 30 days' prior written notice has been given to the Contractor.

17.6 The Owner and Contractor waive all rights against each other and the Architect, Architect's consultants, separate contractors described in Article 12, if any, and any of their subcontractors, sub-subcontractors, agents and employees, for damages caused by fire or other perils to the extent covered by property insurance obtained pursuant to this Article 17 or any other property insurance applicable to the Work, except such rights as they may have to the proceeds of such insurance held by the Owner as fiduciary. The Contractor shall require similar waivers in favor of the Owner and the Contractor by Subcontractors and Sub-subcontractors. The Owner shall require similar waivers in favor of the Owner and Contractor by the Architect, Architect's consultants, separate contractors described in Article 12, if any, and the subcontractors, sub-subcontractors, agents and employees of any of them.

ARTICLE 18

CORRECTION OF WORK

18.1 The Contractor shall promptly correct Work rejected by the Architect or failing to conform to the requirements of the Contract Documents, whether observed before or after Substantial Completion and whether or not fabricated, installed or completed, and shall correct any Work found to be not in accordance with the requirements of the Contract Documents within a period of one year from the date of Substantial Com-

9 A107-1987 **AIA DOCUMENT A107** • ABBREVIATED OWNER-CONTRACTOR AGREEMENT • NINTH EDITION • AIA® • ©1987
THE AMERICAN INSTITUTE OF ARCHITECTS, 1735 NEW YORK AVENUE, N.W., WASHINGTON, D.C. 20006

Sample

contractor's original bid as the "downside" by recording painting and HVAC as unit prices (Articles 3.3.2 and 3.3.3) included in the contract sum, and by requiring him to try to get comfortable with a new team mix (Article 21.1). This provision resulted in the contractor hiring the new painter for his crew, but the HVAC sub wanted too much money to do the work, so the owner accepted the original heating proposal. Because the painting change occurred after execution of the contract, it was recorded as a Change Order for the difference between the contract unit price (Article 3.3.3) and the newly quoted sum.

pletion of the Contract or by terms of an applicable special warranty required by the Contract Documents. The provisions of this Article 18 apply to Work done by Subcontractors as well as to Work done by direct employees of the Contractor.

18.2 Nothing contained in this Article 18 shall be construed to establish a period of limitation with respect to other obligations which the Contractor might have under the Contract Documents. Establishment of the time period of one year as described in Paragraph 18.1 relates only to the specific obligation of the Contractor to correct the Work, and has no relationship to the time within which the obligation to comply with the Contract Documents may be sought to be enforced, nor to the time within which proceedings may be commenced to establish the Contractor's liability with respect to the Contractor's obligations other than specifically to correct the Work.

ARTICLE 19
MISCELLANEOUS PROVISIONS

19.1 The Contract shall be governed by the law of the place where the Project is located.

19.2 As between the Owner and the Contractor, any applicable statute of limitations shall commence to run and any alleged cause of action shall be deemed to have accrued:

.1 not later than the date of Substantial Completion for acts or failures to act occurring prior to the relevant date of Substantial Completion;

.2 not later than the date of issuance of the final Certificate for Payment for acts or failures to act occurring subsequent to the relevant date of Substantial Completion and prior to issuance of the final Certificate for Payment; and

.3 not later than the date of the relevant act or failure to act by the Contractor for acts or failures to act occurring after the date of the final Certificate for Payment.

ARTICLE 20
TERMINATION OF THE CONTRACT

20.1 If the Architect fails to recommend payment for a period of 30 days through no fault of the Contractor, or if the Owner fails to make payment thereon for a period of 30 days, the Contractor may, upon seven additional days' written notice to the Owner and the Architect, terminate the Contract and recover from the Owner payment for Work executed and for proven loss with respect to materials, equipment, tools, and construction equipment and machinery, including reasonable overhead, profit and damages applicable to the Project.

20.2 If the Contractor defaults or persistently fails or neglects to carry out the Work in accordance with the Contract Documents or fails to perform a provision of the Contract, the Owner, after seven days' written notice to the Contractor and without prejudice to any other remedy the Owner may have, may make good such deficiencies and may deduct the cost thereof, including compensation for the Architect's services and expenses made necessary thereby, from the payment then or thereafter due the Contractor. Alternatively, at the Owner's option, and upon certification by the Architect that sufficient cause exists to justify such action, the Owner may terminate the Contract and take possession of the site and of all materials, equipment, tools, and construction equipment and machinery thereon owned by the Contractor and may finish the Work by whatever method the Owner may deem expedient. If the unpaid balance of the Contract Sum exceeds costs of finishing the Work, including compensation for the Architect's services and expenses made necessary thereby, such excess shall be paid to the Contractor, but if such costs exceed such unpaid balance, the Contractor shall pay the difference to the Owner.

ARTICLE 21
OTHER CONDITIONS OR PROVISIONS

21.1 Contractor acknowledges potential replacement of the painting and HVAC subcontractors per the Owner's request, and has provided unit prices in Article 3.3 for this scenario. Further, the Contractor agrees to solicit proposals for these alternative subcontractors starting with the Owner's recommendations. Contract Articles 11 and 12 herein remain unchanged.

This Agreement entered into as of the day and year first written above.

OWNER

(Signature) _____   _(Signature)_ _____

Mary Green   John Green
(Printed name and title)

CONTRACTOR

(Signature) _____

J. Gaston, J & J Construction, Inc.
(Printed name and title)

MITIGATING FUTURE CHANGE ORDER COSTS

The best time to control the cost of future Change Orders is while the owner and builder are still in the honeymoon stage of their relationship. Whereas in hiring your designer, you required him to divulge his Additional Service labor rates in his Proposal Form, you are now negotiating a builder's contract not having asked the equivalent question of him in the Bid Form. This is because of the likelihood that the

A

CUSTOM WET-BAR CABINET

This cabinet group (Photograph A) has been designed to match adjacent cabinets in a radically expanded family room. Because the kitchen was on the floor above, this wet-bar area provides for separate preparation of drinks and snacks on the family room level. Above the counter is a microwave and an appliance garage concealing a blender. Photograph B shows the undercounter refrigerator. This model by Uline is designed for just such a built-in application. Unfortunately, this work center suffers from a common custom-cabinet malady, that is, endgame glitches. In this case, the refrigerator is almost impossible to remove for servicing, because it was installed from the back before the entire cabinet was fixed in place. This requires that the bottom oak rail be cut for the appliance to slide out.

B

designer will have required his compensation to based on a percentage of construction cost, rather than the builder's lump sum. A clause similar to Example 28, Page 3, Article 3.3, probably should have been included in the previous contract (Example 27). It requires no more hassle of the bidders, in deference to simply recording the rates the contractor intends to charge when Change Orders arise. You should be more worried about having him compete for real what-if scenarios through the Alternates in the Bid Form, where the big savings can be found. Although other architects may disagree, I am particularly sensitive to avoiding a situation where the remodeling builders feel that they are having to jump through too many hoops to secure the job. The builders who would seriously gouge an owner on Change Order work are fewer than you might think. Most would be insulted at the suggestion.

When your architect provides the mark-up contract copy for your review, ask that the builder be as specific as possible with the "extra" billing rates for the people who will be on your job. Remember that in your stipulated-sum arrangement, you don't really care what he pays them, until you have to approve of work outside the specified scope. Then the contract clause covering unit prices for Change Order work becomes very important, for it allows you and your designer to quickly decipher the fairness of an extra charge, with little discussion.

VARIATIONS

Notice that Allowances can be set out in the contract (Article 3.3.1) as well as in the Drawings or Specifications, as they sometimes are. If they are expressed elsewhere, the contract language should

point to their location and "attach" the document to the agreement. This may also happen with Alternates, which can be described in the Drawings, the Bid Form, or in language within the Contract. In another job (Example 28, Page 3, Article 3.2.1), all prior descriptions of Alternates are superseded by the new contract wording, and the Bid Form does not become part of the contract documents.

And because Article 3.2.2 speaks of air conditioning, look at Example 28, Clause 1.1.1. For this project, the documents instructed bidders to assume that the new work would be supplied from the mother-system. The consensus of all but one of the bidding subcontractors was that a new second unit was required. Opting for the new unit, the owner approved the architect's making the following changes to the construction documents. All obsolete references to the system in the Drawings were deleted in the shakedown revision and the new HVAC work was called for in the contract (Article 1.1.1). The quoted price for the unit was recorded in Article 3.3 as an Allowance.

When should the work commence? Notice that the sample agreement in Example 27 and another job in Example 28, instruct the builder to begin the work in totally different ways (Article 2.1.1). One way obligates the builder to begin within a calendar-window, which is a good idea if the project is a definite "go" and you want work to begin soon. But if you are not sure when you want work to start, particularly if a six-months-or-so start seems likely, then a "notice to proceed" method is better. From a risk standpoint, the "notice to proceed" scenario offers more protection for the owner during the period between signing and start of construction. I had a rather traumatic job where very negative information surfaced on a builder during this period, and the owners terminated his contract before any work had begun (upon my

---

OTHER HELPFUL CONSTRUCTION CONTRACT CLAUSES

For use in Owner-Contractor, Limited Scope Project, Stipulated Sum Agreement   Form: AIA A107-1987

Page 2

1.1.1.   Provide a new heating and air-conditioning unit in the attic according to all applicable codes. See Article 3.3 herein for the Allowance included in the Contract Sum.

2.1.1.   Commencement: No Work under this agreement is authorized until the Owner provides written Notice to Proceed to the Contractor. Contractor will begin Work within 30 calendar days after receiving Notice to Proceed.

Page 3

3.2.1.   All prior Alternates have been dissolved. Some measures specified in prior Alternates have been incorporated into the drawings as part of the Work and are now included in the Contract Sum.

3.3.   The Contractor's Overhead and Profit on any material or labor Change Order work, shall not exceed the Contractor's discounted trade price plus twenty percent (20%). In addition, any Change Order labor by Contractors own employees are not to exceed the following hourly rates, including Overhead and Profit:

General Contractor, T. Brachaglia: $25/hr
Lead Carpenter, T. Pritchard: $25/hr
Carpenter, K. Healey: $20/hr
Helper, K. Cleary: $15/hr

OTHER HELPFUL CONSTRUCTION CONTRACT CLAUSES

EXAMPLE 28. *This language comes from other remodeling owner-builder contracts (form AIA A07-1987). Each clause has been written to prevent a specific problem from arising during construction.*

---

advice). He successfully argued through several threatened lawsuits and finally in arbitration that the owners are obligated to him from their point of signing the agreement, regardless of how outrageous his behavior is subsequently. Using similar "notice to proceed" language should help mitigate this eventuality, although I know there is no such thing as absolute protection from a person with no scruples and a lawyer in tow.

To get a feeling for the kind of provisions that may be included in the Contract for Construction, review Example 29. Here the property was a large urban rowhome in an upscale but crime-prone area. This,

plus the fact that the owner would be absent during construction, generated many areas of concern from all parties. Like any agreement should, this one sets out mutual expectations, although this Article 21 is likely to be too lengthy for your project.

FRONT MONEY

A primary goal in the Example 29 project was to begin and complete the job during the short time the owner was away. The work was to begin immediately with

CONSTRUCTION CONTRACT LANGUAGE   **Absent Owner in Urban Area**

For use in Form: AIA A107-1987 Page 11, Article 21 Other Conditions or Provisions

21.1   General Contractor agrees that the premises shall be checked and locked whenever leaving or working in remote sections of the residence. Door keys are to be stictly accounted for.

21.2   Contractor agrees to exercise extra care in assuring that construction openings are secured, alarms are reset, and that the premises is protected as much as possible from break-ins or vandalism.

21.3   General Contractor agrees that protecting and shifting furnishings and belongings is included in this Work.

21.4   General Contractor has reviewed installation of all Art Glass and (excepting carrying of the kitchen window units) has included this in the Work.

21.5   General Contractor partner Bo Thorndike agrees that he shall manage no more than one other construction project concurrent to this Work.

21.6   General Contractor agrees to work with his Subcontractors and the Architect to facilitate a mid-August meeting with the Owner where all product selections are documented and presented for final approval before his departure.

21.7   Owner agrees that should Trade Union representatives force the Owner to direct the General Contractor to provide Union workers, then the Contract Sum will be adjusted by Change Order to reflect the differences in costs when fairly documented by the General Contractor.

21.8   An initial amount of $2000 will be paid the General Contractor by the Owner via the Architect, for his use in securing a building permit. On the approximate day that construction begins and following the presentation of the first Payment Request, an additional $5000 will be disbursed directly to the Contractor . This initial $7000 dollars shall be assigned on a pro-rated basis to discreet trade/material line items in the Payment Request, and shall be fully absorbed as payment for work-in-place within sixty (60) days.

21.9   Contractor understands that a 10% retainage will be withheld from each Payment Request line-item. Half of the retainage will be released when the Architect's Substantial Completion punch-list has been satisfied. The Owner will generate another punch list upon return, and the balance of the retainage, constituting Final Payment will be made when it is satisfied.

21.10   Contractor will submit application for Building Permit no later than August 14, 1992.

CONSTRUCTION CONTRACT LANGUAGE

EXAMPLE 29. *This is an excerpt from a builder's redo contract. Here, Article 21 (AIA A107-1987, page 11) is extensive and well considered. The property was a large urban rowhome in an upscale but crime-prone area. This, plus the fact that the owner would be absent during construction, generated many areas of concern. Like any agreement should, this one sets out mutual expectations for the involved parties, although this Article 21 is likely to be too lengthy for your project.*

many workmen and material purchases, and the method of overseas money transfer was unfamiliar. Here, contrary to my usual advice, money was to be paid up front. Because this causes the owner to lose his cash-flow leverage, that is, the builder would not be requesting payment for "work in place," Article 21.8 lays down a schedule whereby the "borrowed" money is paid back to the owner over sixty days. After that time, the owner is back in control of the project, at least from a monetary standpoint. Unless your project is unique, you should try to defer discussion of initial payments until after signing the contract. You have already advised your builder in the Invitation that you will be paying for "in place" work. If he presses for a contract clause requiring front money, review Chapter 8 before you respond.

CHAPTER 8

CONSTRUCTION

NOW IT'S SHOWTIME!

With the builder's contract signed, work can begin. Give yourself a pat on the back! You have passed a critical milestone; your project has moved from planning into production. And coming up, a "r-r-r-really good show!" as my sons would say. The process should now be well-cast and your pros firmly engaged to move it along. The really crucial decisions for you have passed. Although your builder or architect will present you with many small decisions to render during construction, your primary responsibility is the management of the big picture. You must balance the maintenance of a good working environment with protection of the quality of the architecture that is to come. That, and cope with the inevitable noise, dirt, and loss of privacy. As in previous chapters, I will not try to show you how to "build" your job, in the strictest sense of the term, for your time will be more productively spent elsewhere. But it will be very exciting watching how your newly hired superstar makes your ideas take shape around you!

PREPARING FOR CONSTRUCTION

It may be months before the general contractor can fit the job into his schedule. Now is the time for you to get your house ready for construction. If you haven't done it thus far, you need to call the builder and jot down a list of things to do. If he hasn't been required to move and protect furnishings as part of the work, then you may need several weeks to prepare for the builder's arrival. Furnishings can either be moved out of the house for storage, or consolidated into rooms that will not be affected. Often in larger homes, one or two peripheral spaces will warehouse covered belongings behind sealed doors. Ask the builder what will be done to protect the things in your attic, before you volunteer your spouse. If major roof work will be done, dust and debris will rain down, coating everything. Sometimes protective plastic sheeting is laid down inside the attic as part of the quoted roofing work, but you had better check; attics are often neglected. And basements frequently suffer the same fate.

Protecting Your Yard

You may need to take protective measures for exterior objects such as trees, shrubs, patios, driveways, curbs, barbecue grills, and swimming pools. If you have valuable things to worry about outside, and have not previously discussed their protection, don't expect too much of the workmen. Ask the builder's intention and then be prepared to take care of it yourself. If you think more protection work should be included in your job, consult with the designer for an interpreta-

A

FIRM FOUNDATION

Like anything worthwhile, a good redo begins with a firm foundation. This project will get an excavated crawl space floor system. The subcontracted backhoe digs the rough hole (Photograph A), and then the carpenters prepare forms for reinforced concrete footings (Photograph B). Note the trenching (upper left) in Photograph C that will accept a monolithic concrete pour for a patio slab, well after the foundation for the structure is ready to go. Footings are poured in Photograph D and are being marked for the block work to follow. The 12" block (required by local code only) is finished and is being damp-proofed in Photograph E. The "rat-slab" required to dress the soil in the crawl space, and to mitigate radon migration, is in place as well.

tion of the construction documents. Protection of shrubbery to a roofer, for example, probably means simply dropping a tarp over the species as rip-up occurs. If you have a new $200 sapling in a vulnerable spot, you will want to do more. Don't worry about the removal and replacement of fences and plantings for equipment access. The things that are necessary for the builder to do, to get into and out of the project, should be included in the contract price. You will need to talk to the builder about dumpsters, material drop-off and storage, vehicle parking, heavy equipment access, safety (particularly with kids in the area), and security. Let him know about any buried sprinkler systems, drains, or cables, as well as any unique overhead clearances to watch for. Make sure you and the builder walk your property together at the beginning of the job to get a common "feel" for its condition. This will help immensely when he is trying to repair it later.

Wardrobe and Bathroom Planning

Changing closets always brings on some clothing trauma and needs pre-planning. The best solution, I think, is to trim your selections down to the bare necessities, and then buy wardrobe-type cardboard boxes from a moving company. These are roughly 30 inches wide with a metal hanging-rod inside. They can be set out freestanding in any room, closed up during dusty times, and moved easily from room to room. I think I still have two up in my attic, full of clothes, a holdover from the time my wife and I had our floors refinished. You will also probably need a place for folded clothes, shoes, toiletries, and dressing accessories. I have seen the large plastic storage-type boxes (with lids on them) used with some success. The idea is to get all these loose items into as few containers as possible, so they can be covered and relocated several times if needed.

Bathrooms are not a lot of trouble, because there always seems to be another one to switch to. A box of toiletries, extra linen, and some time-shifting is usually enough to get through the construction phase.

Temporary Kitchen Setups

If a remodeled kitchen is in your redo, your pre-construction effort should multiply. You will need to cull your utensils, dishes, and foodstuff down to a minimum, and box the rest for storage elsewhere. Most people are not lucky enough to be getting a kitchen in an entirely new area, and therefore can not have a functioning space parallel to the creation of a new one. Usually a temporary kitchen setup is required either in the construction zone itself, or somewhere else within the balance of the home. What you need to do now will depend on where and what your temporary setup will be. Normally your old sink will be quickly blocked up and plumbed in a different spot, and your old refrigerator and range will be temporarily relocated and supplied with electricity and gas. The best setup is outside the new work area, such as in the old dining room. Although setups in unaltered spaces are harder to provide, largely because of penetrations that need to be made and then reclosed, they preclude your having to clean dust and debris out before preparing meals. Moving some of the old base cabinets and counters into the setup can be a big help.

A setup within the new construction zone is more of a hassle, for you and the builder. Remind yourself that you are saving money by not having a temporary setup elsewhere, or that dollars spent for these kinds of things don't produce tangible results in the end. Most people seem to resort to paper plates and cups only in emergencies. And although "dining out" is a common occurrence, you must plan for long-term food preparation in rather Neanderthal conditions. To prepare a meal, you will have to ferry utensils and foodstuffs from clean areas and then return them afterwards. This requires some container forethought and lots of trial-and-error. Your setup will need to be completely covered by plastic sheeting several times a day, so make sure the builder takes some time to get the "system" right the first time. These covers are his responsibility. In the evening, for example, you will need to move in to the setup area, remove covers, and give it a quick wipe down. Because dishwashers are not usually a part of temporary setups, after the meal you will need to hand-wash dishes in the sink, dry them, and put them away quickly (before dust settles). Nothing but the major appliances, with covers intact, should be left in the construction zone when work begins the next morning. It is rare for you to be without a working sink for more than a day (a good day for takeout pizza and paper plates), but the temporary kitchen setup may have to feed the family for several months.

FRONT-END PAPERWORK

Well before workmen arrive to start the job, your architect should begin organizing the front-end paperwork. Because this is a do-it rather than a plan-it stage, these documents should be as few and simple as possible. I tell builders that legible handwritten information is fine, as long as my forms are used when I provide them. The designer should request the following items from the builder, on behalf of the owner:

- Certificate of Insurance
- List of subcontractors (names, addresses, phone numbers)
- Schedule of Values

Certificate of Insurance

Provision of an insurance certificate is a standard procedure for general contractors. In most cases the contractor will have to present such a document to the local building department for his license to build in the municipality. The license, of course, is the building department's way to protect property owners. License criteria advise the builder about such things as the local inspection and permit requirements. But even though he probably will have forwarded a copy to local officials, he should now call his insurance company and have them issue a new certificate directly to you for this current job. This is the builder's representation that he has insurance, and to the levels indicated. The document should show him as the insured and you as the certificate holder, plus identify the insuring firm with a number to call for more information. If he has employees, he must have Workmen's Compensation, and he should also carry general liability coverage. If you have questions about the type or levels of coverage provided, you should call your insurance advisor, his provider (via the number provided), or your attorney.

List of Subcontractors

This simple request is very important. A typical job may have anywhere from three to ten separate firms subordinated to the general contractor. This list of names, addresses, and phone numbers should be forwarded to the architect and copied to you before any work begins. By this submitted document, the builder says that "this is the team that made up the bid for the job." By contract, he is not allowed to change a sub without your written permission. And further, you have the right to object to any firm on the list and request that it be replaced. This rarely happens, but if

A

B

CLOSET TALK

Closets are often neglected because they hide behind closed doors. Unless you or your designer directs otherwise, you will likely get something similar to Photograph A. This is a standard single "rod & shelf" fitout. In this case, the builder has used an expanding metal rod and bracket system because it is strong and easily installed. Many people prefer the ventilated wire product shown in Photograph B. It has the flexibility to handle most closet requirements and still appears consistently built. For closets that will need to maximize every inch of space, your designer should include the interior design of the space in his redo service. This will be most important in master walk-in closets where double rods and clothes cubbies are common. Sometimes it is hard to resolve the inside-outside design conflicts that are caused by large closets. Notice that in Photograph B, there is a window in the closet, positioned at a height that allows a high-low rod to pass by unobstructed. This was done primarily to solve the unacceptable blank wall that would occur in the exterior elevation. When space is at a premium, new master bathroom-closet combinations are extremely difficult to work windows into. Photograph C shows the closet window being built on the back, right-hand, second-floor wall. A new bathroom is in the same mass, to the left of the window.

C

A

B

JULIA CHILD'S NIGHTMARE

When you redo your kitchen, this is likely to be your fate—at least for several long days. Notice in Photograph A that the stove is covered during working hours, and must be uncovered each time a meal is prepared. Photograph B shows the old sink in its temporary location. It has been rather precariously blocked up until an area across the room is ready for the switch back to the final location.

it were to, the designer would be more likely to recognize a bad apple in the group. The list of subcontractors also provides a way to account for an adequate number of lien releases at the end of the job. But as much as anything else, it is an important cross-checking tool for you. If the builder or architect tells you something about the plumbing work that doesn't quite sound right, the list allows you to discreetly call the sub and ask him a question directly.

Schedule of Values

I allow extra time to go over the Schedule of Values with builders who haven't played on a team before. As you might guess, it is essentially a list of numbers whose total equals the Contract Sum. This values list will be inserted into his Payment Request Form and used again and again. But it should not be a direct copy of the quote that was prepared by the builder in securing the job. The distinction is in the intended use of the categories. The Schedule of Values is the way you, the owner, want to watch expenditures as the job progresses. The builder will be paid as a percentage of completion for each itemized category. Although your designer will be doing the directing on your behalf, the instruction to the builder should be something like, "You need to remix your quote into numbers that will allow us to track the job effectively." Notice I used the word "us," suggesting that the builder will use the new schedule as well. This is very important, because you want to avoid making extra work. If he is smart, he will alter the way he normally bills, to make his payment requests a money-management instrument for you and himself as well. If he is inflexible, the requirement will still remain. He must ask for money using the owner's Schedule of Values, in the Payment Request Form, even if he has to transcribe his list to yours.

If the builder previously gave you a breakdown of his price, at the time you didn't particularly care what the individual numbers were. You will recall that the Bid Form required only a lump sum and several Alternates. Only the cost of the overall package was instrumental in his hiring. But now that he is on the team, you do care about these monetary details. Should some crisis happen in the middle of the job, these values will determine how funds will be divided up. I usually forward the builder several Payment Request Forms and ask him to plug in a new Schedule of Values for me to look over prior to his submission of the first draw request. I rarely engage the owner in this process, although I suggest that you look over your designer's shoulder to ensure he is up-to-speed in his construction-administration skills.

In reviewing the numbers, I first look for overall scope changes. If Alternates have been accepted, then their individual values should be distributed back into the pertinent line items, and no Alternate categories should remain. If large unit prices or Allowances have been set out in the contract, they need to be discreetly set out in this table. If any discussion has taken place about the owner electing to remove large portions of the work, the potential take-out items should not be reduced in deference to other items that are likely to remain. Interior painting is a good example of such a take-out. If the builder originally represented that he had $10,000 in the job for interior painting, and then his Schedule of Values tried to adjust that number down to $7000, then he may be planning a nice $3000 bonus for himself if you elect to take the painting out. This red flag is hard to spot because the total job cost is the same either way.

If any large or unique material purchases have to be made, they also should occur as a separate line-item. Kitchen cabinets, appliances, or long lead-time granite tops might fall into such a group. A category to watch for is frequently labeled "mobilization." This is a way for the builder to take money out of the job quickly, or from the owner's perspective, to take some profit out prematurely. But when hard pressed to justify its amount, the only solid task that emerges is the securing of the building permit. Thus, for most redo work, "mobilization" should be relabeled "permits" and should be around 0.5% to 1% of the Contract Sum.

Other than these kinds of scope and categorization issues, the builder should be trusted to generate his own new numbers within the stipulated sum agreement. If he has become uncomfortable with his quote in a particular area, he needs to be able to set new targets and make it up elsewhere. As in other paperwork items, small is beautiful. Try to encourage him to keep the categories limited enough to fit onto one page. You want him to treat the values in the Payment Request Form as a working tool. I frequently redline a few things in his blank form and fax it back. His first Payment Request should be based on the new (and improved) Schedule of Values.

PRECONSTRUCTION CONTRACTORS MEETING

As soon after conforming the builder's contract as possible, the architect should arrange for a meeting at the project site. The builder, his lead carpenter, all subcontractors, the owner, and the architect should all attend. The purpose of the meeting is to gel the construction team into a group that is not hesitant to pick up the phone. The architect should list some things that he thinks will be problem areas, and precipitate a discussion by the concerned trades. Questions should be encouraged from everyone, and a walkthrough should occur. In keeping with the "your profit is our goal" philosophy in Chapter 3, the message should be explicitly stated: "We expect great work, without hurting anyone financially."

QUALITY VIA CASH-FLOW MANAGEMENT

The single best technique to control construction quality is through the management of cash flow. We all know that the quickest way to get someone's attention is to talk about his money: how much, when, and God forbid, if. Maybe I should revise the axiom to "money is the root of all responsiveness." Most people are not aware that this is an extremely important element that the architect's service brings to projects. There is nothing particularly difficult about cash-flow management because it is built into the AIA contracts and forms. Although you could do it yourself (with this book), it is better handled by your designer.

When you hired the builder, he was advised that he would be paid for "in-place work." This concept is sometimes referred to as leverage. It is very simple. It means that you, the owner, will need to see results before you approve and then pay for them. The overall objective of leverage, then, is to keep cash flow such that the builder is in a constant state of approval-seeking to maintain a continuous project. He should be asking you "is it okay?" rather than your coming to him saying "this is not right" after it is in place and paid for. This ensures that the general contractor pays attention to all the construction documents and works within the roles defined therein. He is forced to share some risk with you. Your money makes you the boss, and this process keeps it that way, even given your neophyte status.

Payment Application Form

Example 30 shows a typical payment form. The cover is a summary of the entire monetary status of the job, and the subsequent page is a detailed breakdown of budget-versus-actual for the builder's Schedule of Values. At a predetermined interval (usually two weeks in remodeling projects) the builder forwards the form to the designer. The architect should review the form for procedural problems, visit the job to confirm the completion percentages claimed, certify the payment amount, and then forward the form to the owner. The builder says, "I need to get paid this much." The designer says, "Looks okay to me." And the owner writes the builder a check. Notice that the form keeps a running account of the Retainage and any Change Orders that have been approved. This form gives you a frozen picture of the job and all the management techniques in use to protect your interests.

Limiting Upfront Payments

I hope I don't have to convince you how risky it would be to write a check to a builder, up front, for one third of the contract sum. I have seen this advocated in remodeling trade books, and am aware that contractors in my area do this to uninitiated owners. This makes the owner a banker for the builder, as well as the boss. As a general rule, you should not pay a builder any money up front. In your particular redo, we have precluded most of these front-money issues by putting the "pay for in-place work" condition on the table during bidding. You see, for stable professional builders, it is simply not necessary for you to take this risk. Their

vendor, subcontractor, and payroll payment cycles are such that they can "carry" the job to the first in-place draw. And if they can't, that means that their credit isn't so hot, and you therefore should be even more reluctant to let them hold your money.

However, on the flip-side, I have seen situations where initial payments should take place. For example, any time the builder will need to make specialized purchases for you, far ahead of the start date, he should not be expected to carry such a cost. Relief should also be given when an inordinate amount of effort must begin on the first day, because of an extremely tight construction window. For these kinds of special circumstances, I suggest two things. First, the designer and owner should try to solve the cash-flow problem by shortening payment application cycles in the front-end, and then settling into the two-week version later on. This could be radical shortening, even to paying at the end of the first or second day, and then maybe at the end of the first week. And second, if initial payments have to be made before work begins, an accelerated repayment schedule should be made a condition of the disbursement. This repayment should be fully accomplished roughly halfway through the job. In Chapter 7, Example 29, Clause 21.8 is just such a cash-flow solution, in this case, cast into the builder's contract. But for either of these special circumstances, you should ensure that these monies be assigned to specific materials or tasks, and that the Payment Request Form be religiously used to request the disbursement. After the builder expresses his problem, the designer and owner should consider several options and then propose a solution. But remember that if his problem isn't truly unique, then he will have to solve his own cash-flow problem, one that he knew about before he bid the job.

APPLICATION AND CERTIFICATE FOR PAYMENT

AIA DOCUMENT G702 (Instructions on reverse side) PAGE ONE OF **2** PAGES

TO OWNER:	Mary and John Green 1492 Columbus Drive Towner, PA 19088	PROJECT: Green Residence
		APPLICATION NO.: **05**
		PERIOD TO: **12-10-94**
		PROJECT NOS.: **G405**
FROM CONTRACTOR:	J & J Construction, Inc. 422 Rock Road Philadelphia, PA 19003	VIA ARCHITECT: Peter Wilson 2134 Harrie Road Wister, PA 19002
		CONTRACT DATE: Jan 8, 1993
CONTRACT FOR:	Renovations	

Distribution to:
☑ OWNER
☐ ARCHITECT
☐ CONTRACTOR
☐
☐

CONTRACTOR'S APPLICATION FOR PAYMENT

Application is made for payment, as shown below, in connection with the Contract.
Continuation Sheet, AIA Document G703, is attached.

1. **ORIGINAL CONTRACT SUM** . . . . $ *72,125.00*
2. **Net change by Change Orders** . . . . $ *5,172.00*
3. **CONTRACT SUM TO DATE** (Line 1 ± 2) . . . . . . $ *77,297.00*
4. **TOTAL COMPLETED & STORED TO DATE** . . . . . . $ *66,067.00*
   (Column G on G703)
5. **RETAINAGE:**
   a. *10* % of Completed Work $ *N/A*
      (Columns D + E on G703)
   b. *10* % of Stored Material $ *N/A*
      (Column F on G703)
   Total Retainage (Line 5a + 5b or
   Total in Column I of G703) . . . . $ *6,606.70*
6. **TOTAL EARNED LESS RETAINAGE** . . . . $ *59,460.30*
   (Line 4 less Line 5 Total)
7. **LESS PREVIOUS CERTIFICATES FOR PAYMENT** $ *41,287.50*
   (Line 6 from prior Certificate) . . . .
8. **CURRENT PAYMENT DUE** . . . . $ *18,172.80*
9. **BALANCE TO FINISH, INCLUDING RETAINAGE** *17,836.70*
   (Line 3 less Line 6) $ *17,836.70*

CHANGE ORDER SUMMARY	ADDITIONS	DEDUCTIONS
Total changes approved in previous months by Owner	*NONE*	*NONE*
Total approved this Month	*5,172.00*	
TOTALS		
NET CHANGES by Change Order	*+ 5,172.00*	

The undersigned Contractor certifies that to the best of the Contractor's knowledge, information and belief the Work covered by this Application for Payment has been completed in accordance with the Contract Documents, that all amounts have been paid by the Contractor for Work for which previous Certificates for Payment were issued and payments received from the Owner, and that current payment shown herein is now due.

CONTRACTOR: John Gaston, J & J Construction Inc.

By: *J. Gaston*   Date: *12/12/94*

State of: **Pennsylvania**
County of: **Montgomery**
Subscribed and sworn to before
me this   day of

Sample

Notary Public: L. Williams
No. 3457843
My Commission expires: Dec 31, 1995

ARCHITECT'S CERTIFICATE FOR PAYMENT

In accordance with the Contract Documents, based on on-site observations and the data comprising this application, the Architect certifies to the Owner that to the best of the Architect's knowledge, information and belief the Work has progressed as indicated, the quality of the Work is in accordance with the Contract Documents, and the Contractor is entitled to payment of the AMOUNT CERTIFIED.

AMOUNT CERTIFIED . . . . $ *18,172.80*

(Attach explanation if amount certified differs from the amount applied for. Initial all figures on this Application and on the Continuation Sheet that are changed to conform to the amount certified.)

ARCHITECT:
By: *P. Wilson*   Date: *12/13/94*

This Certificate is not negotiable. The AMOUNT CERTIFIED is payable only to the Contractor named herein. Issuance, payment and acceptance of payment are without prejudice to any rights of the Owner or Contractor under this Contract.

BUILDER'S PAYMENT APPLICATION FORM

EXAMPLE 30. *This pair of forms is from a typical remodeling project. Page 2 is a detailed status of job cash flow, and page 1 is a summary for conforming signatures. Page 2 column G shows that the job is 85% complete, with $17,230 of effort left in plumbing, electric, front pent, ceramic flooring, and Change Order*

CONTINUATION SHEET

AIA DOCUMENT G703 (Instructions on reverse side)

PAGE 2 OF 2 PAGES

AIA Document G702, APPLICATION AND CERTIFICATE FOR PAYMENT, containing Contractor's signed Certification, is attached.
In tabulations below, amounts are stated to the nearest dollar.
Use Column I on Contracts where variable retainage for line items may apply.

Green Residence

APPLICATION NO.:	05
APPLICATION DATE:	December 15, 1994
PERIOD TO:	12-10-94
ARCHITECT'S PROJECT NO.:	G405

A	B	C	D WORK COMPLETED	E WORK COMPLETED	F	G	%	H	I
ITEM NO.	DESCRIPTION OF WORK	SCHEDULED VALUE	FROM PREVIOUS APPLICATION (D + E)	THIS PERIOD	MATERIALS PRESENTLY STORED (NOT IN D OR E)	TOTAL COMPLETED AND STORED TO DATE (D + E + F)	% (G ÷ C)	BALANCE TO FINISH (C – G)	RETAINAGE (IF VARIABLE) RATE)
1	Permit	$725.00				$725.00	100	$0.00	
2	Demolition	$2,600.00	$2,600.00			$2,600.00	100	$0.00	
3	Foundation	$7,000.00				$7,000.00	100	$0.00	
4	Rgh Framing	$9,300.00	$1,900.00			$9,300.00	100	$0.00	
5	Roofing	$4,900.00	$4,900.00			$4,900.00	100	$0.00	
6	Windows & Ext. Doors	$7,900.00	$7,900.00			$7,900.00	100	$0.00	
7	Siding & Gutters	$6,000.00	$3,500.00	$2,500.00		$6,000.00	100	$0.00	
8	Plumbing	$4,300.00	$2,300.00	$900.00		$3,200.00	74	$1,100.00	
9	Electric	$3,750.00	$1,850.00	$1,000.00		$2,850.00	76	$900.00	
10	Front Pent	$1,750.00					0	$1,750.00	
11	Heat	$3,500.00	$2,500.00	$1,000.00		$3,500.00	100	$0.00	
12	Insulation	$1,900.00	$1,000.00	$900.00		$1,900.00	100	$0.00	
13	Drywall	$5,500.00		$3,700.00		$5,500.00	100	$0.00	
14	Int. Doors & Trim	$3,900.00		$3,900.00		$3,900.00	100	$0.00	
15	Fixtures	$2,600.00		$2,600.00		$2,600.00	100	$0.00	
16	Painting	$800.00					0	$800.00	
17	Ceramic Flooring	$2,200.00			$1,500.00	$1,500.00	68	$700.00	
18	Carpet & Vinyl Floorg	$3,500.00					0	$3,500.00	
19	C.O.'s 001-005	$5,172.00	$500.00	$2,192.00		$2,692.00	52	$2,980.00	
		$77,297.00	$28,950.00	$18,692.00	$1,500.00	$66,067.00	85	$17,230.00	

work. Page 1 shows that as of this fifth Payment Application, $5,172 in Change Orders have been authorized by the owners, and that $6,606 of earned compensation (really from the general contractor's profit) is being held out (the 10% Retainage, item 5) until the job is successfully completed. Page 1 bottom right shows that the architect has certified for owner payment the full amount the builder has asked for (item 8), or $18,172.80.

Change Orders

Aside from payment applications, the other critical documents that will circulate throughout construction are Change Orders (aka COs). These are simply a way to record changes that need to take place. More precisely, Change Orders are the owner's prior approval of both physical and monetary changes to the project. COs alter the Contract Sum (or Time), become a part of the contract documents, and are accounted for in the Payment Application Form. In practice, they can become a dreaded harbinger of bad news. For although changes can accrue as either debits or credits, they are notorious for costing the owner extra money. Keeping your redo cost under control will mean paying close attention to Change Orders.

Many COs are brought forward by the builder because an unforeseen and undocumented task has arisen. Whether such a task was reasonably foreseeable or not is at the heart of determining the legitimacy of the potential contract extra. Unforeseeable work is a valid CO. Had this hidden work been known and included in bid documents, then the extra cost would not be in a Change Order but within the original Contract Sum. Theoretically, you pay either way. Some COs are to be expected in a redo where the existing building may hold many surprises, even for seasoned pros. Comprehensive construction documents by the designer will minimize many of these unpleasant surprises. From a procedural standpoint, the designer should do the paperwork for the team; this is an incentive for the builder to keep him advised of changes. In order to keep his job moving, the builder should forward a proposed work description and cost to the designer, who should review and prepare the CO form (Example 31). The owner reviews the form and authorizes the work by his signature. This process should be done expeditiously enough to allow evaluation and even disapproval of the change.

Remember that you should discuss any potential change directly with the designer and builder, limiting such discussions with workmen on the job. Any change that will require an adjustment to the Contract Sum or Time must be recorded in a CO. A circumstance where you are asked to approve a change after it has taken place is unfortunate, although it does happen. This signals a goof, giving you the right to have the work put back as originally documented. If you are faced with such a situation, you should talk to the designer about the design implications of the in-place work, to see if it can be "worked with". Sometimes a few design changes to unbuilt details elsewhere can make the mistake disappear. But if no new solution can be quickly reached, have it ripped out, for it is not your fault.

Looking at Extra Charges

As agent for the owner, the architect has a responsibility to review the fairness of the costs being charged to the owner. This is part of his cross-checking team role. Change Order prices are always subject to much contention. The builder has no overriding concern for making add-on prices competitive, except for those he has committed to in his contract (see Chapter 7), and he may be honestly unable to give full value to take-out prices because of changes made since his original estimate. The owner, on the other hand, is normally quite shocked at how expensive it is to build anything, and is apt to cry "overcharge" at the drop of a hat. As a frequent middle-man in this debate, I offer the following observations.

The owner's resistance to Change Orders is necessary to thwart the breeding ground for more, and

CHANGE ORDER

AIA DOCUMENT G701

OWNER ✓
ARCHITECT ☐
CONTRACTOR ☐
FIELD ☐
OTHER ☐

Sample

PROJECT: (name, address)	Green Residence Towner, PA 19088
TO CONTRACTOR: (name, address)	J & J Construction, Inc. 422 Rock Road Philadelphia, Pa 19003

CHANGE ORDER NUMBER:	010
DATE:	Janurary 16, 1995
ARCHITECT'S PROJECT NO:	g405
CONTRACT DATE:	October 21, 1994
CONTRACT FOR:	Renovations

The Contract is changed as follows:

Provide additional electric blank-type plates   + $210.00

Credit for owner-supplied lighting fixtures/hardware: - $362.00
    L7 light, power room, allowance $150.00
    L4 light, outside, $65.30 list, trade net: $58.00
    L6 light, pendant, $49.95 list, trade net: $42.00
    Closet door pulls $30.00
    Towel bars/TP holders $70.00
    Vanity knobs, allowance $12.00

Electrical work: installation of lighting is included in contract sum.
This work will be prepaid and completed when fixtures are available through
Owner. Front exterior flood work is extra T&M by J & J Construction. L7 installation
may require extra T&M for moving feed.

Not valid until signed by the Owner, Architect and Contractor.

The original (Contract Sum) (Guaranteed Maximum Price) was . . . . $		72,126.00
Net change by previously authorized Change Orders . . . . $	+	11,022.00
The (Contract Sum) (Guaranteed Maximum Price) prior to this Change Order was . . . . . $		83,147.00
The (Contract Sum) (Guaranteed Maximum Price) will be (increased) (decreased)	-	152.00
(unchanged) by this Change Order in the amount of . . . . $		82,995.00
The new (Contract Sum) (Guaranteed Maximum Price) including this Change Order will be . . $		

The Contract Time will be (increased) (decreased) (unchanged) by   None   ( ) days.
The date of Substantial Completion as of the date of this Change Order therefore is   January 26, 1995

NOTE: This summary does not reflect changes in the Contract Sum, Contract Time or Guaranteed Maximum Price which have been authorized by Construction Change Directive.

Peter Wilson	John Gaston	Mary Green
ARCHITECT 2134 Harrie Road	CONTRACTOR per above	OWNER project address
Address Wister, PA 19002	Address	Address
BY *[signature]*	BY *[signature]*	BY *[signature]*
DATE 1·16·95	DATE 1/18/95	DATE 1·26·95

AIA   CAUTION: You should sign an original AIA document which has this caution printed in red. An original assures that changes will not be obscured as may occur when documents are reproduced.

EXAMPLE 31. *In this example Change Order, a credit is being given back as a result of the difference between product Allowances and final picks, as well as an "extra" for special electric-box plates. Note that this CO also records a simple clarification of the work. Here, because the owner changed her mind after several fixtures were installed, and the electrician has graciously volunteered to reinstall for free, he will be paid prior to actual completion but his promise to return when the owner has found new lights is recorded. Notice that the form keeps a cumulative account of changes. In this case the owners have elected to spend an additional $11,022.00 prior to this CO. This is unusually high; a typical redo will vary by less than 5% of the original Contract Sum.*

CHANGE ORDER

therefore you should make some noise, for effect if nothing else. Indicate how worried you are about the slipping budget, ask the builder to help you out by taking some of the cost out elsewhere, or have him check a unit price that seems out-of-line. But do not accuse anyone of dishonesty. That is a good way to permanently poison a relationship. Also, requiring the builder to write out all the details in the CO price will not only point up glaring problems, but will control overcharging in general. Labor charges, of course, are normally the biggest cost component, and they are relatively easy to get a handle on if you refer to his contractual "extra" billing rates. Unfortunately, owners are rarely invited to consider the things that the builder throws in for free. He doesn't normally make paperwork out of these items, so the portrayal is of a machine that only ratchets in one direction. This is a perceptual mistake. I encourage builders to put in for changes that render credits and "no charge's" to the owner whenever they can. This gives the owner a more balanced picture of the way money flows back and forth across the builder's budget as the redo takes shape.

Job Meetings

Most remodeling projects will require job meetings, where the builder, designer, and owner meet the same time every week at the house. Before work begins, the architect should get a consensus on the best time to fix into everyone's calendar. An hour or two during the typical workday will be best for the builder and designer, although for busy families this may be hard to arrange. Your pros will be prepared to meet at night or on the weekend, if necessary. Each team member should try to put fresh issues "on hold" so they can be

dealt with in the weekly job meeting, although many times the problem will not wait. The overall purpose of the meeting is to manage the ongoing construction, by facilitating a running dialogue between parties. I find that a simple agenda is adequate for job meetings.

- Paperwork
- Problem solving: owner, builder, architect issues
- Quality zones and the budget
- Color, material, and product selections
- Action Items

Paperwork and Action Items

The meeting is the best place to push routine paperwork around, thus avoiding mailing required documents. Payment Requests, Change Orders, and Drawing revisions are the most likely instruments to change hands, often in triplicate. The architect will be the administrator of the meeting, taking notes if necessary. Although in large commercial jobs he usually prepares and distributes a meeting record, for remodeling this is overkill. Because job meetings tend to break up into several walks into the construction zone, I find it best to get the boring stuff done upfront while seated at the table. The meeting should wrap up with the designer summarizing any action items that have been agreed to.

Problem Solving

Each actor will arrive at the meeting with his own agenda, and should be encouraged to get it out early for discussion. The owner, builder, and designer should each talk a little about what they are worried about, what they are presently doing, and what they intend to do before the next meeting. This lets the architect and builder cross-check each other, and keeps the owner focused on useful issues. As problems come up, their solution should be attempted within the meeting, and deferred only as a last resort. The designer should have drawing materials with him to quickly sketch out options for the owner to approve. Builders usually cannot wait around for the architect to go back to his office to draft something up. Most construction problems need quick-and-dirty solutions to fine tune the builder's effort. This is do-it time.

Quality Zones and the Budget

The best way to solve problems is to pre-empt them completely. Each redo has elements that are straightforward, as well as areas that are complicated and critical in nature. If your designer has done a good job, he has maximized your use of your space, and his construction drawings are likely to hold several dimensional dominoes. These are areas that will fall apart if each element isn't constructed to specified tolerances. Sometimes the loss of a half-inch can totally wreck a scheme, because the dimensions are linked in series through many different building systems. The photo on page 238 shows a quality zone whose dimensions allowed for no slop. The critical criteria started at the ridge beam under the old soffit, then followed an angle matching the existing roof rake, onto an underheight wall plate, down through a special compacted window header, so minimal height awning windows would fit over a hearth that had to fit a specific TV size, on a fireplace seat at a minimal sitting position. I can still remember the look on the builder's face when I told him he had to lower the base for the zero-clearance fireplace by 2-1/2″, back to the way it was originally

drawn. He did not understand that those few inches would have meant that the hearth would engage the window casing, which was extra-wide hardwood at the owner's request and would stand out like a sore thumb if not symmetrical.

At other times, a poor installation technique can make the result worse than if no attempt at excellence had been made at all. These areas need to be identified and monitored closely as construction progresses. I call them quality zones. During the first job meeting, the designer and builder should redline the Drawings to highlight any such areas. This is where the builder's and architect's experience is best used. My sense is that the designer is better at identification of the zone, and the builder is better at foreseeing preventative measures. Potential problems should be discussed and the area debugged. The quality zones should remain on the job meeting agenda until their excellence is assured.

The construction budget really needs to be a monetary version of the physical quality zone. The budget should be discussed in each job meeting to keep cost issues on the front burner. You, the owner, should continually reiterate your threshold for pain in the financial area. The builder-designer team can usually still find ways to take money out of the job if so challenged, and if you are willing to rescind some prior decisions. The architect can help make final product selections beneath their Allowances to offset surprise add-ons, but only if this is known to be necessary ahead of time. Therefore, the builder needs to identify potential cost-extra areas and discuss their dollar implications in the initial meeting. You are the one who must initiate a cost-saving initiative to have your budget downside covered, if it is judged to be necessary. At the very least, these potential cost-extra zones should be monitored in each job meeting. As the structure is closed in, and

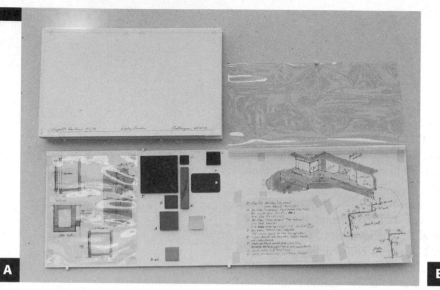

A

B

MANAGING A QUALITY ZONE

Quality comes from the smart use of products and craftsmen. The builder needs to match the right craftsmen to the task. And the architect must be there to debug the details. After the construction contract is conformed, the owner should "redline" complicated construction areas and orchestrate a "skull session" with both his architect and builder. The agenda: "Is there anything that can be done to ensure that we get this area right?" The builder should be asked to recommend smarter solutions; the architect may need to justify or modify some areas of the design. "Can we make it better, or cheaper? Do we need a different subcontractor?" The important thing is for the owner to recognize a potential problem area ahead of time, ensure that positive cross-talk is happening, and reinforce the expectation of quality. Complex media centers should always be a quality zone. This series of photographs chronicles the construction of a fireplace-media center situated in the focal point of a new family–library room and a country kitchen. Photograph A is a mock-up the architect used to make final tile, laminate, paint, and stain selections and secure approval from the owner. Although the owner had wanted a masonry fireplace, the architect proposed the use of this prefab unit (Martin, zero-clearance) because it saved several thousand dollars, its chimney would not sacrifice an important window-over, it would offer three-way viewing of the fire, and it would integrate more easily into a media group. Rough framing dimensions were critical (Photograph B) in allowing the tile to work as planned (Photograph C). Lighting, power, audio, telephone, and cable rough-in locations were important as well. Although appearing simple, 8 x 8 floor tile, two colors of 2 x 2 mosaic and their trim profiles, and 8 x 8 slate were used (Photograph D) on the hearth. The mantle cabinetry needed to match the 1 x 6 oak window casing and combined custom carpentry (Photograph E) with stock cabinet doors. Clearance for electronic equipment and media storage was carefully surveyed and provided. Photograph F shows that the team has built an inviting but durable hearth seat, and the media-fire function sits comfortably in the new light-filled space.

C

D

E

F

mechanical and plumbing systems are roughed out, the likelihood of major hidden costs is reduced.

Color, Material, and Product Selections

Most of your effort during construction should focus on the items that remain undecided. And there usually are many, even as excavation begins. I cannot overstate the importance of these decisions, for even the best-planned redo can be quickly disemboweled by poor product choices. At each job meeting these selections need to be well considered. Your first construction meeting should include an overview of all outstanding product selections. If you have been shopping with your drawing schedules (per Chapter 7), go over which picks are finalized and which are not. A time-line should be established so that selections will not hold up construction. General contractors will want to wait until their subs put the pressure on for final selections. This is way too late in most cases.

The goal should be for the team to show you all products in your dining room using mock-up boards, product-cut packages and samples, and then to rely on showroom visits for the 5% or 10% that you can't immediately approve for purchase. Setting this objective has several important effects. First, it forces use of the designer's recommendations as a starting point, and therefore encourages individual picks to be made within an overall context. Second, it purges supply lines and causes slow-boat or problem products to be red flagged ahead of purchase time. Third, it includes the supplier's purchasing expertise into your professional team, using the specified schedules as "kickoff points." And finally, bringing the product-pick "store" to your table puts the owner's needs first, which is

where all the pros say they want to place it. The following recommendations should be batted about in your first job meeting, as you decide what your particular team approach will be.

Builder Product Purchases

In most instances, products are purchased by the trades that will install them. Subcontractors buy them, mark them up, and bill the general contractor, who charges you a price that is factored for his own overhead and profit. In large commercial work this logic holds up; the guys who know the most about installing the products are the ones who buy them. Here, owners are rarely engaged in the minutia of product selection. Redo owners are the exact opposite; they sweat everything. Plus, in remodeling work, subcontractors seldom have the administrative staff or the desire to do the coordination required for more demanding homeowners. This needs to be a very people-friendly procedure; after all, the owner is shopping for thousands of dollars worth of product that they will see and touch every day for the next ten years. I find that small plumbers and electricians are particularly poor at co-ordinating this process. You should ask your builder to consider purchasing product for the subs.

Many variations exist to satisfy the genuine need to "touch it before you buy it." Plumbing, lighting, appliance, kitchen/bathroom, hardware, and building product showrooms all exist because of this market. But you pay for their overhead. And total reliance on showrooms requires the owner to do a lot of legwork. How product gets purchased is an important business decision, and each builder should be flexible in finding the best cost-service mix for his client. Although it may mean altering agreements with his subs, remodeling builders need to look at fresh ways to help owners shop.

Catalog Cuts

Very early in construction, the builder should have all suppliers prepare a "catalog cut" package to allow each product to be viewed and cross-checked against the drawing schedules (for more about catalog cuts, see Chapter 6, Shopping for Products). The package is nothing more than an organized collection of catalog pages. Even though a similar effort will have been done to originally specify the list, it should be repeated as confirmation. Substitutions should be clearly marked when not available through this supplier, and the spec-versus-substitution cost set out. When the complete product-cut package is ready, it should be forwarded to the designer, who will go over it with the owner. Some of these products may not be approved, with the owner or architect preferring to shop separately, beginning with the builder's recommended sources. The catalog cut package usually reduces the owner's homework to finding only a handful of items, a list short enough to be fun.

Slow-Boat Items

Unique items requiring long lead times should be identified as early as possible, and purchased separately from the remaining off-the-shelf products. I find that builders will wait until the typical order time, even though they know that several of the items will take much longer. These unique items are frequently within the quality zones that the team has earmarked. The photo on page 243 shows such a product. Here a special recessed medicine cabinet has held up drywall finishing, wall tile, and electric for an inordinate amount of time. The redo team and their material suppliers should quickly scan the schedules for such "special handling" products.

PRODUCT CHECK-IN AND APPROVAL

When product arrives at the job site, a well planned check-in procedure should be applied. This procedure should be ironed out in an early job meeting. It should ensure that each item is opened, inspected for shipping damage, viewed by the owner and architect for final acceptance, and then repackaged for job-site protection. You would be surprised at how many unacceptable substitute products get discovered after they are in place. Usually it is because of a casual purchasing process by a subcontractor. They fax a schedule to the supply house, who ships material to the job. Only when the workmen need it do they open the box and put it in. This methodology assumes that the original product schedule is 100% accurate, and that all generic-spec or substitution products are acceptable to the designer and owner. This perfect scenario never occurs. And failure to accept this fact results in workers having to uninstall product, hunt for original packaging, exchange the item, and ultimately point fingers. The owner is lucky if he isn't forced into a Change Order for a restocking or damage charge, or the acceptance of something he isn't happy with.

PROFESSIONAL SELECTION TECHNIQUE

Many redo owners fret over the selection of final finish items. They have reason to worry, because the ultimate quality of their job will depend on the combination of all these decisions. And this is where most homeowners go wrong: they fail to make these decisions "in

A

B

TIGHTLY STRUNG BANJO

Master bathrooms do not have to be enormous to be elegant. They simply must be well planned, as demonstrated in the design-board in Photograph A. A custom ceramic tile shower, lavatory, and water-closet can be worked into the minimal 5' x 8' module, and feel both spacious and upscale. To do this, this bathroom uses a "banjo" vanity top in combination with mirror, window, and lighted valence above. The banjo extends the countertop across the back of the toilet. The wall area above the back splash is totally infilled with window and mirror, which lightens and expands the space. The medicine cabinet on the right is recessed and set into the corner to turn the mirror, stopping just short of the light box at the top. Close coordination between the builder and designer is required for such tight, intricate spaces. The window in Photograph B had to have custom trim designed. The sill was compacted to allow room for the tile backsplash, and the casing was widened to fill the gap between the shower wing-wall at the left. The outlets in the backsplash were first turned to avoid the tile accent band, and one was deleted later. The tile backsplash was held up for the special-order medicine cabinet (Photograph D), so it could terminate flush. The single remaining electrical outlet is being replaced with a beige color to match the tile field in Photograph E. Notice in Photograph C how the bull-nose tile base is being taken around the toekick of the vanity. This top is custom fabricated in Corian with a 1-1/2" bullnose edge.

combination," and with no specific process in mind. The very last thing you want to do is let the builder arrange for the tile, carpet, or painting sub to show up separately, with swatches for your immediate decision. These elements for consideration can be paint colors, wall coverings, floor finishes, granite and solid surface tops, ceramic tile and grout, laminates, kitchen cabinet finishes and pulls, appliance and plumbing fixture colors, hardware finishes, to name just a few. Outside, you may need to select roof shingles, window and door claddings, prefinished sidings, brick, paint, stain, aluminum trim capping, hardware, masonry pavers, light fixture finishes, and gutters. The best way to make these kinds of decisions is with the timely use of composite mock-up boards. This technique is the backbone of many design professions, graphic, interior, architectural, and others. Your architect will normally prepare some of these for you. The point at which he stops should have been set out in his contract. But whether done by your architect, interior designer, or yourself, the methodology to select product finishes should be based on two ideas.

Composite Mock-up Boards

The first idea is to create a portable microcosm of the space to be examined. This means that you have to bring all the important elements into a common format so each product can be viewed in concert with its neighbors. Mock-up boards, sometimes called swatch sheets, are as simple as they are powerful. A swatch sheet can be made of illustration board, foam core sheet, or just an 8-1/2" x 11" piece of paper. Regardless of size or thickness, the board must be white, for your perception of colors and textures is radically influenced by adjacent color and lighting. Then you should attach as many elements as you think you need to the board. Designers, and to a lesser extent, builders, will have access to sample kits that are intended for this purpose (see page 246). The things that seem to defy miniaturization can be simulated somehow, given a little ingenuity. Crude attempts are better than none at all. An existing stone wall for instance, can be simulated by matching several colors against the original, and then using paint chips to stand-in for the primary hues (see page 246, Photograph C). Photographs of furniture may find their way onto a swatch board. Sometimes it makes sense to cut up the architectural prints and color them up as a way to explore or explain application of the picks. Pantone makes a color selection and tear-out system that works well if you have access to their catalogs (available in art supply stores). White art tape and a glue gun are also very helpful. A designer will cut pieces up, lay them on the white background, play with their combinations, and finally attach and label them as a visual record of the design intent. I prefer to armor my mock-up boards somewhat, so they can be left on site for workmen to use, and so the owner can pack them off to a showroom in a purse or briefcase. After your redo is completed, you will find yourself returning periodically to the swatch sheets to retrieve paint ID numbers for touch-ups.

Organizing Product Decisions

The second idea, important for selecting finishes, is the need to approach the problem in a logical order. At the very top of the list must be those strong visual elements that already exist and that must be included in the design scheme. Existing floor finishes and exterior sidings are good examples. These should be mocked up and attached to the swatch sheet as a "given." Also high in the pecking order should be the setting of a selection parti (or if you and your architect have established one already, its reinforcement through final product picks). You may recall from Chapter 5 the importance of such a simple, organizing design concept. In remodeling, I find that I am constantly wanting to mask something unsightly, or highlight a worthy architectural element. Setting a "warm, light, and airy" theme, or one with "dramatic contrasts," is the stuff of good design. Finding the new product to deal with first usually means guessing which is the most costly. Like Deepthroat advised in *All the President's Men,* I suggest you "follow the money." It is no coincidence that the most expensive things offer the fewest finish choices, and the cheapest ones have practically limitless possibilities.

So, where is the money in a new kitchen? Probably appliances are first (for small spaces), cabinets second, countertops third, and flooring fourth. And in selecting finishes for this kitchen, you might construct a mock-up board in that order. Appliances are available in white, almond, black, stainless steel, or paneled to match the cabinets. Make your decision and paste up a catalog photo of the refrigerator (if it is representative of the appliance group). Then move on to cabinets. Pick a door style and finish (maybe keep an alternate to play with), cut up a catalog photo, and attach it to the swatch sheet. If your tops will be laminate and your floor hardwood (and therefore more expensive), next secure and attach a sample (or photo) of finished oak. Then do the counters. If you will have granite tops, reverse the order. By the time you get to paint selections you will have a host of prior decisions that limit what can be tastefully done. This is not a problem because at the bottom end of the financial hierarchy, the choices are many. Many times I find that paint selection is a simple matter of matching and mitigating colors determined by the more expensive products.

As in other job phases, you should encourage your designer to go as far as possible with mock-ups by "spoon feeding" him as much as you can. Providing pictures and samples for swatch sheets falls into this category. Where he leaves off, you or your interior designer can take up the task. For a simple redo, you may need only one mock-up board for the outside and one for the inside. For a large job, you may need to add another swatch sheet for the kitchen, master bathroom, powder room, or any other interior space that will be significantly different. Remember that there is nothing magic about these mock-up boards. Keep them fresh by pulling things off or adding recent "finds." They are simply tools to make and communicate product design decisions.

SOME THINGS ON MY RADAR

As construction proceeds and a redo goes through its weekly cycle of job meetings, experience has taught me that there are reccurring problems to watch for. Since they are not usually within quality zones, they can be easily overlooked until the in-place problem glares back at you. You see, I know that within each set of construction drawings are assumptions and opinions that are little more than educated guesses. Many design issues are subjective in nature, and sometimes full-scale architecture belies paper buildings. In remodeling work, a lot of guessing must take place because of the inability to take the existing structure apart and secure hard answers. Most folks look at a well-crafted set of drawings and erroneously take what is depicted at face value. This goes to the heart of why I throw cold water on the Designer-Owner-Builder Scenario in Chapter 3. To say goodbye to the designer before building begins presumes that you know where

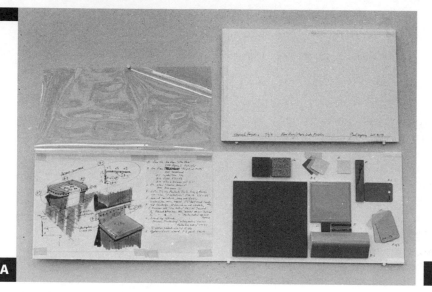

A

B

TRY IT BEFORE YOU BUY IT

A large part of design is about mocking-up a potential solution, and then critiquing it in time to change your mind. Drawings are only one way of imaging a scheme. There are many ways to try things out ahead of time. The best work comes when all the important parameters are considered in concert. From a practical standpoint, this means that it is a mistake to go to a paint store, browse the color swatches, and pick a paint color. This is because the color you pick will, in fact, change when perceived with its ultimate surroundings. Just because you favor mauve doesn't mean it will look okay next to your new tile floor. So for all the color and material choices you will make in your redo, you and your designer should try to bring the important ones, in mini-form, into a common palate. Photograph F shows the sample kits available to the architect for this very purpose. Carpet, tile, laminates, roofing, siding, molded millwork, counter edges, wall coverings, and paint are just some of the design-candy available. Photograph A is a product board for the kitchen in Photograph B. A similar product board for a redo exterior is shown in Photograph D. In this case the existing stonework was color-matched with a paint wheel (Photograph C), and then represented in the product board with a paint color swatch. After product picks are made, they should still be viewed with some skepticism. Testing small quantities before purchasing all of the product is advisable whenever possible.

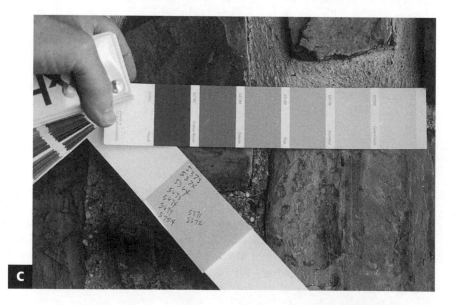

C

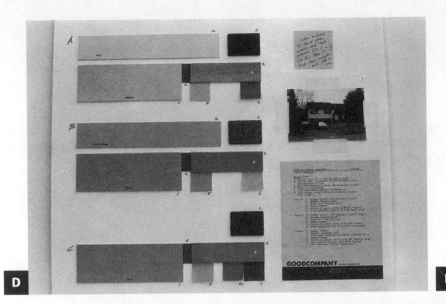

his critical assumptions are. And it also presumes that the only way to receive the architect's experience is via the documents, which is ludicrous, of course. To pack quality into a job, you need to push the technical envelope a little, but you had better have your radar up as construction begins. So a small list follows; if your designer doesn't pick up on these problems, you should call them to his attention.

- Confirmation of assumed dimensions
- Mechanical soffits and chases
- Perceptual surprises after rough framing
- Electric and HVAC device locations
- New and old transitions
- Artistic placement or treatments

Confirming Assumed Dimensions

Beginning with footings, I worry about confirming questionable dimensions, completely through demolition and framing. Old walls are full of surprises, and vertical heights are often not capable of being directly measured. Many times you can't tape off a reliable distance until complete demolition has taken place. Remember, it is common to have the new work completely closed in around the old before radical penetrations are made, which compounds measurement problems. Although I trust the carpenters to lay out the new work according to the drawings, I know that they may not give anyone a heads-up if they encounter a surprise dimension as they make openings into the old structure. More often, they make a seat-of-the-pants decision and keep rolling. Many times three or four inches need to be reallocated. If in the owner's favor, it is a gift to be treasured. I want to be able to put the extra space where it is most valu-

able. But if the dimension must come out of adjacent rooms, it needs to be done judiciously. It will probably need to be spread out over several spaces in series, to keep from penalizing any single room. This may mean moving several interior partitions, which is no fun. I try to cubby-hole the builder or his lead carpenter early on and have him check the critical numbers as soon as possible.

Mechanical Chases and Soffits

Paying attention to piping and ductwork is very important. Although the construction documents will allow clearances for many of them, these are best-guess paperwork efforts, that need further refinement in the field. Sometimes a lot of cosmetic architecture needs to be done to keep overhead soffits and wall chases from imposing on important spaces. The delivery of conditioned air to fine old homes is particularly hard to do well. I used to worry about my inability to accurately foresee where the subcontractors would need to place horizontal and vertical runs in their systems. I now know that much of it is subjective (just like architecture). What I mean is that until the rough framing is in place, and the guy who will do the work is standing there looking at it, precise prediction is practically impossible. Therefore, as these details are worked out in construction, someone needs to be the advocate for quality architecture. Like controlling project costs, there is no one magic bullet for controlling where and how these systems are snaked through the structure. It takes a running dialogue between the designer, builder, and subs. This conversation begins in the drawings where extra space is set out, and continues through rough-out and municipal inspection of the systems. At the first job meeting I usually ask the builder to have his subs provide redlines of where they will route their systems. My predictions are right maybe half the time. For the wrong half, I will have to provide the carpenters with a quick revised framing layout. Then after the framing is in, the builder and I mark where we think the lines will run, given the constraints of in-place studs, joists, and girders. Because further surprises can happen as the systems are roughed in, I ask the builder to advise his subs to let us know immediately if they want to vary from their prior plan.

Perceptual Surprises

The architect should hold a walk-through whenever the builder gets his rough frame up and before any mechanicals are roughed in. This needs to take place with the owner, designer, and builder present, whether falling on a job meeting day or not. The owner may benefit from having another pair of eyes present if he wishes, such as an interior designer. I learned this from a residential development firm. After rough framing, they would invite a whole boatload of professed experts to go through their product lines, and make primarily marketing observations about the architecture. The idea was simple—to critique the work when it was first in physical form, and still rather easily changed. And further, they knew that the guys who had been laboring over the project needed to hear fresh, objective impressions, and then consider further refinements. The architecture always improved as a result, although I frequently had to bite my lip as these expensive gurus talked about my dwelling units, as we called them.

A fresh look at the remodel in rough form will make it better. Just walk through each space and ask some questions like "Any perceptual surprises here? Is this too big or too small? Any views or obstructions

that should be exploited or corrected? Height of windows? Opportunities for final finishes to start or stop? Where will lighting go in this room?" This is likely to be the last time for relatively inexpensive changes, so you should move some furniture in if necessary, to get a feel for the way it will furnish. After plumbing, air conditioning, electric, or drywall is in, will be too late to ask these kinds of questions.

Device Locations

If I could have one single redo-wish granted, I would wish that electric and HVAC subs would care about how their devices appear, as well as how they perform. I would ask for them to think of themselves as players on a team trying to deliver an excellent overall product, someone's home. Thoughtful placement of heating registers, air grilles, and electric devices is very important to maintaining the orderly "feel" of the architecture. Although all subcontractors have a tendency to come into a job with blinders on, and try to get out with as little conversation as possible, the electric and HVAC guys are unique because of the devices they hang. They will locate them on the nearest stud or joist and never ask the carpenter to put in some extra blocking for an off-framing mount. And most builders don't seem to share the designer's and owner's concern; they always need to be asked to have grilles and electric boxes repositioned or squared up.

Because I know my wish will not be granted, I must first suggest that you send a clear signal to your designer and builder that you care about these details. This is a good topic for a job meeting just before rough framing is finished and before mechanical rough-ins. The team should walk the redo and mark important device locations to direct the subs. If you have the luxury of time, make this walk-through distinct from and after the one for perceptual changes. Pay attention to walls with numerous electric boxes at strange intervals. Ask whether some of these can be consolidated into a larger box or be moved entirely. Kitchens and bathrooms always seem to have outlet location problems, particularly in the backsplash. Sometimes it makes sense to leave extra wire coiled in the wall and the box loose until the finish details are finalized. Recessed lighting is often poorly located, so check every fixture for its spatial position. Where these will occur in front of wall cabinets, such as in the kitchen, the fixture itself should wait until cabinets are hung. Using recessed fixtures with "old work" mounts will allow the lighting to be positioned after drywall, to wash specific cabinets on their centerline. You should determine a center-of-table mark on the floor for locating pendant fixtures in eating areas. Wall sconces should get the coiled wire/loose box treatment until the specific fixture is available to hold up and mark its best position.

Any area that gets devices from two different trades may offer unpleasant surprises. Bathroom ceilings may have lights, exhaust vents, and air grilles that need to be better organized. Thermostats near switches often appear misaligned. Heating registers or air grilles in high-visibility positions should be carefully located, often dead-center on small walls. These walk-through marks will require the carpenters to rework a small amount of framing, but this is routine. You are saving them from relocating things later when it is much more difficult. Similar to the plumber's instruction, the builder should serve notice to the electric and HVAC subs to speak up if something prevents them from hitting the marks. After rough-in, the designer should confirm that these devices will appear as planned. Further adjustments after rough-in are to be expected.

New and Old Transitions

Many jobs fall short in "transition" areas. Much of the expertise that remodeling specialists possess has to do with how they will handle seams between old and new structure. This attention to transitions begins in rough framing, where it is often difficult to match up floor levels. The existing building may have settled by an inch or more from one end of the redo to the other. Even if the builder thinks to look for the lowest old-floor level, his efforts will be constrained because new framing may come before demolition of the old envelope. Making his new framing level will yield second-floor spaces with recessed floors. But this is much more desirable than the disastrous reverse—new floors that are too high. It is a simple matter to raise a new floor with various combinations of sheathing layers.

The transition between new trim and the old version must be carefully watched as construction proceeds. Although the construction documents will have specified wall-base and fenestration casing treatment, these paper decisions will always be found lacking. A good set of drawings will make a distinction between the type of finish carpentry to take place in each room, but the provision of interior elevation drawings is never fully provided. You are lucky if you get a decision between "new spec trim" and "existing to remain" on walls designated as north, south, east, and west in the Room Finish Schedule. As much as anything else, these specifications are for bidding purposes. They come into the construction phase as economic goals to be met by the finish carpenters. The lead carpenter should be able to turn to his drawings and find out that "for this room we need to protect the old trim, provide the new 'look-a-like' spec for the new walls, and then change to the 'new-work' trim after the doorway and into the addition." He should then think, "Why shouldn't we do this? What is wrong with this picture?"

The Drawings are a jumping-off point for further attention to the trim carpentry in each room. The trim for spaces where the new and old building engage must be debugged separately. Strange as it may seem, rough-framing and demolition stages are the time to begin worrying about final trim. I have seen workers cut an old baseboard for expediency in breaking-through, and then have to replace all the wall trim in the room as a result. Sometimes the designer may want to add a cased-opening (doorway with trim all around, but no door), for the sole purpose of switching baseboard treatments. And many times, this switch is required to keep the architecture intact and stay on budget.

Before finish carpentry begins and the trim is installed, a job meeting walk-through is a good idea. The trim for new-old rooms should be discussed briefly, with an eye toward the highly visible areas. Sometimes it makes more sense to replace old work, especially if it is in bad shape. Why save money on carpentry, and then pay it to the painter for extra paint preparation in the same spot? Trimwork is one of those interior architectural elements that evoke quality, and therefore is a smart place to spend time and money.

The last "transition" item that you and your designer should worry about concerns final finishes. Most tradesmen will give you predictably excellent work in the interior expanses of the surface, but edge treatments vary widely. This really applies to all special surface treatments, such as ceramic tile, hardwood floors, carpeting, and sheet vinyl. Adequate coverage of these details in the construction documents is always absent, and therefore it should be an ongoing design management concern. I hesitate to say that you should look for these problems prior to installation, because that is frequently too late to provide the elegant solution. For example, a precise matchup of hardwood floors without a taper strip to transition new to old may require the new floor framing to be set at a specific height. This would have to happen months before the floor guy is standing in front of you describing the less-than-perfect solution. My point is that at every opportunity you should ask for an explanation of the way things will "start" and "stop." There is usually a specific product designed to handle the change, and you should ask for a sample.

Artistic Placement or Treatments

Unpleasant surprises frequently arise in design "accent" areas. Most of the motifs that add special character to your home will take place in the final finishing stages of a project. These might be patterns or accents in ceramic and vinyl tile, or wood floors. They could be architectural trelliswork, brackets, dentals, decorative moldings, gingerbread, filigree, or fishscale shingles. I include any treatment that requires a certain amount of artistic placement, such as wall covering accents, painted stencils, or faux finishes. Whether germinated in drawings or in final product selection, extra care must be taken when installation time comes around. Their very purpose is to draw attention to themselves, and placement by a person with an "artistic eye" is very important. Tile patterns are probably the most abused, because of the extra work required to vary the starting and stopping points of the module. The installer's judgment will be colored by the fact that in order to place the accent in its correct visual position, he will have to cut many more rows of tile. I have never met a painter yet who will tell you he couldn't do faux finishes well, but few ever do.

So you must earmark the artistic treatment areas early on, and make sure you give some sort of guidance to the installer. You cannot assume that he will have the "design eye" he needs. Some will, but most will not. Your designer should be better at this than you; your best role is to make sure the "connection" is made at the right time. For tile, probably the way to do it is to catch the installer (and/or builder) with the product on hand, lay out the pieces, and maybe mark up the floor or wall. You should start the conversation with "I am worried about the way the pattern will work here. Have you figured out what you want to do?" Notice I said what "he" wanted to do. You should cause him to think about all the things he should, and arrive at the best conclusion for himself. If he is busy, don't let him off the hook. "When should I show up, so we can go over this before you install?" You will find that most workmen want to do the best job possible even if it takes a little more trouble, but if you autocratically tell them what to do, they will lose the fire. It will become your tile job, not theirs, and you will have to catch all the other small details for them down the road. You want your enthusiasm for excellence to infect them as well.

PROJECT CLOSEOUT

As your project nears completion, several management instruments need to be employed. These are normally provided by your architect, on your behalf. Utilized together, punch lists, the Certificate of Substantial Completion, a Release of Lien, and Final Payment help finish the work and pay the builder for his services. They maintain your control of the job through the crucial final phase. Closing out a redo is often stressful for all parties, and a fair methodology is in everyone's interest.

Punch Lists

A punch list is simply a list of things to do that should be marked off (punched out, as they say) as each item is accomplished. The designer should initiate and maintain punch lists for the team. You should ensure that you, the designer, and builder take the time to walk through each interior space, and around the building and yard, to reach a consensus on each "hit" item. This should not be approached as a critique of the builder's work, but as an accounting of the things left to do. You are making a record that will be left with the lead carpenter for his action. There are always nicks, missed nail holes, and paint spots that need further work. The initial punch list may be three or more pages, and it may need to be revised several times as things are crossed off. Your job, as the owner, is to make the initial punch list reflect all the things that you expect the builder to do before getting paid. The builder would prefer your initial list to be extensive, rather than untimely or sporadic. When the builder indicates that the punch list is taken care of, your team should retrace the original walk-through and check off each item. I find that although the punch list is always used as a starting point to make corrections, there are still many "misses" at the second walk-through. Workmen will fill the nail hole, return to sand it, but forget to retouch the paint. Some builders will place masking tape flags on each "hit" so the carpenters won't miss them. As a last resort, rooms can be punched-out as they are completed so you can occupy and use them separately. Remember though, that once an area is "blessed," any nicks that appear will be considered your kid's fault, not the carpenter's. For large, chaotic jobs, several attempts to clear the final Punch List is routine, so keep your humor, as well as your final check.

Final Payment

When the job is finished enough for you to occupy all the new space, your designer should issue a Certificate of Substantial Completion similar to Example 32. Although there may still be a few items remaining on the punch list, the certificate is simply a way to formalize a completion date in a process that is tapering to closure. This date sets the legal point from which warranties will begin. The builder will be eager to submit his final Application for Payment to the designer for review. This final invoice should include a Payment Affidavit and Release of Lien from the builder and all subcontractors, contingent upon his receipt of Final Payment. The details of this procedure will vary from state to state, but in essence, it is your receipt for construction services that have been "paid in full." The list of subcontractors submitted earlier in the job should be used to assure that an original signature from each one is included. Although the owner has advised the builder that this process must precede final payment (in the Contract for Construction and elsewhere), he has a lot of latitude in this requirement. For simple jobs where the builder and a few subcontractors are well known, phone calls from the subs might be enough to satisfy the owner that there is no second-echelon payment problem. For remodeling jobs, the owner is usually privy to any friction between contractors. Requiring only the builder himself to submit the assurances offered in the Payment of Debts and Claims Affidavit (Example 33), is the middle ground. Unless you direct him otherwise, the architect will withhold his certification of the final payment until lien releases (Example 34) from all subs have been submitted, attached to the builder's Payment Affidavit, and the punch list is complete. This is the safest call.

Builder's Warranties

The best builders are quick to assume responsibility for things that can go wrong with your redo. I work with several who scoff at the idea of a legal warranty, taking the position that if their work doesn't hold up, then they will make it right, regardless of the law or when the complaint is lodged. This posture has never been tested to my mind, because they have never had a hard-cash (nonemployee) obligation of many thousands of dollars to fulfill. I see this as mostly salesmanship, albeit very effective. But the fact is, once your project is over, the builder is responsible to correct all substandard work (including that in subcontracts) for a one-year period starting from the date of Substantial Completion. This is the warranty explicitly worded into the builder's contract (Article 18, Correction of Work), and is therefore the legal minimum. In practice, this year is a little short. Many times it takes a full cycle of summer-winter, plus some observation time, to see the changes that the building and its mechanical systems will undergo. After writing this book I will begin recommending that owners alter their Owner-Builder contract to require an 18-month warranty as a minimum. Because this is non-standard, it should be annotated early in the Invitation to Bid. I understand that many states have laws that further obligate the general contractor. Should it come to this, your lawyer will know the standards he will be held to, outside the contract.

Call-backs

I wish I could "say it ain't so, Joe," but in most projects, the builder will need to be called back in to fix a few

A

B

START TO FINISH

Most people are ready to move right in as soon as they hire their architect. And by the time the builder shows, they have just about decided that it will never happen. But in the first week, when demolition, excavation, and the foundation happen, they are selling tickets to the show (Photograph A)! Then in short order, the ridge beam is set (Photograph B) and the rough frame emerges (Photograph C). This is when they can be overheard bragging about their builder. About the time the addition is closed in and drywall work begins, the pace will begin to slow. Improvements are being made at a smaller, less dramatic scale. After the several months it takes to get the redo ready to bring furnishings in (Photograph D), they will swear the carpenters are loafing. But this is unfair. The crew is sort of like your in-laws. It's nice to have them over, but it's even nicer to have them leave.

C

D

CERTIFICATE OF SUBSTANTIAL COMPLETION

AIA DOCUMENT G704

(Instructions on reverse side)

OWNER ☑
ARCHITECT ☐
CONTRACTOR ☐
FIELD ☐
OTHER ☐

PROJECT:
(Name and address)
Green Residence
Towner, PA 19088

PROJECT NO.: G405

CONTRACT FOR: Renovations
CONTRACT DATE: January 8, 1993

TO OWNER:
(Name and address)
Mary and John Green
1492 Columbus Drive
Towner, PA 19088

TO CONTRACTOR:
(Name and address)
J & J Construction, Inc.
422 Rock Road
Philadelphia, PA 19003

Sample

DATE OF ISSUANCE: April 17, 1993
PROJECT OR DESIGNATED PORTION SHALL INCLUDE:

The entire work consisting of additions and alterations to the owner's residence.

The Work performed under this Contract has been reviewed and found, to the Architect's best knowledge, information and belief, to be substantially complete. Substantial Completion is the stage in the progress of the Work when the Work or designated portion thereof is sufficiently complete in accordance with the Contract Documents so the Owner can occupy or utilize the Work for its intended use. The date of Substantial Completion of the Project or portion thereof designated above is hereby established as
April 17, 1993
which is also the date of commencement of applicable warranties required by the Contract Documents, except as stated below:

A list of items to be completed or corrected is attached hereto. The failure to include any items on such list does not alter the responsibility of the Contractor to complete all Work in accordance with the Contract Documents.

| Peter Wilson | BY | ~P. Wilson~ | DATE 4/20/93 |
| ARCHITECT | | | |

The Contractor will complete or correct the Work on the list of items attached hereto within **fifteen calendar** days from the above date of Substantial Completion.

| John Gaston, J & J Construction, Inc. | BY | ~John Gaston~ | DATE 4.20.93 |
| CONTRACTOR | | | |

The Owner accepts the Work or designated portion thereof as substantially complete and will assume full possession thereof at
(time) on   (date).

| Mary Green | BY | ~M. Green~ | DATE 4/21/93 |
| OWNER | | | |

The responsibilities of the Owner and the Contractor for security, maintenance, heat, utilities, damage to the Work and insurance shall be as follows:
(Note—Owner's and Contractor's legal and insurance counsel should determine and review insurance requirements and coverage.)

Responsibilities for damage to the Work becomes that of the Owner, excepting those items on the attached To Be Corrected Or Completed List (if any).

AIA CAUTION: You should use an original AIA document which has this caution printed in red. An original assures that changes will not be obscured as may occur when documents are reproduced.

CERTIFICATE OF SUBSTANTIAL COMPLETION

EXAMPLE 32. *When the job is finished enough for you to occupy all the new space, your designer should issue a Certificate of Substantial Completion similar to this example. Although there may still be a few items remaining on the punch list, the Certificate is simply a way to formalize a completion date in a process that is tapering to closure. This date sets the legal point from which warranties will begin.*

CONTRACTOR'S AFFIDAVIT OF PAYMENT OF DEBTS AND CLAIMS

AIA Document G706

(Instructions on reverse side)

OWNER ☑
ARCHITECT ☐
CONTRACTOR ☐
SURETY ☐
OTHER ☐

TO OWNER:
(Name and address)

Mary and John Green
1492 Columbus Drive
Towner, PA 19088

ARCHITECT'S PROJECT NO.: G405

CONTRACT FOR: Renovations

PROJECT:
(Name and address)

Green Residence
Towner, PA 19088

CONTRACT DATED: January 8, 1993

STATE OF: Pennsylvania
COUNTY OF: Montgomery

The undersigned hereby certifies that, except as listed below, payment has been made in full and all obligations have otherwise been satisfied for all materials and equipment furnished, for all work, labor, and services performed, and for all known indebtedness and claims against the Contractor for damages arising in any manner in connection with the performance of the Contract referenced above for which the Owner or Owner's property might in any way be held responsible or encumbered.

EXCEPTIONS:

None

Sample

SUPPORTING DOCUMENTS ATTACHED HERETO:

1. Consent of Surety to Final Payment. Whenever Surety is involved, Consent of Surety is required. AIA Document G707, Consent of Surety, may be used for this purpose.

   Indicate attachment: ☐ yes ☑ no

The following supporting documents should be attached hereto if required by the Owner:

1. Contractor's Release or Waiver of Liens, conditional upon receipt of final payment.

2. Separate Releases or Waivers of Liens from Subcontractors and material and equipment suppliers, to the extent required by the Owner, accompanied by a list thereof.

3. Contractor's Affidavit of Release of Liens (AIA Document G706A).

CONTRACTOR:
(Name and address)

J & J Construction, Inc.
422 Rock Road
Philadelphia, PA 19003

BY: *John Gaston*
(Signature of authorized representative)

John Gaston
(Printed name and title)

Subscribed and sworn to before me on this date: 6/12/93

Notary Public: L. Williams, 3457843

My Commission Expires: 3/10/95

AFFIDAVIT OF PAYMENT OF DEBTS AND CLAIMS

EXAMPLE 33. *This completed form is your receipt for construction services that have been "paid in full."*

CONTRACTOR'S AFFIDAVIT OF RELEASE OF LIENS

AIA Document G706A
(Instructions on reverse side)

OWNER	✓
ARCHITECT	☐
CONTRACTOR	☐
SURETY	☐
OTHER	☐

TO OWNER:
(Name and address)

**Mary and John Green
1492 Columbus Drive
Towner, PA 19088**

ARCHITECT'S PROJECT NO.: **G405**

CONTRACT FOR: **Renovations**

PROJECT:
(Name and address)

**Green Residence
Towner, PA 19088**

CONTRACT DATED: **January 8, 1993**

STATE OF: **Pennsylvania**
COUNTY OF: **Montgomery**

The undersigned hereby certifies that to the best of the undersigned's knowledge, information and belief, except as listed below, the Releases or Waivers of Lien attached hereto include the Contractor, all Subcontractors, all suppliers of materials and equipment, and all performers of Work, labor or services who have or may have liens or encumbrances or the right to assert liens or encumbrances against any property of the Owner arising in any manner out of the performance of the Contract referenced above.

EXCEPTIONS:

None

SUPPORTING DOCUMENTS ATTACHED HERETO:

1. Contractor's Release or Waiver of Liens, conditional upon receipt of final payment.

2. Separate Releases or Waivers of Liens from Subcontractors and material and equipment suppliers, to the extent required by the Owner, accompanied by a list thereof.

CONTRACTOR:
(Name and address)

**J & J Construction, Inc.
422 Rock Road
Philadelphia, PA 19003**

BY: *(Signature of authorized representative)*

John Gaston
(Printed name and title)

Subscribed and sworn to before me on this date: **6/12/93**

Notary Public: **L. Williams, 3457843**

My Commission Expires: **3/10/95**

AIA CAUTION: You should sign an original AIA document that has this caution printed in red. An original assures that changes will not be obscured as may occur when documents are reproduced. See Instruction Sheet for Limited License for Reproduction of this document.

LIEN RELEASE

EXAMPLE 34. *Unless the owner directs him otherwise, the architect will withhold his certification of final payment, until releases similar to this one have been submitted by all contractors, and attached to the builder's Payment Affidavit (Example 33).*

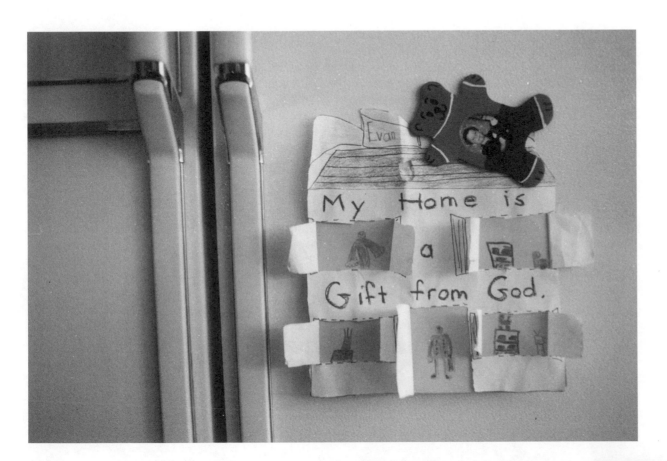

It doesn't take a genius to understand that your home is a special place. Because it can be fun, safe, private, and warm, your home can mold people maybe as much as you can alter it. This is especially true for the little guys, who will take half a century to look back and appreciate the gift.

YOUR HOME

things. This is simply the nature of custom-crafted work. Most problems will be the result of wood members drying out, and the new and old structures settling differently. This will happen to even the most fastidious builder. Drywall screws pop, seams open up, and air conditioning systems need to be better balanced. Sometimes another turn needs to be put on a plumbing fixture to stop a leak. You should not hesitate to call the builder and ask him to correct problems, because he will be as ready as you are. He will want to keep you on his satisfied-customer list, as well as learn what has caused the failure in the first place. Be sure that you don't short-circuit the process; call him first. Do not under any circumstances pay one of his subs directly on a call-back. If you are not sure what degree of performance should be expected, ask the architect for a ruling, which is part of his role. I suggest you keep a log, so you can accurately describe all call-back activities and have a precise record in case you need to go elsewhere for satisfaction.

Total Satisfaction

And speaking of satisfaction, I have to say that although its total achievement should be the team's goal, it is never reached. Although neighbors will rave about your redo, most projects end with a few things that are not quite perfect. I always have a short list of things I am not happy with, and the builder will as well. Because you have been intimately involved with the birth of this tailored dwelling, you will see the warts when others will not. I suggest you view them as you would your children. Love them, and accept their minor blemishes as signs of their crafting by human hands. Then, having done your best, get on with living in your handiwork. Put away the lists and file folders, and let your home wrap itself around your family. Now you can pass the torch on to the architecture, which will encourage you daily to do the things you enjoy.

NOTES

Chapter 2

1. *Remodeling Magazine,* 1993 Cost Versus Value Report, October 1993, Hanley-Wood, Inc. Call 202-383-3845 for reprints.

Chapter 3

1. American Institute of Architects, National Headquarters, 1735 New York Avenue NW, Washington DC.

2. *Kitchen & Bath Business Magazine,* November 1994, p. 24, results of study by Custom Builder Magazine and KBB Magazine, polling 400 custom builders. Who designs the kitchen: Architect 27.6%, Builder 26.2%, Designer where cabinets are purchased 21.7%, Independent Designer 14.9%, Designer on builder's staff 5.9%, Interior Designer 2.4%, Other 1.4%.

3. *Managing,* by Harold Geneen with Alvin Moscow, Doubleday.

4. *In Search of Excellence, Lessons from America's Best-Run Companies,* Thomas J. Peters and Robert H. Waterman Jr., Harper & Row. Publishers, 10 East 53rd Street, NY, NY 10022.

5. *The Second Industrial Revolution,* Dr. Russell L. Ackoff, professor at the Wharton School of Finance and Commerce, University of Pennsylvania. Paper presented at Fordyce House April 20, 1972.

Chapter 6

1. *Kitchen & Bath Source Book,* McGraw-Hill, Sweet's Group, 1221 Avenue of the Americas, NY, NY 10020; annual renewal for Construction Professionals.

INDEX

THE WOMAN IN BATTLE

Wisconsin Studies in Autobiography

THE WOMAN IN BATTLE

The Civil War Narrative of
Loreta Janeta Velazquez, Cuban
Woman and Confederate Soldier

With a new introduction by Jesse Alemán

The University of Wisconsin Press

The University of Wisconsin Press
1930 Monroe Street
Madison, Wisconsin 53711

www.wisc.edu/wisconsinpress/

3 Henrietta Street
London WC2E 8LU, England

Library of Congress Cataloging-in-Publication Data
Velazquez, Loreta Janeta, b. 1842
    The woman in battle : the Civil War narrative of Loreta Janeta Velazquez,
    Cuban woman and Confederate soldier / with a new introduction by Jesse
    Alemán.
    p. cm. — (Wisconsin studies in autobiography)
    Previously published: Hartford : T. Belknap, 1876.
    ISBN 0-299-19420-5 (alk. paper) — ISBN 0-299-19424-8 (pbk.: alk. paper)
    1. Velazquez, Loreta Janeta, b. 1842. 2. United States—History—Civil War,
1861–1865—Personal narratives, Confederate. 3. Women soldiers—Confederate
States of America—Biography. 4. Women spies—Confederate States of Amer-
ica—Biography. 5. Cubans—Confederate States of America—Biography. 6.
United States—History—Civil War, 1861–1865—Participation, Female. 7.
United States—History—Civil War, 1861–1865—Participation, Cuban. I. Title.
II. Series.
E605.V43   2003
973.7'82—dc21   2003050119
[B]

PREFACE

The Woman in Battle's first publishers, Dustin, Gilman, and Company, aptly issued the same text in Richmond, Virginia, and Hartford, Connecticut, in 1876. The book then reappeared in 1970 and more recently as an online facsimile available on the Documenting the American South electronic series compiled at the University of North Carolina, Chapel Hill. Previous reprints did not involve editing, so there is little variation between editions except where blemishes in one copy created word or page omissions in textual reproductions. The following edition is a reprint of an 1876 copy of *The Woman in Battle* in excellent condition.

I have not abridged the book because its greatest strength is its appeal to audiences ranging from general readers and lay historians of the Civil War to academics interested in nineteenth-century American literature, Civil War history, and studies in gender, autobiography, and U.S. Latina/Latino culture. It would be impossible to cut a significant portion of the book without also excluding a major part of Velazquez's story and an important segment of the book's readership. Because of the book's length, though, I have kept extratextual commentary to a minimum. A glossary of battles, people, and places that appear prominently or frequently in the book stands in for specific, extensive endnotes, which would have drawn-out an already expansive text, and, aside from my introductory comments, I have not attempted to verify the narrative with historical documentation, since Velazquez's history and the history of the text are so embattled in a debate over their authenticity. Instead, *The Woman in Battle* stands as readers confronted it in 1876—a sensationalist, secessionist, and suspicious autobiographical account of a Cuban woman who participated in the Civil War as a cross-dressed Confederate.

ACKNOWLEDGMENTS

I am almost embarrassed by the amount of institutional, intellectual, and personal debts I accrued to publish this edition. The Center for Regional Studies at the University of New Mexico granted me financial support to begin the research for this project, and the University's English department approved a year's leave so I could accept the inaugural Latina/Latino Studies post-doctoral fellowship at the University of Illinois at Urbana-Champaign, where I completed the edition. UIUC's Latina/Latino Studies Program provided generous research funds; Victoria González offered extensive staff support along with her friendship; and Nick Rudd of UIUC's interlibrary borrowing office proved to be an indispensable ally. The librarians from the Library of Virginia in Richmond and Duke University's Rare Book, Manuscript, and Special Collections Library were also helpful. Meanwhile, William L. Andrews and Minrose Gwin encouraged the project from the start, provided splendid models of scholarship, and gave me critical advice on the introduction. Elizabeth Young offered exhaustive suggestions for reprinting the book, and the editorial staff at the University of Wisconsin Press saw the book and me through the whole republication process. There are too many friends to thank for hearing, reading, or commenting on my Velazquez research: Hector Torres, Catherine Ramírez, Eric Porter, Andrea Tinnemeyer, Kirsten Silva-Gruesz, and an army of colleagues at the 2000 Recovering the U.S. Hispanic Literary Heritage conference and the 2000 American Studies Association conference. Finally, my family—I hope—tolerated my absent-mindedness, brief visits, and infrequent calls, while Melina read final drafts and always met me at the airport with the sleepy kids in tow. So I leave this edition to them, one last gift from Champaign because I'm coming home now.

AUTHENTICITY, AUTOBIOGRAPHY, AND IDENTITY

THE WOMAN IN BATTLE AS
A CIVIL WAR NARRATIVE

JESSE ALEMÁN

The way to keep a secret, as I had long since found out, is not to tell it to anybody.
—Loreta Janeta Velazquez

When Confederate General Jubal Early came across Loreta Janeta Velazquez's *The Woman in Battle* (1876), he was so outraged by it he wrote to Tennessee Congressman William H. Slemons to protest the book's authenticity. Early attacked the book on several fronts. He noted its factual inaccuracies; its dubious author; and its affront to the honor of Southern men and women. After all, the seemingly pro-Confederate Civil War narrative poses as the autobiography of a Cuban woman who claims to have cross-dressed as Harry T. Buford and fought for the Confederacy. Even though Early had previously encountered women dressed as men in his ranks, he nevertheless objected to Velazquez's account, mainly because the book challenged the supposed gentility of Southern gender codes.[1] "Nearly all the Confederate officers she describes," Early complains, "are drunken, gasconading brutes, whose mouths are constantly filled with obscene language, and the women, especially the young and pretty ones, are ready to throw themselves into the arms of the dashing 'Lieutenant Harry T. Buford,' and seceding without waiting to be asked, all that is dear to women of virtue."[2] Indeed, Early found it downright offensive that a narrative about a woman masquerading as a Confederate soldier would be in circulation, which is why he centered his attack on the authenticity of the book and its supposed author. Early targeted several factual errors in particular to question the book's veracity: Velazquez describes her first husband in a Confederate uniform before the Confederate Army adopted standardized dress; she mistakenly identifies Robert E. Lee as a general before he gained that rank; and she claims to have traveled north from Columbia, South Carolina, to Richmond, Virginia, on a railroad line that did not exist at the time of her adventures.

The anachronisms in the Velazquez text confirmed Early's suspicions about the author. He claimed to have met Velazquez in Richmond and supposedly carried on a correspondence with her, and both experiences led him to conclude that Velazquez and her book were fakes: "If the author of that book is the same with the author of the letter to me, then her style must have deteriorated very much since the former was written. It will be seen, according to the story in the book, Madame Velasquez [sic] received a thorough English education, and the solecisms in grammar contained in the letter do not result from the broken English of a foreigner, but are the blunders of an American whose education is imperfect. Her appearance and voice are those of an American woman, and has no resemblance to those of a cultivated Spanish lady. If she is really Spanish in origin, then her associations with camp life have thoroughly Americanized her." With an ambivalence reminiscent of the Velazquez text, Early could not pinpoint Velazquez's authentic national identity, but he is certain she is not a "true type of a Southern woman," those "fair specimens of the pure and devoted women who followed with their prayers the armies of the Confederate states through all their struggles and trials." Rather, Early implies that only a Yankee hack would have the nerve to imagine a Cuban woman who dressed in men's clothes, took up arms for the South, seduced unsuspecting women, and then wrote about it for money. Velazquez is simply a "pretender," Early concludes, unless her identity can be proven otherwise, and her book "ought not to be patronized by Southern men and women, for it is a libel on both" (Early to Slemons).

Early's doubts are not entirely unwarranted. Edited by C. J. Worthington, a former Yankee naval officer, *The Woman in Battle* offers a seemingly impossible autobiographical account of a Cuban-born woman who came to the United States in the 1850s to receive her education and ended up fighting for the Confederacy in drag. Born in Havana, Cuba, in 1842 to a Spanish father and French American mother, Loreta Janeta Velazquez claims to be a descendent of Diego Velazquez, conqueror and first governor of Cuba, and she also admits to a desire to wage war on the battlefield like her historical heroines: Catalina de Eranso, the sixteenth-century Spanish nun who left the convent to join the conquest of the New World; Appolonia Jagiello, who fought for Poland and Hungary during their mid-nineteenth-century revolutions; and of course Joan of Arc. As Velazquez puts it, "I have no hesitation in saying that I wish I had been created as a man instead of a woman."[3] Moving from Cuba to New Orleans in the 1850s, Velazquez attends an all-girls Catholic school, seduces her best friend's betrothed, and, after eloping, they light out to Mormon territory. Following secession, she harangues her husband to join the Confederacy and also convinces him to take her out for a night on the town in drag. He reluctantly agrees, thinking it a playful adventure, but Velazquez makes the transvestite transformation in earnest. Once her husband leaves for the front lines, Velazquez outfits herself with a wire bodice, dons an army uniform, and takes the name Harry T. Buford to support the Confederate cause. She organizes an Arkansas regiment at her own expense, participates in the battles of Bull Run, Balls Bluff, Fort Donelson, and Shiloh, and then decides to be a spy rather than a soldier.[4] Posing as a Northern woman, she infiltrates the ranks of the Yankee secret service and works as a double agent to support the Confederate cause from the other side of the Mason-Dixon Line. Eventually, the Yankee secret service even hires her to find herself, the "woman who is traveling and figuring as a Confederate agent" (516).

As a spy, Velazquez participates in a host of shady acts: she smuggles contraband across Northern blockades; traffics in counterfeit Confederate money, bonds, and securities; has a hand in bounty-jumping scams; and helps to plot a botched rebellion by Confederate prisoners detained at Johnson's Island. On several occasions authorities arrest Velazquez on the suspicion of being a woman, which is quite an apt charge considering she often spies across gender lines too.

During her first night on the town in drag, Velazquez satirically exposes the drinking, cussing, cigar smoking, and bellicose bravado that characterize masculine public space—the biggest cowards during the war, Velazquez reveals, were the men who were usually the loudest secessionists in the bar. At the same time, Velazquez as Buford enters the privacy of women's drawing rooms to satisfy her "curiosity to know how love-making went from the masculine standpoint" (75). Velazquez/Buford carries on a flirtation with Miss Sadie Giles, "a fair flower of the Arkansas forest" (75), enjoys the courtship of "a pretty widow" in Pensacola (87), and finds some "amusement, too, to carry on a bit of a flirtation with a nice girl" named Miss E. in Leesburg (111) to name only a few of Buford's "conquests" (91). Velazquez never claims to find her flirtations with women sexually stimulating, which would overstep the bounds of Victorian culture. Rather, she claims to be upholding her role as Buford and chastises Southern women who too quickly throw their affections on eligible and dashing young soldiers.

The Woman in Battle is undeniably part pulp fiction, but it is not necessarily inauthentic, as Early would have us believe. Throughout July 1863, for instance, the *Daily Richmond Enquirer* and the *Daily Richmond Examiner* announced that Confederate General Winder sentenced a woman disguised as a Confederate soldier to Castle Thunder. The stories vary somewhat, suggesting that the historical record is not entirely consistent, but on Thursday, July 2, 1863, the *Enquirer* and the *Examiner* reported the arrest of a woman passing as "Lieutenant Bensford" and "Lieutenant Benford," respectively. The *Enquirer* also noted that the woman claimed to be "Mrs. Alice Williams," a British citizen and pro-Southerner who had a husband in the Federal army. By July 11, 1863, the *Enquirer* noted that "Lieut. Buford" (rather than its previous "Bensford") had been released from the Castle and on July 15 even claimed that the female lieutenant was appointed as a clerk in the Confederate prison. The *Examiner* also covered the release of "Lieutenant Buford" (rather than its previous "Benford") on July 11 and explained that her "real name is Mrs. S. T. Williams, and her husband is a 1st Lieutenant in company E, 13th Connecticut regiment, under Banks, in Louisiana. Her father is Major J. B. Roche, of Mississippi, but she was born in the West Indies." By July 16 the *Examiner* reported the "female soldier" had been released and sent to Atlanta, Georgia, after having "ordered everybody about" in the Castle, but on September 16 the *Examiner* heralded the return of "Lieutenant Harry Buford," who "for a time was employed in the secret service, effecting important arrests of spies, and doing some very daring things." The "gay Lieutenant" also sported a new name, "Mrs. Jeruth DeCaulp," after marrying "an officer of the Confederate States Provisional army of that name," the report explains, "first obtaining a divorce from her first husband, Williams, who is in the army of General Grant."[5]

Of course, Velazquez used Lieutenant Harry T. Buford as her *nom de guerre,* and, as Civil War researcher Richard Hall notes, the Richmond reports chronologically coincide with the dates on which Velazquez claims to have been arrested in the Confederate capital and sent to Castle Thunder.[6] Several times in the narrative, moreover, Velazquez takes the name "Mrs. Williams," and she claims to be a British subject when she is held under arrest in New Orleans on the suspicion of being a spy. Equally important, the news reports suggest a connection to the largest documentary discrepancy in *The Woman in Battle*—Velazquez's marriage to her second husband, Thomas C. DeCaulp. According to Hall, DeCaulp did in fact exist and participate in the Civil War. His military file, however, contradicts much of Velazquez's account: DeCaulp did not die in a Federal hospital in Chattanooga, as Velazquez claims; rather, he was captured at Chattanooga and then deserted the Confederate army. His records further indicate that DeCaulp had "been impressed into the Confederacy against his will, deserted, and later fought under the assumed name 'William Irwin' in a Union regiment and was married to the daughter of an English admiral by the name of Rosche."[7] Notice how these pieces of documentary evidence blend into each other, crossdressing, if you will, from one account to another: The news articles describe "Mrs. Williams" as a British subject born in the West Indies, the daughter of J. B. Roche, and the wife of a Federal soldier, though "Mrs. Williams" later returns as "Mrs. Jeruth DeCaulp"; Thomas DeCaulp's military file lists "William Irwin" as his alias, places him in the Union forces, and indicates that he is married to the daughter of an Englishman named Rosche; and after the death of her first husband, William, Velazquez claims to have married De-Caulp, occasionally takes the name "Mrs. Williams," and passes as a British subject while her alleged Cuban birth makes her a native of the West Indies.[8] The coincidences that connect the Velazquez text, the Richmond reports, and DeCaulp's military file indicate that a collusion of truth and lies surround Velazquez's identity and the authenticity of *The Woman in Battle,* making it a combination of fact and fiction that accurately reflects the times of the Civil War but, especially in light of cross-dressing, also speaks to the instability of gender and national identities.

Indeed, as Civil War biographer Stewart Sifakis says of Velazquez, "Little in her work can be even circumstantially supported. Yet there may be an element of truth. She may have done some of the things she claimed, but this will never be definitely known due to her penchant for exaggeration." Historian Sylvia Hoffert agrees, adding the book's authenticity can never be confirmed "simply because there is not enough evidence available to substantiate it." Scholars of women in the Civil War are equally divided. In *The Women in the Confederacy,* Francis Simkins describes Velazquez as a "morally loose" woman whose adventures "have an air of the tawdry and the unreal"; Mary Massey considers the dubious autobiography "a composite picture of several women's experiences, published or rumored at the time and later enlivened by the author's vivid imagination"; and Elizabeth Leonard reads the book as a coauthored venture between Velazquez and Worthington that reveals the complex motivations behind women's desire to dress as men and participate in the war. Meanwhile, Velazquez's authorship still remains vague among researchers. Richard Hall's extensive investigation of *The Woman in Battle* finds enough circumstantial evidence to corroborate the book's veracity, but his documentary proof falls short of confirming Velazquez's authorship, let alone her existence. And literary scholars such as Kathleen De Grave and Elizabeth Young read the book as fiction rather than fact without considering the possibility that Velazquez's identity may be fictional too.[9]

In fact, the ambiguity of *The Woman in Battle*'s authorship poses more problems for the book's authenticity than Velazquez's seemingly impossible adventures. After all, Mary Livermore, a former Union nurse, estimated in her 1888 account that over four hundred women participated in the Civil War in drag, and more recently, Civil War scholars DeAnne Blanton and Lauren M. Cook have extensively documented cross-dressed female soldiers.[10] Meanwhile, there is enough textual evidence to suggest that the book's battle accounts are generally accurate, with only minor slips in details that could be attributed to memory. In Velazquez's account of the Battle of Bull Run, for instance, she remembers that Confederate General Bee rallied his retreating men by exclaiming "'See how Jackson stands there like a stone wall'" (102), thus giving Jackson his famous nickname, but Velazquez neglects to mention Bee's death after his rallying cry. She forgets to describe Harrison Island, "a prominent geological feature" at the center of the Battle of Ball's Bluff, according to Richard Hall, yet her account of the Battle of Fort Donelson recalls a dramatic turn in the weather from summer to winter conditions, a factor often noted in other accounts of the Fort's fall.[11] Details aside, her sense of a battle's significance also rings historically true. The Battle of Bull Run initiates her into the Civil War, as it did the rest of the country, making her realize that, on the one hand, the South can potentially win their independence, and on the other, the country was in for a long, bloody war. She begins to doubt the South's chances for victory, though, after the loss of Fort Donelson, echoing an historical consensus that the Confederacy's loss of the Fort broke rebel morale on the western war front and led directly to the South's defeat at Shiloh. And as with many Confederates, she questions General P. G. T. Beauregard's decision to halt the fighting at Shiloh after a day of battle, a decision that allowed Union troops to regroup, take the battle the following day, and eventually secure western Tennessee.

The Woman in Battle contains enough details to make it a legitimate Civil War narrative, but the authenticity of Velazquez's authorship remains more uncertain, mainly because the documentary evidence surrounding Velazquez's identity reproduces the book's characteristic ambivalence. No direct, contemporaneous reference to Velazquez during the antebellum period or the Civil War has appeared to date, though there are certainly some close encounters. In his 1863 publication, *Three Months in the Southern States,* Lieutenant Colonel Fremantle, a British national, recalls riding the train from Chattanooga to Atlanta and meeting a "goodish-looking woman" who had fought as a private in the battles of Perryville and Murfreesborough; she wore a "soldier's hat and coat, but had resumed her petticoats." Another Englishman, Fitzgerald Ross, notes in his 1865 travel account that he met a "Confederate captain in one of the ladies" while traveling by train from Augusta to Atlanta; she was riding in one of the ladies' cars, no longer in uniform, and "told her adventures in a pleasant quiet kind of way." Civil War historian Ella Lonn claims Ross and Fremantle encountered Velazquez in these brief meetings, and Lonn may be right, but both accounts never name Velazquez directly, and the women the Englishmen come across appear too conspicuous for Velazquez's self-proclaimed sense of secrecy—Ross and Fremantle probably met two different women traversing the South in men's clothing.[12]

As for Velazquez's *nom de guerre,* however, historical records contemporaneous with the war indicate that Lieutenant Harry T. Buford—and variations on the name, including Henry Buford, Bensford, and Benford—was in fact a female Confederate in drag. The Confederate Secretary of War received a request for an officer's commission for "H. T. Buford" on July 27, 1863, which was the same month Richmond newspapers ran the series of stories on the "Lady Lieutenant," Harry T. Buford, aka Mrs. Alice or S. T. Williams.[13] There is even report of a "Laura J. Williams" posing as Lieutenant Henry Benford during the war, raising the possibility that either Velazquez and Mrs. Williams (be it Alice, S. T., or Laura J.) was the same woman passing as Buford or two different women with strikingly similar experiences and stories: Velazquez passed as Harry Buford and married Thomas DeCaulp while Williams posed as Henry Benford and married Jeruth DeCaulp, leaving Civil War scholar Janet Kaufman to conclude that Velazquez "heard of Mrs. Williams after the war and grafted her own autobiography on the other woman's life."[14] Of course, the opposite holds equally true: "Laura J. Williams" could be one of the many pseudo-identities Velazquez used during her days as a spy, perhaps even an English echo of Loreta Janeta Velazquez's more conspicuous sounding Spanish name.

Whatever the case, *The Woman in Battle*'s publication gave birth to Velazquez in postwar historical records. Jubal Early claims to have met her in 1878 but remains uncertain whether she was an American or a "Spanish lady" (Early to Slemons). Early and Velazquez even corresponded, but because Early copied Velazquez's letter and sent it to Congressman Slemons, no original Velazquez letter exists. Another Confederate general, James Longstreet, notes in a letter to Emily Park, dated June 18, 1888, that a woman who served in the ranks as Lieutenant Buford went west after the war, speculated in gold, and then got married before returning south to New Orleans, where Longstreet met her but could not remember her maiden or married name. Longstreet's letter suggests his familiarity with the Velazquez narrative, but while he insists he did not know the cross-dressed Buford during the war, he appears in *The Woman in Battle* and even has a brief interview with Velazquez as Buford (290). Confederate veteran Bromfield L. Ridley's *Battles and Sketches of the Army of Tennessee* (1906) also mentions Velazquez's military service as Buford, though clearly Ridley is referring to the Velazquez narrative rather than Velazquez herself. As he simply puts it, "She has written a book." In fact, all of the biographical information on Velazquez included in recent reference books such as *Who Was Who in the Civil War, American National Biography,* the *Historical Times Illustrated Encyclopedia of the Civil War, The Civil War Dictionary,* and the *Encyclopedia of the American Civil War* relies entirely on the Velazquez narrative, ironically using the dubious autobiography to question Velazquez's authenticity.[15] On the most literal level, then, Velazquez's so-called autobiography in effect created her, as her name and adventures appear in public circulation only after the book's publication.

It is thus significant that the most compelling evidence verifying *The Woman in Battle* and its author appears in an 1876 advertisement that solicited sales agents and subscribers for the book. Authenticating statements from Atlanta newspapers and Confederate veterans accompany the broadside, and even though the newspaper reports and M. D. Lorme McLeod's statement appear to be book reviews that corroborate the narrative more than they verify its authorship, the "unsolicited testimonials" from Hammond, Alexander, Anderson, and Newman confirm the book's veracity and the authenticity of its authorship.[16] Several of the commentators even appear in the narrative, where they are privy to Velazquez's cross-dressed identity as Buford. Dr. J. F. Hammond, whom the ad lists as an assistant surgeon at Atlanta's Empire hospital during the war, affirms Velazquez's identity as Buford, asserts "Her work is founded on facts," and claims to have witnessed her marriage to Thomas DeCaulp at the Thompson House, corroborating his role in *The Woman in Battle* even as he breaks his promise to Velazquez to keep her transvestism and matrimony a secret (335). G. W. Alexander, the Confederate captain in charge of Castle Thunder from 1862–63, similarly attests to have known Velazquez as Buford and declares she "was particularly distinguished for her devotion to the cause, for which she made many sacrifices." One of Velazquez's sacrifices was the prison time she spent in the Castle under Alexander's watch, during which she befriended Alexander and his wife and revealed to them her transvestite identity (278–79). Another Confederate veteran, George Anderson, general of the Eleventh Georgia Regiment and a brigade of Georgia troops, also vouches for the book and Velazquez's identity just as tersely as he reveals her cross-dressed identity in his brief appearance in *The Woman in Battle* (534). Finally, Major John Newman, who does not appear in the Velazquez text, nevertheless proclaims to "have been personally acquainted with her for the past thirteen years," a friendship that may have started when Velazquez enlisted as Buford in Newman's regiment—the Twenty-first Regiment of Louisiana Volunteers (181).[17]

The handbill's documentary evidence was so compelling that the editor of the Richmond, Virginia, *Southern Historical Society Papers* concluded in his 1876 book review: "As to the reality of the experiences of such a personage, there can be no reasonable doubt."[18] Apparently, rebel veterans and Southern readers agreed, taking *The*

Woman in Battle as seriously as any other legitimate Confederate memoir published during Reconstruction. Yet, the historical record tracing Velazquez's identity and authorship remains a myriad of contradictions and connections that demonstrate the instability of identity and its ambivalent representation through language. Velazquez's name, for instance, goes through a series of literal and symbolic misspellings in the broadside alone: The title page announces her as "Loreta Juaneta Velasquez"; J. F. Hammond, who claims to have known her "better than" anyone, spells her name, "Laureta Juaneta Velasquez"; and Alexander refers to her as "J. L. Velasquez." Meanwhile, the Richmond reports change the name of the "lady lieutenant" from "Bensford" to "Benford" before settling on "Buford," while the first name of "Mrs. Williams" is still a toss up between "Alice," "S. T.," and "Laura J." These misnomers may be sleights of literacy, pronunciation, and lies, but General Early's meeting and correspondence with Velazquez proves equally equivocal, for he doubts her identity even as he meets her face to face. And the references to Velazquez in accounts published after 1876, such as Ridley's memoirs, suggest that Velazquez became a popular and contested literary character in Confederate postwar narratives. Perhaps Velazquez's secrecy as a spy "inadvertently complicated the problem of trying to document her career in retrospect," but I suspect that the "lady lieutenant" will always escape us, for the historical records generate more ambivalence than answers when it comes to finding Velazquez.[19] Indeed, her identity depends so much on cross-dressed documentary clothing—news reports, authenticating letters, an advertising pamphlet, and postwar accounts—that Velazquez's very existence, as with the narrative attributed to her, rests somewhere in between history and story, where even a seemingly inauthentic author can nonetheless produce an authentic cultural text that embodies and enacts the prevailing beliefs and anxieties of its historical context.

GENDER AND THE GENUINE THING.

The act of cross-dressing, which is so central to *The Woman in Battle*, may in fact trouble the notion of authenticity altogether in autobiography, authorship, and even identity. Cross-dressing reminds us that

The following are but a few of the many unsought testimonials received from gentlemen of high character, identifying the person and vouching for the character, of Madame Velasquez, also that she was the veritable Lieut. Harry T. Buford, C. S. A., the heroine of this book:

DEAR SIR: It affords me great pleasure to state that no one knew Madame Laureta Juaneta L. J. Velasquez under her assumed *pseudonym* (Lieut. Harry T. Buford) better than I did. I know much of her history, especially that part which relates to the field service. Lieut. Buford was admitted into the Empire Hospital on July 26, 1863: was suffering at the time from a wound. Captain Decaulp was at that time a patient of mine. He afterwards became her husband ; I witnessed their marriage at the Thompson Hotel. I certainly knew her private character, and I cheerfully state, and will make oath, if such a thing should become necessary, that it was good and above suspicion ; her conduct was that of a brave soldier, whose life was at the disposal of home and country. Her work is founded on facts.
J. F. HAMMOND, M. D.,
Asst. Surgeon Empire Hospital, Atlanta.

IT affords me great pleasure to state that I have carefully read the "Woman in Battle," by Madame L. J. Velasquez, *née* Lt. Harry T. Buford, C. S. A. This book is ably written, and will certainly place her among the foremost of heroines in history. After reading her description of scenes, places, and persons on the Pacific slope, which are so true and life-like, I imagine myself once more among them. Madame Velasquez is a lady of unsullied character, and of acknowledged ability.
M. D. Lorme McLeod, M. D.,
Late of Denver, Col., now of Atlanta, Ga.

THE name of Madame L. J. Velasquez, better known as the famous Lt. Harry T. Buford. occupies a conspicuous place in the history of the late unpleasantness as a Confederate spy, and valuable aid to the "Lost Cause."
She went into the army with her husband disguised as a soldier, and won her way to a Lieutenancy by sustaining an unblemished reputation, valiant service in battle, and the discharge of important offices of trust.
She has devoted many years to the preparation of a book to be called the "Woman in Battle." In this remarkable book is recounted all of her daring exploits, by land and sea, while in the service of the Lost Cause. Knowing that Madame Velasquez was in the city, and desiring to see and talk to the famous Harry Buford, of whom I had read so much during the war, I called on her in behalf of the *Constitutionalist*, and interviewed her She is a tall, graceful woman, something over thirty. Her eyes, blue in color, have a way of brightening up and sparkling when she speaks of her native island, struggling Cuba. Although having passed through all the roughness of camp life, among soldiers of every grade, who never even suspected her true sex, she bears the modest demeanor that belongs to woman, and you can't for the life of you detect anything in her deportment or conversation that would be expected from a woman who had gone through her many trials and mingled with so many men. She showed me letters from prominent men in the North, West, and South, commending her and her book.—*Augusta (Ga.) Constitutionalist.*

WOMAN IN BATTLE.—This popular and highly romantic work is one of the most thrilling and interesting books ever published in the United States.
The heroine of the book, Madame Velasquez, *née* Lieut. Harry Buford, of Confederate fame, well known to many of our most prominent men, and who was the most daring and reckless spy that ever entered an enemy's camp, has furnished the material which the distinguished author has woven into history. The lady hero who still survives the dangers and hair-breadth escapes that compassed her mission, will transmit to posterity, through this narrative, a name and character that will place her side by side with the proudest heroines of ancient or modern history The work is filled with engravings and is ably written. Every one should buy and read it.—*Kennesaw Gazette, Atlanta, Ga.*

THE work is well gotten up and elegantly written. and is an embodiment of daring adventures, hair-breadth escapes, etc., that equal the life of any heroine whose exploits have ever been recorded in history. The work will create a profound sensation throughout the Union, as it contains some startling revelations of the corruptions of the "best government the world ever saw."—*Atlanta, (Ga.) Daily Commonwealth.*

Madame L. J. Velasquez, otherwise known as Lieut. Harry T. Buford, of Confederate fame. is well known to the citizens of Atlanta ; among them our Col. Acton. There are numerous certificates from good and reliable judges as to the excellencies and truthfulness of the literary features of the work.—*Atlanta, (Ga.) Daily Constitution.*

Madame J. L. Velasquez (Lieut. Harry T. Buford, C. S. A.) was well known to me during the late war. She was particularly distinguished for her devotion to the cause, for which she made many sacrifices. She was also brave, noble, and generous in disposition, ready at all times to do anything in her power for the Confederacy.
G. W. ALEXANDER,
Proprietor *Washington Gazette*, Washington, D. C.

Madame L. J. Valasquez is a lady of the most unblemished character. I have been personally acquainted with her for the past thirteen years. She has served under me with distinction as a soldier, for three months, and was afterwards promoted for her great efficiency and integrity to the position of 1stLieutenant in the Confederate Service. I therefore take great pride in recommending her to parties to whom her services may be available.
JOHN NEWMAN,
Major of 21st Regiment of Louisiana Volunteers, New Orleans

It affords me great pleasure to certify to the fact that Madame L. J. Velasquez is the person known during the late war between the South and North as Lieut. Harry T. Buford, C. S. A. Her book cannot but be one of unusual interest.
GEO. ANDERSON,
Late Brigadier General C. S. A., Atlanta.

Pennsylvania Broadside 1876 "The Woman in Battle" in the Rare Book, Manuscript, and Special Collections Library, Duke University, Durham, North Carolina

A TRUE HEROINE.

THE WOMAN IN BATTLE:

THE ADVENTURES, EXPLOITS, AND TRAVELS OF

MADAME LORETA JUANETA VELASQUEZ,

OTHERWISE KNOWN AS

LIEUTENANT HARRY T. BUFORD, C. S. A.

The most intensely interesting war book ever published; being the true narrative of
the romantic career of the MOST REMARKABLE WOMAN OF THE DAY; who participated, in
the DISGUISE OF A CONFEDERATE OFFICER, in some of the hardest-fought battles of the
late war, and who played such an important part as a spy and secret-service agent as to win
the applause and admiration of those highest in authority.

Sold Only by Subscription.--Agents Wanted.

One Handsome Octavo Volume of 600 pages, Beautifully Illustrated in the Highest
Style of Art, by 48 Full-Page Engravings, and printed on Fine Laid Tinted Paper, made
expressly for this book.

H. W. KELLEY,

711 Sansom St., Philadelphia, Pa.

Pennsylvania Broadside 1876 "The Woman in Battle" in the Rare Book,
Manuscript, and Special Collections Library, Duke University, Durham,
North Carolina

one of the most seemingly natural identity categories—gender—is only a matter of dress and culturally contingent on factors ranging from fabrics and fashions to region and race. That is, gender is not a natural identity category but a cultural one that identifies masculinity and femininity through readable but arbitrary signs of behavior and dress that fluctuate, especially during times of war. Moreover, cross-dressing suggests that other identity categories, including race and nation, likewise rely on arbitrary markers such as skin color and language to categorize someone as a specific racial or national subject. As the Velazquez text makes clear, identities transgress, transform, and translate into other gendered, racial, or national categories with a simple change of clothing: Velazquez masquerades as a Confederate solider, a Northern woman, and even a Spanish lady just as easily as the book's Yankee editor cross-dresses as the narrative's Cuban female author; North and South collapse in a book ostensibly about the Civil War just as comfortably as Cuba and the Confederacy converge on Velazquez's corselette. Instead of a fixed state of being, identity in *The Woman in Battle* is a series of performances that render authenticity an impossibility. Nonetheless, the Velazquez text does offer an accurate indication of the Civil War's gender crises and the transnational connections between Cuba and the Confederacy as two slaveholding regions waging similar anti-imperialist wars. This level of historical authenticity has less to do with finding a "real" Velazquez and more to do with understanding *The Woman in Battle* and its author as embattled national allegories that offer cultural truths about the instability of gender, race, and nation during the Civil War and in its literature.

In this sense, Velazquez might be considered as a character both in *The Woman in Battle* and in the embattled history surrounding the question of her identity. Velazquez exists but only in disguise as Harry T. Buford, C. J. Worthington, Mrs. Williams, and, ironically, even Loreta Janeta Velazquez, for transvestism reminds us that literal and linguistic clothing fashion self-identity. As gender theorist Judith Butler explains, gender identity amounts to a series of acts that, because they are repeated over time, give the impression of an authentic self, but "Inasmuch as 'identity' is assured through the stabilizing concepts of sex, gender, and sexuality, the very notion of 'the person' is called into question by the cultural convergence of those 'incoherent' or 'discontinuous' gendered beings who appear to be persons but who fail to conform to the gendered norms of cultural intelligibility by which persons are defined." Cross-dressing may not always subvert heterosexual norms, according to Butler, but it does trouble "the reality of gender": "it becomes unclear how to distinguish the real from the unreal. And this is the occasion in which we come to understand that what we take to be 'real,' what we invoke as the naturalized knowledge of gender is, in fact, a changeable and revisable reality."[20]

Butler's gender theory cuts to the core of the authenticity issues surrounding *The Woman in Battle,* as the narrative often collapses the distinction between otherwise clear identity markers. First of all, the book is a cross-dressed production, ostensibly authored by Velazquez but edited by C. J. Worthington. Both confess up front that they had a hand in the narrative. Velazquez allegedly produced an original diary, and Worthington revised and edited it, but no line separates Velazquez's voice from Worthington's revisions. Instead, Velazquez cross-dresses as a Confederate soldier, and Worthington, the Yankee editor, takes on the guise of a pro-Confederate Cuban woman. Moreover, the book self-consciously wavers between fact and fiction to the point that one blends into the other, as when the text accurately recounts specific battle scenes but then parodies the discourses of sentimentality, romance, and seduction plots when Velazquez/Buford romances men or women. In fact, genre confusion compounds the book's gender trouble as it shifts from pulp fiction, diary, spy memoir, historical text, travel account, picaresque novel, and even a queer seduction narrative that reverses the usual heterosexual seduction plot. The multiple narratives make it impossible to categorize the text as the cross-dressed genres demand readers to bracket the issue of autobiographical authority and read Velazquez instead as a character whose cross-dressing highlights the idea that identity is more like a series of fictional performances than a set of genuine facts.

The narrative even connects its generic transformations with Velazquez's gender trouble. Generally, the book makes three movements framed within autobiography. The categories overlap, of course, but the text clearly shifts from battle accounts, in which Velazquez poses as Buford in the South; espionage novel, in which Velazquez more often figures as a woman in the North; and travel narrative, in which Velazquez mostly passes as a woman but ironically enjoys her transvestite reputation abroad among other expatriot Confederates. Similarly, Velazquez moves from a romantic to a realist throughout the narrative: her Joan-of-Arc fantasy for the Confederate cause soon gives way to her opportunism in female attire once she senses the South's defeat. As she explains, "The romance had been pretty well knocked out of me by the rough experience of real life; and although I was better able to appreciate the performances of Joan of Arc at their true value, somehow they did not interest me to the extent they once did" (525). By far, however, Velazquez's most important transformations occur with simple changes of clothing. Fully equipped with wire bodice, lace shirts, shoulder braces, and "pantaloons stand[ing] out to the proper number of inches," Velazquez turns herself into Buford and professes "any woman who can disguise her features can readily pass for a man" (58). Planning an espionage mission in the North, Velazquez as Buford finds it just as easy to transform into a woman, with a "calico dress, a woolen shawl, a sun bonnet, and a pair of shoes much too large for [her]" (132). Ironically, clothing is perhaps the only readable identity marker in *The Woman in Battle,* but Velazquez changes outfits so often that her identity is more fluid than fixed. Or, as Velazquez puts it, "Clothing, and particular cuts of clothing, have a great deal to do towards making us all, men or women, appear what we would like the world to take us for" (185).

It may also be that Velazquez slips in and out of so many disguises that she becomes a counterfeit of herself. Literally, the narrative plays on Velazquez's counterfeit identity by linking her to the trafficking of bogus Confederate greenbacks and bonds, which, as Elizabeth Young notes, challenges Velazquez's pro-Confederate stance and perhaps even explains General Early's reception of the text: counterfeit Confederate currency overinflated an already weak Confederate dollar, making Velazquez's transvestism "an inadvertent reminder that both the literal currency of the Confederacy and its symbolic currency—the pure Southern white woman—may be without foundation."[21] Moreover, while Velazquez counterfeits Confederate bills as a double agent in the North, the Yankee secret service enlists her to find herself, the "woman who is traveling and figuring as a Confederate agent" (516). Colonel Baker, the head of the secret service, even produces a picture of Velazquez, one that a detective on her trail had previously shown her, but it was "a photograph of a very different looking woman" (413). Nevertheless, Velazquez commences to "find herself" and ends up in Cuba, where she decides to participate in a military parade by dressing as "a young Spanish officer who had been educated in England" (566). As it turns out, however, she performs Spanish identity poorly: "my Spanish accent was none of the best," she explains, "my long non-use of the language having caused me to lose the faculty of speaking in such a manner as to do entire credit to my ancestry" (567).

After passing as Buford, a white Northern woman, a Canadian, a French Creole, an English woman, a Spanish officer, a Spanish lady, and as a Cuban woman, there is no genuine "self" for Velazquez to find. Rather, her cross-gender performances turn her into her worst enemy: "I had a not ill-founded distrust of these people," she writes of Copperheads, "who are neither one thing nor another" (431). As a Cuban Confederate, double agent in drag, Velazquez's livelihood depends on her ability to be "neither one thing nor another," and as a cross-genre narrative, the Velazquez text wavers between one thing and another as well. Transvestism thus foregrounds the impossibility of authentic identity and highlights instead the ongoing process of identity (trans)formation that gives new meaning to the idea of "self-writing": words function as symbolic clothes that construct identity in much the same way that autobiography is "a unique, self-defining mode of self-referential expression," as autobiography theorist Louis A. Renza puts it, "one that allows, then inhibits, its ostensible project of self-representation."[22] In this sense, Velazquez's identity is not so much genuine as it narrated through cultural signs that describe gender, historical documents that frame identity, and even the supposed autobiography that recounts her life—all of which can only represent Velazquez, rather than embody her, through the medium of language and are thus subject to all of the impossibilities of fiction.

Genre and the Civil War's Gender Crises.

When we recall that the South's most important first-person female Civil War narrative, Mary Chesnut's *A Diary from Dixie,* as it was originally titled, is not a diary at all per se but a fictionalized diary the author revisited after honing her skills as a fiction writer, then authenticity in autobiographical Civil War accounts becomes more of a problem than a solution.[23] Indeed, contrary to popular belief, authenticity is not even inherent in autobiography. For scholars of autobiography, life writing invites a level of storytelling that highlights the fictional quality of autobiography and the idea that language fashions identity, especially when it is the subject of a narrative.[24] Nevertheless, according to autobiography critic Peaches Henry, there are layers of truth that inform autobiographical narratives. For Henry, autobiographies consist of referential, subjective, and ideological truths. Referential truth refers to the facts and details that usually establish or challenge an autobiography's credibility in the eyes of readers. Subjective truth, however, cannot necessarily be verified by factual evidence, mainly because it describes the personal development or interiority of the autobiographical subject. Finally, Henry describes ideological truth as that "which extends beyond the life of the author but that she wishes to advocate through her life; ideological truth is the personal conviction of an author concerning an aspect of human existence such as human rights, political rights, or social justice."[25] While ideological truth aptly applies to Henry's reading of Rigoberta Menchú's contested *testimonio,* it less clearly fits *The Woman in Battle,* though it does inspire what I want to call the text's cultural truth or ideological authenticity. That is, *The Woman in Battle* is an ideologically authentic cultural text that reflects—through cross-dressing—the gender and national crises the Civil War generated.

As with most wars, the Civil War brought radical if only temporary changes to normative gender codes on both sides of the Mason-

Dixon Line as war culture disrupted the domestic space by sending men to the war front and women into the work force. Of course, some women entered the frontlines as nurses, which in itself generated gender anxiety during the Civil War, especially in the South. What is more, the war forced many upper-class southern white women to become responsible for overseeing the plantation, its crop, and the slaves. As historian Leeann Whites explains, the war made Southern white women, who generally supported secession, independent from the South's old-world gender codes, at times reversing those codes and, more often, suspending them during the war years to the point that Southern white women increasingly became an empowered class exactly at a moment when the war feminized Southern men.[26] Even after the war, Civil War scholar Nina Silber notes, gender remained a significant, albeit troubled, category of national identity that expressed the North's defeat of the South in terms of gendered power relations. "[T]hese notions of gender and sectional power," Silber notes, "presented themselves as images of weakened southern men, hostile southern women, and a disguised Jefferson Davis, all of whom were ultimately suppressed by virile northern soldiers."[27]

This type of gender trouble manifests itself in *The Woman in Battle* as a cultural truth that legitimates the text's transvestism as an authentic symptom of the Civil War. Velazquez's uniform, for instance, suggests a very specific crisis in gender and class during the war. Velazquez wears "half a dozen fine wire net shields" around her chest; over the wire shield, she wears a silk shirt, an undershirt with a shoulder brace, and a heavy belt around the waist "to make the waistbands of [her] pantaloons stand out to the proper number of inches" (58). In effect, Velazquez wears an inverted hoopskirt. As a Victorian outfit, the hoopskirt enclosed women in their own private space, historian Drew Gilpin Faust explains, but as the war progressed, the hoopskirt, and all of the class and sexual trappings, became a causality of the war.[28] Instead, women entered the public sphere to work, nurse soldiers, and when bread got too expensive, to riot in the streets. Velazquez's inverted hoopshirt, then, symbolically indicates the South's collapsing gender roles and class categories. It also mirrors the South's fluctuating power, as Elizabeth Young points out. When the South is heady with secession, Velazquez embodies the South's masculinity by donning a Confederate uniform, but as the South wanes, Velazquez's disguise becomes increasingly disheveled until she sheds her uniform and more often passes as a woman. This process of (re)feminization, Young contends, unintentionally undermines the South's attempt to affirm its masculinity after the war and even suggests that its masculinity was questionable from the start.[29]

Indeed, on the eve of secession, when Velazquez goes out on the town in drag with her first husband, she encounters "some tall talking about the war" in a Memphis, Tennessee, bar. "Every man present was full of fight, and was burning with a furious desire to meet the enemy," she explains, yet it occurs to her that the bellicose bravado is just a performance of barroom masculinity: "but it flashed upon me that some of these loud-talking, hard-drinking, and blaspheming patriots were not so valiant, after all, as they professed to be" (54). One of the less-valiant is her first husband, whom Velazquez has trouble convincing to join the Southern cause, but instead of sending him a hoopskirt and bonnet, as female Confederates in Texas did to men who stayed at home during the war, Velazquez "resolved to forsake him if he raised the sword against the South" (51).[30] Reluctantly, he joins a rebel regiment. Captain DeCaulp, Velazquez's second husband, is more clearly pro-Confederate, but the courtship between him and Velazquez only raises more gender trouble. Disguised as Buford, Velazquez reveals to DeCaulp that his female lover and fellow soldier are one in the same. "'Well, captain, don't you think your lady-love looks the least bit like your friend Harry Buford,'" Velazquez/Buford asks, kneeling in uniform next to DeCaulp's hospital bed. After some confusion, DeCaulp recognizes his fiancée disguised as a man and exclaims, "'I love you ten times more than ever for this, Loreta!'" (332). Ironically, in a heterosexual moment, when Velazquez and DeCaulp confirm their wedding plans in fact, Velazquez's cross-dressing registers a fissure in the construction of Southern masculinity and femininity, with Velazquez wearing Buford's pants and Captain DeCaulp helplessly feminized in a hospital bed.

Other Civil War narratives similarly express the war's gender crises. Scores of patriotic Southern women confessed in their diaries the desire to be men, while Sarah Rosetta Wakeman and Sarah Emma Edmonds, to name two, donned Union uniforms and headed into battle. Edmonds even published her account, *Unsexed,* as it was originally titled.[31] Meanwhile, especially at the start of the war, transvestite tales appeared in the popular press to shore up Yankee patriotism. Published in 1862, for instance, *The Lady Lieutenant* recounts the adventures of Madeline Moore, who assumes soldier's clothes to follow her lover to war and ends up fighting in the Battle of Bull Run. After a series of adventures, though, Madeline forgoes her gender transgressions to nurture and marry her wounded lover.[32] The narrative of Pauline Cushman, a Spanish-French Creole and Union spy, suffered a similar pulp fiction fate. Banking on the popularity of Cushman's exploits, Ferdinand Sarmiento took liberties with Cushman's life and adventures and published the *Life of Pauline Cushman* in 1865, but by then, Cushman had already inspired at least two other pieces of pulp fiction: *Pauline of the Potomac* (1862) and *Dora, The Heroine of the Cumberland* (1864). In both narratives, the main character claims to be Pauline, cross-dresses as a man, and, inspired by patriotism, offers her services as a spy; at the end of both texts, though, romance and marriage return the transvestite heroine to her normal gender roles.[33]

Perhaps because war disrupts the domestic space, there is an American literary tradition of first-person female accounts of cross-dressing during wartime that dates back to Deborah Sampson's participation in the Revolutionary War, and while most of the narratives reflect the gender confusion created by war, they usually end in romance to restore the nation's heterosexual domestic space. After the War of 1812, for instance, *The Female Marine* circulated throughout Boston and narrated the gender-bending adventures of Louisa Baker, later renamed Lucy Brewer, who, after being seduced by a dishonest lover and forced into prostitution, disguises herself as a man, enlists in the United States Marines, and boards the battleship *Constitution* to wage war against England. The seduction narrative becomes a romance plot, however, as Lucy Brewer ends up in a conventional marriage that resolves the gender trouble her transvestism creates.[34] Eliza Allen's 1851 account, *The Female Volunteer,* similarly narrates war's disruption of gender codes but concludes with a romance that reconstructs the domestic space. Inspired by Deborah Sampson and Lucy Brewer, Allen decides to leave her comfortable Eastport, Maine, home in drag to follow William, her working-class betrothed who volunteers to join the U.S.-Mexico War after Allen's father forbids the young lovers from marrying. As "George Mead," Allen fights in the Battle of Cerro Gordo, marches on Mexico City, and even captures the affection of two Mexican sisters as Mexico's capital falls; after the war, Eliza/George follows William to gold rush California, where after a series of hardships, they strike it rich, and Allen reveals her disguise. Allen's new wealth allows her to marry William independently of her parent's permission, but in the end, they forgive her gender transgressions and bless her marriage anyway.[35]

The body of wartime transvestite literature reminds us that cross-dressing is not necessarily a subversive act, since most of the wartime narratives eventually emphasize the sanctity of the domestic space, be it home or nation, and they often conclude with heterosexual romances that resolve the very gender crises the narratives reflect. The Velazquez text, however, is more ambivalent, making it a queer war narrative in more than one sense. As with Eliza Allen, Velazquez rejects her father's wishes and pursues an American lover; she even dresses in drag to follow him to war, as most other heroines do. Yet, there is no domesticity in *The Woman in Battle,* and the heterosexuality of Velazquez's character seems perfunctory as her marriages become increasingly insignificant and her husbands—all four of them—have a tendency to die rather quickly in the narrative, as do the three children of her first marriage. Her last husband does not even warrant a name. At the same time, Velazquez's transvestism allows her to experience proto-lesbian desire, and while not all cross-dressing performances are necessarily homosexual, Velazquez as Buford spends considerable time wooing women. Even when she is figuring as a "widow woman," she seduces a hotel chambermaid to gain access to the quarters of Northern officers (449–50), and while she is touring the Southwest, she likewise spends the night with a drunken woman, who wears "a formidable-looking knife and a six-shooter" around her waist (579). As Elizabeth Young explains, Velazquez prefers to be the seducer rather than the seduced, and she also finds the company of women repulsive, which curtails the possibility of collective female empowerment and, I would add, even suggests the narrative's internalized homophobia.[36] In this sense, *The Woman in Battle* reproduces the Civil War's gender crises as a sexual civil war divides the narrative between heterosexual conventions and homosexual desire, never quite settling on one or the other but offering contradictory messages that place the text within and against the American literary tradition of transvestite wartime narratives.

CUBA, THE CONFEDERACY, AND THEIR CROSS-DRESSED CIVIL WARS

So while the act of cross-dressing challenges the issues of authenticity surrounding *The Woman in Battle* and its authorship, the transvestism Velazquez performs in the narrative also reflects the Civil War's gender crises, offering in effect an authentic representation of how the war disrupted Victorian gender codes in the United States. Similarly, Velazquez's national cross-dressing reflects a cultural truth about the historical relationship between Cuba and the Confederacy during the war years: as they engaged in contemporaneous anticolonial struggles, Cuba and the Confederacy shared the same revolutionary sentiment of independence troubled by the issue of slavery. As early as the 1830s, black slavery in Cuba generated racial and national anxieties for whites who feared the population disparity between blacks and whites would result in a slave rebellion reminiscent of Haiti. So Cuba's landed class increasingly embraced a contradictory anticolonial break with Spain for the possibility of United States annexation as a way of protecting slave interests in Cuba. Admittedly, Cuban revolutionaries espoused conflicting ideas of independence. Some questioned the idea of replacing one empire with another and argued instead for complete national independence, while others extended the idea of independence to all Cubans—free and slave—to generate an anticolonial, abolitionist movement that gained momentum later in the century. By 1850, however, Narciso López led a failed filibuster invasion of Cuba with the hope of annexation, and many, though not all, of his recruits were Southerners. Meanwhile, in Cuba, the Club de la Habana, an organization consisting of Cuba's leading plantation owners, aristocrats, and educated elites, actively pursued annexation. As Tom Chafflin explains, "The United States seemed the best alternative to royalist Spain: an option that promised relative autonomy, a likely end to the slave trade, but immediate protection of Cuban slavery—and all without massive social upheaval."[37]

Cuba attracted competing interest in the United States as well. For the North's market economy, Cuba represented a central shipping port that connected Northern industry with Latin America and Europe, while the island represented a potential slave state or two for the South, especially after the U.S.-Mexico War of 1846–1848 upset the balance between free and slave states. Of course, Northerners and Southerners alike were wary of Cuba's potential to become another Haiti and were equally dubious of Cuba's large, free mestizo population and predominantly Catholic ruling class. Yet, along with the 1854 Kansas-Nebraska Act, which deemed slavery a states' rights issue in the United States's new territories, the Pierce administration produced the Ostend Manifesto, a public proclamation by three leading American diplomats, including incoming President Buchanan, that asserted to the U.S. State Department that "'Cuba is as necessary to the North American republic as any of its present members, and that it belongs naturally to that great family of states of which the Union is the Providential Nursery.'"[38] The "great family," however, was on the brink of family feud, and Cuba became one of the South's adopted siblings.

Hundreds of Cubans, inspired by Cuba's revolutionary anticolonial sentiment and failed filibusters, joined the Confederate ranks, and Cubans already living in the United States also had a vested interest in the war, since a majority of them settled in Southern states such as Louisiana and Florida. Most notably, José Agustín Quintero, a Harvard graduate and member of the Club de la Habana, served the Confederacy as a diplomat who, among other things, negotiated a much needed trade relationship between Mexico and the Confederacy. Meanwhile, Ambrosio José Gonzales, who introduced Quintero to the Havana Club, volunteered his services to the Confederates and ended up as a Colonel and Chief of Artillery under his old schoolmate and friend, General P. G. T. Beauregaurd. Finally, on the Florida home front, the Sanchez sisters joined the action. With their brother enlisted in the Confederate army and their father arrested as a spy, the Sanchez sisters found themselves reluctant hosts to Union soldiers who congregated at the Sanchez house along the St. John's River across from Palatka, Florida. On one occasion, Lola Sanchez overheard soldiers' plans to raid the Confederate camp near St. Augustine, so while her two sisters distracted the Union troops, Lola dashed through dense forest and swamp to relay the plans to the Confederate army. The next day, the rebels held off the Union troops and even captured their gunboat, which they promptly renamed *The Three Sisters*.[39]

Cubans saw a common cause in the Confederacy: namely, they "believed in limited government, the right of self-determination, and in defending a staunch Constitutionalist peoples against invasion by a powerful majority."[40] Thus, Velazquez's assertion that she was a "genuine Southerner" rings historically true even as it plays on the issue of authenticity, for her cross-dressing links Cuba and the Confederacy as two regions involved in related anticolonial conflicts—while the South fends off Yankee imperialism, Cuba struggles to free itself from Spanish dominion. Embattled against two imperial powers that were themselves in competition for the Americas, Cuban and Confederate independence become synonymous causes for Velazquez. At the height of the war, for instance, she vows to fight for Cuban independence in much the same way her Cuban nationalism led her to fight for the South: "I begrudged that this fair island should be the dependency of a foreign power; for I was, despite my Spanish ancestry, an American, heart and soul, and if there was anything that could have induced me to abandon the cause of the Southern Confederacy, it would have been an attempt on the part of the Cubans to liberate themselves from the Spanish yoke" (248). In effect, Velazquez's transvestism goes transnational as it turns Cuba into a Confederate state, likens the North to the Spanish empire, and places the American Civil War within other nineteenth-century colonial struggles in the Americas between imperialism and independence.

As with Southern revolutionary discourse, though, Velazquez's anticolonial independence rests on the contradiction of slavery, and while Cuban revolutionaries in the 1850s supported Cuba's slave interests, the winds of the revolution had changed dramatically by 1876, when *The Woman in Battle* was published. Cubans still espoused a break from Spain, but they increasingly advocated the abolition of slavery as well, seeing little difference between the Spanish yoke that oppressed white Cubans and the slave yoke that held blacks. Indeed, by the start of Cuba's Ten Year's War against Spain in 1868, many Cubans "spoke of a raceless nation," historian Ada Ferrer explains, "in the period that represented the nadir of American racial politics. Thus, the escalation of racial violence, the spread of spatial segregation by race, and the dismantling of political gains made during Reconstruction in the South occurred in the United States precisely as black and mulatto leaders gained increasing popularity and power in Cuba."[41] In this sense, Velazquez's performance as Buford must be read as reactionary rather than revolutionary. That is, her cross-dressing symbolizes a culturally true connection between Cuba and the Confederacy during the Civil War, but it also enacts an ideologically authentic postwar Confederate reaction to radical Reconstruction that imagines an independent Cuba disguised as an independent South to create a new Southern slavocracy that provides an alternative yet equivalent slave system to sustain the white privilege Velazquez enjoyed under Cuba's Spanish colonial rule.

Recall, Velazquez's family owns a sugar plantation in Puerto de Palmas, and Velazquez can trace her name to Cuba's Spanish Colonial history: "Both in Spain and in the Spanish dominions is the name of Velazquez well known and highly honored. Don Diego Velazquez, the conqueror and the first governor of Cuba, under whose superintendence the expedition which discovered Mexico was sent out, was one of my ancestors" (39). From colonization to plantation, Velazquez's name—and its related implication of her pure historical lineage—links her to a legacy of slavery in the Americas that finds a home in her Confederate patriotism. "I am a Cuban, and am a true Southern sympathizer," she writes (502). So she buys a slave named Bob, who legitimates Buford's white Southern masculinity, harkens back to Velazquez's Spanish colonial heritage, and connects them both to an ideology of whiteness propped up by black slave labor at a time when slavery in the United States and Cuba is on the decline. In fact, Velazquez's emphasis on her Old World ancestry marks her distance from Cuba's revolutionary politics, its war against Spanish dominion, and its emerging abolitionist sentiment and positions her instead within postwar myths of the Old South, where the hacienda converges onto the big house; Spanish *criollismo* becomes Southern whiteness; and Cuban revolutionary discourse turns into Southern reactionary rhetoric to radical Reconstruction.

Thus, while the defeat of the South brings an end to Velazquez's performance as Buford, it does not put an end to the narrative. Rather, when Velazquez returns to the United States after a trip to Europe, she finds the South "in the hands of ignorant Negroes" and "white 'carpet-baggers'" (535), so she proposes a colonization trip to Venezuela with the hopes of discovering a new South, one that will remove Cuban whiteness and Southern slavery to Latin America as an alternative to Yankee America. She leads a group of Southern exiles to Venezuela, where, much to their chagrin, they encounter free blacks.[42] As Velazquez puts it, "it would have been just as well to have remained at home and fought the battle for supremacy with the free Negroes and carpet-baggers on familiar ground" (535). She laments that they "were beset by negroes" in Georgetown, Guyana, too (553), while Port Spain, off of Trinidad, proves equally displeasing to Velazquez: "It was a very dingy-looking settlement, with a very ragged and dirty native population. There were a few Englishmen, but the majority of the people were negroes or half-breeds, whose habitations were disgustingly dirty and squalid" (558). Finally, when the ship stops at Puerto Rico, Velazquez simply refuses to go ashore, "not liking the looks of the place" (565).

Ironically, the colonization expedition ends where Velazquez began—Cuba. As scores of other ex-Confederates discovered, though,

Velazquez has little success with finding a potentially new Southern republic in Cuba. In fact, contrary to her earlier dreams of liberating Cuba from Spain, Velazquez aligns herself with the occupying Spanish army and parades as a Spanish officer from England in another transvestite performance that marks her return to the white privilege of her Spanish ancestry but also highlights the instability of Velazquez's Spanish identity and Spain's waning power in Cuba: Velazquez can no longer speak Spanish fluently (567). Faced with radical Reconstruction in the South and abolitionist revolution in Cuba, Velazquez turns to the U.S. frontier, traversing Utah, Nevada, California, Arizona, and New Mexico, and the narrative ends with Velazquez on the road back to the South via Texas, where she claims her father once owned a land grant but lost it with Texas's 1845 annexation.[43] Her homelessness aptly reflects the fluidity of her identity as her transnational transvestism keeps Velazquez on the move between national boundaries and gender categories to the point that her only authenticity is as a symbolic, historical embodiment of a pro-slavery Cuban Confederate with no place in the Americas. After all, Cuba never found its way into the United States as a state; ex-Confederates never quite settled colonies in Latin America; and Velazquez's identity never quite materializes beyond the publication of *The Woman in Battle.*

Velazquez's cross-dressing thus works as a complex trope that defies the search for her real identity but nonetheless makes her narrative an authentic representation of the Civil War's gender crises and the historical connection between Cuba and the Confederacy; in this sense, the book's significance shifts from a suspicious autobiography to a cultural narrative that accurately represents the historical instabilities of the war years. Indeed, the legacy of slavery that troubles the Velazquez text also connects it to another nineteenth-century book embroiled in the question of authenticity, Hannah Crafts's *The Bondswoman's Narrative.* According to literary scholar Henry Louis Gates Jr., the Crafts narrative is perhaps the first autobiographical novel written by a fugitive slave, and as Gates's attempt to verify the book and the identity of its author makes clear, there is a mania if not an industry for authenticating nineteenth-century narratives, especially those by marginal subjects. Yet, cross-dressing vexes Gates's attempt to find the "real" Hannah Crafts and confirm her authorship, let alone her existence. The fugitive slave passes and escapes into the oblivion of whiteness, going "incognegro," Gates speculates, before he could authenticate her.[44] Just as Hannah Crafts dresses as a white man in her narrative to elude slavery, Velazquez dresses as a white man to uphold it, and even as their respective transvestism haunts the authenticity of both texts and their authors, their cross-dressing also reflects the arbitrary distinctions maintaining the embattled history of slavery in the Americas. While Velazquez's gendered and national transvestism collapses the distinctions between masculinity and femininity, North and South, and Cuba and the Confederacy, Crafts's racial cross-dressing reveals Velazquez's sense of whiteness as an equally arbitrary identity marker more fictional than natural. In the end, then, perhaps the most important cultural truth *The Woman in Battle* and its ostensible author offer is that gender, race, and nation are simple matters of clothing that, when cross-dressed, challenge the ideologies of authenticity that determine the battle lines between masculinity and femininity, black and white, North and South, autobiography and fiction, and ultimately, self and Other.

NOTES

1. In 1864, Early sent Mary and Molly Bell to prison in Richmond after a captain accused them of "demoralizing his men." The Bell sisters had been passing for two years among the troops as Tom Parker and Bob Martin before Early sent them packing to prison still wearing their Confederate uniforms. See Elizabeth D. Leonard, *All the Daring of the Soldier: Women of the Civil War Armies* (New York: W. W. Norton, 1999), 243–45.

2. Jubal Early to W. H. Slemons, May 22, 1878, in Tucker Family Papers (no. 2605), Southern Historical Collection, Wilson Library, University of North Carolina, Chapel Hill. Letter used by permission. Further citations from the letter will be given parenthetically as Early to Slemons.

3. Loreta Janeta Velazquez, *The Woman in Battle* (Richmond, Va: Dustin, Gilman & Co., 1876), 130. Further citations from the book will be given parenthetically. See Drew Gilpin Faust, *Mothers of Invention: Women of the Slaveholding South in the American Civil War* (Chapel Hill: University of North Carolina Press, 1996), for a list of similar transvestite expressions found in the diaries of Southern women. "Nearly every female Confederate diarist at some point expressed the desire to be a man," Faust explains (231).

4. According to DeAnne Blanton and Lauren M. Cook, *They Fought Like Demons: Women Soldiers in the American Civil War* (Baton Rouge: Louisiana State University Press, 2002), Louisa Hoffman, Sarah Emma Edmonds (aka Frank Thompson), and a woman described as "Charlie" fought for the North in drag at the Battle of Bull Run (8–9); Francis Louisa Clayton joined the Union ranks at Fort Donelson (10); and the Federal forces at Shiloh included four women in uniform (10).

5. *Daily Richmond Enquirer,* Thursday, July 2, 1863; *Daily Richmond Enquirer,* Saturday, July

11, 1863; *Daily Richmond Enquirer,* Wednesday, July 15, 1863; *Daily Richmond Examiner,* Thursday, July 2, 1863; *Daily Richmond Examiner,* Saturday, July 11, 1863; *Daily Richmond Examiner,* Thursday, July 16, 1863; *Daily Richmond Examiner,* September 16, 1863.

6. Richard Hall, "Loreta Janeta Velazquez: Civil War Soldier and Spy," in *Cubans in the Confederacy: José Agustín Quintero, Ambrosio José Gonzales, and Loreta Janeta Velazquez,* ed. Phillip Thomas Tucker (Jefferson, N. C.: McFarland & Co., 2002), 234.

7. Richard Hall, *Patriots in Disguise: Women Warriors of the Civil War* (New York: Paragon House, 1993), 208–9.

8. In *Women Who Spied for the Blue and Gray* (Philadelphia: Dorrance & Co., 1972), Oscar A. Kinchen recounts Velazquez's exploits, relying mainly on *The Woman in Battle,* yet Kinchen writes, "She was married at an early age to a man named *Rouch* and was living in St. James parish in Louisiana at the outbreak of war between the North and South" (146, emphasis added). Velazquez never gives the surname of her first husband, William, and the name "Rouch" never appears in *The Woman in Battle.* Unfortunately, Kinchen does not provide the source for the Rouch reference, which rings similar to the "Roche" named in the Richmond reports and the "Rosche" in Thomas DeCaulp's military file.

9. Stewart Sifakis, *Who Was Who in the Civil War,* vol. 2 (New York: Facts on File, 1988), 290; Sylvia Hoffert, "Madame Loretta [sic] Velazquez: Heroine or Hoaxer?," *Civil War Times Illustrated* 17, no. 3 (1978): 31; Francis Simkins Butler and James Welch Patton, *The Women in the Confederacy* (Richmond: Garret and Massie, 1936), 81; Mary Elizabeth Massey, *Women in the Civil War* (Lincoln: University of Nebraska Press, 1994), 82; Elizabeth Leonard, *All the Daring of the Solider,* 260; Richard Hall, *Patriots in Disguise;* Kathleen De Grave, *Swindler, Spy, Rebel: The Confidence Woman in Nineteenth-Century America* (Columbia: University of Missouri Press, 1995); Elizabeth Young, *Disarming the Nation: Women's Writing and the American Civil War* (Chicago: University of Chicago Press, 1999).

10. Mary A. Livermore, *My Story of the War* (Hartford, Conn.: A. D. Worthington & Co., 1888), 119–20; Blanton and Cook, *They Fought Like Demons.*

11. Hall, "Loreta Janeta Velazquez": 230.

12. Lieutenant Colonel Fremantle, *Three Months in the Southern States, April–June 1863* (London: William Blackwood and Sons, 1863), 175; Fitzgerald Ross, *A Visit to the Cities and Camps of the Confederate States* (London: William Blackwood and Sons, 1865), 132; Ella Lonn, *Foreigners in the Confederacy* (Chapel Hill: University of North Carolina Press, 2002), 381–82.

13. Leonard, *All the Daring of the Solider,* 257.

14. Janet E. Kaufman, "'Under the Petticoat Flag': Women Soldiers in the Confederate Army," *Southern Studies* 23 (1984): 373. For news reports on "Laura J. Williams," see Felix Gregory De Fontaine, *Marginalia; or, Gleanings from an Army Notebook* (Columbia: De Fontaine & Co., 1864), 65–66.

15. James Longstreet to Emily Park, June 18, 1888, in the James Longstreet Papers, Rare Book, Manuscript, and Special Collections Library, Duke University, Durham, North Carolina. Letter used by permission. Bromfield L. Ridley, *Battles and Sketches of the Army of Tennessee* (Mexico, Mo.: Missouri Printing & Publishing Co., 1906), 495; Stewart Sifakis, *Who Was Who in the Civil War,* vol. 2, 290; *American National Biography,* vol. 22, ed. John A. Garraty and Mark C. Carnes (New York: Oxford University Press, 1999), 317–19; *Historical Times Illustrated Encyclopedia of the Civil War,* ed. Patricia L. Faust (New York: Harper & Row, 1986), 779–80; Mark Mayo Boatner III, *The Civil War Dictionary,* rev. ed. (New York: David McKay Co., 1988), 869; *Encyclopedia of the American Civil War,* vol. 4, ed. David S. Heidler and Jeanne T. Heidler (Santa Barbara: ABC-CLIO, 2000), 2018–19.

16. Pennsylvania Broadside 1876 "The Woman in Battle" in the Rare Book, Manuscript, and Special Collections Library, Duke University. Used by permission.

17. J. F. Hammond is not listed in William B. Atkinson, ed., *The Physicians and Surgeons of the United States* (Philadelphia: Charles Robson, 1878) or Joseph Jones, "Roster of the Medical Officers of the Army of Tennessee," *Southern Historical Society Papers* 22, no. 3 (Jan.–Dec. 1894): 165–280. The mobility of medical personnel during the war may explain the lack of documentation on Hammond. For more on Captain G. W. Alexander, his role at Castle Thunder, and his interaction with Velazquez, see Sandra V. Parker, *Richmond's Civil War Prisons* (Lynchburg: H. E. Howard, 1990), 18, 26–27; find General George Anderson in the

Encyclopedia of the American Civil War, vol. 1, 43; see Arthur W. Bergeron Jr., *Guide to Louisiana Confederate Military Units, 1861–1865* (Baton Rouge: Louisiana State University Press, 1989), 124, for reference to Major John Newman and the Twenty-first Regiment. Newman also appears in *Records of Louisiana Confederate Soldiers and Louisiana Confederate Commands,* vol. 3, pt. 1B (New Orleans: Louisiana Military Records, 1920), 1274, but the enlistment records hold no listing of Harry T. Buford (or near variations of the name).

18. *Southern Historical Society Papers* 2, no. 4 (October 1876): 208.

19. Hall, "Loreta Janeta Velazquez": 237.

20. Judith Butler, *Gender Trouble: Feminism and the Subversion of Gender* (New York: Routledge, 1999), 23, xxiii.

21. Elizabeth Young, *Disarming the Nation,* 179.

22. Louis A. Renza, "The Veto of the Imagination: A Theory of Autobiography," in *Autobiography: Essays Theoretical and Critical,* ed. James Olney (Princeton: Princeton University Press, 1980), 295.

23. See C. Vann Woodward, ed., *Mary Chesnut's Civil War* (New York: Quality Paperback Book Club, 1995).

24. As autobiography scholar Thomas G. Couser puts it in *Altered Egos: Authority in American Autobiography* (Oxford: Oxford University Press, 1989), "If the self is inherently a function— a fiction of language, then autobiography is double so; after all, it is a literary capitalization of the 'I.' Thus, the trend in recent autobiography studies has been to erode the distinction between the self and its textual embodiment.... Autobiography, then, is not seen as *produced by* a preexistent self but as *producing* a provisional and contingent one. Indeed, that self is seen as bound and (pre)determined by the constraints of the linguistic resources and narrative tropes available to the author" (18–19).

25. Peaches Henry, "*I, Rigoberta Menchú* and the Question of Truth-Value in Autobiography," *A/B* 16, no. 1 (2001): 11.

26. Leeann Whites, "The Civil War as a Crisis in Gender," in *Divided Houses: Gender and the Civil War,* ed., Catherine Clinton and Nina Silber (New York: Oxford University Press, 1992), 3–21.

27. *The Romance of Reunion: Northerners and the South, 1865–1900* (Chapel Hill: University of North Carolina Press, 1993), 303. Nina Silber quotes the May 15, 1864 *New York Times* dispatch reporting Davis's capture: "The captors report that [Jefferson Davis] hastily put on one of Mrs. Davis' dresses and started for the woods, closely pursued by our men, who at first thought him a woman, but seeing his boots while running suspected his sex at once. The race was a short one, and the rebel President was soon brought to bay.... He expressed great indignation at the energy with which he was pursued, saying that he had believed our Government more magnanimous than to hunt down woman and children" (29). Suffice it to say that the event symbolically feminized the South and generated discourses of masculine conquest in the North.

28. Faust, *Mothers of Invention,* 223.

29. Elizabeth Young, "Counterfeit Confederate: The Case of the Cross-Dressed Civil War Soldier," in *Passing and the Fictions of Identity,* ed., Elaine K. Ginsberg (Durham: Duke University Press, 1996), 171, 181.

30. For Texas women shaming men into the war, see Faust, *Mothers of Invention,* 181.

31. Sarah Emma Edmonds, *Memoirs of a Soldier, Nurse, and Spy: A Woman's Adventures in the Union Army,* ed., Elizabeth D. Leonard (DeKalb: Northern Illinois University Press, 1999). Even though extratextual material confirms Edmonds's experiences, her narrative conceals most of her gender transgressions. I would also suggest that Edmonds's transvestite performances as a black slave, Irish peddler, and even a Confederate soldier register race, class, and national crises that preoccupied the North during the war. Indeed, the fluidity of identity in Edmonds's memoir challenges the text's claim to authenticity to the point that Edmonds eventually denies her identity. As she explained in a pension application, "There is much mean deception necessarily practiced by a spy that I much prefer every one should believe that I never was beyond the enemy's lines rather than fasten upon me by oath a thing that I despise so much" (Leonard, "Introduction," xxii). For Sarah Rosetta Wakeman's letters, see Lauren Burgess Cook, *An Uncommon Soldier: The Civil War Letters of Sarah Rosetta Wakeman, Alias Private*

Lyons Wakeman, 153rd Regiment, New York State Volunteers (New York: Oxford University Press, 1994).

32. Madeline Moore, *The Lady Lieutenant* (Philadelphia: Barclay & Co., 1863). According to Estelle C. Jelinek, *The Lady Lieutenant* is a plagiarized version of *The Female Officer,* an 1851 narrative recounting Madeline Moore's transvestite adventures in a filibuster campaign against Cuba ("Disguise Autobiographies: Women Masquerading as Men," *Women's Studies International Forum* 10, no. 1 [1987]: 55–56). Long before the Velazquez text, Cuba was cross-dressing as the South in the American imagination and troubling the notion of authenticity in the process.

Lucy Holcombe Pickens's 1854 narrative, *The Free Flag of Cuba,* might thus be seen as a genteel Southern literary response to the pulp fiction about transvestite filibusters. In Pickens's Southern novel, Mabel Royal, a Yankee visiting the South, exclaims, "I regret the growing strong-mindedness of my sex" (108). Following its traditional gender codes, the novel also imagines a happy union between North and South in their interest to help Cuba gain its independence; heroizes the male participants in Narciso López's failed invasion of Cuba; and views American and Cuban filibusters as agents of independence waging a "lost cause" battle against the forces of Spanish tyranny and United States governmental indifference. See Lucy Holcombe Pickens, *The Free Flag of Cuba: The Lost Novel of Lucy Holcombe Pickens, ed. Orville Vernon Burton and Georganne B. Burton* (Baton Rouge: Louisiana State University Press, 2002).

33. Ferdinand L. Sarmiento, *Life of Pauline Cushman* (Philadelphia: J. E. Potter, 1865); [C. W. Alexander], *Pauline of the Potomac, or General McClellan's Spy* (Philadelphia: Barclay & Co., 1862); [C. W. Alexander], *Dora, The Heroine of the Cumberland; or, The American Amazon* (Philadelphia: Barclay & Co., 1864). Another "Pauline" text, *Maud of the Mississippi* (Philadelphia: C. W. Alexander & Co., 1864), does not end in a romance, but its transvestite story nevertheless offers an intertextual narrative that reflects the problem of authenticity and authorship: a hack assumed C. W. Alexander's name and penned *Maud* to capitalize on Pauline's popularity.

34. Daniel A. Cohen, *The Female Marine and Related Works: Narratives of Cross-Dressing and Urban Vice in America's Early Republic* (Amherst: University of Massachusetts Press, 1997).

35. Eliza Allen, *The Female Volunteer* (Ohio: H. M. Rulison, 1851). Two other ostensible autobiographical accounts are worth mentioning because, even though they do not end with marriage, they still warn against war's threat to the national domestic space. In *The Female Warrior* (New York: E. E. & O. Barclay, 1843), Leonora Siddons loses her father in the Texas revolution, so she dismisses her black servant, dresses in a soldier's uniform, and joins General Houston's forces. She falls captive to Mexicans, rebuffs Santa Anna's sexual advances, and then returns to her native state, Alabama, via Cuba, lamenting her gender rebellion. As an ideologically authentic text, Siddons's narrative warns against the domestic dangers, especially to the South, of annexing Texas—the new territory will dismantle the South's patriarchal domestic space, threaten the stability of slavery, and even create an unseemly alliance between Mexico and the South. Sophia Delaplain's *Thrilling and Exciting Account* (Charleston: E. E. Barclay, 1851) narrated similar anti-expansionist anxieties. Rebelling against her father's class pretensions, Sophia dresses as a working-class boy to elope with her lower-class lover, Mortimer Bowers, but on their way to California, freebooters heading for Cuba overtake the ship in a failed filibuster that leaves Sophia and Mortimer prisoners of Cuban authorities, who torture them both and dismember Mortimer before Sophia dresses as a Cuban servant and escapes to the United States, where she regrets rejecting her father's domestic authority.

36. Young, "Confederate Counterfeit," 195–97.

37. Tom Chafflin, *Fatal Glory: Narciso López and the First Clandestine U.S. War against Cuba* (Charlottesville: University of Virginia Press, 1996), 12.

38. David M. Potter, *The Impending Crisis: 1848–1861* (New York: Harper & Row, 1976), 190.

39. Phillip Thomas Tucker, "Introduction," in *Cubans in the Confederacy,* 1–8; Ella Lonn, *Foreigners in the Confederacy,* 378–79.

40. Darryl E. Brock, "José Agustín Quintero: Cuban Patriot in Confederate Diplomatic Service," in *Cubans in the Confederacy,* 44.

41. Ada Ferrer, *Insurgent Cuba: Race, Nation, and Revolution, 1868–1898* (Chapel Hill: University of North Carolina Press, 1999), 4.

42. On January 5, 1867, the New Orleans *Picayune* reported that "Mrs. Mary DeCaulp," who had fought in the Civil War as "Lieutenant Bufort" [sic], joined the expedition to Venezuela as a Southern agent. As with other references to Lieutenant Buford prior to the publication of *The Woman in Battle,* the *Picayune* account does not mention Velazquez's name, though some scholars believe "Mrs. Mary DeCaulp" is Velazquez. See Massey, *Women in the Civil War,* 310; Hall, "Loreta Janeta Velazquez," 235; and Alfred Jackson Hanna and Kathryn Abbey Hanna, *Confederate Exiles in Venezuela* (Tuscaloosa, Ala.: Confederate Publishing Co., 1960), 136.

43. No land title under the name Velazquez appears in Virginia Taylor, *Index to Spanish and Mexican Land Grants* (General Land Office: [Texas], 1976) or Thomas Lloyd Miller, *Bounty and Donation Land Grants of Texas, 1835–1888* (Austin: University of Texas Press, 1967).

44. Hannah Crafts, *The Bondswoman's Narrative,* ed. Henry Louis Gates (New York: Warner Books, 2002); Henry Louis Gates, "Introduction: The Search for a Female Fugitive Slave," *The Bondswoman's Narrative,* lviii.

GLOSSARY

The following list of people, places, and events appear with either some frequency or prominence in *The Woman in Battle.* No attempt has been made to corroborate their reference in the text with documentary evidence beyond the encyclopedic glosses below.

ARMSTRONG, FRANK

Born in Indian Territory in 1835, Armstrong earned a commission as a second lieutenant in the United States Army and was deployed to Utah in 1858 to check the Mormon rebellion. During the Civil War, he participated in the Battle of Bull Run (First Manassas) for the Union but then joined the Confederacy in August 1861. He made brigadier general and continued with the Confederacy until his capture during Wilson's Raid in Selma, Alabama, on April 2, 1865. After the war he became a United States Indian inspector and died on September 8, 1909.

ATLANTA, GEORGIA

Four railroads converged in Atlanta, making it a central hub for Confederate troops, munitions, commerce, and industry. The city was reluctant to secede, but after Lincoln's election, Atlantans burned the new president in effigy, joined the Confederacy, and became one of the South's most strategic cities. Its factories produced consumer goods, wartime supplies, arsenal, and, as the site of the Quartermaster's Depot, Atlanta provided most of the Confederate army's clothing. As the war lingered, Atlanta became a haven for petty criminals and counterfeiters; food became scarce for the twenty-two thousand inhabitants; and in March 1863, rebel war widows looted stores for bacon, flour, and other goods. After an extensive campaign, Atlanta surrendered to Union forces on September 2, 1864, and General Sherman destroyed the city's railroads and factories before leaving Atlanta ablaze.

BAKER, LA FAYETTE CURRY

Born in Stafford, New York, in 1826, Baker moved to New York at the outbreak of the Civil War and offered his services to the Union as a spy. He was sent to Richmond, where he convinced Confederate officials that he would spy on the Federal government; he soon became a leading Union detective used to track Confederate double agents, counterfeiters, conspirators, and insurrection plots along the U.S.-Canada border. He commanded the detectives charged with arresting John Wilkes Booth and his pro-Confederate conspirators, who hatched their assassination plot in Mary Surratt's Washington, D.C., boarding house. By then, allegations that General Baker accepted bribes when he was provost marshal of the War Department challenged his credibility. After President Andrew Johnson fired Baker, he published his memoirs and died the following year, July 3, 1868.

BALL'S BLUFF, VIRGINIA

The Battle of Ball's Bluff (also known as the Battle of Leesburg) was fought on October 12, 1861, near Leesburg, Virginia, thirty-five miles up the Potomac River from Washington, D.C. Under General George McClellan's orders, General Charles Stone led Federal troops across the Potomac to engage the Confederate forces in Leesburg; a small Federal force occupied Leesburg, while Colonel Edward Baker, an inexperienced soldier, commanded the 1,640 men who remained near the bank of the Potomac at the bottom of the hundred-foot Ball's Bluff. Confederates under Colonel Nathan "Shanks" Evans arrived and commenced firing at the open Federal forces. Baker perished in the melee, while Union soldiers died trying to escape onto overcrowded riverboats. The Yankee rout, along with the Baker's death, initiated the congressional Joint Committee on the Conduct of the War, which faulted General Stone for the casualties.

BEAUREGARD, PIERRE GUSTAVE TOUTANT

Born at Contreras Plantation, just south of New Orleans, on May 28, 1818, General Beauregard participated in the Civil War's most significant battles and clashed with most of the Confederacy's leadership. A French Creole, Beauregard attended the French School of New York City before attending West Point, where he graduated second in the class of 1838. The U.S.-Mexico War initiated his first clashes with his military superiors—he believed they did not adequately recognize his service. After holding the position of West Point's superintendent, he resigned from the Federal army in January 1861, joined the Confederacy, and was placed in command of South Carolina's forces. There, Beauregard fired the first official shots of the Civil War: on April 12, 1861, he shelled Federal forces—including his former West Point instructor—at Fort Sumter. The attack brought him accolades, but he fell out of favor with Confederate leaders after the Battle of Shiloh, where he had pushed Grant's troops back to the Tennessee River, but instead of pursuing his advantage, Beauregard ordered a withdrawal, a decision that cost him the battle. Jefferson Davis tried to keep Beauregard out of the field, but by 1864, the Creole general had defeated Benjamin Butler's forces at Drewy's Bluff and assisted Lee on several battlefronts before he was mustered out to Georgia, where he was again barred from taking the field and oversaw the evacuation of Southern troops. After the war, he returned to New Orleans, was pardoned by President Johnson, and, after considering military service in Brazil, Egypt, and Spain, turned to Southern politics; later, he took an active interest in narratives about the Civil War, especially Confederate accounts about the Battle of Shiloh. He died on February 21, 1893.

BEE, BARNARD E.

Born in South Carolina in 1824, General Bee spent his youth in Texas and attended West Point, where he graduated with the class of 1845 before serving in the U.S.-Mexico War. Bee returned to Texas with misgivings about secession, but, when Texas seceded, he joined the Confederacy as a major. He was promoted to brigadier general and fought at First Manassas, where he is best remembered for rallying his troops by pointing out Jackson's "stone wall" stance. The name stuck with Stonewall Jackson; however, shortly after Bee issued his rallying cry, he was fatally wounded.

BLACKBURN'S FORD

On the eve of the Battle of Bull Run, Federal and Confederate forces skirmished at Blackburn's Ford—a shallow crossing point in Bull Run—in a prelude to the Confederacy's victory at Bull Run. Under orders from General Irvin McDowell, Daniel Tyler led a division of Union troops toward the Bull Run crossing, where he met James Longstreet's Confederate forces. On July 18, 1861, they engaged in a brief, intense exchange that left eighty-three Union troops killed or wounded and forced Tyler to retreat to Centerville.

BULL RUN, FIRST BATTLE OF (FIRST MANASSAS)

Fought on July 21, 1861, at Manassas Junction, Virginia, the First Battle of Bull Run changed how Northern and Southern combatants and civilians viewed the war. Before Bull Run, most of the country figured the war would last no longer than ninety days; this over-confidence might explain why President Lincoln sent General Irvin McDowell and a thirty-five-thousand-man army of ill-prepared volunteers to meet thirty-three thousand Confederate troops under Joseph E. Johnston and P. G. T. Beauregard on the banks of Bull Run. The battle initiated everyone into the Civil War. With Yankee civilians and politicians picnicking on the hillside, the opposing armies exchanged command of the field. Union forces outflanked the rebel troops several times, but the Confederates maintained a constant stream of reinforcements until the fighting converged onto Henry Hill, about six miles north of Manassas Junction. There, McDowell tried to flank the Confederates again, when the last rebel support reached the battlefield. After ten hours of fighting, McDowell called for a Federal retreat, and everyone fell into disarray: Union troops scattered away from bullets and shells and soon found the line of retreat at Cub Run bridge blocked; the Confederate army hastened their chase in similar disorder; and the civilians ran for their lives. The battle's nearly nine hundred casualties shocked the country into the realization that it was in for a long, bloody civil war.

BUTLER, BENJAMIN FRANKLIN

Born in New Hampshire in 1818, General Butler had a vexed military career. When South Carolina seceded, Butler led the Eighth Massachusetts Militia, but Lincoln soon relieved Butler of his command after he led an ill-fated invasion of Richmond; he attacked Confederates at Drewy's Bluff in 1864 and was repulsed all the way back to Bermuda Hundred; and later that year he led another failed attack on Fort Fisher, off the shores of Wilmington, North Carolina. He is best remembered for his uncompromising occupation of New Orleans, where he took command on May 1, 1862, and tried to force the largely pro-Confederate population of 168,000 to accept the Federal government. He hanged William Mumford for lowering a U.S. flag and ordered civil servants and clergymen to make oaths of allegiance to the Union. His greatest battle was against the women of New Orleans, who received the occupying Federal soldiers by insulting them, spitting on them, and even emptying their chamber pots on them from second-story windows. Butler responded on May 15, 1862, by issuing General Order No. 28, which declared that any woman who insulted Union officers or soldiers would be treated as a prostitute and charged accordingly. While the order checked the women's behavior, it outraged Northerners and Southerners alike and even drew criticism from the British press. Lincoln relieved Butler of his New Orleans command in 1862 and released him from duty in 1865. After the war, he continued his political career until 1884; then he returned to his legal practice, penned his memoirs in 1891, and died two years later in Washington, D.C.

CAMP CHASE

Located four miles west of Columbus, Ohio, Camp Chase served as a Federal instructional camp, a holding site for paroled Union soldiers returning to service, and a release center for soldiers whose enlistment had expired. The camp began to detain Confederate captives in 1861 and raised stockades a year later to hold the growing number of prisoners. Housing roughly eight thousand prisoners and four thousand Federal soldiers, the 165-acre area strained under its poor drainage system, sanitation problems, and the spread of typhoid and smallpox. Conditions for rebel captives became worse in 1864, when Federals withheld food, clothing, and blankets. An estimated twenty-five thousand Confederates passed though Camp Chase, and at the end of the war the camp held nine thousand prisoners, the last of which were released in July 1865.

CASTLE THUNDER PRISON

In 1862 the Confederate government converted Gleanor's Tobacco Factory, Palmer's Factory, and Whitlock's Warehouse, which were all located on the same city block, into holding cells surrounded by a high fence and watchtowers. Castle Thunder thus emerged in Richmond, Virginia, and served to detain a variety of wartime prisoners. It held Confederate deserters, suspect civilians, political prisoners, and Federal captives; Whitlock's Warehouse detained blacks and women who were held under charges of espionage, Union sympathies, or dressing as men to join the Confederate army. Captain George W. Alexander commanded the prison with an iron fist, and in 1863 the Confederate Congress investigated Alexander's run of the prison, as well as charges that he traded in Federal money and accepted bribes from prisoners. He was exonerated of the charges but lost his command of the Castle, which, like other Civil War prisons, was overcrowded, filthy, and infested with smallpox. Prisoners were evacuated when Union forces invaded Richmond, and while the compound survived the assault, it burned down in 1879.

CHATTANOOGA, TENNESSEE

Nestled along the Tennessee River in a valley of the southern Appalachian Mountains, Chattanooga was strategically important for both armies. What it lacked in river transportation, it made up in train access, as four railroad lines connected the small city to the South's central positions. Surrounded by large mineral deposits, Chattanooga housed two major ironworks and was a prosperous, industrial town on the eve of the war, which may explain why the city's roughly five thousand residents were divided on the issue of secession. The city's strategic importance, however, stabilized its prosperity during the war, so when Tennessee seceded, Chattanooga became a hub, full of barracks, hospitals, and warehouses, which swelled the city's population to twenty-five thousand. The city lasted as a rebel center until the summer of 1863, when Federal forces under General William S. Rosencrans pushed Braxton Bragg's army out of Tennessee; after Grant broke the Confederacy's siege of the town in November, Chattanooga remained under Union control until the end of the war.

Columbia, South Carolina

As the capital of the first state to secede, Columbia was more symbolically than strategically significant for both armies. Located in the center of South Carolina and overlooking the Congaree River, Columbia commanded a large cotton market and was a hotbed of secession. The state convention first convened in Columbia to declare its intention to secede, but an outbreak of smallpox moved the meeting to Charleston. Nevertheless, the 8,052 residents of the capital celebrated secession with bonfires, parades, and thrashing an abolitionist carriage maker. The city opened a Confederate printing operation that employed women to print currency and bonds; a military hospital opened in 1862; and local businesses provided supplies and munitions. As the war progressed, Columbia's population boomed to twenty-five thousand, which strained the city's resources and left many of its inhabitants in relief lines. In February 1865 Sherman's Union troops invaded the city, forcing Wade Hampton's Confederate cavalry to evacuate the capital. Cotton warehouses were emptied, but much of the cotton remained in the streets, where it caught fire—or was set by Sherman's men—and ignited powder in the railroad depot. Fires burned for several days, and after destroying the city's railroads, bridges, and munitions, the Union army marched out of Columbia.

Copperheads

Coined by Republican politicians, "Copperhead" pejoratively described conservative Democratic critics of the Lincoln administration and the war. In a campaign to win public support for the war, Republican pundits likened dissenting Democrats to copperhead snakes and suggested that their opposition to the war marked their disloyalty to the Federal government. Republicans even claimed Copperheads were organized into secret societies based in Cincinnati, St. Louis, and Indianapolis, where they plotted to attack the Union. The public relations campaign in part explains the success of the Republican Party in the 1864 elections, while Democratic dissent generally declined as the war neared its end, especially after the South's defeat appeared imminent.

CORINTH, MISSISSIPPI

Intersected by two railroad lines, Corinth served as a depot for transferring and transporting Confederate troops across the South, and its proximity to key ports along the Mississippi also made it a contested logistical site for both armies. In 1862 Confederate forces under P. G. T. Beauregard retreated twenty-two miles south to Corinth after their defeat at the Battle of Shiloh; Union troops followed, but as they arrived on May 30, 1862, to occupy the city, the Confederate army escaped south by railroad. Skirmishes continued around Corinth—most notably in October 1862, when Generals Earl Van Dorn and Sterling Price attempted to retake the city for the Confederacy—but Corinth remained in Federal hands until the end of the war.

FISK, JAMES

Born in April 1834 in Pownal, Vermont, Fisk became an infamously popular financial speculator who made a fortune after the Civil War in shady stock deals and financial scams, but his career as a double-dealing opportunist began in the 1860s, when he set up shop in Willard's Hotel in Washington, D.C., and secured government textile orders for his Boston company, Jordon Marsh, while smuggling Confederate cotton out of the South for Marsh's northern mills. He also profited from selling Confederate bonds in the London market through a New York agent. After the war he continued with a variety of stock and investment cons until he was shot on January 6, 1872, and died the next day.

Forrest's Raids

From July 1862 through November 1864, Confederate General Nathan Bedford Forrest led cavalry raids throughout Tennessee that harassed Union fronts, broke their supply lines, and inflicted casualties to disrupt the Federal army's advance in the South. The most significant raids occurred against a Union garrison in Murfreesboro in July 1862; against Union lines in western Tennessee between December 1862 and January 1863; and against a Federal depot and storage facility at Johnsonville in November 1864. Forrest's quick raids and hard-fought skirmishes harried Union commanders and raised Confederate spirits, even after Forrest gave up his command in May 1865.

Fort Donelson, Battle of

Ensconced on the banks of the Cumberland River just north of Dover, Tennessee, Fort Donelson and its nearby counterpart along the Tennessee River, Fort Henry, were essential points in the western war theater. The Confederacy commanded both forts until Federal forces seized them in a series of engagements that lasted from February 3 to 16, 1862. Fort Henry fell quickly under the bombardment of navy gunboats, but Fort Donelson was a tougher battle for Union troops, mainly because Confederate forces silenced navy gunboats. Grant's men initially carried the field, but when he left his headquarters, the rebels found an opportunity to break from the fort; they mounted an attack to clear a retreat path, but after pushing Union troops back, they attempted an outright defeat and ended up being forced back into the fort once Grant and reinforcements arrived. While Confederate Generals Pillow and Floyd absconded across the Cumberland, they left General Buckner with Grant's demand for unconditional surrender. The loss of Fort Donelson produced fifteen thousand Confederate prisoners, led directly to the fall of Nashville, and facilitated the rebel defeat at Shiloh, thus turning the tide of the war against the Confederacy.

Grant, Ulysses S.

The eighteenth United States president was born in Point Pleasant, Ohio, in 1822, graduated from West Point in 1843, and saw service under Generals Taylor and Scott during the U.S.-Mexico War. But on the eve of secession he was living in obscurity with his wife in Galena, Illinois, where he was working as clerk in his father's store and suffering from bouts of alcoholism that would follow him into the White House. On June 15, 1861, he became colonel of the Twenty-first Illinois Infantry at Springfield and rose in the ranks as he dominated the western war front. His army prevailed at Fort Henry, Fort Donelson, Shiloh, Corinth, Vicksburg, Chattanooga, and Knoxville, earning Grant the rank of general-in-chief of all Federal armies. With strategic control of the west, Grant consolidated his grand army around Virginia to face Confederate General Lee, but Lee's army exacted a heavy toll on Grant's troops, even as the Confederates suffered great losses. Grant lost scores of soldiers as he tried to implement his siege of Virginia, and critics began referring to him as the "Butcher" rather than his more admiring soubriquet, "Unconditional Surrender" Grant. Yet, his strategy worked, for it cut off Lee's lines of retreat and trapped him between two Federal armies at Appomattox. Lee surrendered to Grant on April 9, 1865, and Grant—in effect ending the war—returned to Washington, where he served two presidential terms (1868–1876) and found success in the publication of his memoirs before he died in 1885.

HAVANA, CUBA

Havana was the central port for the transportation of Confederate goods during the Civil War and also provided a means of breaking the Union's naval blockade of the South. Cuba traded clothing, food, and medicine for Southern cotton, while Havana served as a hub for Southern diplomats heading for Europe. As the Union blockade improved, trade between Cuba and the Confederacy ceased, but they continued to share common interests in slavery, anti-imperialism, and agricultural commerce. On the heels of the U.S. Civil War, Cuba rebelled against Spanish dominion and waged an abolitionist, anti-imperial war against Spain that did not successfully end for Cuba until the late nineteenth century.

INDIANAPOLIS, INDIANA

With strong Unionist sympathies, Governor Oliver P. Morton established Federal training camps, purchased war equipment, and opened a state arsenal at the start of the Civil War. While Indiana organized two full Union regiments, the state was also believed to house a large Copperhead contingent that was ostensibly behind the only Confederate raid of Indiana. In July 1863, General John Morgan crossed the Ohio River with three thousand rebel soldiers in an unsuccessful attack that either miscalculated the amount of Copperhead support or proved their sympathies to be false.

ISLAND NO. 10

Now part of the Missouri shoreline, Island No. 10 was a mile-long islet on the upper Mississippi River that served as a Confederate fort protected by swamplands, the river, and considerable Confederate arms. Along with nearby New Madrid, Missouri, Island No. 10 secured the Mississippi River for the Confederacy through Fort Pillow, Tennessee, making it a key position for both armies. To seize the island, Union forces first captured New Madrid and cut off its supply line to the island; then, with a combination of army and navy attacks, Federal forces trapped the Confederate island and compelled General William W. Mackall to withdraw. On April 8, 1862, island commander Captain W. Y. C. Hume unconditionally surrendered to Union General Foote, who took forty-five hundred rebel prisoners; seized a number of small arms, cannons, and mortars; acquired four steamers; and secured the upper Mississippi River for the next Union offense against Fort Pillow, Tennessee.

JACKSON, MISSISSIPPI

The state capital, Jackson rests on the Pearl River in the center of the state, two and a half hours by train from Vicksburg and the Mississippi River. Wanting to protect its slave interests, Mississippi was the second state to secede, and the 3,798 Jacksonians, including its population of Germans, Irish, Italians, and French, welcomed the rebellion. Despite the war, the city's social and economic life—the latter centered mostly on slavery—remained intact until 1862, when Jackson became a Confederate command post for logistics, railroad transportation, movement of slaves, and troop deployment. Once General Grant captured Vicksburg in 1863, he set his sights on Jackson and the two armies battled for the city throughout the summer of 1863. By war's end, Federal troops had occupied Jackson four times.

JACKSON, THOMAS J.

Even though his service in the Civil War lasted only two years, Lieutenant General "Stonewall" Jackson was perhaps the war's most gifted and enigmatic commander. He was born in 1824 in what is now West Virginia and survived a childhood of destitution, parental deaths, and familial displacements, all of which left Jackson introverted and self-reliant. In 1842 he entered West Point, and what he lacked in scholarship and social graces, he made up with diligent study until he graduated seventeenth in his 1846 class. He earned brevet major for his service in the U.S.-Mexico War, and after a brief command at Fort Meade, Florida, Jackson resigned his army commission to take a position as professor at the Virginia Military Institute in Lexington. His exacting commitment to duty and discipline—reflective of his devout Calvinism—made him unpopular with his young students but also characterized his future strengths as a Confederate commander. Reluctant at first to break from the Union, Jackson joined the Confederacy when Virginia seceded. He earned his famous nickname, "Stonewall," at First Manassas, where he held the Confederate line at the top of Henry Hill like a "stone wall," as General Bee expressed it. Jackson's most significant action came in the 1862 Shenandoah Valley campaign, where his seventeen thousand Confederates vexed and routed sixty-four thousand Union troops out of the valley through a series of long marches, strategic flanks, and concentrated attacks. He continued to outmaneuver and defeat Federal forces for over a year until, on his way back from his only reconnaissance mission during the war, a Confederate brigade mistook Jackson and his staff for Union cavalry and opened fire; three bullets struck the general, leading to the amputation of his arm and his death a few days later, on May 10, 1863.

JONHNSON'S ISLAND PRISON

Located three miles from Sandusky, Ohio, and a mile offshore in Sandusky Bay, Lake Erie, the three-hundred-acre island was selected as a prison camp for officers because of its difficulty of escape, distance from Canada, and access to Sandusky's railroad. It received its first Confederate prisoners in February 1862, after the fall of Forts Henry and Donelson, and continued to receive, detain, and exchange rebel prisoners—mostly officers—with relative efficiency until the end of 1862, when prisoner exchange agreements ceased. The winter months were harsh on inmates, as fresh water became scarce and the Federal government started to withhold blankets and food. Some prisoners were able to escape to Canada, and in 1863, rumors of a conspiracy to rescue the prisoners circulated as Confederate agents in Canada encouraged the prisoners to revolt, secure their escape, aid in the break of rebel prisoners in other Northern camps, and attack the United States from its northern flank. In September 1864, John Yeats Beall, an escaped prisoner, even led a failed attempt to capture the *Michigan,* the only armed Union vessel in the Great Lakes; he was later captured in the United States and hanged. The end of the war emptied the prison, and by June 1865 the post was abandoned.

JOHNSTON, ALBERT S.

Born in Kentucky in 1803, Johnston graduated from West Point in 1826 and began a busy military career. He served in the Black Hawk Indian War and joined the army of the independent Republic of Texas until his resignation in 1840. The U.S.-Mexico War brought him out of retirement to serve under General Zachary Taylor, and ten years later Johnston commanded a U.S. force sent to Utah to quell a Mormon rebellion. When his adopted state, Texas, seceded in February 1861, Johnston resigned from the Federal army, joined the Confederacy, and was made full general in command of the Confederate's western front. In February 1862 he lost Forts Henry and Donelson to General Grant, defeats that compromised the South's western command. But two months later he concentrated his rebel forces in Corinth and surprised Grant at the Battle of Shiloh, where Confederate troops initially carried the day until Johnston was killed in battle.

JOHNSTON, JOSEPH E.

Alongside Sidney Johnston, Joseph was one of the Confederacy's five full generals, but his stormy relationship with Confederate

President Jefferson Davis characterizes Johnston's career. Born in Virginia in 1807, he graduated from the U.S. Military Academy in 1829 and served in the Black Hawk, Creek, and Seminole wars throughout the 1830s before serving under General Winfield Scott in the U.S.-Mexico War. When Virginia seceded and Lincoln announced his plans to check the rebellion, Johnson reluctantly resigned his command as brigadier general in the Federal army and joined the Confederacy. He was put in command of the rebel troops at Harper's Ferry, Virginia, but redeployed them to reinforce General Beauregard at First Manassas, where Johnston's tactical decisions aided the South's victory. Soon, he squabbled over official recognition: Johnston claimed his role at First Manassas was ignored; he felt slighted when Jefferson Davis ranked him as fourth rather than first of the Confederacy's five full generals; and he exchanged acrimonious letters with Davis over rank, leadership, and the direction of the war. The strained relations with Confederate leadership showed in Johnston's performance in battle, as he proved to be ineffective in skirmishes throughout the rest of the war, culminating in the surrender of his army to General Sherman in North Carolina on April 26, 1865. After the war, Johnston penned a memoir that was critical of Davis, and he also served one term as a U.S. Congressman from Virginia (1877–1881). He died on March 21, 1891.

LAKE PONTCHARTRAIN

Approximately twenty-five by forty-one miles in size, Lake Pontchartrain is a lagoon located near Louisiana's Gulf coast. Its shore served as a popular resort before the Civil War, but its canal connection between the Mississippi River and New Orleans made it strategically important for the control of New Orleans.

LEE, ROBERT E.

The Confederate general who would become a postwar living legend was born in Virginia in 1807. His father was a Revolutionary War hero and former governor of Virginia who left for the West Indies in 1812 to escape his debts and never returned; his mother raised Lee until he entered West Point in 1825. He graduated second in the class of 1829; participated in the U.S.-Mexico War under Scott; returned to West Point as a superintendent; accepted command of cavalry troops in Texas; and then took leave to untangle his father-in-law's estate. In 1859 he led a detachment of marines to Harper's Ferry and two years later resigned from the Federal army when Virginia seceded. Made a full general, Lee's initial service in the Confederacy shifted between commanding on the warfront and advising on the home front, until he took command of Joseph E. Johnston's army in May 1862. Beginning with the Seven Days' Battles, Lee's Army of Northern Virginia repulsed the Federal army on several fronts for over a year, despite Lee's ill health and the shrinking number of rebel troops. The tide began to turn for Lee in 1863, especially after Gettysburg, and in 1864 Lee and his Army of Northern Virginia faced General Grant and his Army of the Potomac, an army of men twice the size as Lee's forces. The armies engaged in a series of fierce, bloody campaigns that culminated with the Federal siege of Petersburg, which caught Lee's army in a war of attrition that forced them to retreat to Richmond. Lee then attempted to retreat from Richmond and join Joseph Johnston's forces in North Carolina, but Grant had trapped Lee, forcing his surrender on April 9, 1865, in Appomattox. After the war, Lee accepted the presidency of Washington College in Lexington, Virginia, and traveled the lecture circuit in the South, where he gained legendary status for his heroic failure to defeat the Federal army. He died on October 13, 1870.

LYNCHBURG, VIRGINIA

Located in the hills of the Blue Ridge Mountains nearly forty miles east of Roanoke on the James River, Lynchburg was a major transportation center during the Civil War. Three railroads intersected in the city, while the James River served as an east-west supply line. Recognizing that Lynchburg supplied General Lee's defense of Petersburg and Richmond, General Grant ordered his army to take control of the city, but the Confederate army made a strong stand at the Battle of Lynchburg on June 18, 1864, and held the city for the Confederacy.

Memphis, Tennessee

Memphis was a crucial port for commerce and the cotton market before the war and a strategic city during the war. While its busy port along the Mississippi River kept an open supply line for the South, its four intersecting railroads provided overland transportation for troops. Memphis's 2,263 residents balked at secession—perhaps because much of its lucrative cotton trade was with the Midwest and Northeast—but at the start of the war the Confederacy's sixth largest city produced seventy-two volunteer companies for the rebel army. Memphis became vulnerable to attack when the fall of New Madrid, Missouri, and Island No. 10 left the upper-Mississippi River in Union hands, and by June 6, 1862, Federal forces occupied the city after a brief naval battle.

Mobile, Alabama

Known as the "Paris of the Confederacy" during the war, Mobile ranked second to New Orleans as the most profitable, diverse, and strategically important port in the South. Its lucrative international cotton trade depended on the surrounding river system and Mobile Bay and created a diverse workforce that was half foreign born. As with other prosperous Southern cities, Mobile was ambivalent about secession but supported it with the hope that it would lead to the city's urban growth, and at first the city remained prosperous as the Union's naval blockade could not stop trade between Mobile, New Orleans, and Havana. When New Orleans fell in 1862, blockade running decreased and then halted in August 1864 with the Federal capture of Mobile Bay. Because the city did not suffer a major attack until the war's end, Mobile kept up an active social life and housed five hospitals, but by 1863 the Federal blockade strained the city's economy to the point that women rioted in the street to protest food shortages and inflated prices. Eight months after the Confederacy lost Mobile Bay, Federal forces occupied the city and closed the port to foreign trade, and while Mobile survived the war relatively intact, it never regained its lucrative cotton market.

Montgomery, Alabama

The first capital of the Confederacy, Montgomery was a prosperous city near the Alabama River that relied on its slave-based agri-

lviii   AUTHENTICITY, AUTOBIOGRAPHY, AND IDENTITY.

culture and cotton commerce. Its nine thousand inhabitants were heady with secession, and when rebel leaders convened in the city to draft the Confederacy's Provisional Constitution, Montgomery became the Confederacy's capital until Virginia's secession. Montgomery remained an important rebel center: scores of troops passed through it on the city's railroad line; seven hospitals served the city; and it was a major food supply depot. Montgomery did not face serious threats from Union forces until April 1865, when the city's mayor, Andrew Noble, surrendered it without a fight to General James Wilson's advancing Federal troops.

NEW ORLEANS, LOUISIANA

As the largest and most cosmopolitan Southern city, New Orleans mustered an array of regiments that reflected the city's 160,000 residents. Besides its popular Zouave unit of French Creole soldiers, New Orleans provided a Spanish legion, Polish brigade, Garibaldi legion, Belgian guard, Scotch rifle guard, a Greek unit, and marshaled its Franco-African soldiers into the state militia. The city's diversity generated division over secession, especially since many business members were Northerners engaged in trade with free states, but its citizens united in Confederate sentiment once the port town became the focus of the Union's naval blockade. An historic hub of overland and international trade, New Orleans functioned as a central port for the Confederacy's soldiers, cotton commerce, and blockade-runners for fifteen months before General Farragut's Federal fleet captured the city via the Mississippi River. Mayor John Monroe refused to surrender to Farragut at first but capitulated when he realized the Federal army controlled most of the region's strategic sites. On May 1, 1862, General Butler took command of New Orleans and challenged the city's pro-Confederate stance. Butler hanged William Mumford for lowering the Union flag; issued General Order No. 28, which demanded that anti-Union women be charged as prostitutes; and arrested the city's fiery mayor. New Orleans remained under Union occupation until the end of war, and a year later the city reelected John Monroe as its mayor.

New York, New York

As an urban center where Southern trade and Northern industry converged, New York became divided during the war. Its stream of immigrants made it a hub for troop enlistment and draft dodging, while the city's Irish working class openly rebelled on the heels of President Lincoln's 1863 Enrollment Act, which placed conscription in the hands of the federal government. The Act's three hundred dollar commutation fee practically guaranteed that the city's laborers would be sent off to the front and sparked the New York Draft Riots, which lasted from July 13 to July 17, 1863. While the rioters generally targeted wealthy members of the Republican party, the white mob specifically terrorized blacks in the city for five nights, leaving a total of one thousand people dead. A year later, New York saw more unrest as Confederate agents and their allies in the city plotted to set the town ablaze in response to Sherman's burning of Atlanta. On November 25 and 26, 1864, the pro-Confederate agents set hotels, hay barges, and the shipping harbor ablaze, hoping the conflagrations would spread across the city, but the fires were contained.

Pensacola, Florida

Home to a major naval yard, three forts, lumber mills, and a number of brick producing companies, Pensacola's 2,876 residents were pro-Confederate, but despite the city's three surrounding military forts, minor skirmishes took place around Pensacola during the war as Confederate General Braxton Bragg enjoyed numerical superiority over the nearby Federal troops for over a year into the war. Pensacola soon became expendable as battles in Tennessee and Kentucky depleted Bragg's army and the Union's blockade hampered the transport of supplies to the city and its forts. The Confederate army left Pensacola by May 1862, and Union forces occupied it for a year as a staging ground for attacks on the Confederate coastline.

Polk, Leonidas

Born into a prominent North Carolina family in 1806, Polk attended West Point, where he befriended Albert Sidney Johnston and

Jefferson Davis and graduated in 1827. He resigned his military commission for Episcopal ministry and moved to New Orleans in 1841 after being chosen as Louisiana's bishop. After disunion, Polk tendered his services to the Confederacy, and his West Point friend, Jefferson Davis, gave him command of the western Tennessee and eastern Arkansas front. Polk immediately made a bad decision: he occupied Columbus, Kentucky—on the Mississippi River near the Tennessee-Kentucky border—without authorization from the government and ended up driving Kentucky, a neutral border state, into the hands of the Union. After leading troops at the Battle of Shiloh, Polk became mixed up in petty quarrels with his commanding officer, Braxton Bragg, but because Polk remained in Davis's good graces, the rebel president transferred Polk to the Department of Alabama, Mississippi, and East Louisiana until 1864, when he joined the Army of Tennessee in Georgia and participated in the early days of the Atlanta campaign. While on reconnaissance north of Atlanta in June, he attracted the attention of Federal troops and was killed by artillery fire.

POLK, LUCIUS E.

Brigadier General Polk was born in Salisbury, North Carolina, in 1833; he was the nephew of Confederate Lieutenant General Leonidas Polk. After studying at the University of Virginia, Polk settled in Helena, Arkansas, as a planter. In 1861 he joined the First Arkansas Infantry Regiment, was wounded at Shiloh and Richmond, Kentucky, and made brigadier general. During the June 1864 Atlanta campaign, Polk sustained a serious injury that forced the amputation of his leg, and he retired from the army. He remained in Tennessee until his death on December 1, 1893.

QUANTRILL, WILLIAM CLARKE

Perhaps the most infamous pro-Confederate guerrilla, Quantrill was born in Canal Dover, Ohio, in 1837. He began a career as a schoolteacher and then turned to farming in Kansas before heading west for adventure. He returned to Lawrence, Kansas, on the eve of the Civil War and played somewhat of a double agent, aligning himself with Kansas Jayhawkers (antislavery Unionist) and Missouri's proslavery "Border Ruffians." When the war began, he emerged as the leader of Missouri's guerrillas and led raids and skirmishes against antislavery advocates in Kansas, culminating with his destruction of Lawrence on August 21, 1863. Four hundred and fifty guerrillas sacked the pro-abolitionist town and set it ablaze after killing between 150 and 200 of its unarmed men and boys. The Confederacy wavered in its official recognition of Quantrill and his guerrillas, especially when they became marked men by Union forces. On May 10, 1865, while Quantrill was leading a raid near Taylorsville, Kentucky, Federal troops wounded and arrested him, and he died nearly a month later in a prison in Louisville, Kentucky.

RICHMOND, VIRGINIA

With five railroads, direct access to the James River, and a booming, diverse industrial and agricultural economy, Richmond was a major transportation hub when it became the Confederate capital after Virginia seceded. Its population of 37,910 quadrupled with the addition of military personnel, government staff, camp followers, Southern refugees, and captured Union soldiers, while the city's hospitals and prisons kept the population in flux. The wartime flow of people through Richmond changed it from a genteel city to a rough urban center living under Provost Marshal John Winder's martial law. By 1863 high inflation and food shortages led to a bread riot in April, while Federal forces increasingly assaulted the capital. Lee's Army of Northern Virginia repulsed Union assaults for over three years, but by April 1, 1865, Lee's lines—depleted and exhausted—broke under Grant's offensive. The Federals took possession of the city on April 3, 1865, and a week later Lee surrendered at Appomattox, in effect ending the war.

SHILOH, BATTLE OF

When Confederate and Federal forces clashed around the Shiloh Methodist Church near Pittsburg Landing, Tennessee, on April 6 and 7, 1862, they engaged in perhaps the most strategically decisive battle of the war, one that signaled the Confederacy's defeat by dividing it along the Mississippi River. After Federal forces captured Forts Henry and Donelson, Confederate troops retreated to Corinth, where rebel armies from Mobile, Pensacola, New Orleans, Nashville, and Memphis gathered to check the Union's southern advance. Confederate General Albert Sidney Johnston ordered an immediate attack, one that surprised the Federal troops gathered around Shiloh and gave the Confederacy initial control of the field. Union soldiers retreated in disarray, and Confederates attacked with equal disorganization; to make matters worse, Johnston was killed on the field, so Beauregard took command and called off the fighting after a day of battle. He lost whatever edge his army had on the field when Union reinforcements arrived in the evening, allowing Grant to take the offensive the following morning and force Beauregard to retreat to Corinth. The Union army followed, and, after taking Corinth on June 1, secured Memphis and western Tennessee.

SHERMAN, WILLIAM TECUMSEH

Born in Lancaster, Ohio, in 1820, Sherman graduated from West Point in 1840, served in the Seminole and U.S.-Mexico wars, and moved from one failed business venture to another between California, the Midwest, and the South before the war. He was living in Louisiana when the state seceded and offered his services to the Federal army, where his military career initially proved as inconsistent as his business ventures, until bouts with mental illness forced him to return home. He returned to duty in January 1862, regained his confidence in the war, and worked his way up the ranks, but his success as a commander is also his most infamous legacy. Deciding that psychological and property damage would subdue the South more effectively than conventional warfare, Sherman began a sixty-mile-wide path of destruction across Georgia that began in Atlanta and ended at the seaport town of Savannah. He torched Atlanta's war-making facilities and left the city ablaze; he then cut a path southeastward and burned or looted much of the countryside, targeting Confederate resources such as cattle, cotton gins, and sawmills but also condoning violence against Southern civilians. By the time he reached Savannah on December 20, 1864, Confederate forces evacuated the fortified city, allowing Sherman to offer it to President Lincoln as a Christmas present. Following the war, Sherman became popular on the lecture circuit and published a well-received memoir before his death in 1891.

St. Lucia

One of the several isles that compose the Windward Islands in the Lesser Antilles (or West Indies), St. Lucia was the object of Spanish exploration around 1500, though the native inhabitants, the Caribs, fended off European explorers until the mid-seventeenth century, when the French established a colony after losing many of the other area islands to the British. England and France competed for possession of the island until the early nineteenth century, when St. Lucia finally fell under British control. As with many other Antilles islands, slavery maintained St. Lucia's sugar economy until emancipation in 1833.

St. Thomas

In 1672 the Danish West India Company established a colony on St. Thomas, one of the three American Virgin Islands in the Caribbean. The Danes used the island for slave trading and customs transfers, while the island's Danish, French, German, English, and other European inhabitants profited from cotton, indigo, tobacco, and sugar plantations maintained by slavery. Even after the abolition of slavery in 1848, St. Thomas remained prosperous in commercial trade and was eventually purchased by the United States, along with two other islands, in 1917.

U.S.-Mexico War

Waged between 1846–1848, the U.S.-Mexico War could be considered one of the most important historical causes of the Civil War. While many Northerners felt President James K. Polk's interest in acquiring parts of Mexico revealed his plot to spread slavery, many Southerners felt the North's expansionist spirit marked a turn to imperialism that targeted key trade ports in New Mexico and California. When war broke out in 1846, Northerners and Southerners alike united against Mexico, as the foreign battlefields proved to be training grounds for men like Jefferson Davis, P. G. T. Beauregard, Ulysses S. Grant, Robert E. Lee, Stonewall Jackson, George McClellan, Joseph Johnston, and Albert Johnston. At war's end, the Mexican territory newly acquired under the 1848 Treaty of Guadalupe Hidalgo again raised the debates over slavery, which the Compromise of 1850, the Fugitive Slave Law, and the Kansas-Nebraska Act exacerbated rather than resolved, by creating political rifts and geographical tensions that developed into civil war.

VELÁSQUEZ, DIEGO DE

Born in Segovia, Spain, around 1465, Velásquez joined Columbus's second voyage to the New World in 1494 and by 1511 he was placed in charge of the expedition to conquer Cuba. The conquest of the island lasted three years and decimated the island's indigenous population, but Cuba soon became the economic, military, and exploration hub of the Spanish New World, with Velasquez as the island's first governor. He vied with other successful explorers, such as Hernán Cortés, to maintain his powerful position in the New World, and, though he was dismissed from the government seat in 1521, he regained it in 1523 and died unexpectedly the next year, having successfully, albeit violently, turned Cuba into Spain's most important port location in the New World.

VELÁZQUEZ, DIEGO RODRÍGUEZ DE SILVA Y

Born in Seville in 1599, Velázquez is recognized as Spain's master artist during the Baroque age, if not Spain's greatest artist in general. He was born of aristocratic Portuguese decent on his father's side but chose to use his mother's surname. His earliest paintings after apprenticeship appear around 1620, and, as his skills improved, he found favor and appointments in King Philip IV's Madrid court. He produced a series of royal portraits for the Spanish crown throughout the 1620s and 1630s and often combined realistic, naturalistic, and sometimes classical representation in Baroque settings. *Las Meninas* (1656) is regarded as his masterpiece in its group portrayal of the royal Infanta Margarita, her handmaidens, two dwarfs, Philip IV and Queen Mariana, and the painter himself in front of his canvas. In 1659 Velazquez was admitted into the Knight of the Order of Santiago, and he died in 1660.

VICKSBURG, MISSISSIPPI

Located along the Mississippi River between Memphis and New Orleans, Vicksburg was a prosperous commercial and transportation center before the war with ideal river access and intersecting, overland railroad transportation. During the war, the city became even more important to both armies as it linked the eastern Confederacy with the Trans-Mississippi South and served as a transit hub for troops, supplies, and goods; it was also a key Confederate defense of the Mississippi River. After New Orleans and Memphis fell to Federal forces, rebel troops garrisoned at Vicksburg and withstood a yearlong, hard-fought campaign against Union army and naval attacks until the besieged city surrendered on July 4, 1863, a psychological and tactical blow to the South that coincided with the Confederacy's defeat at Gettysburg.

WASHINGTON, D.C.

As the Federal seat, Washington housed the Executive Mansion (later called the White House); the Capitol; the War Department; the Patent Department; Post Office; and Treasury Building. The District was still predominantly rural on the eve of the war with a fluctuating population of fifty thousand that boomed at the start of the war with the arrival of office seekers, soldiers, volunteers, and camp followers, most of whom congregated around the Capitol and the White House grounds. The war activity in the capital, along with its fluctuating population, made Washington a denizen of political opportunists, Confederate spies, and petty thieves, but even when Confederate General Jubal Early led an unsuccessful raid on the northern part of the city on July 11, 1864, Washington withstood the war relatively unharmed.

WINDER, John H.

Born on the family plantation in Somerset Country, Maryland, in February 1800, Winder graduated from West Point in 1820 and served in the U.S.-Mexico War. When he joined the Confederacy in 1861, he was considered too old for field command and so was made brigadier general and served as provost marshal general of Richmond from 1862 to 1864. He was also put in control of Union prisoners from 1861 to 1865 as commissary general of prisoners. Northerners and Southerners alike criticized Winder's command as tyrannical, and the prisoners under his supervision, especially at the Andersonville prison in Georgia, suffered under the prison's poor conditions. As Federal forces swept through Georgia, Winder worked frantically to move Union prisoners and died of an apparent heart attack on February 6, 1865, leaving the commandant of the Andersonville Prison, Henry Wirz, to answer for Winder's treatment of Union prisoners. Wirz was tried and executed for war crimes.

MADAM VELASQUEZ IN FEMALE ATTIRE.

THE WOMAN IN BATTLE:

A NARRATIVE OF THE

Exploits, Adventures, and Travels

OF

MADAME LORETA JANETA VELAZQUEZ,

OTHERWISE KNOWN AS

LIEUTENANT HARRY T. BUFORD,

CONFEDERATE STATES ARMY.

IN WHICH IS GIVEN

Full Descriptions of the numerous Battles in which she participated as a Confederate
Officer; of her Perilous Performances as a Spy, as a Bearer of Despatches, as
a Secret-Service Agent, and as a Blockade-Runner; of her Adventures
Behind the Scenes at Washington, including the Bond Swindle;
of her Career as a Bounty and Substitute Broker in New York;
of her Travels in Europe and South America; her Mining
Adventures on the Pacific Slope; her Residence
among the Mormons; her Love Affairs,
Courtships, Marriages, &c., &c.

EDITED BY

C. J. WORTHINGTON,

Command the trumpets of the war to sound !
This stillness doth perplex and harass me:
An inward impulse drives me from repose,
It still impels me to achieve my work.
SCHILLER — *The Maid of Orleans.*

PROFUSELY ILLUSTRATED.

RICHMOND, VA.:
DUSTIN, GILMAN & CO.
1876.

ELECTROTYPED AT THE BOSTON STEREOTYPE FOUNDRY,

No. 19 Spring Lane.

TO MY

Comrades of the Confederate Armies,

WHO, ALTHOUGH THEY FOUGHT IN A LOSING CAUSE,
SUCCEEDED BY THEIR VALOR IN WINNING
THE ADMIRATION OF THE WORLD,

THIS NARRATIVE

OF MY ADVENTURES AS A SOLDIER, A SPY,
AND A SECRET-SERVICE AGENT,

Is Dedicated,

WITH ALL HONOR, RESPECT, AND GOOD WILL.

AUTHOR'S PREFATORY NOTICE.

If I expected by this story of my adventures to achieve any literary reputation, I might be disposed, on account of its many faults of style, to ask the indulgence of those who will do me the honor to undertake its perusal. As, however, I only attempted authorship because I had, as others assured me, and as I myself believed, something to tell that was worth telling, I have been more concerned about the matter than the manner of my book, and I hope that the narrative will prove of sufficient interest to compensate for a lack of literary elegance in the setting forth. Mine has been a life too busily occupied in other matters for me to cultivate the graces of authorship; and the best I can hope to do is to relate my story with simplicity and truth, and then let it find its fate, whether it be praise or condemnation.

The composition of this book has been a labor of love, and yet one of no ordinary difficulties. The loss of my notes has compelled me to rely entirely upon my memory; and memory is apt to be very treacherous, especially when, after a number of years, one endeavors to relate in their proper sequence a long series of complicated transactions. Besides, I have been compelled to write hurriedly, and in the intervals of pressing business, the necessities I have been under of earning my daily bread being such as could not be disregarded, even for the purpose of winning the laurels of authorship. To speak plainly, however, I care little for laurels of any kind just now, and am much more anxious for the money that I hope this book will bring in to me than I am for the praises of either

5

critics or public. The money I want badly, while praise, although it will not be ungratifying, I am sufficiently philosophical to get along very comfortably without.

I do not know what the good people who will read this book will think of me. My career has differed materially from that of most women; and some things that I have done have shocked persons for whom I have every respect, however much my ideas of propriety may differ from theirs. I can only say, however, that in my opinion there was nothing essentially improper in my putting on the uniform of a Confederate officer for the purpose of taking an active part in the war; and, as when on the field of battle, in camp, and during long and toilsome marches, I endeavored, not without success, to display a courage and fortitude not inferior to the most courageous of the men around me, and as I never did aught to disgrace the uniform I wore, but, on the contrary, won the hearty commendation of my comrades, I feel that I have nothing to be ashamed of. Had I believed that my book needed any apologies on this score, it would never have been written; and, having written it, I am willing to submit my conduct to the judgment of the public, with a confidence that I will at least receive due credit for the motives by which I was animated.

In the preparation of this book for the press, I have been greatly aided by the gentleman who has consented to act as my editor. Although during the war he was on the other side, he has interested himself most heartily in assisting me to get my narrative into the best shape for presentation to the public, and has shown a remarkable skill in detecting and correcting errors into which I had inadvertently fallen. I take pleasure in acknowledging my indebtedness to him.

The book, such as it is, — and I have tried to make it all that such a book should be by telling my story in as plain, straightforward, and unpretending a style as I could command, — is now, for good or ill, out of my hands, and my adopted country people will have to decide for themselves whether the writing of it was worth the while or not.

EDITOR'S PREFATORY NOTICE.

THE frank egotism of such a narrative as is contained in the volume now in the hands of the reader needs no apology. Self-reliance, self-esteem, and self-approbation, all were necessary for the consummation of such adventures as those herein related ; and, in the opinion of the editor, a chief merit in the book is the perfect unreserve with which its author gives to the world, not only the full particulars of her numerous daring exploits and adventures, but the motives by which she was influenced in undertaking them, and her impressions of men and events. Since the author has not seen fit to do so, the editor does not feel called upon to argue the question of propriety involved in the appearance of a woman disguised in male attire on the battle-field ; but, with regard to some of the transactions in which Madame Velazquez was engaged during the progress of the great civil war, a few words of comment, explanatory rather than apologetic, seem to be required.

Some of these transactions were of a character that, under ordinary circumstances, would admit of no extenuation ; but, in making up a judgment concerning them, several important facts must be constantly borne in mind. One of them is, that Madame Velazquez was acting as the agent of the only government to which she acknowledged allegiance, and that she considered herself as justified in aiding that government by every means in her power, as well by fighting its enemies in the field, as by embarrassing them by such attacks in the rear as are related in her narrative. This plea will, of course, be

7

worth nothing to those who refuse to admit that for any purposes the Confederacy had a right to exist. It is necessary, however, to view matters of this kind from a different standpoint from this. The fact that the Federal Government was compelled to recognize the Confederates as belligerents, and was compelled to hold official intercourse with them, renders argument on this head unnecessary. Admitting that they were belligerents, they were justified, within certain limitations, in doing all in their power to defeat their enemies, not only by opposing them with armies in the field, but by demoralizing them by insidious attacks in the rear, and by hampering their efforts to keep their ranks full, and to provide the ways and means for maintaining the armies at the highest state of efficiency. Whatever view non-combatants might have taken of the war, the men who did the fighting were obliged to consider it, in a great measure, as a trial of skill and valor, and practically to disregard sentimental or political considerations. From a military point of view, therefore, what was proper and justifiable for one side, was proper and justifiable for the other, and will so be considered by impartial critics.

These remarks have particular reference to the portions of this narrative which relate the experiences of Madame Velazquez as a Confederate secret-service agent at the North during the last eighteen or twenty months of the war. It will be noticed that she speaks with undisguised contempt of some of her associates within the Federal lines, — associates without whose aid she could never have accomplished the work she undertook. The unprejudiced reader will have no difficulty in understanding that their position and hers were vastly different. Some of these people were trusted officers of the government, were sworn to loyalty and fidelity, and were in the enjoyment of the full confidence of the public, as well as of their immediate superiors. Others were men who were loud in their protestations of loyalty, but who, while eager to be recognized as stanch supporters of the Federal government, were, for the sake of gain, secretly engaged in aiding the enemy by every means in their power. These people, and the shrewd, sharp woman who made use of them for the furtherance of the work she undertook to perform for the purpose of aiding the government to which she had given her allegiance in carrying on a gigantic contest, are surely not to be judged by the same standard; and that Madame Velazquez does not hesitate to relate the details of her transactions as a Confederate agent and spy, proves that she, at least, does not consider that she has done anything to be ashamed of, and is willing that her conduct shall be freely criticised.

To many readers, the story of Madame Velazquez's experiences in camp and on the battle-field while disguised as a Confederate officer, will, from the peculiarities of her position, have a particular interest. In the opinion of the editor, however, the most important part of the book is that in which a revelation is made, now for the first time, of the exact manner in which the Confederate secret-service system at the North was managed. There is no feature of the civil war that more needs to have light thrown on it than this; and, as the story which the heroine of the adventures herein set down recites, is an exceedingly curious one, it is deserving of the special consideration of the public, both North and South.

The editor of this volume was in the United States naval service from near the beginning to the end of the civil war; and as he gave his adhesion to the Union cause from principle rather than passion, and as he has never, either during the war or since its close, had other than the kindest feelings towards those who took the other side, under a sincere conviction that they were right, he not only had had no hesitation in preparing the narrative of Madame Velazquez for the press, but he feels that he can appreciate the motives which, from first to last, seem to have actuated her. The Southern people made a great mistake when they inaugurated the war; but it does not become those who fought in the Federal ranks to doubt, at this late day, the sincerity or honesty of purpose of the vast majority of them.

The great American civil war was an event that deserves to be judged dispassionately; and to judge it dispassionately, it is necessary that the people of both sections should understand each other better than they did while the conflict was being waged, or, indeed, than they do now. It is especially important that the people of the North, being the victors, and being in a great measure responsible for the present and future good government of the South, and for a proper appreciation there of the advantages of a cordial and fraternal, as well as a political union, should study the war from a Southern point of view. The present volume, the editor believes, is not only a most interesting narrative of adventure of a very exceptional kind, but it is an important and valuable contribution to the history of the war.

Madame Velazquez, whose enthusiasm for the cause of Southern independence induced her to discard the garments of her sex, and to assume male attire for the purpose of appearing upon the battle-field, is a typical Southern woman of the war period; and there are thousands of officers and soldiers who fought in the Confederate armies who can bear testimony, not only to the valor she displayed in battle, and under many circumstances of difficulty and danger, but to her integrity, her energy, her ability, and her unblemished reputation. Upon these points, however, it is not necessary to dilate; her story will speak for itself, and that it is a true story in every particular, there are abundant witnesses whose testimony will not be disputed.

As Madame Velazquez is a typical Southern woman of the war period, so her story furnishes a curious inside view of the Confederacy, and it throws much light on a great number of obscure points in its history. For this reason, if no other, it will deserve the attention of Northern readers, who will find many things stated in it which it is well for them to know. No commendation of any kind is needed to command for it the consideration of the people of the South. From the breaking out of the war to its close, the Confederate cause had no more

enthusiastic or zealous supporter than the woman who was
known as Lieutenant Harry T. Buford. According to her
opportunities, she labored with unsurpassed zeal and efficiency,
and with a disinterestedness that cannot but be admired.

With regard to the part performed by the editor in preparing this work for the press, it may be proper to say a few
words. The manuscript, when it was placed in his hands,
was found to be very minute and particular in some places,
and rather meagre in others, where particularity seemed
desirable. Having undertaken to get this material into
proper shape, correspondence was opened with Madame Velazquez, and a number of interviews with her were had. A
general plan having been agreed upon, it was left entirely to
the judgment of the editor what to omit or what to insert,
— Madame Velazquez agreeing to supply such information as
was needed to make the story complete, in a style suitable
for publication. From her correspondence, and from notes of
her conversations, a variety of very interesting details, not in
the original manuscript, were obtained and incorporated in the
narrative. The editor, also, in several places has corrected
palpable errors of time and place, and has added a few facts
not supplied by the author. These corrections and additions
have been made after consultation with the author, and with
her entire approbation. In preparing her manuscript, Madame
Velazquez seems to have endeavored to narrate the incidents
of her career in the fullest manner possible; and it consequently contains a large amount of matter which can be of but
very little, if any, interest to the general public. It has been
necessary, therefore, while expanding in some places, to make
large excisions in others; but the story is such an extraordinary one, in many of its aspects, that it has been judged
better to give it in too great fulness, rather than to omit what
the purchasers of the book would have a right to find in it.
The excisions have, therefore, been carefully made, and it is
-believed that nothing has been omitted that is of value or
importance. A few expressions that might needlessly give

offence, have either been stricken out or altered, while some, which persons of severe taste may object to, have been permitted to remain as they were originally written, they being in some way characteristic of the writer, or of the circumstances under which she was placed. While Madame Velazquez does not pretend to any literary accomplishments, her style has a certain flavor which is far from unpleasant; and the editor has been careful, in making such changes and alterations as have seemed necessary, to retain the author's own words wherever practicable.

Owing to the loss of her diary, Madame Velazquez was compelled to write her narrative entirely from memory, which will account for the errors to which allusion has been made. Indeed, considering the multiplicity of events, it is very remarkable that she has been able to relate her story with any degree of accuracy. It is possible that, despite the pains that have been taken to make the narrative exact in every particular with regard to its facts, a few errors may have been permitted to remain uncorrected. These errors, however, are not material, and do not in any way impair the interest of the story.

Madame Velazquez is a very remarkable woman, and some account of her personal appearance, other than can be obtained from the portraits of her which are given in this book, will doubtless be appreciated by the reader. She is rather slender, something above medium height, has more than the average of good looks, is quick and energetic in her movements, and is very vivacious in conversation. Her frame is firmly knit, and she is evidently endowed with great powers of physical endurance. Those who have seen her in male attire say that her skill in disguising herself was very great, and that she readily passed for a man. At the same time she is anything but masculine, either in appearance, manners, or address. She is a shrewd, enterprising, and energetic business woman, and in society is a brilliant and most entertaining conversationalist, abounding in a fund of racy anecdotes, and endowed with a mimetic power that enables her to relate her anecdotes in the most telling manner. In New York, Philadelphia, and other Northern cities, as well as throughout the South and West, she has a large number of very warm friends, who hold her in the highest esteem on account of her eminent talents, her fascinating social qualities, and her unblemished reputation. It is to be hoped that the publication of the story of her checkered career will have the effect of increasing, rather than of diminishing, the number of these friends. Her story is a most remarkable one, in nearly every respect. During the war a number of women, on both sides, from time to time, performed spy duty, and several of them are said to have occasionally assumed male attire. Madame Velazquez, however, it is believed, is the only one of her sex, who, for any length of time, wore a masculine garb, or who participated as a combatant in a series of hard-fought battles. Narratives of the adventures of several heroines on the Federal side have been published, but none of them will at all compare in extent and variety of interest with the volume now before the reader, which has an additional claim on the regards of the public as being the only authentic account of the career of a Confederate heroine that has issued from the press.

CONTENTS.

CHAPTER IV.

DISGUISED AS A CONFEDERATE OFFICER.

CHAPTER V.

RECRUITING.

CHAPTER VI.

A WIDOW.

CHAPTER VII.

THE BATTLE OF BULL RUN.

CHAPTER VIII.

AFTER THE BATTLE.

CHAPTER IX.

THE BATTLE OF BALL'S BLUFF.

CHAPTER X.

FIRST EXPERIENCES AS A SPY.

CHAPTER XI.

IN WASHINGTON.

2

CHAPTER XII.

ACTING AS MILITARY CONDUCTOR.

CHAPTER XIII.

A MERRY-MAKING.

CHAPTER XIV.

THE FALL OF FORT DONELSON.

CHAPTER XV.

DETECTION AND ARREST IN NEW ORLEANS.

CHAPTER XVI.

AN UNFORTUNATE LOVE AFFAIR.

CHAPTER XVII.

THE BATTLE OF SHILOH.

CHAPTER XVIII.

WOUNDED.

CHAPTER XIX.

THE CAPTURE OF NEW ORLEANS, AND BUTLER'S ADMINISTRATION.

CHAPTER XX.

A VISIT TO HAVANA.

CHAPTER XXI.

A DIFFICULTY WITH BUTLER. — ESCAPE FROM NEW ORLEANS.

CHAPTER XXII.

CARRYING DESPATCHES.

CHAPTER XXIII.

UNDER ARREST AGAIN.

CHAPTER XXIV.

RUNNING THROUGH THE FEDERAL LINES.

CHAPTER XXV.

THE MILITARY SECRET SERVICE. — RETURN FROM A
SPYING EXPEDITION.

CHAPTER XXVI.

IN THE HOSPITAL.

CHAPTER XXVII.

A STRANGE STORY OF TRUE LOVE.

CHAPTER XXVIII.

AGAIN A WIFE AND AGAIN A WIDOW.

CHAPTER XXIX.

IN THE CONFEDERATE SECRET SERVICE.

CHAPTER XXX.

ON DUTY AS A SPY.

CHAPTER XXXI.

SENDING INFORMATION TO THE CONFEDERATES FROM MEMPHIS.

CHAPTER XXXII.

FORREST'S GREAT RAID. — GOING NORTH ON A MISSION OF MERCY.

CHAPTER XXXIII.

SECRET SERVICE DUTY AT THE NORTH.

CHAPTER XXXIV.

PLAYING A DOUBLE GAME.

CHAPTER XXXV.

VISIT TO RICHMOND AND CANADA.

CHAPTER XXXVI.

ARRANGEMENTS FOR A WESTERN TRIP.

CHAPTER XXXVII.

CHAPTER XXXVIII.

CHAPTER XXXIX.

BLOCKADE-RUNNING.

CHAPTER XL.

AN ATTACK ON THE FEDERAL TREASURY.

CHAPTER XLI.

COUNTERFEITING AND BOGUS BOND SPECULATIONS.

CHAPTER XLII.

BOUNTY-JUMPING.

CHAPTER XLIII.

THE SURRENDER OF LEE.

CHAPTER XLIV.

THE ASSASSINATION OF PRESIDENT LINCOLN, AND END OF THE WAR.

CHAPTER XLV.

A TOUR THROUGH EUROPE.

CHAPTER L.

ACROSS THE CONTINENT.

CHAPTER LI.

MINING IN UTAH AND NEVADA. — THE MORMONS AND
THEIR COUNTRY.

CHAPTER LII.

COLORADO, NEW MEXICO, AND TEXAS. — CONCLUSION.

THE WOMAN IN BATTLE.

CHAPTER I.

CHILDHOOD.

The Woman in Battle. — Heroines of History. — Joan of Arc. — A Desire to emulate Her. — The Opportunity that was offered. — Breaking out of the War between the North and the South. — Determination to take part in the Contest. — A noble Ancestry. — The Velazquez Family. — My Birth at Havana. — Removal of my Family to Mexico. — The War between the United States and Mexico. — Loss of my Father's Estates. — Return of the Family to Cuba. — My early Education. — At School in New Orleans. — Castles in the Air. — Romantic Aspirations. — Trying to be a Man. — Midnight Promenades before the Mirror in Male Attire.

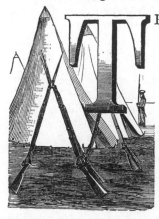

THE woman in battle is an infrequent figure on the pages of history, and yet, what would not history lose were the glorious records of the heroines, — the great-souled women, who have stood in the front rank where the battle was hottest and the fray most deadly, — to be obliterated? When women have rushed to the battle-field they have invariably distinguished themselves; and their courage, their enthusiasm, and their devotion to the cause espoused, have excited the brave among the men around them to do and to dare to the utmost, and have shamed the cowards into believing that it was worth while to peril life itself in a noble cause, and that honor to a soldier ought to be more valuable than even life. The records of the women who have taken up arms in the cause of home and country ; who have braved the scandals of the camp ; who have hazarded reputation, — reputation dearer than life, — and who have stood in the imminent deadly breach, defying the enemy, if not so imposing in numbers as those in which the deeds of male warriors are recited, are glorious nevertheless; and if steadfast courage, true-hearted loyalty, and fiery enthusiasm go for anything, women have nothing to blush for in the martial deeds of those of their sex who have stood upon the battle-field.

Far back in the early days of the Hebrew commonwealth Deborah rallied the despairing warriors of Israel, and led them to victory. Semiramis, the Queen of the Assyrians, commanded her armies in person. Tomyris, the Scythian queen, after the defeat of the army under the command of her son, Spargopises, took the field in person, and outgeneralling the Persian king, Cyrus, routed his vastly outnumbering forces with great slaughter, the king himself being among the slain. Boadicea, the British queen, resisted the Roman legions to the last, and fought the invaders with fury when not a man could be found to lead the islanders to battle. Bona Lombardi, an Italian peasant girl, fought in male attire by the side of her noble husband, Brunaro, on more than one hotly contested field ; and on two occasions, when he had been taken prisoner and placed in close confinement, she effected his release by her skill and valor.

The Nun-Lieutenant.

Catalina de Eranso, the *Monja Alferez*, or the nun-lieutenant, who was born in the city of Sebastian, Spain, in 1585, was one of the most remarkable of the heroines who have distinguished themselves by playing the masculine *rôle*, and venturing into positions of deadly peril. This woman, becoming disgusted with the monotony of convent life, made her escape, and in male garb joined one of the numerous expeditions then fitting out for the New World. Her intelligence and undaunted valor soon attracted the notice of her superior officers, and she was rapidly promoted. Participating in a number of hard-fought battles, she won the reputation of being an unusually skilful and daring soldier, and would have achieved both fame and fortune, were it not that her fiery temper embroiled her in frequent quarrels with her associates. One of her many disagreements resulted in a duel, in which she had the misfortune to kill her antagonist, and, to escape the vengeance of his friends, she was compelled to fly. After traversing a large portion of the New World, and encountering innumerable perils, she returned to Europe, where she found that the trumpet of fame was already heralding her name, and that there was the greatest curiosity to see her. Travelling through Spain and Italy, she had numerous exceedingly romantic adventures; and while in the last named country she managed to obtain an interview with Pope Urban VIII., who was so pleased with her appearance and her conversation that he granted her permission to wear male attire during the balance of her life.

Within the past hundred years more than one heroine has stamped her name indelibly upon the role of fame. All Amercans know how brave Molly Pitcher, at the battle of Monmouth, busied herself in carrying water to the parched and wearied soldiers, and how, when her husband was shot down at his gun, instead of, woman fashion, sorrowing for him with unavailing tears, she sprang to take his place, and through the long, hot summer's day fought the foreign emissaries who were seeking to overthrow the liberties of her country, until, with decimated ranks they fled, defeated from the field.

At the seige of Saragossa, in 1808, when Palafox, and the men under his command, despaired of being able to resist the French, Agostino, "the maid of Saragossa," appeared upon the scene, and with *guerra al cuchillo* — "war to the knife" — as her battle-cry, she inspired the general and his soldiers to fight to the last in resisting the French invaders, and by her words and deeds became the leading spirit in one of the most heroic defences of history.

APPOLONIA JAGIELLO.

Nearer our own time Appolonia Jagiello fought valiantly for the liberation of Poland and Hungary. She had kingly blood in her veins, and her heart burned within her at the wrongs which her native country, Poland, suffered at the hands of her oppressors. When the insurrection at Cracow took place, in 1846, she assumed male attire, and went into the thickest of the fight. The insurrection was a failure, although it might not have been had the men who began it been as stout-hearted and as enthusiastic in a great cause as Appolonia Jagiello. In 1848 she participated in another outbreak at Cracow, and distinguished herself as one of the most valorous of the combatants. After the failure of this attempt at rebellion she went to Vienna, where she took part in an engagement in the faubourg Widen. Her object in visiting the Austrian capital, however, was chiefly to ascertain the exact character of the struggle which was in progress, in order to carry information to the Hungarians. After numerous perilous adventures she joined the Hungarian forces, and fought at the battle of Enerzey, in which the Austrians were defeated, and on account of the valor she displayed was promoted to the rank of lieutenant. After this she joined an expedition under General Klapka, which assaulted and took the city of Raab. When the Hungarians were finally defeated and there was no longer any hope that either Hungary or Poland would gain their independence, Mademoiselle Jagiello came to the United States, in 1848, with other refugees, and for a number of years resided in the city of Washington, respected and beloved by all who knew her. No braver soldier than this lady ever trod the field of battle, while the universal testimony of all who were honored with her acquaintance is, that she was a most womanly woman, and was lacking in nothing that makes true womanhood esteemed by right-thinking people.

JOAN OF ARC.

But, whenever I think of the women who have distinguished themselves in battle, my affections turn to the greatest and noblest of them all, and my imagination fires with a desire to emulate the glorious deeds of Joan of Arc, the Maid of Orleans. A religious enthusiast, as well as a born leader of men, and a martial genius of the first order, this great woman infused, by the power of her matchless eloquence, courage and determination into the heart of a weak, cowardly, and vacillating king, and then, seizing the banner of France, she rallied the defeated and demoralized armies, and led them with terrible effect against the British foe. At last, betrayed into the hands of her enemies, she suffered with all the unbending courage of her heroic nature, a martyrdom at the stake, which, while it embalmed her memory in the hearts of the French people, covered with shame the names of the cowardly ruffians who decreed her death on a pretended charge, because they were afraid to let her live for fear that her existence, even as a prisoner, would be a perpetual menace to them, and a perpetual encouragement to the French people to fight to the death. The statue of Joan of Arc, chiselled by the fair hands of a French princess, stands to-day in the market-place at Rouen where she suffered, and the memory of her glorious deeds as a great-hearted patriot remains to all time as an example of what a woman may do if she only dares, and dares to do greatly.

From my early childhood Joan of Arc was my favorite heroine ; and many a time has my soul burned with an overwhelming desire to emulate her deeds of valor, and to make for myself a name which, like hers, would be enrolled in letters of gold among the women who had the courage to fight like men — ay, better than most men — for a great cause, for friends, and for father-land.

At length an opportunity offered, in the breaking out of the conflict between the North and the South in 1861, for me to carry out my long-cherished ideas ; and it was embraced with impetuous eagerness, combined with a calm determination to see the thing through, and to shrink from nothing that such a step would involve.

My opportunities and my circumstances were different from those of my ideal woman, Joan of Arc, and consequently my story has but little resemblance to hers. I did all that it was possible for me to do, however, for the cause I espoused, and the great French heroine did no more. Happily I escaped her dreadful fate, and live to relate the many adventures that befell me while playing the part of a warrior. So many persons have assured me that my story — prosaic as much of it seems to me — is full of romance, and that it cannot fail to interest readers both South and North, that I have been induced to narrate it for the benefit of those who wish to make the acquaintance of a woman warrior, and to be entertained, and perhaps instructed, by a recital of her adventures. If there are any such, — and I am sure there are, — they will find in these pages an unaffected and unpretending, but truthful, and I hope interesting narrative of what befell me while attached to the army of the Confederate States of America, and while performing services other than those of a strictly military character under the *pseudonyme* of Lieutenant Harry T. Buford.

Hundreds, nay thousands of officers and men in the Confederate service, knew me well under this name, and although my disguise was finally penetrated, and I was forced to resume the garments of my sex, it is probable that a vast number of my late associates will now for the first time learn that the handsome young officer — I was accounted an uncommonly good-looking fellow, when dressed in my best uniform, in those days — was a woman, and a woman who was mentally making some very uncomplimentary notes with regard to much of their very naughty conversation. My experience is, that the language used by the very best men in masculine society is too often not such as pure-minded women would like to listen to, while that of the worst is so utterly revolting, that it is a pity some men cannot always have decent women at their elbows to keep their tongues from being fouled with blasphemy and obscenity. I hope that some of my late associates, when they learn that the Lieutenant Harry T. Buford, whose ears were so often greeted by their profanity and ribaldry, will have enough self-respect to blush with shame at having addressed the language they did to a woman, and a modest woman at that.

What I have just said will give a hint of some of the most unpleasant incidentals of the *rôle* which I undertook to play. I was not to be deterred, however, from carrying out my plans by the bad language I was compelled to listen to, nor by any other of the disagreeable features of camp life. How well I did play my part, happily does not depend upon my own testimony alone, for some of the most distinguished officers of the Confederate army, and many equally distinguished civilians, can and will testify to the truthfulness of the story I am about to relate, and to the unblemished character I bore while in the Confederate service. I not only assumed the garment of my sex once more with the credit of having done the state some important services, and of having labored with efficiency, courage, and energy to secure the independence of the Confederacy, but, with my womanly reputation unblemished by even a suspicion of impropriety; and I take this occasion to say, in a very positive manner, that women, if they will, may pass through the most trying scenes with unblemished reputations, and that they have much more to dread in this particular matter from the scandalous gossip of city, village, and country neighborhoods, than they have from camp associations, with all their license of language and conduct.

THE VELAZQUEZ FAMILY.

I have every reason to be proud of the name I bear, and of the ancestry from whom I inherited it. My father's family is a very ancient one, and the blood which flows in my veins is that of Castilian nobles, whose deeds are intimately connected with some of the most impressive episodes of Spanish history. Reckless as some portions of my own career may seem to unthinking persons, I have the satisfaction of knowing, in my own soul, that by no act of mine has the noble name of Velazquez been brought into discredit, and that at all times, and under the most discouraging circumstances, I have ever upheld my own honor and that of my family.

Both in Spain and in the Spanish dominions on this side of the Atlantic, is the name of Velazquez well known and highly honored. Don Diego Velazquez, the conqueror and the first governor of Cuba, under whose superintendence the expedition which discovered Mexico was sent out, was one of my ancestors, and Don Diego Rodriguez Velazquez, the greatest artist that Spain ever produced, was a member of my family. It will thus be seen that I came of excellent, although somewhat fiery and headstrong stock, and, if in assuming the garments of a man, and endeavoring to do a man's work on the battle-field, I transgressed against the conventionalities of modern society, the reader will, I am sure, charitably attribute some of the blame to the adventuresome blood of old Governor Don Diego, which I inherited, and, which fired my brain and steeled my nerves when there was a prospect held out that, despite the fact of my being a woman, I might be able to enjoy the excitements of the battle-field, and win for myself a warrior's fame.

My father was a native of the city of Carthagena, and he received a very thorough education at the universities of Madrid and Paris. He was an accomplished Latin, French, and German scholar, and spoke all these languages fluently. English he paid but little attention to until after his marriage with my mother. Like all the members of his family, he was a very strict Catholic. Two of his brothers being in the Spanish army, and his tastes inclining him to the life of a civilian, a diplomatic appointment was procured for him, and he went to Paris as an attaché of the Spanish embassy.

It was while residing in Paris that my father became

acquainted with the lady whom he married, and made the mother of his children. My mother was the daughter of a French naval officer, by an American lady, the daughter of a wealthy merchant. She, of course, spoke English fluently, and tried to instruct my father in it. He managed, in time, to understand it very well, but he never spoke it without some accent. My father's marriage occurred a short time before the expiration of his term of office, and after his recall to Spain he took up his residence in the city of Madrid, where three sons and two daughters were born.

MY BIRTH.

In 1840 my father was appointed to an official position in Cuba, and two years later I, his sixth and last child, came into the world in a house on the Calle Velaggas, near the walls in the city of Havana, on the 26th of June, 1842. I was christened Loreta Janeta.

When I was almost one year old, my father fell heir to a large estate in Texas, which was then a part of the republic of Mexico. He accordingly resigned his position as an employee of the Spanish government in Cuba, and in 1844 removed with his family to San Luis Potosi, in Central Mexico. His property consisted of a very large tract of land and immense herds of cattle, and as he was a careful and accurate business man, the probabilities are, that in a short time he would have become one of the wealthiest landed proprietors of that region. Unfortunately we had scarcely been settled in our new home a twelvemonth, when the war between Mexico and the United States broke out. I was too young at the time, of course, to recollect anything of this memorable contest, although it had a potent influence on my own destiny.

THE MEXICAN WAR.

My father, so soon as war was declared, decided to take part in the conflict, and offered his services to the Mexican government to assist in expelling the invaders. His offer was accepted, and he received a commission as an officer in the army. Sending his family to the Island of St. Lucia, one of the British West Indian provinces, where my mother's only brother resided, he took the field, and fought until the end of the war against the forces of the United States. During the conflict his estates were devastated and his property destroyed, and this, combined with the non-success of the Mexican arms, greatly imbittered him against the Americans, and this bitterness he retained till the day of his death.

When the war was ended, and a large portion of the northern part of Mexico ceded to the United States, my father, whose estates were included in this territory, refused to live under a government which he disliked so intensely, and he consequently abandoned his property and went to Santiago de Cuba, where he was rejoined by his family. In the mean time he had fallen heir to another valuable estate at Puerto de Palmas, and settling upon it, he engaged actively in the sugar, tobacco, and coffee trade. The profits on these articles being very large, he speedily acquired great wealth, and was able to surround his family with every luxury.

While we were residing on the Puerto de Palmas plantation, an English governess was employed to conduct my education. I remained under this good lady's instruction until 1849, learning the elementary branches, and acquiring a fair knowledge of the English language. In that year my father, at my mother's urgent solicitation, determined to send me to New Orleans for the purpose of completing my education. I accordingly took up my abode with Madame R., my mother's only surviving sister, who resided in Rue Esplanade, New Orleans. My aunt was rather strict with me, but she took much pains with my education, and for two years I studied under her supervision, mainly devoting myself to acquiring an accurate knowledge of English, so as to be able to read, write, and speak it with fluency. Having become reasonably proficient in such studies as were assigned me by my aunt, I was sent to the school conducted by the Sisters of Charity, to learn the ornamental branches. Here I remained until the romantic clandestine marriage, which did so much towards shaping my future career, took place.

DREAMS OF GLORY.

From my earliest recollections my mind has been filled with aspirations, of the most ardent possible kind, to fill some great sphere. I expended all my pocket money, not in candies and cakes, as most girls are in the habit of doing, but in the purchase of books which related the events of the lives of kings, princes, and soldiers. The story of the siege of Orleans, in particular, I remember, thrilled my young heart, fired my imagination, and sent my blood bounding through my veins with excitement. Joan of Arc became my heroine, and I longed for an opportunity to become such another as she. I built air-castles without number, and in my day-dreams I was fond of imagining myself as the hero of most stupendous adventures. I wished that I was a man, such a man as Columbus or Captain Cook, and could discover new worlds, or explore unknown regions of the earth. I could not even write a social letter to my father to inform him of the state of my health, or my educational progress, without putting in it some romantic project which I had on hand. This propensity of mine evidently annoyed him greatly, for he frequently reprimanded me with much severity, although he took no measures to remove me from influences which were certainly not unattended with danger to a girl of my impulsive and imaginative disposition ; so that it is no wonder I was soon engaged in a romantic *escapade* which gave my family great offence and anxiety.

I was especially haunted with the idea of being a man ; and the more I thought upon the subject, the more I was disposed to murmur at Providence for having created me a woman. While residing with my aunt, it was frequently my habit, after all in the house had retired to bed at night, to dress myself in my cousin's clothes, and to promenade by the hour before the mirror, practising the gait of a man, and admiring the figure I made in masculine raiment. I wished that I could only change places with my brother Josea. If I could have done so I would never have been a doctor, but would have marked out for myself a military career, and have disported myself in the gay uniform of an officer.

CHAPTER II.

MARRIAGE.

My Betrothal. — Love Matches and Marriages of Convenience. — Some new Ideas picked up from my Schoolmates. — A new Lover appears upon the Field. — I Figure as a Rival to a Friend. — Love's Young Dream. — A new Way of popping the Question. — A Clandestine Marriage. — Displeasure of my Family. — Life as the Wife of an Army Officer. — The Mormon Expedition. — Birth of my first Child, and Reconciliation with my Family. — Commencement of the War between the North and South. — Death of my Children. — Resignation of my Husband from the Army. — My Determination to take Part in the coming Conflict as a Soldier. — Opposition of my Husband to my Schemes.

SOME time previous to my admission to the Sisters' school, I was betrothed to a young Spaniard, Raphael R., in accordance with plans which my relatives had formed with regard to me, and without any action on my part. Indeed, my consent was not asked, my parents, thinking that they were much better qualified to arrange a suitable alliance than I was, and that, provided other things were satisfactory, love was something of minor importance, that could very well be left to take care of itself. They were mistaken, however, as other parents have been in similar cases, for, like a good many girls, as soon as I was old enough to do much thinking for myself, I had no difficulty in coming to the conclusion that the choice of a husband was something I ought to have a voice in.

I had been educated under very old-fashioned ideas with regard to the duties which children owe to their parents, for, among my father's country people, children, even when they have arrived at years of discretion, are supposed to be under the authority of their father and mother, and marriages for love, having their origin in a spontaneous affection of young people for each other, are very rare. It is the custom in Spain,

43

and among the Spanish people in America, for the parents to make what they consider suitable matches for their children, and the young people are expected to accept any arrangement that may be concluded in their behalf, without murmuring.

This does not seem to be the proper way of conducting such an important piece of business as marriage, and it is very contrary to the notions which are common in the United States. A good deal, however, could be said in favor of it, and it is certain that quite as large a number of marriages of convenience, such as are usual in Europe, turn out happily as of the love matches which are usual in the United States. The fact is, that the majority of young people really do not know their own minds, and they often fancy themselves in love when they are not. Marriage undeceives them, and then they wish that they had exercised a little more discretion, and had not been in quite such a hurry. On the other hand, in a marriage of convenience, if the parties are at all suited to each other, and are at all disposed to make the best of the situation, they soon become affectionate, and love after marriage is, perhaps, in reality, the most likely to be enduring. As a general principle, however, there can be no doubt that a couple ought to be fond of each other before marriage, and if a young man and young woman of proper age, and with the means to start housekeeping, fall in love, and want to get married, parents do wrong to oppose them unless there are some very serious reasons for so doing.

A marriage by parental arrangement was the last thing in the world to suit a scatter-brained, romantic girl like myself, whose head was filled with all sorts of wild notions, and it is not to be wondered at, therefore, that I rebelled. When I was betrothed to Raphael, however, I had not the slightest notion of objecting; and although I did not feel a particle of affection for him, I accepted him for my future husband, as a matter of course, and received his visits with a proper degree of complacency, if not with any great demonstrations of regard.

I had not been long in the school, however, when, from my association with American girls, I obtained considerable enlightenment on a good many subjects about which I had previously been profoundly ignorant; and concerning this matter of marriage, in particular, I learned that it was not considered the correct thing at all for the parents of a young lady to pick out a husband for her. The girls, when they found that I was betrothed without my own consent, were at a great deal of pains to inform me that this was a free country, and that one of the chief blessings of living in a free country was, that a girl could not be compelled to marry any particular man if she did not choose to do so.

This kind of talk excited me very much, and I began to wish to break my engagement with Raphael, even before a rival stepped in to secure the affections which belonged to him, according to the arrangement my parents had made. I did not see my way very clear, however, and probably would have married him eventually, had not a more acceptable lover put in an appearance. Some of the girls professed to know a good deal about the law, and insisted that if my parents wished to force me to marry against my own consent, I could defy their authority, and appeal to the courts to allow me to choose a guardian. Such a course as this, however, I knew would sever me from my family ; and as I had the fondest regard for my dear father and mother, I dreaded to find myself cut off, disinherited, and thrown upon the charity of strangers. I consequently took no steps to get rid of Raphael until I chanced to make the acquaintance of a young American army officer who was paying particular attention to one of my schoolmates, Nellie V.

A Real Lover.

Nellie was a beautiful girl, of about sixteen years of age, and a very warm regard subsisted between us up to the time of her discovery that I was endeavoring to capture her lover. Her affection for me did not last long after that, and she said a great many disagreeable things about me, for which I have long since forgiven her, as I doubt not she has me for running away with her handsome young officer.

He was indeed a handsome young officer, and his manly and graceful appearance, especially when attired in his brilliant uniform, made such an impression on my heart, that I soon could think of nothing else. I found now that love was a reality, and my thoughts by day and my dreams by night had no other object than the gentleman who, while paying his assiduous attentions to Nellie, never imagined what ravages he was making in the heart of her schoolmate. I learned to hate Raphael, and his attempts to make himself agreeable to me only served to increase my dislike. Of Nellie I soon became savagely jealous, and was ready to cry with rage and vexation whenever I saw her lover paying her any delicate attentions. We, however, to all appearances, continued fast friends, and it was not for several months that she discovered I was her rival. The object of my devotion was also profoundly ignorant of my feelings towards him, and I had not the courage to tell him. At length I became desperate, and determined at the earliest opportunity to acquaint the young officer with the affection I entertained for him.

A DECLARATION OF LOVE.

The wished-for opportunity finally offered. One evening Nellie and I agreed to exchange partners, for the purpose of finding out how much they loved us. Raphael did not fancy this manœuvre a bit, but submitted to it with as good a grace as possible. The officer and myself managed to get out of ear-shot of the other couple, but, now that the opportunity I had sighed for was mine, I was afraid to open my mouth on the subject nearest my heart. I trembled all over, but was determined before we separated to let him know the state of my heart. Finding that I had not courage to speak, I wrote a few words in his pocket diary, which told him everything.

He was intensely surprised; but he declared, with much warmth, that he had long wished to speak with me on this very matter, and would have done so, were it not that he thought I was betrothed, and that under any circumstances there would be no chance for an American to win my affections. My new lover behaved in the most honorable manner, for, as soon as he obtained my consent for him to pay his addresses, he went to my aunt, and asked permission to visit at her house. She granted his request, with the condition that he was to understand that I was betrothed, and would demean himself towards me accordingly. This condition he listened to, but with a determination to pay little heed to it, his main object being accomplished in securing the right to see me without fear of being interfered with.

When my lover began to appear at my aunt's as a pretty constant visitor, Raphael was quick to suspect him as a rival, who was more highly appreciated than himself, and became furiously jealous. I cannot tell what torture I suffered in endeavoring to be amiable to a man whom I hated, in order that I might prevent an explosion which would deprive me of the society of the one I really loved with the most devoted fondness. Finally Raphael, unable to endure the sight of his rival constantly in attendance upon me, and evidently finding extreme favor in my eyes, prevailed upon my aunt to forbid him admittance to the house, on the plea that he was becoming altogether too intimate with the betrothed of another. This gratified Raphael's malignity, and it was a severe blow to both of us. Although we could not meet on the same pleasantly familiar terms as before, we were resolved not to be separated, for we were now too much in love to be willing to give each other up. In spite of my aunt's endeavors to keep us apart, and in spite of Raphael's jealous vigilance, William — for that was my lover's name — found means to carry on a correspondence with me, to meet me at the houses of mutual friends, and to speak to me on the street on my way to and from school. Raphael, who took pains to have us closely watched, informed my aunt of what was going on, and I was accordingly threatened with being locked up in a convent, or with being sent back to Cuba, if I did not conduct myself with more propriety. I was horror-stricken at the idea of either fate, but as I knew my aunt to be a very determined woman, who would certainly carry out her threat if I did not take measures to place it out of her power to do so, I was not long in making up my mind what course to follow, and having fixed upon a plan of action, I only awaited a suitable opportunity to put it into execution.

The opportunity I sighed for was not long in offering itself; for one evening, as I was sitting at my window, in company with a young French creole girl, I saw William pass and look up. I waved my handkerchief in salutation, and he recognized the signal by raising his cap. I then asked the young lady if she would not do me the favor of taking a letter to him, and of permitting us to have an interview at her home. She readily consented; and carrying a hastily written note to William, soon returned with an answer, to the effect that he would meet me in an hour's time. My aunt did not permit me to go out alone in the evening; but as she suspected nothing wrong in the proposed visit to my friend's house, she consented, without hesitation, for me to go under the escort of one of the servants. As my escort, of course, on our arrival at the rendezvous, remained with the servants of the house, I was able to converse with William without fear of espial, or of being interrupted.

A RUNAWAY MATCH.

My lover informed me that he expected soon to be ordered to one of the frontier posts. He declared that he could not exist without me, and proposed that we should elope, and get married privately. As this was my own plan exactly, I gave my consent, without any hesitation, the moment the proposition was made. On a little reflection, however, my conscience began to trouble me, for I knew that I should not be doing right; so I told him I would prefer that he should make an open and straightforward proposition for my hand to my parents. I considered that it was a duty I owed them to ask their consent first, but promised, if they opposed the marriage, that I would not let their disapprobation interfere with the consummation of our wishes. William himself thought that this was the proper and honorable course to pursue, and he accordingly wrote to my father, and asked his permission to marry me. A reply to his request was not long forthcoming, in which he was reprimanded in very harsh terms for daring to make it, knowing me to be the betrothed of another. This settled the matter; and accordingly, on the 5th of April, 1856, we were clandestinely married.

I told no one of the step I had taken, and remained at my aunt's, on the same apparent footing as before, until the following October, meeting William privately, when I could do so without being observed, but taking more pains to prevent our interviews from being noted than I had done previous to our marriage. At length I had a furious quarrel with my aunt on account of Raphael. She reproached me in severe terms for my conduct towards him; and I replied by discarding him, and refusing to have anything more to do with him. My aunt was extremely indignant; and finding me obdurate, threatened to put me in the convent at Baton Rouge. I was terribly frightened at this, and concluded that it was time for me to act with decision. I accordingly informed my husband of the situation, and he came immediately and claimed me as his wife, presenting the certificate of marriage to my horror-stricken relative.

This was a terrible blow to my aunt, but a greater one to my parents, especially to my father, who idolized me. My father's indignation got the better of his affection, and he promptly informed me that I might consider myself as repudiated and disinherited. The pangs this cruel message caused me were intense, but I was consoled with the lavish affection bestowed upon me by my handsome young husband, and with the thought that, in course of time, my parents would relent, and be willing to again receive me as their daughter.

With the exception of my estrangement from my family, there was but one thing that interfered with my happiness. My husband was a Protestant, and desired me to believe as he did. It required a hard struggle for me to forsake the faith in which I had been educated; but eventually I learned to think as my husband did about religious matters, and became a member of the Methodist church.

My separation from my family caused me much grief, but I tried hard not to let my husband see how much I suffered. I entered as far as possible into his thoughts and wishes, and only gratified a natural taste by giving a large portion of my time to the study of military tactics. I longed for a war to break out, and resolved that if one did occur, I would follow my husband to the battle-field, and minister to him, even if I was not allowed to fight by his side.

THE MORMON EXPEDITION.

In 1857 there appeared to be a chance that my martial aspiration would be gratified. The government organized an expedition against the Mormons, and my husband was ordered to accompany it. In the mean time, however, I had become a mother; and much as I desired to accompany the army to Utah, I was forced to acknowledge the impracticability of a journey across the plains with an infant in my arms, and was compelled to submit to remaining behind.

When my baby came into the world I yearned more than ever to be reconciled with my family, and, with my husband's consent, wrote to my mother and to my favorite brother, who, but a few months before, had graduated with distinction from the College de France. This brother had long since forgiven me, and, in confederation with my mother, had labored to soften the heart of my father towards me. On the receipt of the letter announcing the birth of my child, and my earnest desire to be forgiven for my fault, they worked so successfully on the feelings of my father, that, after a somewhat stubborn

4

resistance, he yielded, and consented to have my mother and brother visit me in St. Louis. My brother, after becoming acquainted with my husband, esteemed him highly, and finally the bad feeling which had been caused by my clandestine marriage wore away, my father alone treating me with a coolness which he had never previously shown. When I met him for the first time after my marriage, he turned his cheek to me, saying, "You can never impress a kiss on my lips after a union with my country's enemy," — from which I concluded that it was not so much my marriage without his consent, as my alliance with an American soldier that imbittered him.

After the Mormon expedition had returned, my husband met me at New Orleans, and from thence took me to Fort Leavenworth, then a remote frontier town. The living accommodations at this place were miserable, and the cooking, especially, was atrociously bad. I bore every discomfort, however, without a murmur, out of deference to my husband's feelings, and in every way endeavored to make myself as little of a burden to him as possible. In course of time I became a good American in thought and manner, and despite the inconveniences of life at a frontier post, was as happy as I could wish to be.

In the spring of 1860 I returned to St. Louis, while my husband went to Fort Arbuckle. During his separation from me, our third babe was born and died. In October of the same year he returned, having received a summons from his father — a resident of Texas — to the effect that there was reason to believe a war was about to break out between the North and the South, and desiring him to resign.

About this time my two remaining children died of fever, and my grief at their loss probably had a great influence in reviving my old notions about military glory, and of exciting anew my desires to win fame on the battle-field. I was dreadfully afraid that there would be no war, and my spirits rose and sank as the prospects of a conflict brightened or faded. When my husband's State determined to secede, I brought all my influence to bear to induce him to resign his commission in the United States army, and my persuasions, added to those of his father, finally induced him, very reluctantly, to yield. It was a great grief for him to forsake the uniform he had worn so long with honor, and to sever the bonds which existed between him and his comrades. He much doubted, too, the wisdom of the Southern States in taking the action they did, and wished most sincerely that the political difficulties which caused their secession could be settled in some other manner than by an armed conflict.

As for me, I was perfectly wild on the subject of war; and although I did not tell my husband so, I was resolved to forsake him if he raised his sword against the South. I felt that now the great opportunity of my life had arrived, and my mind was busy night and day in planning schemes for making my name famous above that of any of the great heroines of history, not even excepting my favorite, Joan of Arc. Having decided to enter the Confederate service as a soldier, I desired, if possible, to obtain my husband's consent, but he would not listen to anything I had to say on the subject; and all I could do was to wait his departure for the seat of war, in order to put my plans into execution without his knowledge, as I felt that it would be useless to argue with him, although I was obstinately bent upon realizing the dream of my life, whether he approved of my course or not.

CHAPTER III.

ASSUMING MALE ATTIRE.

A Wedding Anniversary. — Preparing for my Husband's Departure for the Seat of War. — My Desire to accompany him. — His Arguments to dissuade me. — My First Appearance in Public in Male Attire. — A Bar-room Scene. — Drinking Success to the Confederacy. — My First Cigar. — A Tour of the Gambling-Houses and Drinking-Saloons. — The unpleasant Points of Camp Life set forth in strong Colors. — Departure of my Husband. — Donning Male Attire. — My First Suit of Male Clothing. — Description of my Disguise. — The Practicability of a Woman disguising herself effectively. — Some of the Features of Army Life. — What Men think of Women Soldiers.

HE fifth anniversary of our wedding was celebrated in a very quiet fashion at the old Commercial Hotel, Memphis, Tennessee. We passed the day pretty much in our own room, packing trunks and preparing for my husband's departure for Richmond, where he expected to meet some of his old army friends, such as General Robert E. Lee, General Reynolds, Captain Bernard Bee, and Captain Cabell, who had linked their fortunes with those of the South. His hardest struggle had been to throw off the uniform he had so long worn; but, that deed having once been consummated, it was not difficult for me to persuade him to offer his sword to the South, especially when so many of his old friends of the United States army were arraying themselves in antagonism to the flag under which they had once fought.

While preparing for his departure, on the anniversary of our wedding, we talked over the whole situation; and I cannot tell how proud and delighted I felt when he attired himself in his elegant new gray uniform. He never looked hand-

52

somer in his life, and I not only gave full vent to my admiration, but insisted upon broaching my favorite scheme again. My husband desired me to go to Galveston, and to write to my father to meet me there; but my heart was set upon accompanying him to the seat of war, and I would listen to no other arrangement. He used every possible argument to dissuade me from my purpose, representing the difficulties and dangers in the darkest colors, and contending that it would be impossible for him to permit his wife to follow an undisciplined army of volunteers. The situation, he told me, was entirely different from anything I had ever been accustomed to, and that the hordes of rude, coarse men collected together in a camp in an emergency like this, would have but little resemblance to the regular troops in garrison with whom I had been familiar; and that a delicately nurtured and refined woman would find camp life, during such a war as that just commencing, simply intolerable. He was not to be persuaded, while I turned a deaf ear to all his remonstrances, and persisted in arguing the point with him to the last.

First Assumption of Male Attire.

Finally, my husband, finding that his words made no impression, thought he would be able to cure me of my erratic fancies by giving me an insight into some of the least pleasing features of masculine life. The night before his departure, therefore, he permitted me to dress myself in one of his suits, and said he would take me to the bar-rooms and other places of male resort, and show me something of what I would be compelled to go through with if I persisted in unsexing myself. Braiding my hair very close, I put on a man's wig, and a false mustache, and by tucking my pantaloons in my boots, as I had seen men do frequently, and otherwise arranging the garments, which were somewhat large for me, I managed to transform myself into a very presentable man. As I surveyed myself in the mirror I was immensely pleased with the figure I cut, and fancied that I made quite as good looking a man as my husband. My toilet once completed, it was not long before we were in the street, I doing my best to walk with a masculine gait, and to behave as if I had been accustomed to wear pantaloons all my life. I confess, that when it actually came to the point of appearing in public in this sort of attire, my heart began to fail me a little; but I was bent on going.

through with the thing, and so, plucking up courage, I strode along by the side of my husband with as unconcerned an air as it was possible for me to put on.

Presently we crossed over to a bar-room, which we found nearly filled with men smoking and drinking, and doing some pretty tall talking about the war, and the style in which the Yankees were going to be wiped out. To judge by the conversation, every man present was full of fight, and was burning with a furious desire to meet the enemy. I was too frightened and bewildered by the novelty of my situtation to pay very close attention to all I saw and heard, but it flashed upon me that some of these loud-talking, hard-drinking, and blaspheming patriots were not so valiant, after all, as they professed to be. My after experiences fully confirmed my first impressions, that the biggest talkers are not always the best fighters, and that a good many men will say things over a glass of whiskey in a bar-room, who won't do a tenth part of what they say if they are once placed within smelling distance of gunpowder.

I had scarcely time to take a good look at the room and its occupants, when my husband caught sight of a couple of men who had belonged to his regiment, and who were very particular friends of mine. I was dreadfully afraid they would recognize me, but there was no escaping from them, as they came up so soon as they saw us, and I was introduced as a young fellow who was on a visit to Memphis to see the sights and to pick up war news.

TREATING.

My husband treated, he and his two comrades taking something strong, while I, in accordance with the instructions given me before starting out, called for a glass of cider, only a part of which I imbibed. After a little conversation, my husband whispered to me to call for the next treat. I was getting to be somewhat disgusted with the whole business, but was bound not to break down ; so, stepping up to the bar, I invited the party, with as masculine a manner as I could put on, to drink with me. This time I took a glass of sarsaparilla, and when all had their drinks poured out, raising my tumbler, I cried out, " Gentlemen, here's to the success of our young Confederacy."

As I said this, my heart was almost ready to jump out of

my throat. The men, however, gave a rousing cheer, and
one of them yelled out, "We drink that toast every time,
young fellow."

He then put his hand into his pocket, as if about to get his
money to pay for the drinks, but I prevented him, saying,
"Excuse me, sir, this is my treat," and laid a twenty dollar
gold piece on the counter. Each of us then took a cigar, I
watching to see how they managed theirs before daring to
put mine in my mouth. After I had gotten a light, I was not
able to take more than three or four whiffs, for my head began
to swim, and I knew if I kept on I should soon be deathly
sick. As it was, I did not feel at all comfortable, but
thought I could bear up, and said nothing for fear of being
laughed at.

I was very glad to get out of the bar-room, and into the
fresh air again; so, bidding our friends good night, we started
off, I throwing my cigar away at the first opportunity I had
of doing so without being observed. Eager to hear my husband's opinion, I asked him if he did not think I played my
part pretty well. He replied, " O, yes ; " but I could see that
he was very much dissatisfied with the whole performance.
Before returning to the hotel we made a general tour of the
city, visiting all the principal gambling-houses and saloons,
my husband evidently hoping I should be so shocked with
what I saw and heard that I should be ready to give up my
wild scheme without further talk about it.

When we were once more in our room he locked the door,
and, throwing himself on the lounge, said, "Well, don't you
feel pretty much disgusted ? "

To please him I said, " Yes ; " adding, however, " but then I
can stand anything to be with you, and to serve the sunny
South."

" Now, Loreta," said he, " I have done this to-night for the
purpose of showing you what men are like, and how they behave themselves when they are out of the sight and hearing
of decent women, whom they are forced to respect. What
you have seen and heard, however, is nothing to what you
will be compelled to see and hear in camp, where men are
entirely deprived of female society, and are under the most
demoralizing influences. The language that will constantly
greet your ears, and the sights that will meet your eye in
camp, where thousands of men are congregated, are simply
indescribable ; and it is out of all reason that you should even

think of associating in the manner you propose with soldiers engaged in warfare."

This, with a good deal of the same kind of talk, convinced me that he would never give his consent to my project; so I pretended to be satisfied with his arguments, but was, nevertheless, resolved more firmly than ever, so soon as he took his departure, to put my plans into execution. I waited impatiently for him to leave, intending to give him a genuine surprise when next we met, and to show him that his wife was as good a soldier as he, and was bent upon doing as much or more for the cause which both had at heart. For the present, however, I said nothing concerning my intentions.

My Husband's Departure.

On the 8th of April my husband started for Richmond, apparently under the impression that, as I had said nothing for several days about accompanying him, I had abandoned all notion of doing so. He ought to have known me better, and to have been assured that a woman of my obstinate temper was not to be prevented by mere argument from carrying out a pet scheme which promised such glorious results as the one we had been discussing.

My husband's farewell kisses were scarcely dry upon my lips, when I made haste to attire myself in one of his suits, and to otherwise disguise myself as a man, as well as was practicable with such material as I had at hand. The first thing to be done before I made any attempt to play a masculine *rôle* at all prominently in public was, of course, to get some properly fitting clothing. Exactly how to accomplish this without being discovered, or at least suspected, was the great problem now before me. Everything depended, I well knew, upon starting right; and the slightest suspicion at this time, in the mind of any one who happened to see or speak to me, might, and probably would, interfere materially with the success of my operations in the future. I had, however, some time before taken notice of a small tailor's shop on a retired street not very far from the hotel, the presiding genius of which was a not very brilliant-looking German, and I thought perhaps I might run the gantlet of his scrutiny without much fear of detection, especially as I proposed to leave Memphis at as early a day as possible after obtaining my male raiment.

I accordingly went to this German tailor, and ordered two uniform suits, for which I agreed to pay him eighty-five dollars each. As he took my measure he eyed me pretty close, and seemed to imagine that something was not quite right. I was dreadfully afraid he would discover me to be a woman, but resolved, if he did, that I would endeavor to silence him with a handsome bribe for a few days, until he got my suits done and I could leave the city, trusting to be able to disguise myself thereafter so effectually that he would not recognize me again, even if he saw me.

" Ah," said the tailor, looking at me rather sharply, " what you want to go to war for ? You is too young for the fightin' ; isn't you ? What your mammy say to that, eh ? "

I replied, with as careless an air as I could possibly assume, that I was twenty-two years of age, and was a graduate of West Point, following up this information with other fictitious statements which it somewhat staggered me to utter, and which, if he had been a trifle sharper, he would have had some difficulty in crediting.

He, however, was satisfied, or appeared to be, and promised to have the clothing ready in two days. I was afraid to tell him to pad the coat all around in such a manner as to conceal my feminine shape ; this I was compelled to do myself after I got possession of the clothing. With a little alteration, however, the coats and pantaloons made by the German tailor at Memphis answered my immediate purpose, and enabled me to get under way with my grand scheme, but my disguise was really not perfected until I reached New Orleans, and was able to command facilities greater than Memphis afforded.

MY DISGUISE.

As this seems to be a very proper point in my narrative for a description of the means adopted for the concealment of my sex, while I was doing duty in the Confederate army as an officer, I will gratify the curiosity of the reader in that matter before proceeding any farther with the story of my adventures.

My coats were heavily padded in the back and under the arms to the hips, until I reached New Orleans. This served to disguise my shape ; but the padding was very uncomfortable, and I soon made up my mind that it would never do for a permanent arrangement. So soon as I got to New Orleans, I went to an old French army tailor in Barrack Street, who I knew was very skilful, and who understood how to mind his own business by not bothering himself too much about other people's affairs, and had him make for me half a dozen fine wire net shields. These I wore next to my skin, and they proved very satisfactory in concealing my true form, and in giving me something of the shape of a man, while they were by no means uncomfortable. Over the shields I wore an undershirt of silk or lisle thread, which fitted close, and which was held in place by straps across the chest and shoulders, similar to the shoulder-braces sometimes worn by men. A great many officers in the Confederate army have seen the impressions of these straps through my shirt when I have had my coat off, and have supposed them to be shoulder-braces. These undershirts could be rolled up into the small compass of a collar-box. Around the waist of each of the undershirts was a band, with eyelet-holes arranged for the purpose of making the waistbands of my pantaloons stand out to the proper number of inches. A woman's waist, as a general thing, is tapering, and her hips very large in comparison with those of a man, so that if I had undertaken to wear pantaloons without some such contrivance, they would have drawn in at the waist and revealed my true form. With such underwear as I used, any woman who can disguise her features can readily pass for a man, and deceive the closest observers. So many men have weak and feminine voices that, provided the clothing is properly constructed and put on right, and the disguise in other respects is well arranged, a woman with even a very high-pitched voice need have very little to fear on that score. One of the princpal causes of my detection, after having successfully passed myself off as a man to thousands of keen-eyed observers, under circumstances where everything was against the concealment of my sex, was, that my apparatus got out of order, so that I was forced to dispense with it. I was to blame, too, for permitting myself to grow careless, and not always being on my guard.

There were several points about my disguise which were strictly my own invention, and which, for certain good and sufficient reasons, I do not care to give to the public. These added greatly to its efficiency. Indeed, after I had once become accustomed to male attire, and to appearing before any-body and everybody in it, I lost all fear of being found out, and learned to act, talk, and almost to think as a man. Many a time, when in camp, I have gone to sleep when from fifty to sixty officers have been lying close together wrapped in their blankets, and have had no more fear of detection than I had of drinking a glass of water.

CAMP LIFE.

The style of conversation that was common in camp, and the kind of stories told around our fires at night, I will leave to the reader's imagination, hoping, however, that he or she has not imagination enough to compass anything so utterly vile. My favorite amusement was a game of cards, and I preferred this way of entertaining myself, and of beguiling the weary hours, to listening to anecdotes which could only debase my mind. Anything relating to military affairs, to social science, to the deeds of great men or women, or whatever else I could improve myself by listening to, I took great delight in. From my earliest recollection, however, I have had a thorough distaste for vulgarity of language and profanity, and my camp experiences only tended to increase my disgust at the black-guardism which many men are so fond of indulging in. The manner in which too many men are in the habit of referring to the other sex in conversation among themselves is, in my opinion, thoroughly despicable; and I really think that it would be morally and intellectually beneficial to many of my sex, especially those who are the victims of masculine vicious-ness, if they could only listen to some such conversations as I have been compelled to listen to, and learn how little respect or real regard of any kind men have for them.

I would that God would put it into my power to utter such a warning as would be heeded, to the weak and erring of my sex, and which would enable them to fortify themselves against the temptations constantly assailing them. But I suppose no warning would prevent those who are disposed to sin from doing so, although I well know that women, and men too, can resist temptation, and can avoid vileness in living and in lan-guage if they will only choose to do so. I do not pretend to say that I am possessed of firmer nerves, or am less under the influence of the natural emotions of my sex, than many others; but my strong constitution, and the perfect health I enjoyed, enabled me to endure more fatigue and hardship than most women, while my firm-mindedness, and resolute determination to carry my point, enabled me to avoid anything like laxity of conduct. I was compelled to sink my sex entirely, for the least inadvertence would have thwarted my plans, and prevented the realization of all I aimed at.

Many and many a time has the subject of women serving in the army as soldiers been discussed at the mess-tables and around the camp-fires; and officers, who have been in my company for days, and weeks, and months, have boasted, with very masculine positiveness, that no woman could deceive them, little suspecting that one was even then listening to them. I have sometimes been asked my opinion on the subject; but have generally answered evasively, without expressing, in very decided terms, my ideas one way or the other. Some of the men with whom I have been associated have spoken in respectful and even commendatory terms concerning women serving as soldiers; but too many have had nothing but vileness to utter on the subject. I can never forget, although I may forgive, the disgraceful language which some of these individuals have used with regard to this matter; and my experiences in the army will not have been in vain, even if they have taught me nothing more than the utter contemptibleness of some individuals, whom it would be a stretch of courtesy to call gentlemen.

Harry T. Buford
1st Lt Indpt Scouts C.S.A

CHAPTER IV.

DISGUISED AS A CONFEDERATE OFFICER.

Preparing a military Outfit. — Consultations with a Friend. — Argument against my proposed Plan of Action. — Assuming the Uniform of a Confederate Officer. — A Scene in a Barber's Shop. — How young Men try to make their Beards grow. — Taking a social Drink. — A Game of Billiards. — In a Faro Bank. — Some War Talk. — Drinks all around. — The End of an exciting Day. — Making up a Complexion. — A false Mustache. — Final Preparations. — Letters from Husband and Father. — Ready to start for the Seat of War.

 ITHIN three days I managed to provide myself with a very complete military outfit; quite sufficient to enable me to commence operations without delay, which was the main thing I was after, for I was exceedingly anxious to carry out a magnificent idea I had in my mind, and to present myself before my husband, under such auspices that he could no longer find an excuse for refusing his consent to my joining the Southern army as a soldier. My uniform suit having been arranged for, it was an easy matter for me to procure the rest of my outfit without unduly attracting attention, and I soon had in my room a trunk well packed with the wearing apparel of an army officer, and neatly marked upon the outside with the name I had concluded to adopt.

Lieutenant H. T. Buford, C. S. A.

When I saw the trunk with this name upon it as large as life, my heart fairly jumped for joy, and I felt as if the dream of my life were already more than half realized. There was a good deal, however, to be done before I could move any

61

farther in this momentous affair, and while waiting for the tailor to send my uniform suit, I thought and planned until my head fairly ached. At length I hit upon a method of arranging my financial matters which I judged would prove satisfactory, and concluded to call in a gentleman who was a very old and intimate friend of both my husband and myself, and demand his assistance.

A Friend in Need.

This friend, in whom I knew full reliance could be placed, came to my room immediately upon my summons, and having first sworn him to secrecy, I made a full revelation with regard to what I proposed to do. He turned deadly pale when I informed him of my intention to disguise myself as a man, and to enter the army on exactly the same footing as other combatants; but, having recovered from his first astonishment and dismay, he tried to treat the whole matter as a jest, and evidently believed that I was either a little demented, or was indulging in an absurd bit of pleasantry. He was convinced, however, that I really meant business, when he saw the trunk with my military *pseudonyme* upon it, the male garments which the tailor had just sent home, and the accoutrements I had purchased within the past two or three days.

As I had anticipated, he thought it his duty to endeavor to persuade me to abandon my wild ideas, as he called them. He went over all the arguments my husband had used, adding a great many of his own, and painted military associations in the blackest and most repulsive colors. He might as well have talked to the wind, for my heart was fixed on achieving fame, and of accomplishing even more than the great heroines of history had been able to do. I turned a deaf ear to all his remonstrances, and the only answer I gave to his pleadings that I would abandon the thought of unsexing myself, was to insist upon his aid. This he finally promised to give, although most reluctantly, when he found that nothing he could say would move me from my purpose.

My friend suggested that the first thing to be done was, for me to leave the hotel; so, sending for a man, he had my trunk and military equipments carried to the house in which he occupied apartments. My other baggage was prepared for removal, and was taken away to be stored in a place of safety until I should need it again, which I hoped would not be very soon. After paying my bill, and giving the proprietor to understand that I was about to leave the city, my friend managed to get me into my new quarters without my being observed by any one. Telling me that he would take care to prevent any interruption while I was making my toilet, he retired and left me to myself.

I immediately proceeded to change my garments, and ere a great many minutes had elapsed, I was transformed into a man, so far as it was possible for clothing to transform me. When I was ready I called my friend, and asked his opinion of the figure I cut. He admitted that I was not a bad looking specimen of a man, considering I had only been about five minutes, and thought that in time I should be able to do credit to the name I bore and the clothes I wore.

The only regret I had in making up my disguise, was the necessity for parting with my long and luxuriant hair. This gave me a real pang; but there was no help for it, and I submitted with as good a grace as I could muster, while my friend played the part of tonsorial artist with a pair of shears. He trimmed my hair tolerably close, and said that it would answer until I could visit a barber's shop with him, and be initiated into some of the mysteries of such a peculiarly masculine place of resort. Before going to the barber's, however, he made me promenade the room, practising a masculine gait, until I had acquired it tolerably well, and gave me a great number of very minute instructions about the proper manner of conducting myself so that my sex would not be suspected. He particularly enjoined me to watch his actions closely at the barber's, in the drinking saloons, the billiard rooms, and the other places he intended conducting me to, for the purpose of informing me with regard to some masculine habits and ways of acting, talking, and thinking.

At the Barber's.

A carriage having been sent for, we were driven to the shop of an old Virginian negro barber, whom my friend was accustomed to patronize. Entering first, he took off his hat and coat, and hung them up, and throwing himself into one of the barber's chairs, asked to have his hair trimmed and his face shaved. I followed his movements as closely as I was able, and was soon in my shirt sleeves and in possession of another chair, with an obsequious colored individual standing over me, vigorously mixing lather in a cup, which he evidently intended to apply to my face, notwithstanding that I had not the least sign of a beard. I was very much amused, but also a trifle frightened at this manœuvre, for I really did not want to have my face scraped with a razor, and yet scarcely knew whether it would be the correct thing to decline going through the performance. My friend saw the dilemma I was in, and came to the rescue, by informing the barber that his young friend only wanted to have his hair trimmed in the latest style. The negro took the hint, but grinned a little as he put away the shaving apparatus, at which I was almost inclined to believe that he had suspicions with regard to me.

I was somewhat reassured, however, and at the same time gained a bit of information with regard to certain masculine traits, when, as he commenced to trim my hair, he said, " De young gemmen in de military always likes to be shaved, sah, even if dey hasn't any beard. Dey tinks dat it helps to make de beard grow, sah; " and then he laughed heartily, as if he thought he was getting off a first-rate joke at the expense of a large and important class of his customers. For my own part I appreciated the joke immensely, in spite of the embarrassment under which I labored, and assured my colored friend that I had no disposition to force my beard, but thought that it would come of itself in course of time without assistance. The barber took this view of the case himself, and intimated confidentially that in his opinion a good many young fellows in their haste to get beards before nature intended that they should have any, not only give themselves considerable unnecessary pain by hacking their chins with awkwardly handled razors, but interfered materially with the proper and graceful growth of the hirsute adornment when it did begin to make its appearance.

I was entertained, and not a little edified, by the talk with which the barber regaled me while he was cutting my hair ; and, as it was evident from his manner that he took me for a young man, I was greatly reassured with regard to the success of my disguise, and left the shop with an increased confidence in my ability to play the part I had assumed. I was the more encouraged as my friend, when we were once more in the street, told me that I had conducted myself first rate, although he warned me that he was about to take me to a number of places with which I would not be so well pleased as I had been with the barber's shop, and in which I would be compelled to be constantly on my guard. He advised me to watch closely what he did, to treat to drinks or cigars after him, but not to take part in any games.

Strolling down the street, we soon came to the hotel, and entered the bar-room, where my companion met a number of friends, to whom he introduced me as a young officer on his way to the seat of war. I was received with much cordiality, and the whole party speedily engaged in an animated conversation about the coming conflict. I said as little as possible, but tried to take part in the discussion, when I was compelled to speak, in as easy and natural a manner as I could without unduly obtruding myself. Of course, as soon as the first introductions were over, somebody suggested drinks. The men all took whiskey straight; but I did not venture on anything stronger than cider. Soon my companion managed to give me a quiet hint, and I treated the party to drinks and cigars. We then adjourned to the billiard-room, and my friend, taking off his coat, went at a game in good earnest with another member of the party. I had never seen the game of billiards played before, and I soon became intensely interested in watching, from a chair in which I sat in my shirt sleeves, pretending to smoke my cigar, the balls rolling over the table. As the weather was warm, I very soon, after entering the billiard-room, availed myself of what seemed to be the custom of the place, to take off my heavily padded coat, which began to be unbearable, and found myself much more at my ease sitting in my shirt sleeves.

A Visit to a Faro Bank.

The players kept pushing the balls about, until nearly one o'clock in the morning, I sitting all the time watching them intently, and endeavoring to obtain some idea of the game. When one o'clock struck, my friend proposed that we should go to a faro bank; and although I was both sleepy and tired, for it was long after my usual hour for retiring, and I was pretty well used up with the excitement of the day, I felt bound to do whatever my instructor in masculine manners desired me. I knew what the game of faro was, for my father's country people are all extravagantly fond of sports of every kind, while in the army, especially upon lonely frontier stations, a game of cards is frequently the only diversion that officers have. Both before and after my

5

marriage, therefore, I had been accustomed to card-playing, and was familiar with all the principal games. although there were some, like faro, used only for gambling purposes, which I had never seen played in a regular manner.

Before entering the faro bank, my companion cautioned me not, under any circumstances, at the present or any future time, to take part in games like faro, or to drink any strong liquor. Card-playing for money, he said, I could avoid with tolerable ease, but I would frequently be so situated that I would be compelled to drink, and that I had better at once establish a reputation for temperance, and only take something that could not possibly intoxicate. If it was once understood that I never touched whiskey, brandy, or even wine, I could manage to get along very well, even with hard drinkers, and would very seldom be troubled by being forced to imbibe when I did not wish to do so, while all sensible people would respect me. My friend liked very well to take something stronger than water himself, but he felt that what would do for him would not do for me, and that even a very slight indiscretion with regard to such a matter as this might get me into serious trouble and thwart all my plans. His present object was simply to show me some points of masculine life, which it was important I should be acquainted with in order that I might play my part with entire success; for, having failed to dissuade me from my grand scheme, he was exceedingly solicitous that I should acquit myself with credit, and get through without tarnishing my fair fame.

The faro bank was crowded with men, some deeply interested in the play, others looking on, and others standing about talking and drinking. The majority of the men in the room were civilians; but not a few officers, in their brilliant uniforms, were present, and the war seemed to be the one topic of conversation. My friend immediately recognized a number of acquaintances, to whom he introduced me. Among others was a major, who, I thought, eyed me pretty close, but who did not address me particularly, except to exchange the ordinary civilities. This officer, after we had been conversing a few moments, proposed that we should take a drink, and the whole party went up to the bar. All but myself called for brandy; I took cider. Whereupon the major said, with a smile, " Lieutenant, you don't appear to be a heavy drinker ? "

" No," replied my friend for me, " he is quite temperate ;

and it's just as good for him. If he don't begin to drink strong stuff, he'll never want to."

"That's so," said the major; "hard drinking is a bad habit, and I wish sometimes I hadn't acquired it; but when a fellow's in camp, and cut off from civilization, he is apt to take more than is good for him; and when he once gets a start in that way, it is hard to stop." Then turning to me, he said, "What part of the country do you come from?"

"He has just returned from the North," put in my friend.

"Ah, indeed!" said the major. "To what command are you attached, sir?"

"To none, as yet," I replied.

Said my friend, "He is a West-Pointer, and has made up his mind to do some fighting for the South."

"The devil he is!" remarked the major, shaking me heartily by the hand; "I am glad to find him on the right side. This is the kind of fellow we want, and, with a few more of the same sort, we will whip the Yankees inside of ninety days."

Some War Talk.

In a few moments a dozen or more men were gathered around, eagerly shaking my hand and plying me with all kinds of questions. They made such a decided demonstration, that I began to be a little frightened, but stood my ground valiantly, and replied to their queries the best I was able.

Said one, "What do the Yankees think of us people down South?"

"Why," replied I, "most persons say that there will be no fighting, and I do not think they want to fight if they can help it."

"We'll show them about the fighting," said another.

"Yes, lieutenant," said a third, "one Southerner can whip any ten they send down here, and will do it in thirty days at the farthest."

The major now asked, "What do you think about foreign intervention?"

This was something I had never given even a thought to; but I answered very boldly, and in a style that I thought would be appreciated by my auditors, "We don't want any foreign help in a war like this. I reckon we can manage to do our own fighting."

" That's the kind of talk," cried the major.

There was considerable more conversation of this kind, during which the drinking went on pretty freely, I treating the same as the rest, but being careful not to take anything that would upset me. I informed them that it was my intention to recruit and equip a company at my own expense in Rackensack, on the Mississippi, among the country people, and that I had eighty-eight thousand dollars with which to see myself through. This made a great impression, and the major remarked, " You are going to just the right place. The boys down there are first-rate marksmen, and you won't have any trouble in getting as many of them as you want."

The major by this time was pretty full, and he proposed to show me the sights, if I would make a night of it with him. I thanked him, but said that as it was very late, and I was tired from travelling, I would like to retire. My friend seconded my efforts to get away ; which we did finally, after some further argument with my new acquaintances, the major especially showing a disposition to insist upon my going with him to see what he called the sights. Finally we reached the house, where my friend put me into his room, while he went and took possession of another apartment occupied by a friend. It was after four o'clock when I went to sleep, pretty well used up with the excitement and unusual exertion which my masculine *début* had caused me.

The next day I completed my outfit by purchasing a pair of field-glasses, a pair of blankets, a rubber overcoat, and a rubber blanket. On returning to my room I made out a form of attorney in my friend's name, and authorized him to attend to all my business matters for me. I also prepared a lot of recruiting papers on the model of some genuine ones I succeeded in getting hold of, and some muster rolls, and procured a manual of tactics, and before the day was over, was pretty nearly ready to commence active operations.

My friend, thinking that my disguise could be somewhat improved, and a more manly air given to my countenance, obtained a false mustache, and a solution with which to stain my face, in order to make it look tanned. I rubbed on the solution until my skin was about the right tint, and then my friend carefully fastened the mustache on my upper lip with glue. This was a very great improvement, and I scarcely

IN A BAR-ROOM IN MEMPHIS.

knew myself when I looked in the glass, and laughed at the thought of what my husband would say when he saw me in this disguise.

During the day I received two letters; one from my father, informing me that he was about to return to Cuba, which relieved my anxiety lest he should come after me, and the other dated Vicksburg, from my husband. In my reply to the latter, I stated that I was going to Texas, for the purpose of accompanying my father to Cuba. This I thought would prevent my husband from being apprehensive with regard to me, and enable me to get matters under good headway before he could interfere, for I was extremely anxious to give him a first-rate surprise.

Everything was now in proper trim for me to commence operations in earnest; so, packing my trunk, rolling up my blankets in army style, as I had often seen soldiers do, preparing my papers, and getting ready a change of under-wear, and other matters for immediate use in a small satchel, I was ready to start on my campaign with as stout a heart as ever beat in the breast of a soldier.

CHAPTER V.

RECRUITING.

HE plan of action I had fixed upon, after mature reflection, was to raise and equip a battalion at my own expense, taking care to select good material for it, and then to appear at the head of my little army before my husband, and to offer him the command. I pictured to myself again and again the look of astonishment he would put on when he recognized his wife as the leader of a gallant band who were pledged to fight to the death for the cause of Southern independence, and flattered myself with the idea that, so far from being inclined to censure me for my obstinate persistence in carrying out my idea of becoming a soldier, he would be disposed to praise without reservation, and so far from being ashamed of my action, would be proud of it. Whatever view of the matter he might take, however, he would be compelled to yield to my wishes, whether he desired to do so or not, and I would consequently be free to follow the bent of my inclinations without fear of further opposition on his part. My desire was to serve with him, if possible; but if this could not be done, I intended to play my part in the war in my own way,

70

without his assistance. I, however, did not contemplate any further difficulty in obtaining his consent, and even his assistance, in the execution of my plans, and so started out on the war-path with a light heart, and with brilliant anticipations for the future.

With my satchel, containing a change of under-clothing and a few other traps, in my hand, I crossed over to Hopefield, on the Arkansas side of the river, and took the five o'clock train, not knowing exactly where I proposed to bring up. For a time I busied myself with the study of my Manual of Tactics, with the intention of becoming sufficiently posted on certain points to get my recruits into something like military training immediately. Having been the wife of an army officer for a number of years, and having seen some hard service on the frontier, I was, in a measure, pretty well qualified for the work I had now undertaken, especially as I had paid a good deal of attention to the details of military organizations, and had seen soldiers drilled hundreds of times. I had not been in the train very long, before, finding the conductor at leisure, I entered into conversation with him, with a view of obtaining information that might be useful in the furtherance of my designs.

Explaining to this individual, who appeared to take the liveliest interest in my affairs, that I was on a recruiting expedition, I asked him if he could not suggest a good neighborhood for me to commence operations in. He said that Hurlburt Station was as likely a place as I could find to pick up a company of strong, hearty fellows, who would do some good fighting, and advised me to try my luck there. Hurlburt, he told me, was not much of a place, —a saw-mill, a country store, in which the post office was located, a school-house, which was also used as a church, being pretty much all there was of it. The country around, however, was tolerably well settled, and most of the young men thereabouts would, he thought, be rather glad of a chance to have a crack at the Yankees.

HURLBURT STATION.

The train speeded through the swamps, and it was not a great while before we reached Hurlburt Station, where, in accordance with the conductor's suggestion, I alighted. With my satchel in my hand, I made for the nearest house, and inquired of a negro, who was chopping wood, whether his master was at home. The darkey stared at me a bit, evidently attracted by something in my appearance, and then, grinning until he showed all his ivories, said that the old boss was away, but that the young boss was about somewhere. I accordingly told him to call the young boss; and soon up came a well-built, good-looking young fellow, whom I fixed upon immediately as a suitable recruit. In response to my inquiry whether I could stop there a few days, he said, with a laugh, "I guess so, if you can stand our fare. We haven't any accommodation for travellers, but pap never turns anybody away."

I replied, "I guess I can stand your fare, if you treat me well in other respects."

"We'll do the best we can for you," he said. "Come in, and I'll call mammy and the gals."

The house to which he conducted me was a rude affair, constructed with logs daubed over with mud, and with only one door, which appeared to have no other fastening than a wooden latch. I quickly made up my mind that a smart young fellow like Frank Giles — for such, he took occasion to inform me, was his name — would not hesitate very long about making up his mind to abandon these rather dismal surroundings, for the sake of embracing such an opportunity for seeing something of the world, and of participating in exciting adventures, as I proposed to offer him.

As we entered the house, Frank bawled out at the top of his voice, "Mammy, here's a man who wants to stop here."

The old woman put in an appearance in a moment or two, and greeted me with a certain amount of cordiality, saying, in reply to my request for board and lodging for four or five days, "Well, sir, we're poor folks, and ain't got much to give you; but we'll do the best we can, if you choose to stop with us."

I replied that I reckoned things would suit well enough, as I wasn't hard to please, and, in compliance with an invitation to make myself at home, took off my cap, and began to remove my duster.

The old woman and the young fellow both stared at me with open-mouthed astonishment when they saw my uniform, which, up to this time, had been concealed by my long linen duster. When they could recover themselves, they began to deluge me with questions. The old woman seemed rather suspicious of me at first, and evidently surmised that I had some intention of carrying off Frank, and making a soldier of him. As for Frank, the sight of my brass buttons fired him with military ardor immediately, and I perceived that there would be no difficulty whatever in securing his enlistment.

"I guess you're an officer; ain't you?" said Frank, following up this question with another one before I could open my mouth for a reply. "What are you going to do down here?"

"Yes, I am an officer, on a recruiting trip," I answered. "What chance do you think I will have in getting some good fighting fellows in this neighborhood?"

"What army do you belong to?" demanded Frank, apparently a little dubious about the colors I fought under.

"To the army of Virginia," I replied.

"Then I reckon you are for the South?" said he.

"Certainly, sir," said I; "and you swear by the same colors that I do; don't you?"

"Of course I do." And then he commenced a perfect siege of questions about what a soldier would have to do, how long was the war going to last, would there be much fighting, and expressed the liveliest desire to take a hand at licking the Yankees.

I told him that I had the army regulations with me, and would take pleasure in explaining them to him in the morning. I then asked him to give me some water, so that I could clean myself up a bit before supper, as I was pretty well covered with dust and cinders after my ride. He accordingly got me a basin of water, and then left me to go off and hunt the old man, full of eagerness to tell him of the arrival of the recruiting officer, and of his own desire to go soldiering.

A SENSATION AMONG THE WOMEN.

The sudden intrusion of a gallant young officer, in a gay uniform, plentifully decorated with buttons and lace, into the Giles homestead, made an even greater impression on the female than upon the male part of the family. My arrival had clearly created an intense excitement, and I understood very well that I was the subject of the whispered conversation that I heard going on outside. From the manner in which the old woman and her son had addressed me, I knew that they had no suspicions of my being other than what I seemed, but I judged that it would be necessary to be pretty careful how I carried myself before the former, for she was clearly a sharp one, and would be quick to take note of any peculiarly feminine traits of manner I might display. I therefore determined to play the man right manfully, whether I thought myself observed or not; and this I found to be a very good rule to go by throughout the entire period during which I wore my disguise.

While making my toilet, I noticed the old woman and a couple of girls peeping at me through a crack in the wall, and I accordingly, without appearing to notice them, took pains to strut about in as mannish a manner as I could, and to imitate a man's actions and gestures while washing my face and hands and arranging my hair.

After a bit, Mrs. Giles and her daughters came into the room, the girls blushing up to their eyes, and dreadfully abashed, at being compelled to go through with the ceremony of an introduction to the handsome and gayly dressed young officer. The eldest of the two daughters was about sixteen, and was attired in a bright, flaring yellow calico; the youngest was about twelve years of age, and was somewhat less unbecomingly dressed in pink. Both of the girls had put on the best they had to do honor to the occasion, and the eldest, especially, so soon as her first bashfulness wore off, seemed very much disposed to attract the particular attention of the visitor by various little feminine artifices, which I understood very well, and which amused me immensely.

On entering the room, the old woman said, awkwardly waving her hands towards her daughters, " These is my gals, sir."

I bowed in the politest manner, and said, with what I intended to be a particularly fascinating smile, " Good evening, ladies," laying a particular emphasis on the word "ladies;" which had the desired effect, for both of the girls blushed deeper than ever, and the eldest simpered as if she heartily enjoyed it. The daughters, however, were too much confused just yet to do a great deal in the way of conversation; so, for the sake of sociability, and to put the entire party at their ease, I started a talk with the old woman, by remarking that it had been an exceedingly pleasant day.

" Yes," replied Mrs. Giles; " but the craps need rain."

After a few commonplaces of this kind about the weather, and other matters of no particular moment, I thought I might as well proceed to business at once; for I expected that I would have some opposition from the old woman in my effort to enlist Frank. So I said, " Madam, I am trying to enlist your son for a soldier in my company; don't you think you can spare him ? "

She burst out crying, and exclaimed, " O, sir, I can't let my boy go for a soldier and get killed."

The youngest girl, seeing her mother in tears, began to blubber a little also; but the eldest not only did not cry, but she looked at me in such a peculiar way, that I was convinced she wished I would take her instead of Frank.

AN ARKANSAS BELLE.

The idea of having a mild little flirtation with this fair flower of the Arkansas forest rather grew upon me as I noticed the impression I was making upon her susceptible imagination. I had some curiosity to know how love-making went from the masculine standpoint, and thought that the present would be a good opportunity to gain some valuable experience in that line ; for it occurred to me that if I was to figure successsfully in the *rôle* of a dashing young Confederate officer, it would be necessary for me to learn how to make myself immensly agreeable to the ladies. I knew how to make myself agreeable to the men, or thought I did, and I could, if I chose, be agreeable to women in a feminine sort of fashion ; but I had never studied the masculine carriage towards my sex critically, with a view of imitating it, and it was important, therefore, that I should begin at once to do so, in order that when compelled to associate with women, as I assuredly would be to a greater or less extent, I might not belie my outward appearances by my conduct. I flatter myself that during the time I passed for a man I was tolerably successful with the women ; and I had not a few curious and most amusing adventures, which gave me an insight into some of the peculiarities of feminine human nature which had not impressed themselves on my mind before, perhaps because I was a woman.

My 'flirtation with Miss Sadie Giles was not a very savage one, and I hope that ·it did not inflict more damage on her heart than it did on mine. It was immensely amusing to me while it lasted, and I presume, if not exactly amusing, it might at least be deemed entertaining to her. At any rate, I succeeded not only in having a little sly fun at her expense, but I picked up an idea or two that I subsequently found useful.

Noticing that Miss Sadie was developing a marked partiality for me, but was much too bashful to give me any encouragement, except some shy glances out of the corners of her eyes, I commenced to ogle her, and, whenever I had an opportunity, to pay her some delicate attentions, for the purpose of making her think I was just a bit fascinated with her. It soon became very evident that the heart which beat under that yellow calico dress was in a great state of excitement, and Miss Sadie, while not encouraging me by any direct advances, made it very plainly understood that my little attentions were appreciated.

While I was conversing with the old woman on the subject of Frank's enlistment, and trying to convince her that it was better for him to volunteer than to wait to be drafted, — following Miss Sadie with my eyes all the while, and letting her see plainly that I was thinking more of her than of her mother, — I heard the youngest daughter, Fan, who had meanwhile left the room, saying to her father that there was a soldier in the house who had come to take Frank away to the war. The old man made his appearance a moment later, and, shaking me very cordially by the hand, gave me a hearty welcome, and apologized for the meagreness of the accommodations he was able to offer. I judged from his manner and from his language that he had seen better days, and that his education was much superior to that of his wife and children.

Supper was now announced, and we all sat down to a tolerably plentiful repast, the principal features of which were bacon, cabbage, and fried chickens — the latter having been prepared in my honor. Miss Sadie managed to place herself by my side, by a dexterous little manœuvre, which escaped the attention of the family, but which I understood perfectly. I, for my part, strove to play the gallant by helping her bountifully to the bacon, cabbage, and chicken, and by endeavoring to induce her to join in the conversation. She undoubtedly appreciated my attentions at their full value, but was not sufficiently self-possessed to do much talking; indeed, during the supper I could scarcely get anything out of her except a timid yes or no.

The old man, on the contrary, was very talkative, and plied me with all kinds of questions about myself, my errand, the war, and the prospect of a speedy accomplishment of Southern independence. I told him that my name was Buford, that I was a lieutenant in the army, and that I had been sent down

to Arkansas for the purpose of recruiting a company for service
in Virginia. He said that I would have no difficulty in getting all the recruits I wanted, as the young fellows in those
parts were every one eager to have a dash at the Yankees,
and promised to aid me in every way possible.

The apartment in which the supper was served was about
ten by twelve feet, and was used as a kitchen as well as dining and sleeping-room. Everything about it was dreadfully
dirty, and the table at which we were eating, and the bench
upon which Miss Sadie and myself were seated, were both so
greasy that I was much afraid of seriously soiling my new
clothes; and I do not doubt that my agitation on this subject
was attributed by the yellow-calico clad damsel beside me to
the close proximity in which I was placed to her. I ate heartily
of the viands that were set before me, paying more attention,
however, to the chicken than to the greasy bacon and cabbage,
which latter, however, were eaten with great gusto by my
entertainers.

My Mustache in Danger.

Before the supper was over I had a terrible fright, and for
a few moments fancied that I was on the brink of a discovery
that would upset all my plans, and nip my enterprise in the
bud. While drinking a glass of buttermilk, which I greatly
enjoyed, for it was the best thing on the table, and was most
refreshing, my mustache got full of the fluid, and when I attempted to wipe this ornament, which my Memphis friend had
so carefully glued upon my upper lip, and which added so
much to the manliness of my countenance, I fancied that it was
loose and was about to fall off. Here was a terrible situation,
and I cannot undertake to describe what I felt. To say that
I was frightened, scarcely gives an idea of the cold chills that
ran down my back. The ridicule of my entertainers, and
especially of Miss Sadie, was the least thing that I feared, and
I would rather brave any number of perils at the cannon's
mouth than to repeat the emotions of that dreadful moment.
Such a situation as this is ludicrous enough, but it was not a
bit funny for me at that time; and I was on pins and needles
until I could get away, and take means to secure the mustache
firmly on again. I managed, however, to keep a straight
countenance, and to join in the conversation with a tolerable
degree of equanimity, keeping my hand up to my mouth all
the time though, and doing my best to hold the mustache

on. My fright, after all, was causeless, for on examination I found that the hair was too firmly glued to my lip to be easily removed; indeed, I subsequently discovered that it was practically impossible to move it without the aid of alcohol.

After supper, the old man and Frank went off to finish up their work before going to bed, and the women folks busied themselves in clearing the dishes. I had thus a little time to myself, and took advantage of it, first of all, to ascertain about the security of my mustache. To my intense relief I found it as fast as if it actually grew on my lip; and so, with a light heart, I returned to the house, and joined the old woman and the girls.

During the supper, the elder Giles nearly monopolized the conversation, and scarcely gave his wife and children a chance to put a word in edgewise. I saw very plainly that the old woman was worried at the prospect of losing Frank, and consequently prepared to sustain a heavy siege of queries and expostulations from her. Leaving the girls to finish putting away the supper things, she seated herself in the corner, and began pulling vigorously at a pipe filled with some very strong-smelling tobacco, which was far from grateful to my nostrils.

After a variety of inquiries about the war, the duties of a soldier, the chances of being killed, the amount of pay a soldier received, and like matters, she asked whether I had any parents.

I replied that my father was living.

" Ain't he opposed to your going to the war?" said she.

" O, no," I answered; "he knows that it is what a military man must expect; and he not only wants me to go, but he will be disappointed if I do not see some hard fighting, and have a chance to distinguish myself."

" Are you married?" was the next query.

" No, madam," I replied, giving a sharp look at Sadie, who made a pause in her rattling of the dishes to hear what I would say; "I am one of the unfortunate single men."

" You are much better off, young man," struck in the old man Giles, who just then came in; and throwing himself on the bench, began to smoke a very strong pipe rather furiously.

Hearing the girls giggle at this, I glanced over my shoulder, and seeing that Miss Sadie had finished her work, and was apparently anxious to be better acquainted with me, I politely arose and offered her my raw-hide chair. This she blushingly

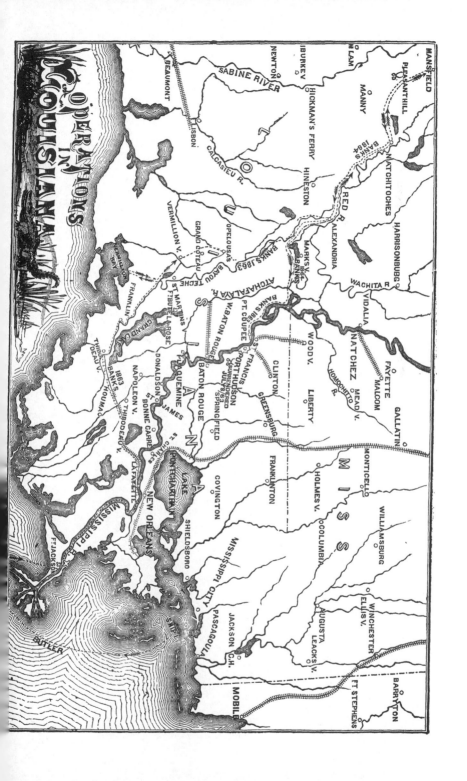

declined, but took a wooden stool, upon which she seated herself quite close to me. I could think of nothing so likely to loosen her tongue, and make her properly sociable, as a reference to religious matters; so I asked her if there were any churches in the neighborhood.

She said that there was no regular church, but that on Sundays a preacher held forth in the school-house; and then, without much difficulty, we got into quite a discussion about religion, and from that to other matters of more immediate interest, if not of so much permanent importance. The old man, I presume, was rather tired, and so, taking advantage of this change of subject in our conversation, he went to bed, and soon was snoring lustily. Finally, Miss Sadie got back to what was the subject uppermost in her thoughts, and began questioning me about my own affairs, by asking if I had any brothers.

"Yes," I replied; "one, older than myself, who is more fortunate, for he is married," — giving a look at her out of the corner of my eye, which I intended her to understand as an intimation that, although not married, I had no objections to being so if I could find a girl to suit me.

"You ought to be married, too," said Miss Sadie, with a simper, and apparently appreciating this kind of conversation much better than the war talk the old man and I had been indulging in.

"How can I get married when none of the girls will have me?" I retorted.

"You git out," was the rather irrelevant remark Miss Sadie made at 'this point, but giving me no reason to believe that she meant her words to be construed literally.

The old woman thinking, I suppose, to flatter me, said, "A handsome young fellow like you, with, I dare say, a pretty fair education, needn't be afraid of the gals not having you."

At this point of the conversation the old man s ~oke, and sang out, "Don't you women talk that man to death. Why don't you git out and let him go to bed?" and then, pointing to a bed in the corner, he told me to turn in there when I felt like it.

THE END OF A DAY'S ADVENTURE.

This was a broad enough hint that Mr. Giles did not want to hear any more conversation that night; so I excused myself to the old woman and the girls, and stepped out on the porch to think a little by myself as to what I had best do next. Here I was at the end of my first day's experience in playing the part of a soldier, with every reason to believe that I had thus far played it most successfully, and that I had really made quite a brilliant start. The prospects were all in favor of the easy accomplishment of my immediate designs, and I saw myself, in imagination, already at the head of a company of stalwart young recruits, appearing in the presence of my astonished husband, and asking him to lead us to battle. That I could successfully pass myself off for a man with both sexes was an assured fact, for the elder Giles and Frank undoubtedly took me for just what I professed to be, and the latter was both willing and anxious to enter himself upon my muster-roll, while the susceptible heart of Miss Sadie was apparently touched in a way that it could never have been had the faintest suspicion of my not being a man crossed her mind. The old woman, too, who, in a matter of this kind, would be quite certain to be a more critical observer than the rest of the family, had no hesitation in believing me to be a gallant young soldier ; so that, taking all things into consideration, I had reason to congratulate myself upon a brilliant opening to my campaign.

My hopes were high, and my heart beat quick at the thoughts that crowded upon me of the future that seemed opening out before me, as under the soft stars of that April night I paced up and down before the house maturing my plans for the morrow, and indulging in romantic imaginings of the glory that awaited me, could I but follow up successfully the career so auspiciously begun. The thought of possible failure only crossed my mind to be banished from it, and I resolved to dare everything to make success a certainty and not a mere peradventure. At length, wearied in mind and body by the fatigues and excitements of the day, I sought the couch which the hospitality of the Giles family had provided me.

When I got back to the room the old woman and the girls had disappeared, and the head of the house was snoring in one corner of the room. I had a large sum of money on my person, and a handsome gold watch; quite enough portable property, in fact, to tempt people so dead poor as my entertainers, and I was somewhat dubious at first about the best manner of disposing of my valuables for the night. I finally, however, concluded to merely take off my coat, vest, and boots, and to put my money and watch under me in such a manner that they could not be touched without my being aroused. My revolver was also examined, and found to be in good shooting condition, and was placed beneath the pillow so that I could easily grasp it in any emergency requiring its use. These preparations completed, I threw myself upon the bed, and ere many minutes, overcome with fatigue, I fell into a deep and dreamless sleep.

6

CHAPTER VI.

A WIDOW.

HE noise of a coffee-mill, operated in a very energetic manner by one of the daughters of the house, and the yelling of half a dozen ill-conditioned dogs, disturbed my slumbers in the morning, at an hour when I fain would have kept possession of my couch, in spite of its unsavoriness. I knew that it was time to get up, but the fingers of sleep pressed heavily upon my eyelids, and I lay for some time half awake and half lost in slumber, not quite certain as to exactly where I was, wondering if camp-life was as rough as this, amused at myself for thinking of such a thing, when I knew that many a soldier would envy me my surroundings, and then dropping off amid a cloud of fancies into a sound doze again. The rather piercing tones of Miss Sadie, calling to Frank, and a fresh outbreak of yells from the dogs, awoke me again, and this time in good earnest. I jumped out of bed, thinking that this kind of laziness would never do if I intended to be a soldier, and pulling on my boots, I stepped out on the porch.

The dawn was far advanced, but the sun was still below the horizon, and the air was dull and heavy with dampness and with the miasmatic vapors of the neighboring swamps. It required some little exertion for me to shake off the lethargy

82

that clung to my limbs, but after a wash in a wooden bowl filled with water, that Frank brought me, I felt refreshed, and ready to begin with proper energy the work of the day. I was not very long in arranging my toilet, using my own soap and towels, which I fortunately had brought with me, for they were articles with which the Giles homestead did not appear to be over plentifully supplied, and was in the midst of a discussion with Frank as to the best method of proceeding in order to enlist the number of men I desired, when the old woman put her head out of the door and squeaked, " Come to breakfast, Mister."

I was in a few moments seated by the side of Miss Sadie, who was still attired in the brilliant yellow calico dress, which was evidently the most esteemed bit of costume her wardrobe afforded. She blushed furiously as I greeted her, but was so evidently partial to me, that the other members of the family could not but take notice of it, and there was not a little sport at her expense. I overheard Frank say to her, in a loud whisper, " You need not stick yourself up for that fellow; he don't want you."

At this I redoubled my attentions, and Miss Sadie showed very plainly by her manner that she was highly flattered by them, so much so, that when Frank, seeing how things were going, whispered maliciously, " I'll tell Bob how you are going on with that soldier," she only turned up her nose, and gave her head a toss in a manner that indicated as plain as words, that Sadie's Arkansas sweetheart had been completely cut out by the military individual seated beside her. It was not altogether bad fun to indulge in a bit of a flirtation with Miss Sadie, for she enjoyed the flattering attentions I paid her immensely, but as I had matters of more importance upon my hands, it was impossible for me to make myself as agreeable to her as she would have liked me to.

RECRUITING.

When breakfast was over, I went out to see the girls milk the cows, and then, after chatting a bit with Sadie, I crossed over to the school-house, where I found half a dozen rather rough fellows waiting to see me, all of whom expressed themselves as extremely anxious to enlist. One very hard-looking specimen, who could not even write his name, wanted very badly to be captain; indeed, they all were quite ambitious to be officers, and I had some difficulty in explaining to them, that in the army, in time of war, where actual fighting was being done, it was a very different thing holding the position of an officer, from what it was in the militia. I, however, encouraged them to believe that they all might be lieutenants, captains, and even generals, some day, if they fought bravely, and succeeded in creating such an enthusiasm among them over the prospect of a brush with the Yankees, to be followed by rapid promotion, that the whole party were soon ready to enlist on any terms I chose to suggest.

After talking the matter over with these men for some time, and explaining the situation in the best style I was able, I wrote out some bills calling for volunteers, one of which I posted on the school-house door, and the rest I gave to Frank, who mounted a horse, and started off to distribute them through the country. During the day I read the army regulations at least a dozen times, and tried to make the men understand what they meant, This was not a very easy matter, but I succeeded in enrolling thirty-six, whom I ordered to report for roll call the next morning. This they did not much fancy ; but on my stating that they were under oath, and bound to obey, they yielded without making any trouble about it, but apparently with no great admiration for military discipline.

My quota was easily filled in four days, and I then proceeded to get my battalion organization complete, and to make preparations for departure. Two of the most intelligent of the men I appointed subordinate officers, one sergeant and the other corporal ; and gave them instructions about drilling the battalion, and maintaining discipline in my absence. Everything now being in proper trim, I sent a messenger ahead to the friend in Memphis who had so efficiently aided my plans, with instructions for him to engage transportation, and then getting my troops into marching order, off we started.

Having seen my little army under way, I lingered for a moment to bid good-by to the Giles family. The old man did not much fancy losing both his boys, — for his youngest son Ira had enlisted as well as Frank, — but he stood it bravely ; the old woman, however, broke down entirely, while both the girls cried, Miss Sadie, I thought, more at the idea of parting with me than at losing her brothers. I, however, begged them to keep their courage up, and to expect the boys home soon, covered with glory, as the heroes of many well-fought fields.

Miss Sadie's hand I squeezed a bit as I said farewell, and I fancy that her lover, Bob, had some difficulty after that in obliterating the impression the young officer had made upon her heart.

On the March.

I determined to march my men to the river, in order to break them in; but before we got to the landing, a good many of them were decidedly of the opinion that soldiering was much harder work than they had calculated upon. None of them showed any disposition to back out, however, and the majority, despite the fatigue of the march, were quite elated at the prospect before them of being able to see something of the world. 1 do not think any of them appreciated the real importance of what they were doing, and looked upon the whole affair much in the light of an excursion, which would be rather jolly than otherwise. Indeed, to tell the truth, I rather regarded the thing in that light myself, notwithstanding that I had seen enough of military life for me to understand something of its serious character.

At the landing I met my Memphis friend with my baggage and equipments and a tent, and with blankets and camp utensils for the use of the men. He also handed me a letter from my husband. This I eagerly read, and much to my disappointment, learned from it that he had gone to Pensacola. I determined, however, to push on and meet him there, for I was bent on carrying out my original idea of surprising him, and of offering him the command of my battalion. I accordingly embarked my men — two hundred and thirty-six in all — upon the steamer Ohio Belle, and issued to them blankets and other articles necessary for their comfort.

My plan now was to go down to New Orleans, where I should be able to procure such stores and equipments as were immediately needed, and where I could perfect my disguise; for, not only did my padded coat not fit me as it ought, but it was almost unbearably warm, and I was anxious to substitute something more comfortable for the padding at the earliest possible moment. My friend accompanied me as far as Vicksburg, where he bade me adieu, the tears springing to his eyes as he did so, for he could not dispossess himself of the impression that I was engaged in a foolhardy and dangerous enterprise, out of which I could scarcely come with credit to myself and friends. He, however, did not attempt to dissuade me, for the time for argument had long since passed, and he knew perfectly well that I was determined to follow my own inclinations at whatever hazard.

On arriving at New Orleans, I landed my men a short distance above the city, and then, with as little delay as possible, purchased my quartermaster and commissary stores, and perfected my private outfit in the manner stated in a previous chapter. Among my other purchases was a fine horse, which I obtained from Dr. Elliott, on Union Street. No finer body of men ever went out of New Orleans than the Arkansas Grays, as my battalion was called. As we passed through Mobile we were heartily cheered, the men waving their hats, and the women their handkerchiefs, and everybody commenting in the most laudatory terms upon our martial appearance. I cannot pretend to tell how proud I was, when I noted how much attention we were attracting ; and if the shadow of a doubt as to the propriety of the course I was pursuing remained in any mind, it assuredly vanished as the cheers of the citizens of Mobile greeted my ears. I felt that, in spite of my being a woman, I was intended for a military leader, and I resolved, more firmly than ever, to let nothing stand in the way of my winning the fame I coveted.

A GENUINE SURPRISE.

At Pensacola we were received by my husband, who came to meet us in response to a telegraphic despatch I had sent him, signed by my *nom de guerre*. He had not the slightest idea who I was, and would not have recognized me had I not revealed myself. So soon as I was able, however, after landing my men from the train, I took him aside where I could speak to him privately, and disclosed my identity. He was intensely astonished, and greatly grieved, to see me come marching into Pensacola at the head of a body of men in such a guise, and said, that although I had done nobly, he would not for the world have had me attempt such a thing. I told him, however, that there was no use of discussing the matter, for I was determined to be a soldier, and then placed in his hands the muster-rolls of my company, to show him how well I could do what I undertook. He was proud of the ability I had displayed in carrying out my plans, and seeing the use- lessness of further argument, took command of the men, and commenced putting them in training. After they were mustered in, and stationed in camp, Thomas C. De Caulp was appointed first lieutenant, and Frank Murdock second lieutenant, while I was ordered back to New Orleans to purchase more stores and equipments.

THE DEATH OF MY HUSBAND.

I had scarcely arrived at my destination when I received a despatch announcing the death of my husband, and requesting my immediate return. Terribly shocked, and nearly wild with grief, I started for Pensacola again, and found, upon my arrival there, that, while drilling his men, my husband undertook to explain the use of the carbine to one of the sergeants, and the weapon exploded in his hands, killing him almost instantly. I was now alone in the world, and more than ever disposed to take an active part in the war, if only for the purpose of revenging my husband's death. Smothering my grief as much as possible, I turned over the command of my battalion to Lieutenant De Caulp, for the double reason that the men were only enlisted for three months, and were to be stationed in Pensacola, or its vicinity, where there was not much prospect of very active service just then, and that I had resolved to go to the front in the character of an independent, with a view of leading a life of more stirring adventures than I probably should be able to do if permanently attached to a particular command.

A PRETTY WIDOW.

During the brief time I had been in Pensacola I had formed the acquaintance of a number of officers who were going to the front, and, as they intended to leave for Richmond shortly, I concluded that it would be better to go in their company, especially as several of them were first-rate fellows, and one or two particular friends of my late husband. I also became acquainted with a good many ladies, one of whom, a dashing young widow, paid my masculine charms the compliment of falling desperately in love with them. This lady did not require any encouragement from me; but finding that, while polite to her, I was rather shy and reserved, and apparently insensible to her attractions, she made a dead set at me, and took pains to let me know, in terms that could not be misunderstood, the sentiments she felt for me.

I was really in no mood for nonsense of this kind, and, to tell the truth, I was not particularly pleased with the decidedly unfeminine advances that were made towards me. The necessity of playing the character I had assumed, however, in a successful manner, pressed upon me, and I felt that diversion of some kind was requisite to divert my mind from the sad and gloomy thoughts caused by my bereavement. I accordingly determined to meet my fair one half way, and paid her numerous attentions, such as taking her to the theatre, and to drive upon the beach. I, however, resolutely refused to accept any of the numerous very broad hints she threw out, to the effect that a little more love-making would be more than agreeable, at which she seemed considerably surprised. Finding, at length, that I either could not or would not understand what she was driving at, she bluntly reproached me for not being more tender in my demonstrations towards her. I put on the innocent air of a green schoolboy, perfectly nonplussed with the advances of a pretty woman, and assured her that I had never courted a lady in my life, and really did not know how to begin. The eagerness with which the widow undertook to instruct me, was decidedly comical, and I learned more about some of the fine points of feminine human nature from her in a week, than I had picked up for myself in twenty years. The courting was pretty much all on her side, and I really had not imagined before that it was possible for a lady to take such an important matter so entirely out of the gentleman's hands. For the fun of the thing I pretended to soften to her, and by the time I was ready to start for Virginia, we were the best possible friends; and although I was careful to make no definite promises, the widow parted from me with the understanding that when the war was over we were to be something more than friends to each other. If I were a man, it would be absurd for me to tell all this, but being a woman, this and other of my love adventures have a comical interest for me, as I doubt not they will have for the reader. If they do not show some of the members of my own sex in the best possible light, it is their fault and not mine.

OFF FOR VIRGINIA.

On the 16th of June I started for Virginia, in company with quite a jovial party of fellows, who were much disposed to make a frolic of their journey. They had a good deal of whiskey with them, and I was constantly importuned to drink, my declining to do so not having the best possible effect on some of them. The conversation became more and more profane and ribald, as the whiskey produced its natural effect; and being almost the only sober person in the party, I was not only intensely disgusted, but the warnings I had received from my husband came into my mind, and had a most depressing influence upon me. Much of the talk was mere meaningless blackguardism, and my ears were saluted for the first time with nastiness in the shape of language, such as it would have been impossible for me to have imagined the tongues of human beings to utter. It was an intense relief to me when, about four o'clock, the train arrived at Montgomery, and I was able to get by myself for a little while.

At the Exchange Hotel I met Mr. Leroy P. Walker, the secretary of war, with whom I had a very pleasant conversation about the prospects of the contest with the North, the political situation, and other matters of interest. The next day I bought a smart and mannerly negro boy, named Bob, of about eighteen years of age. I procured him a proper suit of clothes and a military cap, and then gave him charge of my baggage, with instructions to keep a sharp eye on my effects, to behave himself properly, and to come to me when he wanted spending money. Bob proved an excellent servant, taking care of my clothing in good style, and when we were in camp, attending to my two horses in a very satisfactory manner.

From Montgomery I went to Columbia, South Carolina, where I remained over for several days. During my stay in this place I formed the acquaintance of a very pleasant family, one of the young ladies of which, Miss Lou, seemed to be quite taken with me. I was invited to the house, and passed a number of agreeable hours there, and on parting, Miss Lou gave me her address, requesting me to write to her, and pinned a small C. S. flag on my coat.

On the train bound north, there was another quite jovial party, but, very much to my gratification, not so much addicted to whiskey-drinking, blasphemy, and obscenity, as that with which I had started out. A good deal of the conversation was about wives and sweethearts, and pictures of the loved ones at home were freely handed about. I was rallied rather severely because I could not show a photograph of my sweetheart, and some of the men intimated that I must be a poor kind of a man not to be able to find a girl to exchange photographs with me. I took the sharp things they thought fit to say of me in good part, and replied that I did not doubt of my ability to get a sweetheart soon enough when I wanted one.

A LADY'S MAN.

Before the journey was ended, I had an opportunity to prove myself as good a lady's man as the best of them, for at Lynchburg, where we were compelled to remain over all night, on taking the train for Richmond, an elderly gentleman stepped up, and after inquiring my destination, asked if I could take charge of some ladies. I replied that I would do so with pleasure; but was rather taken aback when I found myself placed in the position of escort to five women and two children. I could not imagine what induced the old gentleman to pick out a little fellow like me, when so many much larger, older, and more experienced officers were present, some of whom were greatly my superiors in rank. I was dreadfully embarrassed, but resolved to play the gallant to the best of my ability, although my heart was in my throat, and I could scarcely find voice to announce myself as Lieutenant Buford, when he inquired my name for the purpose of introducing me.

I was about to inquire whether the ladies had their tickets and checks, when the old gentleman presented them, very much to my satisfaction. Excusing myself for a few moments, I went to attend to checking my own baggage. While I was engaged in this occupation, an officer of my party, who was tolerably full of liquor, approached, and slapping me on the back, exclaimed, " You're a lucky fellow to fall in with such a nice lot of feminines ; won't you introduce me ? "

" Not unless the ladies give their consent," I replied. " If they are willing, and a good opportunity offers, I have no objections."

Just then the bell rang, and I hastened to escort the ladies to the car. My tipsy friend, who was determined to show his gallantry at all hazards, whether his services were agreeable or not, stood ready to lend his assistance ; but as he could not but make himself offensive in the condition he was in, I determined to snub him so completely that he would not have the temerity to intrude on us again. Drawing myself up to my full height, and putting on as severe a manner as I could command, I said, "Excuse me, sir, but these ladies are under my charge, and I am able to take care of them without assistance."

He gave me a rather defiant look, but otherwise took this snub quietly enough, and went into another car, while I joined the ladies feeling several inches taller, and with an increased confidence in myself.

We were soon under way, and had a pleasant enough ride, or at least it would have been pleasant enough had I not been tormented with the fear that they would penetrate my disguise, and discover that I was not what I pretended to be. No suspicions were excited, however, and we finally arrived at Richmond without anything having happened to mar the enjoyment of the journey. On alighting from the cars, I procured carriages to convey the several members of the party to their destination; two of the ladies, however, accompanied me to the Ballard House, where I obtained rooms for them. The youngest of my newly-found female friends, — a very pretty girl, who seemed to have taken quite a fancy to me, — had the room adjoining mine, and I had scarcely established myself in my new quarters, when a waiter knocked at the door and handed me a card from her, asking me to escort her to supper. I laughed to myself at this, and fancying that I had succeeded in making another conquest, determined to get myself up in the best style I could, and to do credit to the uniform I wore by showing her that her appreciation was not misapplied. I dressed myself in my best apparel, and, after a visit to the barber's, I was ready to play the gallant in the best possible manner.

AN EMBARRASSING POSITION.

It was all well enough while I was pacing the corridors of the hotel with mademoiselle on my arm, but I confess that my heart failed me when we entered the dining-room, and I fancied that everybody was looking at us. When the big steward, advancing towards us with his politest bow, said, "Lieutenant, step this way with your lady," and then turning to one of the waiters, told him to attend to this gentleman and lady, it seemed to me as if every eye in the room was fixed on me. I was a rather conspicuous object, it is true, for my uniform, made of the best cloth, and trimmed with buttons and gold lace, was well calculated to attract attention, while the lady on my arm being rather taller than myself, made me even more an object for the curious to gaze at than if I had been alone. The probabilities, however, are, that I imagined myself to be creating a much greater sensation than I was, and it was not a great while before I became accustomed to be stared at, and learned not to mind. My feelings on entering the dining-room, however, were not the less unpleasant for being imaginary, and I was in no mood to develop my talents as a conversationalist for the delectation of my companion.

The young lady was nothing daunted by my silence, and chattered away at a great rate on all imaginable subjects, and finally succeeded in putting me somewhat at my ease. I was just beginning to feel a little comfortable, when in came several persons, my friend, the major, among them, whom I had met in Memphis. They sat down nearly opposite to us, on the other side of the room. I could see by their glances in our direction, and by the laughing manner in which they conversed, that they were discussing my lady and me, and I tried all I could to avoid noticing them. The major, however, at length caught my eye and saluted me, and from a motion he made, I was dreadfully afraid that he intended to come over and join us. My lady at length finished her supper, much to my relief, and I hurried her out of the room as fast as I could, and repaired to the drawing-room, where I excused myself on the plea that I had urgent business to attend to, as I intended leaving the city on the first train. She seemed extremely reluctant to part company with me, and would not let me go until I promised to see her again before I left the city. In bidding her good night, she extended her hand ; and when I took it, she gave mine a squeeze, that indicated as plain as words that a trifle more forwardness on my part would not be disagreeable. I was a little bit disgusted with her very evident desire to capture me, and was very glad to get her off my hands, my determination on parting being not to see her again if I could avoid doing so.

As I strode down the hall, I was overhauled by my Memphis friends, who were very glad to see me, and asked me all kinds of questions about myself, affairs in Memphis, the operations of the Army of the West, and other matters of similar interest. A good deal of the information I gave them was fictitious, while the rest was made up from telegrams, the newspapers, and conversations I had overheard; but it answered the purposes of the moment, and was probably about as near the truth as the greater part of the war talk that was going on around us. I told them that I intended joining Johnston's army, and that I was bound to have a hand in the fight that was coming off, and was anxious to get to the front as soon as possible.

After some further conversation of this kind, the major proposed that we should take a carriage and see the city. We accordingly drove around for a while, seeing the sights, and visiting numerous bar-rooms and gambling-houses, and before a great while the major, who took rather big drinks every time, was very much inclined to be noisy, and to insist upon our making a night of it with him. I had no desire for his company any longer than I could help, and I especially did not desire to go through with the particular kind of performance which he called "making a night of it;" so, resisting his his importunities, I invited another member of the party, a captain, and a very gentlemanly, quiet sort of a fellow, to play a game of cards with me. The major, finding that he could not get us to join him, started off to hunt other companions, while the captain and I returned to the hotel, where we played "old sledge," until one o'clock in the morning.

On going to my room, I found a note from my lady friend, requesting me to visit her in her chamber. This considerably astonished me, and assuredly did not increase my good opinion of her. I was almost tempted, however, to comply, just for the sake of hearing what she had to say to me, but wisely concluded that, situated as I was, it would be more prudent to avoid any further acquaintance with such a forward specimen of my sex.

I slept late the next morning, having forgotten to give directions for being called, and found, much to my satisfaction, on inquiring of the clerk, that my lady had left before I was out of bed. After breakfast, I ordered Bob to have everything ready for our departure by the six o'clock train. While strolling about the street, I was accosted by an officer, who asked me to show my papers. I told him that I had none, but that I was an independent, and had recruited, and put in the field, at my own expense, a battalion of two hundred and thirty-six men. This seemed to highly delight him, for he shook me warmly by the hand, asked me to step over to his office, where he could furnish me with transportation, and otherwise showed a desire to be of service to me. I thanked him, but declined the offer, on the plea that I proposed to pay my own way.

During the day I bought two horses and shipped them, and provided myself with a number of articles necessary for the campaign upon which I was about entering. Returning to the hotel, I paid my bill, had a lunch put up, and my baggage got ready, while Bob blacked my boots and brushed my coat. As ill luck would have it, however, I missed the six o'clock train, and was consequently compelled to remain another night in Richmond. The next morning, however, Bob and I were off in the five o'clock train, the darkey apparently as anxious as myself to see what fighting really was.

CHAPTER VII.

THE BATTLE OF BULL RUN.

Joining the Army in the Field. — Trying to get a Commission. — The Skirmish at Blackburn's Ford. — Burying the Dead. — I attach myself to General Bee's Command. — The Night before the Battle of Bull Run. — A sound Sleep. — The Morning of the Battle. — A magnificent Scene. — The Approach of the Enemy.— Commencement of the Fight. — An Exchange of Compliments between old Friends. — Bee's Order to fall back, and his Rally. — "Stonewall" Jackson. — The Battle at its fiercest. — The Scene at Midday. — Huge Clouds of Dust and Smoke. — Some tough Fighting. — How Beauregard and Johnston rallied their Men. — The Contest for the Possession of the Plateau. — Bee and Bartow killed. — Arrival of Kirby Smith with Re-enforcements. — The Victory Won. — Application for Promotion. — Return to Richmond.

WAS now about to enter upon the realization of all my dreams, to see some real warfare, to engage in real battles, to do some real fighting, and, as I fondly hoped, to have some opportunities of distinguishing myself in a signal manner. I was never in better health and spirit than on that bright summer morning, when I left Richmond for the purpose of joining the forces of the Confederacy in the face of the enemy; and the nearer we approached our destination, the more elated did I become at the prospect before me of being able to prove myself as good a fighter as any of the gallant men who had taken up arms in behalf of the cause of Southern independence. I had only one fear, and that was, that I should be stopped on account of not having the proper papers; but my motto was, "Nothing venture, nothing have;" and I was bent on facing the thing through, and trusting to luck to bring me out all right. Fortunately I had no trouble of any kind, and arrived safely at Clifton, — a supply-station about a dozen miles from the headquarters of the army in the field.

At Clifton I bought a couple of fine horses, and on the 15th of July set out for headquarters, with a view of being assigned to a command where I should have a chance to see some fighting. I sought an interview with a prominent general, but he was in rather a crusty humor; and as he did not seem inclined to talk with me, I concluded not to bother him, but to take my chances as matters might shape themselves for the accomplishment of my designs. His adjutant was more polite, and desired to employ me as a courier; but this did not suit my notions, and I consequently declined. I told him that I was an independent, paying my own expenses, and that the only thing I wanted was an opportunity to take a hand in the coming fight. I suppose he thought that I was entirely too independent for him, for he said no more, but turned away, and went about other affairs.

TRYING TO GET A COMMISSION.

General Beauregard was in command of the entire army; but I felt a hesitation in approaching him, especially after the rebuff I had just received. Thinking that the shortest way to get what I wanted was to obtain a regular commission, I offered an officer, with whom I became acquainted, five hundred dollars for his. He would not sell, however; and I then went over to Brigadier General Bonham, who was holding Mitchell's Ford, and introduced myself to him. General Bonham looked at me sharply, and asked what company I belonged to.

"To none," I replied. "I belong wherever there is work to do."

"Well," said Bonham, "you are the right sort to have around when a fight is going on. If you stay here a little while, I reckon you will be able to find plenty of work."

I took this as a hint that I might make myself at home, and, bowing myself out of the general's presence, went to look after my boy Bob. The darkey was just beginning to have some appreciation of what fighting was really like, and was badly scared. I told him that if he ran off and left me, I would kill him if I ever caught him again; which threat had its desired effect, for he stuck to me through thick and thin.

THE SKIRMISH AT BLACKBURN'S FORD.

At half past twelve o'clock, on the 18th, the enemy made a sharp attack, but did not do any great damage. Kemper's battery, which occupied the ridge on the left of the Centreville road, performed efficient service in holding the Yankees

STARTING TO THE FRONT.

in check. Soon, however, the enemy advanced in strong force, and attacked General Longstreet's brigade at Blackburn's Ford. Our pickets fell slowly back across the Ford, which was crossed by our skirmishers, and for some time a rapid but irregular firing was kept up between the two contending armies. Longstreet, however, soon was in a condition to meet the attack squarely; and bringing about three thousand infantry into position, he succeeded in repulsing the enemy after a sharp skirmish of nearly an hour's duration. Later, Longstreet was re-enforced by Brigadier General Early's brigade, and the enemy finding us too strong for them, was forced to retreat from the field. As they broke and ran, I fired a last shot at them with a dead man's musket, which I picked up. During the greater part of this fight, the men belonging to the two armies who engaged in it were often not more than a few feet from each other, and it seemed more like a series of duels than anything such as I had imagined a battle would be. It was during this affair that I had the pleasure of meeting with a man I had heard a great deal about, — Colonel J. B. Walton, of the Washington artillery. He was a brave man, and a very genial, pleasant fellow.

This skirmish was but the prelude to the great battles of Manassas or Bull's Run, which was fought on the 21st of July, 1861. It served, however, to initiate me, and to make me impatient to see an engagement of real importance, in which I should have an opportunity to make a first-rate display of my fighting qualities. I was the more anxious for a big fight soon, as I had been placed temporarily in command of a company, the senior officer of which had been killed, and I was afraid that if a fight was long delayed I should be superseded, and should be compelled to lose my best chance of distinguishing myself. I had no occasion, however, to be afraid of a fight not coming off, for we had ample information of all the movements of the enemy, and knew that he was about to advance upon us in full force, so that the conflict was likely to begin at almost any moment. I was able, therefore, to take part in the first great battle of the war, under the best possible auspices, and to thus accomplish what had been one of the great objects of my ambition from my earliest childhood. There may have been men who did harder fighting at Bull Run than myself, but no one went through the fight with a stouter heart, or with a greater determination to behave valiantly, and, if possible, to give the enemy a sound thrashing, if only

7

for the sake of affording him an idea of the magnitude of the job he had undertaken in attempting to coerce the Southern people.

BURYING THE DEAD.

On the 18th I assisted, with the rest, to bury the dead, my boy, Bob, rendering us efficient service in the performance of this duty. When night came I was tired out, and, lying down on the bare ground, slept soundly until four o'clock the next morning. When I awoke, I was weary and sore in all my limbs through the unusual exertions I had been compelled to make, and the exposure to the hot sun in the day time, and the damp air and cold ground at night. I was not sick, however; and as I had no doubt that I should soon get used to this kind of rough life, I never thought of giving up, especially as a great battle was impending, upon taking part in which my heart was bent.

At daybreak, on the 19th, I was in my boots, and ready to march. Passing through Ashby's Gap, we reached the little town of Piedmont, on the Manassas Gap Railroad, where we halted. On the 20th, General Johnston arrived at Manassas about noon, and was followed by two Georgia regiments and Jackson's brigade of gallant Virginians. Then came Bernard E. Bee, with the fourth Alabama regiment and the second regiment, and three companies of the eleventh regiment of Mississippians. On account of some delay, or detention on the railroad, it was now found necessary to hold a council of war, and to make some changes in the plans already aranged.

When the troops were once more in motion, I followed Bee's line through a dense wood, as far as Sudley's Road. General Bee, at this place, appointed me a special messenger, and sent me with an order to Colonel Wheat, of the Louisiana battalion, and also to General Evans, whose command was about six hundred yards distant. Evans was an officer whom I had heard much talked of, and whom I greatly desired to see. He was commonly designated, by the officers and men, as " Shanks," and he looked very much as if the kind of liquor he was in the habit of drinking did not agree with him.

It was well known that the Federals intended to attack us in force on Sunday, the 21st, and preparations were made to give them the right kind of a reception when they appeared. Although full of excitement at the prospect of taking part in a great battle, one that, perhaps, would enable us to secure the independence of the South at a single blow, — for the skirmishes in which I had thus far been engaged only seemed to whet my appetite for fighting, and to make me more than ever desirous of seeing what a really desperate-fought battle was like, — I succumbed to the fatigues I had undergone, and passed the greater part of the night, before the terrific conflict at Bull Run, in a dreamless sleep. I had fancied that sleep would be impossible to me under such circumstances; but a very little experience as a soldier was sufficient for me to be able to fall into a soldier's way of doing things, and I soon learned to take my rest as naturally and composedly upon the bare ground as if on the most downy couch, and not even the excitements and anxieties incident to an impending battle could prevent my tired eyes from closing after a long and fatiguing day passed under a broiling July sun.

THE MORNING OF THE BATTLE OF BULL RUN.

On the morning of the day of the battle I was awake at dawn, and ready to play my part in the great drama which was about to begin; and although some of the men around me had been disposed to laugh at the efforts of the little dandified independent to get a chance to display his valor, not one of them was more eager for the fight than myself, or was more bent upon doing deeds of heroism. If I had allowed myself to be irritated by snubs from officers, who behaved as if they thought the results of the war depended upon them alone, I should have gone back to Richmond in disgust several days before the battle came off, and should have resumed the garb of my sex, with a determination never to figure as a man again. I was not to be bluffed by anybody, however; and having come thus far to see and to take a hand in a great battle, I had no thought of turning back for any cause, or under any circumstances, no matter what might be said or thought of me.

I labored under some disadvantages in not having a regular commission, and not being attached to a regular command. This exposed me to slights that would otherwise not have been put upon me, and prevented officers, who would, under some circumstances, have gladly taken advantage of my readiness to attend faithfully to any task assigned me, to avail themselves of my services. On the other hand, my being an independent, enabled me, to a great extent, to choose my own position in the battle, and I probably, therefore, had a better opportunity of distinguishing myself than I should have had otherwise. I was especially bent upon showing some of them, who were disposed to smile at me on account of my *petite* figure and jaunty air, that I was as good a man as any one of them, and was able to face the enemy as valiantly. This I did show them before the day was over, and I was highly elated at the commendations which some of the best soldiers bestowed upon the " plucky little devil," as they called me.

By the time it was fairly daylight, the preparations for meeting the enemy were well advanced, and the sun rose in all his majesty upon a host of men drawn up in battle array, — the brave among them anxious for the fray to begin, the cowards — and there were plenty of them in both armies, — trembling in their boots, and eager for a pretext to sneak away, and hide themselves from the coming danger. The morning was a beautiful one, although it gave promise of a sweltering day; and the scene presented to my eyes, as I surveyed the field, was one of marvellous beauty and grandeur. I cannot pretend to express in words what I felt, as I found myself one among thousands of combatants, who were about to engage in a deadly and desperate struggle. The supreme moment of my life had arrived, and all the glorious aspirations of my romantic girlhood were on the point of realization. I was elated beyond measure, although cool-headed enough, and watched the preparations going on around me with eager interest. Fear was a word I did not know the meaning of; and as I noted the ashy faces, and the trembling limbs of some of the men about me, I almost wished that I could feel a little fear, if only for the sake of sympathizing with the poor devils. I do not say this for brag, for I despise braggarts as much as I do cowards; but, in a narrative like this, the reader has a right to know what my feelings, as well as my impressions, were, upon so important an occasion as my appearance as a combatant upon the battle-field, where the Confederate troops first gave the enemy a taste of their genuine quality, and achieved their first great victory.

The Advance of the Enemy.

As the hot July sun mounted upwards through the almost cloudless sky, and the mists of the morning disappeared before his ardent beams, the approach of the enemy could be distinctly traced by the clouds of dust raised by the tramping of thousands of feet, and, once in a great while, the gleam of the bayonets was discerned among the heavy clumps of timber that covered the undulating plain which the commanders of the armies of the South and the North had selected for their first trial of strategy and of strength. The desultory firing with which the battle opened soon was followed by rapid volleys, and ere the morning was far advanced, the sharp rattling of the musketry, the roar of the artillery, and the yelling of the soldiers, developed into an incessant tumult; while along the entire line, for miles, arose clouds of yellow dust and blue smoke, as the desperateness of the conflict increased, and the men on either side became excited with the work they had in hand.

It soon became apparent that the position in which fortune had placed me was to be the chief point of the Federal attack, and that my immediate comrades would be compelled to bear the brunt of the battle. The gallant Colonel Wheat was severely wounded early in the day, but he succeeded in checking the advance of the enemy, and in maintaining his position, until General Bee, on being informed of the peril he was in, advanced to the Henry House with the Alabama regiment and Imboden's artillery, and from thence crossed the valley to the support of Evans's command. The Federals were in strong force, there being, probably, fifteen thousand immediately in front of us, and they followed up their first sharp attack with some desperate fighting. The commands of Bee, Evans, and Bartow were all soon actively engaged in resisting the advance of vastly superior numbers, and had quite as much as they could attend to to do it. I attached myself to my favorite officer, Bee, and remained with his command during the entire day.

BEE ORDERS HIS MEN TO FALL BACK.

The Federal artillery, which sent its shell showering over us, and bursting in our ranks, creating terrible slaughter, was commanded by an acquaintance of mine, Ricketts. I did the best I could to give him as good as he sent, for the sake of old times when we were friends, and when we neither of us imagined that we would some day be opposed to each other on the battle-field. The Confederates, although greatly outnumbered, succeeded for a long time in maintaining their ground, in spite of the odds against them, and again and again pierced through the enemy's lines. Our men suffered terribly, however, the seventh Georgia and fourth Alabama regiments, especially, being very badly cut up. At length, despite all our efforts, Bee was compelled to give the order for us to fall back, the enemy having been heavily re-enforced by the commands of Sherman and Keyes.

The Federals, doubtless, thought that the victory was theirs when they saw us in retreat. It was a terrible moment, and my heart failed me when I heard Bee's order. I was wrought up to such a pitch of excitement, while the fight was going on, that I had no comprehension whatever of the value of the movements being made by the different commanders. I only saw the enemy before me, and was inspired by an eager desire to conquer him. I forgot that I was but a single figure in a great military scheme; and as, while we stood face to face with the foe, every man on the other side became for the moment my personal enemy, whom I was furious to overcome, so, when by the general's command, we were compelled to fall back, I was overcome with rage and indignation, and felt all the shame and mortification of a personal defeat.

"STONEWALL" JACKSON.

I soon, however, saw the object Bee had in view in his momentary retreat, when he rallied his men in the rear of a house, and gave them a breathing spell, until Wade Hampton's legion and Jackson's brigade could come to their assistance. This movement on the part of Bee afforded me an opportunity to cool off a little, and to observe the ebb and flow of the tide of battle more critically. I ere long was able to understand the general plan upon which the action was being conducted, and to view the combatants as masses to be wielded in a certain way for the accomplishment of definite objects, and not as a mere howling mob, bent only on a momentary success. From this point, therefore, the battle became more interesting than ever, and while none the less exciting, simply as a personal adventure, — for my spirit rose and sank as victory or defeat seemed likely to rest upon our banners, — I was more under the dominion of my reason, and less of my passions, than I had been when the fight commenced.

Bee rallied his men, with a voice of thunder, saying, "My boys, at them again! Victory or death! See how Jackson stands there like a stone wall." This last expression seemed

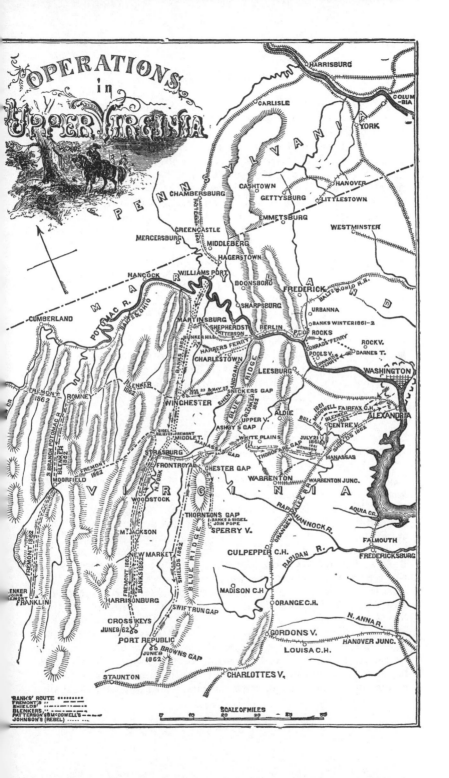

OPERATIONS in UPPER VIRGINIA

SCALE OF MILES

BANKS' ROUTE ••••••••••
FREMONT'S ··········
SHIELDS ─·─·─·─·─
BLENKERS +·+·+·+·+
PATTERSON'S & McDOWELL'S ─ ─ ─ ─
JOHNSON'S (REBEL) ──────

to please the men mightily, for they took it up immediately; and with a cheer for "Stonewall" Jackson, they made another dash at the enemy.

At noon the battle was at its fiercest, and the scene was grand beyond description. The simile that came into my mind was the great Desert of Sahara, with a broiling sun overhead, and immense whirlwinds of sand rolling along over the plain between heaven and earth. The red dust from the parched and sun-dried roads arose in clouds in every direction, while the smoke from the artillery and musketry slowly floated aloft in huge, fantastic columns, marking the places where the battle was being fought with most bitterness. The dry and motionless air was choking to the nostrils, from the dust and smoke which filled it, while the pitiless July sun poured its hottest rays upon the parched and weary combatants. It was a sight never to be forgotten, — one of those magnificent spectacles that cannot be imagined, and that no description, no matter how eloquent, can do justice to. I would not have missed it for the wealth of the world, and was more than repaid for all that I had undergone, and all the risks to my person and my womanly reputation that I incurred, in being not only a spectator, but an actor, in such a sublime, living drama.

The Pinch of the Fight.

At the moment when Bee rallied his men for another grapple with the enemy, I would have given anything could I but have had the strength to make a clean sweep of our opponents, and, by a single blow, end the great struggle. Looking towards the hill which, in the morning, had been occupied by three of our bravest and best generals — Beauregard, Johnston, and Bonham — and their staffs, I saw it covered with men fighting with desperation; all along the valley were dense clouds of dust and smoke, while the yells of the excited soldiery, and the roar of the guns, were almost deafening.

Hard pressed by the greatly superior Federal force, our men at several points wavered and fell back, and at one time there was every prospect of a panic. This disgrace was spared, however, largely by the personal exertions of Beauregard and Johnston, who darted along the line, and succeeded in rallying the men, and in bringing them up to their work again. General Johnston turned the fortunes of the day by charging on the enemy, with the colors of the fourth Alabama regiment at his side. This was the pinch of the fight; for the enemy were bearing down upon us with a large force of infantry, cavalry, and artillery, and the personal example of Generals Beauregard, Johnston, and other prominent officers, who plunged into the thickest of the *mêlée*, had an immense effect in encouraging the men to resist to the last, no matter what the odds against them might be.

The fiercer the conflict grew the more my courage rose. The example of my commanders, the desire to avenge my slaughtered comrades, the salvation of the cause which I had espoused, all inspired me to do my utmost; and no man on the field that day fought with more energy or determination than the woman who figured as Lieutenant Harry T. Buford.

At two o'clock the right of Beauregard's line was ordered to advance — with the exception of the reserves — to recover the plateau, for the possession of which both armies had been fiercely contending. Stonewall Jackson succeeded in piercing the enemy's centre, but his troops suffered terribly in doing so. Bee, while leading his fourth Alabama regiment in a charge, fell mortally wounded about a hundred yards from the Henry House. Fifty yards farther north, Bartow was shot, and was caught, as he fell from his horse, by General Gartrell, then commanding the 7th Georgia, and by his order carried to the rear. His last words were, "Boys, I am killed; but don't give up the field." Colonel Fisher, of the sixth North Carolina regiment, was also among the killed. He was a noble fellow. The conflict now became more bitter than ever, and at one time it seemed that we should be compelled to succumb to the fierce attacks which the enemy were making against us. At this crisis, a courier came up to me with a message for General Johnston, to the effect that the Federals had reached the line of the Manassas Gap Railroad, and were marching on us with a heavy force. Had this information been correct, it would have been all up with us. Fortunately, however, the advancing troops were those of Kirby Smith, and consisted of about two thousand infantry and Beekman's artillery. The arrival of this force decided the fate of the battle, and the Federals fled, defeated, from the field, while our army fell back to Manassas Junction.

After the battle, I appealed to General Jackson for the promotion which I considered that I had fully earned, and he gave me a recommendation to General Bragg for a recruiting commission. This I did not care about, for I thought that I did not need his permission or his aid to do recruiting duty, and determined to wait and see if something better would not offer. I accordingly remained for some time with my acquaintances of the fifth and eighth Louisiana regiment, hoping that another battle would come off at an early day. Finding, however, that there was no prospect of a fight very soon, and becoming tired of inactivity, I determined to return to Richmond, for the purpose of seeing whether it was not possible for me to find some work to do suited to my abilities.

CHAPTER VIII.

AFTER THE BATTLE.

Erroneous Ideas about the War. — Some of the Effects of the Battle of Bull Run. — The Victory not in all Respects a Benefit to the Cause of the Confederacy. — Undue Elation of Soldiers and Civilians. — Richmond demoralized. — A Quarrel with a drunken Officer. — An Insult resented. — I leave Richmond. — Prospect of another Battle. — Cutting a Dash in Leesburg. — A little love Affair. — Stern Parents. —A clandestine Meeting. — Love's young Dream. — Disappointed Affections. — In Front of the Enemy once more. — A Battle expected to come off.

 **I** HAVE remarked in a previous chapter with regard to the men belonging to the battalion which I recruited in Arkansas, that they seemed to be under the idea that they were going on a pleasant holiday excursion, rather than that they were engaging in a very serious business, which would demand all their energies, if the object they had in view was to be secured. I frankly confess that I was not altogether free from the feeling which prevailed, not merely with the young fellows like my Arkansas recruits, who were glad of any pretext for getting away from their rather dismal surroundings, and who thought that fighting the Yankees would be good fun, but with all classes of society. The expression constantly heard, that one Southerner could whip five Yankees, was not mere bounce, but it really represented what nearly everybody thought; and very few had any doubt as to the speedy end of the conflict that had been begun, or that it would end in the recognition of Southern independence. It took time to convince our people that they had no holiday task to perform; but the difficulty of effectively forcing the Federal lines, in spite of victories won by Con-

107

federate arms in the field, combined with the privations caused by the constantly increasing efficiency of the blockade, at length compelled all classes of people at the South to realize the fact that they had a tough job on their hands, and that if they expected to obtain their independence it would be necessary for them to work, and to work hard for it.

In many respects, the victory at Bull Run was anything but a benefit to the South. The panic which overtook the Federal soldiers, so far from communicating itself to the people of the North, only inspired them with a determination to wipe out the disgrace, and they hurried men to the front with such rapidity and in such numbers, that they soon had a force in the field which compelled the Confederates to act upon the defensive, and to think about the means of resisting invasion instead of attempting to assume the aggressive. On the other hand, not only the men who fought at Bull Run, but the whole South, were greatly elated at having won the first great battle; and, overestimating the importance of their victory, they were more than ever impressed with the idea that whipping the Yankees was a remarkable easy thing to do.

RELAXATION IN DISCIPLINE.

The result of all this was, that discipline in the army, instead of being kept up to the best standard, was relaxed, and hundreds of good fighting men, who thought that the war was virtually over, were permitted to go home, while many others lounged round the camps, or went to Richmond, for the purpose of having a good time, when they ought to have been following up their success by further blows at the enemy.

It is easy enough now to see the mistakes that were made, and any narrative of the war would be incomplete were not some note made of them. I do not pretend, however, that I was any wiser at the time than other people, or that I had any better appreciation of the magnitude of the task we had before us. Experience is a bitter teacher; and Experience in this case was too late in giving her instructions for it to do any good.

As for myself, I was just like hundreds of other young officers, eager to fight as much for the excitement of the thing as anything else; but having little comprehension of the real situation, or the gigantic obstacles which stood in the way of the realization of our hopes, I chafed at the inactivity which followed the battle of Bull Run, hoping for another engagement which would enable me to display my valor, but was disposed to have as good a time as was possible while the thing lasted, whether any fighting was going on or not.

The victory at Bull Run, while it elated the whole Southern people, and very greatly excited their hopes and expectations, was most demoralizing to Richmond, to which city the capital of the Confederacy had been removed a short time before the battle came off. Crowds of soldiers, officers, and privates thronged the streets, when they ought to have been on duty in the field; while innumerable adventurers, male and female, were attracted to the seat of government in the hope of making something out of the war, careless of what happened so long as they were able to fill their pockets. Money was plenty, entirely too plenty, and the drinking-saloons, gambling-houses, and worse resorts, reaped a rich harvest. For a time all went merrily; but after a while, as month after month wore away, and no substantial fruits of our brilliant victory were reaped, and the prospect of a severe contest became every day more decided, those who, like myself, had their hearts in the cause, began to be impatient and disgusted at the inactivity that prevailed, and were disposed to do a good deal of growling. I confess that I enjoyed the excitement of life in Richmond at this period hugely for a time, but I soon had enough of it, and was glad to get away.

After the battle of Bull Run I did as much tall talking as anybody, and swaggered about in fine style, sporting my uniform for the admiration of the ladies, and making myself agreeable to them in a manner that excited the envy of the men, and raised me immensely in my own esteem; for I began to pride myself as much upon being a successful lady's man as upon being a valiant soldier.

A LITTLE UNPLEASANTNESS.

The only adventure of any consequence that I had in Richmond, however, was a difficulty with a lieutenant, who started a quarrel with me without the slightest provocation on my part, and who, finding me apparently indisposed to have any words with him, seemed to think that he could insult me with impunity. I stood a good bit of insolence from him on account of his being in liquor, and endeavored to avoid him. As I was much smaller than himself, and so evidently unwilling to quarrel, he probably thought that it was a good opportunity to air the spirit of blackguardism, which is the strongest characteristic of some people, and persisted in following me up. At length I could not stand his insolence any longer, and to put a stop to it slapped his face. He evidently had not expected anything of this kind, for he seemed stunned for a moment, while I walked off, determined to take no further notice of him, unless absolutely compelled to do so. When he recovered himself he gave me a volley of abuse, and threatened to shoot me ; but, fortunately for himself, a friend who had seen the encounter stepped up, and taking him in charge, prevented him from making a fool of himself any further. I thought that perhaps he might attempt to revenge himself in some way for the indignity I had put upon him, but he doubtless came to the conclusion that this was a case where discretion was the better part of valor, and so prudently kept out of my way. I never saw his homely visage again, although I every day appeared in the most public places, where he would have had no difficulty in finding me if he had desired to.

One of Cupid's Mistakes.

Not being successful in getting the kind of appointment I desired at Richmond, I concluded to try my luck elsewhere. I went to Danville, and remained a couple of days, and on my return to Richmond obtained a pass and transportation for the West. When I got as far as Lynchburg, however, I changed my mind, owing to meeting some of the boys from Leesburg, who persuaded me to go there with them, as there was every prospect of another fight coming off soon. This suited me exactly, and to Leesburg I accordingly went, with a full determination to take a hand in a battle if one did come off. The fight did occur, although not so soon as I expected or wished, and I played my part in it as successfully as I had done at Bull Run. In the mean time, however, I splurged around Leesburg in fine style, and enjoyed myself immensely, being quite as successful as I had been in other places in winning the regards of the members of my own sex, not one of whom appeared to have the slightest suspicion that I was other than I pretended to be.

One young lady in particular, Miss E., showed a marked regard for me ; and as she was a very charming girl, our acquaintance would probably have developed into a decided attachment, had I not been sailing under false colors. I was sorry that I could not reciprocate, in a proper manner, the very evident partiality she displayed towards me; and I more than half regretted that I permitted matters to go as far as I did, when I found what an impression I was making on her susceptible heart. It was necessary for me to sustain the character I had assumed, of a dashing young officer; and, situated as I was, it was important that I should make myself as agreeable as possible to the members of my own sex. Apart from this, however, much of the male society into which I was thrown was so very disagreeable to me, that I was glad to escape from it by seeking that of lady friends. It afforded me some amusement, too, to carry on a bit of a flirtation with a nice girl; and I was very much tempted to entertain myself in this manner, without reflecting very deeply as to the consequences. I am very willing to admit that I ought not to have acted as I did in this, and some other similar cases; and if anything should occur to induce me to assume male attire again, I should carefully avoid making love to young ladies, unless I had occasion to do so for the immediate furtherance of my plans. My error in allowing myself to indulge in flirtations with my own sex, arose from thoughtlessness, and from a desire to play my part to the best advantage; and I am sure my readers will forgive me, as I hope the youug ladies, whom I induced to indulge false expectations, will, when the publication of this narrative makes known to the world the whole truth about the identity of Lieutenant Harry T. Buford, C. S. A.

A Cool Reception.

I met Miss E., by accident, in a store, and she was introduced to me by a youug dry goods clerk, with whom I had struck up an acquaintance. After a little conversation on indifferent subjects, she gave me a very pressing invitation to call on her. I said that I would do myself the honor, and accordingly put in an appearance, dressed in my best, at her residence. She received me with many smiles and with great cordiality, and introduced me to her father and mother. As I noticed that the old people were rather inclined to be a little cool, and evidently did not regard me with overmuch favor, I cut short my visit, and, politely bowing myself out, determined, in my own mind, never to enter the house again.

Had I been a man, the conduct of the parents would probably have spurred me to court the favor of the daughter with more pertinacity than ever. I have noticed that parental opposition to a young man generally has this sort of stimulating effect upon him; but, being a woman, I did not look at the thing exactly from a masculine point of view, and, as the French say, *Le jeu n'en valait pas la chandelle.*

I was sufficiently piqued, however, to accept any advances the young lady might make with some degree of favor, and to revenge myself upon the old people, by making myself intensely agreeable to the daughter, in spite of them. When Miss E., therefore, showed a very marked disposition to continue our acquaintance, I was quite ready to meet her half way.

The next day I met her on the street, and she, with a pleasant smile, said, "I hope that you were not offended last night."

"Certainly not," said I. "Why should I be? Nothing has happened to offend me;" just as if I had not noticed the behavior of her parents.

"O, yes, there has," she answered. "Pa did not behave at all polite to you; but then he treats all the young men who come to see me in the same way, so you must not mind him."

She then informed me that, if I wished, I could see her at her cousin's; and as she seemed to be exceedingly anxious to have me call upon her again, I consented to do so. As we walked up the street together she pointed out her cousin's house, and I made an appointment to meet her there the next day, at five o'clock. I then went with her to within a short distance of her home, but declined to go to the door; not that I cared for what the old folks might say or think, but because I thought that perhaps she might get a scolding.

On parting with my little lady, I went immediately to a livery stable, and, hiring a team, ordered my boy Bob to drive past Miss E.'s home, for the sake of showing the old gentleman what kind of style I could put on. Then going to the dry goods store, I took my friend, the clerk, out with me for a turn around the town, but did not inform him with regard to what had occurred between the young lady and myself.

I was punctual in keeping my appointment with Miss E.; and whether it was that my stylish team had impressed her imagination, or that it was really a case of love at first sight, she was even more cordial in her manner towards me than on the previous occasions when we had met.

She asked me innumerable questions about myself, where I was from, who were my parents, and seemed to be particularly anxious to find out all about me.

I made up a story that I thought was suited to the occasion and the auditor; and, among other things, told her that I was the son of a millionnaire, that I had joined the army for the fun of the thing, and that I was paying my own expenses.

This seemed to make a great impression, on her; and, with a very significant smile, she said she wished that the war would soon end, and that I would settle permanently in Leesburg. This was a rather broad hint, and I could scarcely refrain from laughing at it; but restraining myself, and keeping my countenance straight, I asked, "Why do you take such a fancy to me, Miss E., when there are so many elegant, accomplished, and wealthy young men in Leesburg, with whom you have been acquainted for a long time? You know nothing whatever of me."

"It won't be hard for us to become better acquainted," she replied.

"Well," said I, "I don't want to deceive you; but the fact is, I am as good as married already;" and producing a young lady's photograph, which I had in my pocket, added, "I expect to be married to this lady as soon as the war is over."

An Embarrassing Situation.

She turned pale at this, and the tears sprang to her eyes, while I could not but feel regret at having permitted the matter to go thus far. For a time neither of us spoke; and at length, to put an end to a scene that was becoming embarrassing to both of us, I arose, and, extending my hand, said that I must bid her good evening.

She looked at me in a pitiable sort of way, and said, "Will I never see you again?"

I answered that she might, if I was not killed, but a battle was expected shortly, and it was my intention to take part in it. I then said adieu, and precipitately left her, not feeling altogether comfortable about the affair; but judging, as a woman, that the young lady would, before a great while, find herself heart-whole, and be none the worse for having permitted herself to become unduly interested in Lieutenant Harry T. Buford.

So ended my Leesburg flirtation; and a desire to avoid meeting Miss E. again, at least until she had had time to recover her equanimity, as well as my eager wish to see some more fighting, induced me to leave the town as soon as possible.

CHAPTER IX.

THE BATTLE OF BALL'S BLUFF.

T might be supposed that one battle would have been enough for me, and that after having seen, as at Bull Run, the carnage incident to a desperate conflict between thousands of infuriated combatants, I should have been glad to have abandoned a soldier's career, and to have devoted myself to the service of the Confederacy in some other capacity than that of a fighter. Indeed, it so turned out, that the most efficient services I did perform in behalf of the cause which I espoused, were other than those of a strictly military character, although quite as important as any rendered by the bravest fighters when standing face to face to the enemy. But it was, in a measure, due to necessity rather than to original choice, that I undertook work of a different kind from that which I had in my mind when first donning my uniform. We are all of us, more or less, the creatures of circumstances; and when I saw that the fact of my being a woman would enable me to play another *rôle* from that which I had at first intended, I did not hesitate, but readily accepted what Fate had to offer.

The battle of Bull Run, however, only quickened my ardor to participate in another affair of a similar kind, and the months of enforced inaction, which succeeded that battle, had

115

the effect of making me long, with exceeding eagerness, to experience again the excitement which thrilled me on the sultry July day, when the army of the Confederacy won its first great victory. The sensations which, on the battle-field, overcome a soldier who knows nothing of fear, can only be compared to those of a gambler who is playing for enormous stakes. The more noble origin of the emotions experienced in the one case over those excited by the other does not prevent them from being essentially similar, although the gambler, who is staking his all on the turn of a card, can know little or nothing of the glorious excitement of the soldier engaged in a deadly conflict with an enemy, and feeling that its issue depends upon his putting forth his utmost exertions, and that determined valor can alone secure him the victory.

THE PLEASURES OF FIGHTING.

The sensations of a soldier in the thick of a fight baffle description; and, as his hopes rise or sink with the ebb and flow of the battle, as he sees comrades falling about him dead and wounded, hears the sharp hiss of the bullets, the shrieking of the shells, the yells of the soldiers on each side as they smite each other, there is a positive enjoyment in the deadly perils of the occasion that nothing can equal.

At Bull Run, it so happened that I was placed where the fight was hottest, where the enemy made his most determined attacks, where the soldiers of the South made their most desperate resistance, and where, for hours, the fate of the battle trembled in the balance. When at length victory crowned our banners, the enemy fled from the field, and we saw no more of them, and desperate as was the fight, it was, notwithstanding the great number of killed and wounded, unattended with the peculiar horrors, the mere thought of which is calculated to send a shudder through the strongest nerves.

The second battle in which I participated — that at Ball's Bluff — was accompanied by every circumstance of horror; and although in the excitement of the moment, when every faculty of mind and body was at extreme tension, and I was only inspired with an intense eagerness to do my whole duty for my cause, I did not fully realize the enormities of such a slaughter as was involved in the defeat of the Federals at that place, I have never been able to think of it without a shudder, notwithstanding that I have fought on more than one bloody field since. Such scenes, however, are inseparable from warfare, and those who take up arms must steel themselves against them.

In the Field once more.

It was the 10th of October, 1861, when I left Leesburg and went to the headquarters of General Evans, where I met quite a number of acquaintances, and was received with great cordiality by them. A young officer of the eighteenth Mississippi regiment invited me to take up my quarters with him; but as I had all my camp equipage with me, I preferred setting up my own tent. Seeking General Evans, I showed him my papers, and asked to be employed. He accordingly sent me to Colonel Burt, of the eighth Virginia regiment, who, however, told me that as he had no vacancy in his command, he could do nothing for me. I had no other resource now but to await events, and see what should turn up in my favor, feeling a little disappointed at not being able to become attached definitely to some command, but with ample confidence in my own ability to take care of myself, and to find some means of having a hand in the expected battle, whenever it came off.

A Friend of my Youth.

At Hunton's headquarters, I had the pleasure of meeting Colonel Featherstone, of the seventeenth Mississippi regiment. This fine officer I had known when I was quite a small child, and I was decidedly amused at the idea of renewing my acquaintance with him under existing circumstances. He had not the shadow of an idea that the dashing little lieutenant who stood before him was a woman whom he had known as a child. He, however, took a very polite interest in me, and asked where I was from, and a variety of other questions, which I had to draw rather extensively upon my imagination to answer in proper style. I told him that I belonged to Mississippi, and a good deal more of the same kind of fiction, which, if not quite as interesting as the truth would have been, was sufficiently satisfying for the moment.

After we had chatted a little while, Colonel Featherstone invited me over to his tent, and handing out a bottle of whiskey, told me to help myself.

"No, thank you, colonel," I said; "I never drink anything

strong; it does not agree with me, and I accordingly make it a rule not to touch it."

He did not urge me when he noticed that I was very positive in declining; but pouring out a sizable one for himself, said, " Well, a drink of the right kind of liquor, now and then, is a pretty good thing, I think. Here's my regards;" — and, nodding towards me, he swallowed it at a gulp, without winking an eye.

He then said, " Lieutenant, you can turn in here if you wish, if you have not been assigned to quarters. You are welcome to all I have, and can make yourself at home."

I thanked him, and said that there was, fortunately, no necessity for trespassing on his hospitality. Whereupon he said, " If you won't stop with me, come in and see me often. I will be glad to talk to you."

Thanking him again for his kindness, I said good-night, and went over to my own tent, where I found Bob sound asleep. Arousing him, I ordered him to be up by three o'clock in the morning, and to cook plenty of provisions, as we expected something to happen. The darkey knew very well that I meant a fight was probably coming off soon; but by this time he had tolerably well gotten over his first scare, and was beginning to find enjoyment in the excitements of warfare, as well as myself. He grinned, and promised compliance with my order, and I lay down to sleep, convinced from what I had heard during the evening, that my desire to participate in another battle was likely to be gratified very soon.

The Battle of Ball's Bluff.

The next morning, October 22, I was up, and ready for whatever might happen, at an early hour. Having learned that a large force of the enemy, belonging to the command of Colonel Baker, had succeeded in crossing at Edwards' Ferry, and had gained the Bluffs, prompt preparations were made to give them a warm reception.

The brigade under the command of General Evans consisted of four regiments, — the eighth Virginia, and the thirteenth, seventeenth, and eighteenth Mississippi, which were respectively commanded by Colonels Hunton, Burt, Featherstone, and Barksdale. The first brunt of the fight was borne by Lieutenant Colonel Janifer, who, with five companies, was covering the approach to Leesburg.

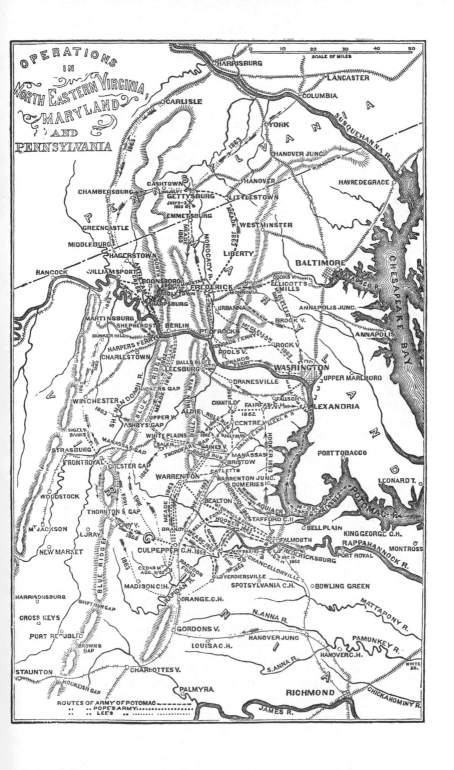

About twelve o'clock, the eighth Virginia regiment advanced to Janifer's assistance, and this, I saw, was my chance if I wished to participate in the battle. My darkey had his fighting blood up too, and was, apparently, as anxious as I was to have a crack at the enemy; for, he said, "Give me a gun, Mas' Harry. I want to shoot, too."

"You'll have a chance to do some fighting pretty soon, Bob, if I am not mistaken," said I, as we pushed forward as fast as we could in the direction of the firing, which became more rapid every moment.

Immediately on top of the Bluff, where the enemy had succeeded in effecting a landing, and for some distance back, there was a tolerably open piece of ground, cut up somewhat by ridges and hollows, and surrounded by a thick growth of woods. This timber for a while concealed the combatants from each other, and it was impossible for us to tell what force we were contending with. The woods seemed to be alive with combatants, and it was thought that the enemy was strongly fortified. Notwithstanding the uncertainties with regard to the number of our opponents, we attacked with spirit, and for a time the fight was bravely carried on by both armies. The enemy certainly fought exceedingly well, especially considering the precariousness of their position, although, of course, we did not know at the time the attack was made that our foes were in such a desperate predicament.

Colonel Burt, with his eighteenth Mississippi regiment, advanced to the attack on the left of our line, while Janifer and the Virginians held the centre. Burt's Mississippians were compelled to undergo a most terrific fire from the enemy, who were concealed in the hollows, but they succeeded in holding them in check, although they suffered severely, and Colonel Burt himself was numbered among the slain before the victory was won.

THE FIGHT AT ITS HOTTEST.

At three o'clock, Colonel Featherstone came up with his regiment, and advanced at a double-quick to the assistance of Burt. The firing now became general all along the line, and the men on both sides seemed to be disposed to fight with the utmost fury. I thought the struggle at Bull Run a desperate one, but that battle at its fiercest did not begin to equal this; and when finally we did succeed in routing the enemy, I experienced a sense of satisfaction and relief that was over-

whelming. For three weary hours the fighting continued
without intermission; and although for a long while the result
was dubious, at length, as the chilly October day was about
closing, the enemy having lost a great number of men and
officers, including Colonel Baker, and being hemmed in on
three sides, were driven in confusion into the river.

Shortly after the fight commenced, I took charge of a company which had lost all its officers, and I do not think that
either my men or myself failed to do our full duty. Perhaps,
if I had been compelled to manœuvre my command in the
open field, I might not have done it as skilfully as some
others would, although I believe that I could have played the
part of a captain quite as well as a good many of them who
held regular commissions as commanders of companies, and a
good deal better than some others who aspired to be officers
before learning the first rudiments of their business, and without having the pluck to conduct themselves before the enemy
in a manner at all correspondent to their braggart style of
behavior when not smelling gunpowder under compulsion.
In this battle, however, fighting as we were for the most part
in the woods, there was little or no manœuvring to be done,
and my main duties were to keep the men together, and to set
them an example. This latter I certainly did.

After the battle was over, the first lieutenant of the company which I was commanding came in and relieved me,
stating that he had been taken prisoner, but had succeeded in
making his escape in the confusion incident to the Federal
defeat. I did not say anything, but had my very serious
doubts as to the story which he told being the exact truth.
He had a very sheepish look, as if he was ashamed of himself
for playing a sneaking, cowardly trick; and I shall always believe that when the firing commenced, he found an opportunity to slink away to the rear for the purpose of getting out
of the reach of danger.

I have seen a good many officers like this one, who were
brave enough when strutting about in the streets of cities and
villages, showing themselves off in their uniforms to the
women, or when airing their authority in camp, by bullying the
soldiers under them, but who were the most arrant cowards
under fire, and who ought tô have been court-marshalled and
shot, instead of being permitted to disgrace their uniforms,
and to demoralize their men, by their dastardly behavior when
in the face of the enemy. My colored boy Bob was a better

soldier than some of the white men who thought themselves immensely his superiors; and having possessed himself of a gun, he fought as well as he knew how, like the rest of us. When the enemy gave way, I could hear Bob yelling vociferously; and I confess that I was proud of the darkey's pluck and enthusiasm.

THE ENEMY PUT TO FLIGHT.

The daylight was beginning to fail, when, at length, the enemy broke, and ran towards the river, a confused mob of fugitives, instead of an organized and disciplined army. I was so wearied that I could scarcely stand. But at this moment I would rather have died than have faltered. All my Southern blood was stirred in my veins, and however little my help might be, I was resolved to give it to complete the victory.

The yells of triumph that broke from our boys, as they saw their foes flying before them, were terrific; and they rushed after them, pursuing them through the woods, and over the open ground, to the very edge of the Bluff. General Evans gave orders to drive them into the river, or to capture them; and every officer and man seemed animated by a determination to make the defeat of the enemy as signal as possible. I advanced my company, in compliance with Evans's orders, until we neared the river, when I called a halt; saying, as I did so, to the boys, "This is warm work, but they are badly whipped, I think."

Looking under me into a little ravine, I espied a Yankee sergeant reaching for a musket, evidently with the intention of treating me to its contents. Levelling a pistol at him, I cried out, "No, you don't! Drop that, and come up here, you scoundrel!"

He obeyed in very short order; and when he had reached me, I said, "What do you mean by that? If it wasn't for having the name of murdering a prisoner, I would shoot you."

He answered, sullenly, "I don't care a d—n whether you do or not;" and I don't believe that he did care much, just then, for he evidently felt badly at having been defeated.

While talking with this prisoner, a number of other fugitives were discovered hid in the gulleys, whom I immediately captured.

" To what command do you belong?" I asked.

They told me that they belonged to the fifteenth Massachusetts regiment, but that the army was under the command of General Stone.

HORRIBLE INCIDENTS.

At the point where I stood the Potomac River was very wide, and it presented a sight such as I prayed that I might never behold again. The enemy were literally driven down the Bluff, and into the river, and crowds of them were floundering in the water, and grappling with death. This horrible spectacle made me shudder; for, although they were my foes, they were human beings, and my heart must have been hard, indeed, could it not have felt for their sufferings. I was willing to fight them to death's door in the open field, and to ask no favors, taking the same chances for life as they had; but I had no heart for their ruthless slaughter. All the woman in me revolted at the fiendish delight which some of our soldiers displayed at the sight of the terrible agony endured by those who had, but a short time before, been contesting the field with them so valiantly, and I could scarcely refrain from making some decisive effort to put a stop to the carnage, and to relieve my suffering foes. For the first time since putting on my uniform I was thrown off my guard, and should certainly have done something to betray my secret had I not fortunately restrained myself in time. Such scenes as these, however, are inseparable from warfare, and they must be endured by those who adopt a soldier's career. The pitiable spectacles which followed our brillant victory at Ball's Bluff, however, had the effect of satisfying my appetite for fighting for a time ; and after it was all over, I was by no means as anxious for another battle, as I had been after the victory at Bull Run.

I have not the ability to give a minute description of the horrid incidents attending the rout of the Federals at Ball's Bluff, even if I had the disposition. As this battle, however, was an important event in my military career, and as it made a very painful impression upon me, some account, even if a very meagre one, of one of the most striking features of the affair, seems to be necessary in order to make my narrative complete.

When the enemy broke before the galling fire which we poured into them, they stampeded for the river, a disordered and panic-stricken crowd. Over the Bluff they went, pell-mell, leaping, rolling, and tumbling, more like a herd of frightened buffalo fleeing from the savages of the plains, than human beings, hundreds being shot down while attempting to cross, and hundreds of others being captured before they could gain the river. I was sick with horror; and as the cold shivers ran through me, and my heart stood still in my bosom, I shut my eyes for a moment, wishing that it was all over, but only to open them again to gaze on a spectacle that had a terrible fascination for me, in spite of its horrors.

ESCAPE OF COLONEL DEVENS.

Directly, one of the prisoners whom I was guarding, shouted, "There goes my colonel!"

"What is his name?" I inquired.

"Colonel Devens, of the fifteenth Massachusetts regiment," he replied, as he pointed to a figure striking out in an attempt to swim across the river.

I said, "I hope the poor fellow will get safely to land, for he has fought bravely, and deserves a better fate than a watery grave."

Colonel Devens, it appears, in the confusion got separated from his men, and seeing no chance of rallying them, or of doing anything to turn the tide of defeat, had, when all hope of ever effecting an orderly retreat was gone, sought to save himself in the desperate manner I have indicated. He was, apparently, a powerful swimmer, for he was soon out of musket-shot, and I believe he managed to gain the other shore. He had my best wishes in the attempt at any rate, for I have not a cruel or vindictive nature, and at this time my womanly sympathies were being awakened in the liveliest manner.

When the rout began, there was but one boat in the river, and this was quickly filled with a struggling mass of humanity, each man being intent only on making good his own escape from the deadly fire of the Confederates. On the bank, a dense crowd of fugitives were throwing away their arms, and divesting themselves of their clothing, some of them, apparently, resolved to save themselves, like Colonel Devens, by swimming. A large number of those who plunged into the river were drowned in the icy waters, and the shrieks of these poor fellows fairly appalled me as I heard them, and rang in my ears for days afterwards.

Our men had orders to keep up a fire from the Bluff, and only too many seemed to delight in the bloody work, as they poured volley after volley into the fugitives. On my left, a Federal captain came charging up the hill at the head of his men, apparently not aware of the full extent of the disaster which had befallen his comrades. As soon, however, as he reached a place where he could survey the field, he saw plainly that it was useless to attempt further resistance, and so he raised a white flag, and surrendered himself and command.

I fired my revolver at another officer — a major, I believe — who was in the act of jumping into the river. I saw him spring into the air, and fall; and then turned my head away, shuddering at what I had done, although I believed that it was only my duty. An officer near me exclaimed, "Lieutenant, your ball took him;" — words that sent a thrill of horror through me.

The most awful episode of the day was the sinking of the boats containing the wounded and dying; and from this I turned away, sick at heart, unable to endure the sight of it.

So ended the battle of Ball's Bluff; and the soldiers of the Confederacy had won another great victory, although at a terrible sacrifice; for many of our bravest officers and men were slain, and a great number severely wounded. I had the satisfaction of knowing that I had done my duty, and had fought as bravely as the bravest. It cost me a pang to think of the noble fellows who fell in defence of the cause they loved, and I particularly mourned the death of the gallant Colonel Burt. I had regrets, too, for the foemen who were so ruthlessly slaughtered, and would willingly have spared them had it been in my power to do so. There were, I think, about nineteen hundred men engaged at Ball's Bluff on the Confederate side, and six pieces of artillery. Exactly how many the Federals had I do not know, but their numbers were certainly equal to ours, if not greater.

When night finally closed upon the battle-field, and put an end to the carnage, I was completely used up by the fatigues and excitements of the day, and not even the terrible scenes which haunted me in my mind's eye, long after I had ceased to gaze upon them, could prevent me from dropping into a sound and dreamless sleep.

CHAPTER X.

FIRST EXPERIENCES AS A SPY.

Reaction after the Excitements of a Battle. — The Necessity for mental and bodily Occupation. — I form a new Project. — War as we imagine it, and as it is. — Fighting not the only Thing to be done. — The Dreams of Youth, and the Realities of Experience. — The Secret of Success. — The Difficulties which the Confederate Commanders experienced in obtaining Information of the Movements of the Enemy. — What a Woman can do that a Man cannot. — A Visit to Mrs. Tyree. — The only Way of keeping a Secret. — I assume the Garments of my own Sex again as a Disguise. — Getting across the Potomac at Night. — Asleep in a Wheat-Stack. — A suspicious Farmer. — A Friend in Need. — Maryland Hospitality. — Off for Washington.

OF too restless and impulsive a disposition to endure patiently the prolonged inaction which seemed inevitable after a battle, it fretted me to be obliged to lounge about camp, or to participate in the too often most demoralizing amusements of the city, as I had been compelled to do for many weeks after the fight at Bull Run. I was disgusted, too, at the difficulties which presented themselves at every step whenever I attempted to get myself attached to a regular command, or to be assigned for the kind of service which I felt best qualified to perform, and which was most in accordance with my tastes. It was an absolute necessity for me to be in motion, to be doing something, and the slow and inconclusive progress of the military movements annoyed me beyond expression. The inevitable reaction, after the intense excitements of the battle of Ball's Bluff, caused a depression of spirits which I felt I must do something to shake off. The terrible sights and sounds of that battle haunted me night and day, for I could not help thinking of them, and the more I thought of them the more horrible they appeared.

I determined, therefore, very shortly after the battle, to put

126

into execution a project I had for some time been meditating, which would require the exercise of all my faculties, and which would give me constant employment for mind and body, such as the routine of camp life did not afford, and which would compel me to concentrate my mind on the invention and execution of plans for the achievement of definite results for the cause of Southern independence.

Before entering upon the career of a soldier, I of course knew a great deal about military life, having been the wife of an army officer, and having resided at frontier stations, but I had nevertheless very crude and superficial notions about the exigencies of warfare. My ideas, however, were no cruder than those of thousands of others, for it is very doubtful whether any but a few veterans understood what would have to be gone through with by soldiers in the field, especially when large armies were operating against each other over an immense stretch of country.

The books I had read, in which the doings of heroes and heroines were recorded, devoted a large space to the description of battles, and these, as a matter of course, being more interesting and exciting than the other portions, it was only natural, perhaps, that the notion should become fixed in my mind that fighting was a soldier's chief, if not only employment.

ROMANCE AND REALITY.

I was soon disillusioned on these points, and, after a very brief experience, discovered that actual warfare was far different from what I had supposed it would be. Neither of the battles in which I had thus far been engaged impressed me at all as I had expected they would, although, in some particulars, they were agreeable disappointments; for there was an exhilaration in an actual, hotly-contested fight that far surpassed anything my imagination had pictured. Battles, however, I found were likely to be few and far between, while there were thousands of disagreeable incidents connected with military life which I had never suspected, and of which my husband's warnings had scarcely given me the slightest hint. The inaction of the camp, when one is day after day hoping and half expecting something startling will happen, only to be subjected to perpetual disappointment, and the dull round of camp duties, and the trivial devices adopted to kill time, after a very brief period become most oppressive.

Not only did I discover that fighting was not the only, or the most frequent, employment of the soldier, but I soon awakened to the fact that, in a great war, like the one in which I was now taking part, it was not always the men who wore the uniforms and handled the muskets who performed the most efficient services. As there were other things besides fighting to do, so there must be other than soldiers to perform necessary portions of the work, and to aid in advancing the interests of the cause.

DREAMS OF DELUSION.

Many of our hopes, anticipations, and aspirations are mere dreams of delusion, which can have no practical fulfilment in this working-day world, and it sometimes costs a pang to dismiss forever a cherished but mistaken idea, and to weave our own web of romance from the parti-colored threads of commonplace reality; it is like parting with a portion of our own being. But, the illusion once dispelled, we are able to step forward more firmly and more resolutely, to act the part which the will of Providence assigns us to play in the great drama of life.

We may regret that the dreams of our youth do not come true, just as we once loved to hope that they would, almost without endeavor on our part; but who shall say that our own life romances, woven out of the tissues of events from day to day, with much labor, doubt, and pain, are not fairer and brighter than any imagination could create? It is good to do one's duty quietly amid the rush of great events, even when the path of duty lies in hidden places, where the gaze of the crowd penetrates not, where applause cannot follow; and one's own satisfaction at duty well and nobly performed, is, after all, the best recompense that can be had.

To be a second Joan of Arc was a mere girlish fancy, which my very first experiences as a soldier dissipated forever; and it did not take me long to discover that I needed no model, but that, to win success in the career I had chosen, I must be simply myself, and not a copy, even in the remotest particular, of anybody else; and that the secret of success consisted in watching the current of events, and in taking advantage of circumstances as they arose.

In a life so novel as that I was now leading, however, it took me some time to become sufficiently informed to be able to do anything effective in the way of shaping my career; I was, of necessity, obliged to go ahead somewhat at random, and to wait and learn, not only what I could do with the best effect, but what there was for me to do. In assuming the garb of a soldier, I had no other idea than to do a soldier's duty: this was my ambition, and I scarcely gave thought to anything else. The experiences of actual warfare, however, soon had the effect of convincing me that a woman like myself, who had a talent for assuming disguises, and who, like me, was possessed of courage, resolution, and energy, backed up by a ready wit, a plausible address, and attractive manners, had it in her power to perform many services of the most vital importance, which it would be impossible for a man to even attempt.

DIFFICULTIES IN OBTAINING INFORMATION.

The difficulty which our commander experienced in gaining accurate and thoroughly reliable information with regard to the movements of the enemy, the rumors that prevailed of the enormous preparations being made by the Federal government to crush the South, an insatiable desire to see and to hear for myself what was going on within the enemy's lines, all stimulated me to make an attempt, the hazardous character of which I well knew; but, trusting to my woman's wit to see me safely through, I resolved that the attempt should be made.

My plans were tolerably well matured when the battle of Ball's Bluff took place, and I should probably have put them in execution before I did, had it not been for the insatiate desire I had to take part in another fight. After that battle, I more than ever felt the necessity for some constant, active employment, for I chafed under the *ennui* of the camp, and felt irresistibly impelled to be moving about and doing something. I accordingly was not long in resolving that the time had now arrived for me to attempt something more than I had yet done, and for me to effect a *coup* that might either make or mar my fortunes, but that, whatever its result might be, would give me the excitement I craved, and demonstrate my abilities, and my disposition to serve the Confederacy in such a signal manner that it would be impossible for those in authority any longer to ignore me.

9

A Woman's Advantages and Disadvantages.

A woman labors under some disadvantages in an attempt to fight her own way in the world, and at the same time, from the mere fact that she is a woman, she can often do things that a man cannot. I have no hesitation in saying that I wish I had been created a man instead of a woman. This is what is the matter with nearly all the women who go about complaining of the wrongs of our sex. But, being a woman, I was bent on making the best of it; and having for some time now figured successfully in the garments of the other sex, I resolved upon resuming those of my own for a season, for the accomplishment of a purpose I had in my mind. This purpose I felt sure I could accomplish as a woman; and although I had a tolerably good appreciation of the perils I should run, I had confidence in my abilities to see myself through, and the perils attending my enterprise were incentives, rather than otherwise, for me to attempt it.

Having obtained a letter of introduction to General Leonidas Polk, and my transportation papers, — for it was my intention, after making the trip I had immediately in view, to visit the part of the country in which his army was operating, as it was more familiar to me, and I thought that I could perform more efficient service there than in Virginia, — I turned in my camp equipage to the quartermaster, and bidding farewell to my friends, started off in search of new adventures.

Stopping in Leesburg, I went, in company with a couple of other officers, to pay a visit to Mrs. Tyree, a brave and true-hearted Virginia lady, who, with her interesting family, had suffered greatly through the devastation of her property by the enemy. We tried, by every argument we could imagine, to persuade her to remove to some safer locality, representing that the Federals, though defeated at Ball's Bluff, were likely to repeat the attack at any time, and to march on Leesburg with a large force. Our appeals were in vain, however, and she answered every argument, by saying, "This is my home, and I will perish in it, if necessary." I heartily wished that I had a force of soldiers under my command at the moment, so that I could compel her to remove for her own sake and that of her family; and when I said adieu to her, it was with the sincerest admiration for her inflexible courage and her devotion to the cause of the South.

MAKING A CHARGE.

THE WAY TO KEEP A SECRET.

Leaving my boy where he would be taken care of, I stated to my acquaintances that I intended to make a journey, and that I expected to be gone about ten days, but did not tell any one where I was going, or what my plans were. No one but myself had the slightest notion as to what project I had on foot, for I felt that success would very largely depend upon my secret being kept to myself, at least until I had accomplished, or had tried to accomplish, what I proposed. What I dreaded more than any dangers I was likely to be exposed to was the ridicule that would probably meet me in case of failure, to say nothing of the probabilities in favor of my sex being discovered, or at least suspected. But ridicule, as well as danger, was what I resolved to brave when putting on male attire, and I really dreaded it less than I did my own heart-burnings in the event of my not winning the desperate game I was playing. The way to keep a secret, as I had long since found out, is not to tell it to anybody; and acting upon this very excellent principle, I have generally succeeded in keeping my secrets — and I have, in my time, had some important ones — until the proper moment for revealing them came. Some people are never happy when possessed of a secret until they have told it to somebody else, of course in the strictest confidence. My experience is that this is a sure way to get the matter, whatever it may be, put into circulation as a bit of general information.

ASSUMING A NEW DISGUISE.

It was necessary, however, for me to have some assistance in getting my enterprise started, just as it had been for me to select a confidant when I first assumed the uniform of an officer; and I would say here that, to the infinite honor of the friend whose aid I sought on that occasion, the secret of my transformation was as faithfully kept as if it were his own; but, as the circumstances were different, a different kind of an agent was in this case selected. My appeal, this time, was to the strongest sentiments of self-interest, and even then my confidant was only intrusted with the knowledge of a change of apparel.

Going to an old negro woman who had washed for me, and who had shown considerable fondness for me, I told her that

I intended visiting the Yankees for the purpose of seeing them about coming and freeing the colored folk, and asked her to let me have a suit of woman's clothes, so that I could get through the lines without being stopped. I made up quite a long yarn about what I proposed to do, and the poor old soul, believing all I told her without a moment's hesitation, consented to aid me in every way she could, her ardor being materially quickened by a twenty dollar Confederate note which I handed her.

She was not long in having me attired in the best she had, — a calico dress, a woollen shawl, a sun-bonnet, and a pair of shoes much too large for me, — and hiding away my uniform where it would be safe during my absence, she started me off with a full expectation that I would be back in a couple of weeks, with the whole Yankee army at my back, for the purpose of liberating all the slaves. The old woman put such implicit faith in me that I really felt sorry at deceiving her, but quieted my conscience with the thought that lying was as necessary as fighting in warfare, and that the prospects were that I would be compelled to do much more fibbing than this before the errand upon which I was about starting would be achieved.

CROSSING THE POTOMAC.

Managing to make my way to the river without attracting any particular attention, I found an old negro who had a boat, and making up a story that I fancied would answer the purpose, I struck a bargain with him to take me across to the Maryland shore for twenty-five dollars. He was eager to get the money, probably never having handled so much before in his life at any one time, but warned me that it would be a risky piece of business, for the weather was very cold, the river broad and deep, and the current strong, and there was considerable danger of my being fired at by the pickets on either bank. I told him that I was not afraid to take all the risks, and that I thought I could stand the cold. I accordingly concealed myself in his cabin until the time for commencing the crossing arrived, neither of us deeming it prudent to start before midnight.

It was after midnight before we were launched in our little craft on the black, swift-running water of the Potomac, and it was quite three hours before we reached the opposite shore. My old ferryman pulled lustily, but it was hard work for him, although the handsome fee he was to receive when his task was accomplished was a decided stimulant. He really had the best of it, however, in having some work to do, for the night air was bitter cold, and I was thinly clad. I would have been glad to have taken a turn at the oars, just for the sake of warming myself, had I believed myself possessed of the physical strength to wield them with efficiency. I was too eager to get over this unpleasant and hazardous part of my journey, however, to incur any delay by attempting to pull an oar, and bore the sharp winds that swept over the water, and at times seemed to cut me to the bones, with what equanimity I could command.

At length we reached the Maryland side of the river, to my infinite satisfaction, for I was numb with the cold, and stiff in all my limbs, from the cramped position in which I had been obliged to sit in the boat, and was heartily glad of an opportunity to tread dry land once more. Dismissing the boatman, and enjoining him not to say anything, I made my way to a farm-house which I espied a short distance from the place of landing, and about four o'clock in the morning, finding no better place to rest my weary limbs, I crept into a wheat-stack, and slept there until daylight.

I scarcely know whether to say that I enjoyed this sort of thing or not. For a thinly clad woman to find no better place for repose during a chilly night in the latter part of October, after having endured the cutting blasts for three hours while crossing the Potomac in an open boat, was certainly hard lines. It is true that, for some months, I had accustomed myself to tolerably rough living, but this was a trifle rougher than anything I had as yet experienced. As there was no one but myself to applaud my heroism, this particular episode did not, and could not, have the same attraction that some even more perilous ones had; and yet, despite the discomforts of the situation, I had a certain amount of satisfaction, and even of pleasure, in going through with it. My enjoyment — if I can designate my peculiar emotions by such a word — I can only attribute to my insatiable love for adventure; to the same overmastering desire to do difficult, dangerous, and exciting things, and to accomplish hazardous enterprises, that had induced me to assume the dress of the other sex, and to figure as a soldier on the battle-field.

When I crept into that wheat-stack, however, I was not in a mood to indulge in any philosophical reflections on the situation, or on my own motives or feelings; I was simply in search of a reasonably sheltered place where I could repose until morning; and having found one, I was not long in closing my eyes, and lapsing into temporary oblivion of the cares and trials of this wicked world.

I managed to get a nap of a couple of hours' duration, when I was awakened by the increasing light, and by the noises of the farm-yard. Adjusting my clothing as well as I could, and shaking off the straw that clung to me, I approached the house, a little dubious with regard to the kind of reception I should get, but trusting to luck to be able to obtain what I wanted. A man came out to meet me, and looked rather sullenly at me, as if he thought me a suspicious character, whom it would be well to have cautious dealings with. My appearance was such that there was certainly good cause for his distrust. The old colored woman's calico dress, woollen shawl, sun-bonnet, and shoes did not come near fitting me, while my slumbers in the wheat-stack had not tended to make me a particularly attractive object. I had no difficulty in believing that I was a perfect fright, and was amused, rather than displeased, at the rather discourteous reception I met with.

Plucking up courage, however, I advanced, and told him that I had been driven out of Virginia, and was trying to get back to my people in Tennessee. I did not give any hint of my political predilections, thinking it more prudent to find how he and his folk stood first. I then asked him if I could not go into the house and warm myself, and get some breakfast, as I was both cold and hungry, and I suppose must have looked so pitiable that he felt compelled to grant my request, if only for charity's sake. He accordingly invited me into the dining-room, and called his wife.

When the woman came, I told a long rigmarole, taking pains to show that I had some money, with which I could, if necessary, pay for what I ate and drank. My story, I saw plainly, did not take very well, and the man was evidently afraid to say much. The woman, however, soon let out on the Yankees with such fiery energy that I understood at once how matters stood, and consequently began to feel more at my ease.

I now began to embellish my story with plenty of abuse of the Yankees, and with such details of the sufferings I had endured on account of my having sided with the South, that their sympathies were at once aroused, and I felt certain that I could easily get all the assistance from them that I wished. Both of them — but the man especially — were eager to know all about the battle. I had told them that I had just come from the neighborhood of Leesburg, and I accordingly gave them an account of the affair, dilating particularly upon the magnificent manner in which the Confederates had whipped the Yankees, and prophesying that, with a little more of this kind of fighting, there would soon be an end of the war.

The woman now invited me to a nice, warm breakfast, which I enjoyed immensely, for I was desperately hungry after my night's adventure. During the meal I showed them a letter, written by myself, for use in such an emergency as this, which, of course, tended to confirm the story I told, and treated them to the style of conversation they evidently liked to hear. After breakfast was over, the woman, taking pity upon my mean attire, insisted upon dressing me in some of her own clothing. I was soon, therefore, in a somewhat more presentable condition than I had been, and, having obtained such information as they were able to give in regard to the best method of proceeding in order speedily to reach my destination, I bade them good-by, sincerely grateful for their kindness, and started for Washington, where I hoped to be able to pick up some useful bits of information, — in fact, to make what the soldiers would call, a reconnoissance in force.

CHAPTER XI.

IN WASHINGTON.

Inside the Enemy's Lines. — Arrival at the Federal Capital. — Renewing an Acquaintance with an old Friend. — What I found out by a judicious System of Questioning. — The Federal Plans with regard to the Mississippi. — An Attack on New Orleans surmised. — A Tour around Washington. — Visit to the War Department, and Interview with Secretary Cameron and General Wessells. — An Introduction to the President. — Impressions of Mr. Lincoln. — I succeed in finding out a Thing or two at the Post-Office. — Sudden Departure from Washington. — Return to Leesburg. — Departure for Columbus, Kentucky.

AVING once penetrated the lines of the enemy, there was, I knew, little to fear. As a Confederate soldier, I was figuring in a disguise which was likely, at any time, to get me into trouble of some sort, and not the least danger I saw was that of being arrested as a spy. When I first undertook to be a soldier, this was an idea that never occurred to me; but a very short experience in actual campaigning taught me that I would have to be careful to prevent the fact that I was disguised from being found out, if for no other reason than that my loyalty to the Southern cause might not be suspected. I relied, however, upon the good fighting I had done, and the other services I had rendered, which were proofs of the genuineness of my devotion, as well as the influence of my friends to get me out of any scrape into which I might fall through the discovery that I was not a man.

Here, in the enemy's country, however, I passed for exactly what I was, with nobody nearer than Memphis who knew me, both as a man and as a woman, and I consequently felt perfectly secure in moving about pretty much as I chose,

CROSSING THE POTOMAC.

having a plausible story on the end of my tongue to tell anybody who might question me. I concluded that, as it was
most likely I would meet in Washington people who knew me
as a woman, — indeed, I relied greatly upon finding some
acquaintance through whom I could be able to obtain the
kind of information I desired, — that it would be safer, and in
all respects better for me to attempt no disguise, but to figure
as myself, and as nobody else.

ON THE ROAD TO WASHINGTON.

The kindness of my friend, the farmer's wife, in furnishing
me with an outfit from her own wardrobe, enabled me to make
a presentable appearance, for, although I was by no means
elegantly attired, my clothing was quite good enough for me
to pass as a lady ; and when I left the farm-house and started
en route for Washington, it was with a light heart, and with
no apprehensions of difficulty, except, perhaps, in getting
back safely, and of being able to resume my disguise again
without being discovered. The prospect of having some
trouble in these respects, however, only gave a zest to the
adventure ; and as I had managed to get safely within the
Federal lines, I had little doubt that I would be able to elude
the Confederate pickets in returning, especially as I understood how matters were managed on the Virginia side, and
knew, or thought I knew, how to elude the vigilance of our
boys.

Between my starting-point on the Maryland side and
Washington, I saw a good many soldiers, from which I judged
that the approaches to the Federal capital were strongly
guarded, and that very efficient means were being taken to
prevent anything like a surprise on the part of the Confederates. This was the most important information I succeeded in obtaining ; and except that I was enabled to form
some estimates of the force that was guarding the Maryland
side of the Potomac it was of no special value, as it was well
understood among the Confederates that the enemy were well
prepared to resist an attack upon Washington, and were concentrating a large army in and about the city.

There were matters better worth knowing than this that I
hoped to discover ; and to discover them, it was necessary for
mè to go to Washington, and when there, to obtain facilities
for conversing with people who knew what I wanted to know.

I had a plan of procedure in my mind in which I had great confidence. but I really trusted more to circumstances than to any definite plan, having ample belief in my own ability to take advantage of anything that might turn up. While on the way to Washington, therefore, I judged it prudent to do as little talking as possible, although I kept my eyes and ears open for any scraps of useful knowledge that might present themselves.

ARRIVAL IN WASHINGTON.

On arriving in Washington, I went to Brown's Hotel, and having learned that an officer of the regular Federal army, with whom I was well acquainted, and who had been a warm personal friend of my late husband, was in the city, I sent him a note, asking him to call on me. He came to see me very promptly on receiving my message, and greeting me with a good deal of cordiality, expressed a desire to aid me in any manner that lay in his power. I told him that I was just from New York, and making up a plausible story to account for my being in Washington, began to question him about the progress of the war. He evidently had not the slightest idea that I was in Washington for any other purpose than what he would have considered a perfectly legitimate one, and consequently spoke without any reserve concerning a number of matters about which he would certainly have kept silent had he suspected that I had just come from the other side of the Potomac, and that my object was to pick up items of information that would be useful to the Confederacy.

He greatly lamented the defeat which the Federals had met with at Ball's Bluff, and from what he said, I judged that the affair was the great sensation of the hour, and that it had caused much discouragement, not only in the army, but among all classes of people at the North. Indeed, my friend was decidedly blue when discussing the subject, and expressed himself in very energetic terms with regard to the rebels, little thinking that he was conversing with one who had played a most active part in the very thickest of the battle. He went on to say, however, that it was expected that the defeat at Ball's Bluff would be more than compensated for very shortly. and that in Kentucky, particularly, the Federals were making great preparations for an active campaign, which, it was hoped, would do material damage to the Confederacy.

I succeeded, by judicious questioning, in obtaining a few

points from him with regard to the operations of the Federal forces in the West; but, although he was tolerably well posted about the general movements, he was apparently not accurately informed with regard to particulars. It is probable, too, that he might have known a good deal that he did not choose to tell, even to me, unsuspicious as he was about my real character.

Something worth Knowing.

The information of most vital moment, however, that I succeeded in obtaining from him was, that active preparations were being made to secure possession of the upper Mississippi, and that a very large fleet was being fitted out for the purpose of blockading the mouth of the river. I instantly surmised from this that an attack on New Orleans was in contemplation, and resolved to bend my energies, during my stay in Washington, to the task of finding out all I could with regard to the actual intentions of the Federal government. I did succeed in obtaining ample confirmation of all my friend told me, and to a limited extent of my guesses. Those, however, who really knew, were very close-mouthed about what particular work was being cut out for the fleet to perform, and the desire seemed to be to leave the impression that it was to undertake blockade duty simply, and to close the mouths of the river to the ingress and egress of vessels. There were some things which I heard, however, that did not exactly conform to this theory, and by the time I left Washington, I was tolerably well convinced that a grand blow was shortly to be struck, either at Mobile or New Orleans, but most likely at the latter city. I pumped, in a quiet way, everybody I met, who was at all likely to know anything; but I was really afraid to push my inquiries too far, or to seem too inquisitive, as I did not care to be suspected as a spy and put under surveillance, especially as I learned that the government was greatly annoyed by the presence of numbers of Confederate spies in Washington, and was disposed to deal vigorously with them if they were caught.

This, it must be remembered, was simply a reconnoitring expedition, undertaken entirely on my own account, without authority from anybody; and while I, of course, wanted to find out all I could, my real object was more to make an experiment than anything else, and I did not wish to spoil my chances for future operations — for I fully expected to visit Washington again on similar service to this — by getting into trouble just then, and consequently making myself liable to suspicion in the future.

After a somewhat prolonged and very pleasant conversation with my friend, he took his departure, promising, however, to call the next day, and as I was a stranger in Washington, — having never visited the city before, — to take me to the different places of interest. This was exactly what I wanted, for I was desirous of being informed, as soon as possible, exactly where the public offices were situated, and the best means of obtaining access to them, and I counted greatly upon this obliging and very gallant gentleman unsuspectingly starting me on the right road for the accomplishment of the ends I had in view.

He made his appearance promptly at the appointed hour the next morning, and took me to see the Patent Office, the Treasury Department, and the War Department. With this latter, especially, I was, as might be supposed, particularly interested; and skilfully hinting to my escort an intense desire to know something with regard to how the operations of a great conflict, like the one in progress, were directed from headquarters, I led him up to making a proposal that he should introduce me to the Secretary of War. In a demure sort of way, I expressed myself as delighted at the honor of being able to meet so great a man, and so, in a few moments more, I was bowing, in my politest manner, to Secretary Cameron.

AT THE WAR DEPARTMENT.

The secretary seemed to be busy, and evidently did not have much time to give to me, and my conversation with him scarcely amounted to more than an exchange of the most ordinary civilities. I made the most of my opportunities, however, for studying his face, and forming some estimate of his character.

I cannot say that the Secretary of War impressed me very favorably. He was abundantly courteous in his manners, but there was a crafty look in his eyes, and a peculiar expression about his mouth, that I thought indicated a treacherous disposition, and that I did not like. I concluded that Mr. Cameron would be a hard man to deal with, unless dealing were made well worth his while; but in spite of his evident knowingness, and his evident confidence in his own abilities,

I left him, feeling tolerably sure that I could prove myself a fair match for him in case our wits were ever brought into conflict.

I was much better pleased with General Wessells, the Commissary General of Prisoners, to whom I was also introduced, than I was with Secretary Cameron. He was very polite, indeed, and I decided immediately that I was likely to make more out of him than I was out of the secretary. On the impulse of the moment, and just for the sake of feeling my ground with him, I said, in a careless sort of way, during our conversation, that I had a brother who was a prisoner, and whom I would like to see, if it could be permitted, notwithstanding that he was on the wrong side. General Wessells very politely said that I could see him if I wished; whereupon I thanked him, and said that I would, perhaps, shortly avail myself of his kindness.

The reader may be sure that while at the War Department I saw and heard all I could, and that I took particular pains to note the movements of everybody, and to observe exactly how things were done, so that in case I should ever be obliged to call there again on any special errand, I should feel reasonably at home, and be able to go about whatever work I had in hand with as little embarrassment as possible.

A VISIT TO MR. LINCOLN.

From the War Department we went to the White House, where my friend said he would introduce me to the President. I really had some dread of this interview, although I experienced a great curiosity to see Mr. Lincoln, and would not have willingly missed such an opportunity as this of meeting him. I had heard a great deal about him, of course, and not much that was favorable, either as regards his character or his personal appearance, and I considered him more than any one person responsible for the war. Mr. Lincoln, however, was an agreeable disappointment to me, as I have no doubt he was to many others. He was certainly a very homely man, but he was not what I should call an ugly man, for he had a pleasant, kindly face, and a pleasantly familiar manner, that put one at ease with him immediately.

I did not have an opportunity to exchange a great many words with Mr. Lincoln, but my interview, brief as it was, induced me to believe, not only that he was not a bad man, but that he was an honest and well-meaning one, who thought that he was only doing his duty in attempting to conquer the South. He impressed me in a very different way from the Secretary of War; and I left the White House, if not with a genuine liking for him, at least with many of my prejudices dispelled, and different feelings towards him than I had when I entered.

My change of sentiment with regard to Mr. Lincoln, as may be supposed, did not influence me in the least with regard to my own opinions concerning the rights and wrongs of the contest between the North and the South, nor did I allow it to interfere in any way with the carrying out of my plans. I was simply trying to do my duty, just as I suppose he was trying to do his, as he understood it; and I was, equally with him, determined to aid, by every means in my power, the particular side I advocated.

After leaving the White House, we visited the Capitol, and listened to the debates in Congress for a while; but as the subjects which the senators and representatives happened to be discussing at the moment were of no particular interest to me, I had more pleasure in looking about the really noble building than I had in hearing them talk.

Our next visit was made to the Post Office, where my friend had some business to transact. Here I succeeded in finding out a number of things I wanted to know, and obtained some really important information, simply by listening to the conversation I heard going on around me, which is a demonstration of the necessity for people who do not want their secrets discovered by the very ones whom it is desirable should not discover them, not to do too much loud talking before total strangers. I was really annoyed at some of the conversation I heard between government officials while at the Post Office, and wondered how the Federal authorities ever expected to prevent the Confederates from finding out their plans if this kind of thing was going on all the time.

My tour around Washington, and especially my visit to the War and Post Office Departments, convinced me, not only that Washington would be a first-rate place for me to operate in, if I could obtain a definite attachment to the detective corps, but that I had the abilities to become a good detective, and would, in a very short time, be able to put the Confederate authorities in possession of information of the first value with regard to the present and prospective movements of the enemy.

Having fulfilled my errand, and accomplished all that I had expected when starting out on this trip, I left Washington as suddenly as I had entered it, giving my friend to understand that I was going to New York. I had as little trouble in getting back to Leesburg as I had in getting away from it, and put in an appearance at the house of the old colored woman, who had my uniform hid away for me, within thirteen days from the time I left it.

In Uniform Again.

Attiring myself once more in the garb of a Confederate officer, I returned the old woman her calico dress, shawl, sunbonnet, and shoes, and in response to her eager inquiries, told her a good deal of nonsense about the Yankees being on their way to free the colored people, and made her believe that they would soon be along. My other suit of female clothing I took up to the hotel with me, and told my boy Bob, who seemed to be very curious about them, that I had bought them for my girl. Bob seemed to be delighted to see me again, as he had been apprehensive, from my long absence, that something had happened, and that I might never return. He was most anxious to know where I had been; but I put a short stop to his questionings on that topic, by giving him orders to have everything ready for an early start on a long journey in the morning. The next day we were *en route* for Columbus, Tennessee, where I expected to find General Polk, under whom I was now desirous of serving.

Like hundreds of others, I had gone to Virginia with the opening of summer, inspired by high hopes and great expectations. These hopes and expectations were far from being realized, although I had succeeded in gratifying some of the most ardent desires that had animated me in setting out, for I had gone through with a number of perilous adventures, such as would have certainly satisfied the ambition of most women. Notwithstanding, however, that the Confederates had won the first great victory, it became apparent, at an early day, that a single battle was not going to finish the war, and that if the South was to achieve its independence, it must go through a long and bloody conflict. My visit to Washington more than confirmed the opinion I had formed, that the Federals were in command of enormous resources in comparison with ours, and that they were settling down to a deadly determination to bring all their resources to bear for the purpose of fighting the thing out to the bitter end. When I took the back track, therefore, nearly six months from the time of starting out, and when the chill winds of winter were beginning to make their severity felt by the poor soldiers, I was prepared for a long and desperate war, which would be a very different thing from the holiday affair which my Arkansas recruits, in common with many others, had expected. I was as resolute as ever in my determination to see the thing out, however, and I experienced even a certain amount of pleasure in the certainty that a prolonged struggle would afford me abundant opportunities for exciting and perilous adventures. There was not a man in the Confederacy who was more willing to fight to the last than I was, or who was willing to venture into greater peril for the sake of the cause ; and, perhaps, if all the men had been as eager to find the last ditch as myself, before giving up, the war might have had a different termination.

This is something, however, about which it is scarcely worth while to speculate now. It is enough to say, that I left Virginia in a different mood from that in which I had entered it. Experience had opened my eyes to a good many things I did not clearly understand before, but although in some particulars I was disappointed, I was certainly not discouraged ; and my head was as full of ideas, and of much better arranged, and more practical plans, than it was when I resolved to become a soldier. I now knew tolerably well what I could do, and the particular kind of work I could do best, and I was as enthusiastic as ever, although, perhaps, in a more sober fashion, to give the cause the benefit of my best exertions.

CHAPTER XII.

ACTING AS MILITARY CONDUCTOR.

At Memphis again. — Ending my first Campaign. — My Friend the Captain and I exchange Notes. — I reach Columbus and report to General Leonidas Polk. — Assigned to Duty as Military Conductor. —Unavailing Blandishments of the Women. — A mean Piece of Malice. — General Lucius M. Polk tries to play a trick on me. — The Path of Duty. — The General put under Arrest. — An Explanation concerning a one-sided Joke. — I become dissatisfied, and tender my Resignation. — A Request to return to Virginia and enter the Secret Service. — Acceptance of my Resignation. — The Lull before the Storm.

FEW days of hard travel, and I was back at my starting-point, Memphis, having made the circuit of the entire Confederacy east of the Mississippi. I was wiser by a good deal of valuable practical knowledge than I was when I set out on my Arkansas recruiting expedition, and I had passed through scenes that made it seem years, instead of a few short months, since I had made my first important attempt at practising essentially characteristic masculine manners with the damsel in yellow calico down there at Hurlburt Station. The mere school-girl romance had been pretty well knocked out of me by the rough experiences of actual warfare. I thought very little just then about Joan of Arc, or indeed, about any of the dead and gone heroes and heroines; but my mind was considerably occupied with my own fortunes, and with those of the cause to which I had pledged myself.

My experiences — I do not allude to the mere hardships of a soldier's life — had not all been of the most pleasurable kind. I had learned much concerning some of the very weak points of human nature; that all men are not heroes who wish to be considered as such; that self-seeking was more common than patriotism; that mere courage sufficient to face the enemy in battle is not a very rare quality, and is frequently associated with meanness of spirit; that it is easier to meet the enemy

10   145

bravely in battle, than it is to exercise one's brains so as to meet him most effectively ; that great names are not always worthily borne by great men, and that a spirit of petty jealousy is even more prevalent in a camp than it is in a girl's boarding-school. These and a good many other things worth knowing, even if the knowledge was not of the most agreeable kind, I had picked up, as well as much information of a different sort, that qualified me to make a second start as something better than an apprentice in the art of war.

Notwithstanding many unpleasant things connected with this, my first campaign, however, I had certainly enjoyed myself immensely, after a certain fashion; for, to have taken part in two such battles as that at Bull Run and that at Ball's Bluff, and to have satisfactorily attempted a trip to Washington for the sake of finding out what they were doing in the Federal capital, were experiences that more than counterbalanced some which I could not reflect upon with equal complacency. If I returned to Memphis a disappointed woman in certain particulars, I also returned a hopeful one, for I knew better now how to go about the work I had in hand; and as it was evident that some of the hardest fighting of the war was to be done in this region, I confidently expected to have abundant opportunity to distinguish myself, both as a soldier and as a scout, and had scarcely a doubt of being employed in such services as I was best qualified to perform.

READY TO MAKE ANOTHER START.

Behold me, then, back in Memphis, ready to commence a second campaign, inspired by a different kind of enthusiasm from that which moved me when I shocked my husband and the friend whom I persuaded to assist me in my enterprise, by my determination to be a soldier, but even more firmly resolved to do my full share of the fighting, and to give the Confederate cause the benefit of all my energy, wit, and courage.

The friend of whom I have spoken I still found in Memphis. He was now captain in the Confederate service, and on my meeting with him he seemed both rejoiced and surprised to see me again. We did not have much of an opportunity to talk matters over, as I was anxious to get to Columbus as soon as possible, but I contrived to find time to relate briefly some of my adventures, and he appeared to be intensely interested

in my recital.   It astonished him somewhat to find that what
I had seen of warfare had not disgusted me with it, and that
I was bent upon being a soldier so long as there was any
fighting to do; but this time, however, he made no attempt to
dissuade me from my purpose, being perfectly well convinced
of my ability to take care of myself.   Wishing each other good
luck, we parted again, and I took the first boat for Columbus,
where I expected to find General Leonidas Polk.

On landing at Columbus, I gave my equipage and the two
horses I had bought at Memphis, in charge of Bob, with directions to keep a sharp eye on them, and went to Barnes' Hotel,
to see if I could come across anybody I knew, and to make
the inquiries necessary for my next movement.

Columbus was one of the liveliest places I had ever visited,
or at least it seemed so that evening.   There was an immense
amount of bustle and confusion, and everything seemed to
indicate that the campaign in this region was being pushed
with considerable energy; although, as I had found out before,
noise and activity in and about headquarters do not always
mean remarkable energy in the field; for an obstinate enemy,
bent on doing some hard fighting, takes a good deal of the
nonsense out of mere cabinet generalship.   Soon after supper
I got my tent up, and the next morning I went in search of
the general for the purpose of presenting my letter.

I REPORT FOR DUTY TO GENERAL POLK.

General Polk, who had been a bishop before the war broke
out, received me cordially enough, although he seemed to be
too busy to do much talking, and after reading my letter,
dismissed me with the rather indefinite observation that he
would see what he could do for me.   This might mean anything or nothing; but as I had no other resource than to wait
and see what conclusion he would come to with regard to me,
I made my bow and retired, determined to be as patient as
my impatient disposition would let me.

While waiting for the general to assign me to duty I visited
the different camps, made a number of acquaintances, and
picked up what information I could about the military situation in the West.   Everybody was expecting hard fighting,
and a desperate struggle with the Federals for the possession
of the Mississippi, as it seemed to be well understood that the
enemy were making great preparations for some heavy work

on this river. It was thought, however, that the defences were sufficiently strong to resist any attacks, and the idea that an attempt would ere a great while be made against New Orleans by way of the Gulf of Mexico, was scarcely entertained seriously by any one. I thought differently; but then I had special reasons for my own opinions, which I did not consider it necessary to communicate to all of my new-made friends, deeming it prudent to keep quiet about my visit to Washington, although ready enough to tell all I knew concerning the military situation in Virginia in exchange for what I learned from them about the condition of things in the West.

The third day after my arrival at Columbus, General Polk sent for me, and told me that he had assigned me to the detective corps. I was considerably elated at this, as I supposed that he intended to employ me in running through the lines as a spy. I had taken a great fancy to this kind of service, and felt myself especially well qualified for it. I wanted something to do that would keep me constantly employed, and especially that would require me to give my whole mind to whatever task I had in hand. There was an element of positive peril in scout duty that had a wonderful fascination for me, and that I felt would give me a keen enjoyment, such as lounging around a camp, with only the disagreeable routine of campaigning, broken by an occasional battle, could never afford.

I AM MADE A MILITARY CONDUCTOR.

I was not particularly well pleased, therefore, when I found that I was to run on the cars as military conductor. This, however, was active duty of a specific kind, and I thought that perhaps it might lead to something better, or might even offer me opportunities for distinguishing myself that I did not suspect. I took it, therefore, without complaining, resolved to do my best while on duty, and to resign the position, and go elsewhere for employment, so soon as I found the service getting too uncongenial. I accordingly went, under orders from General Polk, to Camp Beauregard, where I was directed to relieve Captain Jannett, on the Nashville road.

It was while acting in the capacity of military conductor on this road that some of the most amusing incidents of my career occurred, or, at least, incidents that were amusing enough to me at the time, although I presume that they would seem stupid enough on repetition; for many of the events of our lives that cause the heartiest laughter, depend so much on the surroundings and accessories, that it is difficult to raise even a smile at them when narrated. Nearly every day, however, little controversies would occur between myself and ladies who tried to beguile me with their smiles, little suspecting how well fortified I was against their fascinating arts; and I often laughed heartily to myself at noting the nice feminine wiles that were brought to bear to beguile me from the strict line of my duty. I am afraid that, had I been a man, some of these wiles would have been successful; but as, in spite of my garments, I was compelled to view the arts of my feminine passengers, and would-be passengers, from a feminine standpoint, I am scarcely able to doubt that the military conductorship on this particular line was run on more rigidly virtuous principles, during my term of service, than before or afterwards.

My duty was to run on the trains and examine passes, furloughs, and leaves of absence; and as I could place any one under arrest who was not travelling with the right kind of papers, or who was unprovided with papers of any kind, I was a personage of considerable importance, not only to the officers and soldiers who were going back and forth, but to the ladies, who courted me with remarkable assiduity, with a view of inducing me to grant them favors. The women folk tormented me a good deal more than the men did, for the average masculine had a wholesome dread of the rigors of military discipline, and was consequently manageable, while my own sex relied on accomplishing, by means of their fascinations, what was impossible to the men. They would make all kinds of excuses, and tell all kinds of improbable stories, to induce me to pass them; but as I put a stop to all that kind of nonsense at the very start, and made up my mind to do business on strictly military principles, I soon became anything but popular. Occasionally some of my would-be charmers, finding it impossible to make any impression on me, would abuse me roundly for refusing to grant their request. This, of course, did not have any other effect than to afford me much amusement; but it enabled me to understand why my predecessor seemed so well pleased at being relieved, although I have doubts as to whether he was as strict in enforcing the regulations as myself. Indeed, I have excellent reasons for believing that he was not at all strict.

While the women, as a rule, gave me the most trouble, there were a good many hard customers among the men, with whom it was not easy to have pleasant dealings. Merely obstreperous fellows, however, I could generally manage by letting them see that I was dead in earnest; but there were plenty of officers who were willing to violate orders, and then put the blame, in case there should be any trouble, on my shoulders, and who took it as a personal grievance that I would not let them travel without the proper papers. One malicious scoundrel, because I would not permit him to travel without a pass, trumped up a most scandalous false charge against me, to General Lucius M. Polk, who undertook to look into the matter himself.

Following the Path of Duty.

I did not know or suspect of anything being wrong; and had I been other than resolutely bent upon doing my whole duty, at all hazards, I should probably have fallen into the trap so cunningly laid for me on this occasion. I had seen enough of military life, however, to know that the only safe course for a soldier is to obey orders, no matter who suffers; and, as my orders were to pass no one unprovided with the right kind of papers, I was resolved to carry them out to the letter, under all circumstances, without regard to consequences.

General Polk, bent upon knowing how I was making out as military conductor, and whether I was entirely trustworthy, — it having been reported to him, by the scamp referred to, that I was not, — stepped aboard the train with a ten days' leave of absence in his pocket. He probably thought that I was as good as detected in neglecting my duty, but he found out his mistake before he got through; and if he had not taken the precaution to provide himself with the proper official documents before starting, the ending of the adventure would have been anything but a merry one for him, for I should certainly have arrested him.

A Game of Bluff.

On entering the car, I sang out, as usual, "Show your passes, gentlemen."

The general turned his head, and commenced looking out of the window rather intently, as travellers not provided with passes were very much in the habit of doing. When I reached him, in going through the car, I gently tapped his shoulder, and said, " Have you a pass?"

" No," said he. " Won't you let me go through without one?"

" No sir," I replied; " I cannot pass any one. My orders are very strict, especially with regard to officers and soldiers."

" Well," said he, " don't you think you could go back on your orders for once? Did you never favor a friend in this line?"

" Sir," I answered, rather severely, " I know no friends in connection with my duty, or general orders."

" Well, what are you going to do in my case; for I haven't got any pass," said the general.

I replied, " I will send you back to headquarters, under guard."

" But," said he, " do you know, sir, that I am General Polk?" putting on all the magnificent style he could command as he spoke.

I was considerably nettled, both by his conduct in endeavoring to persuade me to pass him in violation of orders and by his manner, and so said, rather sharply, " I don't care, sir, who you are; you can't travel on this line without a pass, even if you are Jeff Davis himself."

I was, by this time, rather angry, and determined to have no further controversy with him; so I called a soldier to take charge of him, while I finished going through the train.

The conductor, who had seen the whole performance, and who was afraid that I was getting myself into serious trouble, strongly advised me to release the general, and to pass him through as he desired. I told him, however, that I understood my duty perfectly, and that I intended to perform it to the letter, in this as in every other instance; and that if General Polk didn't know better than to undertake to travel without his papers, he would have to bear the consequences.

When we were nearing the station, General Polk beckoned to me, and said, " I have a leave of absence."

I held out my hand, and he produced it from his pocket, laughing as he did so at what he evidently considered a good joke on the military conductor. I looked at it, and returned it, simply saying, " That is all right, sir." The general held out his hand to me with a very cordial smile, and was evidently desirous of doing away with any ill feeling that the incident might have occasioned on my side. I was very badly vexed, however, that he should have attempted to play such a trick upon me, and to have doubted my honor; and I did not receive his greeting with any great amount of cordiality, being resolved, in my own mind, to be even with him some day.

On his return, General Polk explained the whole affair, and apologized very handsomely for having made such a test of my fidelity. I told him very plainly, however, that I did not like that sort of thing, and that I proposed to tender my resignation shortly, as I preferred service in the field to duty like this, where I had to be acting the part of a spy on the people all the time, while being myself subjected to the surveillance of my superiors in a manner that was far from agreeable. He attempted to discourage me from indulging in the idea of resigning; but although I did not care to argue the matter with him, my mind was fully made up to try my luck in some other line of duty.

I AM WANTED IN VIRGINIA.

I was the more anxious to get away, as I had received an urgent letter from my friend, Captain Shankey, asking me to return to Virginia and enter the secret service. This would have suited me exactly, had I been certain of getting the kind of employment I wanted by complying with Captain Shankey's request. But having just come from Virginia, where I had been for a number of months waiting in vain for a fair chance to make myself useful in such a manner that I could take a genuine pride and interest in my work, I was disposed to wait a while and see something of military operations in the West before returning. This call to go East was, however, a good pretext for throwing up a position that was becoming unpleasant, and that promised to be abundantly annoying, without offering any corresponding advantages. It was an additional string to my bow, and I could, at least, consider it while making another effort to tempt Fortune, before putting in an appearance on my old campaign ground again.

It was really, however, my intention to go back to Virginia, so soon as I could get relieved from the duty I was engaged in, and had that object in my mind when I sent in my resignation, although circumstances occurred that induced me to change my plans. My resignation was accepted without much hesitation at headquarters, and once more, after three weeks,

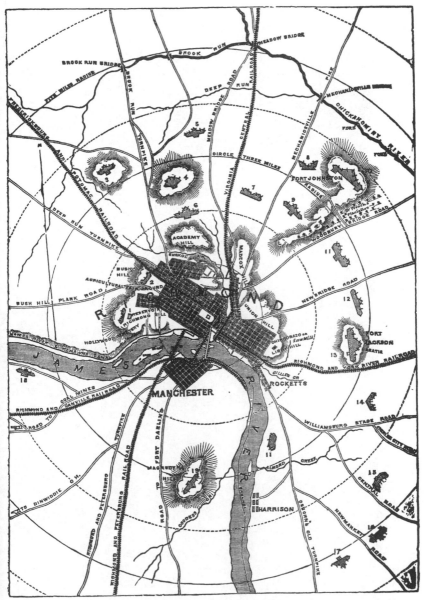

AROUND RICHMOND.

service as a military conductor, I was free to follow my own inclinations.

These three weeks were very fruitful in experiences, and I learned a good many things which I do not particularly care to set down in black and white, but which were worth knowing. Between what I saw and heard, both in the East and the West, I was beginning to understand why things did not move briskly, and why, in spite of successes in the field, the Confederate cause, instead of making headway, was losing ground ; and I was, in a measure, prepared for the disasters which shortly after began to follow thick and fast. But, before disasters did come, there were some bright days, which, in my memory, seem brighter than, perhaps, they really were, from the contrast between them and the dismal times by which they were succeeded. These I enjoyed to the utmost, and when the darkness of defeat and disaster did begin to settle down upon the doomed Confederacy, I, for one, bore up with undaunted spirit to the very last hour, and was willing to fight the thing out even when every hope of success had vanished. But these are matters that do not properly come up for discussion in this place; and what we are now concerned with are the pleasant hours of genuine fun and frolic — the last I saw for many a day — that preceded the bursting of the storm-cloud which was beginning to overshadow the fortunes of the Confederacy.

CHAPTER XIII.

A MERRY-MAKING.

T would, perhaps, have been better for me, in many respects, had I gone back to Virginia ; for the probabilities were that I would, very shortly, if not immediately, have obtained the gratification of my desire for active employment in the secret service corps, and I would, consequently, not only have put in my time to much better advantage than I did, both for myself and for the Confederacy, but I would have been spared a number of particularly unpleasant occurrences which were fruitful of nothing but abundance of disgust on my part. If everything happened to us, however, just as we desired in this world, not only would we not properly appreciate heaven, when we get there, — if we ever do, — but adventure would lose much of its zest. So, the best way, after all, is, perhaps, to take things about as they come, and keeping a sharp lookout for the main chances, do what we can with them to advance the ends we have in view.

My campaign in the West, before I trod Virginia ground again, was certainly adventuresome enough to satisfy all my cravings, were adventure alone what I wanted. While, however, I plunged into adventures for the love of the thing, and cared not what perils presented themselves when I had an object to attain, I was neither reckless nor foolhardy, and wanted to have something definite in view beyond the excitement of the hour.

It was because I thought that there would be a chance for

154

me, ere a great while, in Kentucky, to demonstrate my value either as a soldier or as a spy, — for some heavy fighting was undoubtedly about to begin, — that I determined to defer going East for the present, thinking that Fortune would favor me where I was. So I remained, and began to look about for a good place to commence operations in again. As there was evidently nothing to be had at Columbus that I wanted, I decided to try what could be done at the other end of the Confederate line of operations, — at Bowling Green.

STARTING FOR BOWLING GREEN.

For Bowling Green I accordingly started, my travelling companions being Colonel Bacon and Captain Billingsley. They were both genial, pleasant gentlemen, — gentlemen in every sense of the word, — and I enjoyed their society greatly during the journey.

Soldiers are generally fond of taking a hand in anything in the shape of a frolic that is going on, more especially as a uniform-coat is tolerably sure to be a passport to the favor of the ladies; consequently, when on reaching the little town of Paris, we found that there was some sport in progress in the shape of a hog-killing and corn-shucking festival, we concluded that the best thing we could do would be to stop and have a bit of fun. Well, it was genuine fun, of a downright hearty kind, and all three of us enjoyed ourselves immensely, although, I am afraid that the captain and the colonel appreciated the thing more than I did; for they were both great ladies' men, and this was such a chance as did not present itself every day for them to exert their powers of fascination upon the fair sex. I considered that I had a manly reputation to sustain, too, and I consequently resolved not to be beaten by them in the matter of gallant attentions to the girls of Paris. My previous experience in winning the regards of my sex, induced me to believe that I could, with comparative ease, become the hero of the occasion, in spite of their superiority of official rank and superior dignity of manly carriage. This was the first occasion since my assumption of male attire that I had been offered a fair chance to attempt a bit of rivalry of this kind, and I thought that it would be a first-rate notion to improve the occasion. I determined, therefore, on an active campaign for the smiles of the fair one with the captain and the colonel.

A Favorite with the Ladies.

The welcome which was extended to us was all that could be desired in the way of cordiality, the girls, especially, evidently being delighted to have three dashing officers take part with them in the frolic. It was not a great while, therefore, before each of us had a young lady in charge, and were doing our best to be as agreeable as possible. I had, perhaps, rather the advantage of the colonel and the captain at the start, for I figured as one of those nice little fellows who, for some unaccountable reason, seem to be admired by many women in a greater degree than are more manly-looking men; and as I exerted myself to be as fascinating as possible, my two companions were speedily thrown in the shade, and I found myself the special object of the adoration of the Parisian damsels, very much to my amusement.

The colonel and the captain, however, had the best of me in the long run, for, as I was only playing a part, I was not able to keep up the competition with as much animation as they did; and although the first successes were mine, I was tired out, and ready to retire from the field some time before they showed any disposition to give up. I think that both of my friends perceived that I was trying to outshine them with the Paris girls; but as they did not understand the situation as I did, they were, of course, unable to see exactly where the laugh came in. Could they have but known who I really was, they would, undoubtedly, have been intensely amused, and would have enjoyed the whole performance immensely.

A Village Ball.

The serious business of hog-killing and corn-shucking was supplemented by a feast, at which the viands were chiefly winter apples and cider, and the frolic concluded with a dance in the school-house, which lasted until morning. My two friends and myself were in great demand as partners, and we nearly danced the breath out of our bodies before the affair wound up; which it finally did about daybreak, very much to my satisfaction, for I was nearly used up, having found waltzing all night much harder and more exhausting work than campaigning. The affair, however, was a right merry one, and I enjoyed myself immensely.

When day began to dawn, we took our girls home, and then

sought our beds. It was not long before I was sound asleep, and so worn out with my exertions of the night, that I did not wake up until nearly supper-time.

The next evening we went to a quilting-party, I acting as escort to an old maid who had been compelled to play the part of a wall-flower nearly all the night before, and to whom I determined to pay particular attention, just for the sake of a joke, and to annoy the younger girls, who showed a marked disposition to monopolize all the masculine attentions at her expense. It was very funny to note the dismay which this choice of mine caused in the breasts of those who thought they had a better right to my courtesies. I had the satisfaction of seeing, however, that my politeness was keenly appreciated by the recipient of it, and I redoubled my exertions to make myself agreeable when I noticed the chagrin my conduct was exciting among the rivals of my lady.

As for the lady herself, she had evidently not received so much marked attention from anybody in masculine garb for a long time, and she plumed herself immensely on having made a conquest of the dashing little lieutenant, and was, doubtless, inspired by a higher appreciation of her own powers of fascination than she had ever been before. Repeated attempts were made to win me away from her side, but all in vain; the sport was too entertaining for me to give it up, and I steadfastly resisted all the allurements of the rival beauties, with not a little enjoyment of their discomfiture.

I take the Needle in Hand.

The quilting-party was a very merry and very noisy one, although the fun was not of quite so uproarious a character as that of the previous night. I offered to take a hand at the work that was going on, making a great boast of my skill with the needle. The probabilities are that I could have manipulated that little feminine instrument quite as deftly as most of those present, but did not think it expedient to show myself too handy with it. Taking my place at the frame, therefore, I set about making a figure with something of masculine awkwardness, and succeeded in putting in quite as shocking a bit of work as most men would have done under the circumstances.

While I was doing this, the girls all looked on with great eagerness, praising my work, and endeavoring to flatter me into the belief that I was doing magnificently. When I had completed the figure, I pretended that I thought it much too bad to remain, and offered to pick it out. At this, there was a chorus of indignant remonstrance from all the feminines present, and I was, consequently, compelled to let it stand, the young ladies very prettily professing to be lost in admiration, and my old maid, in particular, smiling on my humble effort with touching sweetness.

There was now an increased effort to win me from my first love; but with a firmness that would have done me infinite credit, had my coat and trowsers rightly represented my sex, I persisted in my preference, leaving it for the colonel and the captain to sustain the credit of the army for gallantry with the other feminine members of the party.

Tokens of Esteem.

My rather excessive politeness to the lady in question was not without its ample reward; for when the time for leaving Paris came, she gave me a substantial token of her esteem and of her keen appreciation of my attentions, by putting me up a lunch, consisting of a fried chicken, biscuits, apples, and two bottles of cider, which, if she is still living, and should have the pleasure of reading this narrative, she will learn were keenly enjoyed by my two friends and myself as we journeyed towards Bowling Green.

So ended the episode of the Paris frolic. It was good fun while it lasted, and it becomes a particularly bright spot in my memory in contrast with the dismal and harrowing scenes by which it was so soon to be succeeded. The Paris girls furnished the colonel, the captain, and myself topics of conversation during a good part of the balance of our journey, and my companions had considerable fun at my expense, on account of my peculiar manner of conducting myself towards the ladies of that village. I took their raillery in good part, of course, smiling to myself at certain amusing incidents, the full significance of which it was impossible for them to understand. Soon, however, all three of us had enough of other things to think of to induce us to dismiss Paris, and the delights of hog-killing, corn-shucking, and quilting-frolics from our minds, and to bend our thoughts to the consideration of matters of more serious interest.

On arrival at General Hardee's headquarters, I went to him,

and showing him my commission, stated that I wanted to go into active service as a scout. He said that he thought there would soon be a chance for me; which was so nearly like the answers I had received from a number of other commanders, that I did not feel especially encouraged by it. It really meant about as much as similar remarks made by others, for nothing came of it, and I was compelled to drift about, looking out myself for something to do to kill time while waiting in hope that the current of events would shape themselves in a manner favorable to my idea.

At this period of the war I could have been employed to very great advantage as a spy, to go to and fro through the lines; and there is no doubt that I could, with comparative ease, have obtained information of the first value to the Confederate commanders. The Federals, as we all knew, were making immense preparations for an important forward movement; and had I been employed as I wanted to be, I could, most likely, have succeeded in saving the Confederates from waiting for defeat to teach them what they ought to have known while making their preparations to meet the enemy.

Perhaps if General Hardee, and others, had known exactly who and what I was, and what were my particular talents in the line of duty I desired to follow, they would have shown a greater disposition to afford me opportunities to signalize myself. They did see, however, that I was ready, willing, and, apparently, able to work; and I scarcely think that they were blameless in not, at least, giving me a fair trial.

THE FIGHT AT WOODSONVILLE.

I was bent, however, notwithstanding the disappointment under which I labored, on showing my devotion to the cause of Southern independence; and, in accordance with my general plan of not letting slip an opportunity of being on hand when there was any real, serious work to be done, I took part in the fight at Woodsonville, on Green River, and faced the enemy as valiantly as anybody. In this fight, Colonel Terry, a brave Texan officer, whom I greatly admired, was among the slain.

The affair at Woodsonville was something of a diversion from the monotony of camp life, but it did not satisfy my ambition or my intense desire for active service; and coming to the conclusion that lounging about Bowling Green and vicinity was much too slim a business for me, I decided to shift my quarters to where there was a somewhat better prospect of hard fighting to be done.   It was by this time evident that the Federals intended making a determined attempt to capture Forts Henry and Donelson, on the Tennessee and Cumberland Rivers, and as I felt confident that our people would make a brave and desperate resistance, I resolved to go and take a hand in the approaching battle, in the hope that something to my advantage would result from it.   If a desire to witness some hard fighting was my chief object in this movement, it was more than gratified, for the horrors of the siege of Donelson far surpassed anything I had yet witnessed, and by the time it was over, I certainly got enough of the excitement of battle to satisfy me for some time to come.   Happily for ourselves, we cannot foresee the future, and in blissful ignorance of the agonizing scenes which I would soon be called upon to witness, I started for Fort Donelson with a comparatively light heart, bent only on so demonstrating my devotion to the cause as would compel the recognition of my superiors.

CHAPTER XIV.

THE FALL OF FORT DONELSON.

The Spirit of Partisanship. — My Opinions with Regard to the Invincibility of the Southern Soldiers. — Unprepared to sustain the Humiliation of Defeat. — The Beginning of the End. — At Fort Donelson. — The Federal Attack expected. — Preparations for the Defence.. — The Garrison confident of their Ability to hold the Fort. — The Difference between Summer and Winter Campaigning. — Enthusiasm supplanted by Hope and Determination. — My Boy Bob and I go to Work in the Trenches. — Too much of a good Thing. — Dirt-Digging not exactly in my Line — The Federals make their Appearance. — The Opening of the Battle. — On picket Duty in the Trenches at Night. — Storm of Snow and Sleet. — The bitter Cold. — Cries and Groans of the Wounded. — My Clothing stiff with Ice. — I find myself giving Way, but manage to endure until the Relief comes. — Terrible Suffering. — Singular Ideas. — A four Days' Battle. — The Confederate Successes on the first and second Days. — The Gunboats driven off. — Desperate Fighting on the third Day. — A breathing Spell. — The Confederates finally driven back into the Fort. — It is resolved to surrender. — Generals Floyd and Pillow make their Escape. — General Buckner surrenders to General Grant. — Terrible Scenes after the Battle is over. — The Ground strewn for Miles with Dead and Dying. — Wounded Men crushed by the artillery Wagons. — The Houses of the Town of Dover filled with Wounded. — My Depression of Spirits on Account of the terrible Scenes I had witnessed.

AM a partisan, by instinct and by education. It is an impossibility for me to limit or divide my affections and predilections; and in choosing a side in a great contest like that which was waged between the South and the North, I must do so with my whole heart and soul. Others, abler than myself, may have done more to promote the cause of Southern independence, and may have labored with greater efficiency; but no man or woman in the whole Confederacy was inspired by a more ardent devotion to the cause than myself, or had greater faith in its ultimate success, no matter what odds it might be compelled to contend against. I trusted to my impulses, perhaps, more than to my reason; but every

11   161

strong partisan must do this, in a greater or less degree, and
if I miscalculated, or was ignorant of the real power of the
North, and of the resources which the Federal government
was able to command, I had plenty of companions in my
error, for there were thousands who possessed far more perfect means of information than myself, who were quite as
eager to enter upon a war without calculating the cost or estimating the consequences.

The fact was, however, that I did not think of calculating
with regard to the probable result of the contest. I had the
most exalted opinion of the invincibility of our Southern soldiers, and of the skill of our generals, and I was unable to
think of them otherwise than as about to enter upon a career
of victory.

Up to the time of which I am now writing, nearly everything had contributed to the encouragement of my original
notions. In both of the great battles in which I had participated the Confederates had been brilliantly successful; and
while the permanent results had scarcely been equal to my
hopes and expectations, my opinion with regard to Southern
invincibility had scarcely received a serious check. My nature and temperament are such, that just as when, amid the
excitement of a battle, each combatant in the opposing army
becomes for the moment a personal enemy, so in the hour of
defeat I am compelled to feel a humiliation as keen as if it
was my own alone. Such a humiliation I was very shortly to
endure; but, in hurrying towards Fort Donelson, I little
knew that I was about to become the spectator of a defeat
so crushing and disastrous as for a time to annihilate in
my bosom all hope, and which gave a death-blow to the
impetuous but untutored enthusiasm with which I had
started out.

I had tasted the sweets of victory, and had felt all the ex-
ultation which fills the breast of the soldier after a hard-
fought battle in seeing the enemy flee before him, and now I
was called upon to taste the bitterness of defeat, and of defeat attended with unspeakable horrors. The capture of Fort
Donelson was the beginning of the end, although I hardly so
understood it at the time; but soon it was followed by other
disasters scarcely less crushing, and the enthusiasm of despair, rather than of hope, was the inspiration not only of myself, but of the whole Southern people during the last three
years of the contest.

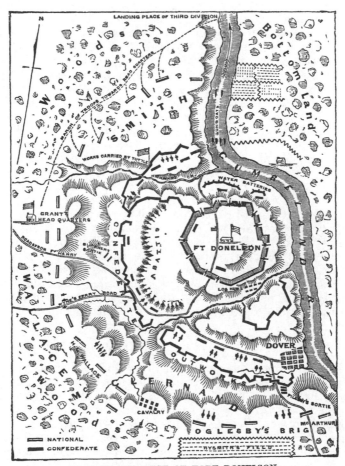

PLAN OF THE SIEGE OF FORT DONELSON.

An Estimate of the Position.

When I reached Fort Donelson, General Pillow was in command, and preparations for meeting the enemy were being pushed forward with all possible energy. Fort Henry, on the Tennessee River, about fifteen miles from Fort Donelson, had been captured by the Federals, and Donelson, every one knew, would be the next object of attack, both by land and water. The fortifications were very strong, although, being built for the purpose of commanding the river, they were weaker on the land than on the water side, and the great duty of the hour was the construction of earthworks for the protection of the exposed side. The labor required for the execution of this task was immense, but every one went at it with a good will, and with a feeling of confidence in our ability to give the Federals the repulse that the garrison of Fort Henry had failed to do, although we were certain that they were about to assail us with a very large force, and that they considered the capture of the position a matter of such vital importance that they would spare no effort to accomplish it. While, however, there was the greatest belief in the impregnability of the position, and in the ability of our garrison, composed of Southern soldiers of tried courage and gallantry, to hold it, even against heavy odds, all felt that a desperate and bloody conflict was about to begin, and nerved themselves for the dreadful task before them.

The Teachings of Experience.

I entered upon this conflict with far different emotions from those which animated me when about to take part in the battle of Bull Run. Then I was inspired by all the enthusiasm of ignorance, and was, perhaps, animated as much by an intense desire to see what a great battle was like, as by any other feeling. I could not get rid of the idea that the rout of the enemy would mean their annihilation, and the triumphant accomplishment of all the ends for which we had taken up arms. I might have known better than this, if I had thought; but I did not think. I only felt, just like thousands of others. The battle of Bull Run, too, was fought in the middle of summer, in beautiful, clear, July weather; and although fighting the enemy through that long, sultry day, with the blazing sun overhead, was no holiday task, and it taxed the energies of officers and men to the utmost to achieve the defeat of the enemy, it was a very different thing from defending a series of earthworks from a combined attack, by land and water, in the dead of winter.

PREMONITIONS OF DEFEAT.

I had seen much of war and its horrors since the battle of Bull Run, and better comprehended now what serious work it was, and what enormous labor would have to be performed, if the hopes and expectations of the summer were to be realized. In fact, I appreciated the situation from the standpoint of a veteran, rather than from that of the raw recruit. Of enthusiasm, or, at least, such enthusiasm as that by which I was originally inspired, I had little or nothing; but I had hope and determination, and was as much bent upon doing my very best as I was the day I was first under fire. There was something most depressing, however, in the idea of figuring in a desperate conflict in midwinter. The whole proceeding seemed unseasonable, and this peculiar feeling, combined with a singular sense of discomfort and constraint at being shut in fortifications from which there was next to no escape, except by driving off the enemy, or surrendering to him, had a powerful effect in dampening my ardor.

At the first intimation of these unpleasant feelings coming over me, however, I shook them off with all the resolution I could command, and determined to show myself in every way worthy of the garments I wore, by doing a full man's work, in preparing for the expected attack. There was a great deal that had to be done, and done quickly, in the way of completing the intrenchments, and I made up my mind to lend a hand, as I felt sure that volunteers would be welcome when hard labor like this was to be performed, even if they were not regarded with the best favor by those in authority at other times.

AT WORK IN THE TRENCHES.

My boy Bob and I, therefore, went into the trenches, and commenced to shovel dirt with all possible energy and good will. In the execution of such a task as this, Bob soon proved himself to be a much better man than I was, and he easily threw two shovelfuls to my one, and was apparently in a condition to keep on indefinitely, when I, finding that I had miscalculated my strength, was compelled to desist. There are some things which men can do better than women, and digging intrenchments in the frozen ground is one of them. I was not a very great while in discovering this most important fact, and concluding that I had better try and make myself useful in some other manner, I repaired, with aching back and blistered hands, to the headquarters of General Floyd, who had just arrived with his Virginians, where I lounged about, waiting for events so to shape themselves that I would be able to show my fighting qualities to advantage, for nature had evidently intended me for a warrior rather than for a dirt-digger.

COMMENCEMENT OF THE SIEGE.

The Federals made their appearance on the afternoon of Wednesday the 12th, and they could be seen at various points through the woods making preparations for commencing their attack by stationing themselves in advantageous positions for the environment of the fort on its land side, while the gunboats were to give us the benefit of their heavy ordnance from the river. These latter we felt very sure of being able to manage with comparative ease, as, indeed, we succeeded in doing; for the fort, as I have before stated, was constructed chiefly with a view to the resistance of an attack upon this side, and our heaviest guns were mounted so as to command the river. The navy, therefore, would have to do some remarkably efficient service if it expected to make any marked impression on us, and the chief anxiety of our officers and men was on account of the comparative weakness of the land defences. But even these, such was the confidence all had in the proverbial Southern valor, it was believed we would be able to hold successfully.

The battle opened on Thursday, February 13, 1862, and, as if to increase the discomforts and sufferings of the combatants, the weather, which had been quite moderate and pleasant, suddenly became intensely cold. On Thursday night, about eight o'clock, a tremendous storm of snow and sleet came on, to the full fury of which I was exposed; for a young officer, who wanted to take French leave for the night, had taken advantage of my eagerness for active service, and made an arrangement for me to go on picket duty for him in the trenches. I was less fitted to stand this kind of exposure than many of my comrades, for, independently of my sex, I was born and brought up in a semi-tropical climate, and although inured to hardships during the months I had been figuring as a soldier, I was but indifferently qualified to endure the sufferings of this terrible night.

ON PICKET DUTY AT NIGHT.

When entering upon a soldier's career, however, I was animated by a stern resolve not to shirk any duty I might be called on to undertake, no matter how arduous or uncongenial it might be; and although I was, on this occasion, really intruding myself where I did not belong, my pride would not have permitted me to back down, even had I fully appreciated, before starting for the trenches, what I would have to go through with before I could return to shelter again. As for the person whose duty I had undertaken to perform, he undoubtedly thought himself particularly lucky in getting rid of such an ugly job, and I fancy that he considered me a fool for the eagerness I displayed to get into a scrape for his benefit. I hope he managed to have a good time during the long hours of that dreadful night, for in spite of what I suffered I bore him no hard feelings.

If repentance for my rashness in resolving to play a soldier's part in the war was ever to overcome me, however, now was the time; and I confess that, as the sleet stung my face, and the biting winds cut me to the bones, I wished myself well out of it, and longed for the siege to be over in some shape, even if relief came only through defeat. The idea of defeat, however, was too intolerable to be thought of, and I banished it from my mind whenever it occurred to me, and argued with myself that I was no better than the thousands of brave men around, who were suffering from these wintry blasts as much as I.

A NIGHT OF HORROR.

The agonized cries of the wounded, and their piteous calls for water, really affected me more than my own discomfort; and had it not been for the heart-rending sounds that greeted my ear every moment, I could, perhaps, have succeeded better than I did in bearing up under the horrors of the night with some degree of equanimity. Every now and then a shriek would be uttered that would strike terror to my soul, and make my blood run cold, as the fiercest fighting I had ever seen had not been able to do. I could face the cannon better than I could this bitter weather, and I could suffer myself better than I could bear to hear the cries and groans of these wounded men, lying out on the frozen ground, exposed to the beatings of this pitiless storm. Several times I felt as if I could stand it no longer, and was tempted to give the whole thing up, and lie down upon the ground and die; but, although my clothing was perfectly stiff with ice, and I ached in every limb from the cold, I succeeded in rallying myself whenever I found these fits of despondency coming over me, and stood my ground to the last.

I understood, from this brief but sufficient experience, what must have been the sufferings of the army of Napoleon, on the retreat from Moscow; and the story of that retreat, which had hitherto seemed to me more like a romance than a narrative of actual occurrences, was now presented to my mind as a terrible reality. I even tried to find some consolation in thinking that, after all, it was only for a few hours that I would be called upon to endure, while the soldiers in that most disastrous retreat were for weeks exposed to all the severities of an almost Arctic winter, in their long march over desert plains, but was forced to the conclusion that reflecting on the woes of others is but an indifferent alleviation of our own.

Fantastic Ideas.

In such a situation as the one I am describing, the most singular ideas run through one's mind. The minutes are lengthened out into hours, and the hours into days, until the reckoning of time is lost; and as the past seems to fade away into a remoteness that makes the painlessness of yesterday appear like the fragment of a happy dream, so the future, when it will all be over, and the commonplace routine of uneventful every-day life will commence again, is as far off as a child's imagination pictures heaven to be. We actually catch ourselves wondering whether it has always been so, and whether it will always be so until we die, and when we die, whether eternity will have anything better to offer. Little incidents in our past lives, of no possible moment, and which had perhaps never been thought of from the date of their occurrence, present themselves suddenly, with astonishing

vividness, to the memory. The mental and the physical beings seem to be engaged in a contest for the mastery, and as
the numbness of the half-frozen limbs increases, the brain
shapes more and more fantastic ideas, and if the terrible contest is too long protracted, and the strain upon the endurance
is not removed, fantasy develops into madness, and madness
swiftly results in death.

More than once I felt myself giving way; more than once
I detected my mind wandering off strangely from the surroundings of the moment; but, by a resolute effort of will, and
by an indomitable determination not to succumb, I succeeded
in sustaining myself until my relief came, and I was able to
seek shelter and the repose I so sorely needed.

THE PROGRESS OF THE BATTLE.

The battle lasted four days and nights, and, although the
Confederates fought with desperate valor, they were at length
compelled to yield, and the humiliation of defeat was added
to the unspeakable sufferings which the conduct of a fierce
and prolonged contest like this, in the middle of a winter of
unparalleled severity, entailed upon them. Fortune, which
had favored the side of the Confederacy in the battles in
which I had heretofore been engaged, was against us now,
however, and in spite of the fierce resistance which the garrison made to the Federal attacks, the result was, that nothing
was left for us to do but surrender.

The results of the first day's fighting were favorable to us,
the Federals being repulsed at all points, and we all felt tolerably sure that we would be able either to drive them off, or
to cut our way through their lines.

THE GUNBOATS BROUGHT INTO ACTION.

On Friday, the forces on the land side, evidently discouraged by their ill luck of the day before, did not attempt any
very serious demonstrations. It was now the turn of the
gunboats to try what they could do towards driving us out
of the fort. The navy, however, did not have any better
success than the army. In the afternoon the boats advanced
up the river, and commenced to shell our works, but they
inflicted on us no particular damage, while our fire told on
them with terrible effect. The contest between the batteries

and the gunboats continued for about an hour and a half, at the end of which time we had the satisfaction of seeing them drift down the river, evidently very badly cut up. So the end of the second day's battle was in favor of the Confederates.

In the mean time, however, the besieging army was receiving large re-enforcements, and was apparently preparing to renew the attack on the land side with increased vigor.

THE CONFEDERATE SORTIE.

With characteristic energy, the Confederate commanders resolved not to wait to be attacked, but to sally from the fort, and strike the enemy a deadly blow. The sortie was gallantly made, and our soldiers fell upon their antagonists with a fury that made them recoil. The contest was conducted with terrible vigor on both sides for some hours, and our men succeeded in driving back the Federals, with great loss. They, however, were unable to follow up their advantage, and there came a lull in the storm of battle, during which both armies seemed to be taking breath, preparatory to renewing the fight with greater ferocity than ever.

At length the Federals rallied, and stormed the intrenchments with a much larger force than before, and, after a severe struggle, the Confederates were driven back into the fort, leaving hundreds of the dead and wounded lying on the frozen ground. By this time our ranks had been so thinned out, that every one felt it would be madness to continue the contest longer against the greatly superior force of the enemy. We had fought, and fought gallantly, doing all that soldiers could do to maintain ourselves; but, in spite of the desperate valor that the garrison had displayed, defeat stared us in the face, and it would have been useless bloodshed to have attempted a prolongation of the battle. The Federals, for this once, at least, were masters of the field, and all we cared longer to do was to get as many of our men as possible away before the surrender took place, and to retrieve the disaster by meeting the enemy under more auspicious circumstances another time.

DEPARTURE OF FLOYD AND PILLOW.

I felt the most profound pity for General Floyd, when he found that further resistance was useless, and that the fort must be given up to the enemy. He actually shed tears, and both he and General Pillow seemed borne down by the keenest humiliation, when, after turning over the command to General Buckner, they embarked their men hurriedly on the boats at night, and effected their escape. Every one knew that they could do no good by remaining, and that, by so doing, they would only give so many more prisoners to the exultant victors; but many of those who were left behind seemed to consider their departure as cowardly, and as an attempt to shirk danger, and greeted them with hisses and groans as they embarked. I was indignant at this, for I knew that they had done all that could have been expected of them, and that for them to participate in the surrender would only increase the extent of the disaster, and add to the importance of the Federal victory.

This was undoubtedly one of the most terrible battles of the whole war, the fact of its having been fought in the midst of an unusually severe winter serving to increase its horrors tenfold. Towards the last, the contest between the besiegers and besieged was hand to hand, both sides contending for the mastery with a ferocity which I cannot pretend to command words to describe. Again and again were the Federals repulsed from the works, and, at some points, they were so much cut up that it seemed impossible for them to rally again. Re-enforcements of fresh troops, however, came continually to the relief of the defeated assailants, while each hour thinned out the garrison terribly. After every repulse, the enemy advanced to the attack with increased force, or made a furious assault in a new place, and by the time General Buckner surrendered the fort to General Grant, the vicinity of the earthworks, for miles around, presented a sickening spectacle of devastation and human suffering.

AFTER THE BATTLE.

In every direction the ground was trampled by thousands of feet, was cut up by the artillery carriages, and was strewn with dead horses and men, and with all kinds of munitions of war. In many of the trenches, especially where the fiercest fighting had taken place, the bodies were heaped together, six or seven feet high, and the faces of the corpses, distorted with the agonies of their death struggles, were hideous to look at. Those who fell, and died where they were shot, were

comparatively fortunate, for their sufferings were soon ended.
It was sickening, however, to think of the many poor fellows
who, after fighting bravely, and falling helpless from their
wounds, had their lives crushed out, and their forms mangled
beyond recognition, by the furiously driven artillery.

All the houses in the town of Dover were filled with the
wounded, and the air was fairly alive with the groans. Dr.
Moore, and other surgeons, did their best to alleviate the sufferings of the victims of cruel war; but the best they could
do was but little. Some of the men, with their limbs fearfully
mangled, pleaded most piteously not to have them amputated,
many of them stating that they preferred death to this new
torture. Others could do no more than groan, or utter such
cries as " God help me ; " while not a few besought the surgeons to kill them, and end their misery. It was no wonder
Dr. Moore said that it was no place for women, and that it
was as much as the strong nerves of a man could do to bear
up under such an accumulation of horrors.

More accustomed to such scenes than most women, and
better able to face the terrible sights by which I was surrounded, I endeavored, notwithstanding I was worn out,
bodily and mentally, and was overwhelmed in spirit by the
fearful disaster which had overtaken the Confederate arms, to
aid, as much as lay in my power, to make the wounded men
as comfortable as possible, until I saw that, if I intended to
escape, I must do so at once.

Although the horrors of a great battle like this affected me
greatly at the time of their occurrence, still the excitement
enabled me to bear up, and it was not until after a battle was
over, and I was compelled to reflect, that I fully realized what
a fearful thing this human slaughtering was. Immediately
after the defeat at Fort Donelson, especially, I was greatly
depressed in spirit, and it was long before I could shake off
the disposition to shudder, and the feeling of intense melancholy, that overcame me to such an extent, that I almost resolved to give up the whole business, and to never allow myself to be put in the way of witnessing anything of the kind
again.

In course of time, however, this feeling wore off, and as,
with restored health, — for I was quite sick from the exposures, fatigues, and horrors of the battle, — my spirits regained
their elasticity, my restless disposition would not let me remain inactive while so many exciting scenes were being

enacted around me, and while the fate of the Confederacy was trembling in the balance. If I did not forget the horrors of Fort Donelson, they erelong ceased to oppress me, and I was as ready as ever to do my share of any fighting that was going on. It was never my disposition to brood over misfortunes, and, although this one affected me deeply for a season, I succeeded in overcoming its effects, and, after a little rest and recuperation, was ready to resume my life of adventure as a soldier of fortune.

CHAPTER XV.

DETECTION AND ARREST IN NEW ORLEANS.

Taking a Rest at Nashville. — Again on the March. — I join General A. S. Johnston's Army. — Wounded in a Skirmish. — Am afraid of having my Sex discovered, and leave suddenly for New Orleans. — In New Orleans I am suspected of being a Spy, and am arrested. — The Officer who makes the Arrest in Doubt. — The Provost Marshal orders my Release. — I am again arrested by the Civil Authorities on Suspicion of being a Woman. — No Way out of the Scrape but to reveal my Identity. — Private Interview with Mayor Monroe. — The Mayor fines and imprisons me. — I enlist as a private Soldier. — On arriving at Fort Pillow, obtain a Transfer to the Army of East Tennessee.

ROM Fort Donelson I went, with what speed I could, to Nashville, and took rooms at the St. Cloud Hotel. I was utterly used up from fatigue, exposure, anxiety, and bitter disappointment; and both I and my negro boy Bob — who had been taken quite sick during the battle — needed an opportunity to thoroughly rest ourselves. It was an immense relief to reach a good hotel, where I could have a shelter over my head, a comfortable bed, and wholesome food; but such was the restlessness of my disposition, and the agitation of my mind, on account of the terrible scenes through which I had just passed, that I could not keep quiet; and scarcely had I recovered a little from my fatigue, than I was eager to be in motion again.

The Excitement in Nashville.

Nashville was in an intense state of excitement over the unexpected result of the attack upon Fort Donelson; and, stimulated, perhaps, as much by the turmoil around me, and by the apprehensions that were felt by every one, lest the Federals should follow up their success by marching on the city, my old eagerness to be an active participant in the contest which was being waged, returned with all its former force, and I was

174

soon as anxious as ever to do a soldier's full duty. If the Federals were to be effectively resisted, and the defeat of Donelson retrieved, there was but one course for the friends of the Confederacy, whether soldiers or citizens, to pursue, and strenuous exertion was the duty which the exigencies of the situation enforced upon every one. I felt that this was not the time for me to shirk the responsibilities I had voluntarily assumed, for if ever my services were needed, they were needed now. After a very brief repose at the St. Cloud, therefore, I was ready to brave the hardships and dangers of the battle-field again.

Sending my negro boy to Grand Junction in charge of a friend, I went to the headquarters of General Albert Sydney Johnston, and upon asking for employment, was put in the detective corps. There was plenty of work for everybody to do, for the fall of Fort Donelson had rendered it necessary that the whole Southern army should fall back for the purpose of taking up a new line, and I had no reason to complain of a lack of activity, although the activity of a retreat was not exactly what I most admired. I was not very long in getting my fighting blood up again; but, unfortunately, my combative propensities, this time, had a somewhat serious result, which compelled me to abandon the line of duty I had chosen, and to disappear from the sight of my new associates.

Wounded.

While participating in a skirmish with the enemy, who were harassing us whenever an opportunity offered, I was wounded in the foot. This lamed me, and compelled me to have the hurt dressed by the surgeon, at which I was not a little alarmed, for I knew that I was now in imminent danger of having my sex discovered. The wound was not a very severe one, and I probably magnified its importance ; but the circumstances were such that it could scarcely have a fair chance to heal speedily if I remained in the field, and dreading the prospect of being for a long period under the care of the surgeon, who would be much more likely to suspect me than any one else, I resolved that the only course for me to pursue was to abandon the army before I got into trouble.

I therefore availed myself of the earliest possible opportunity to take French leave, and quietly slipped away to Grand Junction, where I remained for three days, and then, in company with my boy Bob, repaired to Jackson, Mississippi. At Jackson I hired Bob out, as I wanted to get rid of him for a while, having in my mind certain plans, in the execution of which it would have been an incumbrance for him to have been with me. Bob being disposed of in a satisfactory manner, I hastened, without further delay, to New Orleans, and took up my quarters at the Brooks House.

By abandoning the army, however, and going to New Orleans at this particular juncture, I was, to use a homely phrase, jumping out of the frying-pan into the fire. Rigid as was army discipline, and strict as were the precautions taken to prevent treachery and the surveillance of spies, I had managed to sustain myself in the army as an independent without difficulty, and was on the best possible terms with everybody. In New Orleans, on the other hand, I found the spirit of suspicion rampant. Confidence in the ability of the city to defend itself against the impending Federal attack was expressed on all sides, but the fact that an attempt was undoubtedly to be made, before a great while, for its reduction, and the uncertainty with regard to the exact nature of the blow, or the exact direction from which it would fall, caused an uneasiness that could not be disguised. The Federals were known to be mustering an enormous fleet at the mouth of the river, and a large army on the Sound, and my surmises of months before, based upon what I had heard in Washington, were, apparently, about to be realized.

NEW ORLEANS APPREHENSIVE OF AN ATTACK.

While the city was in this condition of suspense, each man looked more or less askance at his neighbor, and the fear of Federal spies was a feeling that preponderated over all others in the hearts of many. People who, in war time, don't do any fighting, are, according to my experience, as bellicose in their language as they are cowardly in the face of real danger, making up in suspiciousness and vindictiveness what they lack in valor. It was not to be wondered at, therefore, that I speedily got myself into serious trouble, to escape the consequences of which I was compelled to resort to some desperate shifts.

I did not at all appreciate the situation when I went to New Orleans. When I entered Washington it was as a spy, and I consequently had all my wits about me ; but in New Orleans

I thought I was among my friends, and very imprudently neglected ordinary precautions for avoiding difficulties.

During the eight or nine months I had been wearing male attire, I had, as the reader is aware, seen a great deal of very hard service. My clothing was well worn, and my apparatus for disguising my form was badly out of order; and the result was, that I scarcely presented as creditable a manly appearance as I did upon the occasion of my last visit to New Orleans. I had, too, by this time become so much accustomed to male attire that I ceased to bear in my mind, constantly, the absolute necessity for preserving certain appearances, and had grown careless about a number of little matters that, when attended to properly, aided materially in maintaining my incognito. In addition to all this, I was in very low spirits, if not absolutely sick, when I reached New Orleans, and was not in a mood to play my part in the best manner.

My Arrest as a Spy.

I had not been in the city very long before it was noted by prying people that there was some mystery about me, and for any one to have a mystery just then, was equivalent to falling under the ban of both military and civic authorities. I, of course, imagining no evil, was not prepared for a demonstration against me, and was accordingly thunderstruck when I was arrested on the charge of being a spy, and taken before the provost marshal.

Terror, dismay, and indignation struggled for mastery with me when this outrage, as I considered it, was perpetrated. My great secret, I feared, was now on the point of being discovered; and if it was discovered, the probabilities were that I would be unable any longer to continue the career I had marked out for myself. I was enraged at the idea of being charged with acting as a spy, and of having my patriotism doubted after all I had done to promote the cause of Southern independence; and at the same time I appreciated the difficulties and dangers of the situation, and puzzled my brain to devise a plan for getting myself out of a very ugly scrape. Reviewing the matter very rapidly in my own mind, I determined that the best, if not the only plan, was to present a bold front, and to challenge my accusers to prove anything against me, reserving a revelation of my identity as a last alternative.

12

I entered a vigorous protest against the whole proceeding to the officer who made the arrest, and I could see, from his hesitating and indecisive manner, that he was in possession of no definite charge against me, and was inclined to be dubious about the propriety or legality of his action. This encouraged me, and induced me to believe that I might be able to brave the thing through; but I resolved, if I did get clear, to cut my visit to New Orleans as short as possible. My protest, however, was of no avail, so far as procuring an instantaneous release was concerned, for the officer insisted upon my accompanying him to the office of the provost marshal. ·

A DELICATE SITUATION.

While on my way to the provost marshal's, my conductor questioned me closely, but I gave him such answers as evidently increased his uneasy feelings, and I soon saw that he was beginning to seriously doubt whether he was doing exactly the correct thing in making the arrest. Finally, he proposed to release me; but to this I objected in very decided terms, and insisted on knowing exactly what accusations there were against me.

To the office of the provost marshal we accordingly went, and, after a very few questions, that official decided, with gratifying promptness, that there was no justification for holding me, and ordered my discharge from custody.

This appeared to astonish the individual who had made the arrest very much, and it was evident that he was repenting of his rashness, and was anxious to get out of an unpleasant predicament the best way he could.

I enjoyed his discomfiture immensely, and, turning to him with all the dignity I could command, I demanded his name. This, with very evident reluctance, he at length gave me, and making him a stiff bow, I said, in a quiet but threatening manner, " I will see you again about this matter, sir," as I walked out of the office.

MY SEX SUSPECTED.

In spite of my bravado, however, this incident gave me a great deal of uneasiness, for I saw that I was in a dangerous predicament, and was liable at any moment to get into further trouble. I was not much surprised, therefore, although greatly disgusted, when the next evening I was again arrested, this

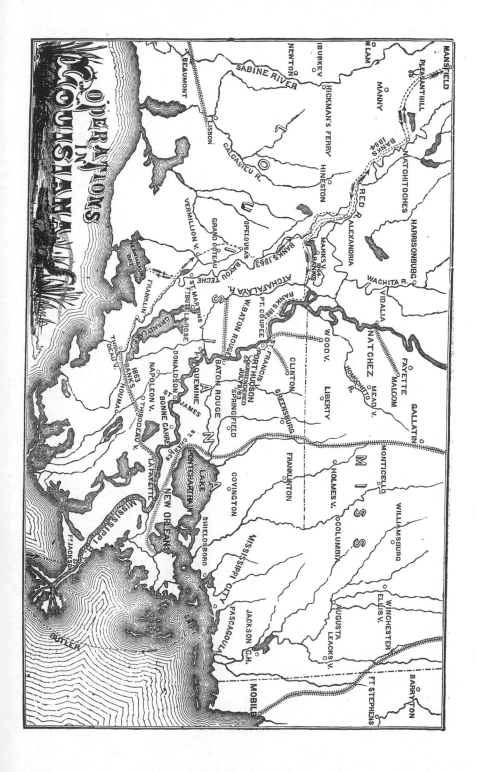

time on suspicion of being a woman. Now what I had so long dreaded was come to pass, and there was nothing to do but to get out of the difficulties which environed me the best way I could.

Being taken before Mayor Monroe, I was interrogated by that individual in a style that I did not at all admire. It seemed to me that he was assuming a certain lordliness of manner that did not sit gracefully upon him, and that was entirely uncalled for by the exigencies of the occasion.

My replies to the queries of the mayor were not satisfactory to him, for his very imperious and pompous bearing made me angry, and rather put me on my mettle. He consequently chose to assume that I was a woman, and ordered me to change my apparel.

I, however, was resolved not to give up without a severe contest, having made up my mind, on assuming male attire, not to acknowledge my sex except in the last extremity, and for the sake of securing ends that could not otherwise be accomplished. So, turning to Mr. Monroe, I said, with a dignified severity quite equal to his own, " Sir, prove that I am a woman ; it will be quite time, when you do that, for you to give me an order to change my dress."

THE MAYOR PUZZLED.

This rather disconcerted the mayor and his satellites ; and, watching their countenances closely, I saw that they were nonplussed, and were doubtful how to proceed, being uncertain whether or not they had made a mistake. My hopes of a prompt discharge, however, were doomed to disappointment, for the mayor, after a brief consultation, decided to remand me to the calaboose, until it should be settled to his satisfaction who I was, and whether I was a man or a woman. To the calaboose I accordingly went, horrified at being subjected to such an indignity, and with anything but pleasant or friendly feelings towards the mayor, and the meddlesome, prying busybodies who had been instrumental in getting me into this trouble.

The circumstances of the case having, in the mean time, become generally known, I was visited the next morning by a local reporter, who showed a very eager desire to find out all he could about me, for the purpose of writing a sensational article for the paper with which he was connected. As may be imagined, this sort of thing did not increase my amiability, or tend to make me bear my misfortunes in a philosophical spirit. I gave Mr. Reporter very little satisfaction, shaping my conversation with him with a view of inducing him to believe that a great mistake had been committed, and that I was the victim of a very unjust persecution.

The reporter was troublesome, but I was not alarmed at him, as I was at my next visitor, Dr. Root, of the Charity Hospital. This gentleman, I knew, would be much more difficult to deal with; and before he got through with questioning me, I was convinced, from his manner, that his mind was made up with regard to me. I felt sure that the easiest and best method, indeed, the only method I could safely adopt, was to confess frankly to the mayor that I was really a woman, trusting that this fact being settled in a manner satisfying to his magisterial dignity, he would have no further pretext for keeping me in confinement, and would order my release.

I therefore wrote a note to his honor, requesting a private interview. This request he granted, and without any more equivocation I told him who I was, and gave him what I hoped would be satisfactory reasons for assuming the garb I wore. My confession having been made, I next endeavored to treat with the mayor for an immediate release, promising to leave the city so soon as liberated, my idea being to return to military life forthwith, as I had had quite enough of New Orleans for the present.

A FINE AND IMPRISONMENT.

Mr. Monroe, however, having gotten me in his clutches, was not disposed to let me go so easily, and he said that he would be compelled to fine me ten dollars, and to sentence me to ten days' imprisonment—a decision that did not increase my good opinion of him, for absolutely nothing had been brought up against my character or my conduct, and I could not, and do not now, see the justice or propriety of such a proceeding.

I thought that this was pretty rough treatment, considering all that I had done to serve the Confederacy. From the outbreak of the war I had been on active duty in the face of the enemy, and had taken part in some of the hardest fought battles in the war, while my persecutor had remained at home enjoying his ease, and taking good care to keep out of danger. To prove this to him, as I could easily have done by procuring testimonials from my numerous friends in the army, would have ruined all my hopes and expectations for the future, however, for, in spite of my present unpleasant situation, I was resolved not to give the thing up. So I concluded that the best plan was to suffer in silence, and to allow the mayor to have what satisfaction he could get out of my ten dollars — I wonder if any of it went into the city treasury ? — and out of keeping me incarcerated for ten days.

Resolving to be as patient as I could, and to be even with Mr. Monroe some day, if ever a good opportunity presented itself, I consoled myself with the idea that my term of imprisonment was a short one, and would soon be over. I was dreadfully tired of it, however, before the hour of release arrived ; and each day my indignation at such an unwarranted outrage increased. The more I thought over the matter the less was I able to see that there was any valid reason for my being subjected to such treatment. At length, after long and impatient waiting, I was free once more ; and now the problem was to get out of New Orleans as quickly as possible, before I was recognized by too many people, and in such disguise that I would be able to follow the bent of my inclinations without hinderance.

Exactly how to manage this, I had some difficulty in determining ; but as the situation was a somewhat desperate one, I was ready to resort to a desperate measure to accomplish my ends. I felt sure that once more with the army I would be safe ; but, with so many suspicious people watching me, it would be, I knew, extremely difficult to get away as I had come, and to enter upon my old career as an independent, without questioning or hinderance. It was therefore necessary for me to smuggle myself, so to speak, among the soldiers again, and I hit upon an expedient for doing so, which, although I felt that it was risky, I resolved to try, and to take my chances for getting out of a new difficulty in case I should fall into one.

I ENLIST.

As soon as possible, therefore, after obtaining my release, I proceeded to the recruiting office at the corner of Jefferson and Chatham Streets, and enlisted in Captain B. Moses' company, of the twenty-first Louisiana regiment. The next day we started for Fort Pillow, to join the balance of the regiment.

In this manner I contrived to get clear of New Orleans, but, as I had no fancy for going on duty as a private soldier any longer than was absolutely necessary, although the regiment of which I was a member was as gallant a one as ever went into battle, and my comrades were, most of them, pleasant, agreeable fellows, my next thought was to resume my independent footing at the earliest moment. I therefore went privately to General Villipigue, and, showing my commission, told a plausible story to account for my enlistment, and asked him to give me employment as an officer. The officers and men of the regiment, of course, knew nothing of my being in possession of this document, or of my previous history. General Villipigue was not able to do anything for me, as there were no vacancies, and I therefore applied for a transfer to the army of East Tennessee, and was very cheerfully granted it.

This was the first time I had ever been regularly mustered into the service, and the step was taken, not from choice, but for the purpose of escaping from the surveillance of Mayor Monroe and the Provost Marshal, two individuals whom, after a very brief acquaintance, I did not particularly care to know more intimately. I had many regrets in parting from the officers and men of the twenty-first regiment, whom I had learned to like very much in the short time I had been with them, but I felt that my interests demanded a removal to another locality. Consequently, so soon as I received my papers, I said adieu to my new friends, and was off with all possible speed.

I was not in a very happy frame of mind, and my physical condition was scarcely better than my mental. The occurrences of the weeks that had just passed had not been of the most pleasurable character, and my personal difficulties in New Orleans, coming as they did when I had not recovered from the mental and bodily suffering caused by the contest at Fort Donelson, did not have the effect of making me view life from its bright side. After the episode of a ten days' sojourn in prison, however, it was a great relief for me to feel that I had my destiny in my own hands once more; and at the prospect of again entering upon a life of adventure that would afford me opportunities for winning distinction, my spirit rose, and I was disposed to dismiss the past, with all its unpleasantnesses, and to make a fresh start with all the energy I could command.

CHAPTER XVI.

AN UNFORTUNATE LOVE AFFAIR.

Again at Memphis. — Public and private Difficulties. — Future Prospects. — Arrival of my Negro Boy and Baggage from Grand Junction. — A new uniform Suit. — Prepared once more to face the World. — I fall in with an old Friend. — An Exchange of Compliments. — Late Hours. — Some of the Effects of Late Hours. — Confidential Communications. — The Course of true Love runs not smooth. — I renew my Acquaintance with General Lucius M. Polk. — The General disposed to be friendly. — My Friend and I call on his Lady-love and her Sister. — Surprising Behavior of the young Lady. — A genuine Love-letter. — A Secret disclosed. — Incidents of a Buggy Ride. — A Declaration of Love. — Lieutenant H. T. Buford as a Lady-killer. — Why should Women not pop the Question as well as Men? — A melancholy Disclosure for my Friend. — I endeavor to encourage him. — A Visit to the Theatre and an enjoyable Evening. — I meet a Friend from New Orleans, and endeavor to remove any Suspicions with regard to my Identity from his Mind. — Progress of my Love-affair with Miss M. — The young Lady and I have our Pictures taken. — I proceed to Corinth for the Purpose of taking Part in the expected Battle. — The Confederate Army advances from Corinth towards Pittsburg Landing.

AVING secured my transportation and transfer papers, I went to Memphis by the first boat, and was erelong once again at my original starting-point, but in a much less enviable mood than when I had last visited it. Then I was dissatisfied with the way in which things seemed to be going, and especially with the — as it appeared to me — very unnecessary and vexatious difficulties that presented themselves whenever I attempted to secure such a position as would enable me to labor with the most efficiency. My confidence in the sacredness of the cause, in the ability of the Southern armies to sustain it, and its ultimate triumph, were, however, unbroken, notwithstanding that I believed precious time was being wasted, and that, through a mistaken policy, the Confederates were compelled to stand upon the defensive,

183

when they ought to have assumed the aggressive, and attacked the enemy on his own ground.

Now, however, things had changed. The terrible disaster at Fort Donelson had been a rude blow to my ideas of Southern invincibility in the field, and if it did not induce me to despair, it certainly opened my eyes to the magnitude of the task we had on hand, and compelled me to recognize the fact, that we were contending with a resolute and powerful enemy, whose resources were enormously superior to ours, and who was evidently bent upon crushing us to the earth, and compelling us to submit to his dictation. All the fine dreams of the previous summer were dissipated into thin air, but there still remained the consolation, that during the bitter struggle yet to come, there would doubtless be plenty of opportunities for me to serve the cause with efficiency, and to win personal glory by my performances.

I had a certain grim satisfaction, too, in thinking that, as things were going, my ambition to do some genuine hard work would scarcely be so lightly regarded in certain quarters as it had been, and that my zeal would consequently be recognized and rewarded as I thought that it deserved to be.

DIFFICULTIES OF MY POSITION.

Apart altogether from the disappointments incident to the military situation, were my private difficulties. My sex had been discovered; and notwithstanding my motives for assuming male attire, and my exemplary conduct while do'ng a soldier's duty, I had been subjected to gross indignities, simply because I chose to perform a man's, rather than a woman's work. This galled me, especially as my secret having once been revealed, it would now be more than ever difficult for me to figure successfully as a man, and I knew that I would constantly be in danger of detection.

Notwithstanding this, however, I was undismayed, and was resolved upon carrying out my original programme, so far as was practicable, and only sought a field of operations where I would be able to follow the bent of my inclinations with as little probability as possible of being interfered with.

Having accomplished my object in leaving New Orleans, and of maintaining a masculine appearance in doing so, I was encouraged to believe that I would be able, by a little discreet management, to get along without a repetition of the troubles

I had encountered in that city, that in the sharp fighting about to occur between the contending armies, I would be able to show my qualities as a soldier to even greater advantage than hitherto, and that amid the excitements of the battle-field and the camp I would forget, or at least cease to think about, the unpleasant things of the past.

So soon as I arrived at Memphis, I telegraphed to Grand Junction for my baggage and my servant, and then went to the tailor, and giving him an order for an officer's uniform suit, with instructions to have it ready at the earliest possible moment, borrowed from him a coat to wear until my new clothing should be ready. I discarded my soldier's jacket with quite as much satisfaction as had inspired me on assuming it, and prepared myself to wait, with what equanimity I could command, the moment when I might be able to figure once more in the eyes of both sexes as the dashing young independent, Lieutenant Harry T. Buford. Clothing, and particular cuts of clothing, have a great deal to do towards making us all, men or women, appear what we would like the world to take us for; and as, although my borrowed coat answered a temporary purpose very well, it did not show me off to the best advantage, I resolved to keep out of sight as much as possible until the tailor had executed his task. I was really not sorry for an opportunity to shut myself up for a day or two, so that I could take a thorough rest, and think, without being interrupted, what was the best plan of action for the immediate future.

MY NEGRO BOY BOB.

The next night, about eleven o'clock, my faithful boy Bob arrived with my baggage, and was delighted to see me again, although my haggard appearance evidently surprised and shocked him. Poor fellow! He little knew what I had passed through since I had parted with him.

"Why, Mas' Harry," he said, "you do look dreadful bad. Has you been sick?"

"Yes, Bob," I replied. "I have been quite ill since I left you, but I am getting quite well now, and am ready to go for the Yankees again."

Bob's eyes sparkled at this, for he was beginning to love fighting almost as much as myself, although the experiences of Fort Donelson had served to extinguish a good deal of the martial ardor that was burning in his heart. I told him enough about my movements since I had seen him last to gratify his curiosity, and to enable him to make satisfactory answers in case any one should question him; and then, giving him orders to call a hack, we drove to the Gegora House, where I took rooms, and prepared to have as good a time as circumstances would permit.

In Uniform again.

My new uniform suit was ready at the appointed time, and I hastened to array myself in it. Making my toilet with more than usual care, and rearranging my mustache and imperial, which had become somewhat demoralized of late, I took a cane in hand, and strolled out to see what was to be seen, not without a little trepidation, but feeling, on the whole, better satisfied with myself and with things in general than I had done for a long time.

After stepping in and out of a number of the principal saloons and drinking-places, I finally came across a friend whom I was really very glad to meet. This was Lieutenant Philip Hastings, a whole-souled fellow, for whom I had an especial liking, and whom I accordingly greeted with great cordiality. Hastings returned my greeting in an equally cordial manner. Shaking me by the hand, he said, " I am glad to see you, old fellow. What is the good news with you? Where are you from? "

" I am just from the Gulf City," I replied.

" Ah," said he; "what is there new there? Did you have a good time? I suppose you were on a leave of absence."

" O, yes," said I; "I always manage to have a pretty good time wherever I go."

A delicate Subject.

Said Hastings, looking at me sharply, " I see you have been raising a new crop of mustaches."

I am afraid that I smiled in a rather sickly manner at this; but putting on as bold an air as I could command, I gave the ornaments of my upper lip a twist, to let him see that they were on tight, and said, " Yes, I have been letting them rush a little; the girls tell me they are an improvement."

Hastings then asked me where I was going; and I replied,

that I expected to join Beauregard's army, but that my plans were a little uncertain, as I was unfortunately an independent, who belonged nowhere in particular; and that, as the commanding officers were getting so confoundedly strict with regard to a good many things, while they were not half strict enough about others of more consequence, I was not sure where I would bring up. I added, that I was at present in the detective corps, and offered to serve him in any way in my power. He thanked me; and then I asked him how he was getting along, and what time he had been stationed in Memphis.

He informed me that he had been on duty there about three months, but that he expected to be ordered to the front very soon.

After a little more conversation of this sort, Hastings said, " I am trying to marry a mighty pretty girl here, but I don't somehow get along with her as well as I could wish. She is a good girl, just as good as they get to be, and she has a deucedly pretty sister, about fifteen years of age, who I think would suit you. They are not rich, but they are mighty nice, and I would like to introduce you."

" Well, Phil," said I, " I am willing — anything to pass the time pleasantly."

" Well, let's take a drink," said Hastings, " and we will go and see them."

AFTER VISITING HOURS.

Hastings had been taking something before I met him, and as I had treated just after we met, this additional drink had the effect of making him rather livelier than the law allowed. He took a brandy smash, and a full-sized one, while I, according to custom, drank cider. Then lighting our cigars, we strolled down the street, my companion bent on making the proposed call. I knew, however, that it must be past visiting hours, and, stopping under a lamp-post, pulled out my watch, and, glancing at it, asked him if he knew what time it was.

" O, it's not late," said he; " about eleven o'clock; they won't be gone to bed yet."

I showed him the dial of the watch, and he exclaimed, " Thunder and lightning! Why, it's one o'clock."

Notwithstanding the lateness of the hour, however, he was very much disposed to insist on going to see the ladies, but

finally I succeeded in persuading him of the impropriety of
such a course, although he yielded very unwillingly. He
then wanted to go and make a night of it somewhere ; and on
my refusing, started off by himself, I being unable to induce
him to go home and get in bed. I did, however, talk him
into letting me take charge of his money, with the exception
of his small change, and on the plea that I had promised to
meet a friend at the hotel, contrived to get away from him.
I disliked very much to let Phil go off by himself in the condition he was in, but as he was just enough under the influence
of what he had imbibed to be troublesome, and was bent upon
having what he called, some fun, my own safety demanded
that I should leave him. My New Orleans experience had
been a severe one, and it was much too fresh in my memory
for me to be willing to run any unnecessary risks of being
arrested on similar charges in Memphis, especially as I felt
certain that it would not be so easy to get out of the clutches
of the authorities a second time, while my future prospects
would, in all probability, be irreparably damaged. So, cau-
tioning my friend to take good care of himself, I went back
to the hotel as fast as I could, and was soon asleep.

Misplaced Affection.

The next morning Phil came around to the hotel to claim
his money, which amounted to over two thousand dollars in
Confederate bills. He did not look as fresh as he might have
done if he had followed the good advice I gave him the night
before, was in a somewhat repentent mood, and, as people
when feeling rather badly through their own indiscretion are
apt to feel, he was very confidential about a variety of private
affairs. During our conversation that morning, he told me
any number of his secrets, and especially gave me to understand that matters were not going as well as could be wished
between him and his lady-love. I had a fancy that the young
lady was, perhaps, offended at something he had said or done
while a little under the influence of liquor, and tried to console him and to encourage him, by offering to aid him in any
way I could towards straightening matters out. I little suspected what the real difficulty was, or I, perhaps, would not
have been so ready in offering my assistance. Alas, poor
Phil ! his affections were bestowed in the wrong direction,
but he lived in hope that things would finally shape them-

selves according to his wishes, and he confidently expected that in time he would be able so to soften the lady's heart towards him, that she would accept his hand. His dreams of happiness, however, were cut short in an untimely manner, for I saw him fall, while fighting bravely, about two weeks subsequently, at the head of his company, at the battle of Shiloh.

Phil took breakfast with me, and after our meal was despatched, we went to a livery stable, and, obtaining a couple of horses, rode out to camp. I dined with him about four o'clock, and then we rode leisurely back to town, and went up to my room, where we smoked and chatted until suppertime.

On going into the supper-room, I noticed that the eyes of a number of people whom I knew, and especially of several ladies by whom I was in some little fear of being recognized, were fixed upon me. I, however, gave my mustaches a savage twist, and putting on as manly a swagger as I was able to command, determined to brave all consequences.

I MEET GENERAL L. M. POLK AGAIN.

My old friend, General Lucius M. Polk, was seated at one of the tables, and I took a seat which brought me nearly back to back with him. He did not notice me when I came in, and I did not care to intrude myself upon him, so did nothing to attract his attention. Soon, however, I said to Hastings, pointing to an old lady in another part of the room, "Lieutenant, there is one of the ladies who were in the habit of visiting Camp Beauregard when I was doing provost duty on the train."

When General Polk heard this, he evidently recognized a familiar voice, and turning round, shook hands with me very cordially.

"Excuse me, general," said I, "but I did not see you when I came in."

"When did you arrive?" said the general.

"Last evening," I replied.

"Where are you from?"

"From New Orleans."

"Is there anything new?"

"No; matters are pretty much as usual. Is there anything new in camp?"

"Well," said the general, "we are expecting to have another battle before long."

"Then," said I, "I am just in time."

"Yes, if you want to have a hand in it," he said. "Are you going out?"

"Probably day after to-morrow," I replied.

"I go at ten o'clock this evening," said the general; and then, turning to the lady with him, he said, "Permit me to introduce you to Mrs. Polk."

I introduced Hastings to the general and his wife, and after a little chat with them, they said good by, and left the room. Hastings and I finished our supper, and then strolled into the bar-room and lighted our cigars.

He was now impatient to have me go with him to call on his girl; so I took his arm, and we sauntered down the street together in the direction of the house which contained the object of his adoration. We stood on the corner for a little while until we had finished our smoke, and then went up to the front door, where Phil rang the bell.

A Social Call.

I always felt a little timorous and unpleasant when compelled to play the *rôle* I had undertaken, in a social way, among members of my own sex; and whether because of my recent adventure in New Orleans, or for some other cause, I felt unusually reluctant to make the acquaintance of Phil's lady friends. Had I then suspected all that I found out afterwards, I would have been even more dubious about the propriety of permitting myself to be introduced.

We took our seats in the parlor, and soon the two young ladies made their appearance. I was introduced; and as I could see that Hastings desired to converse with Miss M., I undertook to make myself as agreeable as possible to Miss E. We did not get along very well together, however, for she was very shy and bashful, while I was far from feeling at my ease, and was conscious of not distinguishing myself very greatly as a lady's man.

After a little while, as our conversation was not very enlivening, Miss E., apparently as much to break the monotony of the performance as anything else, went out, and returned shortly with a servant girl bearing a waiter of apples. This brought the other couple out of the corner where they had been sitting and conversing in a low tone, and the four of us amused ourselves by eating apples and telling fortunes with the seeds. This appeared to afford some amusement to the other three, but I found it rather dull entertainment, and heartily wished that the evening was over. Phil, however, was so wrapped up with his lady, that he was in no hurry to go; but somehow Miss M. did not appear to fancy him by any means as much as he did her, and before a great while they had quite a falling out, and she addressed her conversation chiefly to me, and seemed to have taken quite a liking to me. I was not a little surprised at the warmth of her manner, but supposed that she was merely trying to provoke Phil by a little coquetry, and never imagined for an instant that there was anything serious in it all.

UNEXPECTED CORDIALITY.

When we arose to leave, Miss M. was scarcely polite to Phil, but she looked at me in a very bewildering way; and squeezing my hand a little more than our brief acquaintance warranted, gave me a most pressing invitation to call again.

As we walked up the street, Phil asked me how I was pleased, and then told me all about his falling out with his girl. She, it seems, had insisted, with considerable vehemence, that she did not, could not, and would not, love him, and he was very much disposed to think, from what she said, and from the manner in which she behaved, that some other fellow was cutting him out. He little imagined that his friend, Harry T. Buford, was the innocent and unsuspecting cause of his troubles. I tried to cheer him up as well as I could, and then we parted, he to get his horse for a night ride to camp, and I to go to bed at the hotel.

A SECRET REVEALED.

The next day I received two letters, one of which was from my future husband; for, gentle reader, all these months that, in a guise of a man, I had been breaking young ladies' hearts by my fascinating figure and manner, my own woman's heart had an object upon which its affections were bestowed, and I was engaged to be married to a truly noble officer of the Confederate army, who knew me, both as a man and as a woman, but who little suspected that Lieutenant Harry T.

Buford, and his intended wife, were one and the same person. By this letter, I learned that my lover was then at Corinth, where I expected to meet him in a few days, and my heart jumped for joy at the idea of being able to fight by his side in the battle that was coming off. This I was determined to do, if the thing could be managed.

Under the influence of the pleasurable emotions excited by this letter, and the prospect of again seeing the man I loved after a separation of many months, I wrote a note to the two young ladies I had visited the night before, inviting them to go buggy-riding. I then went to the bank and drew some money, and on my return to the hotel, found an acceptance from my lady friends.

I accordingly hired a couple of teams, one for Hastings, and one for myself; but on arriving at the house, much to Phil's disgust, Miss M. would not go with him, and he took her sister, while his lady, with great apparent satisfaction, seated herself in my vehicle. I felt for him, for I knew that he was terribly disappointed; and with a just received love-letter of my own in my pocket, I was more appreciative of his emotions than I probably otherwise would have been, and made an attempt towards effecting another arrangement. Phil, however, put on a careless air, as if it were all one to him which girl he had, and tipping me a wink, said that he was satisfied as things were.

When we got started, I said to Miss M., "I am afraid I am interfering with my friend's pleasure."

"O," said she, "it's all right. I don't belong to him. He is mad with me, and I don't care if he never gets pleased again."

"You must be mistaken," I said. "I know that he thinks a great deal of you, and he would not offend you for the world. You oughtn't to be hurt at his brusque manner sometimes, for it's just a way he has, and he don't mean anything by it."

"I don't care what his manner is," she put in, rather tartly, "for I don't love him, and wish that he wouldn't bother me."

A GOOD WORD FOR A FRIEND.

This induced me to think that I could put in a good word for Hastings, and, perhaps, soften the heart of the lady towards him. I accordingly began to set forth all his good qualities in the best light, and to try and persuade her that it was worth while to win the affections of such a fine fellow.

So soon as she fairly comprehended what my meaning was, she would not let me proceed; saying, " It's no use of talking to me about Lieutenant Hastings.   I cannot love him, for I am in love with another man, and would give anything in the world if I could only possess his heart."

I thought that this was getting to be rather more confidential than there was any necessity for, considering our short acquaintance; and had I been a man, I suppose it would have been quite the proper thing for me to have become embarrassed.   As things were, however, I was rather amused at the idea of the young lady undertaking to reveal the state of her affections in such an explicit manner, but never suspected what she was really driving at.   I fancied that she was merely trying to draw me out for the purpose of seeing what I would say to her, and thought that her real object, after all, was to stimulate Phil's affections by making him a little jealous. Women, as I have more means than one of knowing, are in the habit of playing just such little tricks as these, and it is astonishing what luck they have in making them succeed.

After considering a moment what I had better say in reply to Miss M.'s bit of confidential communication, I asked if I knew the fortunate individual who had made the conquest of her affections.

" Yes," she replied, looking at me out of the corners of her eyes, and then bashfully dropping her eyelids, and doing her best to blush.

" Well," said I, " if you will tell me his name, I will try and find out for you what his feelings are.   Perhaps if I give him a hint that a nice girl is in love with him, he will try and make himself agreeable."

A REVELATION.

She hesitated, sighed, bit her lips, made a desperate attempt at blushing, and finally murmured, in what was evidently intended to be a sweet, low, and very touching tone of voice, " I will tell you his initials; " and then, after a moment's hesitation, " They are H. T. B."

Before this came out, I was beginning to understand from what direction the wind was blowing; and when this very broad hint was given, I could scarcely contain myself from laughing outright, the situation was so supremely ridiculous.

13

I managed, however, to keep a straight face, and feeling a real sympathy for Phil, and an anxiety to make matters all right for him if I could, I pretended not to understand who the fortunate one could be, and said, "Where does he live? Is he an officer?"

"O, yes," she answered, "and one of the sweetest, handsomest fellows that ever lived. He stops at one of the most fashionable hotels."

I felt immensely flattered at this, as may be conceived, but could not help thinking that, however entertaining it might be to me, it was awful rough on Hastings. I still, however, pretended that I could not understand, the lady all the while wondering, doubtless, what made me so confoundedly obtuse; and after pretending for a few moments to be guessing, I finally said, "Well, I'll give it up; I don't know who it can be." And then, as if a bright idea had just struck me, added, "O, here, just write his name in my diary, if you are too bashful to tell me."

I accordingly handed her the book and a pencil, and she wrote my name, and handed it back, blushing more furiously than ever.

I read the name; and pretending to be astonished, and dreadfully shocked, exclaimed, "O, this cannot be possible!"

"Yes," said she, "you are the object of my affections, and have been for a long time, and I am determined not to love any one else."

This was rushing the thing rather stronger than I thought there was any occasion for; and wondering what on earth the girl meant, I asked, "Since when have I been the object of your affections? I have only been acquainted with you since last night."

"I have loved you ever since last November, when I saw you in the cars. We were strangers then, but I have been longing ever since for an opportunity to make your acquaintance."

I began to wonder how many more susceptible feminine hearts I had unwittingly conquered during my military conductorship; but thinking still of Phil's misfortune, I asked her whether she had ever told him of all this.

She replied that she had, but that, not knowing my name, she was unable to inform him who his rival was, although she had informed him that there was a rival.

Here, thought I, was a nice mess; and I scarcely knew

whether to be amused or disgusted at the perversity of Fate, which made me such an irresistible lady-killer. Miss M. was evidently dead in earnest, and was a nice, attractive-looking, and real good girl, who would have made Phil a capital wife. As for her forwardness in letting me know the state of her affections for me, I could not blame her for that; for I had adopted a similar expedient in my own case, and considered that, although it is, as a rule, a man's place to make the first advances, there is no good reason why a woman who is in love with a man should not take measures to let him know the fact. The conventionalities of society are not always based on reason and common sense, and even where they have a rationalistic basis, people are very apt to quibble about very immaterial points, to the neglect of really weighty matters.

A Question of Propriety.

In the relations of the sexes, there are many points which society insists upon for the sake of the proprieties, which are absolutely absurd when tested by any common-sense standard, while permitting a laxity of manners in others that is far from being conducive to good morals or to the general happiness. Many a woman has lost a good husband through a false modesty, which would not permit her to even give him a hint with regard to her real feelings; for some of the best and most whole-souled men are frequently as timid and bashful as the most timid and bashful women, and require some encouragement before they can be induced to speak; while others are strangely obtuse, and do not even think of being anything more than commonly polite to particular ladies, unless something is done to stimulate them. Such backward and thick-witted men are often the most ardent lovers, and the fondest and best of husbands when they are once aroused. Many a woman, too, is fond of one man while she is being persistently courted by another; and if, as is apt to be the case, the object of her regards refuses to notice her in the manner she wishes, — perhaps simply because he does not like to interfere with another man's love affair, — she has no resource, if she hopes for a happy future, but to declare herself. There was, therefore, no occasion for censuring Miss M.; but the fact that Phil's rival happened to be, of all people in the world, Lieutenant Harry T. Buford, C. S. A., certainly complicated the situation.

I could not resist the temptation to have a little sport at the

expense of Miss M.; but I was really desirous of trying so to
manage matters that Phil would be placed in a better position
with his lady than before. I knew that the worst thing I
could do would be to repel her advances, and concluded that
it was incumbent upon me to at least meet her half way. As
she still continued to address me with some degree of for-
mality as Lieutenant, or Mr. Buford, I — giving her an ogle that
was intended to be very sympathetic, and to indicate how
profoundly my feelings had been wrought upon — suggested
that she should call me Harry. This was said in a very tender
tone, and evidently made a great impression. During the balance of the ride we exchanged confidences in a very lover-
like manner, and by the time we reached home again, Miss M.
was in a very happy state of mind, being convinced that she
had made a conquest of the man she had so long sighed for.
It was all very absurd, of course, and very melancholy from a
certain point of view; but I could not help being amused, although I wished myself well out of the scrape, and resolved to
inform Phil how matters stood immediately.

A Surprise for my Friend.

Having returned our teams to the livery stable, I invited
him to my room, and having settled ourselves for a smoke, I
disclosed the whole situation to him. He was very much surprised, and a good deal cut up by what I told him, and said
Miss M. had often spoken to him of another officer for whom
she had an affection, but that he had never imagined that it
was I.

I told him that I was quite as much surprised as himself,
and that I certainly should not have called upon the lady had
I known what was going to happen.

Phil paced up and down the room a good deal agitated; and
at length he burst out with, "Well, now, lieutenant, ain't
women d—d deceitful things anyhow? but I shan't mind being
gone back on in this way very long. I will leave for the field
in a few days, and I will try and forget her, and, in the mean-
time, I will not call without your consent."

"O, pshaw," said I; "I am not in love with the girl, Hastings, and I don't expect to be. I have no intention of marrying, and I don't propose to interfere with you in the least. So
go ahead, and win the lady if you can, and I don't doubt but
that you can, if you only try hard enough."

"No," said Hastings, "I don't want to marry any girl who don't love me, or who has a fancy for another fellow."

"Well, any how," I replied, "it is kind of pleasant, though, to have a nice place to pass one's leisure hours in, and you might as well visit Miss M., even if you choose to give up the idea of marrying her, as there is, certainly, no necessity for your doing."

THE EXPENSIVENESS OF COURTSHIP.

"But," said Phil, — and I could not help laughing at the sorrowful energy with which he made this declaration, — "a fellow has to make a girl so many little presents, and show her so many attentions, that the thing gets mighty expensive, unless both parties mean business. It takes a sight of trouble to get into the good graces of some women, and then they are so fickle and uncertain, that it is impossible to tell when you have them safe.

"Why," said he, warming with his subject, "women have cost me a small fortune, and I have had mighty little satisfaction with them;" and then, lapsing into a reflective mood, added, "Why do men run after them, any how, when they so often regret it afterwards?" This was a conundrum, for which he, apparently, found no satisfactory answer; for, after a moment's pause, he said, "Well, I guess, it must be ordained, and we'll have to put up with it."

This, I thought, was showing a proper philosophical spirit, even if it was not altogether complimentary to my sex; so I said "Well, Phil, we ought not to complain about women being what they are; we must always remember that our mothers were women."

This appeared to touch Phil in a tender place; for he said, in a softer tone, "That's so; and God Almighty never made anything better than a real good woman. The good ones are better than the best of us men. If any man were to take advantage of my sister I would kill him."

I then suggested that he should not give it up with Miss M. yet, and promised to aid his cause with her as best I could. The result was, that Hastings was feeling a good deal better at the close of the conversation than at the beginning of it, and his little disappointment in love did not in the least prevent him from eating, and evidently enjoying immensely, a very hearty supper.

While at supper, I proposed that we should go to the theatre, and take the girls. To this Phil readily assented, and Bob was accordingly despatched with an invitation. He soon returned, with an answer to the effect that the ladies would be most happy to accompany us.

On our way to the theatre, Miss M. suggested that we should have our pictures taken, and gallantry would not permit me to refuse. So I made an engagement with her for the next day to go to the photographers. I had not seen a play for a long time, and consequently enjoyed the entertainment immensely; and being considerably more interested in it than in the young lady, Phil had no reason to complain of the warmth of my attentions to her. He tried to take advantage of the occasion to reinstate himself in her good graces, but I am sorry to say that he did not make much headway, and Miss M., much to his chagrin, persisted in manifesting a decided partiality for Lieutenant Buford.

AN ALARM.

After the play was over we took the ladies home; and I said good night to Hastings, who started for camp, while I returned to the hotel, where I found a note from my friend, Major Bacon, who was stopping at the Commercial Hotel. I accordingly went to call on him, and found that he had just arrived from New Orleans. This made me feel really uneasy, and I was not a little alarmed when he told me that he had heard of my arrest by the mayor. I was a trifle reassured, however, when I was unable to notice anything in his speech or manner to indicate that he believed me to be a woman; and to quiet any suspicions that might be lurking in his mind, I said, as I twisted my mustache, and put on all the swagger I was able, " I am a queer-looking female, ain't I, major?" And then, to clinch the matter, I invited him to take a drink.

The major replied "Well, you might manage to pass for one, if you were to put on petticoats;" but, rather to my astonishment, he did not seem to be particularly interested in the matter; and as I was not especially anxious to make it a subject for conversation, we soon began to talk about something else.

The next day, in accordance with my promise, I went to the photographers with Miss M., and we had our pictures taken, and made an exchange. From that time, up to the date of my departure from Memphis, I was an almost daily visitor at her house, and was looked upon by her and her friends as an accepted lover, although I certainly was not as explicit in my language on the subject of matrimony as accepted lovers are usually supposed to be under the necessity of being. On the contrary, I tried to put in a good word for Phil as often as I could, until I saw that it was no use pleading for him, as the young lady seemed to have taken an unconquerable aversion to him. That she should have discarded such a really worthy fellow for me was a source of serious annoyance to me; and one reason why I kept up my acquaintance with her was, in the hope of doing him a service.

At length, all the officers in Memphis were ordered to proceed to Corinth without delay, and then every one knew that a big battle was expected to come off shortly. As a consequence, the greatest excitement prevailed, and many of the officers found it hard work parting from their friends. In order to avoid a scene with Miss M., I wrote her a note, bidding her farewell, which was not to be delivered until after I left the city; and, jumping aboard the train, was soon on my way to Corinth

On arriving at Corinth, I found great preparations being made, and everything nearly ready for a forward movement. I met a considerable number of old friends, some of them old Virginia comrades, whom I had not seen for a very long time. We exchanged very cordial greetings, but otherwise we had not much time to give to each other, they having important duties to perform, while I was eagerly endeavoring to obtain some official position that would enable me to participate in the coming fight in a manner advantageous to myself. All the commanding officers, however, were too busy just then to attend to me; and so I resolved to follow the army to the field in my independent capacity, and take my chances there.

The order to advance being given, the army moved out of Corinth in the direction of Pittsburg Landing, animated by the expectation of being able to fall upon the enemy, and deliver a crushing blow at a moment when it was least expected.

CHAPTER XVII.

THE BATTLE OF SHILOH.

A Surprise upon the Federal Army at Pittsburg Landing arranged. — A brilliant Victory expected. — I start for the Front, and encamp for the Night at Monterey. — My Slumbers disturbed by a Rain-storm. — I find General Hardee near Shiloh Church, and ask Permission to take a Hand in the Fight. — The Opening of the Battle. — Complete Surprise of the Federals. — I see my Arkansas Company, and join it. — A Lieutenant being killed, I take his Place, amid a hearty Cheer from the Men. — A Secret revealed. — I fight through the Battle under the Command of my Lover. — Furious Assaults on the Enemy's Lines. — The Bullets fly thick and fast. — General Albert Sydney Johnston killed. — End of the first Day's Battle, and Victory for the Confederates. — Beauregard's Error in not pursuing his Advantage. — I slip through the Lines after Dark, and watch what is going on at Pittsburg Landing. — The Gunboats open Fire. — Unpleasant Effect of Shells from big Guns. — Utter Demoralization of the Federals. — Arrival of Buell with Re-enforcements. — General Grant and another general Officer pass near me in a Boat, and I am tempted to take a Shot at them. — I return to Camp, and wish to report what I had seen to General Bureaugard, but am dissuaded from doing so by my Captain. — Uneasy Slumbers. — Commencement of the second Day's Fight. — The Confederates unable to contend with the Odds against them. — A lost Opportunity. — The Confederates defeated, and compelled to retire from the Field. — I remain in the Woods near the Battle-field all Night.

ORT DONELSON was to be avenged. After the capture of that position, the Federals had swept in triumph through Tennessee, the Confederates having been compelled to abandon their lines in that state and in Kentucky, and to seek a new base of operations farther south. The Federals were now concentrating in great force at Pittsburg Landing, on the Tennessee River, their immediate object of attack evidently being Corinth, and General Albert Sydney Johnston, who was in command of the entire Confederate army, resolved upon striking a vigorous blow at once, with a view of turning the tide of victory in our favor before the enemy were as-

200

sembled in such strength as to make it imperative for us to act upon the defensive, and to fight behind our intrenchments. The experiences of more than one well-fought field had shown how well nigh irresistible the Confederate soldiers were in making an attack, and the general knew that it would be necessary for him to be the assailant, if he expected to get all the work out of his men they were able to do.

The reports which we received from our scouts, and from the country people, indicated either that the Federals were unaware of the strength of the Confederates in their immediate neighborhood, or else that, flushed with victory, they were over-confident, and were taking comparatively few precautions against a surprise. These things were the common talk of the Confederates for days before the battle took place; and while not a little astonishment was expressed at the temerity of the enemy, considerable jubilation was felt at the idea of our being able to gain a comparatively easy victory, which would put an end to the invasion, or at least so stagger the Federals, that subsequent operations against them would be unattended with any great difficulties.

A Surprise in Preparation.

We all knew that a surprise was to be attempted, and all felt confident of its success, although some hard fighting was expected before the rout of the Federals could be achieved. Hard fighting, however, was something from which the Confederate soldiers did not shrink at any time, and on this occasion every one was anxious to repair the disaster of Fort Donelson, and to teach the enemy a lesson they would not be likely to forget in a hurry.

At the prospect of a battle, and especially of a battle in which the chances of winning a brilliant victory would be on the side of the Confederates, I was as eager to participate, notwithstanding the severity of my recent experiences, as I was the first time I faced the enemy. If I thought of Fort Donelson, and the retreat of Johnston's army after the fall of that position, it was only with a desire to be revenged for the sufferings my brave comrades and myself had endured, and my thoughts rather turned to Bull Run and Ball's Bluff, where Southern valor had so signally displayed itself, and where I had assisted in defeating the enemy, and in sending them flying, a routed and panic-stricken mob, from the field.

My love for such excitement as only a great battle can give, too, overpowered all lesser emotions, and my mortification at the indignities I had endured at the hands of Mayor Monroe and his satellites in New Orleans, was overcome by the thought that, notwithstanding the fact that I was a woman, I was as good a soldier as any man around me, and as willing as any to fight valiantly and to the bitter end before yielding. The fighting blood of my ancestor, old Governor Don Diego, was making itself felt in my veins as I prepared to follow Hardee's corps to the scene of action with all possible expedition.

OFF FOR THE FIELD.

Obtaining a pass from the provost marshal, I put my tent in an army wagon, and then Bob and I mounted our horses and started for the field, on Saturday, April 5. 1862. The roads were in a horrible condition from the heavy spring rains, and we made rather slow progress, — much too slow for my impatient spirit, — and I was very tired when, at nightfall, I reached a village of half a dozen scattered houses called Monterey, about half way between Corinth and Shiloh Church, a little Methodist meeting-house, just outside the Federal picket lines.

It was necessary for me to halt here until morning; so, obtaining sufficient forage for my horse from a Mississippi regiment, I prepared to camp for the night, and hoped to get a sound sleep, to fit me for the hot work of the next day.

THE NIGHT BEFORE THE BATTLE OF SHILOH.

My animals having been fed, I took off the saddles, and raking up a quantity of leaves, arranged my bed by spreading a saddle blanket to lie upon, and placing a saddle for a pillow. Then throwing myself on this extemporized couch, I wrapped myself in an army blanket, and was soon lost in slumber as profound as would have visited me had my accommodations been of the most luxurious description.

I was not destined, however, to have a quiet, uninterrupted slumber, such as I needed, for ere long I was awakened by the rain, which began to fall in torrents, and which compelled me to seek some more sheltered spot in which to finish the night. My first care was for my horse, and covering him well with the blanket, I went as fast as I could to one of the deserted houses of the village, and stopped there until the rain was over.

It was quite three o'clock before the shower ceased, and it was high time for me to be moving if I expected to take part in the opening of the battle, as I was exceedingly anxious to do. I therefore ordered the horses to be saddled, and was in a few moments ready to start. A soldier very generously offered me a cup of army coffee, which, although perhaps it was not quite equal in strength and flavor to some I had tasted in the best hotels, was swallowed with great relish, and with many benedictions on the giver, whose courtesy I rewarded by a good-sized drink of brandy, from a flask I carried for the benefit of my friends. His eyes fairly sparkled with delight as he gulped it down, and he smacked his lips as if he had not had such a treat for many a day. Then mounting my horse, I set off at a smart pace for General Hardee's headquarters.

I found the general stationed near Shiloh Church, and rode up and saluted him just as he was mounting his horse. Showing him my pass, I said that I wanted to have a hand in this affair. Hardee looked at the pass, and replied, " All right; fall in, and we'll see what can be done for you."

COMMENCEMENT OF THE FIGHT.

The fighting had already commenced between the skirmish lines of the two armies while I was conversing with the general, and the troops were hurrying forward to attack the Federals before they could gain time to prepare themselves for an effective resistance.

In obedience to Hardee's command, I fell in with his men, and we advanced briskly upon the enemy's camp. It was a complete surprise in every respect. Many of the enemy were only half dressed, and were obliged to snatch up the first weapons that came to hand as the Confederates rushed out of the woods upon them. The contest was brief and decisive, and in a few moments such of the enemy as escaped the deadly volleys which we poured into them were scampering away as fast as their legs could carry them. We took possession of their camp, with all its equipage, almost without resistance, and I thought that this was an excellent good beginning of the day's work, especially as I had the pleasure of eating a capital hot breakfast, which had been prepared for some Federal officer. I enjoyed it immensely, for I was decidedly hungry after my early morning march, the cup of coffee tendered by my soldier friend not having proved as satisfactory as something more substantial might have done.

I had scarcely finished eating when I came across General Hardee again. He was in a high good humor at the course events had taken thus far, and said to me, in a jocular sort of way, " Well, lieutenant, what can I do for you ? "

I replied that I was anxious to do my share of the fighting, and wanted to be stationed where there was plenty of work to be done.

The general laughed a little at my enthusiasm, but just then his attention was called away for a moment, and I, glancing down the line, spied the Arkansas boys whom I had enlisted at Hurlburt Station nearly a year before. I was immediately seized with a desire to go into the fight with them; so I said, " Ah, there is my old company, general; with your permission, I will see the captain. Perhaps he can give me a chance."

I Rejoin my Arkansas Boys.

Hardee nodded an assent, and, giving him a salute, I started off at full speed to the rear, where I got my commission out of my pocket, and then darted along the line, closely followed by Bob, my idea being to avoid being stopped by giving the impression that I was bearing an order from the general. Dismounting from my horse, I forced my way through the ranks until I reached Captain De Caulp, who shook me heartily by the hand, and was evidently delighted to see me, as we had not met since I parted from him in Pensacola the previous June, when starting for Richmond. My pleasure at the interview, especially at meeting him again under such circumstances as those I am describing, was of a very different and much more intense kind than his, for reasons that will appear hereafter.

It was no time then, however, to exchange compliments, for there was hot work before us if the brilliant successes of the first assaults upon the Federal position were to be followed up to a satisfactory issue. I therefore told Captain De Caulp that I was anxious to have a hand in the fight, and especially to go into the thing with this company, if it could be permitted, and asked him if he could not assign me to some duty. I spoke in such a way, and in a sufficiently loud tone for the

other officers and the men to understand that I belonged to
the special corps, and was doing a share of the fighting just
for the love of the thing. Some of them evidently did not
know who I was, and were inclined to regard me as an in-
truder; for I heard a soldier behind me say, "What little
dandy is that?" Some one replied, "Why, don't you know?
That's the fellow that raised the company," — a bit of information that undoubtedly raised me immensely in the estima-
tion of the interrogator, as well as in that of others who had
joined the company since I had left it.

Among Old Friends.

Notwithstanding the number of strange faces that met my eyes
as I glanced along the ranks, I saw enough old acquaintances to
make me feel very much at home, and I was delighted beyond
measure in an opportunity to take part in a great battle along
with my own company that I had raised over in the Arkansas
swamp, that I had marched through New Orleans and Mobile
in such gallant style, and that I had so astonished my late
husband by appearing in Pensacola at the head of, and resolved to prove myself worthy of them, and to show that,
even if I was a little dandy, I was as good a soldier as the
best of them when any hard fighting was to be done. Indeed, all the circumstances were such as to inspire me to distinguish myself by some unusually gallant action, and I
resolved that, if it were possible to do so, the occasion should
be made a memorable one for us all.

Captain De Caulp told me to remain with him, and to wait
and see what would happen for my advantage; for as some
desperate fighting was yet to be done, there would very
probably be some need of my services before the battle was
over. In the mean time, and until there was a special call
upon me, I could fight on my own hook, or act as a sort of aid
to him. He then sent his orderly to the rear with the boy
Bob and the horses, with directions to conduct them to the
camp.

Glancing over the field, I saw the eleventh Louisiana regiment, with a friend of mine, and a brave officer, Colonel
Sam. Marks, at its head, going for the enemy in gallant
style, and in a short time the order came for us to advance.
I was all oak, as the boys would say, and there was not upon
the whole field a prouder or more determined upholder of the

fortunes of the Confederacy, or one who was more bent upon retrieving past disasters, and of inflicting upon the Federals a blow from which they would not be able to recover, than myself. I considered it a rare piece of good fortune that I was able to take part in what all hoped and expected would be a decisive battle with my own company, — as fine a body of men as were in the field, — and there were special reasons for feelings of jubilation at the idea of being permitted to fight by the side of Captain De Caulp.

The Secret Out.

The secret might as well be told now as at any other time, I suppose; so the reader will please know that Captain De Caulp and I were under an engagement of marriage, having been in correspondence with each other since my departure from Pensacola. I had his letters in my breast pocket, and his photograph in the lining of my coat, while, I doubt not, that he had about him memorials of my unworthy self; and if he cared as much for me as I was led to believe he did by the fervency of his epistles, I was the especial object of his thoughts when, in obedience to the command to advance, we dashed at the enemy. He little suspected, however, that the woman to whom his heart and hand were pledged was by his side as he led his men into that bloody fray; for, as I have before explained, he had an acquaintance with me both as a woman and as a man, but did not know that the two were the same.

An Inspiring Situation.

The situation was a singularly inspiring one for me, as may readily be imagined; it was, in fact, such a situation as I doubt whether any woman had ever been placed in before; and yet it seemed the most natural thing in the world that I should be there, and that I should try to distinguish myself by deeds of valor, for the sake of winning the approving smile of the man who, of all others, I was anxious should give me his approbation..

It may be thought that, even if I felt no fear for myself, as a woman I should have had some tremors when beholding my lover advancing into the thick of a desperate fight, at the head of his men. The idea of fear, either on his or on my own account, however, never occurred to me at the time,

although, on reflecting over the matter afterwards, it struck me that some slight emotion of that kind would perhaps have been proper under the circumstances. We cannot think of everything at once, however; and just at that time I was intent only on defeating the enemy before me, and proving myself a good fighter in the eyes of Captain De Caulp and his command. As for him, I desired for his sake, even more ardently than on my own account, that the occasion should be a glorious one, and I had a strange delight in following him into the thickest of the mêlée, and in watching with what undaunted spirit he bore himself throughout the long and sternly-fought battle.

We had not been long engaged before the second lieutenant of the company fell. I immediately stepped into his place, and assumed the command of his men. This action was greeted by a hearty cheer from the entire company, all the veterans of which, of course, knew me, and I took the greeting as an evidence that they were glad to see their original commander with them once more, and evidently anxious to do a full share of the heavy job of work that was to be done before the field could be ours. This cheer from the men was an immense inspiration to me; and the knowledge that not my lover only, but the company which I had myself recruited, and thousands of others of the brave boys of our Southern army were watching my actions approvingly, encouraged me to dare everything, and to shrink from nothing to render myself deserving of their praises.

A FURIOUS ASSAULT.

Our assaults upon the enemy were made with irresistible fury, and we rushed through their lines, literally mowing them down like grain before the mowing machine. It was grander fighting than I had ever witnessed before, surpassing even the great sortie at Fort Donelson in desperateness and inspirational qualities. The bullets whistled through the air thick and fast, cutting the trees, and making the branches snap and fly, splintering the fence rails, striking the wagons, or sending some poor soldier suddenly to the earth. A corporal who was by my side was shot through the heart by a Minie ball. He fell heavily against me, and all my clothing was reddened by his blood. His only words were, " Damn the Yankees ! they have killed me." · He was a very handsome young man, only about twenty-two years of age, and his death perfectly infuriated me, as it did his other comrades.

The Federals never succeeded in recovering from the surprise of the morning; and although they stood their ground most stubbornly in some places, their entire line was gradually driven back towards the Landing, and each succeeding hour of the fight made their total defeat more of a certainty than ever.

General Albert Sydney Johnston Killed.

Shortly before three o'clock in the afternoon, our commander-in-chief, General Albert Sydney Johnston, was numbered among the slain. His death, however, was carefully concealed from the army, and was known to but few until the battle was over. He was a great soldier, and his loss was an irreparable one; for had he lived to superintend the conduct of the battle to the end, it is scarcely possible that he would have failed to push his advantages to the utmost, or that he would have committed the mistakes which turned a brilliant and decisive victory into an overwhelming and most maddening defeat.

Close of the First Day's Battle.

When the sun set that day the Confederates were successful at every point, and although they had suffered terribly, they had forced the enemy's lines back almost to the Landing, so that there was nothing now left them to do but to make a final successful stand, or else be crowded over the bluffs into the river, just as I had seen them crowded, six months before, at Ball's Bluff. That they could have made a final effective resistance, had the Confederates finished the day's work in the spirit they had begun it, was scarcely within the range of possibility; and I confidently expected, as the daylight declined in the sky, to witness a repetition, on a larger scale, of all the horrors of the Ball's Bluff battle. There was absolutely no escape for the Federals; and their only hope was to hold their last rallying ground, and to gain time until the arrival of re-enforcements, which would enable them to recover their lost ground, and to assume the offensive against our victorious, but worn and shattered army. Why the Confederate advantages were not pushed that night, before General Buell could arrive with his fresh troops, and the

14

Federal army either captured or annihilated, as it assuredly would have been, was a mystery to me then, and is now.

During the afternoon, I succeeded in gaining a good deal of very important information from several prisoners, and particularly from a sergeant belonging to the twenty-seventh Illinois régiment. I did this by inducing him to believe that I was only in the Confederate army under compulsion, and that I intended to desert at the first opportunity. I got out of him pretty much everything he knew about the Federal situation, who the different commanders were, and even how the forces were posted; and, in full confidence that all I told him was the literal truth, he took out his diary and wrote a short note to his colonel, which he intrusted to me to deliver for him. From this prisoner I learned how desperate were the straits of the enemy, and how anxiously they were awaiting the arrival of Buell with re-enforcements, and I was, consequently, in despair, for I saw our brilliant victory already slipping from us, when General Beauregard, who had succeeded to the command after the death of Johnston, issued the order from his headquarters at the little Shiloh church, for us to halt in our advance, and to sleep on our arms all night, instead of pursuing the routed enemy, and compelling them either to surrender or to take to the river, as we compelled them to do at Ball's Bluff.

A FATAL MISTAKE.

When I heard Beauregard's order, I felt that a fatal mistake was being committed; and, in utter desperation at the very thought of losing on the morrow all that we had gained by the most determined and desperate fighting through that long and bloody day, I could not resist the temptation of making an effort to find out for myself exactly what the situation within the enemy's lines really was, and was willing to run all the risks of being caught and shot as a spy, rather than to endure the suspense of a long night of uncertainty.

My station was with the advanced picket line, I having persuaded the captain to post me in a manner most favorable for carrying out my designs. I did not dare to tell him all I proposed to do, for fear that he would consider it his duty to prevent me, but gave him to understand that I intended, under cover of the darkness, to creep up as close as I could, with safety, to the Federal lines, with a view of trying to find out something concerning their movements. He hesitated somewhat at even permitting me to do this much without the knowledge of the colonel, but finally gave a tacit consent. I also refrained from telling my full design to my immediate companion of the picket station, and made up a story about my intentions, which I thought would keep him quiet, and also promised to give him a drink of good whiskey when I got back if he would mind his own business and not attempt to interfere with me.

I Make a Reconnoissance.

I accordingly stole away, and creeping as noiselessly as I possibly could through the underbrush, approached the Landing. The command of General Wallace was stationed at this end of the Federal line, and I had a good deal of trouble to get past his pickets, being compelled to pause very frequently, and to keep close to the ground, watching favorable opportunities for advancing from one point to another. I finally, however, did manage to get past them, and gained a tolerably good point of observation near the river, where I could see quite plainly what was going on at the Landing.

It was just as I had anticipated. The Federals were crowding about the Landing in utter disorder, and were without any means of crossing the river. They were completely in a trap, and so evidently keenly appreciated the fact, that the capture of the entire army ought to have been an easy matter. One more grand charge along the entire line, in the same brilliant fashion that we had opened the battle, and every officer and man on this side of the river would either have been slain or taken prisoner, while we would have gained possession of the Landing, and have prevented any of the expected re-enforcements from crossing.

Beauregard's Mistake.

At this moment, I felt that if I could only command our army for two good hours I would be willing to die the moment the victory was won, while it maddened me to think that our commander should have permitted such an opportunity for inflicting a perfectly crushing defeat on the enemy to pass by unimproved. Beauregard, certainly, could not have understood the situation, or he would inevitably have pursued his advantage ;

and yet I could not understand how he could help knowing, not only that the Federals were in desperate straits, but that fresh troops were hurrying to their assistance, and that in the morning the battle would, assuredly, be resumed with the odds all in their favor.

ARRIVAL OF FEDERAL RE-ENFORCEMENTS.

While I was watching and chafing under the blunder that I was sure had been committed, a steamboat with re-enforcements arrived at the Landing. These fresh troops were immediately formed, and despatched to the front. Another detachment came, before I withdrew, overwhelmed with grief and disgust at the idea of our victory coming to nothing, simply because there was not the requisite energy at headquarters to strike the final blow that was needed, in order that our hard fighting might have its proper reward.

There was, evidently, somebody on the Federal side who was bent on retrieving the disaster; for the hurried movements of the new troops, and the constant firing which the two gunboats — Tyler and Lexington — kept up, indicated an aggressiveness that augured unfavorably for our tired and badly cut-up army when the fight should re-open in the morning. The two gunboats had moved up to the mouth of Lick Creek, and about dark commenced throwing shells into our lines in a manner that was anything but agreeable, and that demoralized our men more than any kind of attack they had been compelled to stand up under. I had been under musketry and artillery fire a number of times, and did not find the sharp hiss of the bullets, or the scream of the shells, particularly pleasant. There was something horrible, however, about the huge missiles hurled by the gunboats, and they excited far more disagreeable sensations than either musket or rifle bullets, or the favors which the field artillerists were in the habit of bestowing. These shells could easily be seen in the air for some seconds, and each individual that beheld them had an uncomfortable feeling that they were aiming directly at him, with a strong probability of striking. Sometimes they burst in the air, scattering in every direction; oftener they burst just as they struck, and the pieces inflicted ugly wounds if they happened to hit anybody, and occasionally they would bury themselves in the ground, and then explode, tearing holes large enough to bury a cart and horse in.

There was something almost comical in the way the soldiers, who had fought, without flinching, for hours in the face of a terrific artillery and musketry fire, attempted to dodge these shells. The hideous screams uttered by them, just before striking, seeming to drive all the courage out of the hearts of those against whom they were directed. Facing this kind of attack, without being able in any way to reply to it, was much more trying than the toughest fighting; and the rapidity with which the gunners on board the boats kept up their fire about dusk, undoubtedly had a great effect in checking the Confederate's advance, and in saving the badly-beaten Federal army from utter rout.

During the whole of the night the Tyler and Lexington threw their shells steadily, and at frequent intervals, in the direction of our army; but now that the fighting was over, and our men were trying to rest for the work of the morrow, it was comparatively easy to keep out of their way, and they consequently did not do much damage. A heavy rain storm, in the middle of the night, had much more to do with making the situation an unpleasant one than the firing from the gunboats, as it drenched every one to the skin, and seriously disturbed the slumbers of the wearied soldiers.

GENERAL GRANT'S PERIL.

While surveying, from my post of observation in the bushes, the movements of the routed Federal troops at the Landing, a small boat, with two officers in it, passed up the river. As it drew near the place where I was concealed, I recognized one of the officers as General Grant, and the other one I knew by his uniform to be a general. Grant I had seen at Fort Donelson, and I had met with pictures of him in some of the illustrated papers, so that I had no trouble in knowing him in spite of the darkness. The boat passed so close to me that I could occasionally catch a word or two of the conversation that was passing between the Federal commander and his associate, although, owing to the splashing of the oars, and the other noises, I could not detect what they were talking about.

My heart began to beat violently when I saw Grant, and my hand instinctively grasped my revolver. Both he, and the officer with him, were completely at my mercy, for they were within easy pistol shot, and my first impulse was to kill them, and run the risk of all possible consequences to myself. I did even go so far as to take a good aim, and in a second more, had I been a little firmer-nerved, the great Federal general, and the future President of the United States, would have finished his career.

It was too much like murder, however, and I could not bring myself to do the deed, although it would have been as justifiable as any killing that takes place in warfare. Any soldier, however, will appreciate my feelings; for those who are bravest, when standing face to face with the enemy, will hesitate to take deliberate aim at a single man from an ambush. I therefore permitted Grant to escape, although I knew it was better for my cause to slay him than would be the loss of many hundreds less important soldiers. Indeed, had Grant fallen before my pistol, the great battle of Shiloh might have had a far different termination; for his loss would have so completed the demoralization of the Federals, that another rally would, in all probability, have been an impossibility. To have shot him, as I at first intended to do, would almost certainly have insured my own destruction; for large numbers of the Federals were so near me that I could plainly hear them talking, and escape would have been almost out of the question. I would, however, have been willing to have made a sacrifice of myself, had I not been influenced in the course I did by other considerations than those of prudence. At any rate, I permitted my opportunity to slip by unimproved, and ere a great many moments the boat and its occupants were out of my reach, and I saw the two generals go on board one of the gunboats.

After I got back to my camp I could not help thinking that I had committed an error; but on reflecting over the matter in cooler moments, I was not sorry that I had resisted the temptation to pull the trigger when I had my finger on it. If I had fired, what would have been the consequences, so far as the results of the war were concerned? The Federals would have lost their ablest general, almost at the beginning of his career. Would they have found another man who would have commanded their armies with the brilliant success that Grant did? These are momentous questions, when we think of the events that have occurred since the battle of Shiloh. Much more than the life of a single man was probably dependent upon whether I concluded to fire or not, as I pointed my pistol at the men in the boat that April night.

After the boat had passed by, I was strongly tempted to go

to the Federal camp and announce myself as a deserter, taking my chances of being able to get back again, or, at least, to give the slip before many hours, should my sincerity be suspected, and a close watch be put over me. This, however, I thought rather too risky a proceeding, under all the circumstances, and therefore concluded to get back to my post again. I succeeded in doing this, although not without considerable difficulty; and not caring to let my comrade know all that I had seen and thought, I told him that my errand had been an unsuccessful one, as I had not been able to get near enough to the Federal lines to discover anything of importance. To insure his keeping quiet, I said that I would go and get him a drink of that whiskey I had promised him, which made his eyes sparkle with delight, and started off to inform my captain with regard to what I had found out, and to ask his advice about what I had better do.

What had Best be Done?

Captain De Caulp was seriously perplexed at my report; but he said that attempting to instruct the general of an army was a risky business, and the probabilities were, that should I go to headquarters with my story, I would get into serious trouble. He further suggested that, perhaps, the general was as well informed with regard to the movements of the enemy as myself, if not better, and was making his arrangements accordingly; all of which did not relieve my mind of its premonitions of impending disaster, although it convinced me that, for my own sake, I had better hold my tongue. In spite of everything, however, it was as much as I could do to refrain from attempting to let Beauregard know how matters were, and of running all the risks of his displeasure. I finally came to the conclusion that the responsibilities were his, and not mine, and I had no fancy for being put under arrest, and of ruining all my future prospects by going through with my New Orleans experiences again, under circumstances that would almost inevitably expose me to indignities worse even than those I had suffered at the hands of his honor Mayor Monroe.

I accordingly reluctantly concluded to wait and see what the result of the next day's battle would be, declaring energetically to Captain De Caulp, that if we were defeated, I would never raise my sword in the army of Tennessee again.

I knew that there would be some hot work in the morning, whatever the final result of the battle might be, and felt the necessity of getting what rest I could, if I was to do a soldier's whole duty. Wrapping myself in my blanket, therefore, I threw myself upon the ground, and tried to sleep; but I was so agitated and apprehensive for the morrow, that slumber was an impossibility. Again and again as I tossed about, unable to close my eyes, I more than half repented of my resolution not to report the result of my spying expedition at headquarters; but being convinced not only of the inutility, but the danger to myself, of such a proceeding, refrained from doing so. Several times I fell into an uneasy doze, but the sound and refreshing slumbers that I so sorely needed would not visit my weary eyelids, and daybreak found me as wide awake as ever, but certainly not fit to endure the fatigues and perils of a fierce battle in such a manner as to do myself any credit. I resolved, however, although I felt that we were rushing on defeat, to face every danger, and endure every trial with the bravest and most enduring of my comrades, so long as the slightest hope of success remained, and if finally defeat seemed inevitable, to make off with what speed I could for the purpose of trying my luck in some other quarter.

Commencement of the Second Day's Battle.

At daylight the gunboats began to fire more rapidly than they had been doing during the night, and with such admirable execution that a prompt attack upon the part of the Confederates was rendered impossible. The second day of the battle, therefore, opened favorably for the Federals, and we lost the advantage we might have gained by assuming the offensive, and hurling our forces on the enemy, with that *elan* for which our Southern soldiers were famous, and which had served them so well on many important occasions. The opportunity thus lost was never regained ; for although the fortunes of the fight seemed to waver, it was easily to be seen that victory was no longer with the Confederates, and that the grievous mistake of the night before, in not promptly following up our success, and finishing our work then and there, would have all the terrible consequences I had feared.

The Federal general, Nelson, formed his troops in line of battle on our extreme left, and threw out his skirmishers for over a mile. Our whole force was soon engaged; but the Federals steadily advanced, and we were compelled to retire before them, our worn and exhausted men fighting desperately as they went. About ten o'clock we succeeded in making the cover of a woods, which enabled us to rally with effect, and our forces were hurled against the enemy with such fury, that they began to retreat in disorder; but, being supported by re-enforcements, they were ultimately able to hold their ground.

About this time a heavy cannonading commenced, and the battle began to assume the phase of an artillery duel. On our side, Terril's battery did excellent service, and succeeded in holding the enemy at bay, giving the infantry a breathing spell that they sorely needed. For more than two hours the artillery and musketry fire continued at short range; and the Confederates kept up to their work in such gallant style, that the enemy wavered again, and one grand charge might have routed them. Before such a charge could be made, however, heavy re-enforcements arrived, under the command of General Buell, as I understood; and these fresh troops, formed by brigades, attacked us at double-quick, and drove us back half a mile, breaking our lines, and throwing us into inextricable confusion.

DEFEAT.

By two o'clock, the whole of this part of the field was cleared, and the battle was practically lost to the Confederates, although the fighting was obstinately continued elsewhere for an hour or two longer.

All my worst anticipations had come true; and the Federal army, which was almost annihilated the night before, had not only saved itself, and recovered its lost ground, but it had inflicted upon the Confederates a most disastrous defeat. This was the only name for it, for we were worse beaten than the Federals were at Bull Run; and the fact that we were not pursued on our retreat, only proved that the Federal commanders, like our own at Bull Run, were either incapable of appreciating the importance of vigorous action under such circumstances, or were unable to follow up their advantages.

When I saw clearly that the day was lost, I determined to leave the field, and half resolved that if I succeeded in getting well away from our beaten army, I would give the whole thing up, and never strike another blow for the Confederacy as a soldier. I was scarcely able to contain myself for rage, not at the defeat, but at the inexcusable blunder that caused it; and was worked up to such a pitch, that I felt willing to die, as if there was nothing now worth living for. The Fort Donelson disaster, which I had hoped would be retrieved, had now been followed by another even more terrible; and the success of the Confederate cause was more remote, and more uncertain, than ever. It made me gnash my teeth with impotent fury to think of these things, and to have all my high hopes so suddenly dashed to the ground, just when the prospects for their realization seemed so bright.

A Valuable Prize.

About five o'clock I found my boy near the hospital. He had my horse, and another fine animal that he had picked up. In reply to my query, Bob said that he had found him in the woods without a rider. He was branded " U. S," and had an officer's saddle on; and as he seemed, from outside appearances, to be superior to my own steed, I concluded to take possession of him. Mounting him, I tried him over a fence, and a large log, which he cleared like an antelope; so deeming him a prize worth securing, I turned over my own horse to Bob, and started him off on the road to Corinth. The boy, however, mistook the road, and went plump into the Federal camp at Purdy, thus depriving me of his valuable services.

As for me, I remained in the woods all night, the roads being perfectly blocked up with the retreating army, trying to shield myself as best I could from the furious storm of rain and hail that came on, as if to add to the miseries which the wretched soldiers of the Confederacy were compelled to endure on their weary march back to Corinth. Although I had escaped from the two days' fighting unhurt, I was so utterly worn out and wretched, that I really did not care a great deal what became of me, and was almost as willing to be taken prisoner by the Federals as to return to Corinth, with a view of again undertaking to exert myself in what was now beginning to appear the hopeless cause of Southern independence. I managed, however, after the worst of the storm was over, to find a tolerably dry place, where, completely used up by the fatigues I had undergone, I fell into a sound sleep.

CHAPTER XVIII.

WOUNDED.

The Morning after the Battle of Shiloh. — My Return to Camp. — A Letter from my Memphis Lady-love. — A sad Case. — My Boy Bob missing. — I start out to Search for him. — A runaway Horse, and a long Tramp through the Mud. — Return to the Battle-field. — Horrible Scenes along the road. — Out on a scouting Expedition. — Burying the Dead. — I receive a severe Wound. — A long and painful Ride back to Camp. — My Wound dressed by a Surgeon, and my Sex discovered. — A Fugitive. — Arrival at Grand Junction. — Crowd of anxious Inquirers. — Off for New Orleans. — Stoppages at Grenada, Jackson, and Osyka on Account of my Wound. — The Kindness of Friends. — Fresh Attempt to reach New Orleans. — Unsatisfactory Appearance of the military Situation.. — The Passage of the Forts by the Federal Fleet. — A new Field of Employment opened for me. — I resume the Garments of my Sex.

ESTED, but scarcely refreshed, by a brief slumber on the damp ground, and with thoughts of the most gloomy description filling my mind, I mounted my horse at daybreak and started to ride back to Corinth. I was in rather different spirits from what I was two days before, when, inspired by brilliant hopes, and full of confidence that with this, the first great battle of the spring campaign, the disasters of the winter would be more than repaired, and that our Confederate army was about to enter upon a career of victory which would, most likely, long before the ending of the summer, establish our independence, I had hastened to the field, eager only to be able to join in the fight in time to have a chance of distinguishing myself before the Federals should be completely wiped out. The attack was, indeed, made as brilliantly and as successfully as I had anticipated that it would be, and at the end of a hard day's fighting, victory was fairly within our grasp. At the end of another day, however, we were a broken and disorganized mass of fugitives, straggling back to our camps, and thinking ourselves lucky that the Federals were not enterprising enough to pursue us before we could reach our intrenchments.

219

There was a hope, indeed, that we would be able to hold Corinth, and, by inducing the Federals to attack us in our fortifications, regain something of the advantage we had lost. The defeat, therefore, bad as it was, was not so desperate an overthrow as the one at Fort Donelson; but, although I felt this, and felt that if we could but hold our ground a little while all might be well, I was so despondent over the way things seemed to be going, that I had little heart to continue in the contest any longer. At the same time I was loath to give the thing up, and could not help reflecting that the true spirit of heroism required me to bear adversity with fortitude, and to seek to advance the interests of my cause, no matter how unpropitious the times might seem.

REFLECTIONS AFTER THE BATTLE.

I was more than ever anxious now, however, to enter upon the line of duty for which I esteemed myself particularly fitted; for, now that the excitement of the battle-field was over, and defeat once more compelled reflection, I could not help thinking that I was doing no very material service by plunging into the thick of a fight, as much for the enjoyment of the thing as anything else, whereas I could be worth many soldiers to the Confederacy if intrusted with certain duties of equal responsibility and danger, which I could perform much better than any man. How to obtain an assignment to this kind of duty, however, was what puzzled me, and it really almost seemed that a first-rate opportunity of distinguishing myself as a secret service emissary would never be offered.

Resolving in my own mind all manner of plans for the future, but unable to determine what my next move had better be, I made my way back to camp feeling, as I reflected on my brilliant expectations of a few days before, as if I were returning from a fool's errand, although I cannot say that I was sorry on account of having taken a hand in the fight, for throughout the two days I had borne myself as gallantly as the best, while simply as a personal adventure, the battle was a memorable affair for more reasons than one. It was at least something for me to have stood by the side of my expected husband throughout the long and bloody contest, and to have given him proofs of my valorous disposition, such as he could scarcely help remembering, with pleasure, in the future, when he learned that the little independent lieutenant, and the woman who was engaged as his wife, were one and the same person. So far, at least, my participation in the battle was a source of satisfaction to me, although it did not diminish my distress at so soon again being called upon to witness another hard-fought field lost to the Confederacy.

A LOVE LETTER.

On arriving at camp I found a mail awaiting me. Among my letters were some from my friends in the army of Virginia, and one from my little Memphis lady, which read as follows : —

"MEMPHIS, TENNESSEE, April 2. 1862.

"MY DEAR HARRY: Yours was handed to me the next morning by our trusty and faithful old servant David, and I hastily opened it, knowing it to be from you by the handwriting. My dear, I am afraid that this will appear unintelligible, being wet with tears from beginning to end. When your letter was handed to me we were at breakfast, and grandpa was reading the "Appeal," wherein it was stated that all officers and soldiers away from their commands should report for duty. I was afraid that you would have to go, but some hope remained until your fatal letter convinced me that my suspicions were too well founded. Alas, how vain are human expectations! In the morning we dream of happiness, and before evening are really miserable. I was promising to myself that one month more would have joined our hands, and now we are to be separated — yes, perhaps for years, if not forever; for how do I know but that the next tidings may bring intelligence of your being killed in battle, and then, farewell to everything in this world; my prospects of a happy future will vanish, and although unmarried, I will ever remain the widow Buford until death.

"And is it possible my dear Harry can doubt for one moment of my sincerity; or do you think that these affections can ever be placed on another, which were first fixed upon your dear self, from a convincing sense of your accomplishments and merit? No, dear Harry, my fidelity to you shall remain as unspotted as this paper was before it was blotted with ink and bedewed with tears. I know not how others love, but my engagements are for eternity. You desire me to remind you of your duty. My dear, I know not of any faults, nor am I disposed to look for any. I doubt not that the religious education you have received in your youth will enable you to resist the strongest temptations, and make that everlasting honor to the army, Lieutenant Buford, although not afraid to fight, yet afraid to sin. However terrifying it may be to meet death in the field, yet it is far more awful to appear before a just God, whom we have offended by our iniquities. There are no persons in the world accused more of irreligion than the military, while from the very nature of their employment none are more obliged to practise every Christian duty. They see thousands of their fellow-beings hurried into eternity without a moment's warning, nor do they know but that the next day they may themselves meet the same fate. My dear Harry, never be ashamed of religion; a consciousness of your own integrity will inspire you with courage in the day of battle, and if you should at last die in defence of the right in your country's cause, the Divine favor will be your comfort through eternity. In the mean time my prayers shall be constantly for your safety and your preservation in the day of battle, and my earnest hopes will be fixed upon your happy return.

"I will visit my aunt this fall in Alabama; she being your friend, will be some consolation to me in your absence. Let me hear from you as soon as possible, and as often, and never doubt my fidelity: consider me yours already, and I am satisfied. I hung your handsome picture opposite to mine in the drawing-room, over where we used to sit and chat together. Grandpa says that it does not flatter you, as we were both lovesick. What ideas the old folks do get into their heads, just as if they had never loved in their time. I have not seen the captain since; I think that his command is ordered away.

"Farewell, dear Harry, and may the wisdom of God direct you, and His all-wise providence be your guard. This is the sincere prayer of one who prefers you before all the world. Grandpa and auntie wish to be remembered to you kindly. I wrote to brother that you would hand him a letter.

"Your loving intended till death,

"M——."

I give this as a favorable specimen of the love-letters I was in the habit of receiving during my military career, and I have the less hesitation in doing so as it is one that no woman need be ashamed of having written. I could not help laughing a little as I read it, and yet I felt really sorry for the writer, and reproached myself for having permitted my flirtation with her to go to the length it did. The case was a particularly sad one, for the reason that the man who loved her devotedly, and who would doubtless in time have succeeded in curing her of her misplaced affections for the fictitious Lieutenant Buford, was among the slain at Shiloh. There was no braver soldier belonging to the Confederate army engaged in that bloody battle than Phil. Hastings, and his death was doubly a source of regret to me, as by it I lost a warm-hearted and sincere friend, and also an opportunity to undo the wrong I had unwittingly done him through capturing the affections of the girl he loved, by endeavoring to make matters right between him and her.

At the time of the receipt of this letter, however, I had something of more pressing importance to think of than explanations with Miss M. My boy had not put in an appearance, and suspecting that he must have lost himself, I started out to search for him; but, although I made diligent inquiry, I could not obtain any intelligence of him. This vexed me extremely, for Bob had become an invaluable servant, being very handy and entirely trustworthy, and I felt that he would be indispensable to me in the movement I now had more than half determined to make, with a view of trying to win the favors of Fortune in a somewhat new field of action.

My Horse gets Away.

To make matters worse, when about five miles from Corinth my horse broke from me, and stampeding out of sight, left me to get back the best way I could. I was now in a pretty fix, with scarcely any money about me, and with miles of terribly rough and muddy roads to traverse before I could regain my quarters. There was nothing, however, to do but to bear up under my misfortunes as bravely as possible, and so plunging through the mud, I tried to make my way back to Corinth with what rapidity I could.

The first camp I made was that of the eleventh Louisiana regiment, in which I had a number of friends. The Louisiana boys imagined that I had just come from Memphis, and they gave me a very hearty welcome, although they were not feeling particularly good over the result of the battle. Obtaining a horse from the quartermaster, I started back to the battle-field in company with Captain G. Merrick Miller, who desired to bury the dead of his company.

The Battle-field Revisited.

The road was lined with stragglers, many of them suffering from severe wounds, who were slowly making their way back to their respective camps, and as we reached the scene of the late action the most ghastly sight met our eyes. The ground was thickly strewn with dead men and horses, arms and accoutrements were scattered about in every direction, wagons were stuck in the mud and abandoned, and other abundant evidences of the sanguinary nature of the conflict were perceptible to our eyes. I could face the deadliest fire without flinching, but I could not bear to look at these things, and so, after having made a number of vain inquiries for Bob, I rode back to camp, and said good-by to my Louisiana friends, leaving them under the impression that I intended to take the train.

This I probably might have done had I not fallen in with some cavalry who were about starting out on scouting duty, and been tempted to accompany them. This was the kind of work that I had a particular liking for ; and as I had no definite plan for the immediate future arranged, and was desirous of finding Bob before leaving Corinth or its neighborhood, I concluded to try whether a little cavalry service would not be productive of some adventure worth participating in. An adventure of importance in its influence on my future career, sure enough, it did bring me, although it was not exactly what I anticipated or desired.

Burying the Dead.

It was about dark when we set out, and we spent the night hovering about in the neighborhood of the enemy, but without anything noteworthy occurring. The next day we had a little brush with a party of Federals, and after the exchange of a few shots were compelled to retreat. After this, we came across some dead men belonging to the tenth Tennessee regiment in the woods. Carefully removing the bodies to a field near by, we put them in a potato bin, and with a hoe, which was the only implement we could find suited to our purpose, we covered them, as well as we were able, with earth.

WOUNDED BY A SHELL.

While engaged in this melancholy duty, the enemy were occasionally firing shells in different directions, apparently feeling for us. We paid no special attention to them, as the Federals seemed to be firing at random, and, so far as we could judge, did not notice our party. Soon, however, a shrapnel burst in our midst, killing a young fellow instantly, and wounding me severely in the arm and shoulder.

I AM SEVERELY WOUNDED.

I was thrown to the ground, and stunned with the suddenness of the thing. One of the soldiers picked me up, and stood me on my feet, saying, " Are you hurt? "

" No, not bad," I replied, in a vague sort of way, but my whole system was terribly shocked, and I felt deathly sick. Before a great many moments, however, I perfectly recovered my consciousness, and by a resolute effort of will, endeavored to bear up bravely. I found, however, that I was unable to use my right arm, and soon the wound began to pain me terribly.

The soldier who had picked me up, seeing that I was too badly hurt to help myself, lifted me on my horse, and started back to camp with me. It was a long ride, of nearly fifteen miles, and I thought that it would never come to an end. Every moment the pain increased in intensity, and if my horse jolted or stumbled a little, I experienced the most excruciating agony. My fortitude began to give way before the terrible physical suffering I was compelled to endure ; all my manliness oozed out long before I reached camp, and my woman's nature asserted itself with irresistible force. I could face deadly peril on the battle-field without flinching, but this intolerable pain overcame me completely, and I longed to be where there would be no necessity for continuing my disguise, and where I could obtain shelter, rest, and attention as a woman. My pride, however, and a fear of consequences, prevented me from revealing my sex, and I determined to preserve my secret as long as it was possible to do so, hoping soon to reach some place where I could be myself again with impunity.

By the time we reached camp my hand and arm were so much swollen, that my conductor found it necessary to rip the sleeve of my coat in order to get at the wound for the purpose of bathing it in cold water. The application of the water

15

was a slight relief, but the hurt was too serious a one for such treatment to be of permanent service, so an ambulance was procured, and I was taken to the railroad and put on the train bound South. The cars stopped at Corinth for two hours, and, feeling the necessity for some medical attendance as soon as possible, I sent for a young surgeon whom I knew intimately, and telling him that I was wounded severely, asked him to try and do something to relieve my suffering.

My Sex Discovered.

He immediately examined my arm, and, as I perceived by the puzzled expression that passed over his face, he was beginning to suspect something, and guessing that further concealment would be useless, I told him who I really was. I never saw a more astonished man in my life. The idea of a woman engaging in such an adventure, and receiving such an ugly hurt, appeared to shock him extremely, and he declared that he would not take the responsibility of performing an operation, but would send for Dr. S. This frightened me, for I had witnessed some specimens of that surgeon's method of dealing with wounded soldiers, and I insisted that he was too barbarous, and that he should not touch me. He then proposed to send for Dr. H., but I objected to this also, and finally, at my urgent solicitation, he consented to make a careful examination himself, and try what he could do.

My shoulder was found to be out of place, my arm cut, and my little finger lacerated — a disagreeable and exceedingly painful, but not necessarily a very dangerous wound. The surgeon applied a dressing, and put my arm in a sling, after which I felt a great deal more comfortable, although the pain was still intense; and he then endeavored to induce me to stop at Corinth until I was in better condition for travelling. Now, however, that my sex was discovered, I was more than ever anxious to get away from my old associates, in the hope of finding some place where I could remain until I got well, and able to commence operations again in a different locality, without being annoyed by the attentions of impertinently curious people. I therefore insisted upon pushing on to Grenada, and he, finding that argument was useless, and, perhaps, appreciating my reasons for getting away as soon as possible, very kindly went and procured transportation papers for me, and before the information that a woman, disguised as an officer, was among the wounded on the train, we were, to my infinite satisfaction, speeding out of sight, leaving behind us the camp occupied by a defeated army. The thought that our brave army should be resting under the cloud of a most humiliating defeat was a mental torture, which even my intense physical suffering could not pacify, and I was heartily glad to be able to take myself off from a locality which had so many unpleasant associations.

While on the train I suffered a great deal, although I was as well cared for as circumstances would permit, and it was an immense relief when we reached Grand Junction, for the hotel proprietor there was an old and true friend of mine, and I felt sure of receiving from him all the attention it was in his power to bestow. I found, however, that it was almost an impossibility to get any accommodation whatever, on account of the crowds of people who filled the place. The wives and other relatives of officers and soldiers had come to await the result of the battle ; and as the news that the Confederate army had been defeated had preceded me, every thing was in confusion, and everybody plunged in the deepest grief.

WAITING FOR THE LOVED ONES.

Some of the waiting ones had already received their wounded friends, or the corpses of the slain, while others were nearly wild with anxiety on account of husbands, or brothers, or lovers who had not yet been heard from. Alas ! many of them were lying stretched, stark and stiff, on the bloody field at Shiloh, where they had bravely fought for the cause they loved.

I was asked a thousand questions about the battle, and was pressed with a thousand anxious interrogatories about particular persons, and endeavored to answer as well as I could, notwithstanding the pain which my wounded arm and shoulder caused. Many of the women could not prevail upon themselves to believe that the Confederate army had been again defeated, and indulged in the fiercest invectives against the invaders. The intense grief of these stricken people affected me even more than the terrible scenes incident to the battle and the retreat, and, as I was not in a fit condition to endure anything more of anguish, and as it seemed to be impossible to obtain a room where I could be quiet and free from intrusion, I determined to push on to Grenada, without more delay, although I was anything but able to endure the excitement and discomfort of several hours' ride by rail.

Having reached Grenada, I took a good rest by remaining there for two days, and was greatly benefited thereby, for rest and an opportunity to cool off from the excitement I was in, were what I particularly needed if I expected to make satisfactory progress with the healing of my wound. I was visited by a great many of the ladies of the place, who presented me with bouquets, delicacies of various kinds, and bandages for my wound, and who otherwise overwhelmed me with attentions, for which I hope I was duly grateful. Not only the natural restlessness of my disposition, which my wound aggravated to such an extent that it was an impossibility for me to keep quiet, but a desire to get as far away from the army of Tennessee as possible, before the fact that Lieutenant Harry T. Buford was a woman became generally known, induced me to move on with all the speed I could make, and I consequently started for New Orleans before I was really fit to travel. The result was, that when I reached Jackson, I found myself too ill to proceed farther, and was compelled, much against my will, to make another stop.

The hospitalities I received at Jackson, I will always remember with the warmest feelings of gratitude. I was really very sick, and my wounded shoulder and arm were terribly inflamed, and I scarcely know what I should have done had not a widow lady and her daughter taken a fancy to me, and waited on me until I was able to be on the road again. These ladies treated me like a young lord, and I shall ever think of them as having placed me under a debt that I can never repay.

At Jackson, I made the acquaintance of General Price's quartermaster, who was stationed there. This gentleman I afterwards met in Wyoming Territory, but he did not recognize me, as, indeed, it was scarcely possible that he should.

On the Move Again.

So soon as I thought myself able to endure the fatigues of travel, I insisted upon being on the move in spite of the remonstrances of my friends, and made another start for New Orleans. I had, however, miscalculated my strength, and was compelled to make another halt at Osyka, near the Louisiana line. At this place resided one of the best friends I ever had in the world. He is, in truth, one of Nature's noblemen, and I wish that our country had more like him. My fervent prayer is, that he may have long life, health, and abundant prosperity, and that every blessing may be showered upon him and his family. With this kind friend I remained a couple of days, and was treated with the greatest kindness, a kindness that would scarcely permit of my departure, when, feeling in better health and spirits than I had been since the battle, I announced my intention of continuing my journey. Resisting all importunities to make a longer stay, however, I insisted upon going, and stepped on board the train bound for New Orleans, determined to reach that city this time at all hazards.

By this time my wound was healing quite nicely; and although it pained me considerably still, the feverishness which had attended it was gone, and I began to feel myself once more, and with restored health began to busy myself in making plans for the future. Exactly what course next to pursue I could not quite determine, but I felt very confident that if I once reached New Orleans, and could prevent myself from being interfered with by my old friends, the provost marshal and Mayor Monroe I would very soon find some congenial employment.

On the train there were a great many wounded men, some of them old friends of mine whom I was glad to meet with again. The trip, therefore, was a pleasant one in some respects, notwithstanding its melancholy aspects, and we had a tolerably lively time discussing the late battle, and the chances of the Confederates being able to make headway in the future against the force which the Federals were bringing against them in every direction. We were obliged to acknowledge that the outlook was not a particularly promising one, and more than one expressed the belief that New Orleans would be the next object of attack. There was a good deal of confidence felt, however, that a Federal advance against the Gulf city, if it should be attempted, would be repulsed in a manner, that would, in some degree, compensate for the Confederate defeats at Fort Donelson and Shiloh. This confidence, on the part of my companions, I was scarcely able to share, for, not only had my late experiences shaken my belief in the invincibility of the Confederate army, but I knew better than they did that the Federals intended to assail New Orleans, and I felt very certain, that if the assault

was made, it would be with a force that our people would
find well-nigh irresistible. I, however, kept my thoughts to
myself, but resolved that so soon as we arrived in the city, I
would exert myself with a view of obtaining a full understanding of the situation, and decide according to circumstances what course it would be best for me to pursue.

BACK IN NEW ORLEANS.

In New Orleans I met a number of old friends, James
Doolan, Frank Moore, Captain Daugherty, and others, all of
whom were first-rate fellows, and all quite certain that in case
the Federals should put in an appearance, they would be given
a warmer reception than they bargained for. I admired their
enthusiasm, although I was not as well able to share it as I
would perhaps have been some months before, and I resolved
to see for myself, as much as I was able, exactly what the
defences of the city amounted to. I accordingly went about
the camps as much as I could, in a quiet sort of way, making
mental notes of all I observed, and I very soon came to the
conclusion that the military situation was one that I did not
like a bit. I knew, however, that the river defences were
strong, and I hoped, rather than expected, that they would
be able to repel any attack that would be made.

I was not long, however, in concluding that New Orleans
would be a good place for me to go away from at as early a
day as possible, for I had no notion of witnessing another
triumph of the enemy if I could help it. I was, however,
far from being strong enough to go on active duty, and
thought that the best thing I could do was to remain where I
was until my health was entirely restored, and to employ this
enforced leisure in maturing a definite plan of action for the
future, for, with returning health, my desire for active
employment, either in the field or on detective duty, returned
with all its original force, and I could not induce myself to
entertain the idea of resuming permanently the garments of
my sex, and of abandoning the service of the Confederacy so
long as there was any work to be done.

When the news came that the Federal fleet had passed
Forts Jackson and St. Philip, I at first thought of leaving as
quickly as I could ; but a little reflection induced me to change
my mind, for I saw clearly that if the Federals took possession of the city, I would, as a woman, have a grand field of

operation. I therefore resolved to remain and see the thing out, and the uniform of Lieutenant Harry T. Buford was carefully put away for future use if need be, and the wearer thereof assumed the garments of a non-combatant feminine for the purpose of witnessing the entry of the victors into the captured city.

CHAPTER XIX.

THE CAPTURE OF NEW ORLEANS, AND BUTLER'S ADMINISTRATION.

Capture of Island No. 10. — The impending Attack on New Orleans. — The unsatisfactory Military Situation. — Confidence of Everybody in the River Defences. — My Apprehensions of Defeat. — The Fall of New Orleans. — Excitement in the City on the News of the Passage of the Forts being received. — I resolve to abandon the Career of a Soldier, and to resume the Garments of my own Sex.   Appearance of the Fleet opposite the City. — Immense Destruction of Property. — My Congratulations to Captain Bailey of the Navy. — Mayor Monroe's Refusal to raise the Federal Flag. — General Butler assumes Command of the City. — Butler's Brutality. — I procure the foreign Papers of an English Lady, and strike up an Acquaintance with the Provost Marshal. — Am introduced to other Officers, and through them gain Access to Headquarters. — Colonel Butler furnishes me with the necessary Passes to get through the Lines. — I drive an active Trade in Drugs and Confederate Money while carrying Information to and fro. — Preparations for a grand final Speculation in Confederate Money. — I am intrusted with a Despatch for the "Alabama," and am started for Havana.

OLLOWING close upon the defeat at Shiloh came the fall of Island No. 10, a disaster of great moment to the Confederacy, for the strength of its fortifications had been much relied upon to check the advance of the Federals down the Mississippi River; and the loss of the position almost simultaneously with the Shiloh affair was well calculated to inspire gloomy apprehensions for the future.   I heard the news that Island No. 10 had been captured, after reaching New Orleans, and the fact that the enemy had been successful in forcing so strong a defence with comparative ease, taken in connection with the radical inefficiency of many of the military preparations being made for the defence of the city, prevented me from sharing the extreme confidence so many people expressed, and that so many undoubtedly felt, with regard to the entire safety of New Orleans.   If a strong fort like Island No. 10 could be taken, why should not the Federals, especially if they made the attack with a proper vigor, be able to overcome any resistance the defences of New Orleans — in many respects not by any means so strong — would be able to make ?

Exactly when or where the blow would be struck, however, it was impossible to tell. The general impression was that the attack would be made by the army under General Butler, and how really formidable the Federal fleet was, few, if any, had any real notion. I suppose that scarcely any one imagined the ships would make an unsupported effort to pass the fortifications below the city, or that they would succeed in doing so in case the attempt was made. I knew little or nothing about the river defences, or the preparations that were being made to receive a naval attack, from my own observations, but from what I understood with regard to them, I felt tolerably assured of their efficiency, and my chief concern was about the inefficiency of the measures adopted to resist a land attack.

The Federal Fleet passes the Fort.

The Federal fleet, however, to the surprise of every one, succeeded in overcoming the obstructions in the river, and in passing the two principal forts, after a desperate battle, and then New Orleans was at the mercy of the naval gunners, specimens of whose methods of fighting had been exhibited to me at Fort Donelson and Shiloh in such a manner as to inspire me with a wholesome dislike for the kind of missiles they were in the habit of throwing. The gunboats I had encountered at Fort Donelson and Shiloh were, however, very different affairs from the ships which fought their way past Forts Jackson and St. Philip, — a broadside from a frigate like the Hartford ought almost to have routed an entire army ; and when I saw these splendid vessels appearing off the levee, I began to have a greater respect for the power of the Federal government than I had had before, and a greater appreciation of the weakness of the Confederacy.

But while I was thus compelled to appreciate more forcibly than I had done the enormous difficulties in the way of a successful termination of the contest, I was no more in a mood for surrendering than I was at the beginning. Indeed, defeat and disaster only nerved me to make greater exertions than ever, and I held in utter contempt those weak-hearted people who, when the news that the fleet had passed the forts and was on its way up to the city reached us, were willing to regard the game for which they were playing as lost, and the Confederate cause as practically overthrown. I was for fighting the thing out so long as we had a foot of ground to fight on, but I saw very clearly that if anything was to be gained now, in the face of the heavy disasters that were overtaking us, stratagem as well as force would have to be called into play, and that we would be compelled to combat the enemy's strength with cunning.

I DETERMINE TO FIGURE AGAIN AS A WOMAN.

I felt particularly that the time was now come for me to make a display of my talents in another character than that of a warrior, and the arrival of the fleet in front of the city found me in the anxious and angry crowd on the levee, not inelegantly attired in the appropriate garments of my sex — garments that I had not worn for so long that they felt strangely unfamiliar, although I was not altogether displeased at having a fair opportunity to figure once more as a woman, if only for variety sake.

Strange to say, the capture of New Orleans did not affect me near so unpleasantly as the defeats at Fort Donelson and Shiloh, and I felt nothing of the depression of spirit that overcame me after these battles. This may have been because I was getting accustomed to defeat now, and was consequently able to bear up under it more philosophically, although it is more than probable that it was because I was not one of the combatants, and consequently did not have that overpowering individual interest that a combatant must feel if he cares anything for his cause. I experienced less of that peculiarly disagreeable feeling of personal chagrin and disappointment that oppresses a soldier belonging to a beaten army. The fact, however, that when the Federals obtained possession of the city I would probably be able to do some detective duty in a style that would not only be satisfying to my own ambition, but damaging to the enemy, and of essential service to the Confederacy, really enabled me to behold the approach of the fleet with a considerable degree of what almost might be called satisfaction. As a woman, and especially as a woman who had facilities for appearing as a representative of either sex, I knew that I would be able to observe the enemy's movements, and ferret out their plans in a signally advantageous manner; and, confident that my cunning and skill would enable me to perform an important work, I was really anxious to see the enemy occupy the city, in order that I might try conclusions with them, having ample confidence that I would prove myself a match for the smartest Yankee of them all.

I was the more willing to try and distinguish myself in a new field, as I had amply demonstrated to my own satisfaction, and to that of thousands of the best fighting men of the Confederate armies, that I lacked nothing of the valorous disposition of a soldier, and that I could stand without flinching before the hottest fire of the enemy, and I aspired to win fresh laurels by performing services of a kind that would require an exertion of all my intellectual faculties, and that would, if I were to be even reasonably successful, bring me more real credit, and more enduring fame, than almost any performances in the field that I might undertake. After nearly a year of service, I was just beginning to appreciate the fact that I occupied a unique position, and that my efforts would be almost profitless, alike to me and to the Confederate cause, if I was content merely to figure as an additional combatant when the actual clash of battle came; and while I did not regret, for a great variety of reasons, my experiences in the field, I was very well satisfied to abandon, for a while at least, a soldier's life for the purpose of undertaking work more naturally congenial than campaigning, and for which my sex, combined with my soldierly training, peculiarly fitted me. My experimental trip to Washington satisfied me that it was as a detective, rather than as a soldier, that my best successes were to be won; and now that one of my most important surmises, based upon almost the barest hints obtained on that trip, was proven to have been well founded, I was inspired by a special zeal to carry out intentions which I had been revolving in my mind ever since my visit to the Federal capital. These intentions I had intended to carry out long before, and had I accepted the invitation to return to Virginia, which I received some time before the battle of Fort Donelson, I doubtless would, long ere this, have been actively employed in passing through the Federal lines in search of information. The acceptance of that invitation was, however, delayed, and finally abandoned, and circumstances prevented my making a very serious effort to become an active *attaché* of the detective corps up to the date of the fall of New Orleans. With the capture of that city, however, I concluded that my great opportunity had come, and that now it depended upon myself, rather than upon the favor or whim of some commanding officer, whether I should give the cause the benefit of my best talents or not. The opportunity I embraced with the utmost eagerness, and with a resolve to make myself as troublesome as possible to the conquerors of New Orleans.

General Lovell, who was in command, so soon as he saw that the fleet had passed the forts, posted up to the city in hot haste, and began to make preparations for leaving, and for destroying all the cotton and other property that would be likely to be particularly useful to the enemy. The wildest excitement prevailed when it was understood that New Orleans was about to fall into the hands of the Federals, and great wrath and indignation were excited by what was believed to be the inefficiency of the defence. Without waiting to argue the matter, however, with the angry citizens, General Lovell turned over the responsibility of making terms with the victors to Mayor Monroe, and got away with the remnant of his army as fast as he was able.

The Fleet appears off the City.

Late in the morning of the 25th of April, 1862, the Federal fleet could be seen coming up the river, but it must have dampened the enthusiasm of the Yankee sailors somewhat to find steamboats, cotton, and all kinds of combustible property blazing for miles along the levee. It was a terribly magnificent spectacle, but one the like of which I earnestly hoped I might never witness again, for it fairly made me shudder to see millions of dollars worth of property being utterly destroyed in this reckless manner, and it impressed me more strongly with an idea of the horrors of warfare than all the fighting and slaughter I had ever seen done. There seemed, however, to be no help for it, and General Lovell was probably justified in giving the order he did, and thereby diminishing the value of the prize which the Federals had won.

It was about one o'clock when the fleet came in front of the city, and the vessels, one by one, dropped their anchors. A demand for a surrender was brought on shore by Captain Bailey, who went up to the City Hall to have a conference with the mayor. I was on the alert to commence operations as soon as possible, and, desirous of being in favor with the captors, I sought an opportunity to speak to Captain Bailey, and to welcome him to the city. He shook hands with me, and said that he would see me again; but he had no time for conversation just then, and as my object was accomplished by introducing myself to his notice as a pretended friend of his cause, I did not make any endeavor to further attract his attention.

Mayor Monroe behaved nobly when he was asked to surrender the city. He said that the city was without defence, and at the mercy of the conquerors, but that it was not within his province as a municipal officer to surrender. He declined to raise the United States flag over the public buildings, or to do anything that would seem a recognition of the right of the Federals in any way to regulate affairs in New Orleans by anything else than the law of force. When I read his reply to Farragut's demand for a surrender, I readily forgave my private grievance against him. The mayor having positively refused to have anything to do with displaying the United States flag, or with lowering the flag of Louisiana, the raising of the stars and stripes on the public buildings was done by the sailors from the Federal fleet.

Mumford pulls down the Flag from the Mint.

The United States flag which was raised upon the mint was pulled down again by Mumford, who paid the penalty of his life for the act after Butler took command of the city. The execution of this young man was an outrage on civilization, and a crime on the part of the man who ordered it which entitles his memory to execration. Mumford told me himself that he perpetrated the act through a mistaken idea that the flag had been displayed by some traitor, and that he was not aware at the time that the Federals had assumed control of the city. The execution of Mumford was a fair specimen of the many dastardly actions perpetrated by Butler during the reign of terror that he inaugurated, and that will cause his name to be remembered with hatred in New Orleans, and, indeed, throughout the whole South, long after the ordinary passions of the war have died out.

When Butler took command, which he did on May 1st, he issued orders stopping the circulation of Confederate currency, directing the people to resume their usual avocations, and giving everybody to understand that he intended to have his own way.

It is not necessary, in a merely personal narrative like this, to go into any details with regard to Butler's rule in New Orleans. The execution of Mumford for what, according to the worst construction that could be put upon it, was a very venial offence, and what in reality was a mere act of indiscretion, utterly unworthy of notice, after the Federals were in full control of the city, and his infamous " woman order," are specimens of the manner in which he conducted himself, and they were acts that speak too loudly for themselves to require comment.

PLANS FOR CIRCUMVENTING BUTLER.

I soon perceived that with such a brute as this man Butler to deal with, it would be necessary for me to be extremely circumspect, and to bring my best strategic talents to bear, if I expected to accomplish anything. I was well acquainted with the city and environs, and knew exactly how to go about slipping in and out through the lines; but to carry on such operations as I proposed with a reasonable degree of safety and assurance of success, it was necessary — especially after the deposition of Mayor Monroe, by Butler's order, and the placing of the city under martial law — for me to keep all my wits about me, and to take care to be on good terms with those in authority.

I therefore set to work with due diligence and persistency to gain the confidence of the Federal officers. Some of them I found to be very pleasant, gentlemanly fellows, who were disposed to make themselves as agreeable as possible to everybody, and who were much gratified to hear any one — especially any woman — express Union sentiments. Many of them did not at all approve of the offensive manner in which Butler conducted himself, and some of his orders were carried out with a great deal of reluctance by those intrusted with their execution. With some of these officers I soon managed to get on very friendly terms, and they were always so polite and considerate in their treatment of myself and others, that I greatly regretted the necessity of deceiving them.

I, however, had objects in view with which my private friendships and personal feelings could not be permitted to interfere, and in all my conversations and communications with the officers of Butler's command, I never lost sight of opportunities to serve the Confederate cause. Following up the line of policy I had determined upon when I introduced myself to Captain Bailey, I professed strong Union sentiments, and took occasion, whenever in the presence of officers or soldiers, to denounce the cause I loved, and the welfare of which I was so anxious to promote. This line of conduct had the desired effect, for I soon became known as one of the few stanch advocates of the Federal government in New Orleans, and not only secured myself from molestation, but gained the entire confidence of our new rulers. My Southern friends, who could not understand what I was driving at, were, of course, alienated from me, much to my regret and sorrow; but this could not be helped, for it was absolutely necessary, in a matter of this kind, that I should have no confidants, and should depend entirely upon myself. My secret, so long as I was the sole possessor of it, was safe, which it assuredly would not have been under such a system of espionage as that established by Butler, had I intrusted it to any one, or had I failed in the slightest particular to sustain the character of a devoted Unionist, which I had assumed. It was better for me to risk the temporary loss of my friends, in the hope and expectation that the vindication of my conduct would come with time, than to risk anything by an incautious word, or even look; and I accepted the consequences of a thorough performance of the duties I had assigned myself without hesitation, and with a resolute determination to give Butler as much annoyance as was in my power.

I PROCURE SOME FOREIGN PAPERS.

I had a stroke of good luck in the very beginning. An English lady, with whom I had become slightly acquainted, was on the point of returning to her own country, having come to the conclusion that Old England was a quieter, and on the whole more agreeable place of residence, just at that time, than America, for a person who, like herself, had no interest in the contest that was being carried on, but who was pretty certain, if she remained, to suffer numerous inconveniences and hardships. This lady was decidedly friendly, however, to the Confederate cause, as, indeed, were all the foreign residents of New Orleans, and she would willingly have aided it in any way that she could without getting herself in trouble. As matters stood, however, she was anxious to get away as soon as possible, the capture of the city by the

Federals, with its attendant horrors, combined with a prospect that the Confederates would before long probably make a desperate attempt to regain it, not having the most soothing effect upon her nerves. Hearing that she was about to leave, I went to her, and expressed a desire to purchase her passport and other foreign papers, confident that, armed with such documents as these, I would be able to make a fair start against the Federal authorities, and gain some immediate advantages that would probably be otherwise out of the question. The lady readily consented to part with the papers for a fair price, being glad to get the money I offered for them, and she either believed, or affected to believe, the story which I told to account for my eagerness to possess them. There was, in fact, however, no particular necessity for romancing to any great extent on such a subject as this; for in the terror and confusion incident to the abandonment of the city by the Confederates and its occupation by the Federals, and in the great uncertainty with regard to what the near future would bring forth, it was the most natural thing in the world that a lone and unprotected woman like myself should desire to have the means at hand of escaping from any claims to allegiance that either party might present; and of invoking the protection of some foreign power.

A TALK WITH THE PROVOST MARSHAL.

Armed with my British papers, I went to the office of the provost marshal for the purpose of striking up an acquaintance with that gentleman, he being the person it was most immediately important for me to have dealings with, and to gain the confidence of. On requesting an interview, I was ushered into the provost marshal's presence, and introducing myself to him under the name I had decided to assume, told him that I was heartily glad to welcome the army of the United States to New Orleans, and that I hoped this wretched contest would soon be at an end, and the stars and stripes acknowledged everywhere once more.

He seemed to be a little surprised, and even suspicious, at my warmth of manner, and giving me a rather keen look, which I bore without flinching, he asked me, with some brusqueness, but at the same time not impolitely, if I had taken the oath yet.

This was a rather delicate question, and as I had not, and

did not intend to take the oath he alluded to, I concluded to waive it, and avoid giving a direct answer. I therefore replied that I was a Northern woman, and that my father was a New Yorker, but that, being in New Orleans at the time of the establishment of the blockade, I had been unable to communicate with my friends at the North and in England, or to get away. This was all plausible enough, and the provost marshal accepted it as a genuine statement of my case, apparently without hesitation, although he did not let me off without some cross-questioning.

"Have you a family?" said he.

"No, sir," I replied, with as sad and mournful an expression as I could put on, "I am a widow; my husband was an Englishman, and on his death he left me in quite comfortable circumstances. I have, however, lost everything by these wretched rebels, who have destroyed my property, and robbed me without mercy." While indulging in this recital of my troubles I wiped my eyes with my pocket handkerchief, tried my best to squeeze out a tear or two, and looked as sorrow-stricken as I possibly could.

The provost marshal, if he did not exactly overflow with sympathy, appeared desirous of doing what he could for me, and asked where I lived.

I replied that, owing to my reduced circumstances I was unable to keep house, as I had been doing up to the breaking out of the war, and that I was occupying a rented room, which, small as it was, I was doubtful about being able to keep unless I heard from my friends soon, or was able to obtain some employment by which I could make a little money. I then told him what my number was, and after some further conversation, chiefly about my poverty, the wrongs I had suffered from the rebels, and the difficulty of making ends meet, I informed him that I had come from England to New Orleans with my late husband, some years before the war, and that I proposed to return there so soon as I received a sufficient remittance. The provost marshal expressed a willingness to aid me in any way that lay in his power, and I bowed myself out of his presence, feeling tolerably confident that I had produced the impression I wished, and that, if I managed matters discreetly, he and I would have no difficulty in getting along with each other.

The next day I met the provost marshal again. He appeared to be quite pleased to see me, and introduced me to

16

two officers of the thirty-first Massachusetts regiment. They were both gentlemen, with whom it would have been a pleasure for me to have formed a real friendship under any other circumstances; but, as my only object in making their acquaintance was that I might be able to use them as instruments for the accomplishment of my purposes as a Confederate agent, I of course did not permit my personal liking for them to interfere with the grand objects I had in view. They, on their side, appeared to be not a little gratified to find at least one woman in New Orleans who professed a decided partiality for the stars and stripes, — for such women were rare in those days, — and they showed a marked inclination to continue the acquaintance. I accordingly invited them to call upon me, and soon managed to establish such friendly relations with them that, through their influence, I gained access to headquarters.

General Butler I fought shy of, for I did not like his looks, and concluded to have as little to do with him as possible. I met his brother, Colonel Butler, however, who was the power behind the throne, and who managed most of the transactions which had any money in them, which the general could not have openly touched without exciting comment, and probably getting himself into trouble. Both the general and the colonel were decidedly on the make, and were bent on improving the chances which the practically unlimited control of one of the richest cities on the continent gave them for bettering their fortunes. The colonel, however, could attend to mere pocket-filling operations to better advantage than his brother, and it soon became well understood that he was the one to apply to, if any favors from headquarters were desired.

I obtain Passes to go through the Lines.

From Colonel Butler I obtained permits to go to Mandeville, on the other side of Lake Pontchartrain, and even to visit Mobile, without being searched. With these papers in my possession, I set about preparing for a career of some activity in the way of running through the lines and communicating with the Confederate authorities. Having the same desire as the two Butlers to earn a dollar or so when I could, and, if possible, without stealing, I engaged quite extensively in the drug business, while performing the duties of a special messenger and bearer of Confederate despatches. Drugs of all kinds were very scarce within the Confederate lines, and consequently brought enormous prices; so that any one who could manage to smuggle them past the Federal outposts was certain of reaping a handsome profit. I succeeded in obtaining a good quantity of this kind of merchandise from the different hospitals, and, as I could carry many dollars' worth about my person without attracting particular attention, I much more than made my expenses on the several trips I undertook to Mandeville and beyond. Confederate money was also cheap, as well as plenty, in New Orleans, as everybody had some of it; while, under Butler's orders, it could not be used. It therefore offered fine opportunities for speculation to any one who could carry it to where it was of more value than it was in New Orleans just at that time. I therefore invested quite heavily in Confederate promises to pay, and, as with the drugs, contrived to make the speculation pay handsomely.

Having made several trips with success and with much profit, I began to think that I was, perhaps, making out with my enterprises entirely too well; and, apprehensive of getting into some difficulty which I might not be able to get out of as easily as I could wish, — for I saw a number of indications of trouble ahead, — I resolved, while on one of my expeditions, after a consultation with my Confederate friends, to return to New Orleans, for the purpose of buying up a quantity of the proscribed money, and then to leave for good, getting out of Butler's power while I had a fair chance of doing so. This arrangement fell through, however; for I was persuaded to make a trip to Havana, for the purpose of carrying a despatch to the Confederate cruiser, the "290," or "Alabama," as she was otherwise called, and of transacting some other business of a secret character for advancing the interests of the Confederacy. This commission I accepted with eagerness, and returned to New Orleans with what haste I could, with the despatch secreted on my person, for the purpose of taking the first vessel for Havana.

CHAPTER XX.

A VISIT TO HAVANA.

A Trip to Havana. — My Purposes in making the Journey. — The Results of a Year of Warfare. — Gloomy Prospects. — A Gleam of Hope in Virginia. — The Delights of a Voyage on the Gulf of Mexico. — The Island of Cuba in Sight. — The Approach to Havana. — I communicate with the Confederate Agents and deliver my Despatches. — An Interchange of valuable Information. — The Business of Blockade-running and its enormous Profits. — The Injury to the Business caused by the Capture of New Orleans. — My Return to New Orleans and Preparation for future Adventures.

HE idea of making a trip to Havana was very agreeable to me for a number of reasons. My health was not so robust as it had been, and my wounded arm, although it had healed up, was still very sore, and hurt me severely at times. It was an impossibility for me to keep quiet so long as I was in the midst of associations calculated to excite me and to stimulate the combativeness of my nature, and I needed more than anything else, for restoration to perfect health, such a rest as a sea voyage alone could give. There was, it is true, some risks in visiting Havana at this season, but I was acclimated, and did not worry myself much with fears of yellow fever or other diseases, my mind being too intently fixed on a variety of other matters that I esteemed of more consequence.

The most important reason for my wishing to take a run over there was, a desire to make the acquaintance of the Confederate agents, and to learn something of their methods of transacting business in the way of sending communications through the lines, for, even when the blockade could not be run with goods, it was often possible to smuggle important information past the Federal cruisers, and, some of the post lines were so complete, that, in spite of the vigilance of their enemies, the beleaguered Confederates managed to maintain

HAVANA.

correspondence very regularly with their friends of the outside world.

My brief experience had convinced me that I had peculiar talents for the kind of work in which I had been engaged since the advent of Butler and his forces in New Orleans, and my only regret was, that I had not made a persistent effort to take it up sooner. I determined now, however, to qualify myself as quickly as possible for the business of a spy and a bearer of despatches, for I felt assured that there would be plenty of employment found for me before the war was over, and that if I proved myself skilful and reliable, the Confederate authorities would avail themselves of my services with an alacrity they had not shown when I was skirmishing around in the character of a little dandy independent lieutenant, seeking to have a hand in every fight.

A DISCOURAGING OUTLOOK.

The military situation in some of its aspects was gloomy enough. In the West we had occasional successes, but their permanent value was little or nothing, while the enemy was steadily advancing and making the beleaguerment of the Confederacy more complete every day. The loss of New Orleans was a bewildering blow, from which there was no recovery but by the retaking of the city, and the prospects that we would be able to do this very soon were not particularly promising. In the mean time the Federals were evidently working resolutely to gain possession of the Mississippi River throughout its entire length, and strong as were the fortifications at Vicksburg and other points, I had not that faith in their invincibility I once would have had. I had seen too many positions proclaimed invincible and defended with valor, fall before the Federal attacks, for me to have anything of my old-time faith in the irresistible valor of Southern soldiers or the masterly generalship of Southern commanders. The old boast which I was accustomed to hear so often at the outbreak of the war, that one Southerner could whip five Yankees, had turned out to be mere boasting, and nothing more. The Federals, while they did not have all the dash and *elan* of the Confederates, had proved their fighting qualities on too many well-contested fields for the old-fashioned talk about the superiority of Southern prowess to be in order; and they had a way, when they once captured an important position, of staying there, in spite of all efforts to dislodge them, that did not promise at all well for the future of the cause.

Were it not that the news from Virginia was in some degree encouraging, I should have been almost willing to have concluded, that we were indeed nearing the last ditch, which some of our orators were so fond of alluding to. There, however, the Confederate soldiers were indeed winning laurels, and the capture of Richmond was as apparently as far off as it was when I turned my back upon it to seek my fortune in the West. If our brave boys under Lee, therefore, could only improve the summer as the winter had been improved in the West by the Federals, there would be some hope that, after all, we might win the desperate game we were playing, and accomplish substantially all for which we took up arms.

EFFECTS OF THE BLOCKADE.

In the mean time, however, things were in a bad way in many respects in the beleaguered Confederacy. The coast blockade was now fully established, and the enemy's lines were drawn so close along the principal avenues of communication with the outside world and the interior, that our commerce was completely killed, and our people were already suffering for many of the necessities of life, while the requirements of warfare with a powerful enemy, amply provided with resources, were impoverishing them more and more every day. Whole districts' had been devastated by the manœuvrings of the different armies, and the suffering among the poorer classes throughout the entire South was very great, while many persons, who were possessed of ample wealth before the war, were now feeling the pinchings of poverty, and were learning what it was' not to know where the next meal was coming from.

It was truly a pitiable condition of affairs; and the worst of it was, that there was no promise of speedy amendment. If these were the results of one year of warfare, what would be the condition of things, should the conflict be prolonged for another twelvemonth? Alas! it was prolonged, not for one more year merely, but for three; and when the dreadful day of total irremediable defeat — to which some of us, at the time which I am now referring to, were already uneasily and unwillingly looking forward — finally came, the South was literally exhausted, as no other country ever had been before.

While I could not help reflecting deeply on the discouragement of the situation, and feeling uneasy with regard to the
future, it was not my disposition to brood over possibly
imaginary misfortunes, or to allow myself to be unnerved by
disasters that might never happen. I believed in making the
most of the present, and I knew that the only way in which
success ever could be achieved, would be by those who really
had the interest of the cause at heart laboring incessantly,
and in the face of every discouragement, with all the energy
at their command. The difficulties of the situation, indeed,
inspired me with a sort of enthusiasm which I had not felt
before, and the particular sort of duty which I had now taken
up was so decidedly congenial, and promised to be so full of
exciting adventures, that there was a positive enjoyment to
be got from it, such as mere campaigning did not yield.

OFF FOR HAVANA.

I started off for Havana, therefore, in anticipation of a
particularly pleasant cruise, which would not only be beneficial to my health, but which would afford me an agreeable change of scene, and at the same time give me facilities for carrying on the line of operations I proposed to the
best advantage.

Leaving the turbulent current and the muddy banks of the
Mississippi behind me, the vessel upon which I embarked
was soon ploughing her way through the beautiful blue waters
of the Gulf of Mexico, pointed towards my native city — a
city that I had not visited since I left it years ago, when a
child, to go to New Orleans for the purpose of completing my
education. It was upon these waters, and in their vicinity,
that my adventure-loving ancestors had achieved renown and
wealth in making explorations and conquests of the New World
discovered by Columbus. Not far from the track of the ship
in which I was now speeding towards Havana had sailed the
expedition fitted out by old Governor Don Diego Valazquez,
which discovered Mexico, and prepared the way for the brilliant exploits of Cortez and his followers, while the whole
Gulf and its surrounding shores were alive with memories
of the valiant deeds of the valiant people of my father's
race.

Nothing more delightful than a cruise on the Gulf of Mexico
during the summer season can be imagined. The water is

deeply, darkly, beautifully blue, — a blue totally unlike that of the Atlantic Ocean, and one of the loveliest of colors, — and to sail upon the broad bosom of this sea of sapphire, for three or four days in fine weather, with just breeze enough to make the spray fly from the tops of the waves, is one of the rarest enjoyments that life affords. I certainly enjoyed it, and every warm sea breeze that fanned my cheeks brought health, strength, and exhilaration of spirits with it. This was just what I wanted to revive me after the trials and sufferings — physical and mental — of the past twelve months, and to prepare me for the trying duties yet to be performed.

APPROACHING CUBA.

At length, far in the distance, the lofty Cuban highlands were seen, resting like a faint blue cloud on the horizon, but taking shape as we approached, until, from the misty outlines, the mountain forms began to disclose themselves, and finally cities, villages, and even single houses and trees were revealed. It seemed like going into another world; for anything more unlike the low, flat, and unpicturesque country which I had just left, could scarcely be imagined, and I not only felt proud of my beautiful native island, but I wondered not that Spain should cling with such tenacity to this the fairest, and now the only really important portion of the great dominion which her valorous sons had centuries before conquered for her in the New World. At the same time, I begrudged that this fair island should be the dependency of a foreign power; for I was, despite my Spanish ancestry, an American, heart and soul, and if there was anything that could have induced me to abandon the cause of the Southern Confederacy, it would have been an attempt on the part of the Cubans to have liberated themselves from the Spanish yoke.

As we approached Cuba, and as the beautiful island seemed to rise out of the sea before us, revealing more and more of its surpassing loveliness, I wondered within myself whether such an attempt would not some day — and some day soon — be made, and more than half resolved that should the Cubans strike a blow for independence, I would join my fortunes to theirs, and serve their cause with the same assiduity that I was now serving that of the Confederacy.

After a voyage which had been to me one of uninterrupted pleasure, our ship dropped anchor before the city of Havana.

No city on the globe has been more fitly named; for this harbor is unsurpassed, and nestles beneath the shadow of the vine-clad hills,—a broad, land-locked basin, in which the navies of the world might float. While not insensible to the beauties of the spectacle which the place of my nativity and its surroundings presented to the eye, I was too full of other thoughts just at that moment to give myself up to the enjoyment of it, as I might have done at another time, and was as eager to get on shore and execute my commission, as if my brief sojourn on shipboard had been a thraldom to me instead of a source of real pleasure.

Landing in Havana.

I, therefore, landed at the earliest possible moment; and making my way through streets that seemed strangely familiar, and among people speaking my native tongue, which sounded most oddly after the long years since I had been accustomed to hear it habitually spoken, I succeeded in finding the Confederate agent, into whose trusty hands I had been directed to place my .despatches for the " Alabama." This important commission having been satisfactorily executed, my chief responsibilities were at an end, and I was at liberty to gratify my curiosity and my desire to learn all that could be learned that was likely to be of service to me in any future enterprises in which I might be engaged.

I confidently expected to visit Havana again, and, perhaps, many times before the end of the war, and therefore was anxious to make the most of the present opportunity for gaining all the information I was able that would in any way aid me in the successful prosecution of such exploits as I might hereafter think it expedient to undertake.

The friends of the Confederacy, with whom I was thrown in contact, were eager to obtain all the news they could with regard to the progress of events, the present situation of affairs, and the prospect for the immediate future. I was able to tell them a great many things that surprised them, and to give them much important information that would never have reached them through the ordinary news channels. There was much, of course, that I did not tell, for a great variety of reasons, and they were evidently puzzled to understand how I came to be possessed of such extensive and such accurate information. I was, of course, particularly reticent about the part I had been playing during a greater portion of the past year, and represented myself to be just what I then appeared, — a woman, who was engaged in the perilous task of running the lines for the purpose of carrying information. My evident accomplishments, and my thorough knowledge upon many points about which they were but meagrely informed, however, greatly increased their respect for me, and enabled me to gain confidences that otherwise might have been withheld.

In Communication with Confederate Agents.

From Messrs. Infanta & Co., and other prominent persons, I succeeded in learning much that was well worth knowing; and before the time came for me to say adieu to Havana, my brain was teeming with plans which I was all eagerness to execute. I found that the friends of the Confederacy were completely in the ascendent in Havana, and that more than one of its capitalists were deeply interested in the profitable but hazardous business of blockade-running; although, through a variety of circumstances, this city was not the headquarters of the extensive trade which the misfortunes of the South were building up, and which promised to yield almost fabulous profits should the war continue for any length of time, as these good money-loving people evidently desired that it should.

I could not help thinking, however, when I heard of the enormous sums of money which a single cargo yielded, in event of its being able to elude the Federal cruisers and the blockading fleet, and reach a Southern port, of the suffering and impoverished people at whose expense the blockade-runners were heaping up riches, and I wished heartily that I had some way of making them devote a portion of their wealth to the relief of the victims of cruel war, and to the advancement of the cause. I could not help acknowledging, however, that their money was fairly earned, and that while accumulating magnificent profits by their operations, they were doing a great deal in a certain way towards sustaining the Confederacy in the mighty struggles it was making for independence.

The capture of New Orleans had been a great surprise to every one in Havana, as it doubtless was to the friends of the Confederacy everywhere; and it was the cause of innumerable and bitter regrets, for it effectually put a stop to blockade-running in that quarter, and, consequently cut off many opportunities for tolerably easy money-making, which those in the business had hitherto enjoyed. · Every one agreed that it was by far the most damaging blow that the Federals had yet succeeded in striking at the Confederacy, and not a few believed that it was but the prelude to greater disasters, and to a final overthrow of the attempt which was being made to secure a permanent severance of the South from the North. All, however, were agreed that, so far as they were concerned, obedience to the adage, to make hay while the sun shines, was the only true policy; and that, while the perils of blockade-running would now be greatly increased, the profits were so enormous as to warrant all the risks, and that the business would, therefore, be prosecuted with more energy than ever, while it would be necessary to adopt a more perfect and certain system of communication with the Confederate authorities. I was able to give a great number of valuable hints with regard to the best way of managing things; and, in return, was supplied with many points which I would be likely to find useful, both immediately and in the future.

My stay in Havana was of short duration; and having accomplished my errand, and learned all that I could, I proposed to return to New Orleans.

BACK IN NEW ORLEANS.

The return trip was as agreeable as the one out, and it greatly refreshed and benefited me, so that when I again set foot on the levee at New Orleans, I felt in better condition than I had been in for a long time, and was prepared for any amount of hard work; and of hard work there was likely to be plenty to do, for Butler was tightening his grasp on the people, and was disposed to make his rule over them as little gratifying to their feelings as possible. That my old business of smuggling drugs, and other matters needed by the Confederates, and of conveying information back and forth, would have to be carried on — if it were carried on at all — under a pressure of much greater difficulties than formerly, was soon very apparent. I was not one, however, to be appalled by difficulties, but was rather excited by them to exert myself to the utmost; and it afforded me an immense amount of satisfaction that, in a quiet way, I would be able to accomplish many things for which Butler would have been highly pleased to have strangled me, could he have discovered what I was about.   And I did manage to do several tolerably good strokes of work before New·Orleans became too unpleasant a place for me to abide in, and I was forced to the conclusion that it was best for me to take up my quarters elsewhere, outside of Butler's jurisdiction.

CHAPTER XXI.

A DIFFICULTY WITH BUTLER. — ESCAPE FROM NEW ORLEANS.

Butler's Rule in New Orleans. — A System of Terrorism. — My Acquaintance with Federal Officers. — I resume the Business of carrying Information through the Lines. — A Trip to Robertson's Plantation for the Purpose of carrying a Confederate Despatch. — A long Tramp after Night. — Some of the Incidents of my Journey. — The Alligators and Mosquitoes. — Arrival at my Destination, and Delivery of the Despatch to a Confederate Officer. — My hospitable Entertainment by Friends of the Confederacy. — My Return to New Orleans. — Capture of the Bearer of my Despatch, and my Arrest. — I am taken before Butler, who endeavors to extort a Confession from me. — Butler as a Bully. — I refuse to confess, and am ordered to be imprisoned in the Custom-House. — My Release, through the Intercession of the British Consul. — I resolve to leave New Orleans, for fear of getting into further Trouble. — A Bargain with a Fisherman to take me across Lake Pontchartrain. — My Escape from Butler's Jurisdiction.

WAS astonished, sometimes, at my own good luck in keeping clear of controversies with the military authorities; for Butler was bent on crushing out every indication of sympathy with the Confederacy, and he was most savage and relentless in his punishment of those who defied his mandates by attempting to hold communication with the Southern soldiery, who were only waiting for a proper opportunity to rescue New Orleans, and who were therefore anxious, of course, to understand exactly how matters stood in the city, in order that they might take advantage of a suitable moment, if any should present, for relieving its unpopular ruler of his responsibilities. The peculiar situation of New Orleans, on a narrow strip of land between the river and Lake Pontchartrain, and with numerous bayous, lakes, and other water ways in close proximity, was such as to make the passage back and forth of Confederate agents a much easier matter than it would have been under some circumstances. It was, however, a dangerous business always, and a number of persons, of both sexes, who undertook to defy Butler by communicating with their friends in the interior, or who employed themselves in smuggling goods or intelligence through the lines, were caught and punished ; sentences calculated to inspire terror in those who were capable of being terrified being imposed, without regard to the sex or social standing of the offenders.

A favorite punishment, for those who managed to fall under the displeasure of the commanding general, was a sojourn, for periods of time varying according to Butler's notions of the gravity of their offences, on Ship Island, a desolate strip of sand on Mississippi Sound, which had been used by the Federal forces as a rendezvous before the attack upon the city.   Butler was compelled to live on this sandbank for a number of months, before Admiral Farragut made it possible for him to take up his abode in one of the finest residences of New Orleans, and he appeared to have contracted such an intense dislike to the place, that he could imagine no worse fate for those who were imprudent enough to defy his will, than to send them there.   I came very near being obliged to make Ship Island my home for a time under orders from Butler, and only escaped such a fate through my address and courage, and the thoroughness of the preparations I had made to meet such an emergency.

RUNNING THE LINES.

Unlike many others, I settled myself down resolutely to the business of running the lines, and was not satisfied with making a trip or two, and then either ceasing operations altogether, or else waiting until suspicion should die away before making another attempt.   I considered myself as much in the Confederate service as I was when I wore the uniform of an officer, and I felt it my duty to be, like a soldier, always vigilant, and always ready to do the enemy all the damage I possibly could.   I therefore went about the prosecution of my plans systematically, taking all proper precautions, of course, to avoid detection, but trusting a good deal to luck and to my ready wit to get me out of any difficulty into which I might happen to fall.

I had very few friends or acquaintances, for I did not care to be extensively known, being well aware that the more people there were whose attention was attracted to me, the

CIENFUEGOS.

more likelihood there would be of suspicion attaching to my movements. At the same time I was anxious to avoid any appearance of mystery, and took particular pains to let myself be seen frequently, and to leave the impression that I was what I pretended to be — a widow, in reduced circumstances, who was only waiting to receive money from England in order to return to that country. I kept up a sort of acquaintance with a few officers of the Federal army, to whom I had been introduced, which I was the more pleased to do as they were very pleasant gentlemen, and contrived, by frequent allusions to the subject, to fix in their minds the idea that I had been robbed, and otherwise outrageously maltreated by the Confederates, and that the arrival of the Federals was a source of infinite satisfaction to me.

From these officers I sometimes succeeded in obtaining information that was worth having by judiciously keeping my ears open, or by asking an apparently innocent question at the proper moment. I was, however, very careful not to appear to question them, or to do anything that would in the slightest degree arouse their suspicions. My acquaintance with them was kept up for the purpose of having it understood at headquarters, and among the officers generally, that I was one of the few women in New Orleans who professed Union sentiments. My means of gaining intelligence were such as these gentlemen had little idea of, and were of such a character that there was no necessity for me to risk anything by imprudent conversation with them. Indeed, it was very evident sometimes, judging from their conversation, that I was very fully informed about a great many things with regard to which they knew little or nothing.

I do not know whether or not Butler and his satellites ever suspected me, up to the time they caught me. When I was finally detected, and arraigned before the general, he tried his best to play the bully, and to frighten me into making some admissions, and he intimated that I had been under surveillance for a long time. This, however, was probably all brag, or at least I chose to understand it as such; and as I did not frighten at all to his satisfaction, he did not succeed in making a great deal out of me.

Not a great while after my return from Havana, I undertook to go to Robertson's Plantation, for the purpose of sending some despatches, as well as some verbal information, to the Confederate forces stationed at Franklin. It was necessary for me to make the trip after nightfall, and to walk the entire distance of seventeen miles; and that such a tramp could scarcely be a particularly pleasant exercise, those who are acquainted with the country around New Orleans need not be reminded. I was not to be deterred, however, any more by the personal inconveniences involved in my undertaking the expedition, than I was by any perils I was likely to encounter, and set off, therefore, resolved to accomplish my errand, if its accomplishment were possible.

A Long Walk after Night.

I had not much difficulty in getting past the outposts, and once sure that I was out of sight and sound of the Federal pickets, I started off at a steady pace, bent upon getting over as much ground as I could before daylight came and rendered it necessary for me to be more cautious in my movements. I made pretty good time, but did not get along as fast as I would have done had I been in male attire, and long before I reached my destination I heartily wished that it had been possible for me to have donned a masculine habit in safety; for a woman's skirts are not adapted for fast travelling on a Louisiana highway, on a sultry summer's night, with only the stars and the fire-flies to lighten the pathway.

It was a terribly lonesome walk. After getting past the pickets, I did not meet with a single human being throughout the whole of my long and weary journey. The only sounds to be heard were the barking of the alligators, or the splashing of one of these monsters as he plunged into the stream at my approach. I was frequently startled by the sounds made by these horrid animals close at hand after a considerable interval of silence, but pushed on resolutely despite them, and despite the swarms of mosquitoes, which seemed to increase in number as I proceeded, and which occasioned me infinite annoyance. Whenever I sat down to rest, which I was compelled to do a number of times before my journey was completed, these venomous insects attacked me with the greatest fury, and my face and hands were terribly bitten before I was able to escape from them. These were some of the delights of my long night walk for the purpose of fulfilling my mission as a bearer of despatches, and it was an immense relief to me when, just about daybreak, I reached my destination, foot-sore and completely tired out, but satisfied with having accomplished my errand without having been interrupted.

THE DESPATCH DELIVERED.

I found some Confederate soldiers preparing to cross the lake, and, going to one of them, who seemed to be in command of the party, I told him a number of things which I had thought it more prudent not to commit to writing, and desired him to pass the word along. Then, waiting until the boat was ready to set sail, I gave him an enclosure containing my despatches, asking him, if possible, to deliver it at headquarters, or if he was unable to do this, to drop it at the earliest moment in the post-office.

I cautioned him particularly, and with the greatest earnestness, to be exceedingly careful of the package, as it contained matters of vital importance, upon which a great deal was dependent. He promised a faithful compliance with my instructions, and jumping into the boat, he and his companions shoved off from the shore, and were soon lost in the heavy mist that rested upon the surface of the lake.

My responsibilities, so far as the custody of the despatches was concerned, were now at an end, and with a light heart, but tired limbs, I sought some place where I could obtain refreshment, and the repose I so badly needed, before I attempted to return to the city. Going to a house near by, I asked for something to eat, and an opportunity to rest myself. Two gentlemen appeared and gave me a very cordial welcome, for they understood, without questioning me, what my errand was, and they were anxious to do all in their power to make me comfortable.

FRIENDS IN NEED.

I was in a most dilapidated condition, and was anything but a presentable object, or one calculated to figure with advantage at the breakfast-table of a respectable family. My clothing was heavy with the night dews, and my skirts were bedraggled with dirt; my shoes were nearly worn through, and were covered with mud; and, taking me altogether, I was as forlorn a looking creature as could be imagined.

My entertainers, however, knew how to excuse appearances; and, understanding the situation thoroughly, they would not permit me to make any excuses or apologies, but

17

insisted on my accepting such hospitalities as they had to offer, and promised to procure me a change of clothing, so that I might make a somewhat more presentable figure.

They accordingly gave me a room where I could make my toilet, and sent a servant to wait on me, while they applied to a lady of the neighborhood for some clothing that I might wear while my own was being dried and cleansed. The lady complied with their requests with the greatest alacrity, and sent me the best her wardrobe afforded, being anxious to serve me in any manner in her power. As she was in entire sympathy with the cause for which I was laboring, she refused to receive any compensation, or to take back the clothing, when, at nightfall, I prepared to resume my own, which, by diligent brushing and rubbing, had been gotten into tolerably good condition again for the purpose of returning to the city.

A wash, a change of garments, and a substantial breakfast refreshed me immensely, and made me feel like another person. As it was impossible for me to attempt to reach New Orleans without running too many risks of discovery, or, at least, of being suspected, except under cover of the night, and as I was sorely in need of rest, my new-made friends insisted that I should remain where I was until the proper time came for me to return.

Return to New Orleans.

I therefore went to bed, and slept a good part of the day, and about eleven o'clock at night they provided me with a horse, and escorted me to as near the outposts as I deemed it safe for them to go. On our way, I gave them a number of points about the situation of things in New Orleans, and informed them how they might, in various ways, be of service to the Confederacy, if they were disposed to extend the active workers all the aid that was in their power. When the time came for bidding them farewell, I thanked them in the warmest manner for their kindness to me; but they assured me that the obligations were all on their side, and that they were only too glad to assist, in any manner possible, a brave woman, who was willing to venture, as I had done, for the purpose of advancing the welfare of a cause which was a common one with us all.

After parting with the gentlemen, I made my way into the city on foot, being as successful as on the night previous in eluding the pickets. Having once got within the Federal lines again, I hastened to the French market, where I obtained some breakfast, and where I remained until the streets began to be filled with people, before venturing to return to my room. My idea was to have any one who might happen to take particular notice of me think that I had been marketing. So, soon as I concluded that it would be safe for me to show myself, I passed up St. Peter Street to Rampart Street, and from thence to my room. On reaching my apartment I locked myself in, and went to bed to take a good rest.

In the afternoon of the same day I wrote a note to one of the officers of the thirty-first Massachusetts regiment, whose acquaintance I had made shortly after the Federal occupation of the city, and he very politely answered it by calling upon me. It was my intention to let him know that I had been out of the city, so that, in case any one should have been making a note of my movements, with a view of reporting them at headquarters, there would be somebody on hand who would be able to give my version of the case, and thus probably prevent any investigation, and stifle suspicion. I therefore, after a little general conversation, gave my visitor to understand that I had been out of town; and on his inquiring my whereabouts during my trip, I told him that I had been to Carrolton, on a visit to a friend. He believed every word I told him, without the slightest hesitation; and after some further talk about matters of no moment, he went away, leaving me tolerably well satisfied with having successfully accomplished my errand, and with having taken all proper precaution to avoid getting into any trouble about it.

Before Butler.

Unluckily for me, however, the very thing upon which I had not calculated, and which I had no power to prevent, occurred. The officer to whom I had intrusted my despatch was captured, and the document was found upon his person. Through some means, which I could not surmise, the provost marshal was informed that I was the writer of the despatch, although the name signed to it was not the one he knew me by. A negro was found, too, who swore that he had seen me walking along the river, outside of the lines, and the result was that I was placed under arrest, and taken before Butler himself. Butler was not the handsomest man I ever saw in my life, and he certainly looked the tyrant that he was. It was a favorite amusement with him to browbeat people who were brought before him, and he was remarkably skilful in terrifying those who were weak enough to submit to being bullied by him into making just the admission he wanted them to make. I had heard a good deal about his peculiar methods of dealing with those who had incurred his displeasure in any way, and particularly with those who were suspected of furnishing the Confederates with information concerning the situation within the Federal lines, and I was therefore prepared, in a measure, for the ordeal which I was now compelled to undergo.

I was determined to admit nothing that could not be distinctly proved against me, to sustain to the last the character I had assumed, and to fall back upon the protection which I felt sure my British papers would afford me as a last resort. I promised myself that, so far as any attempt to bully me, or to overcome me with threats were concerned, the general would find me more than a match for him; and the only trepidation I suffered in going before him grew out of my uncertainty with regard to the extent of his information about my proceedings. I felt, however, that it would be a safe course to admit nothing, and to compel Butler to produce his proof, if he had any, before making any acknowledgment whatever.

A CONTEST OF WITS.

Sure enough, when I was brought into his presence, he proceeded on the theory that I was the person he wanted, and that I was guilty of the charge made against me. He evidently thought the case was a perfectly plain one, and that I would not attempt a denial. I, however, kept cool, and refused to look at the matter from his point of view; and, as none of the witnesses who appeared were able to swear positively to my identity as the woman who had acted as the bearer of the despatch found on the Confederate officer, I began to think that I was going to get clear without a great deal of trouble.

Butler, however, was not one from whom it was easy to get away when his suspicions were once aroused, and I saw plainly that he was convinced of the fact that he had captured the right person this time, and that his prisoner was a spy who had been giving him serious annoyance. He was, therefore, resolved not to let me slip through his fingers if he could help it; and finding that he could not absolutely prove anything

BEFORE BUTLER.

against me, he concluded to try whether it would not be possible to force me into committing myself.

When, therefore, instead of ordering my release, Butler settled his podgy figure back in his chair, and, apparently, making a vigorous attempt to look straight at me with both eyes at once, — an impossibility, by the way, — said, with a harsh, grating voice, and with what was intended to be an intensely satirical manner, "Well, madam, you have shown your hand nicely; I have been wanting you for some time past, and I propose to send you to Ship Island," — I felt that the real ordeal was but just commencing.

Without permitting myself to be disconcerted, either by his manner or by his threat, I replied, "I guess not; the law does not permit you to sentence any one on mere hearsay or belief, and no evidence has been produced against me."

"Are you not guilty?" said Butler, blinking his eyes, and trying to look as savage as possible.

"That is for you to prove, if you intend to punish me," I replied. "It is very certain you have not succeeded in proving it yet."

"Come, come, madam, I don't want any of this nonsense," struck in Butler, sharply. "I know you, and your tricks; and as your little game is played out, you might as well confess, and be done with it."

"There is no difficulty about your finding out who I am," I retorted. "My name, and residence, and circumstances are well known to your officers, and have been ever since the capture of the city. You have no proof against me, and I have nothing to confess."

"Do you mean to say," continued the general, "that you are not the writer of that letter, or that you did not smuggle it through the lines?"

"I don't mean to say anything about it," I answered; "and I don't mean to confess what I didn't do."

By this time Butler, seeing that he was not making much headway with me, began to get angry, and he roared out, "Well, madam, if you won't confess without compulsion, I'll see whether I can't compel you. I'm tired of this sort of thing, and I'm going to make an example of you for the benefit of the other female spies who are hanging about this city."

I replied, as cool as possible, "You may get yourself into trouble, sir, if you attempt to punish an innocent woman on a false and scandalous charge like this, when there is not a particle of evidence to sustain it."

This appeared to infuriate Butler more than ever; and, turning to one of his officers, he gave an order that I should be locked up in a cell in the Custom House until my case was investigated further.

When I heard this order I turned to him with all the dignity I could command, and said, " One word, sir; you will please to understand that I am a British subject, and that I claim the protection of the British flag."

Butler, who displayed a particular antipathy to foreigners, and especially to the English, on all occasions, blurted out, " We will see about that; I don't care for Johnny Bull; " and then turning to the officer he said, " Take that woman to the Custom House."

This ended the investigation, and I left the presence of the general, feeling tolerably well satisfied with having got the best of him thus far, but dubious about the ultimate issue of the affair, for I was confident that he would make an endeavor to fasten the charge on me in such a manner that there would be no escape; and I knew that if he once got possession of the right clew, he could easily obtain plenty of evidence against me; for, notwithstanding all my precautions, there were necessarily a number of persons in the city who were, to a greater or less degree, informed with regard to my movements, and some of them, I feared, might tell what they knew if they were put under cross-examination, backed up by a liberal use of threats.

I, however, was not disposed to vex myself with troubles before they came, and preserved my equanimity, trusting to my usual good luck to bring my present difficulties to a satisfactory conclusion. The officer in whose charge I was placed was a gentleman in every respect, and he treated me in the most courteous manner while escorting me to the Custom House, apologizing for being compelled to perform so unpleasant a duty; and, on our arrival at the building which was to serve as my prison, he procured a nice camp bed for my cell, and in other ways tried to make me as comfortable as circumstances would permit. He ordered that my meals should be sent me regularly, and promised that an effort would be made to prevent my incarceration from being any more unpleasant than was absolutely necessary.

The behavior of this gentleman was in striking contrast to

that of his chief, and I felt very grateful to him, as I did, also, to several unknown ladies, who sent me a number of little luxuries that aided materially in making my imprisonment endurable. Before the officer left me, I asked him if I could not be permitted to have the use of writing materials. He said that he had no authority to grant such a request, but that he would see what could be done for me, as it would give him pleasure to oblige me by every means in his power.

A friend of mine, Sergeant B., hearing that I was imprisoned, came to see me, and on my expressing a great desire to have some pens, ink, and paper, he promised to procure them and slip them in to me. He also said that he would carry any message I might desire to send to my friends outside. I thanked him, and requested him to try and let me have some writing materials as soon as possible. He therefore procured them, and I immediately wrote a note to Mr. Coppell, the British consul, in which I explained my situation briefly, and asked his assistance.

Mr. Coppell called upon me at once, and I, claiming that I was a British subject, and under imprisonment by General Butler's personal order, although nothing whatever had been proven against me, asked his protection and his influence for a release without more delay. He promised to do what he could for me, and asked for my proofs of British citizenship. I therefore gave him my trunk key and the number of my room, with a description of the papers I had purchased in view of just such an emergency as this, and he having obtained them went to Butler's headquarters to demand my liberation.

RELEASED FROM PRISON.

I do not know what passed between the consul and the general, but the result of the interview was an order for my release, and I accordingly walked out of the Custom House under Mr. Coppell's escort, and with all the rebel in me exultant at having got the better of Butler.

I understood plainly that my operations as a spy in New Orleans were now at an end, and that the safest and best thing I could do, if I did not want to get into further trouble, would be to leave the city at the earliest possible moment. There was, however, no longer any necessity for keeping my rebel sympathies concealed, and I was really glad of an opportunity to let them be seen. As we were going out of the

Custom House I heard some one bragging how they were going to thrash Johnny Bull, and I could not resist the temptation of turning to Mr. Coppell, who must also have heard the remark, and saying, " That fellow must be crazy. He and his friends had better wipe out secession first, before they talk about whipping Johnny Bull." I said this loud enough for everbody to hear me, and it made the speaker and others around us furious, and elicited several retorts, at which we only laughed. This was a foolish proceeding on my part, but I could not help taking a bit of womanly revenge on my enemies for what they had done to me.

Having obtained my freedom again, I prepared to forsake New Orleans, and applied for a pass. This, however, was refused me ; and I saw that if I intended to get out of Butler's power so as to be able to resume operations.either as a spy or as a Confederate officer, it would be necessary for me to run the blockade. Situated as I was, and under suspicion of being a spy, this, I was well aware, would be a particularly risky thing to attempt; but there was no alternative left me except to either attempt it, or else remain in the city in idleness, and in constant danger of having some of my many previous transactions, in the way of carrying information to the Confederates, found out. I felt very certain that if Butler did succeed in discovering who I was, and in fastening upon me, beyond a doubt, any charge of a similar nature to the one I had just eluded, I would not get off so easily as I had done in my first controversy with him, and I therefore concluded that I ran a greater risk in remaining in New Orleans than I did in attempting to leave it surreptitiously.

Having made up my mind to leave, and to leave as expeditiously as I conveniently could, I proceeded to make the necessary arrangements, taking care to attract as little attention as possible. The provisioning of New Orleans was a serious problem with the military rulers of the city ; and in order to keep the markets supplied, even in a moderate degree, with the necessities of life, they were compelled to permit some intercourse with the surrounding country, and boats for the conveyance of food even ran between New Orleans and Mobile, under certain stringent regulations, which, however, were unable to prevent them from being used by the agents of the Confederate States in a manner that Butler did not approve. Communication, therefore, between the city and country was always possible, although to attempt anything of the kind without a pass, subjected the wayfarer to a liability of being suspected and punished as a spy.

I had made a goodly number of trips in different directions, sometimes with passes and sometimes without, and consequently knew exactly how to proceed, and what were the difficulties to be overcome. The chief danger to be apprehended I knew would be from the Federal patrols, who were becoming more and more vigilant every day, as resolute efforts were being made to break up the Confederate spy system, and the illicit traffic which many persons of both sexes were engaged in carrying on, to the great discomfort of the Federal occupants of the city. I had also something to fear lest any agent whom I might employ to aid me in making my escape should prove treacherous, either through hope of gain or a desire to win the favor of Butler. On this last score, however, I had comparatively few apprehensions, as I was prepared to pay a good round sum to any one who would be willing to perform for me the services I needed, and I knew well that some of the stanchest adherents of the Confederacy were to be found among the poor white population of New Orleans and vicinity. I knew that if I could once make the other side of Lake Pontchartrain I would be safe, and that there would be fewer risks to run in attempting an escape in that direction than in any other. I accordingly laid my plans for a trip across the lake, with a view of striking a point near the railroad, so that I could reach Jackson with the least inconvenience.

Going down to the lake, I found a fisherman who was pursuing his avocation under a permit from Butler, and taking advantage of an opportunity to speak to him when our conversation could not be overheard, I asked, " Do any rebels ever cross the lake without papers ? "

" Yes," said he, " sometimes."

" Do you think that you could take me over if I were to make it worth your while ? " said I.

" Are you a reb ? " he questioned, looking at me sharply.

" They say I am," I answered.

" Well, I might take you over if you will pay enough."

" I'll give you a good deal more than you can get for any job you do for the Federals."

" All right, then," said he ; and without more argument we struck a bargain, and arranged time and place of meeting, my boatman giving me some directions how to proceed so as to avoid attracting attention, from which I inferred that this was not the first time he had been engaged in running the blockade.

Going home, I put on two complete suits of clothing, as it would not have answered for me to have carried any baggage, or even a small package, and secreted about my person all the Confederate money I had purchased, about nine thousand dollars in greenbacks, and my jewelry. At the appointed time I was at the rendezvous, and saw my boatman waiting. Fearful, however, of being apprehended just as I was about to start, I did not show myself at first, but crept cautiously through the bushes until I could see whether any one was observing my movements. Finding the coast apparently clear, I made a signal to the man, and he approached and took me into the boat.

Getting away from New Orleans.

In a moment more the sail was hoisted, and we were speeding over the lake before a good breeze, which promised, ere a great while, to waft me beyond Butler's jurisdiction, and enable me once more to give the Confederacy the benefit of my services.

I had a reasonable amount of confidence in the fidelity of the boatman, but at the same time was determined to be prepared against any attempt at treachery on his part. I had, accordingly, provided myself with a six-shooter, and had taken pains to see that it was loaded, and all in condition for instant use, before leaving my room. On taking my seat in the boat I placed my hand on this weapon, and was resolved to put it to the head of the man if he showed the slightest indication of a desire to betray me. I had no fancy for a sojourn on Ship Island, and would, without the slightest hesitation, have used my revolver freely before submitting to a capture. The man, however, was faithful enough, and with the prospect of a liberal reward before him, he was only eager to reach the other side of the lake as soon as he could, and to avoid the Federal patrols in doing so.

Fortune favored us, and it was not long before we were out of the reach of immediate danger, and in a fair way to make the Mississippi shore without being interfered with. On landing I paid the boatman his money, according to the bargain I had made with him, and started off for the nearest railroad station for the purpose of going to Jackson. Thus ended my career in New Orleans as a Confederate spy. It was a successful one, taking all things into consideration, but I was not sorry to get away, and considered myself fortunate in being able to make my escape with as much ease as I did.

CHAPTER XXII.

CARRYING DESPATCHES.

Uncertainties of the Military Situation. — I go to Jackson, Mississippi. — Burning of the Bowman House in that place by Breckenridge's Soldiers. — The unpleasant Position in which Non-combatants were placed. — A Visit to the Camp of General Dan. Adams, and Interview with that Officer. — I visit Hazlehurst, and carry a Message to General Gardner at Port Hudson. — Recovery of my Negro Boy Bob. — General Van Dorn's Raid on Holly Springs. — I resolve to Return to Virginia. — The Results of two Years of Warfare. — Dark Days for the Confederacy. — Fighting against Hope.

N leaving New Orleans I had no very definite plans for the immediate future, my hurried departure, as well as my lack of knowledge with regard to the exact details of the military situation, having prevented me from forming any. I was, therefore, rather at a loss exactly how to proceed, but did not doubt of my ability to find a field for the display of my talents ere a great while. I was now more intent than ever upon being employed on detective and scouting duty, for which my recent residence in New Orleans had been an excellent schooling; so excellent, indeed, that I considered myself as well out of my apprenticeship, and as quite competent to assume all the responsibilities of the most difficult or dangerous jobs that might be thrust upon me.

I did not doubt that there would be plenty of work for me to do, for throughout the entire West military matters seemed to be in a very mixed condition, and the different armies, both Confederate and Federal, so broken up and scattered, that it must have taxed the energies of the commanding officers on both sides to have kept the run of each other's movements. The Federals, by their victories at Fort Donelson and Shiloh, and several other points, had succeeded in forcing both the first and second Confederate lines of defence, and in penetrating to the heart of the portion of the Confederacy west of the mountains, but they had not been able to complete the conquest they were aiming at; and the possession of the Mississippi — that coveted prize for both parties — was something for which there was still to be done some hard fighting.

I judged that matters ought soon to be approaching a crisis somewhere, although exactly what definite aims the belligerents were driving at, if, indeed, they had any just then, I could not comprehend. I resolved, if a grand movement of any kind was coming off, that I must have a hand in it in some shape; but that if something of importance was not attempted before a great while I would return to Virginia, and see what fortune had in store for me there. I judged, however, that I would not have much difficulty in finding work to do in the west, if I went about looking for it in the right way; and I knew of no better locality in which to seek the information I needed before commencing operations in the field again than Jackson.

To Jackson, therefore, I went, with what haste I could, and arrived just in time to witness an occurrence for which I was sincerely sorry. This was the burning of the Bowman House by Breckenridge's men, who were infuriated at being told that the proprietor had permitted the Federals to occupy the hotel, and that he had entertained them at one third less than he had charged the Confederates who had claimed his hospitalities. The unfortunate man was in reality not to blame in the matter, for the Federals had occupied his house without his consent, and he had taken just what they chose to give him, thinking it better to pocket less than his dues than nothing; and fearing to make any complaint, either about their presence in the hotel, or the money they offered him, lest they should take it into their heads to play him some such trick as the Confederates subsequently did.

THE SUFFERINGS OF NON-COMBATANTS.

This incident will serve to show the desperately unpleasant position of the non-combatants throughout this whole region at this and later periods of the war. They were literally between two fires; and no matter how peaceably disposed they might be, they could satisfy neither party, and were made to suffer by both. The proprietor of the Bowman House was forced to witness a fine property destroyed before his eyes through the reckless and unthinking anger of men who never stopped to inquire whether he was guilty or not of any offence against them or their cause before taking vengeance upon him. He was reduced to poverty by the burning of his hotel, and I could not help feeling the keenest regret for the occurrence, although I recognized it as one of the inevitable calamities of warfare.

I was, myself, in the hotel when it was fired, and barely succeeded in escaping from the building with my life. Not expecting any such occurrence, I had taken rooms, and was proceeding to make myself comfortable, when, all of a sudden, I found that it was in flames, and that it would be as much as I could do to get out unscathed. The men who fired the building did not give the proprietor an opportunity to make explanations, or if they did, they refused to believe him. Knowing what the passions of men engaged in warfare are, and how little consideration they are disposed to give those who are suspected of aiding the enemy, I was not altogether surprised at this action, but I thought the officers in command might have succeeded in restraining their soldiers until the exact truth of the matter could have been ascertained.

The next day after this occurrence I visited the camp of General Dan. Adams, from whom I gained a number of points which were useful to me in making my arrangements for the future. He gave me a tolerably definite idea of how things stood, and advised me what course to take if I wanted to go into active service again. Among other things, he said it was understood that the Federal General Grierson was on a raid in the direction of Natchez, but he thought he would most likely have a speedy stop put to that kind of performance. As for himself, he told me that he had been ordered to re-enforce General Joe Johnston at Big Black, and that he expected to start for that point shortly. Exactly what was on foot he did not know, but thought it likely that the Federals were about to make an attempt on Vicksburg, and that Johnston intended to be well prepared to receive them in his best style.

Several times already had the Federals made attacks of greater or less importance on Vicksburg, which city was now the most important position held by the Confederacy, and commanding the Mississippi River as it did, its possession was considered a matter of the most vital importance. The fall of Vicksburg, everybody knew, would practically give the Federals possession of the river throughout its entire length;

and as such a calamity would, just at this particular junction, be an even greater blow to the Confederate cause than the fall of New Orleans had been, every exertion was being made to render it impregnable. That sooner or later the Federals would make a more determined effort than they had done previously to take this post, appeared to be certain; but the natural advantages of the position were such, and the fortifications in course of construction were so strong, and were being rendered stronger with each succeeding day, that the utmost confidence in the ability of the garrison to hold it was felt by every one.

This confidence, unfortunately, was as ill-founded as had been that felt with regard to other posts; and although the siege of Vicksburg was a heavy task for the Federals to undertake, they did undertake it, and they succeeded in their efforts after a protracted and desperate conflict, in which the Confederates, although ultimately compelled to surrender, won fresh laurels for their pertinacity in fighting, until all hope of prolonging the contest was gone.

Having heard all that General Adams had to say, I took the train for Hazlehurst, and from there I went to a portion of Logan's command and took a look at things, stopping all night with the family of Mayor Wallis. It was here that Lieutenant Colonel Blackburn, of General Grierson's command, was killed subsequently, when that Federal officer made his great raid in April, 1863.

From Hazlehurst I pushed on towards Port Hudson with a message for General Gardner, but was met at Clinton by the special courier of that commander, and delivering the message to him, I hastened back to Jackson.

On my arrival at Jackson I heard of my negro boy Bob, for the first time since I had lost him, just after the battle of Shiloh. I therefore proceeded to Grenada, where I found the darkey, who appeared to be heartily glad to see me again after such a long separation. Bob, it seems, had gone plump into a Federal camp, having missed his road, after I had started him off for Corinth; but not liking the company he found there, had slipped away at the earliest opportunity, and had wandered about in a rather aimless manner for some time, seeking for me. Not being able to hear anything of me, he had made up his mind that I was dead, and was quite surprised to see me turn up again alive and well.

At Jackson I found General Lowering in command, and heard that General Van Dorn had surprised the Federals at Holly Springs, and had captured the entire force there, and an immense quantity of supplies of every description. This event took place on the 20th of April, 1863, and was one of the most brilliant affairs of the whole campaign. The Federals had made Holly Springs a base of supplies, and had collected there everything that was needed for the maintenance of the army in the operations against Vicksburg; but Van Dorn, by one bold and skilfully executed movement, succeeded in giving the impoverished Confederates provisions and munitions of war which they sorely needed, and in damaging the Federals more than a hard-fought battle would have done.

FACING EASTWARD AGAIN.

From Grenada, I returned once more to Jackson, and found the place in considerable excitement over the prospective army movements; but as there did not seem to be much for me to do in the particular line of business I desired to take up, I now determined to put my old intention of returning to Virginia into execution; and as having once made up my mind to a certain line of action, I was not in the habit of long delaying over it, I was soon speeding eastward again on my way to Richmond:

I should have mentioned, that after leaving New Orleans, I resumed male attire at the earliest possible moment, and figured once more as Lieutenant Harry T. Buford. Perhaps if I had gone to General Johnston, or some other commanding officer of high rank, and frankly stated that I was a woman, giving at the same time a narrative of my exploits, and furnishing references as guarantees of the truthfulness of my story, I would have obtained the kind of employment I was looking for, with permission to use the garments of either sex, as I might deem expedient for the particular errand I had in hand. I sometimes thought that this was what I should have done; but I could not overcome my repugnance to making any one a confidant of my secret, even if by so doing I would have advanced my own interests. In the then condition of affairs, when the different commands were fully organized and disciplined, my position as an independent was even more anomalous than it was at the commencement of the war, and as in the conduct of the peculiar operations then in progress, the generals were necessarily obliged to be particular in whom they confided, it was scarcely to be wondered at that one who, like myself, was endeavoring to play the part of a free-lance, should receive comparatively little countenance.

I appreciated the situation, and yet I could not help being disappointed, that one who had done so well by the Confederacy as myself, and who was so willing to undertake difficult and hazardous tasks, should get such little encouragement, and so I resolved to abandon the west, for the present at least. In Virginia, I thought that I would be likely to have a better chance for distinguishing myself, if only for the reason that the operations of the contending forces were confined to a more limited space than they were in the region I was leaving. I had an idea, too, that in case my claims to consideration at the hands of the authorities were not admitted with the promptness I desired, I would be able to do some business in the way of running through the lines on my own account, just for my own satisfaction, and for the sake of showing what I was capable of.

Once past the Confederate pickets, I believed that I could easily reach Washington; and I felt certain that a skilful spy, such as I esteemed myself now to be, could, without great difficulty, find out plenty of things which the Richmond authorities would be glad to know, and for the furnishing of which they would be glad to extend me such recognition as I desired. The military situation in Virginia, too, was more satisfactory than it was in the west, and I had a hankering to be where the Confederates were occasionally winning some victories. Since I had been in the west, I had witnessed little else than disaster, and I greatly desired to take a hand in a fight when the victory would rest with the Confederates, if only for the sake of variety.

My experiences since leaving New Orleans had not been particularly fruitful, for although I performed several services in satisfactory style for officers to whose notice I brought myself, no opportunity had offered for me to do anything of special moment, or to show the full extent of my capabilities, and, as there did not seem, from the condition things were in, that anything was to be gained by remaining, I was not sorry to leave for the scene of my first exploits as a Confederate soldier.

18

The war had now been in progress nearly two years, and, although the South had not been conquered, affairs were beginning to look decidedly blue for us. All our fine expectations of an easy achievement of our independence had long since vanished, and the situation every day was getting more and more desperate. The country was becoming exhausted, and had not its natural resources been enormous, our people must, ere this, have given up the contest. As it was, with a large portion of the male population in the field, and with heavy drafts being constantly made upon it to fill the ranks of the armies, the cultivation of the ground was neglected, and the necessities of life every day became scarcer and dearer. We were shut out, too, owing to the stringency of the Federal blockade, from anything like regular intercourse with Europe, and all kinds of manufactured articles, and the food we had been accustomed to import, were held at such enormous figures, that they were utterly beyond the reach of any but the most wealthy. The suffering among the poorer classes in all parts of the South was very great, and in those portions which had been devastated by the tramp of the different armies, many of the people were very nearly on the verge of starvation.

A SERIOUS QUESTION.

It was fast becoming a serious question, how long the contest could be prolonged, unless some signal advantage could speedily be achieved in the field by the Confederate forces. It is impossible to express in words how eagerly all classes looked for the achievement of some such advantage, and how bitter was the disappointment, as month after month wore away, and in spite of occasional victories, the people saw, day by day, the Federals drawing their lines closer and closer, and slowly, but surely, closing in upon them.

We were now entering upon the desperate stage of the war, when the contest was conducted almost against hope, and had the South been inhabited by a less determined race, or one less animated by a fixed resolve to fight to the very last, and until it was impossible to fight any longer, the Federal forces would have succeeded long ere they did in compelling a surrender of the Confederate armies. The men who commanded the armies, however, were not the sort to give up until they were absolutely defeated, and it was starvation, rather than the Federal arms, that at length forced the contest to the conclusion it reached, by the surrender of the armies under the command of Lee and Johnston.

Bad as was the situation at the time of which I am writing, and worse as it was shortly made by the surrender of Vicksburg, and other disasters in the west, and by the lamentable conclusion of Lee's invasion of Pennsylvania, the Confederates fought on for two years longer, with a heroic contempt for defeat, that won for them the admiration of the world. History does not record any such magnificent resistance as the South made; and however opinions may differ with regard to the original merit of the quarrel, not even the bitterest enemies of the Confederate cause can refuse to admit that it was defended with splendid courage.

But it is no part of my purpose to produce a history of the war. The story of the great contest has been written by abler pens than mine. I only aim at giving in plain language an unadorned narrative of the personal experiences of a single adherent of the Confederacy — experiences which gain their chief interest from the fact that they were different in a marked degree from those of any other participant in the war on either side, and I can only hope that the story of my adventures has proved sufficiently attractive to the reader to induce a perusal of it to the end.

CHAPTER XXIII.

UNDER ARREST AGAIN.

Commencement of a new Campaign. — Return to Richmond, and Arrest on Suspicion of being a Woman. — Imprisonment in Castle Thunder. — Kindness to me of Major G. W. Alexander and his Wife. — I refuse to resume the Garments of my Sex. — I am released, and placed on Duty in the Secret Service Corps. — General Winder, the Chief of the Secret Service Bureau. — A remarkable Character. — General Winder sends me with blank Despatches to General Van Dorn to try me. — A Member of the North Carolina Home Guards attempts to arrest me at Charlotte. — I resist the Arrest, and am permitted to proceed. — The Despatches delivered to Van Dorn in Safety. — My Arrest in Lynchburg. — The Rumors that were in Circulation about me. — I am pestered with curious Visitors. — A couple of Ladies deceived by a simple trick. — A comical Interview with an old Lady. — She declares herself insulted. — An insulting Letter from a general Officer. — My indignant Reply, and offer to fight him. — I obtain my Release, and leave Lynchburg.

WAS now about to commence a new campaign, and to enter upon experiences of another kind from those through which I had just passed. The condition of affairs was materially different in an infinite number of ways from what it had been when I first sought the Confederate capital with rather vague dreams of glory floating through my brain, but with considerable confidence that the Federal forces, against whom the brave boys of the South were marching, would melt away before them, and that I and my comrades in arms would, ere many days, have the flag of the Confederacy floating from the dome of the Capitol at Washington, and, perhaps, indulge in a march through a portion of the North, just for the sake of convincing the Yankees that they had been rash in meddling with us.

Well, we met the forces sent out against us by the Federal government, and long before the close of the day they were running back as fast as their legs would take them to their intrenchments before Washington. The flag-raising on the Capi-

276

tol, and the march through the North, were deferred by those who were managing affairs on our side to a more convenient opportunity, and the grand chance for winning the great stakes for which we were fighting was lost, never to be regained. Just as at Shiloh, the hesitation to follow up a brilliant victory, and make it complete by the capture or annihilation of the enemy, lost us the field, and inflicted upon us a most humiliating defeat, so at Bull Run, a similar hesitating policy lost us not merely the substantial results of victory, but inflicted upon us four years' of slaughter, during which the Federals closed in upon us gradually, until at length they were able to crush us.

I mean no disparagement to the brave soldiers and the skilful commanders on the Federal side, when I express the opinion that, as a rule, the Confederates were better fighters, and were better officered, than their opponents. There was inefficiency somewhere, however, in the management of military affairs on our side. We never seemed to be able to follow up our successes, or to gain permanent results from our victories, no matter how brilliant they might be. The Federals, on the other hand, had a way of staying, when they once got to a place, that was most disheartening; and one after another the strongest and most important of the Confederate posts fell into their hands, never to be regained, until finally they won the grand prize for which, during four long, weary years, vast armies had contended in vain, and, by the capture of Richmond, virtually ended the contest.

At the time of which I am writing, however, the capture of Richmond, although constantly threatened, was a long way off yet, and some trying days were to come before the abandonment of the capital would give the signal to Southern hearts, weary of strife, but hoping against hope, that even Hope itself was dead.

Richmond, however, was a very different place from what it was on my last visit to it, as I soon found to my cost. Martial law was in force in its most rigorous aspect, and General Winder, the chief of the secret service bureau, and his emissaries, were objects of terror to everybody, rich and poor. Beleaguered as Richmond was, every person was more or less an object of suspicion, and strangers, especially, were watched with a vigilance that left them few opportunities to do mischief, or were put under arrest, and placed in close confinement, without scruple, if Winder or his officers took it into their heads that this would be the most expeditious way of disposing of them.

UNDER ARREST IN RICHMOND.

It is not surprising, therefore, that almost immediately upon my arrival in Richmond I fell under the surveillance of Winder as a suspicious character, and was called upon to give an account of myself. My story was not accepted in the same spirit of credibility that some rather tough yarns I had manufactured in the course of my career, for the purpose of satisfying the curiosity of inquisitive people, had been. The fact that my secret had already been several times discovered, was against me to begin with; then my disguise was not in as good order as it had been when I first assumed it; and my papers were not of such a definite character as to inspire respect in the minds of the Richmond police authorities. There was, evidently, something suspicious and mysterious about me; and, suspicion having once been excited, some lynx-eyed detective was not long in noting certain feminine ways I had, and which even my long practice in figuring as a man had not enabled me to get rid of; and the result was, that I was arrested on the charge of being a woman in disguise, and supposably a Federal spy, and was conducted to Castle Thunder, to reflect upon the mutabilities of fortune, until I could give a satisfactory account of myself.

I thought that this was rather hard lines; but as good luck often comes to us in the guise of present tribulation, as matters turned out it was the very best thing that could have happened to me, for it compelled me to reveal myself and my plans to persons who were willing and able to aid me, and to tell my story to friendly and sympathetic ears.

The commander of Castle Thunder was Major G. W. Alexander, a gentleman who, ever since I made his acquaintance through being committed to his custody as a prisoner, I have always been proud to number among my best and most highly-esteemed friends. Major Alexander, and his lovely wife, both showed the greatest interest in me, and they treated me with such kindness and consideration that I was induced to tell them exactly who I was, what my purposes were in assuming the male garb, what adventures I had passed through, and what my aspirations were for the future. They not only believed my story, but thinking that my services to the Confed-

eracy merited better treatment than I was then receiving at the hands of the authorities, interested themselves greatly in my behalf.

Both the major and his wife — but the lady, especially — seemed to be shocked, however, at the idea of a woman dressing herself in the garb of the other sex, and attempting to play the part of a soldier; and they eagerly urged me to resume the proper costume of my sex again, assuring me that there would be plenty of work for me to do, if I were disposed still to devote myself to the service of the Confederacy. The major, however, was evidently impressed with the narrative I had given him of my exploits, and was convinced that if regularly enlisted in the secret service corps I would be able to render assistance of the first value. He, however, was urgent that I should abandon my disguise, and represented, in forcible terms, the dangers I ran in persisting in wearing it.

To these remonstrances I turned a deaf ear. I had passed through too many real trials to be frightened by imaginary ones, and I did not like to change my costume under compulsion. I accordingly refused positively to put on the garments of a woman, except as a means of gaining my liberty, and with the full intention of resuming male attire at the earliest opportunity.

Major Alexander, therefore, finding me fixed in my determination to have my own way, undertook to have matters arranged to my satisfaction without putting me to the necessity of discarding my disguise, in representing my case to General Winder, and inducing him to give me a trial in his corps.

IN THE SECRET SERVICE.

General Winder ordered my release, and, assigning me to a position in the secret service corps, he proceeded to play a very characteristic trick upon me, for the purpose of testing my fidelity and my abilities. The trick was neatly played; but I got the best of the general to such an extent that he was tolerably well convinced that I was both trustworthy, and that I was quite wide awake enough to take good care of myself even against such a sharp practitioner as himself.

General Winder was one of the most remarkable men I became acquainted with during my whole career as an officer and a spy in the Confederate service. He was a venerable, pleasant-looking old gentleman, with white hair, and a rather

agreeable expression of countenance that was well calculated
to deceive superficial observers with regard to his real character. He had a most confiding, plausible way about him, and
an air of general benevolence, that completely masked the
hardness of his heart, and imposed so on his victims, that,
until they found themselves fairly caught in his cunningly-laid
traps, they were unwilling to believe him to be the desperate
old sinner he really was. Calculated as General Winder was
to leave a favorable impression at first glance, he would not
bear inspection. No man of strongly-marked character can
long conceal his real self from those who are accustomed to
study human nature; and a very slight acquaintance with
Winder sufficed to convince me that he was a dangerous man
to trifle with, and that cruelty and rapacity were among his
predominant traits. His eyes were hard, cold, and piercing,
and there was a wicked twist about his mouth that was far
from being reassuring. I do not believe that man had such a
thing as a conscience; that he was utterly unscrupulous with
regard to the means he took for the accomplishment of his
ends, I know. He was a most valuable officer, however, and
I doubt whether another individual in the whole Confederacy
could have been found who would have commanded the secret
service corps with the signal ability he did.

General Winder plays a Trick on Me.

Such was the new commander under whom I was now to go
on duty, and who, when he consented to release me from
prison, and give me employment, prepared as pretty a trap
as was ever devised for catching an innocent. The trap was
sprung in first-rate style, but the intended victim was agile
enough to slip through the wires, and the result was that General Winder had nothing but his trouble for his pains. I
believe it would have delighted him to have caught me, much
more than it did to have it proved, by his ingeniously-arranged
device, that I was all that I pretended to be, and that the
probabilities were all in favor of my being able to become a
most efficient ally.

I was a little taken in by Winder's plausible manner at first,
and I really did not have a fair chance of studying his character before I was compelled to submit myself to the test
which he prepared for me. From what I saw and heard
of him, however, I easily arrived at the conclusion that he was

a hard customer to deal with, and that I would have to be unusually wary if I wanted to avoid getting into trouble with him. I had, however, unlimited confidence in my own abilities, and accepted the commission he gave me as a secret service agent with a determination to carry out my instructions to the letter at all hazards.

Furnishing me with transportation, General Winder started me off with despatches for General Earl Van Dorn. The despatches were simply a lot of blank papers, and a letter explaining the little game Winder was playing with me.

A North Carolina Militia-man tries to arrest Me.

Unsuspicious of any evil intentions on the part of the white-headed, benevolent-looking old gentleman, I hastened to execute my orders, but suddenly found myself brought up at Charlotte, N. C., with a round turn, as the sailors say. Winder had telegraphed to the provost marshal at Charlotte to have me arrested; and accordingly, when the train stopped at that place, a gawky member of the North Carolina home-guard put in an appearance, took me into custody, and demanded the papers I had in my pocket. It now flashed upon me that Winder had put up a job on me, and I resolved that he should not have the satisfaction of succeeding, if I could help it.

I accordingly measured my captor with my eye, and saw at a glance that he was not the brightest-witted specimen ever created, and concluded that if I only put on enough dignity I would have no serious difficulty in getting the best of him. It was evidently somewhat of a novelty for the tar-heeled home-guarder to arrest an officer; and while he felt the importance of the occasion immensely, he was in some degree of trepidation, especially when he saw that I was not disposed to acknowledge his authority.

I refused to give up the papers, and demanded, in the severest manner I could command, what right he had to undertake to make the arrest of an officer of the Confederate army travelling under orders. He showed me his orders, which I was forced to acknowledge were correct, but still declined either to give up the papers or to submit to an arrest.

I, however, promptly offered to return to Richmond with them, and report at headquarters to General Winder.

This completely nonplussed him, and he was in a terrible quandary. His orders to arrest me were positive, and he was confident that there was something wrong about me. My prompt offer to return and see Winder, however, convinced him that there must be some mistake, and he was in an agony to know what course he had better pursue.

I pitied the poor fellow's perplexity, but could scarcely help from laughing in his face at his desperate stupidity. He blinked his eyes at a terrible rate, and great drops of sweat oozed from his forehead, which he wiped off with the sleeve of his jacket, as he tried to argue the matter with me. I, however, would not give in in the least, and seeing that he did not have the slightest comprehension of the duties of his office, and was puzzled to know what to do, I suggested that a telegraphic despatch should be sent back to headquarters, asking for further instructions. This settled the case effectually; and with a little further parley I was released, and was soon on my way again. I don't know whether Winder ever took any notice of this most admirable exhibition of inefficiency on the part of the gallant defender of the homes of Charlotte, but I thought that if I were in his place, I would take some pains to discipline this particular tar-heel into some adequate appreciation of the necessity for obeying orders, no matter who was hurt. The adventure afforded me considerable amusement, when I was well through with it, and I could not but laugh whenever the comical expression of the puzzled North Carolinian presented itself to my mind's eye.

Without more interruption or delay I proceeded on my journey, and finally reached General Van Dorn, to whom I delivered my package of supposed despatches. He read Winder's letter, and looked through the lot of blanks which had accompanied them; then, glancing at me, he burst into a laugh, which indicated that he saw something funny in the proceeding, and after a few questions, he ordered me to return. This might be good fun for Van Dorn and Winder; but I did not particularly admire having been sent all this distance on such a fool's errand, and was very much disposed to resent it. A little reflection, however, told me that it was none of my business what the pretended despatches were, and that as I had accomplished my errand according to order, and without falling into the snare that General Winder himself had evidently set for me, I had every reason to be satisfied, and would probably find, on getting back to Richmond, that he was satisfied also.

I was anxious to reach Richmond at as early a day as possible, for I heard a number of rumors which induced me to believe that another great battle was shortly to be fought, and I was immediately seized with a furious desire to be on hand for the purpose of taking part in it. Despite the terrible scenes through which I had passed, despite the severe wound I had received, and from which my arm was still stiff, the prospect of joining in another fight had an irresistible fascination for me. I found, however, on reaching Richmond, that there was no present chance for a battle, and consequently settled myself down as contentedly as possible to do whatever work might be assigned me in the secret service department.

It seemed to be an impossibility for me now to avoid getting into continual trouble about my disguise. Not only were a number of people fully informed of all the particulars of my career since the outbreak of the war, but it began to be whispered about among the soldiers and citizens that a woman dressed as a man had been discovered, and some highly-exaggerated rumors with regard to my exploits were diligently circulated. My having received a wound, shortly after the battle of Shiloh, appeared to be a particularly attractive episode to the minds of many people; and my performances at that battle were believed, in some quarters, to have been of a most extraordinary nature. Indeed, I do not know but that some people thought me the commander-in-chief of the Confederate forces on the occasion, while I was credited with exploits of unparalleled heroism.

INCONVENIENCES OF CELEBRITY.

This sort of rather indefinite celebrity might have amused me, and pleased my vanity, were it not the source of much annoyance. Not only did the report that this woman-soldier had come to Virginia have a tendency to attract attention to me, and to excite suspicions that might never have occurred to any one, but the extraordinary vigilance that was exercised on all sides to prevent spies from pursuing their occupations in safety, and to prevent deserters from escaping, was sure to occasion me troubles of various kinds. I felt out of the reach of serious danger, it is true, having been assigned to duty in the secret service corps by General Winder; but the fact of my being in this corps would not prevent my arrest and detention at any time if somebody should take a fancy to believe that I was not all that my outward appearances represented.

I was vexed, therefore, but scarcely surprised, when, shortly after my return from my trip to Van Dorn's headquarters, on taking a run over to Lynchburg, I was again arrested on the charge of being a woman in disguise. My sword was taken from me, and I was otherwise treated with a good deal more rudeness than I thought there was any occasion for; and this treatment had the effect of making me obstinate, and indisposed to give my captors any satisfaction with regard to who I was, and for a considerable time I stood out strongly for my rights as an officer in the Confederate army. I was subjected to a brief examination before his honor the mayor, but refused to commit myself; and it very soon became apparent that my captors were in somewhat of a quandary as to the best course to pursue with regard to me. It was finally, however, decided to hold me for the present, and I was assigned to tolerably comfortable quarters, where I proceeded to make myself as much at home as I could.

THE FUN COMMENCES.

Now the fun commenced. It having become rumored about that a woman, disguised as a Confederate officer, had been arrested, all the curiosity-seekers of the town became immensely excited, especially as the most exaggerated reports of my heroic deeds on the battle-field and elsewhere were in circulation, and everybody — the women in particular — evinced the most eager desire to see the heroine of innumerable bloody conflicts.

I began to be pestered with visitors, who plied me with all sorts of questions, some of them most insulting ones, but which I was compelled to refrain from getting angry at for fear of betraying myself. My position was a most unpleasant one, and it required very skilful management for me to play the part of a man to advantage. What gave piquancy to the situation was, that, while it was generally believed I was a woman, and the particular woman whose exploits had reached their ears, my visitors were none of them quite sure which sex I belonged to, and all their efforts were directed to solving the mystery.

While the attentions I received from the good citizens of Lynchburg, and particularly from the women folk of that town, were all in a greater or less degree annoying, some of my interviews with the visitors who persisted in calling upon me were decidedly amusing, and caused me much hearty laughter.

On one occasion I heard feminine voices and footsteps approaching, and prepared myself for the ordeal which I would be compelled to go through with. During the two years and more I had been wearing male attire, I had not only learned the general carriage of a man, but had picked up a good many little masculine traits, which I had practised until I was quite perfect in them. I relied greatly upon these to aid me in maintaining my *incognito*, for they were eminently characteristic, and well calculated to throw a suspicious person off guard. So, when I heard these visitors coming, I stuck my feet up on the window-sill, and, just as they were opening the door, I turned my head, and spit.

This action attracted the attention of the youngest of the two ladies who were entering, immediately; and I heard her say in a whisper to the elder, " O, ma, that can't be a woman! See how he spits!" I saw that my little ruse was a success, and laughed inwardly at the impression it made on the ladies.

They were a mother and daughter, and had evidently come to remonstrate with me, in good set terms, about the impropriety of my costume. One little peculiarly mannish gesture, however, so completely confounded them that they did not venture to approach the subject they had in their minds except in the most roundabout way. They were very nice people, and were disposed to be as kind to me as they possibly could; but I did not think proper to give them any satisfaction with regard to what they were most concerned about; and, after a somewhat embarrassed conversation, during which they offered to serve me in any way in their power, they took their departure as wise as they came.

Comical Interview with an Old Lady.

Not long after, I had another visitor of a somewhat different kind. This was a motherly old lady, who seemed to consider that her years and experience gave her a right to speak to me in plain words, whether I was a man or a woman. She accordingly, without any ceremony, began to subject me to a very rigid cross-examination; but I replied to her questions in a manner that was anything but to her satisfaction. The result was, that both of us at length began to be somewhat vexed, and, as I could not understand what right she had to undertake such a task as that she was then engaged in, and considered her behavior impertinent in the extreme, I resolved to say a few words that I thought would settle her.

Finding that she could not obtain any definite answers to her questions, she finally said, "Well, all I've got to say is, that if you really are a young man, you deserve credit for what you have done to advance the interests of the cause. If you are a woman, however, you are disgracing your sex by dressing yourself up in men's clothes, and attempting to be a soldier. If you wanted to serve your country, you might have found some other way of doing it, and you ought to be ashamed of yourself."

This made me a little mad, but I kept cool, and, shrugging my shoulders, said, in as deliberate a manner as possible, looking the old lady straight in the eyes, "Well, madam, as you seem to be in doubt about my sex, and are apparently exceedingly anxious to find out whether I am a man or a woman, allow me to suggest that the facts of the case can very readily be established to your satisfaction. Suppose you —" But it would be cruelty to the reader to give the rest of my reply, so I will leave it unrecorded.

It had an astonishing effect, however, on my visitor. She got red in the face, her eyes flashed, and, muttering something that I did not hear, she bounced out of the room, leaving me to enjoy a hearty laugh at the comical termination of the adventure. My irate visitor went down stairs in hot haste, and, in a terrible state of excitement, informed the mayor that that nasty little fellow had insulted her. The supposed insult I explained in such a way that the laugh was fairly turned upon the ancient dame.

If such occurrences as these had been the only annoyances to which I was subjected, no particular harm would have been done, but, rather, considerable amusement would have been afforded me. To my surprise and indignation, however, I received one day the following letter from a general officer, with whom I was acquainted, and whom I had hitherto regarded as something of a gentleman: —

"LIEUTENANT HARRY T. BUFORD, C. S. A.

"Dear Sir: If you will accept a position on my staff as one of my aids, I can obtain for you your release from the civil authorities. You will have a pleasant time. I will furnish you with a fine horse, and you can share my quarters and my mess."

The meaning of this did not require explanation. It stung me to the heart, that a man who had fought with me on the same field of battle should offer me such an indignity, situated as I was; and I was so overcome with rage at the insult that I would have killed him, without thought of the consequences to myself, could I have reached him. I replied instantly to his note, stating that I would meet him at any time and place he might designate, and that I would either kill him or he would have to kill me, for I was resolved that no man should insult me with impunity. I heard no more from him; and when I gained my freedom once more, he was gone. At that time the writer of this insulting note was single, but now he is married; and it is only for the sake of his noble little wife and his family that I refrain from branding his name with infamy. I am informed that he always speaks of me with the highest respect; but, as I have no respect for him, I care not what his opinion of me may be.

Finally, I obtained my release; and having had quite enough of Lynchburg, and being anxious to escape from the gaze of the impertinently curious people, who watched my every motion, I took my departure without any delay.

CHAPTER XXIV.

RUNNING THROUGH THE FEDERAL LINES.

At Charlotte, North Carolina. — Arrival of Longstreet's Corps, on its Way to re-enforce Bragg's Army. — I obtain Permission for myself and other Officers to go on the Train southward. — I arrive in Atlanta, Georgia, and receive Letters from several Members of my Family. — I learn for the first time that my Brother is in the Confederate Army. — I receive Information of the Officer to whom I am engaged to be married, and whom I have not seen since the Battle of Shiloh. — I make an Attempt to reach him, but am unable to do so. — Failing in an Endeavor to become attached to General Armstrong's Command, I determine to undertake an Expedition through the Lines. — Finding a Supply of female Garments in a deserted Farm-house, I attire Myself as a Woman. — My Uniform hid in an Ash-barrel. — An Invasion of the Dairy. — I start for the Federal Lines.

ROM Lynchburg I went to Charlotte, North Carolina, where the home-guard officer had attempted to arrest me while carrying through General Winder's blank despatches to Van Dorn. I had some curiosity to meet this individual again, as I thought I would like to make his acquaintance. I did not have the pleasure of seeing him, however; but I did see quite a number of officers and soldiers who had collected at this point, under orders to return to their commands without delay, and who were waiting for transportation. Many of these were old friends and acquaintances of mine, and I proceeded to make myself at home among them, and also among the good people of Charlotte, taking particular pains, according to my usual custom, to be as agreeable as I could to the ladies; for, notwithstanding my recent little unpleasantness with the Richmond and Lynchburg authorities with regard to my right to wear male attire, I still was inspired by some ambition to achieve a reputation as a ladies' man. I succeeded as well as I usually did when attempting to play this *rôle*, and managed to enjoy myself immensely,

288

although I am not aware that I inflicted any irreparable damage upon the hearts of the fair ones of Charlotte.

This was in the summer of 1863. General Lee had invaded Pennsylvania, had been defeated at Gettysburg, and had returned to Virginia, to resume again the defence of Richmond. His army was shattered, but defiant still, and, as events proved, was quite competent to do as hard fighting as it ever did, and to ward off the always impending Federal attack on the Confederate capital for a good while to come. But, with the battle of Gettysburg, the important work of the summer in that quarter had culminated, and the attention of the entire Confederacy was now anxiously directed to Eastern Tennessee, where the Federal General Rosecrans was pushing forward, with the evident intention of striking a damaging blow somewhere, and perhaps of forcing his way into Georgia. It was in resisting the forces of Rosecrans, therefore, that distinction was to be won, and not by remaining in the neighborhood of Richmond. As I always liked to be where the heaviest fighting was going on, I concluded that I ought to set my face southward if I hoped to win any laurels.

Hearing that Longstreet's corps had been detached from Lee's army before Richmond, and ordered to re-enforce Bragg, I concluded to wait in Charlotte until it made its appearance on its way southward, and, if possible, travel with it to its destination. A good many of the officers waiting in Charlotte were anxious to take advantage of this opportunity to obtain transportation back to their commands, but it was reported that no one would be permitted to go on the train except Longstreet's own men. It would have been a very serious disappointment and some trouble to many who did not know when they would have such another chance to reach the scene of action, and there was a good deal of growling at the prospect that a prolonged stay in Charlotte might be necessary, when their services were so much needed elsewhere.

I, however, had made up my mind to make a determined effort to go, at every hazard, despite the orders to the contrary ; and I proposed to some of the officers, who were impatient to get off, that we should have an interview with General Longstreet, and endeavor to impress upon his mind the imperative necessity we were under of rejoining our regiments immediately. There was a difference of opinion,

19

however, about the expediency and propriety of this course, and no one was willing to take the responsibility of doing the necessary talking. As no one else would undertake the task of interviewing Longstreet on the subject, I resolved to represent the situation to him myself.

An Interview with Longstreet.

After the arrival of his corps in Charlotte I watched for a good opportunity, and at length espied him engaged in conversation with General Jenkins. I therefore went up, and, making a salute, stated to General Longstreet that a number of officers who were ordered to join their regiments immediately were unable to proceed for lack of transportation, and asked if we might not go on with him; for, if we did not, great inconvenience would be caused to ourselves and to the army. The general hesitated somewhat, but after asking me several questions about who we were, how many there were of us, where we were going, &c., he acceded to my request. I made known the success of my mission to the rest, and so, jumping on board the train, we managed to get through.

I was determined, however, that in case Longstreet refused, I would wait until the very last minute, and then jump on the engine or tender, believing that, in an emergency like this, the best plan is to take the law into one's own hands. It is true that, had I attempted this, I might have been put off; but I did not think this very likely, but rather thought that I would probably win the favor of the general, by showing him that I was bent upon getting to the front at the earliest possible moment. At all events, I was willing to have taken the chances of getting through in proper style.

On reaching Atlanta, I had the gratification of receiving a number of letters from relatives from whom I had not heard for many months. There were two from my father, one from my sister in Matanzas, and one from my brother, in the trans-Mississippi department. This was the first time in nine months I had heard from my brother, and it was the first intimation I had that he was in the army. It was a great delight for me to receive these letters, as, though I had been long separated from my relatives, they were often in my thoughts, and I remembered them with the tenderest affection. I was, as may be supposed, particularly well pleased to learn that my brother was in the Confederate service, but I was glad that he was so far off that there was not much danger of my meeting him; for I felt certain that he would object, in no measured terms, to my course in assuming male attire for the purpose of doing a share of the fighting, and feared that we might quarrel about it.

SOME GOOD NEWS.

Shortly after my arrival in Atlanta, however, I heard something that delighted me even more than the receipt of the letters from my near and dear relatives. This was that Captain De Caulp was near Spring Hill with Van Dorn. This bit of particularly interesting information I obtained from a soldier of the third Arkansas regiment. I had not seen the captain since the battle of Shiloh, where I fought by his side, or at least under his eye, during nearly the whole of the conflict, succeeding in winning his commendation for my courage, without exciting any suspicion in his mind that I was the woman upon whom his affections were bestowed. So soon as I heard that he was in my vicinity, I was seized with an intense desire to meet him again; for I was greatly in love with him, and it afforded me the keenest delight to hear praises of myself from his lips, and he all the while thinking that he was addressing them to a third party.

I don't suppose, since the commencement of the world, so strange a courtship as ours was ever carried on. It is certain that not many women have had the same opportunities as myself to find out, from their own lips, exactly how fond of them their expected husbands really are. The situation, I confess, had a wonderful fascination for me, for there were intensely romantic elements in it, that addressed themselves, in the strongest manner, to my imagination. To have been able to fight by the side of my lover in one of the greatest battles of the war, and to be praised by him for my valor, were of themselves matters for intense satisfaction; and I often imagined how it would be after the war was over and we would be able to compare notes and relate our adventures to each other. But, alas! before the war would be over there was much that both of us would be compelled to endure of toil and suffering; and the peaceful, happy home that my fervid imagination pictured was but a dream, and nothing more.

At the time of which I write, however, a desire to see Captain De Caulp again was the uppermost thought in my mind, and I was almost more than half resolved to give him a surprise by revealing myself to him. Whether to do this or not was a question that I debated with myself most seriously while on my way to join him. The fact that I was a woman had now been so often discovered, that it was probable he might at any moment learn that his expected wife and Lieutenant Harry T. Buford were one and the same; and, not knowing what he might think of the course I had pursued in assuming male attire, I dreaded having any one but myself discover my secret to him. In addition to this, I loved him most fondly; and, although inspired by a sense of the duties I owed to the cause for which I had taken up arms, I endeavored to control my feelings, and to regard my marriage with Captain De Caulp as not to be thought of until the time came for both to forsake the battle-field, and to think no more of warfare but as something we were done with forever.

Cupid's Tyranny.

I would have been less than human, however, if sometimes I did not desire most ardently to be with him, and to hear from my lover's lips the terms of endearment which are the sweetest music a woman's ears can be greeted by, and to be courted by him as other women were by the men who had won their affections. I knew that, in many respects, it would be better for me to remain at a distance from Captain De Caulp; but I was moved by an inscrutable impulse at this time to go to him, and I was almost willing, if he should say so, to abandon the army, and to permanently resume the garments of my sex. I did not propose, however, to do this if it could be avoided, and the leading idea in my mind was, in the event of my concluding to reveal myself to him, to go through the rest of the war with him, and to fight constantly by his side, as the Italian heroine, Bona Lombardi, did by the side of her husband, Brunaro. The course which I would ultimately pursue, however, I finally determined should be governed by circumstances, but that, at all events, I would make an effort to see my lover again.

So soon as I found that Captain De Caulp was near at hand, I took the train for the point nearest to where I learned that Van Dorn's command was stationed. Getting off at Tyner's

Station, I obtained a horse, and started off in the direction of Chickamauga. At this point I fell in with General Pegram's cavalry, and had the great pleasure of seeing the handsome General Frank Armstrong, an officer for whom I entertained an intense admiration.

I remember once saying to Major Bacon, who at that time had not the slightest idea who I really was, "I wonder how any woman could help falling in love with Frank. If I was a woman, I would be in love with him." Indeed, I fear that if my affections had not already been engaged, General Armstrong would have captured them. General Armstrong was a tall, fine looking man, dark complexioned, with regular and very handsome features, jet black hair and eyes, and with mustache and side whiskers that became him immensely. His uniform always fitted him exactly, and was exceedingly becoming to him. He was not a gay or dashing sort of man, but firm and decisive in his manners and appearance, and he always seemed to be what he was, — a true officer and gentleman. From General Pegram I learned that it would be very difficult, and, indeed, almost impossible, for me to reach Van Dorn, and I therefore concluded to remain where I was, and to endeavor to become attached to General Armstrong's command. After waiting for some time, however, and finding that there was no chance for me to do this, I turned back as far as Ringold. At this place I met some of the officers and men of the tenth Tennessee regiment, with whom I was acquainted, and from whom I obtained some ideas with regard to the general situation of affairs, which induced me to make rather different plans from those which I had been endeavoring to carry out.

In a Quandary.

In fact, I was in somewhat of a quandary, and scarcely knew exactly what to do with myself so as to dispose of my time to the best advantage. I saw plainly, as matters were then, that it would be exceedingly difficult, if not impossible, for me to join Van Dorn's command, whereas, if I waited patiently for a little while, Captain De Caulp would most likely come my way, and I would be able to meet him sooner by waiting for him than by going after him. I was too impatient, however, to pass my time in idleness, and felt as if I must do something for the cause and my own credit as a soldier.

It really appeared to be more trouble than it was worth to endeavor to persuade any of the general officers to assign me to the particular kind of duty I desired; and, as I had been decidedly successful in more than one expedition, planned and executed by myself, and on my own responsibility, I resolved to undertake another one, just for the sake of keeping myself busy, and of seeing what would come of it. . I felt very confident that if I could make a big hit, my services as a spy would be in heavy demand, for there was evidently going to be some close fighting, and the movements of the enemy would need watching at every point.

My Washington trip, just after the battle of Ball's Bluff, suggested a general method of procedure; but in a great number of ways the present situation was a far more difficult and dangerous one, and would require the exercise of all the wits I had — wits that had been tolerably well sharpened by over two years of severe experience, both as a soldier and as a spy. I was even more reckless now than I was then, but my recklessness was that of a veteran, who scorns danger when there is a necessity for braving it, but who does not expose himself any more than there is occasion for, or run himself against rifle bullets just for the fun of the thing. While well aware of the risks I incurred, however, I had an unlimited faith in my own tact and skill, and did not doubt my ability to accomplish my proposed adventure in safety, and with satisfactory results.

PLANNING AN EXPEDITION.

My idea now was to run through the lines, and take a good view of the situation from the Federal standpoint, and I knew that the safest and best way of doing this — if, indeed, not the only one — was to go as a woman; for, in the proper attire of my sex it would be easier for me to pass the pickets, and avoid being suspected of having any end in view to which objection could be taken. The only difficulty in the way of accomplishing my object was in procuring suitable clothing without attracting attention. As there were a number of houses in the vicinity from which the people had fled, some of them in great haste, when they found themselves likely to be in the midst of contending armies, it occurred to me that in all probability I would be able to find what I wanted in some one of them.

I, therefore, commenced a search, and soon came to a dwelling that promised to supply me with everything I needed: for, from such views of the interior as I could get, the people seemed to have gone off, and left nearly all their goods behind them.   I, accordingly, concluded to make an investigation, to see if my surmises were correct, and forced my way in through one of the back windows.   Sure enough, I found an abundance of female clothing to select from, and proceeded forthwith to appropriate the best outfit the wardrobe of the absent mistress of the establishment afforded, never doubting but that, as she must be a good Confederate, she would highly approve of my conduct, could she be informed of the use .to which her dresses and underwear were being put.

TRANSFORMATION.

Having completed my toilet, and transformed myself from a gallant young Confederate officer into a reasonably good-looking woman, I packed a carpet-bag with a change of clothing, and other articles, such as I thought might be useful on a journey.   Before making a start, however, there were several matters to be attended to.   My uniform was to be disposed of, and, as I was a trifle hungry, I thought that if any provisions were obtainable, a good meal would aid me materially in getting along comfortably.

My uniform I folded up carefully and put into a pillow-case, and in looking about for a place to bestow it, where it would be least likely to be discovered or disturbed, I concluded that an ash-barrel which I found would answer my purpose exactly.   I therefore put the pillow-case, containing the garments, into the barrel, and, covering it with ashes, placed it, with the mouth turned towards the smoke-house, in a corner where it would not be apt to attract attention.

This arrangement being effected, I next went into the dairy in search of food, and found enough to supply the demands of my hunger, although the bill of fare was, perhaps, not all that I would have desired, had I been permitted any choice in the matter.   I succeeded, however, in making a tolerably hearty meal, by eating some raw ham, and all the preserves I could find.   Having despatched such eatables as I was able to lay my hands upon, I picked up my carpet-bag, and made directly for the enemy's lines.   I knew that the bold way was the best way, in the execution of such an enterprise as that upon which I was now starting, and that the correct plan was to strike directly for headquarters, with a plausible story to tell, rather than to attempt to slip past the pickets and run the risk of being detected, and of being compelled to give an account of myself, under suspicion of being upon some objectionable errand. Until actually within the Federal lines, however, I would be, so to speak, between two fires, and would stand a chance of being used quite as roughly by my friends as by the enemy; and it was important, therefore, for me to make the distance I had to go as quickly as I could, and yet to avoid appearing in too much of a hurry, in case any one should happen to see me. I judged that I would be able to pass the Confederate lines without any very great trouble, as I was not able to note any picket posts in the vicinity of the house which had so conveniently been left standing by its owners, with everything in it that I wanted for the particular errand I was on. But I knew that it would not do to rely too much on appearances in such a situation as this, and that I was liable to have an individual armed with musket or sabre put in an appearance at any moment, and demand to know who I was, and what I was prowling about there for.

The dangers attending the enterprise, however, gave it a certain pleasurable excitement, such as it otherwise would not have had, and I enjoyed it, after a fashion, immensely — even more than I did the excitement of a battle. In a battle, a single combatant, no matter how valorous he may be, is lost in the crowd; and as his individuality is, in a large measure, merged in that of his regiment or brigade, so the dependence of the issue upon single, personal effort is something that it is difficult to appreciate. In attempting such a bit of work, however, as I now had on hand, my own personality necessarily asserted itself in the strongest manner. The plan of action was mine; its execution depended upon myself; mine alone was the peril; and should I succeed in accomplishing my first point, in gaining the Federal lines in safety, the prosecution of my enterprise would be a contest of wits between myself and those with whom I was brought in contact, and from whom I expected to gain the information I was after. For these reasons I found a keener enjoyment in the performance of spy duty than I did in doing the work of a soldier; and, although I would not have missed, on any account, the experience I underwent during the first two years of the war, especially those incident to being a participant in such hard-fought battles as Bull Run, Ball's Bluff, Fort Donelson, and Shiloh, my career during the latter part of the great contest, when I was, for the most part, acting as a spy within the enemy's lines, was in many ways much the most interesting to myself. Whether the narrative of it will prove the most interesting portion of this volume, I, of course, cannot tell. I hope, however, that the reader, having followed the story of my fortunes and misfortunes thus far, will have sufficient curiosity to keep with me to the end.

CHAPTER XXV.

THE MILITARY SECRET SERVICE. — RETURN FROM A SPYING EXPEDITION.

The Duties of Spies. — The Necessity for their Employment. — The Status of Spies, and the extraordinary Perils they run. — Some Remarks about the Secret Service, and the Necessity for its Improvement. — I reach the Federal Lines, and obtain a Pass to go North from General Rosecrans. — On my Travels in search of Information. — Arrival at Martinsburg, and am put in the Room of a Federal Officer. — A Disturbance in the Night. — "Who is that Woman?" — I make an advantageous Acquaintance. — A polite Quartermaster. — All about a pretended dead Brother. — How Secret Service Agents go about their Work. — A Visit to my pretended Brother's Grave, and what I gained by it. — I succeed in giving one of Mosby's Pickets an important bit of Information. — The polite Attention of Federal Officers. — I return to Chatanooga, and resume my Confederate Uniform. — A perilous Attempt to reach the Confederate Lines. — What a Drink of Whiskey can do. — I become Lame in my wounded Foot, and am sent to Atlanta for medical Treatment.

HE position and duties of spies are little understood by persons who have had no actual experience of warfare, and who, consequently, are unable to understand the multitude of agencies it is requisite for the commanders of armies and the heads of governments, which may find it necessary to make an appeal to arms in order to settle their differences, to resort to for the accomplishment of the ends they have in view. Just as the quartermaster, the commissary, the paymaster, and the surgeon are as important as the generals, — if any fighting worthy of the name is to be done, and warfare is to be an affair of science and skill, instead of a mere trial of brute force, — so the spy, who will be able to obtain information of the movements of the enemy; who will discover the plans for campaigns and battles that are being arranged; who will intercept despatches; who will carry false intelligence to the enemy, and who, when he does become possessed of any fact worth knowing, will

298

prove himself prompt and reliable in taking it, or sending it to headquarters, is indispensable to the success of any movement.

The spy, however, occupies a different position from that held by any other attaché of an army. According to all military law he is an outlaw, and is liable to be hung if detected — the death of a soldier even being denied him. Nothing has been left undone to render the labors of the spy not only perilous in the extreme, but infamous; and yet the spy is nothing more nor less than a detective officer, and there cannot be any good and sufficient reason assigned for the discredit which attaches to his occupation. It is simply one of the prejudices which, having no substantial foundation, have been carefully fostered by military men for their own purposes, and it is high time that it should be given up by sensible people.

SPIES AND THEIR LABORS.

During the war a vast deal of the most important kind of work was performed by spies on both sides, and these secret emissaries, men and women, labored with a diligence, a zeal, and an intelligence in the execution of tasks of enormous peril, that was rarely equalled, and never surpassed, by those who had the actual work of fighting to do. The fate of more than one battle was decided, not so much by the valor of the soldier, as by the movements which the generals were able to make through information furnished them by spies; and more than one commanding officer has testified, in hearty terms of approbation, to the efficiency and fidelity of the secret service agents who have aided him.

The spy must, of necessity, perform his work amid the most perilous environments. Self-preservation is the first law of nature and of armies; and it is the duty of a general to make it an exceedingly dangerous business for the secret emissaries of the enemy to penetrate his lines for the purpose of picking up useful bits of knowledge. There is no reason, however, why, in this civilized age, when, as every one knows, spies are freely employed by all commanders, and their services are appreciated at the highest value, this class of agents should not have their status fixed in a more satisfactory manner than it is. The agent of a secret service bureau ought to have the same immunity that any other combatant has. We shoot guerrillas, or unauthorized combatants, and so, perhaps, we might continue to hang unauthorized spies; but a regular

attaché of a secret service bureau should have some recognized rights, which even the enemy would be bound to respect.

I admit that there are difficulties in the way of any such
arrangement as this ; for, from the peculiar manner in which
a spy carries on his operations, it is often necessary that he
should be known to be what he is to no one but his confidential superior, and in the prosecution of some of the most important enterprises it is impossible for him to carry about him,
in any shape, evidences of who or what he is ; still, something
might be done to improve the barbarous methods now in
vogue of dealing with military detectives ; for it is preposter-
ous to attempt to regard them in the light of outlaws, when
they are acting as much under the orders of responsible superiors as are the men who shoulder the muskets.

Having been for a long period a spy myself, and a very
successful one, and having been engaged in many as hazardous
and responsible enterprises as usually fall to the lot of a secret
agent of a belligerent power, I naturally feel a, so to speak, professional interest in this matter. Otherwise, however, it does
not concern me personally what may be. done, or left undone,
in the way of organizing the detective forces of the armies of
the future. I am well out of the business, with a consciousness of having served the cause I advocated with zeal and
efficiency ; and as I did not fear danger while engaged in
secret service duty, so I feel no compunctions in relating the
particulars of a number of transactions which, at first sight,
the reader may think were not to my credit. All I ask is, that
fair-minded persons, who will do me the honor to peruse this
portion of my narrative, will remember that the circumstances
were not ordinary ones. I was mixed up in a good deal of
most rascally business ; but it was my associates, and not
myself, who were deserving of condemnation. Their motive
was gain, and gain at the expense of a government and people
that trusted them, and to the detriment of a cause which they
professed to hold sacred. I, on the other hand, was the secret
agent of the enemy, who considered that pretty much anything
was fair in war, and that I was justified in inflicting all the
damage to the enemies of my cause that I was able, whether
by fighting them with arms in my hands in the open field, or
by encouraging treason within their own ranks. That I
associated with traitors, and strove to make men betray the
cause to which they were bound by every tie of honor and

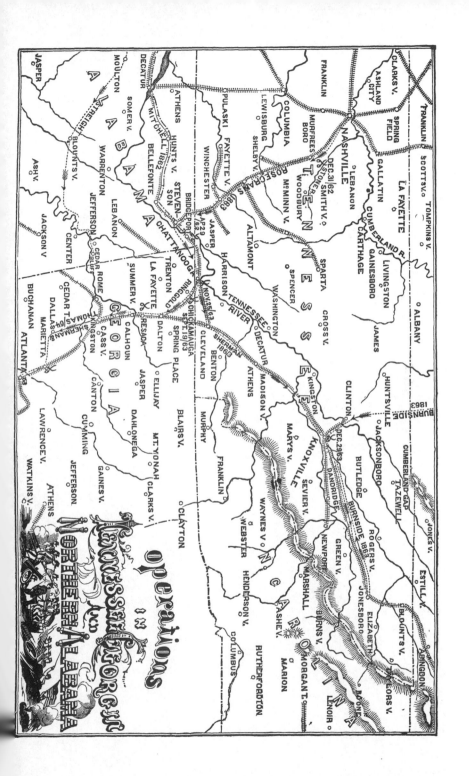

Operations in Tennessee Georgia and Northern Alabama

duty, did not render them less despicable to me; and I even now shudder to think of the depravities of human nature which my career as a secret agent of the Confederate government revealed to me.

WITHIN THE FEDERAL LINES.

But it will be enough to speak of these things when the proper time comes; and my special task just now is to relate the prosecution of my adventures after quitting the farm-house, where I had succeeded in obtaining the clothing I needed for the accomplishment of the particular enterprise I had on hand.

Luckily for me no one observed my movements, and I made my way to the nearest Federal picket station without interruption. I gave my name as Mrs. Williams, told as much as I thought the officer in charge ought to know about me, and asked to see General Rosecrans. I was accordingly ushered into the general's presence, and gave him a somewhat more detailed account of myself.

I represented that I was a widow woman, who was endeavoring to escape from the Confederacy, and who desired to go to her friends in the North; and, judging from appearances, I quite won upon the sympathies of the Federal commander. He asked me a great number of questions, which I answered to his satisfaction, and he then dismissed me, with a pass permitting me to go North. I could not help smiling at the ease with which I deceived General Rosecrans, and said to myself, as I retired from his presence, " My good old fellow, I'll teach you what we Southern women are good for before I am done with you."

Having got my pass, I started off, with a general notion of seeing all I could see, and finding out all I could find out, watching all the time for an opportunity for the execution of a grand *coup*. Picking up information here and there, some of which was of no little importance, I travelled as far as Martinsburg, and had a considerable notion of proceeding to Washington, to see whether a second visit to that city would not be even more productive of results than my first. Circumstances occurred, however, which detained me in Martinsburg, and my trip to Washington was, therefore, deferred to another opportunity, and when the opportunity arrived the reader may be assured that I made good use of it.

It was after night when I reached Martinsburg, and the only unoccupied room in the hotel where I stopped was the one belonging to a Federal quartermaster, that officer having been called away to Washington. The landlord, accordingly, put me in there, and I proceeded to make myself as much at home as possible in the quartermaster's quarters. As luck would have it, however, the officer returned during the night, and after I had retired, and finding the door bolted, he commenced a furious knocking.

A DISTURBANCE.

I was asleep when he began to make this noise, and it caused me to wake with a start. I had no idea who it was, but thought some drunken fellow was making a disturbance. I therefore concluded not to take any notice, thinking that when he found he could not get in he would go away. The quartermaster, however, was angry at finding his room occupied, and being unable to obtain a response, finally said, "Open the door, inside there, or I will break it open!"

I thought that it was high time for me to speak now, and so said, in a half terrified tone of voice, "Who are you? What do you want?"

Finding that his apartment had a feminine occupant, he lowered his voice somewhat, and said, "Excuse me, madam," and walked to the office, where he gave the clerk some sharp words for permitting any one to take his room.

I heard him say, "I would like thundering well to know who she is;" but the clerk was unable to give him any satisfactory information, and the upshot of the whole matter was, that he was obliged to sleep in the parlor, the clerk apologizing for the inconvenience caused him, by saying that he did not know he was going to return so soon.

The next morning I overheard the quartermaster say to the old negro porter, "Uncle George, do you know who that woman is that they put into my room last night?"

"No, sah; I doesn't know, sah," replied the darkey.

"What train did she come on?"

"On the western train, I believe, sah."

"Was anybody with her?"

"Not as I knows of. I didn't see anybody with her, sah."

"Is she good looking?"

"Yes, sah; she's a pretty good looking lady, sah."

This was flattering; and the compliment was the greater as it was evidently not intended for my ears, and I resolved to myself that Uncle George's good taste should be properly rewarded.

This conversation served to give me a hint as to the kind of man I had to deal with in the quartermaster, and I doubted not that if my good looks made anything like as favorable an impression on him as they apparently had done on Uncle George, I would have but little difficulty in inducing him to ʸell me a good many things that it would be highly advantageous for me to know, but which it would not be exactly according to the regulations of the Federal army for him to reveal to a Confederate spy.

Having made my morning toilet, and having, in anticipation of striking up an acquaintance with the quartermaster, endeavored to make myself as attractive as possible in outward appearance, I left my room, and went and took a seat in the parlor. It was not long before I saw my gentleman, or one whom I suppose to be he, walking past the door, and looking at me with a rather curious gaze. I, however, took no notice of him, concluding that it would be more to the purpose to let him make the first advances, something that he was evidently not indisposed to do.

Breakfast was announced as ready before a great while, and with the announcement came the quartermaster's opportunity to introduce himself to me. Advancing towards me, he bowed very politely, and said, "Are you Mrs. Williams?"

"Yes, sir," I replied; "that is my name."

Smiling as agreeably as he could, he said, "I owe you an apology, madam, for the disturbance I made at your door last night. I was not aware that there was a lady in possession of the room."

"O, sir," I said, "no apology is necessary, I assure you. Indeed, I rather owe you one, for I fear I must have caused you some inconvenience."

"O, not at all, madam. On the contrary, when I learned that a lady had possession of the apartment, I regretted exceedingly that I had made so much noise. We officers of the army, however, are inclined to become rather rough in our ways, owing to the associations we are thrown in with, and to our absence from female society. We forget, sometimes, that we are civilized human beings, and don't know exactly how to behave ourselves under circumstances where rudeness is inexcusable.

" O, pray, sir, don't apologize," I answered; " I am sure that an officer of our brave army would not be intentionally rude under any circumstances." I thought that this would do to start the idea in his mind that I was a stanch Federal.

Just then a colored woman appeared, and asked us whether we would not walk into breakfast; and my new-made friend very politely said, " As you are a stranger here, will you permit me to escort you to the breakfast-room? "

" Certainly, sir," I replied; and taking his arm, we walked into the room together, my escort finding a seat for me beside himself at one of the pleasantest tables.

During the progress of the meal, my friend manifested the greatest interest in me and my movements, and by a series of questions, he elicited the information that I was from Cincinnati, that I was uncertain how long I would remain, and that I was in search of a brother, whom I greatly feared was either killed or wounded, as he had not been heard of for an unusually long time.

CONCERNING A BOGUS BROTHER.

The little game I was playing with the quartermaster will serve as a very fair specimen of the methods which a secret service agent is compelled to use for the purpose of gaining such information as is desired. A spy, or a detective, must have a quick eye, a sharp ear, a retentive memory, and a talent for taking advantage of small, and apparently unimportant points, as aids for the accomplishment of the object in view. While making the journey which had brought me as far as Martinsburg, I had, of course, kept my eyes and ears open, and had consequently accumulated quite an extensive stock of knowledge which I thought might be useful some time. Among other things, I had learned the name of a Federal soldier belonging to General Averill's command, and I made a mental note of it for future reference. I cannot recollect, at this distance of time from the incident, whether I accidentally saw this name in a newspaper, or whether I overheard it mentioned in conversation between people near me in the cars. How I obtained it, however, is a matter of small consequence, for that I might have done in a thousand ways. At all events I had the name, and my purpose now was to use it as a means of making the Federal officer by my side at the hotel table useful to me.

My friend asked me what company my brother belonged to, but I said that I could not tell him that. All I knew was, that he was under Averill, and that, as the command had been engaged in some sharp fighting lately, his family, as they had not heard from him, were becoming exceedingly anxious.

I believe that I wiped the semblance of a tear from my eye as I told all this, and looked as distressed as possible, in the hope of working on the quartermaster's sympathies. He proved as sympathetic as I could have desired; and bidding me not to distress myself unnecessarily, but to hope for the best, he promised to undertake to find out for me where my brother was, if still alive, or, if it should turn out that he had been killed, where he was buried.

Accordingly, when we had finished breakfast, he escorted me back to the parlor, and then, saying *au revoir*, he went immediately to headquarters to inspect the roll of the command. Before a great while he returned, and, with a very sorrowful countenance, stated that it gave him pain to tell me that my dear brother was dead.

" O, that is awful ! " I cried, and began to go on at quite a rate, actually, I believe, squeezing out a few real tears.

My friend tried to soothe me as well as he could, and finally, becoming calm, in response to repeated requests to do so on his part, I asked him where Dick was buried, and declared that I must visit his grave.

That I should desire to see, and to weep over, the grave of my dear departed brother, seemed to the quartermaster both reasonable and natural, and he said that he would get an ambulance and take me to the burial-place.

At my Supposed Brother's Grave.

Before many moments, therefore, the vehicle was in attendance, and my friend and I drove out to where my supposititious brother was buried. It was now my turn to question ; and my escort proved to be so exceedingly communicative, that before we returned to the hotel, I was informed of the exact number of troops in the neighborhood, their positions, their commanders, where the enemy were supposed to be located, who they were commanded by, the results of the recent conflicts, and a variety of other matters of more or less importance. The

20

man was as innocent and as unsuspicious as a new-born babe, and I could scarcely keep from laughing sometimes at the eagerness he displayed in telling me all manner of things that, had he been possessed of ordinary common sense, he would never have revealed to any one, much less to a total stranger, with regard to whose antecedents he knew absolutely nothing.

Some of the information thus obtained I knew would be of vital importance to the Confederates, could it be conveyed to them immediately. I therefore made my arrangement, and that night slipped through the Federal lines, and told all that I had to tell to one of Mosby's pickets. With that extraordinary good luck which so often attends bold adventures, I succeeded in getting back without being observed or suspected, and my escort of the morning was never the wiser by the knowledge that his silly talkativeness had produced such good results for the Confederacy.

I remained about a week in Martinsburg, and enjoyed myself immensely. Not only my friend, the quartermaster, but a number of other officers paid me very marked attentions, and I was soon quite a rival to the belles of the place. I did not have another opportunity to communicate with the Confederate forces ; but this week was not an idle one, nevertheless, and by the time it was ended, I was in possession of a large number of facts that were well worth knowing. While still undecided whether to push on farther or not, I received some intelligence which induced me to think it better to return.

When I announced that I was about to depart, my friends, the officers, expressed the greatest regret. The quartermaster said, " We shall miss you greatly ; you have made yourself so agreeable since you have been here, that we shall scarcely know what to do without you."

I said that I was sorry to go, but that my family was anxious for my return ; and as I bade the quartermaster good-by, I declared that I had half a mind to turn detective, for the purpose of catching the rebel who killed Dick. The quartermaster insisted that I should write to him when I got home ; and on his stating that he had a notion to come and see me when the war was over, I gave him a pressing invitation to do so, thinking that he would have a good time in finding me.

But when I got back to Chattanooga, I had some trouble in making any farther progress ; but by representing myself as a soldier's wife, and expressing an extreme anxiety to see my husband, I was permitted to remain within the Federal lines, but was not afforded any particular facilities for finding out anything worth knowing. My anxiety now was to regain the Confederate lines at the earliest possible moment. As I knew the country pretty well, I felt certain of being able to find the farm-house where I had left my uniform, if I could only get a chance to go to it. Fortune favors the brave in a majority of cases, and ere long I was enabled to reach the house, but only to find that it had been burned, and, with the exception of the smoke-house and kitchen, was a mass of charred ruins.

I confess that my heart sank within me when I saw that the house had been destroyed, for I would have been in a nice predicament, and without my masculine garments would have been even more unwelcome among the Confederates than I was among the Federals. To my great joy, however, I discovered the ash-barrel just where I had placed it and unharmed, and in a few moments I had discarded my feminine raiment, and was once more in the guise of a Confederate officer. The costume I wore, however, was not one in which I could appear with impunity in that neighborhood, and it was necessary, therefore, that I should make haste to get where it would be regarded with friendly feelings.

Ere many moments I was crawling through the underbrush and under the fences, with my coat and cap tied up in a bundle, so that I could drop them in case of necessity. In this way I worked myself slowly and cautiously along for several hours during the night, in the direction of the Confederate outposts. When it was light enough for me to see with reasonable distinctness, I made a reconnoisance, and concluded that I must have been within the Confederate lines for more than an hour.

To my left I saw the railroad track tolerably close to the road I was on, and the smoke of the camp was clearly visible. I then crept back into the bush and made for the nearest camp, not wishing to be stopped either by friend or foe at this particular point. Before I reached the point I was aiming at, however, I was compelled to take a rest, for the kind of travelling I had been doing was the hardest kind of hard work, and I was tolerably well used up. Drawing on my coat, therefore, I sat down and began to think what story it would be best for me to tell in order to obtain such a reception as I desired. After turning over the matter in my mind, I concluded to represent myself as an escaped prisoner belonging to Morgan's command.

BACK IN THE CONFEDERATE LINES.

Having thoroughly arranged my plan of action in my mind, I walked up boldly to a picket, whom I saw sitting on a horse at some distance, and saluting him, and telling him that I was unarmed, asked to see the officer of the guard. The officer soon came riding out of the woods towards me, and asked who I was. I told him that I was an escaped prisoner, and that I belonged to Morgan's command, and produced my transportation papers and the letter to General Polk, which had been given to me in the early part of the war. The officer read the papers, which he apparently did not find particularly satisfactory, and scanned me very closely, as if he thought that there was something not quite right about me.

I was much afraid lest he should suspect something, for I had no mustache, and having become somewhat bleached, was not by any means so masculine in appearance as I had been at one time. I, however, bore his scrutiny without flinching, and he apparently did not know what to do but to receive me for what I appeared to be. He accordingly told me that I should have to wait where I was until the relief came, when he would conduct me to camp.

I told him that I was terribly hungry and tired, having walked from Chattanooga since early in the previous evening without food or sleep, and that I would like to get where I could obtain some breakfast. As a means of softening his heart, I pulled out a little pocket flask of whiskey, and asked him if he would not take a drink. His eye brightened at the sight of the flask, and he accepted my invitation without a moment's hesitation. Putting it to his lips, he took a good pull, and when he handed it back there was mighty little left in it. This little I gave to the sergeant, who appeared to relish the liquor as highly as his superior did. The whiskey had the desired effect; for the officer told me he guessed I had better not wait for the relief, and detailed a man to show me the way to camp.

On our arrival at camp, the man took me to the officer's tent, where I made myself as much at home as I could until the master appeared. It was not long, however, before he followed me, and to my great satisfaction, an excellent breakfast was in a short time placed on the table.

After breakfast, the boys, having heard of the arrival of an escaped prisoner, I was speedily surrounded by a crowd of eager questioners, who were anxious to hear all the news from the Federal army. I tried to satisfy their curiosity as well as I could, and told them that the Yankees had received heavy re-enforcements, and were preparing to make a grand movement, and a variety of other matters, part fact and part fiction. Having got rid of my questioners, I took a good sleep until noon, and then, borrowing a horse, rode down to Dalton, where I learned that Captain De Caulp was sick at Atlanta, and resolved to make an effort to get there for the purpose of seeing him.

I was spared the necessity, however, of being obliged to make any special plans for the accomplishment of this end, for I managed to severely hurt the foot which had been wounded shortly after the battle of Fort Donelson, and became so lame that it was decided to send me to Atlanta for medical treatment.

CHAPTER XXVI.

IN THE HOSPITAL.

N army is made up of all kinds of people, — the rougher element of masculine human nature, of necessity, predominating; and not the least of the evil effect of a great war is, that it tends to develop a spirit of ruffianism, which, when times of peace return, is of no benefit to society. A man who is instinctively a gentleman, will be one always, and in spite of the demoralizing influences of warfare; but one who is only a gentleman by brevet, and whose native blackguardism is only concealed on ordinary occasions by a superficial polish of cultivation, will be apt to show himself a blackguard at the earliest opportunity amidst camp associations. Such men are usually cringing sycophants before their superiors, bullies to those who are under them, shirks when fighting is going on, and plunderers when opportunities for plunder are offered. It is creditable to the American people, as a class, that the great armies which contended with each other so earnestly during four long, weary years of warfare, were disbanded and dismissed to their homes with so little injury to society; for, under the very best auspices, war is not calculated to make men good citizens, while it is pretty certain to make those who are ruffians and blackguards already, worse than they were before they took up arms.

During the time that I wore the uniform of a Confederate officer, I was, of course, brought into contact with all sorts of

310

people, — blackguards as well as gentlemen, — and had some pretty good opportunities for studying masculine character. The warnings that had been given me with regard to the most peculiarly unpleasant and disgusting features of camp life, I very speedily discovered were only too well founded; and had I been possessed by a less fervid enthusiasm for the cause, or a less resolute determination to carry out my purpose, I might at an early day have given the whole thing up in disgust. I got accustomed, however, in time to rough, profane, even dirty language, and did not mind it; or, at least, did not permit myself to be annoyed by it. The best and most highly esteemed of my acquaintances in the army permitted themselves a license of language and conduct that they would not have ventured upon in the society of ladies; but this, while it shocked me somewhat at first, I finally came to regard as a matter of course; and when I heard things from the lips of those whom I knew to be gentlemen at heart, which offended my ears, I regarded the annoyance I felt as one of the penalties of the anomalous position I occupied, and very speedily learned to bear with it.

It was different, however, with another class of men, who seemed to take delight in showing, on every possible occasion, what consummate blackguards they were. These I ever regarded with loathing and contempt; and I hope that some of them will undertake the perusal of this narrative, in order that they may know what I think of them.

KEEPING THE PEACE.

With the ruffianly elements of an army it was exceedingly difficult for decent, peaceably-disposed people to get along on any terms. An indisposition to quarrel was regarded as an evidence of cowardice; and as your genuine bully delights in nothing more than in tormenting one whom he imagines will not fight, a reputation for being willing to fight, on the shortest notice, is an excellent thing to have by one who desires to avoid getting into difficulties.

Situated as I was, it was especially important that I should not quarrel if I could help it; but I was not long in finding out that, as quarrelling was necessary sometimes, the bold course was the best, both for the present and the future, and that by promptly resenting anything approaching an insult, I would be likely to avoid being insulted thereafter. I, therefore, very speedily let it be known that I was ready to fight at a moment's notice, if there was any real occasion for fighting; but, at the same time, that I desired to live peaceably with everybody, and was not inclined to quarrel if I was let alone. The result of this line of policy was, that, as a general rule, I got along smoothly enough, but occasionally I could not avoid an angry controversy with somebody; and when I did become involved in anything of the kind, I usually tried to give my antagonist to understand, in plain terms, that I was not an individual to be trifled with.

On my arrival at Atlanta, I unfortunately had a little unpleasantness, which caused me very serious disquietude for a time, owing to the peculiar situation in which I was placed, and which might have had some ill results, either for the person who started the quarrel or for myself, had it not been for the good judgment and consideration of one or two of my friends, who persuaded me not to resort to any extreme measures.

I was expecting to see Captain De Caulp, and was very anxious with regard to him, as I did not know exactly what his condition was, and feared that he might be seriously ill. It was my intention to go to him, to devote myself to him if he should need my services, and perhaps to reveal myself to him. Indeed, I pretty much made up my mind that our marriage should take place as soon as he was convalescent; and, in view of such an event occurring shortly, I was in no humor for a mere bar-room squabble with a drunken ruffian, and would have avoided such a thing at almost any cost, could I have had warning with regard to its probability. More than this, in addition to the lameness of my foot, I was really quite sick, and at the time of the occurrence ought to have been in bed under the doctor's care, and was consequently less disposed than ever to engage in a brawl.

A DRUNK AND DISORDERLY GENERAL.

Unsuspecting any trouble, however, I went to the hotel, and registered my name, and was almost immediately surrounded by a number of officers, who were eager to learn what was going on at the front. Among them was General F.,— I do not give his name in full for his own sake,— an individual who thought more of whiskey than he did of his future existence, and who was employing his time in getting

drunk at Atlanta, instead of doing his duty at the front by leading his men.

He saw that I was a little fellow, and probably thought, on
that account, he could bully me with impunity; so, while I
was answering the thousand and one questions that were put
to me, he began making offensive and insulting remarks, and
asking me insolent questions, until I longed to give him a
lesson in good manners that he would not forget in a hurry,
and resolved that I would make an effort to chastise him
if he did not behave himself.

This was one of the class of men for which I had a hearty
contempt; and, as I neither wished to be annoyed by his
drunken insolence, nor to quarrel with him if I could avoid it,
I left the office and went into the wash-room. The general evidently considered this a retreat due to his prowess,—prowess
which he was careful not to make any great display of within
the smell of gunpowder, — and he followed me, apparently
determined to provoke me to the utmost. I, however, took
no notice of him, but, after washing my hands, came out and
took a seat in the office beside my esteemed friend, Major
Bacon—a thorough gentleman in every sense of the word.

My persecutor still following me, now came and seated himself on the other side of me, and made some insolent remark —
which I do not care to remember. This excited my wrath, and
I resolved to put a stop to the tipsy brute's annoyances. I
accordingly said to him, " See here, sir, I don't want to have
anything to do with you, so go away and let me be, or it will
be worse for you."

At this he sprang up, his eyes glaring with drunken fury,
and swinging his arms around in that irresponsible way incident
to inebriety, he began to swear in lively fashion, and said,
" What'll be worse for me? What do you mean? I'll lick
you out of your boots! I can lick you, or any dozen like
you."

Nice talk, this, for a general, who was supposably a gentleman, wasn't it? I merely said, in reply, " You are too
drunk, sir, to be responsible. I intend, however, when you
are sober, that you shall apologize to me for this, or else make
you settle it in a way that will, perhaps, not be agreeable to
you."

He glared at me as I uttered these words; but my firm
manner evidently cowed him, and turning, with a coarse,
tipsy laugh, he said, to an officer who was standing near

watching the performance, "Come, colonel, let's take another drink; he won't fight;" and they accordingly walked off towards the bar-room together.

This last remark enraged me to such a degree, that I declared I would shoot him if he came near me again. Major Bacon tried to pacify me, and said that I had better let him alone, as he was not worth noticing. ˙After considerable persuasion I concluded that there was very little credit to be got by following up a quarrel with such a blackguard, and made up my mind to have nothing to do with him, if it was possible to avoid him.

The general did not come near me until after supper, when I met him again at the bar. As I had not undertaken to punish him for his behavior to me, he evidently thought that I was afraid of him; and, without addressing me directly, he began to make insulting side remarks, aimed at me. I was on the point of going up and slapping his face, when Major Bacon and Lieutenant Chamberlain, thinking that it was not worth while for me to get into trouble about such a fellow, induced me to go to my room.

Already quite ill, and far from able to be about, the excitement of this unpleasant occurrence made me worse, and I passed a night of great suffering from a high fever, and from my sore foot, which pained me extremely. The major waited on me in the kindest manner, bathing my foot with cold water, and procuring some medicine for me from the hospital steward, and towards morning I fell into a sound sleep, which refreshed me greatly, although I was still very sick.

In the morning Major Bacon ordered me some breakfast, of which, however, I was able to eat but little. While I was breakfasting, he said, "How are you off for money, lieutenant?"

"I have only twenty-four dollars in my pocket just now," I replied, "but I intend to send to Mobile for some to-day."

"Well," said he, "you may need some before yours comes, so here's one hundred and fifty dollars at your service. I will have to leave at five o'clock, but before I go I will try and see that you are in good hands, and in a way to be well taken care of."

The major then went out, and about two o'clock returned with Dr. Hay, who prescribed for me. During the afternoon I was visited by a number of my friends, who appeared to be solicitous for my welfare, and who did their best to cheer me up. I was too sick, however, to enjoy their company much, although I appreciated their kind intentions. I really felt sad at the idea of being forsaken by Major Bacon, who would gladly have staid by me had he not been under positive orders to leave. When the time came for him to go, he shook me by the hand, and said, " Lieutenant, my boy, I will have to leave you now. Lieutenant Chamberlain and the doctor will take good care of you, and I hope you will be up soon."

I asked the major to write to me, and he promised to do so, and bidding me good-by, he took his departure. After Major Bacon had gone, Lieutenant Chamberlain took charge of me, and I shall ever be grateful for the unwearied kindness of his attention. There was nothing I desired, that was procurable, that he did not get for me, and had I been his own relative he could not have done more to promote my comfort.

In the Hospital.

As I got worse instead of better, however, it was concluded that the hospital was the best place for me, and to the Empire Hospital I accordingly was sent, by order of the chief surgeon of the post. I was first admitted into Dr. Hammond's ward, and subsequently into that of Dr. Hay. Dr. Hay, who was a whole-souled little fellow, is dead, but Dr. Hammond is still living, and I am glad of such an opportunity as this of testifying to his noble qualities. During the entire period I was under his care in the hospital, he treated me, as he did all his patients, with the greatest kindness.

O, but these were sad and weary days that I spent in the hospital! I cannot tell how I longed, once more, to be out in the open air and the sunshine, and participating in the grand scenes that were being enacted not many miles away. My restless disposition made sickness especially irksome to me, and I felt sometimes as if I could scarcely help leaving my bed, and going as I was to the front, for the purpose of plunging into the thickest of the fight ; while at other moments, when the fever was strong upon me, I almost wished that I might die, rather than to be compelled to toss about thus on a couch of pain.

There was one consolation, however, in all my sufferings, which sustained me, and made me measurably patient and contented to endure the irksomeness of the restraint which my illness placed upon me, — I was near the man I loved, and hoped soon to have an opportunity to see and to converse with him. I learned soon after my admission to the hospital that Captain De Caulp was in Dr. Benton's ward, adjoining that under the charge of Dr. Hay; and to be under the same roof with him, and the probability that ere long I would be able to see him again, helped me to bear up under the suffering I was called upon to endure. I resolved that if Captain De Caulp was willing, our marriage should take place so soon as we were able to leave the hospital; and I busied myself in wondering what he would say when he discovered what strange pranks I had been playing since we had been corresponding as lovers. I almost dreaded to reveal to him that the little dandified lieutenant, who had volunteered to fight in his company at Shiloh, and the woman to whom he was bound by an engagement of marriage, were the same; but I felt that the time for the disclosure to be made had arrived, and was determined to make it at the earliest opportunity.

CHAPTER XXVII.

A STRANGE STORY OF TRUE LOVE.

Sick-bed Fancies. — Reflections on my military Career. — I almost resolve to abandon the Garb of a Soldier. — Difficulties in the Way of achieving Greatness. — Warfare as a laborious Business. — The Favors of Fortune sparingly bestowed. — Prospective Meeting with my Lover. — Anxiety to know what he would think of the Course I had been pursuing in figuring in the Army as a Man. — A strange Courtship. — More like a Chapter of Romance than a grave Reality. — My Recollections of an old Spanish Story, read in my Childhood, that in some respects reminds me of my own Experiences. — The Story of Estela. — How the Desires of a Pair of Lovers were opposed by stern Parents. — An Elopement planned. — The Abduction of Estela through the Instrumentality of a Rival. — She is carried off by Moorish Pirates, and sold as a Slave. — Her Escape from Slavery, and how she entered the Army of the Emperor disguised as a Man. — Estela saves the Emperor's Life, and is promoted to a high Office. — Her Meeting with her Lover, and her Endeavors to make him confess his Faith in her Honor. — The Appointment of Estela as Governor of her native City. — The Trial of her Lover on the Charge of having murdered her. — Happy Ending of the Story. — I am inspired, by my Recollections of the Story of Estela, to hear from the Lips of my Lover his Opinion of me before I reveal myself to him. — Impatient Waiting for the Hour of Meeting.

WHILE tossing upon my sick-bed in the hospital, I was compelled, for very lack of other occupation, to think of many things that, under ordinary circumstances, busied as I habitually was with innumerable ambitious schemes, would never have pressed themselves upon my mind with the force they now did. This was a strange life I had been leading now for more than two years, and yet it was the kind of a life that, from my earliest childhood, I had ardently longed to lead. I had some understanding now of what the great discoverers, adventurers, and soldiers, who were the idols of my childish imagination, had been compelled to go through with before they won the undying fame

317

that was theirs, and I comprehended, to some degree, how hard a thing it was to win fame.

For myself, I had played my part in the great drama of war with what skill I could command; and, although I had not played it altogether unsuccessfully, the chances that fame and the applause of future ages would be mine, seemed as remote as ever. Warfare, despite all that was terrible and horrible about it, was, to the majority of those who participated in it, a most commonplace, practical, and far from exciting business, in which the chances for eminent distinction seldom appeared, and in which Fortune showered her favors only on a chosen few. And yet there was an almost irresistible fascination in being an active participant in the great events upon which the destinies of a continent were hanging, and the possibility that, at any moment almost, something might occur by which the humblest among the host of combatants would be immortalized, gave a zest to the hard work, and an inspiration to exertion.

Had I continued in health, the probabilities are that the idea of abandoning the cause I had chosen before the close of the war, would never have been permitted to take lodgment in my brain, and I would have gone on from one adventure to another, in spite of every discouragement and disappointment, hoping always that I would be able to achieve something great. Now, however, lying upon my sick-bed, I could not but confess to myself that I was disappointed, and that I was following a will-o'-the-wisp in striving to gain for myself a great name by heroic deeds. Although I had no regrets for the course I had pursued, and as I reviewed in my mind the momentous events in which I had been an active participant during the two years I had been wearing a Confederate officer's uniform, my heart beat proudly at the recollection of them, I nevertheless almost concluded that I had had enough of this, and that it was time for me to exchange my uniform for the attire of my own sex once more, and in good earnest, with the intention of never resuming it again.

THOUGHTS OF LOVE.

These were sick fancies, and I felt ashamed of myself at times for my weakening in the resolution I had formed to see the thing through at all hazards, in some shape, and, if there was a possibility of doing it, of making for myself a great name as a soldier. But there were other influences at work to make me doubtful of the propriety of my longer continuing the hazardous experiment of passing myself off as a man. In an adjoining ward of the hospital was my lover, to a speedy meeting with whom I was looking forward with many fond anticipations. How would he regard my conduct? And should he, as I hoped he would, be proud of my efforts to advance the Confederate cause by doing a soldier's duty, would he be willing that I should longer continue to wear my uniform, especially if we should conclude to have our marriage solemnized at an early day? These were questions that pressed themselves upon me, and that, even more than the dispiriting influences of a sick-room, made me half repent that I had ever assumed male attire, and made me more than half resolve to permanently abandon it so soon as I was out of the hospital.

I was curious, however, rather than apprehensive, with regard to the effect of the disclosures I would have to make when I met Captain De Caulp. There was nothing that I had done that I need blush for, while he had himself been the witness, on one momentous occasion, of my prowess as a warrior, and I longed to hear him repeat to me, as a woman, the praise he had so freely bestowed upon me as a man when we fought side by side at Shiloh.

What a strange courtship ours had been! The only time we had met since our engagement was on the field of battle, and in the midst of scenes of carnage, and here we both were now, sick in adjoining wards of the same hospital; I, longing to be with him, but unable to go to his side; and he, all unconscious that the woman he loved was so near; sighing, doubtless, for the time to come when our futures would be united, but never dreaming that the future he sighed for was so near at hand. It was like a romance, and it was in the scenes of a romance, the memories of which floated through my mind as I thought over the situation, that I alone could find any similitude to it.

I recollected, as I reviewed the circumstances of my own case, an old Spanish *novela*, which I had read when a girl, and which had long since passed out of mind with other childish memories, but the incidents of which now came back to me with singular vividness, on account of a certain resemblance they had to points in my own career. The author's name I forgot, but I distinctly remembered the story, which was one of a collection in an old book I was fond of perusing when at home under my father's roof at the Puerto de Palmas plantation in Cuba.

THE STORY OF ESTELA.

The name of the heroine of this tale was Estela, and she was beloved by a handsome, rich, and gallant young man, — all the heroes in these old Spanish novels are young, handsome, rich, and of high birth, and all the heroines are marvels of beauty, — and for a long time the course of true love ran smoothly enough. At length, however, a young grandee, of enormous wealth, also became enamoured of Estela; and although he failed to win the affection of the lady, he succeeded, without any difficulty, in becoming the choice of her parents; not that they had any objections to Don Carlos, — which I believe was the name of Estela's lover, — but that his rival promised to be a more splendid match for their daughter. Don Carlos was, therefore, forbidden to hold any correspondence with the object of his adoration, but, as Estela continued true to him in spite of her parents' opposition, they were accustomed to meet surreptitiously, through the agency of the lady's waiting-maid and the gentleman's page, who arranged secret interviews for them.

Now, it so happened that while the pair were thus carrying on their secret courtship, the page of Don Carlos took sick and died. It was not many days, however, before a handsome youth applied to be taken into his service, who proved himself so zealous and faithful that he was soon intrusted with all his master's secrets. This youth, however, was a woman, who had fallen in love with Don Carlos, and who, unable to attract his attention in any other way, had resorted to this means of bringing herself to his notice, and of being near him, in the hope that something would occur to enable her to win his love.

The heroines of these old Spanish romances seem to have had a decided fancy for masquerading in male attire, and it is not unlikely that this propensity on their part had some effect in encouraging in me a desire to assume the dress of the other sex for the purpose of seeking adventures. I can call to mind many more stories than the one I am endeavoring to give a brief outline of, in which the women attempt, for the accomplishment of different ends, to figure as men, and it is

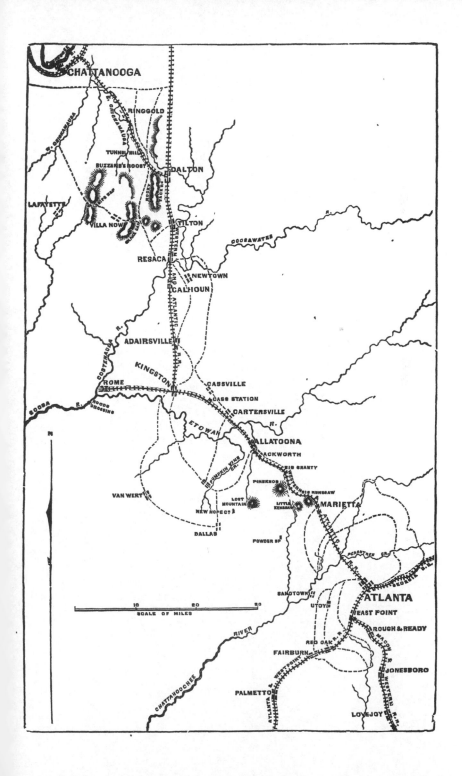

scarcely possible that I was uninfluenced by a perusal of the narratives of their exploits.

The new page, as I have stated, easily gained the entire confidence of Don Carlos, and was employed as the messenger between him and his lady-love. She, however, soon found that he was so much absorbed in Estela, that it was useless to hope to win him, unless her rival could be removed; and she accordingly set about devising a plan for the accomplishment of this end. An opportunity soon offered; for the parents of Estela, despite her unwillingness, were determined that she should accept the hand of the lover of their choice, and made their arrangements for a speedy wedding. Estela, of course, informed Don Carlos of this, and he, seeing that his bride would be lost to him unless he acted with decision, persuaded her to consent to an elopement with him to another city, where their marriage could take place.

The fictitious page was, of course, informed of all that was proposed by the lovers, and felt that the time had now come for her to interfere. Don Carlos and Estela, having arranged for the elopement to take place on a certain night, the lady wrote a letter to her parents, stating that, unable to endure the idea of marrying, at their dictation, a man whom she did not love, she had ventured to incur their displeasure by uniting herself with Don Carlos, for whom, as they well knew, she had long borne a tender regard.

The page, to whom had been intrusted the task of conducting the lady to a rendezvous, where her lover would be waiting with horses to bear them away beyond the reach of pursuit until the marriage should take place, basely betrayed the trust confided to her, however, and, instead of delivering Estela to her lover, took her to where some Moorish pirates were in waiting, by whom she was seized, and carried off to Algiers, to be sold as a slave. The pirates, as a precaution against treachery, insisted upon the page going with them; and thus Estela became informed that her betrayer was a woman, and also learned the reason for her conduct.

On the disappearance of Estela being discovered, the only clew to the mystery was the letter she had written, announcing her intention of eloping with Don Carlos; and that gentleman, who had been waiting anxiously and impatiently for her, and who was lost in wonder at her non-appearance at the rendezvous, was accused of having spirited her away, and perhaps of having murdered her. He was not only overwhelmed

21

with anguish at such a charge being brought against him, but was sorely perplexed to know what had become of the lady; and, as day after day passed by, and no tidings of her were received, he at length forced himself to believe that she had proved false to him, had accepted the page for a lover, and had fled with him. In the mean time the indignation against him increased, and the suspicions that he was the murderer of his mistress grew into certainty in many minds. His trial, on the charge of murder, was therefore ordered; but, determined not to be made the victim of a false woman's treachery if he could avoid it, he made his escape from prison, and, flying to Italy, entered the army of the emperor, Charles V., as a common soldier.

In the mean while, Estela, after passing through many strange adventures in the land of the Moors, at length succeeded in making her escape, in male attire, and she, too, joined the army of the emperor, which was then besieging some Moorish town. In a skirmish which occurred soon after, she had the good fortune to save the life of the emperor, who, finding that she was a person of education and talents, appointed her — little suspecting her to be a woman — to an important position near his own person. Estela soon became the emperor's favorite officer, and he delighted in heaping honors upon her, she, all the while, longing only for an opportunity to return to her own country, for the purpose of seeking her lover.

One day, however, she was amazed to behold a soldier in the ranks who reminded her greatly of Don Carlos, and, on engaging in conversation, found that it was indeed he. She, therefore, took him to her tent, and, by degrees, succeeded in inducing him to tell his story. That he should have suffered so much on her account, grieved her exceedingly; but her womanly pride was touched that he should suspect her honor, and she resolved to try and induce him to have a better opinion of her than he professed, before revealing herself. Appointing Don Carlos to the post of secretary, she engaged him, almost daily, in conversation about his lost love, and endeavored, by various means, to persuade him that Estela might be guiltless.

The melancholy of Don Carlos, however, increased the more the matter was talked about. He could not help confessing that he still loved Estela tenderly, despite her unworthiness, but it was impossible to induce him to think that she

was not unworthy.   That he still loved her, was some consolation to Estela, but it piqued her that he should be unwilling
to admit that there might be some explanation of her strange
disappearance that would relieve her of blame.   While devising in her mind some plan for bringing Don Carlos to
reason, she learned that the governor of her native city had
suddenly died.   This suggested a means of accomplishing
her purpose, and she accordingly applied to the emperor for
the vacant office.   Her request was granted, and she set off
immediately to take possession of the governorship, Don
Carlos going with her, feeling sure that, as one of the new
governor's household, he would be free from molestation on
account of the old charge against him, or, at least, that he
would be able to receive a fair and impartial trial.

So soon as the new governor was installed, and it was found
that Don Carlos was in his suite, the parents of Estela, and
other prominent citizens, stated what the accusations against
him were, and demanded that he be brought to trial, and
punished according to law.   The governor promised that
strict justice should be done, and appointed a day for the trial
to take place, refusing, however, to permit Don Carlos to be
sent to prison, and promising to be responsible for him.

Up to the time of the trial the conferences between the
governor and the secretary were frequent, and Estela redoubled her efforts to make her lover acknowledge, not only
that he loved, but that he still had infinite faith in his lady.

This, as I recollect it, was the most intensely interesting
and exciting part of the story, and it made a strong impression on my imagination.   I thought the lady cruel in unnecessarily prolonging the misery of her lover, and at the same
time, although I was but a child when I read the story, I
could not but appreciate the feelings which induced her to
desire that Don Carlos should confess that he had banished all
unworthy suspicion of her from his mind before she cleared
up the mystery of her disappearance.

At length the confession was forced from the unhappy
man, that, as Estela had never given him reason to think, by
any levity of conduct, that she was capable of loving another
than himself, much less that she was capable of basely for-
saking him for one less worthy, he still, in his inmost soul,
had faith in her honor, and that the dream of his life was,
that he might be able to be reunited to her.

The day of trial came, and Estela, as the chief magistrate

of the city, sat upon the bench, with the other judges, to hear the case. The various witnesses who appeared related the story of Estela's disappearance; her letter, announcing her proposed flight with Don Carlos, was produced; the servants who had been cognizant of the clandestine meetings of the lovers related in detail all they knew about the frequent interviews Don Carlos had had with Estela, without the knowledge of her parents; to all of which the accused could oppose nothing but a simple denial of his guilt.

The disguised Estela, in her character of governor, said, with a frown, and with pretended severity, that, had she known there was such a weight of evidence against Don Carlos, she could never have given him her protection, or have continued him in his office of secretary. The only way in which his innocence could be proved, in the face of such testimony, was by the appearance of Estela, but that, if she could not be produced, it would be necessary to pronounce condemnation.

The miserable man now threw himself at the feet of the governor, and besought him to remember how, long before either of them had any reason to believe they would be called upon to appear before each other in the character of accused and judge, he had told his whole story, and had confessed his love for Estela, despite the reason he had for believing that she had acted basely to him, and how, but a brief time before, he had not only acknowledged his unaltered affection, but his faith in Estela's honor, and besought that true justice might be done, despite what seemed to be an accumulation of evidence against him.

Estela, moved by these entreaties, and overcome by the confession of enduring love and of faith in her honor, made in the presence of a great assembly, was unable longer to restrain herself, and she therefore proclaimed that, notwithstanding the evidence, as she knew Don Carlos to be innocent, she would order his release. This excited a loud murmur of discontent; whereupon the governor, commanding silence, revealed herself to the marvelling crowd as the lost Estela, and, throwing herself in the arms of Don Carlos, asked his pardon for the severe tests she had put him to for the purpose of proving that his affection for her was the same as ever.

The lovers were married without delay, and, as the hero and heroine of a novel ought to be, they were happy ever afterwards, the emperor giving to Don Carlos the governorship of the city in place of Estela, — who preferred to relinquish masculine duties with masculine attire, — and otherwise making the reunited pair the recipients of favors which testified, in a practical manner, his esteem for them.

This is but a feeble and incomplete recital of a very pretty story, and is only entitled to a place in this narrative of my own adventures, because it was so much in my thoughts at the particular period of which I am now writing, and because it inspired me to imitate Estela's example so far as to seek to obtain a confession of love from Captain De Caulp, before I should reveal myself to him. I was filled with an eager desire to hear what he would say of me to his friend, the supposed Lieutenant Buford, and having arranged in my mind what I should say to him when we met, I waited, with ill-disguised impatience, for the time to come when I could put my plan in execution, trying to imagine, all the while, what would be the effect upon him when the whole truth was made known.

It was a weary while waiting, though, for the hour of meeting to come, and, had my physicians permitted it, I would have left my sick-bed to go to Captain De Caulp long before I was really able to be on my feet. Dr. Hammond, however, knew better what was good for me than I knew myself, and he constrained me to remain under his care until he should be able to pronounce me able to care for myself once more; and, as there was no use in resisting his orders, I obeyed them perforce, with what patience I could command.

CHAPTER XXVIII.

AGAIN A WIFE AND AGAIN A WIDOW.

Convalescence. — I pay a Visit to my Lover. — A friendly Feeling. — A Surprise in Store for him. — I ask him about his matrimonial Prospects, and endeavor to ascertain the State of his Affections towards me. — An affecting Scene. — The Captain receives a Letter from his Lady-love. — "She has come! She has come!" — The Captain prepares for a Meeting with his Sweetheart. — A Question of Likeness. — A puzzling Situation. — I reveal my Identity. — Astonishment and Joy of my Lover. — Preparations for our Wedding. — A very quiet Affair proposed. — The Wedding. — A short Honeymoon. — Departure of my Husband for the Front. — My Apprehensions for his Health. — My Apprehensions justified in the News of his Death in a Federal Hospital in Chattanooga. — Once more a Widow.

FTER a weary waiting, which I thought would never end, both Captain De Caulp and myself were convalescent. At the earliest moment that I could obtain permission to leave my ward I went to see him, being naturally more impatient for a meeting than he was; for, although we had exchanged greetings through our physicians, it was simply as friends and officers of the Confederate army, and not as lovers, and he had no suspicion whatever that his sick neighbor of the hospital was other than the young lieutenant whose acquaintance he had formed at Pensacola, and who had fought beside him at Shiloh.

He was extremely glad to see me, however, much more so than I expected he would be; but the fact was, it had been so long since he had had a chance to chat with any of his old friends, that it was a genuine pleasure to him to have any one call on him for the sake of a lively talk over old times. I found him sadly reduced and worn by the severe illness through which he had just passed; but, although he was weak, he was evidently improving, and in a fair way for a rapid recovery.

When I came in and stood by his bedside, he smiled, and held out his hand, and said, " I am mighty glad to see you again, lieutenant. It is like meeting a brother."

A DELICATE SUBJECT.

I said that I was rejoiced to meet him again, and would have called on him much sooner had the doctors permitted it. I then asked him how he was coming on, about the nature of his sickness, and matters of that kind, and gradually drifted into a conversation about things in general,— the progress of the war, the people we knew, matters at home, — and so led him up to the subject about which I particularly desired to speak with him. After some little preliminary talk, which would enable me to bring the question in naturally, without exciting suspicion that I had any but a merely friendly interest in the matter, I said, "Captain, are you married yet? You know you told me some time ago you were engaged, and were expecting very shortly to ask the lady to name the day."

" No," said he, " the wedding has not come off yet, but I hope it will very shortly. I should have gone home for the purpose of getting married if I had kept my health, but this spell of sickness has knocked all my plans in the head."

" Does the lady know that you are sick?" I asked. " Have you heard from her recently ?"

" I doubt whether she does," he replied. " I have been expecting to hear from her for some time, and have been greatly disappointed that I· have not. The last letter I had stated that she would meet me here ; but for several months I have been unable to communicate with her, and am unable to even guess where she is, or why she has not come to me."

He then raised up, and took the letter he referred to out of a package, evidently made up of my epistles, and read it to me. He also showed me a picture of myself, which he produced from some hiding-place in his pocket, and handed it to me, saying, " That is the woman I love ; what do you think of her ? "

A PORTRAIT AND ITS ORIGINAL.

This was almost too much for me ; and all trembling with emotion, I handed it back to him, saying, " She is a fine-looking woman ;" and wondering he did not observe the resemblance between the portrait and the original before him.

"Yes," said he, "and she is just as good as she is good-looking. I think the world of her, and want to see her again — O, so bad!"

"Have you known her long, captain?" I asked, with a trembling voice, and scarcely daring to trust myself to speak, for these words, and the tender tone in which they were spoken, made my heart leap with joy, and brought tears to my eyes. I was afraid that he would notice my agitation, and in some way surmise the cause of it; and I did not want him to do this, for I was not yet ready to reveal myself, but desired further to hear what he would say about me before I told him my secret. So I turned away, and pretended to be attracted by some object in another part of the room while I wiped the tears from my eyes, and attempted to recover my composure before I confronted him again.

" Yes," he went on, " I have known her for a long time. She is a widow, and her husband was an excellent friend of mine." Then, apparently suddenly recollecting the circumstances under which he first made my acquaintance in the character of a Confederate officer, he said, glancing quickly and eagerly at me, " Why, you ought to know her; her husband was the first captain of our company ; you recollect him, surely."

" O," said I, as if rather surprised at this revelation, " she is his widow, is she ?"

" Yes," said Captain De Caulp; " you have met her, have you not?"

I could scarcely help smiling at the turn this conversation was taking; and still wondering whether my lover would be shrewd enough to detect the likeness between the picture he was holding in his hand, and fondly gazing at, and the original of it who was sitting by his bedside, I said, " Yes, I have had a slight acquaintance with her, but you, probably, have known her longer than I have. When did you see her last?"

" I have not seen her for three years," he replied.

" Have you been engaged to her that long?"

" O, no; I did not become engaged to her until about six months after the death of her husband. He was killed, as you know, at Pensacola, just after the war commenced, by the bursting of a carbine."

" Well, if you have not seen her all that time, how have you managed to do your courting?"

" O, that was easy enough. After her husband's death, we had some correspondence about the settlement of his affairs, and we kept on writing to each other after these were arranged. I always had a great liking for her, as I thought that she was a first-rate woman, of the kind that you don't meet every day; and, consequently, after about six months, I asked her to marry me. She was a sound, sensible, patriotic woman, who admired me for going to the front more than she would have done had I remained at home to court her, and she accepted me without hesitation."

THE PLEASURES OF COURTSHIP.

" I understand the situation now, and I hope you have secured a prize. It seems to me, however, that it would be pleasant for both parties if you could do a little courting in person before you get married; and if I were you, I would try and go to her."

" I intend to go to her just as soon as I have health and strength to travel, for I feel that I must see her."

" Yes," said I, " you ought to go for your own sake as well as for that of the lady. You have done enough hard fighting for the present, and you are entitled to take a rest."

" I don't intend to leave the army permanently unless I am obliged to; but, as you say, I need a rest, and I am determined that I will go home and get married if it costs me my commission. I am now improving rapidly, and I trust that God will restore me to perfect health soon."

" What would you give," — and my voice was so choked with emotion that I could scarcely utter these words, — " What would you give if you could see your lady now? "

" O," said he, — and his eye sparkled, and the color flushed into his cheeks as he spoke, — " I would almost give my existence in heaven."

I could not bear to hear any more; but dreading lest he should notice my agitation, and inquire the cause of it, I made a hasty excuse for concluding the interview, and saying goodby, left the room so abruptly that he must have seen there was something the matter with me.

It would be foolish in me, in attempting to tell this story of the culmination of my strange courtship, to make a secret of the emotions that filled my breast at the results of this interview with Captain De Caulp. I felt that I loved him

more than ever, and that he was more than worthy of me. I
wept the first genuine womanly tears I had shed for many a
day, but they were tears of joy, — of joy at the thought that
I had such a lover as this, and that the day of our union was
certainly not far distant.

The next morning I wrote him a note in my proper person,
stating that I had arrived, and was coming to see him. On
the receipt of this he was nearly wild with excitement, and it
was as much as Dr. Benton could do to keep him in his bed.
Burning with anxiety to see what the effect upon him of the
letter would be, I followed hard after the bearer, and waiting
until he would have a fair opportunity to master its contents,
I passed by the door in such a manner that he could not fail
to see me. So soon as he caught sight of me, he called out, in
an exultant tone, " Lieutenant, come in. I want to talk to
you;" and holding out the note, which I had written but a few
moments before, towards me, he said, with the happiest smile
I ever saw on a human face, " She has come, — she has come,
and will be here soon ; congratulate me, my friend."

An agitating Occasion.

I was greatly agitated, not only at the sight of his extreme
happiness, but because I felt that the dreaded hour was now
come when I must reveal my secret to him. I loved him most
fondly ; and it was but yesterday that I had heard from his
own lips assurances of his affection for me, the verity of which
it was impossible for me to doubt; and yet I dreaded whether
his feelings towards me might not change when he heard my
story. I felt that they ought not, and I did not believe that
they would; but I had heard so many men, and good men too,
speak harshly with regard to women undertaking to play
the *rôle* that I had, that my very love gave encouragement to
my fears lest Captain De Caulp—when he learned I had been
in the army ever since the outbreak of the war, and from
before the date of our engagement, disguised as a man —
would regard my course with such disapproval that he would
refuse to consider the motives which induced me to adopt
the course I had taken.

The situation was, for me, painful beyond expression; and
although I felt that the secret must now be told, I scarcely
knew how to tell it, or how to begin an even ordinary friendly
conversation with him. The disclosure which I was about to

make was, moreover, one that was meant for no other ears than his, and was certainly not a proper one for the public ward of the hospital. My first care, therefore, was to get him to a place where we could converse without being overheard, and so I said, " Captain, I congratulate you heartily, and I hope to have the pleasure of meeting with your lady. As you expect to have a visit from her soon, and as you will doubtless want to talk over a great number of confidential matters, don't you think that it would be better if the doctor were to move you into a private room ? "

He said, " Yes ; thank you for the suggestion ; that is just what I would like. I wish you would tell the doctor I want to see him."

I accordingly conveyed his message with all possible despatch, and the doctor very cheerfully granted his request, and had him taken to a private chamber. A barber was then sent for, and he was shaved, and made to look as nicely as possible ; and it touched me deeply to notice what pains he took to make himself presentable, in view of the expected arrival of his lady-love, whom, by the anxious manner in which he glanced at the door, he was evidently looking for every minute, and almost dreading her arrival before he was ready to receive her.

A REVELATION TO BE MADE.

So soon as we were alone together, I said gravely, " Now, captain, I have something of great importance to say to you before your sweetheart comes."

He looked at me wonderingly, evidently impressed by my manner, and apparently half fearing that something had occurred to defeat his expectations.

I then knelt by the bedside, and taking from my pocket a picture of himself that he had sent me, and his last letter, said, " Did you ever see these before ? "

He glanced at them, recognized them, and turned deadly pale. His hand trembled so that he could scarcely hold the picture and the letter, and looking at me with a scared expression, he gasped, " Yes, they are mine ! Where did you get them ? Has anything happened ?

" No, no, captain," I exclaimed. " You must not be frightened ; nothing has happened that will be displeasing to you."

"But I don't understand," he said; "how did you get these?"

"Ah!" I said, "that is my secret just now. You know you told me last night, when you showed me the portrait of your lady, that you had not seen her for three years; are you so very sure of that?"

He still failed to comprehend what I meant, and stared at me in astonishment. I, therefore, went to his pocket, and got the picture, and, placing it in his hand, said, "Now take a good look at that, and tell me if you have not seen somebody very much like it inside of three years."

He looked at the picture, and then at me, with a most puzzled expression, unable to say anything, until I, oppressed with his silence, and unable to endure longer a scene that was becoming most painful to both of us, said, "Well, captain, don't you think that the picture of your lady-love looks the least bit like your friend Harry Buford?"

RECOGNITION.

A light seemed to suddenly break upon him; he gasped for breath, and sank back overcome on his pillow, the great drops of perspiration standing out all over his forehead. Then, raising himself, he looked me hard in the face, and, grasping my hand tightly, exclaimed, "Can it be possible that you are she?"

"Yes," said I, clasping his hand still tighter, "I am, indeed, your own Loreta. It was your sweetheart who fought by your side at the great battle of Shiloh; and not only on that occasion, but ever since the outbreak of the war she has been doing a soldier's work for the cause of the Confederacy. Can you love her a little for that as well as for herself? or will you despise her because she was not willing to stay at home like other women, but undertook to appear on the battle-field in the guise of a man for the purpose of doing a man's duty?"

"I love you ten times more than ever for this, Loreta!" he said, with a vehemence that brought tears of joy to my eyes.

I then went into a long explanation of my reasons for acting as I had done, and gave him an outline of my adventures, reserving the details for a future time when he would be stronger and less agitated. He suggested that I should not reveal the

secret to any one else just at present; whereupon I proposed that we should continue as we were until the war was over, I to make such arrangements, however, as would enable me to be near him. He would not listen to anything of this kind, but said, " No, my noble lady, I can never permit that; I cannot consent to part from you again until I have called you by the endearing name of wife." He then burst into tears, and, leaning his face on my shoulder, said, between his sobs, " O, Loreta, can it be possible that you have been so far from me, and yet so near to me, all this time ? "

This interview had agitated both of us greatly, and, as Captain De Caulp was still very weak, I was somewhat fearful of the consequences to him; so I tore myself away, after promising to see him again soon, and requesting him to compose himself, and not let his excitement retard his recovery.

The crisis was past for me, and all was well. I had the strongest assurances that a woman could have of the undivided love of as noble a man as ever breathed; and to say that I was supremely happy, but faintly expresses what I felt as I left the chamber of Captain De Caulp. It all seemed like a dream to me, but it was a happy one, and I desired never to awaken from it. I was of too practical and decided a disposition, however, to give way to mere sentiment on such an occasion as this; and the fact that my lover was still confined to a sick-bed rendered it the more important that I should be about, and making such preparations as were necessary for our approaching marriage.

I felt quite strong enough to leave the hospital, and told Dr. Hay so. He was a little dubious about it; but finally consented that I should go out on condition that I would take good care of myself, and not attempt to enjoy out-of-door life too much of a sudden. As he was himself about going out as I was prepared to leave the hospital, I walked down the street with him, holding his arm. As we were sauntering along, I asked him, " Doctor, how do you like Captain De Caulp ? "

" O, very much, indeed ! " said he. " He is a perfect gentleman in every respect, and a man of very polished manners and superior talents. He is of foreign extraction, I think."

" Yes," said I, " I believe he is. I have known him for five years, and I think a great deal of him. I was with him at the battle of Shiloh, and he behaved like a true hero."

"Ah, indeed!" said the doctor; "I knew that you were acquainted, but I did not know that you had served together during the war."

"Do you think he will soon be well?" I inquired. "He seems to be getting along quite nicely."

"O, yes, if he takes proper care of himself. He has had a pretty hard time of it, but I don't see any reason why he should not be in a fair way for recovery now, provided nothing occurs to set him back. He will have to look out, and not expose himself too much, however, for a while yet."

At the corner of White Hall Street I left the doctor to go to the depot. He said, as I parted from him, "You must be careful, and not exercise too much, lieutenant, or you will suffer for it. You are scarcely fairly on your feet as yet."

I promised to take care of myself, and went to the depot, arriving there just as the down train was coming in. I met a number of persons with whom I was acquainted, and after some conversation with them, took a turn as far as General Wash. Lee's office, where I had a chat about the way things were going at the front. I then returned to the hospital, and asked for my discharge. This was granted me, and I also obtained a ticket to go to Montgomery, where I had some business to attend to.

On my arrival at Montgomery, I found that the person I wanted to see was at Camp Watts. I accordingly went there; and having seen him, arranged the business I had made the trip for, and then returned to Montgomery, where I remained all night. The next day I returned to Atlanta, and went immediately to the hospital to visit Captain De Caulp. To my great joy I found him out of bed, and so much improved that he was confident of being well enough to walk out.

We, therefore, went down to the Thompson House together, and I engaged a room, and set about making preparations for my marriage.

I was anxious that the affair should pass off as quietly as possible, and particularly desired not to give any opportunity for unseemly gossip or talk; and on discussing the matter with Captain De Caulp, we came to the conclusion that it would be better to tell the whole story to Drs. Benton and Hammond, and to ask them to witness the ceremony, under a promise to say nothing to any one about the fact of my having worn the uniform of a Confederate officer. We, however, resolved to take no one else into our confidence, although there were several good friends of both of us in the town, whom we would have been glad to have had at our wedding.

I procured a sufficiency of woman's apparel for my wedding outfit, by purchasing at a variety of places, under the pleas that I wanted the garments for some persons out of town, or for presents to the girls at the hotel — in fact, making up whatever story I thought would answer my purpose. My *trousseau* was, perhaps, not so complete or so elegant as it might have been under some circumstances, or as I could have desired; but then, the particular circumstances under which the wedding was to take place were peculiar, and neither the bridegroom nor the bride was disposed to be over ceremonious, or to make much ado about trifles. So long as the captain and myself were satisfied, it did not much matter whether any one else was pleased or not; and we both concluded that a very modest wardrobe would be all that I would need, the main thing being that I should be dressed as a woman when the ceremony took place, for fear of creating too much of a sensation, and, perhaps, of making the clergyman feel unpleasant should I appear before him, hanging on the captain's arm, in my uniform.

My arrangements having all been made, we concluded to inform the friends whom we had agreed to invite; and accordingly we walked to the hospital together, when the captain called Dr. Benton into his private room, and astonished him by telling him that he was going to be married, and by asking him to attend the wedding. I broke the news as gently as I could to Dr. Hammond, who scarcely knew what to make of it at first, but who, when I made him clearly understand the situation, gave me his hearty congratulations, and promised to be present when the happy event came off.

A WEDDING.

The next day Captain De Caulp and I were married in the parlor of the hotel by the Rev. Mr. Pinkington, the post chaplain, in as quiet and unpretentious a way as either of us could desire. The clergyman and our kind friends wished us all manner of happiness; and we both looked forward to a bright future, when, after the war was over, we could settle down in our home, and enjoy the blessings of peace in each other's society. Alas! if wishes could only make us happy, there would be but little misery in this world of ours. Neither Captain De Caulp nor myself, as we stood up that day, and pronounced the words that made us man and wife, had any but pleasant anticipations for the future, and little imagined how brief a time we would be permitted to be together.

I was very desirous of resuming my uniform, and of accompanying my husband to the field. I wanted to go through the war with him, and to fight by his side, just as I had done at Shiloh. He, however, was bitterly opposed to this; and, with my ample knowledge of army life, I could not but admit the full force of his objections. He contended, that, apart from everything else, I had served my country long enough as a soldier, and that I was under some obligation now to think of him as well as of myself, and no longer to peril life, health, and reputation by exposing myself, as I had been doing. He said that he would fight twice as hard as before, and that would answer for both of us, although he was not sure but that what I had done ought to count in his favor, — as man and wife were one, — and procure him a release from further service.

I very reluctantly yielded an assent to his wishes, although, if I could have looked a little into the future, I either would have prevented his going to the front at all, or else would have insisted upon going with him. Indeed, he ought not to have gone when he did; but he knew that the services of every man were needed, and so soon as he was at all able to be on duty, he felt as if he was shirking his share of the work by remaining at the rear when so much hard fighting was going on.

Our honeymoon was a very brief one. In about a week he thought himself well enough to report for duty; and he insisted upon going, notwithstanding my entreaties for him to remain until his health was more robust. Had he been really fit to endure the exposure and toil of campaigning, I would never have offered to stay him by a word; for my patriotism, although perhaps not of so fiery a nature, was as intense now as it was when I besought my first husband to permit me to accompany him to the field; and I considered it the duty of every man, who was at all able to take a hand in the great work of resisting the advance of the enemy, to do so. But Captain De Caulp, I knew, was far from being the strong man he once was,

ALBERT SIDNEY JOHNSON.

W. J. HARDEE.

BRAXTON BRAGG.

BENJAMIN F. CHEATHAM.

and I feared the consequences should he persist in carrying out his resolve.

He did persist, however, in spite of all I could say; and so, when I found that further argument would be useless, I prepared his baggage, and bade him a sorrowful adieu. Alas! the adieu was a final one, for I never saw him afterwards; and within three short weeks of my marriage, I was a widow again!

Death of my Husband.

Before reaching his command, Captain De Caulp was taken sick again; and before I obtained any information of his condition, he had died in a Federal hospital in Chattanooga. This was a terrible blow to me, for I tenderly loved my husband, and was greatly beloved by him. Our short married life was a very happy one, and its sudden ending brought to nought all the pleasant plans I had formed for the future, and left me nothing to do but to launch once more on a life of adventure, and to devote my energies to the advancement of the Confederate cause.

Captain De Caulp was a native of Edinburgh, Scotland. His father was of French descent, and his mother was a Derbyshire woman. He was very highly educated, having studied in England and France with the intention of becoming a physician. His fondness for roaming, however, induced him to abandon this design; and in 1857 he and his brother came to this country, and travelled over the greater part of it until 1859. In the last-named year he joined the United States army, but on the breaking out of the war, he came South, and offered his services to the Confederacy. From first to last he fought nobly for the cause which he espoused, and he died in the firm belief that the Southern States would ultimately gain their independence.

Few more honorable, or truer, or braver, men than Captain De Caulp have ever lived. He was tall in stature, with a very imposing presence. His hair was auburn, and he had a large, full, dark, hazel eye. He was a very powerful man, but as gentle as a child, and exceedingly affable in his disposition, and remarkably prepossessing in his manners. At the time of his death he was about twenty-nine years of age. I made an endeavor to procure his body for the purpose of sending it to his relatives in Scotland, in accordance with his last request; but, owing to the exigencies of the military situation, — the

22

Federals being in possession of Chattanooga, — I was unable to do so.

Captain De Caulp's brother was also in the Southern army, and also held the rank of captain. He died in Nashville just after the close of the war, leaving a wife, who died in New York.

CHAPTER XXIX.

IN THE CONFEDERATE SECRET SERVICE..

Altered Circumstances. — The Result of two Years and a half Experience in Warfare. — The Difference between the Emotions of a raw Recruit and a Veteran. — Difficulties in the Way of deciding what Course it was best to pursue for the Future. — I resolve to go to Richmond in Search of active Employment of some Kind. — The military Situation in the Autumn of 1863. — Concentration of the Armies at Richmond and Chattanooga. — Richmond safe from Capture. — The Results of the Battle of Chickamauga. — Rosecrans penned up in Chattanooga by Bragg. — The Pinch of the Fight approaching. — Hopes of foreign Intervention. — An apparently encouraging Condition of Affairs. — I go to Richmond, and have Interviews with President Davis and General Winder. — I am furnished by the latter with a Letter of Recommendation, and start on a grand Tour through the Confederacy. — Arrival at Mobile, and meeting with old Army Friends.

HEN, under the influence of the grief caused by the sudden death of my second husband, within so brief a period after our marriage, I felt impelled to devote myself anew to the task of advancing the cause of the Confederacy by all the means in my power, the circumstances were all materially different from what they were when, the first time I was made a widow, I started for Virginia, full of the idea of taking part in whatever fighting was to be done. It was no longer possible for me to figure as successfully in the character of a soldier as I had done. My secret was now known to a great many persons, and its discovery had already caused me such annoyance that I hesitated about assuming my uniform again, especially as I believed that, as a woman, I could perform very efficient service if I were only afforded proper opportunity.

At the time of my first husband's death, I was full of an idea which had filled my brain ever since I could remember, and

339

was bent upon accomplishing it at all hazards. I had attired myself in the uniform of an officer, had enlisted a large body of men by my own unaided exertions, had marched them from Arkansas to Pensacola, and was firmly resolved to see some fighting, and to win some military glory, if any was to be won. My desire was that my husband should command the battalion I had raised, and should permit me to serve with him. His death, however, frustrated my plans, and threw me on my own resources. I was then inspired, not only with a desire to win personal distinction, but to avenge him; and I started for the front with the vaguest possible idea concerning what warfare really was, or what I was to do. My main thought, however, was to see a battle, and to take part in one. I had been reading all my life about heroic deeds, and dreaming day and night about the achievement of glory, and was, perhaps, more impressed with the notion of becoming a second Joan of Arc than anything else.

After nearly two years and a half experience of warfare, these early ideas, when I reflected upon the hap-hazard manner in which I had started out, appeared ludicrous enough in some of their aspects, and yet I would have given a great deal could I have been impressed with some of my original enthusiasm, when, a second time a widow, I made up my mind again to take part, in some shape, in the great conflict which was yet far from its close.

The Lessons of Experience.

I had seen enough of fighting, enough of marching, enough of camp life, enough of prisons and hospitals, and I had passed through enough peril and suffering to satisy any reasonable human being. These experiences, however, while they had made me weary of war, would also, I well knew, especially qualify me to perform any work I might undertake in a most satisfactory manner, and would render my services much more valuable than they could have been in the early days of the contest. It was a feverish desire to be in motion, to be doing something, to have occupation for mind and body, such as would prevent me from dwelling on my griefs, more than any ambitious designs or aspirations for personal distinctions, that now impelled me to seek for employment in some shape, under the Confederate government, which would enable me to do something further to advance the interest of the cause to which I had already given myself, heart and soul, during more than two of the best years of my life.

That I did not feel exactly the same enthusiasm now that I did in the spring of 1861, was due, not to any feeling of coldness towards the cause, nor to any lack of disposition to do anything in my power to win the final victory, which I still hoped, in spite of every discouragement, would crown our efforts, but to circumstances which every veteran soldier will appreciate. These circumstances were the more potent in my case from the fact that I was a woman, and in endeavoring to carry out my notions with regard to the best way of making my services of the utmost value, was consequently hampered in many ways that men were not. For having dared to assume a man's garb, for the purpose of doing a man's work, I had been treated with contumely, on more than one occasion, by those who ought at least to have given me credit for my intentions, and although my comrades of the camp and the battle-field — or at least all of them whose good opinion was worth having— esteemed me for what I had done, and for what I tried to do, bestowing ample praise upon me for my valor and efficiency as a soldier, I was getting out of the notion of subjecting myself to the liability of being locked up by every local magistrate within whose jurisdiction I happened to find myself, simply because I did not elect to dress according to his notions of propriety.

A PERPLEXING SITUATION.

I was a little dubious, therefore, with regard to what course it was best for me to pursue, especially as, apart from all other considerations, my health was not so robust as it had been, and my husband's fate was a warning to me not to expose myself as I had been in the habit of doing, at least until I had fully regained my strength. On reviewing the whole subject in my mind, I became more than ever convinced that the secret service rather than the army would afford me the best field for the exercise of my talent, although I almost more than half made up my mind to enter the army again, and try my luck, as I had originally done, disguised as an officer, in case I found it impossible to become attached to the secret service department in the manner I wished.

I finally concluded that the best thing for me to do was to go to Richmond, and if nothing else availed, to make a personal appeal to President Davis, feeling assured that when he heard my story he would appreciate the motives which animated me, and would use his influence to have me assigned to such duty as I was best qualified to perform in a satisfactory manner.   This resolve having once been made, I prepared, without more delay, to visit the capital of the Confederacy, leaving behind me Atlanta, with its mingled memories of pleasure and pain.

The Progress of the War.

The military situation at this time — the autumn of 1863 — was of painful interest, and the fate of the Confederacy seemed to hang trembling in the balance.   In Virginia, General Lee was defending Richmond with all his old success, and was holding one immense army in check so effectively that the prospect of ever entering the Confederate capital as conquerors must have seemed to the enemy more remote than ever.   In the West and South, however, the Confederates had lost much, and the question now with them was, whether they would be able to hold what they had until the Federals were tired out and exhausted, or until England and France, wearied of the prolonged contest, consented to aid in terminating it by recognizing the Confederacy, and perhaps by armed intervention.

It was known that there were dissensions at the North, and that there was a strong anti-war party, which it was expected would, ere long, make its power felt as it had never done before; and if the South could hold out for a season longer, would insist upon a peace being concluded upon almost any terms.   Great expectations were also built upon foreign intervention, which every one felt had been delayed longer than there was any just reason for, but which it was thought could not but take place shortly.   Every little while exciting rumors were set afloat, no one knew how or by whom, that either France or England had recognized the Confederacy, and many bitter disappointments were caused when their falsity was proved.   The people, however, hoped on, getting poorer and poorer every day, and eagerly watching the progress of the campaign around Chattanooga.

The Mississippi River was now entirely in the hands of the Federals, and not only were the trans-Mississippi states, as far as any effective military or political co-operation was concerned, lost to the Confederacy, but the question now was whether the war was not to be transferred from the ground west of the mountains to the rich fields of Georgia. Bragg had been compelled to fall back with most of his forces to Chattanooga, and had been expelled from that place, which was now in the hands of the Federals. All efforts on the part of the Federals to advance beyond Chattanooga, however, had utterly failed, and the opinion, at the time of which I am writing, was gaining ground that they had been caught in a trap, and would, in a short time, be incapable of either advancing or retreating.

While I was in the hospital, Bragg gained his great victory at Chickamauga, and great hopes were excited that he would be able to follow it up with effect, and succeed in destroying the army of Rosecrans. Had he succeeded in doing this, the war would have had a different ending, and the independence of the South would have been secured. It was felt by everybody that the pinch of the fight was approaching, and that in the neighborhood of Chattanooga, rather than in that of Richmond, would the decisive battle of the war be fought, and, it was hoped, won for the Confederacy.

It was at Richmond and at Chattanooga that the contending forces were massed, although there was plenty of fighting going on elsewhere, and some of these minor campaigns were of great importance in their influence on the fortunes of the war, and did much to enable the Confederacy to prolong the contest for nearly eighteen months.

Much as we had lost, the situation was not an altogether discouraging one for the Confederacy. Richmond was apparently more secure than it had been two years and a half before, and nearly all the honors of the war in that vicinity had been carried off by the Confederates. Lee was making himself a name as one of the greatest generals of the age, while the Federals, although they changed the commanders of their army continually, were making no headway against him, and were in constant fear of an invasion of their own territory. In the South, Bragg had just achieved a great victory over Rosecrans, and had him now penned up in Chattanooga, from which it was next to impossible for him to escape in either direction, and to keep him there, and either fight him or starve him into surrendering before sufficient re-enforcement to enable him to assume the offensive, was the task the Confederate army had before it.

Well, matters did not turn out as it was expected they would. Bragg's victory at Chickamauga was a fruitless one, except so far as it delayed the Federal advance from Chattanooga, and the army of Rosecrans was neither starved nor beaten into subjection. On the contrary, Rosecrans was superseded, and Grant was put in his place, to follow up the victories he had won at Fort Donelson, Shiloh, and Vicksburg; and the army was so greatly re-enforced that it was enabled to press forward and menace Atlanta, and finally to capture it. The results of that capture are well known.

OFF FOR RICHMOND AGAIN.

The capture of Atlanta, however, was a long way off when I started for Richmond for the purpose of making a definite offer of my services to the Confederate authorities there, and was apparently as little likely to occur as was that of Richmond. Bad as the condition of things, in many particulars, was, I was in a more hopeful frame of mind than I had been for a long time, and I was anxious to labor, as I felt that I was able to labor, in behalf of the cause.

Had I then known as much as I knew not a great while after, I would not have put myself to the trouble of going to Richmond for the purpose of asking for work, but would at once have executed the project which I had frequently contemplated, and which I had more than once been on the point of carrying into effect, and would have gone directly north, and have put myself in communication with, the friends, sympathizers, and agents of the Confederacy there. This was the true field for me to operate in, although I had no idea, at this time, what opportunities a residence at the North would give me for aiding the cause in a most efficient manner. It was chance rather than design that finally took me within the jurisdiction of the Federal government, and enabled me to do more to baffle its efforts to crush the Confederacy by my operations in the rear of its armies in one year, than I had been able to do in three while endeavoring to fight them face to face.

INTERVIEWS WITH PRESIDENT DAVIS AND GENERAL WINDER.

With only the most indefinite plans for the future, and little suspecting what exciting and perilous adventures fate yet had in store for me, I proceeded, on my arrival in Richmond, to call on General Winder, and took measures to procure an interview with President Davis. From General Winder I did not obtain much satisfaction; and Mr. Davis, while he was very kind to me, did not give me a great deal of encouragement. I represented to President Davis that I had been working hard for the Confederacy, both as a soldier and a spy, and that I had braved death on more than one desperately fought battle-field while acting as an independent, and that now I thought I was deserving of some official recognition. Moreover, I had lost my husband through his devotion to the cause, and, both for his sake and for my own, I desired that the government would give me such a position in the secret service corps or elsewhere as would enable me to carry on with the best effect the work that he and I had begun.

Mr. Davis was opposed to permitting me to serve in the army as an officer, attired in male costume, while he had no duties to which he could properly assign me as a woman. I left his presence, not ungratified by the kindness of his manner towards me, and the sympathy which he expressed for my bereavement, but none the less much disappointed at the non-success of my interview with him.

Failing to obtain any satisfaction from Mr. Davis, I returned to General Winder, but got comparatively little encouragement from him. He finally, however, consented to give me a letter of recommendation to the commanding officer of the forces in the South and West, and transportation. This was not exactly what I wanted, but it was better than nothing; and I thought that, armed with such a letter, I could scarcely fail to accomplish something that would be satisfactory to myself, and of value to the cause.

On another Grand Tour.

Having obtained this important document I started off, and, for the last time, made a grand tour of the entire Southern Confederacy. Stopping from point to point, I gathered all the information I could, and thoroughly posted myself with regard to the situation, — military, civil, and political, — and endeavored to find a place where I could commence active operations with the best chance of achieving something of importance.

I, however, during the course of a long journey, failed to meet with the grand opportunity I sighed for, and met with no adventure worthy of particular record, until finally I reached

Mobile — a city I had not visited since I marched through it in 1861 at the head of my gallant battalion of Arkansas Grays.

On arriving at Mobile, I took up my quarters at the Battle House, with the intention of taking a good rest, for I was weary with much travel, and, if possible, of arranging some definite plan of action for the future. I was resolved now to make a bold stroke of some kind, and on my own responsibility if necessary, trusting that my usual good luck would accompany me in any enterprise I might undertake.

In Mobile I met quite a number of officers whom I had met on the various battle-fields where I had figured, and received the kindest and best attentions from them all. This was most gratifying to me; and the flattering commendations that were bestowed upon me served to mitigate in a great degree the disappointment I felt on account of the non-recognition of the value of my services in other quarters.

I may as well say here, that in mentioning the disappointments I have felt at different times at not being able to obtain exactly the kind of official recognition I desired, I do not wish to appear as complaining. That I did feel disappointed, is true; but reflection told me that if any one was to blame it was myself. By entering the army as an independent, I secured a freedom of action and opportunities for participating in a great variety of adventures that I otherwise would not have had, but I also cut myself off from opportunities of regular promotion. When I resolved to start out as an independent, I was animated by a variety of motives, not the least of which was, that I believed I would be able to maintain my disguise to better advantage, and would have better opportunities for escaping any unpleasant consequences in case of detection than if I attached myself regularly to a command. I was right in this, and am now convinced that, on the whole, the course I pursued was the wisest one.

Not having been attached to a regular command, at least for any great length of time, it was impossible for me, however, to secure that standing with those who were best able to reward my services that was necessary, while the full value of my services could only be made known by my taking a number of people into my confidence, and this I had great objections to doing. As matters turned out, the peculiar experiences through which I passed, during the first two years of the war, were of the utmost value to me in a great many ways in the prosecution of the very important work in which I subsequently engaged; and I consequently had no cause for regret at having followed the line of action I did. At the time of which I am writing, however, I could not know what the future would bring forth; and although, without being aware of it, I was about to enter upon a series of enterprises of great moment, all my plans seemed to have gone amiss, and I certainly was not in the most pleasant state of mind imaginable.

In writing this narrative, it has seemed to me that the only proper method is to represent events as they actually occurred, and to record the impressions they made upon me at the time of occurrence, and not as they were colored by subsequent developments. My ideas and feelings under particular circumstances are as much a part of my story as the narrative of actual events, for my proceedings were guided and influenced by them; and this would scarcely be a fair record of my career while in the Confederate service did I not make some mention of them.

CHAPTER XXX.

ON DUTY AS A SPY.

I receive a mysterious Note requesting me to meet the Writer. — I go to the appointed Place, and find an Officer of the Secret Service Corps who wants me to go through the Lines with Despatches. — I accept the Commission, and the next Day go to Meridian for the Purpose of completing my Arrangement and receiving my Instructions. — A Visit to General Ferguson's Headquarters. — Final Instructions from the General, who presents me with a Pistol. — I start for the Federal Lines, and ride all Night and all the next Day. — A rough and toilsome Journey. — I spend the Night in a Negro's Cabin. — Off again at three o'clock in the Morning with an old Negro Man for a Guide. — We reach the Neighborhood of the Federal Pickets, and I send my Guide back. — I bury my Pistol in a Church. — I am halted by a Picket-guard and am taken to Moscow. — A Cross-examination by the Colonel in Command. — Satisfactory Result for myself. — On the Train for Memphis. — Insulting Remarks from the Soldiers. — A Major interferes for my Protection. — Off for General Washburn's Headquarters.

SHORTLY after my arrival at Mobile, I received a rather mysterious note in a masculine hand, asking me to meet the writer that evening at the corner of the square, but giving no hint whatever of the purpose of the invitation. I hesitated for some little time about taking any notice of the request, thinking that if the writer had any real business with me, he would seek me out and communicate with me in a some less mysterious way. On a little reflection, however, I concluded that it would be best for me to meet the gentleman, whoever he might be, according to the terms of his invitation, and to find out who he was and what he wanted. I felt tolerably well able to take care of myself, although I was aware that the circumstances of my army career being rather extensively known, I was especially liable to annoyances of a peculiarly unpleasant kind from impertinent people. Anything of this sort I was resolved to resent in such a manner that

348

the offender would have occasion to beware of me in the future.

The fact, however, that I was travelling under credentials from General Winder, and was in a manner an attaché of the Secret Service Department, rendered it not improbable that this was an application for me to undertake some such enterprise as I for a long time had been ardently desirous of engaging in. The more I considered the matter, the more I was disposed to take this view of it, and accordingly, at the hour named, I was promptly at the rendezvous, wondering what the result of the adventure would be.

A Mysterious Conference.

My surmise proved to be correct. I had scarcely arrived at the corner of the square, when my correspondent, who I discovered was Lieutenant Shorter, of Arkansas, advanced towards me, and said, " Good evening. I am glad to see you. How have you been?"

" I am quite well," I replied; and waited for him to introduce the subject concerning which he was evidently desirous of conversing with me.

After a few inconsequential remarks on either side, he said, " I see that you received my note."

" Yes."

" Well, you must excuse me for asking for a secret interview like this, but the matter I wanted to talk to you about is of great importance, and, as in these times, we don't know whom to trust, it was necessary that I should have an opportunity to carry on our conversation without danger of being watched or overheard. You have had considerable experience in running through the lines, and in spy and secret service duty, have you not?"

" Yes," I replied ; " I have done something in that line."

" You have usually been tolerably lucky, haven't you?"

" Yes, I have had reasonably good luck. I got caught once in New Orleans, but that was because the parties to whom I had delivered my despatches were captured. Butler tried his hand at frightening me, but he did not succeed very well, and I managed to slip away from him before he had any positive evidence against me which would have justified him in treating me as a spy."

" Well, you're just the kind I want, for I have a job on hand that will require both skill and nerve, and I would like you to undertake it, especially as you seem to háve a talent for disguising yourself."

I concluded that I would find out exactly what he wanted me to do, before I gave him any satisfaction; so I said, "What kind of a job is it? I have risked my neck pretty often without getting very many thanks for it, and I don't know that I care a great deal about running all kinds of risks for little glory, and no more substantial reward."

"O, come, now," said he, "you must not talk that way. Now is the very time that your services will be worth something; and this bit of business that I am anxious for you to undertake, is of such a nature, that it would not do to give it to any but a first-rate hand."

"Well, what is it? When I know what you want me to do, I will be better able to say whether it would be worth my while to do it."

"Wouldn't you like to take a trip through the lines?" said the lieutenant.

"That depends," said I. "What do you want me to make the trip for?"

"I will tell you that, when you tell me whether you will go."

I considered a moment, and then said, "Yes, I will go, if it is for anything to serve the cause."

"That's the way to talk," said he. "I am in the secret service, and I want you to take a despatch through the lines and give it to a certain party. It will be a big thing if you succeed, as I think you will, or I wouldn't have picked you out for the business."

"Well," said I, "I will make an effort, and do my best to succeed."

"O, you must succeed," said the lieutenant; "for there will be the devil to pay if the Feds discover what you are up to, and you will have to do your prettiest to prevent them from even suspecting that you are up to any unlawful tricks."

"I'll do my best, and I can't do any more than that; but as I have fooled them before, so I guess I can again."

"Well," said he, "that's all right. Now, what I want you to do is, to meet me to-morrow evening at Meridian. I will have everything ready for you, and will give you your instructions, and you be prepared for a hard journey. In the mean time, keep quiet, and don't whisper a word to anybody."

We then said good night and parted, I going back to the hotel to do a heap of thinking before I went to sleep. Lieutenant Shorter, beyond saying that I was to go through the lines, and endeavoring to impress upon me the great importance of the enterprise, had given me no hint of where I was to go, or what the exact nature of my errand would be, and I consequently had to depend upon myself in making such preparations as were necessary. Having considered the subject as well as I was able, I concluded to procure a very plain suit of woman's clothing, and to make up a small bundle of such few extra articles besides those upon my back, as I thought I would require. My arrangements having been all made, I started for Meridian the next day, and on my arrival at that place found Lieutenant Shorter waiting for me at the depot. Under his escort I went to the hotel kept by a Mr. Jones, and was received with great cordiality by him and by his wife. The lady especially was most attentive to me, and did everything in her power to make me comfortable.

I appreciated her kind attentions the more highly as I was far from being well, and felt that I was scarcely doing either myself or the others interested justice in undertaking such an enterprise, under a strong liability that I might be taken seriously sick before concluding it. I had a great deal of confidence, however, in my power of will, and having promised Lieutenant Shorter that I would go, I was determined to do so, especially as he represented the business as being most urgent.

What I was to do.

Having obtained a room where we could converse privately, the lieutenant proceeded to explain what he wanted me to do, and to give me directions for proceeding. He said that he had captured a spy belonging to the Federal General Hurlbut's command, and had taken from him a paper containing quite accurate accounts of the forces of Chalmers, Forrest, Richardson, and Ferguson, and their movements. This he had changed so that it would throw the enemy on the wrong scent, and I was to take it to Memphis and deliver it to the Federal General Washburn, telling him such a story as would induce him to believe that I had obtained it from the spy. He also had a despatch for Forrest, which he wanted me to carry to the Confederate secret agent in Memphis, telling me where to find him, describing him so that I would know him,

and giving me the password which would enable me to communicate with him without difficulty.

" Now," said Shorter, when he had finished all his explanations, " you see that you will have to keep your wits about
you, for if you let the Feds get their fingers on these papers
it will be all up with you. When you reach Memphis, deliver
this bogus account of the movement of our troops to General
Washburn immediately, and get him and his people well
impressed with the idea that you are on their side ; then, at
the earliest possible moment, give this despatch for Forrest
to our agent. I will know by the success of the movement
that Forrest is to make whether you are successful or not."

After some further conversation about the best plan of
proceeding, and further explanations about what I should do,
Lieutenant Shorter suggested some changes in my dress, his
idea being, that I should personate a poor countrywoman,
who had lost her husband at the outbreak of the war, and who
was flying into the Federal lines for protection. He also gave
me letters to the different Confederate commanders whom I
would meet on my road, directing them to assist me, and put
in my hand the sum of one hundred and thirty-six dollars in
greenbacks which had been taken from the captured spy.
This, he thought, would see me through, but in case it should
not prove sufficient, he said, that if I made my wants known,
any commanding officer I met would supply me with funds,
and that after I reached Memphis I would find plenty of
friends of the Confederacy upon whom I could call for
assistance.

Everything being in readiness for my journey, the next
morning I took the train for Okolona, where, procuring a pass
from Captain Mariotta, the provost marshal, I hired a conveyance, and drove to the headquarters of General Ferguson.
On showing my order for assistance to the general, he received
me with the greatest politeness, and invited me into his
quarters, where he gave me some information and additional
instructions, and reiterated Lieutenant Shorter's cautions to
be vigilant and careful, as I was on a mission of great
importance.

The general then handed me ninety dollars, and presented
me with a pistol, which he said was one of a pair he had
carried through the war. The money he was sure I would
need, and the pistol might be a handy thing to have in case I
should be compelled to defend myself, for my journey would

take me through a rough country, and I might chance to meet with stragglers who would give me trouble. He advised me, however, not to use the weapon except in case of absolute necessity, and especially not to carry it with me into the Federal lines, for if it was discovered that I had it about me, it might excite suspicions that I was a spy, when such a thing would not otherwise be thought of.

A fine horse having been provided for me, I said adieu to General Ferguson, who wished me good luck, and started off with an escort who was to conduct me to a point somewhere to the north-east of Holly Springs, from whence I would have to make my way alone, getting into the Federal lines as best I could.

A ROUGH JOURNEY.

In spite of the fact that I was quite sick, and sometimes felt that I could scarcely sit upon my horse, I rode all that night and nearly all the next day, through lonesome woods, past desolate clearings, — occupied, if at all, by poor negroes, or even poorer whites, all of whom had a half-terrified look, as if they were expecting every moment to have a rapacious soldiery come tramping through their little patches of ground, and appropriating whatever was eatable or worth taking, — through gullies and ravines, and over the roughest kind of roads, or sometimes no roads at all. At length we reached a negro's cabin, which, although it was but a poor shelter, was better than nothing at all, and feeling too ill to proceed any farther without rest and refreshments, I resolved to stop there all night.

The inhabitants of the cabin were not very much inclined to be over communicative, and apparently did not want me for a lodger, and their abode was not one that I would have cared to make a prolonged sojourn in. I was too much of a veteran campaigner, however, to be over fastidious about my accommodations for a single night, and was too sick not to find any shelter welcome. From what I could learn from these people, I was not very many miles from the Federal lines, and I secured their good will, to a reasonable degree, by promising to pay well for my night's lodging, and what was given me to eat, and finally succeeded in inducing them to bestir themselves to make me as comfortable as circumstances would permit. I also struck up a bargain with an old man who appeared to be the head of the household, such as it,

23

was, to act as a guide for me in the morning, and to conduct me to the neighborhood of the Federal pickets.

I wished my escort now to return to General Ferguson's headquarters, but, as he suggested that the negroes might prove treacherous, we both concluded that it would be best for him to remain until I was fairly started in the morning on my way to the Federal lines. A supper which, under some circumstances I would scarcely have found eatable, was prepared for us, and I partook of it with a certain degree of relish, despite the coarse quality of the food, being too tired and hungry to be critical or squeamish. Then, completely used up by my long and toilsome ride, I retired to the miserable bed that was assigned me, and ere long was in happy obliviousness of the cares and trials of this world.

About three o'clock in the morning I was up and ready to start, after having made a hasty toilet, and after a breakfast which served to satisfy my hunger, but which certainly did not tempt my palate. My escort now bade me good-by, and was soon out of sight, on his way back to camp, while I, mounted on a little pony, and with the old negro to lead the way, faced in the opposite direction.

Through woods, over fields, along rough country roads, and often along mere pathways that could not be called roads at all, making short cuts wherever we saw a chance to do so, often dubious as to exactly where we were, and dreading lest we should come suddenly upon some picket-station, and thus lose a chance of making a proper diplomatic approach, the negro and I pursued our way for several hours during the damp and dismal gray morning twilight.

APPROACHING THE FEDERAL LINES.

Not having the most implicit confidence in my guide, I took care to keep him in front of me all the time, and had my hand constantly upon the pistol which General Ferguson had given me, and which I was resolved to use upon my colored companion in case he should be inclined to act treacherously. Fortunately there was no occasion for any violence, and our journey continued without interruption, except such as was caused by the rough nature of the ground, until, at length, I spied through the trees a little church. It was now broad daylight, although the sun was not yet up, and the surroundings of this building, as it was seen through the fog-laden

ENTERING THE FEDERAL LINES.

atmosphere, were dismal enough. I surmised, from what my
guide had told me before we started out, that the Federal
pickets must be somewhere near, and I concluded that it was
time for me to get rid of the darkey; so I said to him, " Isn't
that the church where you said you saw the Yankee
soldiers ? "

" Yes, miss, dat's de place; dey's jes' beyond dat church a
bit, or dey was las' week."

" Well, I want to find them; but I guess, if you don't want
them to catch you, you'd better get back as quick as you can."

" O Lord, miss, I doesn't want dem to catch me, sure."

" Well, then, you will have to travel off as fast as you are
able; if you don't, they will have you, and will run you off,
and give you to the abolitionists."

I said this in a very severe way, and it evidently made an
impression on the darkey, who probably thought the abolitionists were cannibals, who would proceed to use him as a substitute for beef. He opened his eyes as big as saucers, and
his teeth chattered so that he could scarcely say, " Good-by,
miss," as he darted off, clutching the ten-dollar Confederate
bill that I had handed him in payment for his services.

Watching the old negro until he was out of sight, I rode up
to the church, and dismounting, entered the building. My
first care now was to get rid of my pistol, as I thought it
would most probably be taken from me if the Federals found
that I had it; and the discovery of it, secreted upon my person, would be not unlikely to cause me to be suspected of
being a spy, which, of course, was the very thing I was most
anxious to avoid. Raising a plank in the flooring, I put the
pistol under it, and covered it well with dirt. My intention
was to return this way, and I expected to get the weapon,
and give it back to General Ferguson. Circumstances, however, induced me to change my plans; and as I have never
visited the spot since, if the church is still standing, the pistol
is probably where I placed it, for I buried it tolerably deep,
and smoothed the dirt well over it, so that it would not be
likely to be discovered except by accident.

As I stated before, my disguise, as I had arranged it with
Lieutenant Shorter, was that of a poor countrywoman, and
the story I was to tell was, that I was a widow, and was flying
for protection to the Federal lines. Having disposed of the
pistol, I sat down for a few minutes to think over the situation, and to decide upon the best method of procedure with

the first Federal soldier I met. Experience had taught me, however, that no settled plan, in a matter of this kind, amounts to much, so far as the details are concerned, and that it is necessary to be governed by circumstances. I resolved, therefore, to regulate my conduct and conversation according to the character and behavior of those I chanced to meet; and so, having first ascertained that my papers were all right, I mounted my pony again, and started in the direction where I supposed I would find the Federal camp.

MEETING A FEDERAL PICKET.

Letting my pony take his own gait — and he was not inclined to make his pace any more rapid than there was necessity for — I travelled for a couple of miles before I saw any one. At length a picket, who had evidently been watching me for some time, stepped out of the woods into the road, and when I came up to him, he halted me, and asked where I was from, and where I was going.

" Good morning, sir," I said, in an innocent, unsophisticated sort of way. " Are you commanding this outpost?"

" No," he replied; " what do you want?"

" Well, sir, I wish you would tell the captain I want to see him."

" What do you want with the captain?"

" I have got a message to give the captain, but I can't give it to any one else."

" He is over there in the woods."

" Well, you just tell him that I want to see him quick, about something very important."

The soldier then called to his officer, and in a few moments up stepped a good-looking young lieutenant, whose blouse was badly out at the elbows, and whose clothing generally bore marks of very hard service. Although his attire was not of the most elegant description, he was a gentleman, and, as he approached me, he tipped his hat, and said, with a pleasant smile, " Good morning, madam; what is it you wish?"

" Are you the captain?" I queried.

" I am in command of this picket guard," he replied.

"Well, captain," said I, "I want to go to Memphis, to see General Washburn. I have some papers here for him."

This made him start a little, and he began to suspect that

JAMES LONGSTREET.

JUBAL EARLY.

THOMAS J. (STONEWALL) JACKSON.

ROBERT E. LEE.

he had a matter of serious business on hand, and, evidently with a different interest in me from what he had felt before, he inquired, with a rather severe and serious air, " Where are you from, madam ? "

" I am from Holly Springs. A man there gave me these papers, and told me that if I would get them through he would pay me a hundred dollars."

" What kind of looking man was he, and where did he go after he left you ? "

" I mustn't tell you that, sir ; the man said not to tell anything about him, except to the one these papers are for, and he would understand all about it."

" Well, madam, you will have to go with me to headquarters. When we get there I will see what can be done for you."

His relief came, not a great while after, and off we started for headquarters. As I had informed my new-made friend that I was hungry, having ridden for a considerable distance since very early in the morning, he stopped with me at a white house near the road, and sending the guard on, went in with me, and asked the woman, who appeared to be mistress of the establishment, to give me some breakfast. Quite a comfortable meal was soon in readiness, and while I was eating, the lieutenant busied himself in trying to ascertain something about the number and position of the Confederate troops. I told him that there seemed to be a large force of them near Holly Springs, but beyond that statement,—which was, I believe, far from being the truth, — I am afraid he did not find me a very satisfactory witness. I am sure that such information as I did give him was not likely to be of very great use.

Unpleasant Attentions from the Soldiers.

After I had finished my breakfast, the lieutenant took me to Moscow, on the Memphis and Charleston Railroad, and here, for the first time, I was subjected to very serious annoyance, and first began to appreciate the fact that I was engaged in a particularly risky undertaking. The soldiers, seeing me coming into the town mounted on a ragged little pony, and under the escort of an officer, jumped at the conclusion that I was a spy, and commenced to gather round me in crowds.

"Who is she?" some one asked.

"O, she's a spy that the Illinois picket captured."

"You're gone up!" yelled some fellow in the crowd.

"Why don't they hang her?" was the pleasant inquiry of another.

These and other cheering comments greeted me on all sides, and some of the brutal fellows pushed against me, and struck my pony, and otherwise made my progress through the streets exceedingly unpleasant, notwithstanding the efforts of the lieutenant to protect me.

Finally we reached the building occupied by the colonel in command, and I was ushered by that official into a private room, in the rear of the one used as an office. The lieutenant accompanied me, and related the manner of my coming to the picket station, and the story which I had told him.

UNDER CROSS-EXAMINATION.

The colonel then proceeded to cross-question me, being apparently desirous of finding out whether I was possessed of any information worth his knowing, as well as whether I was exactly what I professed to be. I flattered myself that I played my part tolerably well. I knew very little about the movements of the Confederates, or their number, but, under the process of rigid cross-questioning to which I was subjected, I said just enough to stimulate curiosity, pretending that what I was telling was what I had picked up merely incidentally, and that, as I took no interest in the fighting that was going on, except to desire to get as far away from it as possible, I really knew scarcely anything, except from rumor.

As for myself, I stuck close to one simple story. I was a poor widow woman, whose husband had died about the time of the breaking out of the war; I was for the Union, and had been badly treated by the rebels, who had robbed me of nearly everything, and I had been anxious to get away for some time with a little money I had collected, and had finally got tired of waiting for the Federal troops to come down my way, and had resolved to try and get through the lines; that a man had promised I should be paid a hundred dollars if I would carry a despatch to General Washburn, at Memphis, and had assisted me to get off; that I was to deliver the papers to General Washburn only, and was to tell him alone certain things that the man had told me; I had some friends in Ohio, to whom I was anxious to go, and I hoped that General Washburn, after I had given the despatch to him, would pay me the hundred dollars, and furnish me with a pass to go North.

The colonel tried to make me vary this story, and he several times pretended that I had contradicted myself. He was tolerably smart at a cross-examination, but not by any means smart enough for the subject he had to deal with on this occasion. I had the most innocent air in the world about me, and pretended, half the time, that I was so stupid that I could not understand what his interrogatories meant, and, instead of answering them, would go off into a long story about my troubles, and the hardships I had suffered, and the bad treatment I had received. The colonel then tried to induce me to give him the despatch, saying that he would pay me the hundred dollars, and would forward it to General Washburn. This I refused to do, as I had promised not to let anybody but the general have it, if I could help it. Neither would I tell who it was that had intrusted me with the despatch, or give any clew to the message for the general he had intrusted me to deliver by word of mouth.

In fine, the colonel was practically no wiser when he had finished than when he commenced, and so, finding that no information worth talking about was to be obtained from me, he said, "Where will you go, if I give you a pass?" at the same time winking at the lieutenant.

"I want to go to Memphis, sir, to give this paper to General Washburn, and I hope that the general will be kind enough to send me on to Ohio."

"Have you any money?"

"Yes, sir; I have about one hundred and fifty dollars."

"Confederate money, isn't it?"

"No, sir; it's greenbacks. I wouldn't have that rebel trash; it isn't worth anything."

"Well, madam," then said the colonel, "you will remain here until the train is ready to start, and I will see, in the mean time, what I can do for you."

The colonel then went out; but the lieutenant remained, and engaged in a general sort of a conversation with me for some time. About noon, he suggested that perhaps I was hungry, and went and procured me something to eat. The train came in at one o'clock, and I proceeded to the depot under the escort of the two officers; the colonel, in response to my request that the soldiers should not annoy me as they had done in the morning, assuring me that he regretted anything of the kind had happened, and promising that he would see that I was protected from insult. Whether the presence of the colonel was the sole cause of the difference in their behavior or not, I cannot say, but the soldiers kept their distance as we were going to the depot, and only stared at me. When we reached the depot, the colonel procured me a ticket, and gave me five dollars, and I overheard him say, in an undertone, to the lieutenant, "You get in the rear car, and keep an eye on her movements. I think that she is all right, but it would be just as well to watch her."

The lieutenant said, "O, there's no doubt in my mind but she is all right."

This little conversation made me smile to myself, and served to convince me that I would have no trouble in getting along nicely with my friend the lieutenant.

The colonel moved off, and the lieutenant and I stepped aboard the train, a half dozen soldiers who were near making such comments as, "She's gone up." "I guess she'll hang." "Hanging's too good for a spy." I took no notice of them, however, but seated myself on the opposite side of the car from where they were standing. The lieutenant was overwhelmingly polite, and after having got me fixed comfortably in my seat, he said, in a low tone, "I may go up with you as far as my camp, if I can get any one to hold my horse."

I thought that this would be a good chance to improve my acquaintance with him, and perhaps do something for the furtherance of my plans; so I said, "O, I would be so glad if you would. I would so much like to have company." And I smiled on him as sweetly as I was able, to impress him with the idea that I profoundly appreciated his courtesy. The young fellow was evidently more than half convinced that he had made a conquest, while I was quite sure that I had. If he had known what my real feelings were, and with what entire willingness I would have made a prisoner of him, could I have got him into the Confederate lines, perhaps he would not have been quite so eager for my society.

When the lieutenant left, the soldiers began to crowd about the windows of the car, for the purpose of staring at me, and using towards me the same kind of abusive language as that which I have already quoted. I came to the conclusion that there must be rather lax discipline when a woman, situated as I was, who was especially under the protection of the officers of the command, and whom the colonel had given orders should not be insulted in any way, could be subjected to such continued ill usage as this. I was the more indignant, as there were several officers standing by, who took no notice of the behavior of the men, and made no effort whatever to prevent them from indulging in what, under any circumstances, was a mean and cowardly pastime. At length, provoked beyond measure, I called to an officer near, who wore a major's uniform, and said to him, "I would thank you, sir, to do something to stop the men from insulting me. I am travelling under a pass from the colonel, and he promised that I should not be annoyed in this manner."

The major very promptly came forward, and pushing some of the soldiers away from the windows, said, "Men, keep quiet, and do not insult this lady. She is on our side; she is Union." And then, turning to me, he remarked, "O, you mustn't mind them. You see, they have got it into their heads that you are a spy. They won't trouble you any more."

It struck me, as the major was making this little speech, that the soldiers were wiser than some of their officers, although I did not feel any more amiable towards them on that account. I, however, thanked the major for his promptness in coming to my protection, and we passed a few words, the idea entering my head that if I could fall into a conversation with him I might be able to beguile him into giving me some points of information worth having. Before, however, we had an opportunity to do more than exchange the ordinary civilities of the day, the train began to move, and I was unable to improve my acquaintance with him.

CHAPTER XXXI.

SENDING INFORMATION TO THE CONFEDERATES FROM MEMPHIS.

My Friend, the Lieutenant, concludes that he will make himself better acquainted with me. — Indiscreet Confidences. — Some of the Traits of human Nature. — The Kind of Secrets Women can keep. — Women better than Men for certain Kinds of Secret Service Duty. — The Lieutenant wants to know all about me. — I suspect that he has matrimonial Inclinations. — He is anxious to discover whether I have any wealthy Relations. — I am induced to think that I can make him useful in obtaining Information with Regard to the Federal Movements. — The Lieutenant expresses his Opinion about the War. — Arrival at Memphis. — Visit to the Provost Marshal's Office. — General Washburn too ill to see me. — I enclose him the bogus Despatch I have for him with an explanatory Note. — The Lieutenant escorts me to the Hardwick House, and I request him to call in the Morning. — Procuring a Change of Dress through One of the Servants, I slip out, and have an Interview with my Confederate, and give him the Despatch for General Forrest. — On returning to the Hotel, I meet the Lieutenant on the Street, but manage to pass him without being observed. — Satisfactory Accomplishment of my Errand.

CONCLUDED that my friend, the lieutenant, had deserted me, for which I was inclined to be sorry; for he was apparently an agreeable enough young fellow, and I was rather anxious than otherwise to have his company as far as Memphis. If any doubts as to my being " all right," as the colonel had expressed it, still lingered in his mind, I thought that I would not only be able to remove them before our journey's end, but that I might be able so to insinuate myself into his confidence that I could learn something from him. I also wished him to go to Memphis with me, for I felt that if I put in an appearance there, under the escort of a Federal officer who would vouch for me, my status with the people at headquarters would be more satisfactory than if I went alone. In performing spy duty, there is nothing like having a friend at headquarters to introduce

you, and to certify to your intentions being such as would meet
with approbation.

As matters turned out, the lieutenant not only did accompany me, but he let out many things that he ought to have
kept quiet about, knowing, as he did, the manner in which I
had come into the lines, and having no assurance whatever
beyond my bare word that I was not a spy. To be sure, the
information I obtained from him with regard to the main object
of my errand was not very momentous, for I was afraid to say
too much on points relating to my errand; but I, without any
difficulty, learned enough to enable me to know exactly how
to go to work to find out a great deal more. Besides this, he
was really of much assistance to me in other ways, and saved
me considerable trouble at headquarters — for all of which I
hope I was duly thankful.

About keeping Secrets.

It may be thought that an officer of the experience of this
one — he had been through the war from the beginning —
would have understood his business sufficiently by this time
to have known how to hold his tongue concerning matters that
it was desirable the enemy should not become informed of,
when in the society of a person whom he well knew might be
a spy. If all the officers and men in an army, however, were
endowed with, not wisdom only, but plain common sense, the
business of the secret service agents would be a very much
more difficult and hazardous one than it really is. The young
fellow was only a lieutenant, with no great responsibilities,
while some of my most brilliant successes in the way of obtaining information have been with generals, and even with
their superiors, as the reader will discover, if he feels sufficient interest in my story to follow it to the end.

The fact is, that human nature is greatly given to confidence; so much so, that the most unconfiding and suspicious
people are usually the easiest to extract any desired information from, provided you go the right way about it. This may
seem to be a paradox; but it is not: it is merely a statement
of a peculiar trait of human nature. Women have the reputation of being bad secret-keepers. Well, that depends on
circumstances. I have always succeeded in keeping mine,
when I have had any worth keeping; and I have always found
it more difficult to beguile women than men into telling me

what I have wanted to know, when they had the slightest reason to suspect that I was not a suitable recipient of their confidence. The truth seems to be, that while women find it often troublesome, and well nigh impossible, to keep little and inconsequential secrets, they are first-rate hands at keeping great ones.

For certain kinds of secret service work women are, out of all comparison, superior to men. This, I believe, is acknowledged by all detectives and others who have been compelled to employ secret agents. One reason for this is, that women, when they undertake a secret service job, are really quicker witted and more wide awake than men; they more easily deceive other people, and are less easily imposed upon. Of course there is a great deal of secret service work for which women are not well fitted, and much that it is scarcely possible for them to perform at all; but, as a rule, for an enterprise that requires real *finesse*, a woman will be likely to accomplish far more than a man.

I was just thinking that my lieutenant had deserted me, or that he was in another car for the purpose of keeping an eye on me unobserved, when he appeared beside me, having jumped on the rear end of the car as it was starting.

He said, " You have no objections to my occupying the same seat with you, have you, madam ? "

" O, no, sir ! " I replied; " I shall be exceedingly glad to have the pleasure of your society, so far as you are going."

" Well, I only intend going up to my camp now, but I have half a mind to run on as far as Memphis — that is, if my company will not be disagreeable to you."

" I will be very greatly pleased if you will go through with me. It has been a long time since I have met any agreeable gentlemen, and I particularly admire officers."

As I said this I gave him a killing glance, and then dropped my eyes as if half ashamed of having made such a bold advance to him. The bait took, however, as I expected it would; and the lieutenant, giving his mustache a twist, and running his hand through his hair, settled himself down in the seat with a most self-satisfied air, evidently supposing that the conquest of my heart was more than half completed, and began to make himself as agreeable as he knew how. *Finesse* was certainly not this youth's most marked characteristic, and he went about making himself agreeable, and endeavoring to discover who I was, where I came from, and all about me, in such an awkward, lubberly manner, that it was mere play for me to impose upon him.

MATTERS MATRIMONIAL AND OTHERWISE.

He had not been seated more than a minute or two before he blurted out, " I guess you're married — ain't you? "

" No, sir; I'm a widow."

" Is that so? Well, now, about how long has the old man been dead? "

" My husband died shortly after the breaking out of the war. I have been a widow nearly three years."

" Well, that's a pretty good while to be a widow; but I reckon men are scarce down your way. Got any children? "

" No, sir; unfortunately I have no children."

" Well, that's lucky, anyhow."

I did not exactly understand whether he meant that it was lucky for me, or for him, in case he made up his mind to marry me. I, however, thought it a good occasion for a little senti-ment, and so, giving a sigh, said, " Children are a great com-fort, sometimes."

" Yes, I suppose so," said he; " especially when they are your own. I don't care much for other people's children, though."

" Are you married, sir? " I suggested, in a rather timid tone, and giving him another killing glance.

" Not much," he replied, with considerable force; " but I wouldn't mind being, if I could find a real nice woman who would have me." And with this he gave me a tender look that was very touching.

" O, there ought to be plenty of women who would gladly have a fine, handsome officer like you."

" Do you think so, now, really? Well, I'll have to look round. By the way, where do you come from? Do you be-long down South? "

" No, sir," I replied; " I am a foreigner by birth, but my husband was an American, and lived in Ohio until shortly be-fore the war."

" Is that so, now? You're English — ain't you? "

" No, sir; my parents were French and Spanish."

" I guess you must speak those languages, then? "

" Yes, sir; much better than English."

" Well, said he, " I'm mighty glad I met you."

"Thank you, sir. I may say the same to you."

He then remarked, "I don't believe you'll have any difficulty in getting through to Memphis, or any trouble after you reach there. I will be glad to assist you any way I can."

I thanked him for his kind intentions; and he then, in a hesitating sort of a way, said, "I hope you won't feel offended if I inquire how your finances are."

"O, no, sir; no offence at all. I am sorry to say that my funds are rather low."

"Well, I'll see you fixed all right until you can hear from your friends. How long do you expect to remain in Memphis?"

"No longer than I can possibly help; for I want to get back to Europe, where I have friends who will take care of me, at the earliest opportunity."

"I'm mighty sorry you are going to make such a short stay. I was hoping that we might become better acquainted. It isn't often that we meet with real ladies in these parts."

An Anxious Inquirer.

He then proceeded to inquire who my relatives in Europe were, where they lived, whether they were wealthy or not, — he seemed to be especially anxious on this point, — how old I was, whether I had ever thought much about getting married again, and so forth. I answered his queries as promptly as he could have wished, and perhaps more to his satisfaction than if I had told him the exact truth in every instance.

At length the whistle blew, and the train stopped at his camp. He jumped up, and rushed out, without even saying good-by; and while I was wondering where he had left his politeness, I saw him running as fast as he could go, and presently dodge into a tent. In a moment or two more out he came in his shirt sleeves, and ran for the train, with his coat in his hand, and jumped on board just as we were starting. I turned around, and watched him as he got into the car behind me, and saw him put on a rather better looking uniform coat than the out-at-the-elbows blouse he had been wearing, and a paper collar and black necktie. These last I considered as particularly delicate attentions to myself.

When he had completed his toilet, he came forward, and, seating himself beside me, said, "I will allow myself the pleasure of going through to Memphis with you."

I assured him that I was pleased beyond measure, and came to the conclusion that it would be my fault if long before we reached Memphis I did not stand so well in his good graces that I would be able to make a most useful ally of him in carrying out my plans for the benefit of the Confederacy.

"Do you see that field over there?" said he, pointing to a good sized clearing. "That's where our boys had a fight with Forrest."

"Did you run fast?" I asked, rather maliciously.

"We had to run," said he; "they were too many for us."

"O, what a pity," said I; "you ought to have whipped them;" and thought, at the same time, that there would be some more hard running done if I ever succeeded in getting to Forrest the despatch I had for him.

"We'll whip them yet," said the lieutenant. "We've had some big successes lately in Virginia, Missouri, and Arkansas, and we'd treat them worse than we do here if we only had a few more men."

"Why," said I, "there seems to be a great many of you."

IMPORTANT INFORMATION.

"O, there's not half enough to do anything. They've got us scattered along this railroad in such a way that it's almost as much as we can do to hold our own, when any kind of a crowd of rebs puts in an appearance."

This was interesting; but I did not think it prudent just then to question him any closer on such a delicate subject, trusting that before we parted he would let out, of his own accord, some other facts worth knowing; so I merely said, "O, this war is a terrible thing. It makes me sick to think of so many being killed and wounded."

"That's so," he replied. "It is bad, but now we've begun it, I guess we'll have to fight it out."

"What do you think they will do with that miserable fellow, Davis, if they catch him?" said I.

"Well, I'm for hanging Jeff, and all his cabinet. We'll just string up the leaders, and let the little people go, if they will promise to behave themselves."

This made my blood boil; but I controlled my feelings, and remarked, "O, I don't believe they will hang him. They've got to catch him first, you know; and then the government at Washington is disposed to be lenient, isn't it?"

" Yes, that's just what's the matter. Between the milk-and-water policy of the government, and the speculators who have been allowed to do pretty much as they please, it has been hard work carrying on the war at all. We western men have done nearly all the hardest fighting, and we've got the least credit for it. So far as I am concerned, if I had known that it was the niggers we were going to fight for, I never would have raised my sword."

" O, you don't believe in slavery, do you ? " said I, with the view of increasing his confidence in me.

" No," said he ; " but the niggers are better off where they are, and are not worth fighting for, anyhow."

I tried to draw him out on this subject, but for some reason he did not seem inclined to talk about it any more ; and he branched off into anecdotes of army life, the fights he had been engaged in, and a variety of matters that were entertaining enough, but do not merit being placed on record. This conversation amused me, and gave me a good number of points worth knowing in the particular business in which I was engaged, until at length the train reached Memphis, and my escort assisting me to alight, requested me to wait on the platform for him while he engaged a carriage.

In a few moments he returned with a close-bodied carriage, and when I was seated in it he ordered the driver to go to the Hardwick House.

" O, nó," said I ; "I must go to General Washburn's headquarters first, and deliver my despatch and message."

" Just as you like," said he ; " but I thought that you might prefer to arrange your toilet before seeing the general."

" No," I replied ; " I must see him immediately, as I was told that this was a matter of great importance. The general won't mind my looks."

A QUEER WAY OF DOING BUSINESS.

The driver was accordingly directed to take us to headquarters, and before many more minutes I was ushered into the presence of the provost marshal, to whom I stated my errand. The fact of the lieutenant being with me undoubtedly prevented a great many questions being asked, some of which it might not have been agreeable, or even possible, for me to answer, and I accordingly was more than ever impressed with the value of having him for an acquaintance, especially as he put in a word now and then which had the effect of establishing me on a satisfactory footing with the provost marshal. That official, when he had heard my story, said, " Madam, I am sorry, but the general is very much indisposed, and cannot see you. I will be glad to receive anything you may have for him, and to give him any message from you."

" O, sir, I must see him. It is impossible for me to communicate what I have to say to any one else."

" Did the person who confided the paper to you give you any private instructions ? "

" Yes, sir, and he was very particular in telling me to communicate with the general in person, and with no one else."

" Well, madam, I am sorry for you; but, as I said before, the general is unable to see you, and you will either have to leave the paper and your message with me, or else call again."

This struck me as being a decidedly odd way of doing business. Here I was professing to be a despatch-bearer, with a confidential message from a spy within the enemy's lines, and the probabilities all in favor of my business being of extreme importance ; and yet, the officer who assumed to represent the general placidly requesting me to call again, just as if I was some one who had stepped in to ask a favor of him. I concluded that if matters were managed in this kind of style at headquarters, Memphis would not be a very difficult place for me to operate in, or for the Confederates to operate against, if they thought it worth their while. I knit my brows, looked vexed and perplexed, tapped the ground with my foot, and pretended to be thinking deeply about what course I had better pursue. After a few moments' consideration, I concluded that the best thing I could do was to get the bogus despatch off my hands, and thus be free to attend to other business of more importance ; so I said, " That is too bad, for I promised to see the general himself, as the man was so particular that I should; but if he won't see me, I suppose I will have to write to him."

The provost marshal accordingly furnished me with a sheet of paper, and I sat down at his desk and scribbled off a brief note to the general, telling him enough about the source from which I had obtained the despatch to induce him to believe in its genuineness, and intimated that if he wanted to know more he could send for me. This note and the despatch I enclosed in the same envelope, and handed it to the provost marshal, with a request that it might be given to the general immedi-

24

ately. I fully expected that when General Washburn received these enclosures he would have me brought before him for the purpose of interrogation, and was much surprised when he did nothing of the kind.

The provost marshal took the envelope back into his private office, and on his return he asked me where I was going to stop. I replied that I did not know yet; whereupon he suggested that there was a nice private boarding-house near the Catholic church. I objected to going there, however, and said that I would prefer to locate myself at the Hardwick House for the present. To the hotel I accordingly went, under the escort of my friend, the lieutenant, and registered myself as Mrs. Fowler, not at all grieved at not having seen the general, and quite satisfied not to see him in the future if he did not wish to see me, for I considered the material part of my errand now practically accomplished.

The lieutenant, when he saw me fairly established in comfortable quarters, asked me to excuse him, saying that, as I seemed to be short of funds, he would see if he could not obtain some for me. I thanked him very much, made all manner of apologies for giving him so much trouble, and as a broad hint that I did not want to see any more of him that day, asked him to call in the morning, as I was feeling quite sick, was tired out with my journey, and would retire to rest after getting some supper. He was not a fool, and understood that I did not desire his company ; so, taking his leave, he said that he would give orders for something to eat to be brought up to my room, and would come to see me again in the morning if I would permit him.

He had not been gone a great while before a servant appeared with a very nice supper. This I ate with immense relish, for I was desperately hungry, at the same time making certain inquiries of the servant for the purpose of enabling me to judge whether it would be safe or prudent to attempt to communicate that night with the spy for whom I had the despatch which was to be forwarded to Forrest. It was now nearly dark, and I decided that no better time for meeting the spy could be found. I accordingly asked the servant to try and borrow for me some rather more presentable articles of attire than those I had on, as I desired to go out for the purpose of making a few purchases, and was really ashamed to go into the streets dressed as I was. My real reason was that I was afraid the lieutenant, or the provost marshal, or some one who had seen me, should happen to meet me while I was out, and as, dressed in the rather outlandish fashion in which I had appeared at the picket station, they would not fail to recognize me, suspicions might be excited which would result in spoiling all my plans.

The servant, whose zeal in my behalf was stimulated by a five-dollar greenback, was not long in appearing with a reasonably decent-looking dress, bonnet, and shawl. I then attired myself with as much speed as I could command, and after having the dust and dirt brushed off my shoes, was ready to start.

A Conference with the Spy.

It is scarcely necessary to say that I was well acquainted with Memphis, and consequently knew exactly how to go and where to go in search of my man. Fortunately for me, the place was not a very great way from the hotel, and persuading the accommodating servant to show me out the back door, under the plea that, meanly attired as I was, I was ashamed to be seen by the officers who were standing about the front of the building, I was not long in reaching it.

I knocked at the door, and the very man I was looking for came to let me in. I had never seen him before, but I knew him immediately by the description I had of him. Giving him the password I was admitted, and he eagerly inquired what I had for him. I handed him the despatch which he was to convey to Forrest, and gave him the verbal instructions which Lieutenant Shorter had ordered me to convey to him, and urged the necessity for his making haste in reaching Forrest at the earliest practicable moment. He, however, said that he thought that a movement of the Federal troops was in contemplation, and that he would like to find out exactly what it was before starting, and as I seemed to be on good terms at headquarters, he urged that I should endeavor to obtain the information for him. I consented to try what I could do, while he promised not to delay his departure longer than two days, at the farthest.

Before parting, I represented the danger to both if we should be seen in conference, and said that I would prefer not meeting him again if some means of communicating with him without a personal interview could be devised. He, therefore, suggested that if I obtained the desired information I should write him a note and deposit it in a certain place which he designated. I consented to this and took my departure, wishing him good luck. On my way back to the hotel, the prudence of my change of dress was sufficiently demonstrated, for on turning a corner I nearly ran against my friend the lieutenant and another officer, who were walking slowly along the street. My heart leaped into my mouth when I saw who it was, but as there was no retreat, I trusted to the darkness and my change of costume, and glided by them as swiftly and quietly as I could, and fortunately was able to gain my room without discovery.

My errand was now accomplished, and in as satisfactory a manner as could be desired, and the only apprehension I had was lest the spy to whom I had given the despatch for Forrest might not succeed in getting off in safety. If he should be arrested and the document found on him, the finger of suspicion would not unlikely point to me as the original bearer of it. I thought, however, that he was probably well able to take care of himself, and being too much of a veteran to allow myself to be worried about possibilities that might never come to pass, I went to bed feeling that the responsibility of the business was well off my shoulders, and was soon in happy obliviousness of cares of every kind.

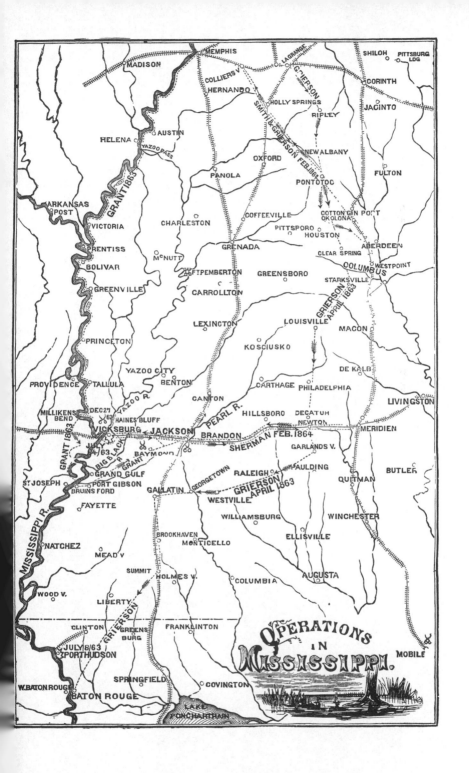

CHAPTER XXXII.

FORREST'S GREAT RAID. — GOING NORTH ON A MISSION OF MERCY.

A Friend in Need is a Friend indeed. — The Lieutenant aids me in procuring a new Wardrobe. — I succeed in finding out all I want to know about the Number and the Disposition of the Federal Troops on the Line of the Memphis and Charleston Railroad. — A Movement made in Accordance with the bogus Despatch which I had brought to General Washburn. — Forrest makes his Raid, and I pretend to be alarmed lest the Rebels should capture me. — The Lieutenant continues his Attentions, and something occurs to induce me to change my Plans. — I have an Interview with an Officer of my Brother's Command, and learn that he is a Prisoner. — I resolve to go to him, and leave for the North on a Pass furnished by General Washburn. — At Louisville I have an Interview with a mysterious secret Agent of the Confederacy, who supplies me with Funds. — On reaching Columbus, Ohio, I obtain a Permit to see my Brother. — Through the Agency of Governor Brough my Brother is released, and we go East together, — he to New York, I to Washington.

HE next morning the lieutenant made his appearance bright and early, and said that he had raised a hundred dollars for me, by representing me as a Union woman who was flying from persecution in the Confederacy, and who had brought important information into the lines. This money I regarded as lawful spoils of war, and therefore had no hesitation in accepting it. Expressing my gratitude to my friend for his zeal in my behalf, I said that he would place me under still further obligations if he would aid me in obtaining some better clothing than that I had on. He expressed the greatest desire to oblige me, and taking half of the money, he invested a good portion of it in a stylish bonnet, a handsome piece of dress goods, and a pair of shoes. He also presented me with a number of little articles, which I was given to understand were meant for testimonials of his individual regard.

373

During the day I was called upon by several officers and others, and one lady—an officer's wife—loaned me a dress to wear until mine should be finished. Taking my piece of goods to the dressmaker's, I stated that I was in a great hurry, and she accordingly promised to have it finished by the next evening. Thus I was in a short time fitted out in good style, and was able to figure to as great an extent as I desired in such society as Memphis afforded just at that time.

My new friends were extremely anxious to know exactly what was going on within the rebel lines, and asked me all sorts of questions. I endeavored to gratify their curiosity as well as I could without committing myself too much, and in return made an effort to find out what I was so desirous of knowing about the contemplated movement of the Federal troops.

I did not have a great deal of trouble in learning very nearly everything that was to be learned about the number and disposition of the troops along the line of the Memphis and Charleston Railroad, and also that the force at Colliersville was being materially strengthened in apprehension of an attack in that quarter. This information I promptly communicated to my confidant, who started for Forrest's headquarters without more delay. The concentration of the Federal force at Colliersville, I had every reason to believe, was induced by the despatch I delivered to General Washburn. At any rate, it had the effect of leaving a gap in the Federal line beyond Grand Junction for Forrest to step through ; and, when in a day or two, intelligence was received that he was on a grand raid through Western Tennessee, I knew that the plot in which I had been engaged had succeeded in the best manner.

FORREST'S RAID.

I made a great to-do when the news of Forrest's raid was received, and pretended to be frightened lest an attack should be made on Memphis, and the rebels should capture me. The fact is, that Forrest, before he got through, did come very near the city, and some of my new acquaintances were just as much frightened in reality as I pretended to be. He, however, did not make any demonstration in the city, but after a brilliant campaign of several weeks slipped by the Federals again, carrying back with him into Mississippi sufficient cattle and other booty to amply repay him for his trouble.

I thought that I had reason to congratulate myself upon the success of the enterprise in which I had been engaged. Taking it altogether, it was as well planned and as well executed a performance as any I ever attempted during the whole of my career in the Confederate service.

My friend, the lieutenant, whose regard for me really increased with each succeeding interview, was obliged to return to his camp, after having assisted me in obtaining a new outfit. In a day or two, however, he returned, having obtained a ten days' leave of absence, and he began to increase the zealousness of his attentions. On his return to Memphis he brought with him a fine horse, which he claimed to have captured, and said that it should be reserved for my use, if I would accept of it, so long as I remained in the city. I was not at all averse to having a good time, although I was beginning to wonder how I was ever to get back to my starting-place again, and I rode out a number of times with the lieutenant, and accepted his escort on all occasions that he offered it.

A CHANGE OF PLANS.

It was while attending church on the Sunday following the arrival, on leave, of this rather over-attentive young gentleman, that something occurred which caused a very material alteration in my plans, which induced me to abandon my design to return to Mobile, and which resulted in my entering upon an entirely new field of operations. I, of course, at the time, had no idea whatever how things were going to turn out, but if all had been arranged beforehand they could not have turned out more in accordance with my desires.

During the service I noticed in the congregation a Confederate officer in citizen's clothes, whom I knew by sight, and who belonged to my brother's command. He did not know me, especially as a woman, although he had seen me a number of times attired in the uniform of a Confederate officer. I was most desirous of communicating with him, for the purpose of inquiring about my brother, of whom I had received no intelligence whatever for a number of months ; so, after the service was over, I watched him as he left the church, and seeing him turn the corner, said to the lieutenant, " Let us take a walk down this street." Keeping him in sight, I saw him turn down towards the Hardwick House, and consequently suggested to the lieutenant that it would perhaps be as well to return to the hotel instead of indulging in a promenade. My escort thought that I was disposed to be whimsical; but I did not bother myself very greatly about his opinion of me one way or the other, being now only intent upon devising some means of obtaining an interview with the disguised Confederate.

On reaching the hotel I found that the man I was after had disappeared, and I was considerably perplexed to know what course to pursue. I was afraid to send him my card, for fear of compromising him in some way, as I thought it highly probable that he was stopping at the hotel under an assumed name. I was bent on securing an opportunity to converse with him, however, and hoped to be able to meet him, and to attract his attention before evening, but failing in this, I was resolved to find out what I could about him from some of the servants, and to send him a note requesting a private interview, giving him a sufficient hint as to who I was to induce him to think that he would be in no danger. Fortunately, however, I was not compelled to resort to any such expedient as this, for, on going in to dinner at five o'clock with the lieutenant, I saw him at one of the tables, having apparently just sat down.

A STRICTLY PRIVATE COMMUNICATION.

The lieutenant was conducting me to the seat which we usually occupied, but I said, as if seized with a sudden freak for a change of locality, " Suppose we go over to this table to-day. I think we will find it pleasanter; " and, before my Federal friend had time to object, I had walked him across the room and seated myself beside the Confederate, indicating for the lieutenant to take the seat on the other side of me. When the waiter came up to get our orders for dinner, I asked him to bring me a couple of cards.

All this time I took not the slightest notice of the Confederate, but chatted with the lieutenant in the liveliest and most animated manner possible; my object being to so engage his attention that he would not think of observing what I was doing for the purpose of letting the gentleman on the other side of me know that I was interested in him.

On one of the cards I wrote some nonsense, which I sent by the waiter, after having shown it to the lieutenant, to another officer whom I saw on the opposite side of the room. On the other one I wrote, " Meet me at my room, at half past ten o'clock this evening, unobserved. Important." This I made a pretence of slipping in my pocket, but dropped it on the floor instead, touching the Confederate officer as I did so, and half turning towards him in such a manner that he could readily understand that I was endeavoring to attract his attention. While this was going on, the lieutenant was watching to see what would be the effect of the jesting remark I had written on the first card on the gentleman across the room to whom I had sent it. He laughed and nodded, and the lieutenant and I did the same,— all of us, apparently, being satisfied that there was a capital joke in progress; which indeed there was, but not exactly the kind of one they imagined.

The Confederate officer, when he looked down and saw the card on the floor, quickly dropped his napkin on it, and stooped to pick it up. He found an opportunity to read my message before he left the table, but I took no further notice of him whatever, until just as he was about to retire, when I turned slightly, and looking him full in the face, gave him a meaning glance, so that he could understand that there was no mistake about the matter.

At the hour named on the card the Confederate officer came to my room, evidently very much perplexed, and uncertain what the end of the adventure would be. I hastened to apologize for the liberty I had taken, and to place him at his ease by explaining matters.

I said, " You will pardon me, sir ; but this is Lieutenant B., of Arkansas, is it not ? "

" Yes, madam, that is my name," he replied.

" You need be under no apprehension, sir. I know you, although you do not know me. I am the sister of Captain ——, and I am exceedingly anxious to learn where he is and how he is, for I have not been able to hear from him for a very long time."

NEWS FROM MY BROTHER.

The announcement that I was the sister of Captain ——, was evidently an immense relief to Lieutenant B., whose face brightened up immediately. He stated that he was very much pleased to meet me, but that he was sorry to have to tell me that my brother had been captured by the Federals about four months before, and was now a prisoner at Camp Chase.

This was unpleasant news, and it determined me to give up the idea of returning to Mobile, but to go North and visit my brother, for the purpose of assisting him in any way possible. From what I had learned during my late stay in Memphis, too, I was very well convinced that, as a secret service agent, I would be able to operate with far more effect at the North than I would if I remained in this region of country; which was an additional inducement for me to travel northward, rather than to essay the hazardous experiment of regaining the Confederate lines without having some definite object in view.

I had quite a lengthy conversation with Lieutenant B. about my brother, and about affairs generally; and having announced to him my intention of visiting the North, and perhaps of acting as a secret service agent if I saw opportunities for doing anything for the advancement of the Confederate cause, I obtained from him quite a number of hints about the best methods of proceeding, and he gave me the names of persons in different places who were friends of the Confederacy, and with whom I could communicate. He also advised me to talk with certain parties, whom he named, in Memphis, who could advise me, and give me much valuable information.

The next day I conferred with some of the persons whom he had mentioned, and having become thoroughly posted, I began to prepare for my departure. My friend, the Federal lieutenant, whose attentions had been getting more and more ardent every day, was, or pretended to be, very much cut up when he heard that I intended to leave. I promised, however, to write to him so soon as I arrived in New York, — having given him to understand that that city was my immediate destination, — and intimated that I might possibly correspond regularly. He, in return for the very slight encouragement which I gave to his hopes that we might meet again when the fighting was all over, procured for me a pass and transportation from General Washburn, and off I started, leaving Memphis, where I was liable at any time to be recognized, and consequently get into trouble, with but little regret. As for the lieutenant, I certainly appreciated his attentions to me, but I thought that any heart pangs he might feel at parting would scarcely be so severe that he would not be able to recover from them in course of time.

My first object was to see my brother, to give him such assistance as I was able, and to discover whether I could not do something towards having him released. I had not seen him for a number of years, and, as the reader will remember, had only learned of his being in the Confederate army some little time before my second marriage. He was the only relative I had in the country, and I felt very anxious about him, fearing greatly that he might be sick, or suffering for some of the necessities of life. I therefore pushed forward as rapidly as I could, and made no stoppage of any moment until I reached Louisville, Kentucky, where I took a room at the Galt House, and communicated with a Mr. B., a gentleman whose name had been given me as one in whom I could confide, and to whom I could appeal in case I was in need of assistance.

A Mysterious Friend of the Confederacy.

I told Mr. B. who I was, and what was my errand, and informing him that I was short of funds, asked whether he could not do something for me. He said he would make an effort in my behalf, and accordingly a gentleman, who declined to tell me his name, but who said that he was a Confederate, called that evening to see me at my room. He was greatly afraid of being seen with me ; and before he would leave, after we had finished our conversation, I had to go out into the hall, and down as far as the stairway, to see that all was quiet, and no one looking, before he would venture out.

We had a long talk about, not only my immediate errand in behalf of my brother, but about the political and military situation generally. As Mr. B. had told me that I could trust him implicitly, I had no hesitation in informing him, that after having seen my brother, and made an effort to procure his release, my intention was to operate as a secret service agent, as I had had considerable experience in that line of duty. I did not think it necessary or proper to entertain him with a recital of the enterprises in which I had been engaged, but told him just enough about myself to let him understand that my pretensions were genuine, and that I really meant business. He, for his part, posted me very thoroughly about the best method of going to work, not only for procuring the release of my brother, but for picking up information of value to the Confederate authorities, and gave me the names of a number of persons in New York and Washington, as well as in the West, with whom it would be well for me to become acquainted as early as possible. He also gave me hints of various enterprises, of more or less consequence, that were on foot, and assured me that I could be of the greatest service to the cause if I would co-operate with the Confederate agents at the North.

Before taking his leave, he suggested that I should retire early, and be ready to go by the first train in the morning, and said that he would see that I was provided with funds. The name of this gentleman I could never discover, although I had considerable curiosity on the subject. He was very much of an enthusiast on the subject of the Confederacy, and was evidently an efficient secret worker for the cause ; but he was either excessively timid, or else he believed that he could do more to advance the interest of the cause by being, as far as practicable, unknown even to those with whom he co-operated.

Early the next morning I was awakened by a knock on my door, and some one outside asked if I was going on the early train. I replied that I was, and hastened to dress myself for the journey. As I was dressing, I was somewhat startled to see a large envelope on the floor, which must either have been pushed under the door or thrown in over the transom during the night. On opening the envelope I found in it five hundred dollars in greenbacks, and letters to a couple of persons in Columbus, Ohio. This money was very acceptable, for I had very little cash with me, and it enabled me to resume my travels with a mind comparately free from care.

Before leaving Louisville, however, I managed to get rid of some of my cash, for, as I was about starting for the train, I met a Confederate army friend, Lieutenant H., with whom I had a hurried conversation. He informed me that he was an escaped prisoner, and was endeavoring to make his way South, hoping to be able to get within the Confederate lines before being discovered. I gave him some advice about the best method of proceeding ; and as I knew that he was short of funds, or most likely would be before he got among his friends again, I pressed fifteen dollars upon him, for which he was overwhelmingly grateful.

I got off on the early train, in accordance with the understanding with my unknown friend of the evening before, and in due time arrived at Columbus, Ohio, and took a room at the Neil House. Here I felt tolerably secure, as no one knew me, and I was sufficiently far away from the seat of war to come and go as I chose without rendering myself liable to suspicion.

I concluded, before delivering the letters I had received in Louisville, that I would try and see what my own unaided efforts would do for my brother. I therefore, the next day, called upon the general in command, — I have forgotten his name, — and introducing myself, said, that if it was allowable, I would like very much to visit that rebel brother of mine.

The general asked me if I had a brother in the prison; and I told him that such was unfortunately the case, but that, notwithstanding he was on the wrong side, I could not help having an affection for him, and was desirous of assisting him in case he should be in need.

The general asked me a number of questions about myself and my brother, in answer to which I gave him to understand that I was from New York, was a strong Unionist, and had only recently heard that my brother was a prisoner, although I was aware that he had entered the rebel army shortly after the breaking out of the war. Having satisfied himself that I was all right, the general, without hesitation, gave me the desired permit, and, with a profusion of thanks, I bowed myself out of his presence.

On reaching the Todd Barracks, where the prisoners were confined, I found a one-armed major in command. He was very polite indeed, and entered into quite a conversation with me, during which he told me that he had lost his arm in the Mexican war. When my brother came, the major gave us his own private room, so that we might talk together without fear of interruption.

MEETING WITH MY BROTHER.

My meeting with my brother was a most affectionate one. It had been a very long time since we had seen each other, and there was much that each of us had to say. I disclosed to him part of my plans, and instructed him how to talk and act towards me. He was to call me his Union sister, and was to speak of me as a New Yorker. I expressed considerable hope that I would be able to effect his release, and stated that

I would go on to Washington for the purpose, if necessary, and see the president and secretary of war.

This proceeding, however, I found to be unnecessary, for Governor Brough, of Ohio, a hearty, pleasant-spoken, and good-natured old gentleman, happened to be stopping at the same hotel with me, and I contrived to obtain an introduction to him.   I cultivated the acquaintance of the governor with considerable assiduity, and he took quite a fancy to me, so much so, that he promised to use his influence to obtain a parole for my brother.   This promise the governor kept, and in a short time the prisoner was released and ordered to proceed East, and to report first to General Cadwalader, at Philadelphia, and then to General Dix, at New York, the idea being that he was to remain with me in the last-named city.

In company with my brother, therefore, I proceeded East, and went to New York, where I left him, while I went on to Washington, for the purpose of seeing what could be done in the way of aiding the Confederate cause by a series of operations at the Federal capital.

CHAPTER XXXIII.

SECRET SERVICE DUTY AT THE NORTH.

New Scenes and new Associations. — My first Visit to the North. — The Wealth and Prosperity of the North contrasted with the Poverty and Desolation of the South. — Much of the northern Prosperity fictitious. — The anti-war Party and its Strength. — How some of the People of the North made Money during the War. — " Loyal " Blockade-runners and Smugglers. — Confederate Spies and Emissaries in the government Offices. — The Opposition to the Draft. — The bounty-jumping Frauds. — My Connection with them. — Operations of the Confederate Secret Service Agents. — Other Ways of fighting the Enemy than by Battles in the Field. — I arrange a Plan of Operations, and place myself in communication with the Confederate Authorities at Richmond, and also with Federal Officials at Washington and elsewhere. — I abandon Fighting for Strategy.

WAS now introduced to entirely new scenes, new associations, and a new sphere of activity. I had never before been farther north than Washington, and my visit to the Federal capital was the hasty and secret one made shortly after the battle of Ball's Bluff, the particulars of which are recorded in a previous chapter. It was almost like going into another world to pass from the war-worn Confederacy to the rich and prosperous states which adhered to the Federal government; and, when I saw the evidences of apparently inexhaustible wealth around me, and contrasted them in my mind with what I was leaving behind in the yet unconquered Confederacy, I confess that my heart began to fail, and I despaired of the cause more than I had ever done before.

In a great portion of the South the towns and villages were few and far between, the forests large and dense, the population thin and scattering, while the most imposing of the Southern cities were far less splendid than New York and

383

Philadelphia, and such prosperity as they had at one time enjoyed was now all but destroyed, through the rigidness of the Federal blockade. Back of the Northern cities, too, was a rich, highly cultivated, and thickly populated country, with numerous large towns, abounding in wealth, and with apparently as many men at home, attending to the ordinary duties of life, as if there was no war going on, and no huge armies in the field.

Not only was there no blockade to put an end to commerce, and to cause a deprivation of many of the necessaries of life, but commerce, as well as all manner of home industries, had been greatly stimulated; so that the war—while it was starving the South, and forcing the male population into the field, until there were scarcely left enough to carry on absolutely needful trade and tillage—actually appeared to be making the North rich, and thousands of people were literally coining money with government contracts, and by means of innumerable industries brought into being by the great conflict.

The Strength of the Federals.

The subjugation of the South was therefore simply a question of time, if matters continued as they were, and the Federals would achieve the ends they had in view by sheer force of numbers and practically inexhaustible resources, no matter how valiantly the Confederate soldiers might fight, or how skilfully·they might be led. Was this subjugation of the South inevitable, however? This was the question that addressed itself to my mind, and upon the determination of which the course it would be best for me to pursue in the ·future would have to depend.

I was not very long in coming to the conclusion that a triumph of the Confederate cause was not by any means an impossibility, provided the right means were used to bring it about. I also speedily satisfied myself that the interests of the cause could be advanced just as much by diligent and zealous workers at the North, as by the men who were fighting the battles of the Confederacy in Virginia, Georgia, Tennessee, Mississippi, and Arkansas; and I was so well convinced that at last I had found the best field for the exercise of my own peculiar talents, that I greatly regretted not having made my way into the midst of the enemy's country long before.

For very nearly a year now I had done very little that was at all satisfactory to myself, or at all really helpful — that is, helpful in a large and positive way — to the Confederate cause; whereas, all this time I might have been carrying on a series of important operations at the North. It looked, indeed, like a great waste of time; but, if it was wasted, I resolved to do my best to redeem it, by the activity of my performances in the future; and I had great reason to hope that these performances would be productive of not unimportant results.

It required but a slight acquaintance with the condition of affairs to discover that the surface indications of wealth, prosperity, and overpowering strength at the North were delusive. The North certainly was wealthy and powerful; but, unfortunately for the Federal government's efforts to conquer the South, and to put a speedy end to the war, the people were very far from being united.

United Public Sentiment at the South.

At the South there were few, if any, genuine adherents of the Federal government, and public opinion was united on the subject of achieving independence. At the period of which I am writing — the winter of 1863–64 — there may have been, and doubtless were, many persons who were heartily tired of the war, and who would have been glad of peace on almost any terms. The vast majority, however, were still in favor of fighting the thing out, in spite of poverty, and in spite of the privations of every kind which they were compelled to suffer.

At the North, on the other hand, the majority of the people had entered upon the war with reluctance; many who did go into it with considerable enthusiasm, with the idea of preserving the Union, were disgusted when it became day by day more apparent that the emancipation of the slaves was a part of the policy of the government; many who went into it for the sake of seeing some fighting were heartily tired, and wanted to stop; and many more, who were eager enough to begin a fight, simply out of animosity to the Southerners, sickened of the thing when their pockets were touched by the enormous advance in prices, and by the heavy taxes which the prolongation of the contest necessitated, and were quite willing for peace at almost any price.

25

In addition to these elements of discord, there was a large, influential, powerful, and wealthy anti-war party, composed of people who were, and always had been, opposed to the war, and who numbered among them many who were not only opposed to the war, but who were warm and earnest friends of the South. These latter believed that the government had no right to coerce States which desired to leave the Union to remain in it, and they were bitterly antagonistic to any and all attempts to subjugate the South, and did everything in their power to baffle the efforts of the government to carry on the war efficiently. These people constantly aided, with their money and their influence, the Confederate agents who were working and scheming for the advancement of their cause at the North, and did a great deal to embarrass the Federal government.

Besides these, there were a great number of weak-kneed, or indifferent people, who had no opinions of their own worth speaking of, and whose chief anxiety was to be on the winning side. These were for the war or against it, as the tide of battle turned in favor of the Federals or the Confederates. The news of a tremendous defeat inflicted on the Confederates, or of the capture of an important position, would excite their enthusiasm, and make them talk loudly of fighting the thing out until the rebels were whipped; while a season of prolonged inactivity, or a succession of Confederate victories, caused them to look gloomily on the situation, and to suggest that there had been about enough fighting, that it was about time prices were coming down a little, and that as the war had been going on so long, without any practical results, there was not much use in killing more men and spending more money, when there was no more chance this year than there was last of a speedy end to the contest. In this class the Confederates found many allies.

The Presidential Campaign.

At the time of my arrival at the North the anti-war party was concentrating its strength for the approaching presidential campaign, and many men who were prominent in it were decidedly confident that the next election would place a president in the White House, whose views about the proper policy to be pursued towards the South would be radically different from those of Mr. Lincoln. If an anti-war president could be elected, — and there were many reasons to believe that such a thing would be possible, — a speedy wind-up of the war, on terms satisfactory to the Confederates, would almost certainly follow his inauguration.

This being the situation, it was as much for the interest of the Richmond government that the political dissensions existing within the Federal lines should be kept alive, and the success of the anti-war party promoted by every possible means, as it was to win victories on the battle-field. Indeed, it was much more important; for victories cost men and treasure, which the Confederacy could not well spare, and even more was to be gained by fighting the enemy on his own ground with the ballot, than there was by shooting him on Confederate soil with the bullet.

It was an important part of the duty of the Confederate agents at the North to aid, by every possible means, the success of the anti-war party, and to this end they labored incessantly and effectively in various ways; but, outside of the field of politics, there was an immense amount of highly important work being done, the like of which my brief experiences in New Orleans had barely given me a hint of.

CONFEDERATE SPIES AND AGENTS IN GOVERNMENT EMPLOY.

Many officials in the government employ were either secret service agents of the Confederacy, or were in the pay of such. There was not a public building at Washington that did not contain a person or persons who was not only willing, but eager to do much more than furnish information to the commanders of the Confederate armies and to the Richmond authorities, as far as it was possible to do so without placing themselves in peril. In all of the large cities were men and women, many of them in government employ, who were in constant communication with the Confederate agents, and in all of them were merchants who were rapidly growing wealthy by sending goods of all kinds, including arms and ammunition, to the South, either by having them smuggled through the lines, or by shipping them to some neutral port for the purpose of having them transferred to blockade-runners.

Some of these merchants made no pretensions, but sold to whoever would buy, having the avowed intention of making all the money they could by every safe means. They simply asked no questions, but took their cash, and shipped according to order. Others were blockade-runners, pure and simple, and their only anxiety was to keep their operations concealed from the government detectives.

Millions of dollars' worth of goods, however, were sold for the Southern market by men who were loud in their protestations of loyalty to the Federal government, who bitterly denounced the South, in public and in private, who contributed largely to aid in carrying on the war, and who enjoyed, in the fullest manner, the confidence of the government, and of those of their fellow-citizens who honestly believed that the war was a just one.

I will not say that all of these men were hypocrites and traitors, for I am confident that very many of them were not. Some, however, — and those not the least influential and wealthy, — had different opinions about things in general, and the war, in particular, in public and in the social circles which they frequented, and in their counting-rooms, when certain people called on them for the purpose of buying goods. They were more than anxious to sell to any one who would buy, but in case the buyer was known to be, or was suspected of being, a Confederate agent, the question of the moment was, to sell without being found out. Of course, some of them were detected occasionally, but there was generally a way to be found for dealing with these gentlemen with tender consciences and highly loyal reputations, by which their goods could be purchased for cash, and their reputations spared, at the same time.

THE CONSCRIPTION.

Another element in the situation was, the intense opposition to the conscription which was going on for the purpose of recruiting the armies — the supply of volunteers having long since failed. This opposition, before my arrival at the North, had culminated in bloody riots in New York and several other places, which caused the greatest alarm, because they indicated, in a very positive manner, that there was a very large disaffected class in the population, which, if excited to take up arms, might be able to start a new and formidable rebellion within the Federal lines. Many of those, too, who professed to favor the war were opposed to the conscription; that is, they were opposed to being conscripted themselves, although they were willing enough that other people should go and do their fighting for them.

The most obnoxious feature of the draft, however, had been in a measure overcome by the different states, cities, and towns offering liberal bounties for men to enlist. In this manner most of the quotas were filled, but the payment of bounties — a demoralizing proceeding, under any circumstances — opened the way for the most shameless and gigantic frauds. The story of the bounty jumping during the last two years of the war, is not one that any patriotic American citizen can read with complacency or satisfaction, and for pure infamy I think that it surpasses anything that the future historian of the war will be compelled to put on record.

Bounty Jumping and other Frauds.

I had a good deal to do with these bounty-jumping frauds, and with a number of other matters very nearly as bad, — or, perhaps, in the opinion of the reader, worse, — and it may be thought that I was as culpable as those whom I now denounce. To those who are only willing to consider such a subject as this from one point of view, I have simply nothing to say; but fair-minded persons, North and South, will, however, freely admit that my actions as a secret agent of the Confederate government are not to be put in comparison with those of the dealers in human flesh and blood, the counterfeiters, and others who did what they did solely from motives of gain. At any rate, acting as I was under orders from the only government the authority of which I acknowledged, and animated only by an ardent desire to advance the interests of the cause which I had espoused, I felt that I was justified in embarrassing the enemy by any means in my power, and that the kind of warfare which I carried on in the rear of the Federal armies was just as legitimate as that which was carried on face to face with them in the field.

It was not pleasant for me to be brought into the relations I was with some of the most consummate scoundrels who ever escaped the gallows or the penitentiary, and it is impossible for me to reflect upon some of the features of my career as a Confederate secret service agent at the North with anything but regret that I should have been forced by circumstances to do what I did, or to associate with the men I did. There is nothing, however, in this portion of my career that I am ashamed of; and I have no hesitation whatever in giving to the world a plain, unadorned statement of the enterprises in which I was engaged during the last eighteen months of the war. So far as my own performances are concerned, this narrative shall be as full and as complete as I can make it; and if I fail to go into exact and minute details about certain important transactions, it will be simply because I feel that I am under obligations not to betray my confederates, no matter how unworthy they may have been. To some of these people I am under no obligations whatever, and shall consequently not hesitate to speak plainly concerning them; but with regard to others, I prefer to err on the honorable side by saying too little, rather than to rest under the imputation of betraying confidences.

Arranging a Plan of Operations.

It took me some little time, of course, to master the entire situation; but a very brief residence at the North enabled me to see that there was a vast amount of most important and valuable work to be done within the Federal lines, and that it was exactly the kind of work that I could do with the very best effect. I arranged my plans, therefore, for a series of operations in behalf of the Confederate cause, and, at the earliest practicable moment, placed myself in communication with the Richmond authorities, and with the various secret service agents in the Northern States and in Canada, and also with Federal officials of various kinds, with whom I desired to establish confidential relations, not only for the purpose of preventing their suspecting me, but to gain through them information otherwise unobtainable.

Having once established myself on a satisfactory footing with those who were managing matters at the rival capitals, it became a comparatively easy matter to go ahead with some degree of boldness, and to follow up a systematic scheme of action; and I flatter myself that, having once gotten fairly started, I performed the tasks I undertook with a praiseworthy degree of thoroughness, and with not altogether unimportant results.

The story of this portion of my career will differ materially from that which has preceded it. I have now to tell, not of battles and sieges, but of stratagems and wiles; and, as the results of warfare are determined even more by strategy than by actual hard fighting, I believe that the reader will find the ensuing pages equally entertaining with those which have preceded them, and probably more so.

CHAPTER XXXIV.

PLAYING A DOUBLE GAME.

Studying the Situation. — I renew my Acquaintance with old Friends of the Federal Army. — Half-formed Plans. — I obtain an Introduction to Colonel Lafayette C. Baker, Chief of the United States Secret Service Corps. — Colonel Baker and General Winder of the Confederate Secret Service compared. — Baker a good Detective Officer, but far inferior to Winder as the Head of a Secret Service Department. — I solicit Employment from Baker as a Detective, and am indorsed by my Friend General A. — Baker gives a rather indefinite Answer to my Application. — I go to New York, and fall in with Confederate Secret Service Agents, who employ me to assist them in various Schemes. — Learning the Ropes. — I send Intelligence of my Movements to Richmond, and am enrolled as a Confederate Agent. — I have several Interviews with Baker, and succeed in gaining his Confidence. — Baker's Surprise and Disgust at various Times at his Plans leaking out. — The Secret of the Leakage revealed.

ON going to Washington I had no very definite idea of what I would do, or, indeed, what I could do. I was now about to work under different auspices from any under which I had hitherto been placed, and it was necessary for me to look around a bit and study the situation. In a general sort of way I hoped to get access to the different departments, so that I would be able to find out what was going on, and to place myself in communication with persons who would be able to give me such information as I desired. It was also important that I should make the acquaintance of, and be on friendly terms with, officers of the army and others who would have the power to help me in case I wanted to run through the lines, or in event of my getting into any trouble through meddling with affairs that the government might not desire an irresponsible outsider like myself to know too much about.

The visit I had paid to the prison where my brother was confined, made me think deeply about the privations and sufferings endured by the brave Southern boys captured on a

392

hundred battle-fields, and now in the hands of the Federal authorities. The more I thought of them the more I was moved by an intense desire to do something to secure their release; and more than one crude suggestion of a plan for the accomplishment of so desirable an end floated through my mind, without, however, my being able to decide upon any definite method of procedure.

I hoped, on going to Washington, to find there some one with whom I was acquainted, and through whom I might fall in with those who could aid me in the execution of my designs. On my arrival in the Federal capital, therefore, I made inquiries concerning the prominent officers of the army there, thinking that, most probably, I would be able to meet some of my military friends of the good old days before the war, and I was not long in learning that General A. and Captain B. were both on duty in or near Washington.

Unconscious Confederates.

I will remark here, that I designate these gentlemen by the two first letters of the alphabet, because I desire to avoid giving any clew to their real names. They were both men of unimpeachable honor, and, had they suspected in the least what my designs really were, I believe that they would immediately have procured my arrest, in spite of any private friendship they might have had for me. I made use of them for the furtherance of my plans in the interest of the Confederacy, but they neither of them, on any occasion, wittingly gave me any information that they should not have given. On the contrary, they declined to be of any assistance to me in visiting the departments or in going to the front, on the plea that the stringent rules in force would not permit them to do so. I obtained points from them occasionally in conversation, for it is impossible for any one, not even a detective or a spy, to be as close-mouthed on all occasions as is desirable; but the chief aid which they extended was in introducing me to people whom I could use, and in maintaining intimate and friendly personal relations with me, by which I was enabled to gain a standing in certain quarters without trouble.

The general, when I introduced myself to him, appeared to be very glad to see me, and asked me innumerable questions about myself, my friends, and my adventures since we last had seen each other. I had a plausible story ready to tell him, in which fact and fiction were mingled with some degree of skill, and expressed myself with considerable bitterness concerning the rebels, wishing that I could do something to aid in securing a speedy termination of the war by their defeat. After a very pleasant intercourse with the general, I parted from him, with a request that he would do me the honor to call on me at the hotel, which he promised to do.

The next day I met Captain ·B. in the street, and we exchanged greetings. He, too, promised to call upon me. This promise he kept, and I had quite a long talk with him on general topics, preferring to see more of him before attempting to make him useful.

I saw both the general and the captain several times after that, and in the course of conversation with one of them, I forget which, he happened to say something about Colonel Baker which excited my interest, and induced me to make particular inquiry concerning him. I had never heard of this individual before, but I now speedily learned that he was the chief government detective officer, and that he was uncommonly expert in hunting down rebel spies, and in putting a stop to their performances. I immediately concluded that Colonel Baker was a personage whom it was eminently desirable that I should become acquainted with at the earliest possible moment, and that it would be much more advantageous for me to make his acquaintance through the introduction of one of my military friends, than through finding him on my track just when I had some enterprise for the benefit of the Confederacy in process of consummation.

Whichever of the two it was that I had my original conversation with about Baker, it was the general who made me acquainted with him, and who spoke of me in such a manner as to put me in the good graces of this terrible man at the start.

Getting Acquainted with Detective Baker.

Colonel Lafayette C. Baker occupied at Washington a somewhat similar position to that held by General Winder at Richmond, although he scarcely had the large powers and extensive authority of the chief of the Confederate secret service department. In fact, Colonel Baker was a detective officer more than anything else, and he had comparatively little to do with military matters. The chief employment of himself and his assistants was to hunt down offenders of all kinds ; and he was much more successful in this than he was in procuring information for the use of the war department, although he prided himself considerably on his own performances as a spy, and upon several not unsuccessful secret service expeditions into the Confederacy that had been made by his directions, and in accordance with his plans.

I confess that I came into the presence of so formidable an individual with some degree of trepidation; but I very soon learned to regard him as not half so ferocious as he looked, and as very far from being as difficult and dangerous a personage to deal with as he was made out to be. There is nothing like having a reputation for ferocity, and other terrible qualities, if you want to make people afraid of you, and Colonel Baker's reputation — how gained it would be somewhat difficult to tell — did him good service in exciting terror among those who were disposed to do things which it might not be pleasant for a government detective to find out.

Colonel Baker differed as much from General Winder in appearance as he did in other respects. Winder was a far more highly educated man, and he had all that peculiar polish of manners that can only be attained by education, and by constant association with refined and educated people. He was a rather imposing looking man, too, and a casual acquaintance with him was calculated to leave the impression that he was a very pleasant and good-natured old gentleman. Under his smooth exterior, however, was a deep scheming and far-reaching mind, and a hard and cruel disposition, and he was a much more dangerous individual to fall into the ill graces of than Baker. Baker was a man who, under some circumstances, I might have taken a genuine liking to; but the more I saw of Winder the less I liked him, and the more I was afraid of him.

BAKER'S APPEARANCE AND CHARACTER.

Baker was a tolerably fair-looking man, after a certain fashion. He was a returned Californian, having resided in San Francisco for a number of years before the war, and having been a member of the famous vigilance committee which made such short work with the rogues of that city in 1856. He had the bronzed face and the wiry frame of a western pioneer, and his manners were marked by a good deal of far-western brusqueness. His hair was dark and thick, and he wore a full and rather heavy beard; but his eyes were the most expressive feature of his face. These were a cold gray, and they had a peculiarly sharp and piercing expression, especially when he was talking on business. He also had a particularly sharp and abrupt manner of speaking at times; and more than once, when I have had reason to think that he might have knowledge of some of my transactions as a Confederate secret service agent, I have felt cold creeps all over me as he looked me straight in the eyes and spoke in that cutting tone of voice he was in the habit of using on occasions.

Colonel Baker was, in my opinion, a first-rate detective officer, and nothing more; for something more is necessary in the chief of a secret service department in time of war than to be a good hand at hunting down offenders. Give him a definite object to go for, and a very slight clew, and he would, in the majority of cases, accomplish a creditable piece of work. He had, however, very little skill in starting enterprises for himself. General Winder, in his place, would have made Washington a much more uncomfortable residence for Confederate spies and agents than it was during the war; and the fact that I was able to play double with the colonel, as I did for nearly a year and a half, and to carry on, as I did, a number of important operations on behalf of the Confederacy, so to speak, under his very nose, was not very creditable to him, all the circumstances being taken into consideration.

Colonel Baker, however, was not without his good qualities, even if he was far from being as great a personage as he thought he was. He was stern and severe, but he was a kinder man at heart than General Winder, although he lacked the intellectual attainments of the Confederate officer. With regard to the relative honesty of the two, it is perhaps as well that I should express no opinion.

APPLICATION FOR A POSITION IN THE FEDERAL SECRET SERVICE.

On being introduced to Colonel Baker by General A., I asked him if he could not give me a position in his detective corps in some capacity, explaining as my reason for making such a request that, having lost everything through the rebellion, I was in urgent need of obtaining some remunerative employment by which I could support myself. In the course of the conversation with him, I told pretty much the same story that I had to the Federal officers at Memphis. I was of Spanish extraction, and all of my friends and relatives were either in Spain or Cuba. My husband, who was a United States army officer, — this I put in for the sake of obtaining the corroboration of my friend, the general, who had been acquainted with my first husband, but who apparently was not aware of the fact that he was in the Confederate service at the time of his death, — had died about the outbreak of the war, and I had been plundered, and otherwise so badly treated by the rebels, that I had been compelled to come North, where I had resided for a considerable period, but without being able to do much in the way of supporting myself. I was well acquainted throughout the South, having travelled a great deal, and having met a great many prominent people, and I did not doubt but that I possessed much information that would be of value to the government, and believed that I could obtain more, as I thought that I had talents which would enable me to do good service either as a spy or simply as a detective.

In the course of a somewhat lengthy conversation with Colonel Baker, I expressed myself with considerable bitterness with regard to the rebels, and the treatment I professed to have received at their hands, and endeavored to impress him with the idea that I was quite as anxious to engage in spy duty for the purpose of being revenged on them, as for the cash I expected to earn by the faithful performance of the particular tasks which might be assigned me.

Baker asked me a good many questions — not particularly skilful ones it seemed to me — about myself, my family, how long I had been at the North, what induced me to take up with the idea of joining the secret service corps, what employment I had hitherto been engaged in, and a variety of other matters. To his interrogatories I replied promptly, and with seeming frankness, and I left his presence tolerably confident that he believed all I had told him, and that I had made a good impression. As for the general, he seemed to be deeply impressed, and advocated my cause strongly, urging Baker to give me an engagement without further delay. The colonel, however, was cautious — he would see about it; he would talk further with me on the subject; he did not know that he had anything he could give me to do just at present, but he might have need of me shortly, and would let me know when he wanted me, and all that sort of thing.

After we left, the general promised to speak to the colonel

again, and said he thought he could induce him to give me an engagement, but that, at any rate, he would try.

This interview with Colonel Baker convinced me that he was the man to begin with, if I wanted to get admission behind the scenes at Washington, and if I wanted to execute any really masterly *coup* at the North in behalf of the Confederacy. As a member of his corps, I would not only be able to do many things that would be impossible otherwise, but I would have ample opportunities for finding out a good many things that were going on, with regard to which the world at large was happily ignorant. As for Baker himself, I made up my mind that he was an individual wise in his own esteem, but with no comprehensive ideas, whom it would not be difficult to fool to the top of his bent. All that it would be necessary for me to do, in case he employed me, would be the performance of some real, or apparently real services for him, to secure his fullest confidence, while at the same time I could carry on my real work to the very best advantage.

Having waited about Washington for a week or two, without hearing anything from Colonel Baker, and the general having told me that there was no chance for me just at present, I decided to return to New York, as I thought, from a hint given me in a letter from my brother, that I might be able to commence operations there. I resolved, however, to cultivate Baker's acquaintance at the earliest opportunity, but thought that perhaps it would be best not to trouble him again until I had some definite scheme to propose.

CONFERENCES WITH CONFEDERATE AGENTS.

When I reached New York, and saw my brother, he was expecting every day to be exchanged; and he told me that he had been visited by several Confederate agents, who wanted him to try and carry some documents through when he went South. He was afraid, however, to attempt anything of this kind, and, besides, did not think that it would be honorable under the circumstances. Without saying anything about my plans to him, therefore, I went and saw the agents in question, told them who I was, referred them to people who knew me in the West, and in a general way disclosed to them my schemes for aiding the Confederacy. I did not, however, tell them about my interview with Colonel Baker, or that I had the intention of becoming an employee of his. This, I thought, was a matter I had best keep to myself for the present, for fear of accident.

These agents were exceedingly glad to see me, and had several jobs of work cut out which they were anxious that I should attend to. They did not strike me as being very important, but I thought that they would do to begin with, and that they would aid me in becoming acquainted with the Confederate working force in the North. I, therefore, promised to give them my aid so soon as my brother should leave for the South.

They then evinced a great eagerness to have me persuade my brother to carry some despatches through; but I said that it would be useless to ask him, and that the most I could expect of him was, that he would take a verbal message from myself to the officials who knew me in Richmond, to the effect that I was at the North, endeavoring to aid the Confederate cause by every means in my power, and filled with zeal to do whatever was to be done. It required considerable persuasion to induce my brother to do even this much, but finally, to my great satisfaction, he consented.

Secret Service Operations.

Shortly after this my brother went South on a cartel of exchange, and in due time I received information that my message had been delivered, and that I was recognized as a Confederate secret service agent.

In the mean while I made a large number of acquaintances among the adherents of both the Federal and Confederate governments, and did a great deal of work of one kind or another. None of my performances, however, for several months were of sufficient importance to warrant special mention in these pages, and their chief value to me was, that they kept me employed, and taught me what kind of work there was to do; and how to do it. During this time I visited Washington frequently, and always made it a point to see Colonel Baker, to whom I furnished a number of bits of information, the majority of which were of no particular value to him, although several were of real importance, and aided him materially in his effort to break up certain fraudulent practices, and to bring the rogues to justice.

By this means I retained his favor, and succeeded in gaining his confidence to a degree that the reader will probably think rather astonishing, considering my antecedents, and the kind of work that I was engaged in *sub rosa*. It should be borne in mind, however, that Baker did not know, and could not know, anything of my previous history; that I had been highly recommended to him, and that I was constantly proving useful to him. Wherein he failed in astuteness, was in permitting me to carry on the peculiar operations I did, almost under his eyes, and to make use of him, and of the machinery of his office, for the accomplishment of my plans.

At each succeeding interview I could see that Baker was becoming more and more favorably impressed with me, and I did not doubt that I would finally succeed in securing him as an unconcious ally of myself and my co-workers.

My grand opportunity at length did arrive, and the cunning secret service chief fell into the trap laid for him as innocently and unsuspectingly as if he had never heard of such a thing as a spy in his life. The colonel, as I have before remarked, was not a bad sort of a fellow in his way; and as I had a sincere regard for him, I am sorry he is not alive now, that he might be able to read this narrative, and so learn how completely he was taken in, and by a woman, too. He was a smart man, but not smart enough for all occasions.

One of Baker's Grievances.

I have heard Colonel Baker frequently complain bitterly of the manner in which so many of his neatly laid plans were revealed to the very persons whom he was most anxious should know nothing about them, almost as soon as they were arranged; and I have endeavored to console him, and to suggest reasons for the phenomena, but was never able to quite make him understand the mystery. The reader of this narrative will know, as Colonel Baker never was able to, why some of his arrangements for capturing certain people who were making themselves troublesome to the government which he represented came to nothing; and it is to be hoped that other detectives, who are wise in their own conceit, will be edified by the revelations herein made.

In the chapters immediately following, I will relate the particulars of a series of operations, which, in many respects, were the most important of my career. The grand scheme which I labored to promote was a failure, but the work which I was assigned to do, in connection with it, was thoroughly well done, and, had the others performed their part as well as I performed mine, the ending of the war would probably have been very different from what it was. It would, however, scarcely have been possible for me to have worked with the signal efficiency I did, had I not secured the aid of Colonel Baker; and, that the chief detective officer of the Federal government should have been induced, unconsciously and unsuspectingly, to assist a rebel enterprise of the dangerous character of this one, was one of the most curious of the many curious things that happened during the war.

Before embarking in this enterprise, I succeeded in making the acquaintance of a number of influential people in Washington and elsewhere, and was engaged in operations of no little importance, the recital of which will, I think, prove both entertaining and edifying to the public, as it will show what consummate scoundrels were filling high places under the Federal government during the war, and how the people who believed the war to be a just one, and were making every sacrifice to carry it on, were betrayed by some of these most trusted servants.

As these operations, however, were connected with others of a much later date, I will, in order not to break the thread of my story, defer narrating them at present, merely stating here that the detection of the gigantic frauds that were being perpetrated was one of the most creditable events of Colonel Baker's career. I say this, notwithstanding that I was working against him at the time, and was implicated in the transactions alluded to. My position with regard to these matters was very different from that of the men with whom I co-operated. I did certain things, and would do them again under similar circumstances, because I think that in time of war it is right and proper to take every advantage of the enemy; but I had so little regard for my chief associates, that, although I took good care to keep out of Baker's sight, and had no desire to have him capture me, I could not help wishing, when I heard that he had his clutches on them, that he would succeed in having them punished according to their deserts.

It was most discreditable in certain of the principal officers of the government, and in certain members of Congress, that

26

these people were permitted to have such opportunities for wholesale swindling, and that after they were detected, they were not only not brought to punishment, but some of them were even continued in office. Colonel Baker was indignant, and justly so, that his efforts were brought to nought through the interference of politicians, who were more afraid of having discredit brought on the party they represented, by the exposures which he made of corruption and scoundrelism in high places, than they were solicitous for honesty and efficiency in the administration of some of the most important affairs of the government. Baker was not only interfered with, and his plans balked, but his opponents even went so far as to persecute him, by bringing a charge of conspiracy, and by compelling him to defend himself in the courts.

I have known Colonel Baker to do some things that were scarcely defensible, but, with regard to this matter, I have the best means of knowing that he was entirely in the right, and that, had he been permitted to do as he wished, he would have effectually stopped rascalities of the worst kind, and have performed services that would have entitled him to the lasting gratitude of his countrymen. It was utterly disgraceful that he should have been subjected to persecutions for doing his simple duty, especially as his investigations were commenced, and for a considerable time carried on, at the instance of the very men who turned upon him so soon as his labors threatened to create a public scandal that might be disadvantageous to the political prospects of some of them. They were willing enough to hunt down, and to punish rascality, so long as they and their friends were not injured in any way, but so soon as Baker began to prove himself in earnest, and determined to bring the rascals to justice, no matter who might be hurt, the very men who had secured his services turned upon him, took sides with the rogues, and did their best to destroy him.

CHAPTER XXXV.

VISIT TO RICHMOND AND CANADA.

MAGNIFICENT scheme was on foot during the summer and fall of 1864, for making an attack upon the enemy in the rear, which, if it had been carried out with skill and determination might have given a very different ending to the war. As it was, the very inefficient attempt that was made created an excitement that almost amounted to a panic, and seemed to show how effective a really well-directed blow, such as was intended, would have been. Such schemes as this, however, are always extremely difficult of execution, and this one was particularly so, on account of the necessity which existed for the most profound secrecy in all the movements, up to the very moment when the blow was to be struck. A large extent of country was to be operated upon, several distinct movements, of equal importance, were to be carried on at the same time, the failure of any one of which would imperil everything, and a neutral soil was to be the base of operations.

403

That a considerable number of persons should be informed of the essential points of the proposed campaign could not be avoided, and, of course, each person admitted to the secret diminished the chances of it being kept; for, even were traitors less plenty than they usually are, the fact that we were arranging our plans and making our preparations in the midst of enemies, or of half-hearted friends, rendered it scarcely within the range of possibility ·that some unlucky word or indiscreet expression would not give some one a hint of what was going on, and enable preparations to meet the attack to be made.

Besides all this, two great difficulties in the way of success existed. There was no thoroughness of organization, — it was impossible, under the circumstances, that there should have been, — and there was no recognized leader whose authority was admitted by all, and who had the direction of all the movements.

The " Copperheads."

The blow, therefore, was to be, to a very great extent, a random one, struck in the dark, and with no assurances whatever that the results expected from it would follow. We were utterly unable to tell how much we could count on in the way of active assistance from the Southern sympathizers, or " Copperheads," as they were called. For my own part, I did not rely greatly upon anything they could or would do, and am now very well satisfied that it was a piece of supreme folly to have expected anything from them.

These people were really traitors both to the South and the North, and in the long run they did the cause of the Confederacy far more harm than they did it good. They professed to believe that the South was right, and yet they were not willing to take up arms for her, or, with very few exceptions, to do anything practical for her that would render themselves liable to get into the least trouble with the Federal government. They annoyed the government by their captious criticisms of all its actions, by opposing the prosecution of the war in every way that they could with safety to themselves, and by loud expressions of Southern sympathy. All they accomplished, however, was a prolongation of the war, and the disfranchisement of nearly the entire white population of the South after the war was ended; for to them, more than to the Southerners themselves, was due the imposition of the hard terms which were the price of peace. To the " Copperheads," therefore, as a class, the South owe little or nothing; and, according to my view, they were the kind of friends that people in difficulties had best be without.

THE PROJECTED ATTACK BY WAY OF THE LAKES.

The great scheme to which I have alluded was no less than an attack upon the country bordering upon the great lakes; the release of the Confederate prisoners confined at Johnson's Island in Lake Erie, near Sandusky, Ohio, and at other localities; their organization into an army, which was to engage in the work of devastating the country, burning the cities and towns, seizing upon forts, arsenals, depots, and manufactories of munitions of war, for the purpose of holding them, if practicable, or of destroying them; and, in fine, of creating such a diversion in their rear as would necessitate the withdrawal of a large force from the front.

A DIVERSION IN THE REAR OF THE ENEMY.

It was expected, in event of the success of the plan, that the Federal forces would be placed between two fires, and that the commanders of the Confederate armies in the South and in the North would be able between them to crush the enemy, and dictate terms of peace, or at least give a new phase to the war, by transferring it from the impoverished and desolated South to the rich, prosperous, and fertile North. As I have before stated, much reliance was felt by many on obtaining something more than mere sympathy from the " Copperheads." I, for one, however, had no great expectations that any considerable number of recruits would be gained on Northern soil, and founded my hopes more on the personal efforts of true and tried Southern men, than upon assistance of any kind from those who were not closely identified with Southern interests.

While the plans for the proposed grand attack in the rear was maturing, I was asked to attempt a trip to Richmond, and consented without hesitation. I was to consult with, and receive final instructions from the Richmond authorities, with regard to the proposed raid on the lake shores, and was also to attend to a variety of commercial and other matters, and especially to obtain letters and despatches for Canada.

Now was my time to make use of Colonel Baker; and I accordingly resolved to see what I could do with him, without more delay. Having received my papers and instructions, therefore, I went to Washington, and called on the colonel, who received me as politely as he had been in the habit of doing of late, and asked what he could do for me; for he saw, by my manner, that I had some definite project on hand, and began to believe that I really meant serious business.

In order to understand the situation from Colonel Baker's point of view, it may be necessary to state, that more than once rumors that attempts to liberate the Confederate prisoners were to be made, had been in circulation, and that Baker, as I knew, was exceedingly anxious to effect the arrest of some of the more active of the Confederate agents engaged in this and similar schemes.

A Confidential Talk with Baker.

I told him, therefore, that I had obtained information to the effect that a noted Confederate spy had been captured, and was now in one of the prisons, from whence he could doubtless find means to communicate with Confederates outside. My proposition was that I should go to Richmond, where, by passing myself off as a Confederate among people with whom I was acquainted, I would not only, in all probability, succeed in finding out exactly who this man was, and where he was, but what he and his confederates were trying to do. I suggested, also, that I could most likely pick up other information of sufficient value to pay for whatever the trip would cost the government.

When I had explained what I proposed to do, Baker said, " I am afraid if you attempt to run through the lines the rebs will capture you; if they do, they will use you rough."

I replied, " I am not afraid to take the risk if you will only give me the means of making the trip, and attend to getting me through the Federal lines."

" It will be a troublesome thing to get you through our lines," said Baker, " for it don't do to let everybody know what is going on when a bit of business like this is on hand; and, after you pass our lines you will have to get through those of the rebels, and that you will find no easy job, I can tell you, for they are getting more and more suspicious and particular every day."

" O, as for that," said I, " I can, if it is necessary to do so, go to Havana, where my relatives are living, and try and run through from there. I believe, however, that I can get through from here if I make the right kind of an effort; at any rate, I would like to make the attempt, if only to show you what I am capable of."

The colonel laughed at my enthusiasm, and said, " Well, you are a plucky little woman; and as you seem to be so anxious to spy out what the rebs are doing, I have half a notion to give you a chance. You must not blame me, however, if you get caught, and they take a notion to hang you ; for, you know, that is a way they have of dealing with people who engage in this sort of business, and your sex won't save you."

" O," said I, " I don't think that my neck was ever made to be fitted in a noose, and I am willing to risk it."

The result of the conference was, that Colonel Baker finally consented to let me try my luck, and he gave me a variety of instructions about how to proceed, and about the particular kind of information I was to endeavor to obtain. I saw very plainly that he did not entirely trust me, or, rather, that he was afraid to trust me too much ; but I attributed his lack of confidence in me to the fact that I was as yet untried, and consequently might be led by my enthusiasm into underrating the difficulties of the task I was undertaking, rather than to any doubt in his mind with regard to my fidelity. I resolved, therefore, to give him such proofs of my abilities, as well as of my fidelity, as would insure me his entire confidence in the future.

BAKER CONCLUDES TO SEND ME TO RICHMOND.

It having been determined that I should make the trip, Baker told me to get ready for my journey immediately, and, in the mean time, he could procure me the necessary passes to enable me to get through the Federal lines, and money to meet my expenses.

When we next met, he gave me five thousand dollars in bogus Confederate bills, and one hundred and fifty dollars in greenbacks, which he said ought to be enough to see me through all right. I suggested that if the Confederates caught me passing bogus currency, they would be apt to deal harder with me than they would simply as a spy. Baker laughed at this, and said that that was one of the risks I must run, but that he did not think there was any danger, as these bogus notes passed more readily in the Confederacy than the genuine ones did, which he could only account for on the supposition that the Confederacy was a bogus government. He seemed to think that this was rather a good joke, although I was not able to see exactly where the laugh came in, and am afraid that I must have struggled hard with the faint smile that I attempted.

Everything being ready, off I started, and had but little difficulty in getting through the Federal lines on the passes furnished me by Baker. To get through those of the Confederate forces was a more troublesome operation; but, as when I came to the outposts, I was able to declare my real errand, I was not seriously impeded, and once in Richmond I was, of course, perfectly at home.

In Richmond.

On my arrival in that city, I immediately communicated with the authorities, delivered the messages and despatches submitted to me, sent letters to merchants in Wilmington and Savannah, as I had been directed to do, and gave all the information I could about the condition of things at the North, the proposed raid, and other matters.

While waiting to hear from the men in Wilmington and Savannah, and for the preparation of such instructions as I was to carry back from the Richmond people, I found myself falling short in funds, and accordingly tried to see what could be done with Baker's bogus Confederate notes. I had no difficulty in passing them, and consequently invested the entire batch in greenbacks, but, as the United States promises to pay were worth more, even in Richmond, than those of the Confederacy, I did not make an even exchange, by a great deal. Indeed, the greenbacks which I pocketed by this operation amounted to a very moderate sum, all of which I knew would be required for my return journey.

Within a few days I heard, by special messenger, from the parties in Wilmington and Savannah. This man delivered to me a package which was to be taken through to Canada, and also orders and sailing directions for certain blockade-runners, and drafts which were to be cashed, and the money disposed of in certain ways for the benefit of the Confederate cause. I also received directions from parties in Richmond to confer with the Confederate agents, and, if agreeable on all sides, to visit the prisons; it being thought that, as a woman, I would be able to obtain admission, and be permitted to speak to the prisoners, where a man would be denied.

Then, freighted with my small, but precious package, several important despatches, and other papers, and a number of letters for Confederates in Canada, I started to return. I would have been a rich prize for the Federals, if they should capture me; and, while on my way back, I wondered what Colonel Baker would think and say, in case some of his emissaries should chance to lay hands upon me, and conduct me into his presence, laden with all this contraband of war.

RETURN NORTH BY WAY OF WEST VIRGINIA.

In consideration of the value of the baggage I was carrying, it was thought to be too great a risk for me to attempt to reach the North by any of the more direct routes, and I was consequently compelled to make a long detour by way of Parkersburg, in West Virginia. This involved a long and very tiresome journey, but it was undoubtedly the best course for me to pursue.

The wisdom in choosing this route was demonstrated by the result, and I succeeded in reaching Parkersburg without being suspected in the least by any one. At that place I found General Kelley in command, and from him procured transportation to Baltimore, on the strength of my being an attaché of Colonel Baker's corps, which was a very satisfactory stroke of business for me, as it saved both trouble and expense.

The instructions under which I was moving required me to go to Baltimore, and from there inform the different parties interested of my arrival, and wait to hear from them as to whether they were ready to meet me at the appointed places, before proceeding farther. I was also to wait there for some drafts for large sums, which were to be cashed in New York, and the money taken to Canada. This involved considerable delay, which was particularly unpleasant just then, as I was getting very short of funds, and was, moreover, quite sick, the excitement I had gone through with, — for this was a

more exciting life even than soldiering, — and the fatigues of
a very long and tedious journey, having quite used me up.

SHORT OF FUNDS.

On arriving in Baltimore, fearing that I would not have
enough money to see me through until I could obtain a remittance, I went to a store kept by a lady to whom I was told to
appeal in event of being detained on account of lack of funds,
and explaining who I was, and the business I was on, asked
her if she would not assist me. She looked very hard at me,
asked me a great many questions, and requested me to show
her my papers. I said that this was impossible, as not only
my honor and life were at stake, but that interests of great
moment were involved in the preservation of the secrets I
had in possession.

This, I thought, ought to have satisfied her; but it apparently did not, for she evidently regarded me with extreme
suspicion. Her indisposition to trust me might have been
caused by my rather dilapidated appearance, although my
soiled travelling dress ought to have been proof of the fact
that I had just been making a long, and very rough journey.
Finally, another lady coming in, she walked back in the store
with her, and I, supposing that she did not intend to take any
more notice of me, arose to go out. She, however, seeing
this movement, called for me to wait a moment. Shortly
after she returned, and, handing me a sum of money, said,
"I am a Union woman; but as you seem to be in distress, I
will have to aid you. This is as much as I can afford to give."

I, of course, understood that this speech was intended for
any other ears than mine that might be listening, and, merely
giving her a meaning glance, walked out of the store, without
saying anything further.

Having obtained this money, I went back to Barnum's
Hotel, where I was stopping, feeling considerably relieved, so
far as the exigencies of the moment were concerned, but not
knowing to what poverty I might yet be reduced before I
received my expected remittances. At first I was very
much vexed at the behavior of the lady in the store, as I
thought that the statement I made her, and the names of persons I mentioned as having referred me to her, ought to have
gained me her confidence at once. On reflection, however, I
came to the conclusion that she might not be so much to

blame after all, as she was obliged to be careful, on the one hand, not to be imposed upon, and, on the other, not to be caught having secret dealings with the Confederates.

ILLNESS.

That night I was so sick that I had to send for a doctor. I offered him my watch for his services, stating that I was out of funds, and was detained in Baltimore through the non-arrival of money which I was expecting. He, however, refused to take it, and said that I might pay him if I ever was able, but that it would not matter a great deal one way or the other. The next day I was considerably better, and was able to go about a little, and I continued to improve with rest and quiet.

While stopping at Barnum's Hotel, I became acquainted with a young captain in the Federal army, and, as I made a practice of doing with all Federal officers, — I did not know when they might be useful to me, — I courted his friendship, and told him a story about myself similar to that I had told on several other occasions with which the reader is familiar, and was especially bitter in my denunciations of the rebels. The captain was so affected by my pitiful narrative, that he introduced me to General E. B. Tyler, who was very affable and courteous, and who, learning that I was anxious to travel northward, and was short of money, kindly procured for me a pass to New York.

Finally, I received notice that one of the blockade-runners, with whom I was to communicate, was at Lewes, Delaware, and, on proceeding to that place, found an English brig, the captain of which was anxiously waiting to receive instructions as to what port he was to sail for. The cargo was principally powder, clothing, and drugs, and the captain was exceedingly glad to see me, as he wanted to get away as fast as he could, there being a liability that the Federal authorities might pounce upon him at any moment. I accordingly gave him his sailing papers, which contained directions for him to proceed to Wadling's Island, on the north of Cuba, where he was to transfer his cargo to another vessel, which was to run for any port it could make in the Confederacy. The captain handed me the cards of several houses in Liverpool and Havre, which were extensively engaged in blockade-running, and I bade him adieu, wishing him a safe and pleasant trip.

This errand having been satisfactorily despatched, I went to Philadelphia, where I took a room at the Continental Hotel, and telegraphed for my papers, money package, &c., to be forwarded to me from New York by express. The next morning I received, in reply to this, my expected drafts, and also the following characteristic letter: —

"QUEBEC, CANADA.

"MRS. SUE BATTLE: You will find enclosed a card of your government agent here, B——. Any orders you have for your government, if forwarded, we will execute and despatch quickly, according to your instructions. Messrs. B. & T. have several clippers, which they will put in the trade, if desired. I will drink your ladyship's good health in a bottle of good old Scotch ale. Let us hear from you at your earliest convenience. I will await your answer to return to Europe.

With great respect, and with hopes of success,
"I am, madam, yours truly,   R. W. L."

BACK IN NEW YORK.

I now proceeded, without further delay, to New York, where I was met, at the Desbrosses Street ferry, by my associate in that city, who conducted me to Taylor's Hotel, where he had engaged a room for me. He said that he had been getting somewhat anxious for my safety, the more especially as he was informed that the detectives had received some information of my doings, and were on the watch for me. This made me a trifle uneasy, as I did not know but my friend, Colonel Baker, had discovered some facts about me which had served to convince him that I was not likely to be as valuable a member of his corps as he had supposed I would when he started me on my Richmond trip. Since my return to the North I had been endeavoring to keep myself concealed from Baker and all his people, as I did not wish to renew my acquaintance with the colonel until I had visited Canada. That accomplished, I proposed to see him again, and to make use of his good offices for the purpose of putting into execution a still more daring scheme.

My New York accomplice said that he did not think I was in any immediate danger, although I would have to take care of myself. He himself had seen one of the detectives who were on my track, and, while I was evidently the person he was after, the description he had of me was a very imperfect one; so that, by the exercise of a little skill, I ought to be able to evade him. To put him on the wrong track, my accomplice had told this detective that he thought he knew the person he was searching for, and had procured a photograph of a very different looking woman, and given it to him.

Having cashed my drafts, and gotten everything ready, I started for Canada, carrying, in addition to valuable letters, orders, and packages, the large sum of eighty-two thousand dollars in my satchel. Mr. L., the correspondent whose letter has been quoted, was requested, by a telegraphic despatch, to meet me on my arrival in Canada.

Under ordinary circumstances, the great value of the baggage I was carrying would not have disturbed my peace of mind; but I knew that, in addition to the money I had with me, my capture would involve the officers of the Federal government obtaining possession of papers of the utmost importance, from which they would scarcely fail to gain quite sufficient information concerning the proposed raid to put them on their guard, and enable them to adopt measures for preventing the execution of the great scheme. It was not comfortable, therefore, for me to feel that the detectives were after me, and to be under the apprehension that one of them might tap me on the shoulder at any moment, and say, in that bland tone detectives use on such occasions, " Come, my good woman, you are wanted."

A DETECTIVE AFTER ME.

I was absolutely startled when, on approaching the depot, my companion, pointing to a man in the crowd, said, " There, that is the fellow to whom I gave the photograph. He is looking for you; so beware of him." Then, thinking it best that we should not be seen together by Mr. Detective, he wished me good luck, and said good-by, leaving me to procure my ticket, and to carry my heavy satchel to the cars myself.

I watched the detective as well as I could without looking at him so hard as to attract his attention, and saw that he was rather anxiously surveying the people as they passed into the depot. I was really curious to know how he managed to get on my track; for, although he might not be sufficiently posted about me for purposes of identification, it was evident that he was working on some tolerably accurate information with regard to my movements. I also wondered whether Colonel Baker had any suspicion of me ; but made up my mind that he scarcely could have, or else this officer would have been better posted.

After getting into the cars I lost sight of the detective until the arrival of the train in Rochester, and was congratulating myself that, not seeing the original of the photograph, he had remained in New York. At Rochester, however, to my infinite horror, he entered the car where I was, and took a seat near me.

When the conductor came through, after the train had started, the detective said something to him in a low tone, and showed him a photograph. The conductor shook his head on looking at it, and made a remark that I could not hear. I did, however, hear the detective say, " I'll catch her yet," to which I mentally replied, " Perhaps."

This whispered conference reassured me a little, as it showed that the officer was keeping his eye open for the original of the photograph which he had in his pocket, while the woman whom he was really after was sitting within but a few feet of him. I concluded that I would try and strike up an acquaintance with this gentleman, in order to find out what he had to say for himself, and because I thought that perhaps I could say or do something to make him even more bewildered than he was already.

I, therefore, picked up my shawl and satchel and removed to the seat immediately back of him. The window was up, and I made a pretence of not being able to put it down, so that after a bit the detective's attention was attracted, and he very gallantly came to my assistance. When he had closed the window, I thanked him, with a rather effusive politeness, and he, probably feeling a trifle lonesome, and also, perhaps, a trifle discouraged, seated himself beside me, and opened a conversation.

He was a short, thick-set man, with a dull, heavy expression of countenance, deep-set eyes, thick eyebrows, and a coarse and rather scrubby mustache. He did not have the appearance of being a very brilliant genius, but then, as I well knew, it did not do to place too much reliance upon mere outward appearances, especially with members of the detective force.

After passing the compliments of the day we launched into a general conversation, I attempting to speak with a touch of the Irish brogue, thinking that it would induce him to believe me to be a foreigner. I would have addressed him with a Spanish accent, but was fearful that it would help to betray me, Baker as well as others having been told that I was of Spanish extraction, while I did not know as yet how much real information the secret-service chief might have with regard to me, or whether this fellow was one of his officers or not. I was playing a rather desperate game, but I felt tolerably sure of being able to deal with the gentleman. I confess, however, to having felt considerable anxiety, although I strove to conceal it from my companion.

"You are going to Canada, are you not?" inquired my new-made friend.

"Yes, sir."

"Do you live there?"

"O, no, sir. I live in England. I am only going to Canada to visit some friends."

"Have you been in America long?"

"Only about eight months."

"How do you like this country? Don't you think it is a finer country than England?"

"O, I like living in England much better than I do here, and expect to go back so soon as I get through with my Canada visit. There is too much fighting going on here to suit me."

"O, you need not mind that; besides, the war will soon be over now."

"Do you think so?" I queried. I am afraid just with the least touch of sarcasm, and for fear he might have noticed something unpleasant in my tone, added, "I will be glad when the fighting is over. It is terrible to hear every day of so many men being killed."

"O, that is nothing; we get used to it."

"Yes," I mentally said, "it may be nothing to such a shirk as you, for you will take precious good care to keep your carcass out of danger."

The detective now took out of his pocket the photograph which my associate in New York had given him, and which I was anxious to see, and handing it to me, said, "Did you ever see anybody resembling this? I am after the lady, and would like very much to find her."

"She is very handsome," I replied. "Is she your wife?" — looking him straight in the eyes as I said this.

"Wife! no," said he, apparently disgusted at the suggestion that he was in pursuit of a faithless spouse. "She is a rebel spy, and I am trying to catch her."

"Why, what has she been doing? She looks like a very nice lady, and I hardly could think she would do anything wrong."

"Well, she has been doing a good deal that our government would like to pay her off for. She is one of the smartest of the whole gang." This I thought was rather complimentary than otherwise. "I am on her track now, however, sure," — "Yes, the back track," I thought — "and I am bound to catch her."

"Well, if she has been doing anything against the law, I suppose she ought to be punished; but I hope you won't treat her unkindly if you do succeed in catching her."

"She will have to look out for that. It don't do to show any mercy to these she devils; they give us more trouble than all the men together."

"But perhaps this lady is not a spy, after all. She looks too pretty and nice for anything of that kind. How do you know about her?"

"O, some of our force have been on the track of her for a long time. She has been working for these Copperheads and rebel agents here at the North, and has been running through the lines with despatches and goods. She came through from Richmond only a short time ago, and she is now on her way to Canada, with a lot of despatches and a big sum of money, which I would like to capture."

"Doubtless you would," I thought; and then said aloud, "I wonder how you can find out so much, when there must be a great many people coming and going all the time. Supposing that this lady is a spy, as you say, how do you know that she has not already reached Canada?"

"Maybe she has," he replied, "but I don't think so. I have got her down pretty fine, and feel tolerably certain of taking her before she gets over the line."

This was a highly edifying and entertaining conversation to me, and I would willingly have prolonged it indefinitely, for the purpose of trying to get some points from my companion which might prove useful. As he, however, seemed inclined to change the subject, I was afraid to seem too inquisitive, and we conse-

₁ₑₙtly dropped into a general conversation, of no interest to the reader.

The detective seemed determined to be as polite to me as he could; and on leaving the cars he carried my satchel, containing eighty-two thousand dollars belonging to the Confederate government, and a variety of other matters which he would have taken possession of with the utmost pleasure, could he have known what they were. When we passed on board the boat I took the satchel from him, and thanking him for his attention, proceeded to get out of his sight as expeditiously as I could.

When the custom-house officer examined my luggage, I gave him a wink, and whispered the password I had. been instructed to use, and he merely turned up the shawl which was on my arm, and went through the form of looking into my satchel.

THE DETECTIVE BAFFLED.

On reaching the Canada shore I was met by Mr. L., who gave me a very hearty greeting; but I cautioned him to say as little as possible just then, as we might be watched. Glancing back, I saw my friend the detective, anxiously surveying the passing crowd; and calling Mr. L.'s attention to him, I said, "Do you see that heavy man with the black eyebrows and scrubby mustache, who looks as though he had lost something?"

"Yes. What of him?"

"He has been travelling on the train with me all day, and has been exceedingly polite and attentive. He is a detective, and I am the individual he is after, but he isn't half smart enough to catch me."

I then, as we moved off, related my adventure with the detective to my Canadian friend. He thought it a capital good· joke, and said that I seemed to be tolerably well able to take care of myself.

On my arrival in Canada I was welcomed with great cordiality by the Confederates there, who were eager to know all about my trip, how things were looking at Richmond, whether I had letters for so and so, and anything else that I was able to tell them. I distributed my letters and despatches according to instructions; mailed packages for the commanders of the cruisers Shenandoah and Florida, which I had received with especial injunctions to be particularly careful of, as they

27

were very important; and then proceeded to the transaction of such other business, commercial as well as political, as I had on hand.

As this was my first visit to Canada, there was much for me to do, and much to learn. I therefore became acquainted with as many people as I could, and found out all I could about the methods of transacting commercial and financial business, who the proper parties to deal with were, and everything else worth knowing that I could think of.

PLANNING FOR THE GREAT RAID.

There were a good many matters of more importance than trade and finance, however, which demanded my immediate consideration, and many and long were the conferences held with regard to the proposed grand movement on the enemy's rear. There were a number of points about this grand scheme that I would have liked to have been informed of; but those who were making the arrangements for the raid were so fearful of their plans in some way getting to the ears of the Federal authorities, that they were unwilling to tell me, and other special agents, more than was absolutely necessary for the fulfilment of the duties intrusted to us. This excessive caution was, perhaps, demanded by the peculiarities of the situation; but it is certain, in my opinion, that could there have been a more definite understanding between the various co-workers, the chances of success would have been very largely increased. I, for one, could have performed my part with far more efficiency — although I did all that it was arranged that I should do — had I been trusted more largely with the details of the proposed movement.

As it was, I was merely furnished with a general idea of the contemplated attack, and was assigned to special duties in connection with it. These duties were to visit Johnson's Island, in Lake Erie, and, if possible, other military prisons, for the purpose of informing the Confederates confined in them of what was being done towards effecting their release, and what was expected of them when they were released. I was then to telegraph to certain agents that the prisoners were warned, and such other information as I might deem it important for them to be possessed of, in accordance with an arranged system of signals. This being done, I was to proceed to the execution of other tasks, the exact details of which, however, were made dependent upon circumstances, and upon directions I might receive from the agents in the States, under whose orders I was to act.

This plan for a grand raid by way of the lakes excited my enthusiasm greatly, and I had very strong hopes of its success. I knew how desperate the situation at the South was getting to be, and felt that a diversion of this kind, which would excite terror in the hearts of the people of the North, and which would probably cause a considerable force to be withdrawn from the front, would help the Confederate cause at this particular juncture more, even, than a series of brilliant victories on the well-trodden battle-grounds of the South. A large number of the people of the North were, I knew, getting heartily sick of the war, and I thought that it would only need a brilliant movement for transferring some of the fighting and some of the desolation to Northern ground, to cause the anti-war policy to demand that peace should be had at any price. Whether the proposed raid would have accomplished all that was expected of it, can, of course, never be determined. It is probable. however, that I, as well as others interested, underrated the difficulties of executing such a complicated scheme. Be that as it may, something could have been done, more than was done, had everybody been as enthusiastic and as determined as myself, and had there been no traitors with us. The scheme failed, when it should have been, at least, partly successful; but it need not have failed so utterly as it did, had it been managed with wisdom, backed up by true daring.

CHAPTER XXXVI.

..ANGEMENTS FOR A WESTERN TRIP.

I return to Washington for the Purpose of reporting to Colonel B
Apprehensions with Regard to the Kind of Reception I am likely to
have from him. — The Colonel amiable, and apparently unsuspicious. —
I give him an Account of my Richmond Trip, and receive his Congrat-
ulations. — General A. calls on me, and he, Baker, and I go to the
Theatre. — A Supper at the Grand Hotel. — Baker calls on me the next
Morning, and proposes that I shall visit the Military Prisons at John-
son's Island and elsewhere, for the Purpose of discovering whether the
Confederate Prisoners have any Intentions of escaping. — I accept the
Commission, and start for the West. — Reflections on the Military and
Political Situations.

N my return from Canada, I went first to New
York, where I delivered such matters as had
been committed to my care for my associates
there, and after a conference with them, hurried on to Washington, for the purpose of
seeing Colonel Baker.

It was not without many apprehensions that I concluded to face the colonel again, for I did not know
how much information he might have about me by
this time, and it really seemed like walking into the
lion's den. That his officers were aware of some of
my movements, as they were following me up rather too
closely for comfort, was certain; but whether they had yet
succeeded in identifying the rebel spy and secret-service
agent with the woman whom Baker had employed to go on a
confidential mission to Richmond, was not so clear. Taking
all things into consideration, I concluded that Baker and his
men must be rather in a mist about me; for the detective,
whom I had met on the cars, was evidently working somewhat in the dark, which could hardly have been the case had
his chief suspected me of playing a double game with him.

If Baker, however, had the least suspicion with regard to

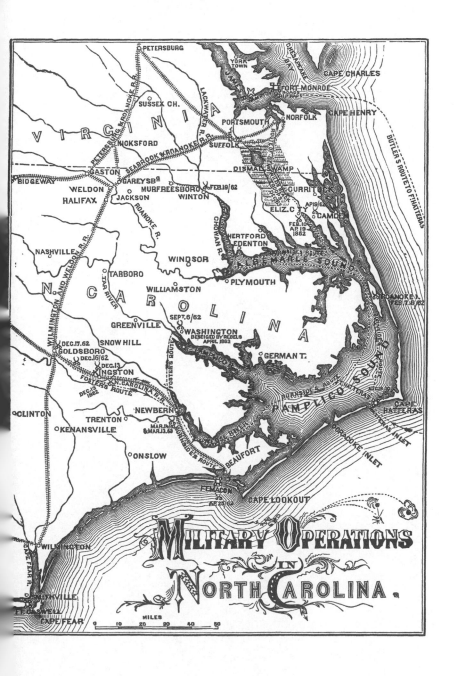

me, the fact of my very prolonged absence would, I knew, be liable to increase it, although under ordinary circumstances there would have been no difficulty in explaining this to his satisfaction; for he well knew that the errand he had sent me on was a difficult as well as a perilous one, and that it was not to be accomplished quite as easily as a trip between Washington and New York.

Making all allowances for the probabilities in my own favor, however, I confess that I experienced some trepidation at the idea of facing the colonel, and 1 wondered not a little what he would do with me in case he did happen to know who I really was. It was of such great importance, however, that I should gain immediate admittance to the military prisons, and I knew that such admittance could be gained by going there as one of Baker's corps, whereas it might otherwise be impossible, that I determined to take all the risks, so far as my own safety was concerned, and to try and have the colonel my ally in making the preparations for what, if properly carried out, would be one of the most brilliant episodes of the war, so far as the Confederates were concerned, and that would not unlikely have the effect of bringing the contest to a speedy termination.

The idea of being able to use the chief of the Federal detectives for the advancement of the Confederate cause was one that gave me enormous satisfaction, and I more than once fancied what a capital good joke it would be for me, after I succeeded in getting beyond Colonel Baker's reach, to inform him how badly he had been taken in, and to ask him what he thought of me and of my performances from a professional point of view.

REPORTING TO BAKER.

While on my way to Washington for the purpose of meeting him, and of making a report of my Richmond trip, my prospective interview was anything but a joking matter. The thing had to be done, though; so, stifling my fears, I, on my arrival in Washington, walked boldly into the colonel's presence, and announced myself as having just got back from Richmond.

Baker received me with proper cordiality, and congratulated me on my safe return. There was nothing whatever in his manner to indicate that he had the slightest suspicion of

me. This was reassuring; still I could not be quite certain
but that, having once got me into his power, he intended to
find out what I had to say for myself before beginning a less
agreeable conversation.

I, however, did not propose to commence saying disagreeable things if he did not; and so, presuming that he imagined
me to have just returned from the Confederate capital, I proceeded to make such a report of my doings as I thought would
suit him.

I told him that I had obtained the name of the spy whom
he was anxious to discover, and such a description of him as
would enable me to identify him without any difficulty, if I
could get to see him. The information I had obtained with
regard to him induced me to believe that he was at Johnson's
Island, but of this I could not be certain.

I then went on to say that it was understood in Richmond
that arrangements were being made for a grand stampede of
the rebel prisoners, and that this spy, in some way, found means
to communicate with the Copperheads and the rebel secret-
service agents. This was the story which it had been arranged
between my confederate and myself I should tell Baker, for
several reasons. There was the least bit of truth in it, and,
in endeavoring to throw a detective like Baker off the scent,
a little truth mingled with the fiction would be likely to
accomplish the object better than a story which was all
fiction. As there had been rumors more than once of
attempted stampedes of the prisoners, it was concluded that
Baker would not be likely to regard this one as of any very
great importance, especially if he had no inkling of the
grand raid which was to take place in connection with the
release of the prisoners, while at the same time he would be
anxious to find out whether a stampede was really to be
attempted, and if I managed right, would most likely employ
me to make the investigations for him.

This explanation is worth making, for its own sake, as it will
give the reader an idea of my method of working, and at the
same time will serve to show that I was not revealing to the
colonel any secrets which it was my duty to keep from him.

BAKER FALLS INTO THE TRAP.

Baker fell into the trap just as innocently as if he had been
a young man from the country, instead of the chief detective

officer of a great government which was engaged in a gigantic contest. On my suggesting my willingness to follow the thing up by visiting the prisons for the purpose of finding the spy, and if possible discovering the facts with regard to any conspiracy that might be on foot, he did not give me any definite answer at once, but said he would think about it; but I saw plainly that he considered the idea as rather a good one, and did not doubt that he would speedily make up his mind to send me.

When we had finished talking over this matter, I proceeded to give him a detailed account of what I saw and heard in Richmond. I said that the rebels were very strict and very suspicious, and would not allow any one to go to the front, or to visit the prisons or the public buildings. I was, however, able to pick up quite a number of facts that might be useful, and then went on to tell him a well-connected story, partly true and partly false, about the way things looked, and the way people talked; what the forces in the field, and their locations were; how the blockade-runners managed to get in and out of port; what I had seen and heard on the road as I was going to and fro, and so on. None of the real facts that I gave the colonel were of any importance, although I magnified them as much as I could, but they served to give an air of plausibility to my narrative, and to convince him that I was quite an expert spy, considering that I was a mere beginner.

Baker asked me numerous questions, which I answered to the best of my ability, so far as was consistent with the good of the Confederate cause; and when we had concluded our conversation he praised me very warmly, said that I was a plucky little woman, that he had thought I had vim enough to go through if any one could, that I had done a good service to the country, and a variety of other nice things, which had the effect of making me feel quite pleasant and quite at my ease with him again; being reasonably certain, although not absolutely sure as yet, that he was harboring no malevolent intentions towards me. Baker also remarked, that not hearing anything of me for such a long time, he had been getting somewhat uneasy about me; to which I replied, by telling him how and why I had been detained; and the explanation appeared to be entirely satisfactory, for he said no more on that point.

I was curious to know exactly how well he was informed

with regard to my real movements, and had half a dozen questions on the end of my tongue which I wanted to ask him. I concluded, however, that this would be going rather too far, and would do no good, while it might have the effect of exciting suspicions where none at present existed. I did, however, venture to inquire whether he had told any one that I was attached to the corps.

"No, no," he replied, "certainly not, and I don't want you to tell any one either. If I employ you for anything, it will be for strictly confidential business, which must be between ourselves. I would·rather that even my own people should not know anything about you as a secret-service agent."

Having finished our business talk, I asked for my friends General A. and Captain B., and was informed that the captain was in the field, but that the general was in the city, and would doubtless be glad to see me.

On reaching the Kirkwood House, where I had taken a room, I sent my card to the general at Willard's Hotel, and he came immediately to see me. While we were chatting, in came Baker, who, I judged by his manner, had something which he wanted to say to me, and surmised that it was a consent that I should visit the prisoners.

"Ah, general," said he, "I see that you are bound to continue your attentions to our little friend here. She hasn't been in Washington many hours, and you have found her out already. I guess, however, that she likes me better than she does you, for she came to see me as soon as she arrived."

The general looked a trifle surprised at this, and said, "Why, Baker, you must be getting to be a lady's man! I didn't know that you were particularly inclined that way."

Baker laughed at this, and said, "She is a first-rate little woman, and I wish there were more like her. She has just made a very successful trip to Richmond, and has brought me some important items."

"Is that so?" said the general. "Why, I did not know that she belonged to your corps."

"Neither does she in a regular way; but as she knew a good deal about Richmond, and was acquainted with a number of people there, I thought I would let her make a trip, especially as she was extremely anxious to try her luck."

The general congratulated me on my success, and then proposed that we should all three go that evening to Ford's Theatre. Baker assented, .and I was quite willing, as I thought an evening's entertainment in witnessing a good play would brighten me up a little. Besides, I was anxious, to cultivate the acquaintance of these two men, and was especially solicitous to have all possible opportunities of conversing with the colonel, with a view of inducing him to accede to my proposition for a visit to the military prisons. Baker and the general then said good-by, for the present. and went away together.

About seven o'clock in the evening the general returned alone, and as he was escorting me to the carriage I asked where Baker was. The general replied that he had been compelled to go unexpectedly to the executive mansion, on some business, but would probably join us in the theatre.

An Evening at the Theatre.

This aroused all my apprehensions of danger again, and I became fearfully uneasy lest all the colonel's fine words should merely have been intended to draw me out and conceal some sinister designs towards me. I stifled my fears, however, as well as I could, and after we got to the theatre tried to converse with the general in an agreeable and natural manner. I was startled by the least sound, however, and was unable to avoid turning round to look every time any one came in, almost expecting every moment that Baker, or one of his officers, would appear for the purpose of arresting me.

My fears proved to be groundless. Baker did come in soon after the play commenced, and taking a seat beside me, made an apology for not joining the party sooner, but begging to be excused, as he had been compelled to go up to the White House, for the purpose of having a talk with the president and the secretary of war. There was nothing in his manner then or afterwards to indicate that he was suspicious of me, and both he and the general, while the play was in progress, were apparently greatly absorbed in what was occurring on the stage.

As for myself, I found it impossible to get interested. I was uneasy for my own safety, knowing that I was playing a desperate game, and was even more anxious lest the grand scheme which I was endeavoring to promote should fail through any fault or misdirection of mine. My thoughts, too, wandered to our brave men in the field, and to the sufferings of the poor prisoners. I almost reproached ᵐ ᵃᶫ making an appearance of indulging in an evening's recreation in company with two Federal officers, while so many thousand Confederates were enduring so much, but consoled myself with the reflection that I was not doing this for mere pleasure, but was engaged in the performance of an important task, which might be greatly promoted through my acquaintance with these men. Finally, to my great relief and satisfaction, the play came to an end, and the curtain dropped for the last time.

As we passed out, the general proposed that we should go to the Grand Hotel and have some supper. I did not care to do this, but thought it best to accept the invitation.

At Supper.

We had a really superb repast — one of the finest I had ever sat down to ; and as I was hungry, I ate quite heartily. In the way of drinkables, I confined myself to lemonade, but the gentlemen took wine. The general, who was quite fond of his toddy, drank rather more than was good for him, and soon became very talkative and a trifle noisy. He was one of those men, however, who never forget to be gentlemen, and he neither said nor did anything offensive. Finally, he began spinning some long yarn, during which Baker took an opportunity to whisper to me that he would probably want to see me in the morning. I nodded assent, although my fears began to rise a little, but I hoped that instead of demanding a different account of my doings from that which I had already given him, the colonel would give me my commission for a trip to the West.

After we had finished our supper, we returned to the Kirkwood, where I bade them good night, at about a quarter before twelve, at the drawing-room door ; and as soon as they were gone, hastened to my own room to obtain the rest of which I stood in so much need, for I was tired out with the fatigues of travel and the excitement and anxieties of the day.

The next morning, just as I was sitting down to breakfast, the waiter brought me a note from Colonel Baker, in which he stated that he would call to see me at the hotel about half past ten o'clock, and requested me to await him at that hour. Still being uncertain whether Baker's intentions towards me were amicable or not, it was not without some trepidation that I looked forward to this interview. I did not know him then as well as I did subsequently, or I would scarcely have been so much afraid of him. It did not take me a very great while to discover that he was not a prodigy of astuteness, but at this time, as the reader is aware, I had had comparatively little to do with him. I knew that if he was not sharp he ought to have been, holding the position that he did, and I also knew that I had good cause to dread falling into his hands, or even being suspected by him. Not only were some of the members of his corps eagerly looking for me, but I was about engaging in a particularly hazardous enterprise which it would have made Baker's fortune to have gotten an inkling of, and I did not know — even presuming that Baker himself was unaware of the fact that I was a Confederate spy — how soon he or some of his men might succeed in identifying me with the troublesome woman they were searching for, or how soon they might discover something about the plot which I was aiding to carry out. The situation, therefore, was a delicate one for me, for much more than my own safety was dependent upon the chief of the United States secret service continuing in the belief that I was exactly what I represented myself to be, and retaining his confidence in me.

Thus far, to be sure, I had been able to detect nothing in Colonel Baker's manner to indicate that his suspicions were excited in the least, although I had watched him narrowly. But, as I knew that, as a detective, it was a part of his business to mask his thoughts and feelings, and not to give even a shadow of a hint that he had been preparing a trap until the moment he was ready to spring it and secure his victim, I felt that I could not place too much reliance on his friendly looks and behavior. On the other hand, I had much confidence in my own power of reading character and detecting motives, and, in watching Colonel Baker, during my late interviews with him, I was not working in the dark, as I might have been doing under some circumstances. I knew that there was good reason to believe not only that he might suspect me, but that he might be possessed of accurate information about me, and I accordingly studied his behavior towards me from this standpoint. The result was a reasonable conviction with regard to my present safety, and yet nothing like a feeling of absolute certainty. As for the future, I, of course, could know nothing as to what that would bring forth, but was prepared to venture everything.

At the appointed time, Colonel Baker made his appearance, and said " Good morning " with a pleasant smile, in which there was apparently not a shade of malice or unfriendliness. After asking me how I had liked the play, and making a few other unimportant remarks, he said, " Well, my little woman, I have made up my mind to let you try your skill as a detective once more, if you are in the same mind you were yesterday."

" Yes," I replied, " I am just as anxious now as I was then, and I think I can not only find that spy for you, but that I can discover whether there really is any intention among the rebel prisoners to make a break."

" That is just what I want you to do.   I think that a woman can manage a job of this kind better than a man anyhow, and I believe that you are just the woman to manage it in first-rate style."

" Thank you, colonel ; I can at least try."

About that Spy.

" Yes, that's it ; try and find out all you can.   I want you to pick out this man for me if he is at Johnson's Island, as you seem to think he is, and if you succeed in finding him, telegraph to me immediately.   If he is not at Johnson's Island, you had better try and find out if any of the prisoners know anything about him; it is possible, you know, that he may be in some other prison, or, indeed, that he may have escaped.   At all events, make every effort to find him."

" You know, colonel, I am acquainted with a good many people down South, and I may come across somebody I know, or somebody that knows somebody I know, and by representing myself as a disguised Confederate, I may be able to get the prisoners to talk plainer than they would to a stranger or a new visitor."

" Well, I will leave it to you to manage the thing the best way you can think of.   It would not be a bad idea, however, if you were to pass yourself off as a Confederate secret-service agent, and if you were to intimate that something was likely to be done soon to procure the release of the prisoners, you might be able to induce them to say whether they have any plans of their own, or whether they are in communication with any one outside."

" That is about my idea of working ; but the only difficulty will be in getting a chance to talk to any of the men privately."

" O, I'll arrange that for you by giving you a confidential letter, which, however, you must be careful not to let any one see except the commanding officer. If those fellows are up to any tricks, I want to know all about it at once. There has been a good deal of talk at different times about the prisoners attempting to stampede, but it has been pretty much all newspaper sensation, with nothing in it."

" But, you know, colonel, something of the kind might be attempted; and if a stampede or an insurrection should take place, it would create a good deal of excitement just now."

" Yes, yes ; that's so. If there is anything on foot I want to discover it, and I want you to find out all you possibly can, and let me know immediately."

" Well, you can rely upon me, and I think you will find me as shrewd as most of your detectives are."

" If you will only keep your eyes and ears well open, and open your mouth only when you have business to talk about, I will most likely find you a good deal shrewder."

" Why, colonel, you don't appear to have the best opinion in the world of some of your detectives."

" O, yes, they do pretty well ; some of them are really first-rate men; but they are not as smart as they ought to be for the kind of service they are in."

" I suppose some of those rebel spies give you a good of trouble in keeping the run of them."

" O, you haven't any idea of it. Half the people of Washington and its immediate vicinity are rebel sympathizers, and would be spies if they dared, and knew how. And then they are at work all through the North and in Canada. Some of my people are after a spy now who has been travelling between Richmond and Canada, but they don't seem to be able to lay their hands on her. If they don't catch her soon, I have half a mind to let you try what you can do, if you succeed well with your present trip."

The conversation at this point, I concluded, was getting to be rather too personal, and I thought it best to change the subject, although I could not help smiling at the idea of Baker employing me to catch myself. That, I thought, would be entirely too arduous a task for me to undertake in my then rather feeble state of health, although there might be both amusement and profit in it. Forbearing, however, to enter upon this interesting theme, I asked the colonel when he desired me to start. He said by the first train, if I could get ready; and handing me my confidential letter and two hundred dollars, he asked whether there was anything more he could do for me.

I said that I could think of nothing, but would proceed to get ready for my journey immediately. He then shook hands and left, after wishing me a pleasant trip, and expressing a hope that he would soon receive a good report from me.

When the colonel was gone, I went up to my room to pack my travelling satchel; and feeling perfectly satisfied from my late conversation with him that I was safe for the present so far as he was concerned, I laughed heartily at the absurdity of the situation, and wondered with myself whether I would have dared to attempt anything of this kind at Richmond with old General Winder. I had no difficulty in concluding that if fate had compelled me to play tricks with Winder, as I was doing with Baker, I would have been forced to proceed in a less open and free and easy style about it, and congratulated myself most heartily that I had so easy a customer to deal with under existing circumstances.

Calling a carriage, I was soon at the Baltimore depot, and on board the train. Having to stop at the Relay House for the western bound train, I made an effort to see the Confederate agent who was stationed there, as I had a number of things I wanted to say to him. He was an old Southern acquaintance of mine, and there were a variety of little matters that I could have whispered in his ear that would have been useful, and, at the same time, that I would not have cared to confide to every agent with whom I happened to come in contact. There is a good deal in knowing who one's friends really are in transacting such delicate business as that I was then engaged in. Unfortunately, my friend was away; and as I was in too much of a hurry to wait for his return, I was forced to forego the pleasure of seeing him.

WESTWARD HO !

Once on board the Western train, I had a long journey before me, and had plenty of time to think over affairs generally. I planned and schemed until my brain fairly whirled, and I was glad to chat a little with some of my neighbors, or to gaze through the car windows at the gorgeous scenery that met my eyes at every turn in the road, and to try and think for a while only of its beauties, as a rest from the wild thoughts that filled my mind.

Try as I might, however, I could not avoid thinking of the situation, the prospects of the Confederacy, and the chances of success for the grand scheme, the execution of which I was endeavoring to assist. What if we failed? or, if we succeeded in our first effort, would we be able to accomplish all we intended and expected? These were questions I could not answer. What I dreaded most was, the possible effect of a raid by way of the lakes on the Confederate sympathizers and the anti-war party. Would it stimulate them to make greater exertions than ever to bring the conflict to a close, or would this, bringing the war to the doors of themselves and their neighbors, turn them against us? I confess that I had fears of the latter result, for I had a not ill-founded distrust of these people, who are neither one thing nor the other; and I believed that had the Copperheads wielded their influence, as they might have done, they could either have prevented the war in the beginning, or could have forced a conclusion long ago.

What power the opponents of the war were able to exert would, however, be determined very shortly. A presidential election was coming off in a few weeks, and the greatest excitement with regard to the political battle that was being waged prevailed. Nearly everybody admitted that the defeat of Mr. Lincoln for a second term would mean that a majority of the people of the North were ready and anxious to abandon the contest, and to let the seceding Southern states go in peace. The fact that the Democratic candidate was a Federal general, who had been commander-in-chief of the armies, and who professed to be willing and anxious to carry on the war, did not please me very well, for it indicated to my mind, very plainly, that the anti-war people were afraid to oppose Mr. Lincoln and the war party on a square issue.

I, however, was nothing of a politician, and did not profess to understand the ways of politicians, they being a class of men for whom I had no special admiration. But I could not help thinking that the Confederate government and the people of the South were basing too many hopes on what the Democrats would be able to do at this election. I knew that they in many ways were doing what they could to secure a Democratic victory; but, for my part, I relied far more on bullets than on ballots to give the South the victory, and I expected more from the great raid, for which I was now working, than I did from the election of General McClellan.

Neither the raid nor the election turned out as it was hoped they would, but just about that time barren hopes were pretty much all that Confederate patriotism and enthusiasm were fed on, and they were rapidly getting starved for lack of more solid meat. The failure of the contemplated raid in the rear, and the re-election of Mr. Lincoln, put an end to all expectations of such a division of sentiment at the North as would be of any benefit to the Confederacy, and there was nothing to be done but to fight the thing out to the bitter end.

The period which preceded the overthrow of the Confederacy was, however, one of brilliant campaigning and desperate fighting, and was the time when the Confederate agents and spies at the North labored with the greatest assiduity. The performances of these agents and spies have never yet been related as they deserved to be, and this narrative of my adventures, personal as it is in its nature, and limited as it necessarily is in its scope, will, I trust, be regarded as a not uninteresting or unimportant contribution to a history of some of the least understood phases of the great conflict.

CHAPTER XXXVII.

JOHNSON'S ISLAND. — PREPARATIONS FOR AN ATTACK ON THE FEDERAL REAR.

On the Way to Sandusky. — I am introduced to a Federal Lieutenant on the Cars, who is conducting Confederate Prisoners to Johnson's Island. — He permits me to converse with the Prisoners, and I distribute some Money among them. — Arrival at Sandusky. — First View of Johnson's Island. — I visit the Island, and on the Strength of Colonel Baker's Letter am permitted to go into the Enclosure and converse with the Prisoners. — I have a Talk with a young Confederate Officer, and give him Money and Despatches, and explain what is to be done for the Liberation of himself and his Companions. — Returning to Sandusky, I send Telegraphic Despatches to the Agents in Detroit, Buffalo, and Indianapolis. — How the grand Raid was to have been made. — Its Failure through the Treason or Cowardice of one Man.

T Parkersburg I met General Kelley again, and had a talk with him, in which he laughingly suggested that I seemed to be in as much of a hurry to go West as I had been to go East the last time he saw me. I remarked, that in war times the enemy had a way of putting in appearances at various points of the compass, and that we had to go for him wherever he happened to be, if we didn't want him to come to us. I also hinted, with a little maliciousness, that perhaps the reason why the war had lasted so long was because so many of our generals instead of going after the rebels wherever they were to be found, insisted on waiting for them to come to places where it would be most convenient to fight them. The general said there was some truth in that; and that if all the generals were as smart about doing what they had to do as I seemed to be, the rebels would have been whipped long ago.

It is pleasant to have commendation even from those we are fighting against, and I felt flattered at the general's good opinion of me, although I knew that he was really not aware what good cause he had to commend my smartness. I won-

28   433

dered what he would say about me if he should suddenly discover what kind of an errand I was then really on, and how, as one of Colonel Baker's secret agents, I was aiding in the execution of a plot, that, if successful, would cause a panic at the North such as had never yet been dreamed of. But such things at such a time were not even to be looked out of the eyes, much less hinted at with the lips, and I parted from the general, with Cincinnati as my next objective point, with a full expectation that ere long he would hear of me, or at least of my work, in a way that would astonish him.

Making the Acquaintance of an Officer in Charge of Confederate Prisoners.

After leaving Cincinnati *en route* for Sandusky, I was introduced by the conductor to a lieutenant who had in charge twenty-seven Confederate prisoners. These he was taking to Sandusky to be placed on Johnson's Island, and I, consequently, thought that he might be an advantageous person to know, and that if I could manage to get into his good graces I might in some way advance the interests of the scheme I was engaged in by means of him.

This officer was a rather flashy young man, who evidently thought that he cut a very dashing figure in his uniform, and whose mind was given rather to reflection on his own importance than to the acquisition of useful knowledge. He was not, however, without a certain amount of good sense, and he made a far from disagreeable travelling companion, for we speedily got tolerably well acquainted, and he not only was very attentive, but he entertained me not a little by his conversation.

Not knowing what use I might have for him, I tried to be as cordial as possible, and long before we reached Sandusky we were on the best of terms. I did not find out a great deal from him that was worth knowing, for the reason, perhaps, that he did not know anything. He, however, permitted me to have a talk with the prisoners, whom I questioned as to what commands they belonged to, when they were captured, and other matters, and gave them each a dollar apiece out of Colonel Baker's money. Beyond asking them questions, I did not say a great deal to them, for I could not know how far they were to be trusted; but I looked much more than I said, and several of the more intelligent among them exchanged significant glances with me, which intimated that they understood that I had a purpose in view in cultivating the acquaintance of the lieutenant so assiduously, and was disposed to befriend them by any means in my power.

As to the lieutenant, he took such a decided fancy to me, and was so excessively gallant, that he insisted upon paying all my incidental expenses along the road. To this I could not, under the circumstances, permit myself to make any objections, but I was unable to avoid wondering whether it was his own cash or that of Uncle Sam's he was so very free with. That, however, was no concern of mine, and it would have been even more impolite for me to have asked him the question than to have declined to permit him to pay my bills.

It was midnight when we reached Sandusky. The lieutenant, attentive to the last, put me in the hotel coach, and requesting me to keep an eye on his satchel, he excused himself for a few minutes until he could dispose of his prisoners. I do not know what he did with them; but while I was waiting for him, I was also wishing heartily that they would manage to give him the slip and escape. Before a great while, however, he made his appearance again, and jumped in the coach. We then drove to the hotel, where he registered my name and procured me a room. After seeing me safely installed in my quarters he said good-night, and expressed a hope that he would have the pleasure of escorting me to breakfast in the morning.

First Sight of Johnson's Island.

When I awoke the next morning I went to the window, and, drawing the blinds, looked out upon the lake, seeing in the distance what I supposed to be Johnson's Island. This little piece of ground, rising off there so serenely and beautifully from the bosom of the lake, was to be the scene of my next great effort in behalf of the Confederacy, — an effort that, if crowned with success, would bring me more credit and renown, and would do more to promote the success of the cause, than all the fighting and campaigning I had done. On it were thousands of brave Confederates, who were sighing for their homes in the sunny South, sighing to be once more on the battle-field fighting for Southern independence, and, all unconscious that the moment was approaching when one good blow rightly struck would not only put an end to their irksome captivity, but would go far to secure all that they had taken up arms for, — all that they had suffered for on the battle-field and in the prisons of the enemy. It was a great responsibility that rested upon me, this preparing the way for the grand attack which was to transfer the seat of war to these beautiful lake shores, that was to effect the release of these prisoners, and that was, perhaps, to end the war ; and I trembled to think that, perchance by some trifling slip or mistake, the whole scheme might miscarry and come to nothing.

When I was dressed, I rang the bell for the chamber-maid to take my card to the lieutenant, to let him know that I was ready for breakfast. When the woman came, I asked her if that was Johnson's Island, where the rebel prisoners were kept. She replied that it was, and that she wished they were away from there. I asked her why, and she said she was afraid they would break loose some time and burn the town. I told her I guessed there was no danger of anything of that kind happening, as there ought to be soldiers enough to guard them. She did not appear to be at all sure upon this point, but seemed to think that a general stampede of the prisoners was a very likely thing to happen. I was of about the same opinion, although I did not tell her so, but followed her down stairs to the drawing-room, where I found my lieutenant waiting to take me in to breakfast.

During the progress of the meal the lieutenant said that he would have to go over to the island with his prisoners, but that he would be back about eleven o'clock, when, if I would permit him, he would get a team and we would take a drive. I thanked him, but declined, on the plea that my engagements would not permit of my accepting his kind invitation, although I might be able to do so at some future time. He said he was sorry, but that he was afraid he would not be able to permit himself the enjoyment of my company much longer, as it would be necessary for him to return the next day, at the latest. I professed to be sorry, but was not very much so, for I wanted to get rid of him, having come to the conclusion that he was not likely to be of much more use to me, while if he pursued me with his attentions he might prove a serious impediment to the proper execution of my plans.

So soon as he was well out of sight, I went to the telegraph office, and sent despatches to the Confederate agents at Detroit and Buffalo, announcing my arrival, and received their responses. This duty performed, I started for the boat that was to carry me over to the island.

While crossing to the prison camp, where so many of my comrades were confined, my mind was filled with a thousand suppositions as to what might happen. The least accident might bring the whole great scheme to nothing, and I felt a nervousness and a dread of consequences at the idea of undertaking the task before me that I had never experienced when facing the enemy on the battle-field. So far as any personal danger was concerned, I was no more sensible of fear than I was when the bullets were flying thick and fast around me ; but it was a terrible sensation, that of feeling that the fate of a magnificent campaign was in my hands, and that upon my good management would depend whether it could ever be inaugurated or not. The sensation was such as a general might feel when making the first movement in a great battle upon which the fate of a nation depended. I did not lose anything of my coolness or my resolution, but I could not help being oppressed, in some degree, with the weight of my responsibility, and could not help wondering whether I would succeed in doing, in good style, what I had been assigned to do, or if, after I had finished my part of the work, my associates would have the skill and courage to do theirs.

In the Johnson's Island Prison Camp.

On arriving at the island, I showed my letter from Baker to the commanding officer, and explained to him that I was searching for a rebel spy, who was supposed to be engaged, or to have been engaged, in some plots which the authorities at Washington were desirous to learn the particulars of. My credentials were recognized as correct, and I was accordingly admitted, without hesitation, into the enclosure, and permitted to speak freely to the prisoners.

My greatest fear now was that some of the Confederates would recognize me, and would say or do something incautiously that would lead to my detection. I was known to a good many in the Confederate service, both officers and men, as a woman, and to a great many more as a man, and there was no telling but that some one among the prisoners might be heedless enough to claim acquaintance with me, and thus spoil everything.

Glancing around the enclosure, however, I could see no signs of recognition on any of the faces of the prisoners, although a number of them were gazing curiously at me, and after a bit

I began to breathe a little freer, and to be able to inspect the
men rather more closely, with a view of picking out a suitable
one to communicate with.

At length I spied a young officer whom I had known slightly when I was figuring as Lieutenant Harry T. Buford, and
who I knew to be a particularly bright, intelligent fellow. I
concluded, therefore, to speak to him, and calling him to me,
asked him a few immaterial questions, until we had walked
away out of ear-shot of the others.

CONFERENCE WITH A CONFEDERATE PRISONER.

When we were where no one could overhear us, I said, " I
am a Confederate, and have got in here under false colors ; I
have something important to say to you."

" I hope you have some good news for us."

" Yes, it is good news ; at least I hope you will think it is,
for it concerns your liberation."

" Well, that is good, if it can be done, for we are mighty
tired of this, I can tell you."

" It will depend a great deal on yourselves whether anything can be done ; but if the prisoners will only co-operate
in the right spirit, at the right moment, with our friends outside, not only will they secure their release, but they will be
able to hit the Yankees a staggering blow."

His eyes sparkled at this, and I saw that he was willing and
eager to engage in almost any enterprise that promised to
secure his liberation, and I was only fearful that in his excitement he would do something incautious, that would interfere
with the successful prosecution of our scheme.

I therefore said, " You must be very careful, keep cool, and,
above all things, don't give a hint as to who I am. Say that
I am a Yankee, if anybody asks you, and pretend that this
conversation was only about how you are treated, and whether
you do not wish that the war was over, whether you expect
to be exchanged soon, and matters of that kind."

" I will fix that all right. What is it that the boys outside
are going to do for us ? "

" I have a despatch here which will tell you what are the
arrangements, what the signals outside will be, and what you
are to do when you see them. Give it to the party it is addressed to, and consider yourselves under his orders until
your liberation is effected. When you are once outside of the

A PRISONER ON JOHNSON'S ISLAND.

prison you will find plenty to help you, and will be able to effect some kind of an organization."

" Well, don't you want to see the party that the despatch is for? "

" No, it won't do for me to talk to too many; and it is better for a number of reasons, in order to avoid any suspicion, that I should not be seen in conversation with him."

" Well, I'll give the despatch to him in any verbal message you may send."

I then dropped on the ground a package containing eight hundred dollars, and said, " There is some money ; conceal it as quick as you can, and distribute it among the men as far as it will go."

He thereupon sat down on a block of wood in front of me and commenced whittling a stick, while I stood close to him with my back to the guard, and with my skirts covering the package. Watching a favorable opportunity, when the guard was looking another way, he seized the package and slipped it into his boot, and then went on whittling in as unconcerned a manner as possible.

I then told him that I would leave Sandusky the next day at the latest, and that with the delivery of the despatch I held in my hand, which contained full and minute directions, my part of the business would be finished, and that the consummation of the scheme would depend upon himself and the others. I cautioned him to be exceedingly wary, and to take none of the prisoners into his confidence unless he was perfectly sure of their thorough reliability.

He promised to be discreet, and then wishing him good by and success, I shook hands with him, passing the despatch as I did so.

The precious paper once in his possession, he started off, whistling and whittling as he went, while I hurriedly returned to the office, when I told the commander that I was unable to find the man I was looking for, and thought that I would have to visit some of the other prison camps.

He said he was sorry, and hoped that I would have better luck next time. We then walked together towards the boat, conversing in general terms about the prisoners and the war. At the landing we met the lieutenant, who seemed to be rather surprised to see me there. He exclaimed, " Why, have you been visiting the prisoners ? If I had known that you wanted to see them, I would have escorted you over to the Island."

I did not care to tell the young man that, under the circumstances, I preferred to dispense with his escort, and so only said, " O, yes. I thought I would like to take a look at them; and I can tell you, some of those rebels are sharp, if they are backwoodsmen. If you don't look out, they will be getting away from you some day."

The officers both laughed, and the lieutenant said, " I guess not ; they are always talking about doing that, but they never do it; we have them too fast."

This was a point which I did not care to argue with him just then, so saying adieu to the commander of the prison, the lieutenant and I stepped aboard the boat, and were soon on our way back to Sandusky.

As we were crossing to the town, the lieutenant again proposed that we should take a drive that afternoon. I, however, excused myself, and gave him to understand that I had engagements which would prevent me from meeting him again. The young man, therefore, to my infinite relief, — for his attentions were beginning to be troublesome, — stated that he would return to Cincinnati by the first train ; and, when I parted from him in the hotel, I sincerely hoped that he would do so, for I did not wish to have him watching my movements.

I now wrote a letter to Colonel Baker, in which I stated that the man I was looking for was not at Johnson's Island, and that I thought I would go on to Indianapolis, and visit the prison camp there. After I had dined, not seeing the lieutenant, I inquired for him, and was told that he had gone. Being, therefore, in no danger of meeting him again, I went to the telegraph office, and sent despatches to the Detroit and Buffalo agents, to notify them that I had visited the prison and executed my commission there, and one to St. Louis, in accordance with the instructions under which I was acting, for the agent there to send certain parties to meet me at Indianapolis.

The next morning I was off for Indianapolis, to continue the search I had begun in Sandusky, although I desired very much to remain in the last named city for the purpose of watching the progress of events, and, perhaps, of taking part in any fighting that might occur. I very well knew that by acting as a spy and as a bearer of despatches I was performing much more valuable service than I would as a soldier, and yet, at the prospect of a battle, all my fighting blood was up, and I could scarcely restrain my desire to be an active participant in the great and exciting scenes I thought were about to take place.

I afterwards wished that I had remained, for I felt confident that had I been in Sandusky when the appointed time for striking the blow came, and had been intrusted with the direction of affairs, there would have been no such miserable fizzle as actually did occur.

THE PROPOSED LAKE SHORE RAID, AND THE CAUSE OF ITS FAILURE.

The general plan, as the reader has already been told, was to organize a raid along the lake shores, to release the prisoners, to gather about us all the Southern sympathizers who could be induced to join us, and to make such a diversion in the Federal rear as would compel the withdrawal of a large force from the front. We also placed great reliance on the effects of the panic which, it was hoped, would be created, and also on British intervention, which it was expected would be brought about by a border war, in which it would be impossible to prevent trespass upon British territory.

In addition to this, the Indians were to be stirred up to acts of hostility all along the frontier, from the lakes to the gulf.

The prisoners, as they effected their escape, were to act according to circumstances. Those at Sandusky, and at places nearest to that point, were to unite with the outsiders, and form an army to operate along the lake shores, and as far into the adjacent country as they could penetrate, while others were to endeavor to effect a junction with Price and Quantrell in Missouri, and to march under their orders.

The execution of this scheme was to begin at a certain time, after the prisoners had been made acquainted with such details of the general plan as were necessary to be known by them, by the capture of the Federal gunboat Michigan, and of such other steamers as the Confederates could overpower by stratagem or force. This being done, the prisoners on Johnson's Island were to be notified by a pre-arranged signal, and were to make a break and overpower their guards, with the assistance of the boats. The prisoners once free, the organization of both military and naval forces was to be proceeded with as rapidly as possible, and all the damage done to the enemy that could be done with the means at hand.

In pursuance of this plan, the Confederates in Canada seized the lake steamers Indian Queen and Parsons, and started for Sandusky. On arriving off that place, however, their signals were unanswered; and after waiting as long as they dared, they were forced to the conclusion that something unexpected had occurred to interfere with the success of the plans, and had no recourse but to make their escape as rapidly as they could, well knowing that the Michigan, if she ever got her guns to bear on them, would blow them out of the water in very short order.

The scheme fell through, not because the party from Canada did not keep their engagement, or were not willing and anxious to do all that they had the power to do, but because one of the men who went to Sandusky for the purpose of seizing the Michigan turned traitor. I may, perhaps, be doing this person an injustice in applying this harsh name to him; but if he was not a wilful traitor, he was a fool, and too weak and cowardly to have been intrusted with such responsible and weighty duties as he was.

Arrangements had been made to secure the attendance of all, or nearly all, the officers of the Michigan at an entertainment, and during their absence the vessel was to have been seized. Before this entertainment could come off, however, the man to whom I' have alluded was either recognized as a Confederate, or else he made some drunken utterances that excited suspicion. At all events, he was arrested, and on a search being made, papers were found in his possession which gave the Federal government full information with regard to the plot, and enabled them to take means to meet it. All this might have happened, and yet no one been seriously to blame; but this man, on the papers being found on him, confessed everything, and revealed, not merely the particulars of the scheme, but who his associates were.

He should have permitted himself to have been torn limb from limb before doing this, as I would have done, had I been captured, sooner than I would have revealed anything to the enemy.

The failure of this raid caused much disappointment at the South; and the Confederates in Canada, by whom it had been planned, and to whom its execution was intrusted, were greatly censured, and were accused both of treachery and lack of courage. These censures and accusations were unjust, for they did all they could do; and if they were to blame for anything, it was in confiding in a person or persons who were unworthy of confidence.

The excitement which the capture of the Sundusky party, and the discovery of what it was that they and the Confederates proposed to do, caused at the North, showed how great would have been the panic that the successful execution of the scheme would have caused. I cannot express the disgust and indignation I felt when I heard that the plot had failed, and how it failed ; and it was on this account, as much as anything else, that I left the country for a time, and refused to have anything more to do with my late associates and their schemes, although I was still intent upon doing all I could to advance the interests of the Confederacy.

CHAPTER XXXVIII.

IN THE INDIANAPOLIS ARSENAL. — FAILURE OF THE PROJECTED RAID.

I deliver Despatches to Agents in Indianapolis. — Waiting for Orders. — I obtain Access to the Prison Camp, and confer with a Confederate Officer confined there. — I apply to Governor Morton for Employment, and am sent by him to the Arsenal. — I obtain a Situation in the Arsenal, and am set to Work packing Cartridges. — I form a Project for blowing up the Arsenal. — Reasons for its Abandonment. — I receive a suspicious Number of Letters. — How I obtained my Money Package from the Express Office. — I go to St. Louis, and endeavor to obtain Employment at the Planters' House, for the Purpose of enabling me to gain Information from the Federal Officers lodging there. — Failing in this, I strike up an Acquaintance with a Chambermaid, and by Means of her pass Key gain Access to several Rooms. — I gain some Information from Despatches which I find, and am very nearly detected by a Bell Boy. — I go to Hannibal to deliver a Despatch relating to the Indians. — Hearing of the Failure of the Johnson's Island Raid, I return East, and send in my Resignation to Colonel Baker.

O N my arrival at Indianapolis, I found two men from St. Louis awaiting me, they having been sent there in compliance with my telegraphic despatch from Sandusky. I had a long talk with them about the condition of affairs, and delivered the despatches I had for them. One of them — a tall Missourian — was to go to the borders, to operate with the Indians, and the other was to report to Quantrell, on some business of a secret nature. I had no idea what the despatch which I handed to this second man was about, and, as he did not seem disposed to tell me, I did not ask him.

In compliance with my orders, I was now to wait in Indianapolis until I should receive directions to proceed elsewhere, and was to occupy my time in obtaining access to the prison çamp for the purpose of conversing with the prisoners, informing them of the movements that were in progress, and encouraging them to make an effort to escape, as no rescue could be attempted in their case.

444

Exactly how to get into the prison enclosure was something of a problem, as, for a number of good and sufficient reasons, I was desirous of doing this without figuring as Colonel Baker's agent, as I had done at Sandusky. Where there is a will there is a way, nearly always, and I speedily found a very easy way to accomplish my object.

OBTAINING ADMISSION TO THE INDIANAPOLIS PRISON CAMP.

Walking out towards the prison camp, the day after my arrival, I determined to try and get in, on some plea or other, and only to fall back on Baker's letter as a last resource, when all other means failed. Not very far from the enclosure I met a cake-woman, who, I surmised, was permitted to go among the prisoners for the purpose of trading with them. It occurred to me that, with a little management, I could obtain admission along with her; so, going up to her, I purchased a few cakes, and said, " Why, do you go into the prison, among those dirty rebels ? "

" O, yes," she replied; " I go in there to sell them cakes."

" I did not know that they let any one in."

" Yes; the officers all know me, and the sergeant always looks through my basket, to see that I haven't anything contraband."

" I would like mighty well to go in there, and see how the rebels look. Do you think they would let me in with you ? "

" Yes; you come along with me; I'll get you in."

When we came to the gate, therefore, and while the sergeant was examining her basket, the old woman said, " Sergeant, this is my sister. She came with me to see how the rebels look ; she never saw one."

The sergeant laughed, and passed us both in, without further parley.

The cake-woman went into the quarters, where she soon had a crowd of men round her, investing their cash — and precious little of it they had — in the contents of her basket. Looking around me, I spied a major belonging to Lee's army, whom I had met in Richmond, but who had never seen me in female attire, and, going up to him, I had a hurried conversation with him, in a low voice.

I told him that now was the time for the prisoners to make a break, if they wanted to gain their freedom, as there were no troops at hand worth speaking of.

He wanted to know whether there was not danger of being retaken.

I replied, that I did not think there was, if they made a bold dash, and all worked together. I then told him what was being done elsewhere, and explaining as well as I could the general plan of operations that had been arranged, suggested that they should try and reach the southern part of the state, and, after crossing the river, report either to Price or Jeff Thompson. I then gave him some money, and hurriedly left him, to rejoin the old cake-woman, whose basket was by this time emptied, and who was prepared to leave.

This duty having been satisfactorily performed, I wrote a letter to Colonel Baker, informing him that the man I was looking for was not at the Indianapolis camp, but that I had information which led me to think I would find him at Alton. I, therefore, proposed to go to that place, and if he was not there, I would give the whole thing up as a bad job, and return East.

An Application to Governor Morton for Employment.

I had no intention of going to Alton, but being under obligation to remain for some time — how long I could not know — in Indianapolis, I was desirous of employing myself to the best advantage. Exactly what to get at, however, was not an easy thing to determine. After considering the subject in all its aspects, I resolved to go to Governor Morton for the purpose of asking him whether he could not give me some employment. My idea was, that perhaps, through the influence of the governor, I could obtain a clerkship, or some position which would afford me facilities for gaining information.

I accordingly called on the governor, to whom I represented myself as a poor widow, whose husband had been killed in the war, and who had no means of support. Governor Morton treated me kindly enough, although I speedily made up my mind that he was by no means as amiable and good-natured an individual as my rather jolly friend, Governor Brough, of Ohio.

After hearing my story, he said that there was nothing he could do for me, but that it was very possible I might be able to obtain employment at the arsenal, as there were a good many women working there.

This, it struck me, was a most capital idea; and, therefore, asking the governor to give me some kind of a note or recommendation, — which request he complied with by writing a few lines, — I left him, to see what I could do at the place where they were manufacturing munitions of war to be used against my Confederate friends.

I do not know whether it was the governor's note that aided me, or whether they were really in want of hands, but I was told that I could have work, if I desired it. The ordnance officer — a German, whose name I have forgotten — said that I was to commence work on Tuesday, the day I applied to him being Saturday.

A PROJECT FOR BLOWING UP THE ARSENAL.

At the appointed time I appeared at the arsenal, and was sent into the packing-room, where I was instructed in the mystery of packing cartridges. There were about eighteen girls working in the same room, most of whom were rather light-headed things, interested in very nearly everything except the business they were paid for. A good part of their time was employed in writing, reading, and discussing love-letters, which they were interchanging with the soldiers in the field, and a number of them had a good many more than one correspondent.

The society of these girls was no pleasure to me whatever, especially as I had things of much more importance to think of than their love affairs. Immediately on Governor Morton suggesting that, perhaps, I could obtain employment at the arsenal, the idea of blowing up that establishment entered my mind. After going to work, I looked about me to see how this could be done, and very soon perceived that the thing was possible, and without much risk to myself, provided I took proper precautions.

I found, however, that I would not be able to blow up the arsenal without destroying a number of lives, and I shrank from doing this. It was a great temptation to me, however, especially when I reflected that I was really in the Confederate service, and that it was a part of my duty to do everything in my power to injure the enemy. I could not, however, get it out of my head that there was a wide difference between killing .people in a fair fight and slaughtering them in this fashion; and so, to get myself out of the way of a temptation that was constantly growing stronger and stronger, I suddenly left, after having been at work about two weeks.

Had it been possible for me to have destroyed the arsenal without loss of life, I would most assuredly have done it; but the circumstances being what they were, it has been a great satisfaction to me ever since that I did not attempt anything of the kind, just as it has been a satisfaction to me that I did not kill General Grant when I had an opportunity to do so on the night after the first day's fight at Shiloh. I doubt, however, whether there would have been a great many men, either Confederates or Federals, who would have been so considerate in similar situations, especially if the deed could have been performed without risk to themselves. I am confident that I could have fired the Indianapolis arsenal without serious danger of being detected, but I do not suppose any one will think the worse of me that I did not do it.

The great number of letters I received from nearly every quarter, within a very brief period, excited curiosity and remark. After my first few visits to the post office the clerk began to take notice of me, and he would say something nearly every time I called for my mail about the extent of my correspondence. What he said was in a joking sort of a way, and under some circumstances I should have thought nothing of it; but not knowing, from day to day, what might happen, it caused me some uneasiness to attract this kind of attention, both for my own sake and for the sake of my correspondents. I very well knew that did the Federal authorities suspect me the least of being a Confederate agent, there would be no hesitation whatever about opening my letters; and if some of them had been opened, there would have been fine revelations; for, although many of them were obscurely worded, so as not to be readily understood except by myself and the others interested, it would have been a comparatively easy matter to have gained from them a knowledge of some of the most important secret Confederate operations; and this would not have been pleasant for me and some of my associates.

For these, as well as other reasons, I was anxious to leave Indianapolis at as early a day as I possibly could, but was unable to move for lack of orders, and also for lack of cash. My funds, in fact, were running very low, so low as to give me considerable uneasiness lest I should be unable to meet my expenses; and I anxiously awaited a remittance, which, as is apt to be the case with remittances that are anxiously awaited,

READING DESPATCHES.

was a long time in coming. Finally, I received information that a money package had been forwarded to me by express; but on applying at the office for it, I was told that it could not be delivered unless I was identified.

This was a perplexing predicament; but I had gotten myself out of worse ones, and thought that I would be able to find a way to obtain possession of the precious package. Returning to the hotel, therefore, I selected an envelope from one of my letters, and writing a letter to myself, as if from my brother, stating that such and such a package had been forwarded to me, I took it to the manager of the packing department at the arsenal, and requested him to go with me to the express office for the purpose of identifying me. He did this without hesitation, but was considerably astonished to see me receive such a large amount of money, and said, " Why, your brother must be a very rich man ! "

" O, no, he is not rich, but he has been thinking of investing some of his spare cash in real estate for some time, and I told him of a good thing in corner lots, which I urged him to try and do something with."

As an explanation of my money package this was a trifle thin, but it was sufficient for the purpose, especially as it was no concern of his whether I had rich relations or not.

Within a day or two I received orders by telegraph to proceed to Cairo, which I did forthwith, and found, on reaching that place, letters of instruction which directed me to go to St. Louis, and to stop at the Planters' House for the purpose of seeing if I could not find out something about projected Federal movements from the officers who were making it their headquarters.

From the tenor of my instructions I judged that I would not be able to do much by going to the table as a guest, which would also have been inconvenient, as it would have necessitated my providing myself with a large amount of different kind of clothing from that which I was then wearing. I was figuring as a widow woman in greatly reduced circumstances, and, so far as baggage was concerned, was, as the soldiers would say, in light marching order. It occurred to me, therefore, that the best plan to pursue was to try and obtain a situation at the Planters' House as a chambermaid. On reaching St. Louis, instead of going to the hotel, I took lodgings at a private house for a few days, until I could mature my plans.

29

On applying for employment as a chambermaid, I was told that there was no vacancy, and that there was not likely to be any; and I saw very plainly, from the manner of the individual with whom I conversed on the subject, that he had no intention whatever of giving me a situation.

NONPLUSSED.

This rather nonplussed me, and I was unable to determine what device to adopt next. Some of the information which I was requested to obtain was very important, and I had been urged to use every effort to get it. I did not like to give the thing up without having exhausted all my resources. I accordingly tried in a number of ways to find out what I wanted to know, but was entirely unsuccessful. All that I succeeded in discovering of any consequence was some knowledge of the personal habits of the officers who were lodged at the Planters' House, and of the times when they were least likely to be in their rooms. My only chance, therefore, seemed to be to gain access to their quarters when they were out, and to the accomplishment of this I put my wits to work.

When applying for employment in the hotel, I struck up a sort of acquaintance with one of the chambermaids, of whom I made a variety of inquiries as to the nature of the duties, and of my chances of getting a situation. This woman had seemed disposed to be quite friendly, and I, therefore, concluded to cultivate her acquaintance. I was not long in becoming intimate with her; and, as I made her a number of little presents, and otherwise displayed a marked liking for her, she speedily took a great fancy to me.

Having, as I thought, secured her friendship, I called upon her one evening and invited her to go out with me. She consented to do this, and we went up to her room together for her to arrange her toilet. While she was dressing I slipped her pass key in my pocket. This being secured, the next thing was to find an opportunity to use it.

When we returned I had no great difficulty in inducing her to extend an invitation for me to stop all night. We accordingly slept together. In the morning she got up, dressed herself, and then, missing her key, began an industrious search for it, I all the time pretending to be asleep. Unable to find it, she went out, and I heard her ask one of the other girls to lend her a key, saying that she had lost hers.

So soon as she was well out of the way, I got up and dressed myself, and when I thought that the officers, whose rooms I wished to visit, were likely to be away, — and I knew that if they had breakfasted and had left the hotel they would scarcely be back until lunch time, — I slipped down stairs to execute my dangerous errand.

Luckily I met no one, and contrived to get into three rooms, where I read a number of despatches and orders, one or two of which were of some importance, but did not succeed in discovering what I was chiefly in search of. I, however, mastered the contents of such papers as I could lay my hands on, for I was bound to have something to show for my labor, even if I did not get all I wanted.

NEARLY CAUGHT.

On coming out of the third room, I came very near being caught by a bell boy, who turned into the corridor just as I had finished locking the door. Putting on a sort of bewildered look, as if I had lost myself, I said, in an innocent sort of a way, " Which is the servant's staircase ; I think I must have got into the wrong hall."

The boy was not particularly bright, and, giving the required direction, I made off as fast as I could, not a little satisfied at having escaped so easily. On the stairway I met the chambermaid, who was bringing me up a cup of coffee. This I drank, and then bade her good-by, glad of an opportunity to get away without attracting more attention.

On reaching my lodgings I wrote out the substance of the information I had obtained, and forwarded it to the proper agent, with a statement to the effect that it seemed impossible for me to learn anything more. In reply to this note I received a despatch by telegraph, directing me to go to Hannibal, where I would find a package awaiting me, which I was to deliver according to directions which would be enclosed.

I took the boat for Hannibal, and on reaching that place found Major T., of the Confederate army, rather anxiously looking for me, as he had received information that orders would be sent him from New York in an enclosure directed to me. Obtaining my package from the express office, it was found to contain a despatch from Richmond, with orders for the major to treat with the Indians, and to aid in the endeavors that were being made to excite them to acts of hostility against the Federal government all along the frontier, from the British Provinces to Mexico.

END OF WESTERN TRIP.

The delivery of this despatch to Major T. was the last transaction of the western trip which I made under the auspices of Colonel Baker. Not more than a day or two afterwards I learned of the failure of the attempt to release the Johnson's Island prisoners, and consequently of the grand scheme, the success of which I had been laboring so hard to promote.

I did not know who was to blame for this failure, but I felt that if all the rest had done their duty as efficiently as I had done mine, success would have crowned our efforts. I, therefore, resolved to return East, and to dissolve all connection with my late co-workers, and with more than half a mind to have nothing more to do with such schemes, or schemes of any kind that would require confederates, in the future. I was beyond measure indignant when I learned, as I did before I reached Philadelphia, that the whole thing had fallen through, owing to the blundering cowardice and treachery of one individual. I did not pretend to restrain my wrath, but the agent whom I met at Philadelphia, after I had become cooled off a little, persuaded me that there was no use in getting discouraged by this misadventure, bad as it was, and that there was still plenty of important work for the Confederacy to be done.

I, however, was so decidedly unwilling to engage in any similar enterprise, at least just then, that it was proposed that I should attempt something in the blockade-running line. By doing this, it was represented, I could not only aid the cause, but could make a handsome profit for myself if I managed rightly, as my commissions alone would amount to considerable. The proposition made to me looked feasible; and, allowing myself to be persuaded, I wrote a letter to Colonel Baker, resigning from the secret service, under the plea that I had obtained other employment of a more remunerative and more congenial character.

I really had not the courage to face Baker again after the trick I had played upon him, having no idea what he might know, or might not know, about my connection with the projected raid which had been so effectually nipped in the bud by the arrest of the men in Sandusky who were endeavoring to seize the gunboat Michigan. From the tenor of the letter which he sent me in reply, however, I judged that he neither knew nor suspected anything against me, and I concluded that I would finally have occasion to make use of him again, as I could not tell what work I might have to do before the war was over.

CHAPTER XXXIX.

BLOCKADE-RUNNING.

Making Preparations for going into Business as a Blockade-runner. — The trade in Contraband Goods by Northern Manufacturers and Merchants. — Profits versus Patriotism. — The secret History of the War yet to be told. — This Narrative a Contribution to it. — Some dark Transactions of which I was cognizant. — Purchasing Goods for the Southern Market, and shipping them on Board of a Schooner in the North River. — How such Transactions were managed. — The Schooner having sailed, I go to Havana by Steamer. — On reaching Havana I meet some old Friends. — The Condition of the Blockade-running Business during the last Year of the War. — My Acquaintances in Havana think that the Prospects of the Confederacy are rather gloomy. — I visit Barbadoes, and afterwards St. Thomas. — While at St. Thomas the Confederate Cruiser Florida comes in, coals, and gets to Sea again, despite the Federal Fleet watching her.

HAD proven myself so efficient in managing matters that required to be managed with skill, boldness, and discretion, during the time I had been co-operating with the Confederate agents at the North, and especially during my late Western trip, that my associates were more than ever anxious to avail themselves of my services. They fully appreciated my feelings over the failure of the Johnson's Island raid, after I had performed the part assigned me so successfully, but they contended that I would not be acting an heroic part to forsake the fortunes of the Confederacy just at this juncture, when, although things were looking exceedingly gloomy, there was a chance that success might yet be achieved if all the friends of the cause would stick together, and labor with even more than their old energy to achieve success in the face of every opposition.

It was a comparatively easy matter to persuade me to continue to act as a Confederate secret service agent, although I was too angry over the Johnson's Island matter to be willing

454

to place myself in peril very soon again by attempting to play a double game, as I had been doing with Colonel Baker and other Federal officials. I was willing to risk as much as any one when there was a fair chance of accomplishing anything, but I was not willing to undertake enterprises of extraordinary peril, and to run the chance of being betrayed through either the stupidity or the treachery of those who professed to be working with me.

I did not know how much information Baker might have with regard to my recent doings, but thought that it would be rather remarkable if he and other government detectives had not discovered something which it was not especially advantageous to me that they should be informed of. I had no very great opinion of their smartness, but, considering all that I had been doing, the peculiar relations which I held to Baker, and the opportunities which the arrest of the Confederate agents in Sundusky had given for them to obtain the full particulars of the plot, and the names of those prominently concerned in it, I did not care to cultivate the acquaintance of Baker and the members of his corps any further just then, and was not sorry to have an opportunity to leave the country for a time.

Buying Goods for the South.

This opportunity was afforded in a proposition that I should purchase a quantity of goods in Philadelphia and New York to fill Southern orders, and should go to the West Indies with them as a sort of supercargo, for the purpose of arranging for their shipment to different Southern ports. I was also to supervise the shipment of a variety of goods of various kinds from Europe.

It was thought that, as in the cases of the proposed raid, a woman would be able to do a great many things without exciting suspicion, that it would be hazardous for a man to attempt. It was daily getting to be more and more difficult to smuggle goods, especially merchandise of a bulky nature, through the blockading fleet. The tribulations of the blockade-runners, however, did not begin when they approached the beleaguered ports of the Confederacy. There were great difficulties in the way of purchasing goods, especially at the North, and of getting them shipped in safety, and then, in the majority of cases, they had to be taken to some point in the West Indies to be re-shipped, all of which involved trouble, expense, and risk.

The purchase and shipment of goods at places like New York and Philadelphia required particularly discreet management. There were, doubtless, some merchants and manufacturers who would not knowingly have sold to Confederate agents, or for Confederate uses in any shape. For such, I had and have every respect, for they were entirely honest and consistent in their opposition to the secession of the Southern States. I am very much afraid, however, that these were few in number, and I know that the prospect of cash payments and handsome profits caused many men, who were loud in their profession of loyalty to the Federal government, and bitter in their denunciations of the South, to close their eyes to numerous transactions of a doubtful character when opportunities for making a good round sum, without danger of detection, were presented.

CONTRABAND TRADING.

Some Northern merchants and manufacturers sold goods, either immediately or at second hand, to Confederate agents innocently enough, being deceived as to the nature of the transactions. No dealers could be expected to maintain a corps of detectives for the purpose of watching their customers and of tracing out the destination of the goods purchased from them, and thus the most ardent and enthusiastic supporters of the Federal government were liable to be imposed upon. That some of these men were honest I know, for I am aware of instances where the sale of goods has been refused, on the plea that there was reason to believe that the intention was to send them South. These refusals have been made where the sales could have been effected with entire safety and with perfect propriety, so far as outward appearances went.

These very fastidious people were not numerous, however, and in the majority of business houses the practice was to welcome all customers, and to ask no questions. In many large establishments, the chiefs of which were noted for their "loyalty," confidential clerks could be found with whom it was possible to transact any amount of contraband business, especially if the cash was promptly forthcoming. Some of these people, I am sure, were well aware of what their subordinates were doing; with regard to others, I am in doubt, but think that they could scarcely have been ignorant of what was going on, and only wanted to be able to say, in case of any difficulties occurring, that they, personally, were not to blame.

There were, of course, numerous manufacturers, merchants, jobbers, brokers, and others, who were eager to make money wherever it could be made, and whose only object in concealing their transactions, so far as the Southern market was concerned, was to avoid getting into trouble. Some of these people were loyal to the Federal government after a fashion, while others were as undisguised in their expressions of sympathy for the South as they dared to be. Political partisanship was, however, not a very strong point with either set; they considered it legitimate to make money by the buying and selling of goods, without regard to what the politicians at Washington and elsewhere might think or do; and, so long as they bought and sold in a reasonably honest manner, their consciences did not trouble them. With such as these, I and my associates found it easy to deal.

If it was easy, it was not always satisfactory to deal with people of this kind; and during the last year of the war, especially, some of the largest transactions were with houses that had reputations to lose, and that were managed by men who aimed to stand high in the regards of the government, and with those of their fellow-citizens who supported the government. To do business with such houses required some *finesse*, but, except in rare instances, it could be done, without a great deal of trouble, and, as I am convinced, in a majority of cases, with the approbation of the heads of the concerns.

CIRCUMSTANCES ALTER CASES.

Looking at this buying and selling from a Southern point of view, it was not only legitimate and proper, but it was a violation of every natural or political right for the Federal government to interfere with it. From a Northern point of view, however, it was giving aid and comfort to the enemy, and it was discreditable, according to the extent which those engaged in it professed to be in favor of coercing the South, and of sustaining the government in the prosecution of the war.

The sale of goods for the Southern market, and the active or surreptitious encouragement of blockade-running, were, however, very venial offences compared with some others that were committed by people at the North, who professed to be eager for the subjugation of the South. Now that the war is over, a good many who made money by supplying the South with contraband articles, other than munitions of war, can afford to laugh at the perils they then ran, and to tell, without fear, of the kind of business they were engaged in. As the reader, however, will discover, there was an immense amount of evil and rascality going on, and some of the most trusted officers of the government were engaged in transactions concerning which there could not possibly be two opinions.

VILLANY.

With some of these transactions I had considerable to do, and I was cognizant of undiluted villany that unveiled depths of human depravity such as I never would have believed to be possible, had I not been brought in such close contact with it.

It may be thought by some who read this part of my narrative that I was as much in fault as those with whom I consented to associate for the purpose of accomplishing the object I had in view. I do not despair, however, of finding readers, even in the Northern States, who will be able to take a liberal and charitable view of my course, and to consider that I was acting as best I knew how to promote the success of a cause which I felt to be a just one, and that I considered myself as justified in doing the Federals all the injury I could, and in promoting the interest of the Confederacy by every means in my power. I am willing, therefore, to brave the censure of some, and the only partial approval of others, for the sake of making my narrative complete, and of putting upon record some very curious features of the great contest between the North and the South.

These things have, many of them, never been told before, although dark hints with regard to them have been dropped from time to time. They, however, are far from being unimportant, as they exerted an influence, more or less potent, on the progress of the war, and no history of the great contest will be complete unless they are understood and a proper consideration given them.

In fact, there is a secret history of the war, records of which have never been committed to paper, and which exists only in the memories of a limited number of people. That this secret history will ever be written out with any degree of fulness is scarcely possible, for reasons that will readily be understood; but some idea of what it will be like, should it ever be written, may be gathered from these pages. When I concluded to give to the public a narrative of my adventures, I determined to make it as complete as possible, so far as I myself was concerned, for, during the whole four years I neither said nor did anything that I am not willing the world should know. With regard to my associates, Confederates and others, who were mixed up with me in certain transactions, the case, however, is different. I deem it proper, in certain cases, to refrain from mentioning their names, as many of them are still living, and might yet get into trouble through my utterances. I kept faith with them when we were acting together, and will do so still, although some of them were villains of the blackest dye, who richly deserve any punishment that the law against which they offended is capable of inflicting upon them.

Having consented to make a trip to the West Indies, I commenced my preparations immediately, and was soon as deeply engaged in commercial matters as I had recently been in some of not quite so peaceful a character. Having once got started, I speedily found trade, and especially this kind of trade, quite as exciting as warfare, while it had certain attractions, in the way of prospective profits, that fighting certainly did not possess.

I had some few transactions with Philadelphia houses, but they were none of them very important, and most of my fitting out was done in New York, where I, and those with whom I was connected, labored for a number of weeks, with all possible zeal, being resolved to make the venture a profitable one for ourselves, as well as of advantage to the Confederacy.

FITTING OUT A SCHOONER.

The first thing done was the chartering of a schooner and the engaging of a warehouse. In this warehouse our goods were stored until we were ready to load. The watchman was perfectly aware that we were engaging in contraband traffic, but, as he was paid handsomely for holding his tongue, he kept his own counsel and ours. When everything was ready, the schooner was loaded at Pier No. 4, North River, and she sailed for Havana with a regular clearance, one of my associates making matters all right at the custom-house, so that the vessel had no difficulty in getting away.

The greatest trouble we had was not in getting our schooner to sea, but in making our purchases without exciting suspicion that we intended to find our market in some Confederate port. To do this required circumspect management; but some of those with whom I was co-operating had done this sort of thing before, and knew how to go about it; while I was not long in learning all the tricks of the trade, so as to be able to perform the part assigned me with as much shrewdness as any of them.

According to the plan which we arranged, I was to pretend that I intended opening a store, and was to visit some of the largest houses, and obtain their prices and terms of payment. The terms varied from sixty to ninety days, or so much off for cash. At one of the most extensive dry goods establishments in New York, — Messrs. C—— & Co., — I inquired for a Mr. B——, who, on being informed that I had been sent to him by certain parties, whose names I mentioned, introduced me to a confidential clerk, who undertook to fill my orders, and deliver the goods in accordance with my instructions. He understood the whole matter thoroughly, and, from various expressions he let drop in conversation, I had no difficulty in concluding that his firm was doing a big contraband trade, although the principals, like many other prominent merchants, were taking especial good care not to be known as having anything to do with it.

The leading members of this firm were very prominent as upholders of the Federal cause, and it would have been ruin to them had it been found out that they were surreptitiously shipping goods to the South. I never was quite able to make up my mind whether they really knew what was going on or not. At any rate, all the arrangements for carrying on a contraband traffic were very complete in their establishment, and any one going there with proper credentials was sure of receiving every attention. If these gentlemen did not know what their employees were doing, they were much less shrewd than they had the credit of being; and I am afraid that a love of gain was a more powerful incentive in their bosoms than loyalty to the cause for which, in public, they professed so much devotion, and for which they professed a willingness to make almost any sacrifices.

With some houses we had less difficulty even than with the one mentioned, and with others' much more; and in several places we were compelled to make our purchases under more or less plausible pretexts, and to arrange for having our goods delivered so that those from whom we obtained them would have no idea what their destination was.

It was a troublesome matter getting our cargo together, but finally, after many anxious days and nights, during which we expected every moment to be pounced upon by the Federal authorities, our schooner was loaded with wines, drugs, boots, shoes, buttons, and military goods. I also filled several private orders, and, among other things, purchased a handsome sword and belt and a fine pair of pistols. These I obtained through a sergeant stationed at Governor's Island, whose acquaintance I made, and who proved useful to me afterwards in a variety of transactions, which will be narrated in their due order.

The Schooner gets safely off.

Everything being ready, the schooner set sail, and succeeded in reaching her port without being overhauled. So soon as she was off, I prepared to start by the steamer for Havana, having orders for coffee and other supplies to the Confederate agent there. These goods had been shipped from Antwerp, and other places in Europe, and from New York, and they were to be sent from Nassau to Brownville, Texas, under consignment to the Confederate quartermaster or agent there, who, if I recollect rightly, was a Captain Shankey.

This trip to Havana was scarcely as pleasant as the one I had made to that city from New Orleans in the summer of 1862. The Atlantic Ocean I found to be a great deal rougher than the Gulf of Mexico, and, for nearly half the voyage, the weather was very stormy. The result was, that I was too sick to have much enjoyment for a couple of days; but, having recovered from my attack of *mal de mer*, I began to enjoy myself, and felt benefited by the sea air. I was not sorry, however, when the shores of my beautiful native island began to appear in the distance, and felt much satisfaction when our vessel steamed in under the guns of the Moro Castle, and anchored off the city of Havana.

A Second Visit to Havana.

In Havana I found a number of my old acquaintances of 1862, who were as busily engaged as ever in running the blockade, although the difficulties and dangers of the business gave them much discomfort. The profits of a successful trip, however, were so great that they could afford to brave them, and to submit to large losses through the vigilance of the Federal cruisers. In fact, despite the annoyances experienced from the blockaders, who were becoming exceedingly keen in their scent after prizes, blockade-running was yet a very paying business, and the men engaged in it would have been quite willing that the war should have continued indefinitely, so long as their ventures yielded as handsome results as they did.

What gave these people the most uneasiness at the time of which I write, was, not the stringency of the blockade, but a prospect that the war would speedily come to an end. They watched the course of events critically and anxiously, but from a very different standpoint from that of myself and my associates, North or South, and I was not a little startled by the evident belief that the collapse of the Confederacy was near at hand. The cold-blooded way in which they considered such a calamity, and the purely pecuniary light in which they regarded it, shocked me, and greatly excited my indignation. I could not but acknowledge the force of much of their reasoning, however, although their total indifference to the fate of the Confederacy, except so far as it affected their opportunities for money-making, had the effect of reviving my enthusiasm, and of making me more than ever resolved to labor for the success of the cause while a glimmer of hope remained.

A Trip to Barbadoes.

Having transacted my business in Havana, I started for Bridgetown, Barbadoes, to make arrangements there for the shipment of goods. I went from Havana to St. Thomas in the steamer Pelyo, and from St. Thomas to Bridgetown in a British steamer. The purser of the last-mentioned vessel was particularly attentive to me; indeed, I had not had so persistent an admirer since the time I was escorted to Memphis by the Federal lieutenant, whose fancy for me I turned to such good purpose in carrying out my plans. The purser gave me his photograph, and made me promise to write to him. The photograph I kept, and have given it a proper place in my collection of curiosities, but the promise to write I am afraid I broke. I hope the purser, who was a very good fellow in his way, did not break his heart in consequence.

At Bridgetown I was received very kindly by the friends of the Confederacy there, but was disappointed at finding that Mr. M——, the gentleman whom I was to see, was absent. I, however, left my orders with his secretary, and started to return to New York by way of St. Thomas.

At St. Thomas I was compelled to wait some days for the steamer, during which time the Confederate cruiser Florida came in under the noses of the Federal fleet, coaled, and put to sea again. One of the Federal men-of-war which was watching her was deluded into giving chase to a mail steamer, and the Florida succeeded in slipping off, and getting out of harm's way before she discovered her mistake — a performance which afforded me exceeding great delight.

While in St. Thomas I succeeded in contracting a loan with Messrs. V—— & Son, a Belgian firm, on account of the Confederate agents in Canada, and, this being done, I was ready to return to New York by the first steamer.

CHAPTER XL.

AN ATTACK ON THE FEDERAL TREASURY.

The Bounty-jumping and Substitute-brokerage Business. — Rascalities in high Life and low Life. — Bounty-jumpers and Substitute-brokers not the worst Rogues of the Period. — High Officials of the Government implicated in Swindles. — Baker's Raid on the treasury Ring, and the Charges of Conspiracy brought against him by Members of Congress and others. — A Committee of Congress exonerates the guilty Parties, and blames Baker for exposing them. — What I know about these Transactions. — Money needed to carry on the Confederate Operations at the North. — Federal Officials countenancing the Issue of counterfeit Confederate Bonds and Notes. — I go to Washington for the Purpose of getting in with the Treasury Ring. — A rebel Clerk introduces me to a high Official, who, on Condition of sharing in the Profits, introduces me to the Printing Bureau of the Treasury. — The Trade with England in bogus Federal and Confederate Securities. — Making Johnny Bull pay some of the Expenses of the War.

N my return to New York, circumstances occurred which called my special attention to the operations of the bounty-jumpers and substitute-brokers, and having no other schemes on hand, I was induced to interest myself in the business of reducing the strength of the Federal armies in the field, by preventing the re-enforcements demanded by the government from reaching the front.

The efficiency of the services rendered the Confederacy by these substitute-brokers and bounty-jumpers, cannot be over-estimated. Large armies existed on paper; but while the generals in command kept constantly and uninterruptedly calling for more men, they failed to receive them in such numbers as were requisite for keeping their ranks full, and many important movements were rendered ineffectual, and thousands of lives were needlessly sacrificed, simply because the recruiting system adopted by the government was far better calculated for giving abundant employment to rogues of the worst class, than it was for keeping the strength of the army up to the proper standard.

The majority of these rogues were Northern men, who, if they had any political principles at all, were Federals. The fact was, however, that they did not care the toss of a button which side won, so long as they were able to make money out of the contest. The war, to them, was a grand opportunity for driving all manner of schemes for their individual profit, and the longer it was likely to last, the better they were pleased, giving no thought whatever to the enormous destruction of life and property that was going on, or to the incalculable misery that was caused to thousands of people, all over the land, every day it was waged.

DEMORALIZATIONS OF WARFARE.

I presume that such villanies as it will now be my task to relate are the inevitable accompaniment of every great armed conflict; and if it could be clearly understood that warfare, no matter for what just causes it may be undertaken, inevitably breeds corruption, in its most aggravating forms, and that the longer it lasts, the more does demoralization spread among all classes of society, right thinking people would be apt to hesitate more than they do about encouraging appeals to arms for the settlement of national and international differences.

I doubt whether a good many of the people of the North who supported the Federal government in its efforts to conquer the South, under the belief that their cause was a just one, and worth making sacrifices for, had any adequate idea of the rascality, in high quarters and low quarters, that was one of the results of the war. We read about certain scandalous doings in the newspapers; but, apart from the fact that many of the worst rascalities of the period never were brought to light, it was impossible for the good, patriotic people who contributed their money and goods, and who prayed, day and night, for the success of the Federal cause, to understand the infamies that were being practised around them, as I, who was in some sort the confederate of the villains, and who consequently was able to study the situation from the inside, could not help doing.

Had these infamies been confined to a comparatively few obscure men in the large cities they would have been bad enough, and would have been sufficiently demoralizing in their influences to make it a subject for profound regret that opportunities for their practice should have been afforded.

30

Bad as they were, however, the substitute-brokers and the bounty-jumpers were not the worst villains of the period. Men high in public station, and occupying offices of the greatest responsibility, were engaged in robbing the government and in swindling the public, to an extent that was absolutely startling to me when I obtained cognizance of their doings, and, for the purpose of carrying out my plans, became an accomplice in some of their transactions.

THIEVES AND COUNTERFEITERS IN THE TREASURY DEPARTMENT.

The treasury department itself — where the Federal currency, and the interest-bearing bonds, upon which was raised money to carry on the contest, were manufactured — was the headquarters of a gang of thieves and counterfeiters, who carried on their operations for months, within my own knowledge, in a most barefaced manner, and who, when at length detected and brought to bay, were able, not only to escape punishment, but to retain their positions, and to find apologists in their official superiors and in prominent members of Congress.

I really did not know what to make of it when I read the report of the committee of Congress, which not only exonerated certain treasury officials, whose misdeeds were discovered by Colonel Baker, but which actually insinuated that the detective was engaged in a conspiracy against them. I knew only too well how guilty they were, and I knew that Baker had ample evidence against them, although he was not informed of a tithe of the villanies they had committed. That the secretary and the solicitor of the treasury should take sides with them, and that a congressional committee, composed of statesmen who claimed to be honest and patriotic, should, in the face of the evidences of their guilt which were produced, sustain them, and endeavor to punish Baker for having detected them, are things that I have never yet been able to understand.

That they were protected, and that attempts were made to punish Baker, are, however, facts that cannot be denied; and certainly, of all the disgraceful things which occurred during the war, this was one of the most disgraceful.

No person has a better right to speak plainly and emphatically on this subject than myself, and no person who reads this narrative will suppose for a moment that I am influenced by any partiality for Colonel Baker in making the statements I do with regard to the matters at issue between him, the officers of the treasury, and the congressional committee. I know that the men were guilty of the offences with which they were charged by Baker, for I was one of their associates, although I claim that the peculiarity of my position entitled my conduct to be judged by a very different standard from theirs; and during the whole time that the investigation was going on, I was in mortal terror lest Baker should discover that I was implicated.

WHO PROTECTED THE ROGUES.

My opinion of Colonel Baker's character, or of his qualifications for the position he held as chief of the United States secret service corps, is not the most exalted; and I have too vivid a recollection of the fears I felt, and of the trouble I had in keeping out of his way at the period to which I am alluding, to have the most amiable feelings towards him. I was pleased, for my own sake, but I was astonished beyond measure, when I learned that his efforts to break up certain practices in vogue in the treasury department resulted as they did, and came to nothing, in the peculiar manner that they did. It was almost incredible that Secretary Chase, Solicitor Jordan, and Mr. Garfield, and the other members of the congressional investigating committee, should have taken the peculiar stand that they did; and, even at this late day, I am unable to imagine any sufficient reason for their conduct that will be at all to their credit.

Baker's raid on the treasury department was a very remarkable episode, from whatever point of view it may be regarded; and the probabilities are that, had he been able to continue his investigations, he would have found out some things that would have startled the country. He, as it was, found out quite enough to prove that an investigation was sadly needed; but it must have stung him to the quick to find himself, instead of being rewarded for his skill and zeal, placed in the position of a criminal, while the scamps whose doings he exposed were protected by all the power of the government.

I have stated that most of those engaged in the bounty-jumping and substitute-brokerage business were conscience-less Northern men, who were only intent upon making money by every means, and at all hazards. A number of Confederates, myself included, were, however, associated with them in many of their transactions, just as we were associated with some other rogues, for the purpose of embarrassing the Federal government, and for the prosecution of the various schemes we had on hand, up to the very hour of the downfall of the government to which our adherence was given.

Making the Federal Treasury pay Confederate Expenses.

To carry on our operations, money, and a great deal of it, was needed, and we had little or no hesitation in making the Federal treasury pay our expenses, as far as we were able to. A large portion of the funds used in purchasing substitutes, and in carrying on the bounty-jumping frauds, was furnished by Confederate agents, who obtained a good deal of their cash, directly or indirectly, from the United States treasury. How this was done, it is my purpose to explain.

I had little or nothing to do with the bounty-jumpers until after my return from the West Indies. My relations with the officials of the treasury department, however, commenced not a great while after my arrival at the North, and it was mainly my transactions with them that made me so much afraid of being discovered by Colonel Baker, and so extremely anxious to stand well in his good graces. I am convinced that my intimate relations with Baker, as one of his employees, and the confidence in me which I succeeded in inspiring in his mind, alone saved me from detection when he went to work to find out what was worth finding out in the treasury department. Whether, in case he had discovered the game I was playing, and had attempted to bring me to punishment, the secretary, the solicitor, and prominent members of Congress would have rushed to my rescue with the same alacrity that they did in the case of those whom Baker succeeded in laying his hands on, is one of those interesting questions that must remain forever unanswered. I am very glad, however, that, as matters turned out, there was no occasion for me to appeal to them for aid.

When I first learned of the uses which some of my Confederate friends were making of the facilities of the Federal treasury for obtaining cash, I was rather shocked; and it took some time to convince me that even the license of warfare, and the right we had to injure our adversaries in every manner possible, made such things permissible. When I found out, however, that not only were counterfeit Confederate bonds and notes freely manufactured at the North, without any interference on the part of the government, but that Federal officials actually made use of this bogus Confederate paper whenever they found it convenient to do so, I had no hesitation in coming to the conclusion that we would be perfectly justifiable in retaliating, and that we had the same right to raid on the Federal treasury, and to injure the Federal credit, that the Federals had to try and swamp our finances.

Bogus Confederate Securities.

It was Colonel Baker who decided me to go into this business. That individual always seemed to have a plentiful amount of bogus Confederate bills on hand, to be used on occasion. On my Richmond trip, as the reader will recollect, he gave me a considerable sum in this kind of money, to assist in paying my expenses, all of which was just so much saved to the Federal government, — or, perhaps, to Baker individually, — for I was travelling in the capacity of a Federal secret service agent. On numerous similar occasions Baker found it convenient to meet the expenses of his spies within the Confederate lines with promises to pay, supposed to have been issued in Richmond, but in reality manufactured and given to the world in New York and Philadelphia. He seemed to regard it as quite a proper way of fighting the rebels, to put as many counterfeit Confederate notes as possible into circulation; and, when I discovered that he was of this way of thinking, I was not long in deciding that we rebels had a right to make the thing even by circulating as many bogus United States notes and bonds as we could, especially as we would serve the double purpose of aiding the Confederate and injuring the Federal government, and as, moreover, we would be assisted by prominent Federal officials.

Having made my arrangements with parties in Philadelphia and New York, and having obtained the information necessary for me to make my initial movements, I went to Washington, and, first of all, had a talk with Colonel Baker, giving him some information — real or fictitious, as the case may have been — which I thought would amuse him, and assist in convincing him that I was overflowing with zeal for the Federal cause. This interview with Baker was in accordance

with a general plan I had laid out, for, especially when I had
any business of real importance on my hands when visiting
Washington, I thought it best to call on him and give an
account of myself, than to have him or his men getting sight
of me unexpectedly, and perhaps wondering what I was up to.

A Confederate Spy in the Treasury Department.

Baker's vigilance having thus been disarmed, I went to a
clerk in the Treasury Department, and telling him briefly
what I wanted, but without giving him the details of the
whole scheme, I asked him to assist me in gaining access to
the private rooms in the building where none but the officials
in charge, and the employees immediately under them, were
ever allowed to go, except by written permits signed by the
secretary.   These rooms were chiefly those of the printing
bureau, where the Federal bonds and currency were manufactured, although I also wanted opportunities for visiting
such other portions of the department as I might think
expedient.

This clerk was a Confederate sympathizer, like a number
of other Federal employees of various grades, and he carried
his sympathies so far as that he was willing and anxious to
aid the Confederacy by every means in his power, so long as
he could do so with safety to himself.   He was not the sort
of a man I had much liking for; but in the kind of work I was
engaged in prosecuting, it did not do to be too fastidious
about the characters of one's associates.   Moreover, he had
proved himself, during a long period, to be a very efficient
spy, and was constantly in communication with the Confederate agents, giving them information which often was of extreme importance.

It was probably through him that my associates first
learned what was going on in the printing bureau, but of
this I am not certain.   At any rate, they knew that he was
the best person to apply to for the sake of getting such an
introduction to the private rooms of the treasury building,
as it was necessary for me to have, as he was thoroughly
posted with regard to the villanies that were being practised
there.

In response to my application to this clerk for assistance,
he gave me a letter of introduction to a man occupying a very
high and very responsible position; so high and so responsi-

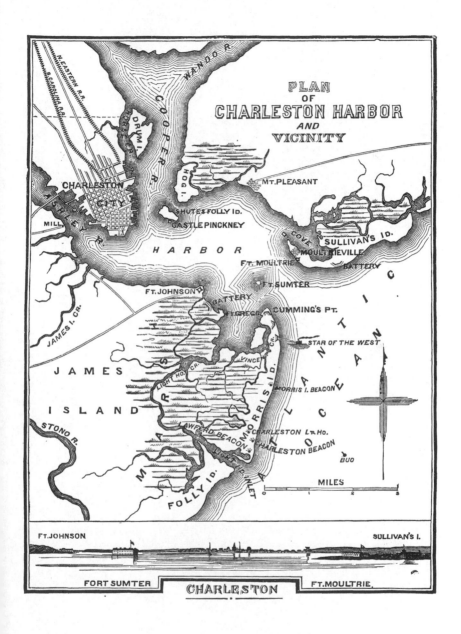

PLAN
OF
CHARLESTON HARBOR
AND
VICINITY

ble that I was astonished, beyond measure, on being referred to him on such an errand, who, he said, would accomplish for me what I wished. This letter was so worded that the party to whom it was addressed would understand. that I wanted to talk with him about matters that it would not do for everybody to be cognizant of, and I was told that I might speak with the most perfect freedom to him with regard to the business I had in hand.

ONE OF THE BIG VILLAINS.

I accordingly went to this official, and presented the letter of introduction, wondering not a little what he would say and do when he read it. His conduct satisfied me at once that he was implicated in unlawful schemes, and that he was exactly the man for my purposes. When he read the letter he turned as pale as a sheet, and then red, while his hand trembled so much that I was afraid some of the people in the room would notice it.

He read the letter through two or three times before he was able to obtain sufficient composure to trust himself to speak. He finally, however, said a few commonplace things to me, which meant nothing, and were intended for the ears of those around us rather than for mine, and then requested me to give him my address.

I did this, and then, in obedience to a hurried gesture, took my departure, without attempting to have any further conversation just then, but feeling well assured that I could speedily be afforded ample opportunity for an exchange of views with him.

That evening my new acquaintance called on me at my hotel, and, although we both for a time fought shy of the main subject, I readily perceived, from the general tenor of his conversation, that he had, since my visit to his office, been making particular inquiries with regard to me. He remarked, among other things, that he had heard Colonel Baker mention my name several times, and always in highly commendatory terms. This was very satisfactory intelligence, for it convinced me that I really stood well with the secret-service chief, as something I could only guess at from that individual's manner.

At length he said he thought he understood my object in making his acquaintance, and, although he was not quite certain what I wanted, he would endeavor to aid me by any means in his power.

I then told him, plump and plain, that I and my associates had full information with regard to what was being done in certain of the treasury bureaux, and that we had it in our power to set the detectives to work in such a way that all those engaged in swindling the government would be arrested and brought to punishment. Instead of doing anything of this kind, however, we proposed to share the profits of such fraudulent transactions as were going on in the treasury department. As the agent and receivers of the others interested, I wanted to get possession of one or more of the electrotype impressions of the bond and note plates, such as were used for fraudulent issues ; and I also desired to obtain facilities for visiting the printing bureau, whenever I might find it expedient to do so, for the sake of conferring with certain parties there, and in order that I might have an eye generally on what was going on.

My friend saw that I "had him," to use a slang phrase that is very appropriate in such a connection as this, for it expresses the situation exactly.

He hesitated, however, as well he might, before yielding to my request; and after some immaterial talk, which expressed nothing but his fears, he said, " Well, if I oblige you in this, I will place my honor and my reputation in your hands. I have never yet stepped aside from the duties of my office since I have been sworn in, and what assurances have I that you will not betray me ?"

I knew exactly how much of this to believe, and so I said to him, " I don't care, sir, what you may or may not have done before this. I am satisfied, however, that you are the proper person to assist me in the matter under discussion, and if you do you shall have your share of the profits. You can rely upon my secrecy, for I will be implicated as well as yourself; but, independently of that, I think that my character for reliability is sufficiently well known for you to have no hesitation in trusting me."

" Yes, I know your reputation for skill and secrecy; you seem to have played it finely with Baker. I am glad somebody has managed to get ahead of that fellow, for he has been making himself an infernal nuisance about here."

This was said with considerable bitterness, and I could not help smiling, both at the words and the manner ; for there was something absolutely comical in the idea of my friend and those in league with him considering Baker's negligence a grievance. I, however, said nothing on that point, but merely remarked that Baker appeared to be a tolerably capable officer.

My friend possibly did not care to argue about Baker, for he went on, without noticing the remark, to say that he would have to swear me to secrecy.

I laughed at this, and ridiculed the idea of my oath being worth any more than my word under the circumstances.

He, therefore, abandoned all notion of attempting to bind me, except by the responsibilities I would incur in connection with himself and the others interested, and began to talk business in a straightforward manner.

This suited me exactly, and it was not long before we had matters arranged to our mutual satisfaction.

He agreed to furnish any capital that might be needed to commence operations, or to do any preliminary bribing that was necessary, and was to have a percentage of whatever profits were made. As for getting possession of a fraudulent plate or plates, I would have to talk about that to the people to whom he would introduce me ; but he did not doubt, if I managed right, I could get all that were necessary for our purposes.

CERTAIN BUSINESS SUGGESTIONS.

There were other things to be done, however, besides printing bogus notes and bonds ; and he thought that a thriving business could be carried on in the genuine articles, which might be abstracted and returned, after being turned over a few times in the market, so as to yield a sufficient profit to pay for the risk and trouble. The bogus bonds, he thought, could be printed in Washington, and seemed rather anxious that they should be ; but I said that I doubted whether my associates would consent to that; at any rate, I could not undertake to make definite arrangements without consulting them. The idea was to float these bonds, as far as possible, on the European market ; and it was thought that it could readily be done, as they could be sold at rates that would defy competition on the part of the government agents who were working with the genuine articles.

Having come to an understanding, and arranged a general plan of action, my friend said that he would give me a note which would obtain for me the freedom of the treasury building, but that I would have to be exceedingly careful of it, and take particular pains not to let any one but the person to whom it was addressed see it.

I, of course, made all necessary promises, and he, accordingly, wrote a note, which he signed with a private mark instead of with his name, and told me to call the next day at the treasury, and give it to a certain prominent official connected with the printing bureau. He then took his leave, and I had little or nothing to do with him afterwards, his share of whatever profits was made being paid to him by some one else.

My arrangement with the parties at whose instance I went to Washington on this business was, that in event of my being able to make a satisfactory bargain with the officials in the treasury department, I was to be the receiver and bearer of whatever they might confide to my care in the way of bonds, notes, bogus plates, and other matters, and was to travel to and fro between Washington, Philadelphia, and New York as a confidential manager, while brokers in the two last-named cities and elsewhere were to do the financiering.

The scheme was an immense one, although it did not reach its full proportions all at once; and it included not only dealing in genuine — borrowed for the purpose from the treasury — and bogus Federal securities, but Confederate bogus bonds also. These bonds were to be, as far as practicable, put upon the English market, at the best rates that could be gotten for them, and our — that is, the Confederate — share of the proceeds was to go into a general fund, to be used for advancing the interests of the cause. As for the Britishers, we considered them fair game, when selling them either kind of bogus securities, for we regarded their conduct as treacherous to both parties in the great contest, and thought that they might as well be made to pay some of the expenses of conducting it.

From first to last the British government had deluded the people of the Confederacy with false hopes of recognition and interference; and, as at the time of which I am writing, it was becoming daily more apparent that it did not propose to interfere unless it could do so without risking anything, the feeling against it, especially among the Confederates at the North and in Canada, who were constantly in correspondence with agents in England and on the continent, was getting to be very bitter.

It was determined, therefore, to go for Johnny Bull's pocket, and a lively trade in bogus Confederate and Federal securities was started and kept up for a considerable time, which, among other things, involved my making a trip to London, at a very critical time, as the reader will learn anon.

CHAPTER XLI.

COUNTERFEITING AND BOGUS BOND SPECULATIONS.

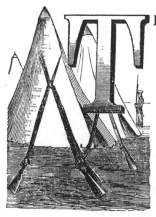

THE day after receiving the note to which reference has been made in the preceding chapter, I took it to the person in the printer's bureau, to whom it was addressed. This individual did not appear to be the least surprised to see me, and it was evident that he had been apprised of the fact that I intended to make him a visit, and what the visit would be for.

He proceeded to business at once, when he had read the note, by requesting me to call the next day at his office, when, he said, the matter would be arranged to my satisfaction. He was not disposed to be talkative about the situation ; and, as I found out shortly

476

afterwards, certain persons under him in the bureau were the active agents in the swindling transactions that were going on, his plan being to avoid, as far as practicable, any palpable participation in them.

This man, however, was at the head of the ring, and was responsible for all the rascalities that occurred in connection with the important bureau with which he was connected. Without his knowledge and consent, the things I am about to relate could never have happened. What the nature of his influence with the secretary of the treasury and with prominent members of Congress was, I cannot undertake to say. It was, however, sufficient, not only to screen him from punishment, but even to secure his retention in office after his misdeeds had been exposed.

GROSS IMMORALITIES IN THE TREASURY DEPARTMENT.

The abstraction of currency and bonds for speculative purposes, and the permitting electrotypes of the plates used for printing bonds and currency, to be taken and disposed of to outside parties, for the purpose of enabling them to print bogus issues, were not his only offences. He and another official, who occupied a very prominent and responsible position in the treasury department, had several abandoned women employed under them, at large salaries, and with whom they were in the habit of carousing in their offices at midnight. Indeed, so shameless and abandoned were both the men and the women, that their doings became a public scandal, and did much to bring about an exposure of their official misdeeds.

Before I knew anything of these matters, Colonel Baker pointed out these women to me as the pets of these two men, and told me about their introducing them into the treasury building, and taking them to the Canterbury saloon in male attire. This was some time before Baker commenced the investigations which created such a sensation by revealing to the public the vice and corruption that ruled in the treasury department. Baker then said he was certain that villanies of no ordinary character were going on, and that he proposed some day to try and find out what they were.

The fact that Baker had his eye on these officials, and others whom I knew were guilty of transactions, that, if the laws were properly administered, would consign them to the penitentiary, induced me to conclude that I had best have nothing to do with them; and, accordingly, I severed my business relations with the printing bureau, after giving those interested a hint to beware of the colonel.

This hint was disregarded, for the reason that the scamps knew that he could not commence an investigation into the affairs of the treasury department without the consent of Secretary Chase, and this consent, for reasons which to them were good and sufficient, they did not believe would ever be given.

Baker requested by Mr. Chase to Commence an Investigation.

It so happened, however, that Mr. Chase, of his own motion, called Baker in to assist him in discovering some suspected wrong-doing in the department, and that individual, having then obtained the requisite authority, immediately went to work with even more than his accustomed zeal to find out what was wrong in the printing bureau.

Baker, however, was either somewhat obtuse, or else the person to whom I have alluded as at the head of the ring, and his confederates, were successful in getting him on the wrong track, for the first man he laid his hands on was Dr. Stewart Gwynn. This old gentleman was an eccentric inventor, who had a lot of queer, original ideas about proper methods of printing the currency and bonds. Mr. Chase believed that he was a great genius, and it is possible he may have been. I regarded him, however, as a mere catspaw for the others, and have never thought that he was guilty of any intentional wrong doing.

Dr. Gwynn was arrested by Baker, and was lodged for a number of months in the old capitol prison. Nothing criminal, however, was proved against him, although it was shown very conclusively that some of his schemes were not very profitable to the government. Much sympathy was felt for this old man; and I, among others, went to Mr. Chase to beg for his release.

I had quite a long talk with Mr. Chase on this occasion, and he was very emphatic in stating that the method in vogue in the treasury department for printing notes and bonds was an effectual check on counterfeiting. I, of course, knew very well what a serious delusion he was laboring under, and it would have given me great pleasure to have undeceived him, could I have done so with safety to myself and those with whom I was associated.

Having captured Dr. Gwynn, Baker next made an exposé of the conduct of the other treasury official whom I have mentioned, and certain female employees of the department, but he did not get at the facts with regard to the bogus plates, and other matters of equal importance, until a considerable time after. Indeed, I am not sure that it was his investigation that brought the worst practices of the printing bureau to light, but think that some one else had a hand in making that revelation.

BAKER DISGUSTED.

It is probable that the manner in which he was treated by those who should have supported him, after proving how the two men mentioned were conducting themselves with the female employees, may have disgusted him with the whole business, and discouraged him from prosecuting his investigations any further. The exposé with regard to the women created a great excitement when it got into the newspapers ; but the implicated treasury officials had sufficient influence to brave public opinion, and to retain their positions in spite of the clamor for their removal that was raised. Indeed, so great was the prejudice against Colonel Baker, in certain quarters, that, I have no doubt, many very good people actually believed the parties accused by him were innocent, and were the victims of a conspiracy.

Besides this, the public attention at that period was tolerably well occupied with war matters ; and Baker, having been bluffed off, the scandal was forgotten in a short time. Baker, however, was very sore over the treatment he received from Mr. Chase, Mr. Jordan, Mr. Garfield, and others ; and was especially indignant that the rogues who were robbing the people should not only be permitted to go unpunished, but should be actually protected in their villanies by their official superiors.

With these matters, however, I had nothing to do, having discontinued my operations in connection with the treasury before Colonel Baker commenced to examine into the gross mismanagement of affairs in that important department.

In accordance with my agreement with the printing bureau official, I called at his office at the appointed hour, and was

referred by him to one of his subordinates. With this man I
made an arrangement for a conference under a certain cedar
tree in the eastern part of the Smithsonian Institution grounds,
at nine o'clock in the evening.

This man and his father were printers in the bureau, and
were confederates in the dishonest practices that were going
on, by which the government was defrauded of immense sums,
and by which immense quantities of bogus notes and bonds
were foisted on the public. One of these men had a mistress,
who was employed to do some work about the printing presses.
This woman conveyed the electrotype duplicates of the plates
to parties outside, and performed other services of a similar
character, for which she was paid handsomely.

A SECRET CONFERENCE UNDER A CEDAR TREE.

Some time before the appointed hour I strolled into the
grounds of the Smithsonian Institution, and after finding the
cedar tree, hid myself in some bushes near by, not being at
all certain that some trick would not be played upon me; for
it occurred to me that perhaps these people might not fancy
my having anything to do with the matters we were negotiating about, and would take a notion to have me put out of the
way in some manner.

My apprehensions, however, were groundless, for I had
approached them in such a manner that they were compelled
to trust me, whether they wanted to or not; and their only
idea was, with the assistance of myself and associates, to make
the grandest haul on the treasury that had ever yet been attempted.

Ere a great while I heard footsteps approaching, and presently some one coughed in a significant manner, which I inter-
preted as a signal for me. I accordingly looked out from my
hiding-place, and saw the man I was expecting. Having assured myself that he was alone, I went up to him, and said,
" Good evening."

" You are here, are you ? " said he.

" Yes, I am always punctual on business ; punctuality is the
road to wealth."

We then sat down together on the grass to arrange our
plans.

The scheme I had to propose was quite a modest one, all
things taken into consideration. It was, that I, as receiver

and bearer for certain other parties, should be given electrotype duplicates of bond and currency plates, such as we had information were manufactured by certain parties in the treasury department. For them we would either pay so much, or would share the profits.

My new acquaintance, however, was in favor of going into business on quite a grand scale. He suggested, in rather indefinite terms, that he had a scheme for bleeding the treasury, which would, if proper management was used, be an even more expeditious and safer method of making money than by issuing bogus paper; but he seemed to be a little hesitating about confiding all the details to me.

I therefore said, after we had talked for some time without coming to any conclusion, " Well, sir, what are your plans? I have no notion of rendering myself liable to imprisonment for the plans of another person, unless I know all about them, and understand exactly what risks I run, and what I am likely to gain. If it were not for the sake of a great object I have in view, I would not engage in this business on any terms, and would not risk my life and reputation as I am and have been doing."

" What is your object? "

" That is a personal secret, and it has nothing to do with any one individual."

A WAY TO GET RICH.

" Well," said he, " this plan of mine is the biggest thing that has ever been tried on yet, and I am certain we can manage it, if we only go to work in the right way. I have facilities for carrying on an affair of this kind such as are possessed by no other man in Washington ; I know all the men in every department, and know exactly who can and who cannot be trusted. I am acquainted with every private entrance to the public buildings in this city, and am familiar with a great part of the rascality that is going on every day and every night."

" If that is so, you certainly have advantages, and if your scheme is a practicable one, I will take it into consideration."

He then went on to tell me how he proposed using government money and bonds, which were to be taken from the treasury for certain speculative purposes, and also for floating bogus bonds, both Federal and Confederate, upon the English market. He was to manage the matter in the

31

treasury department, I was to act as go-between, and certain brokers and others in Philadelphia and New York were to attend to the outside business.

When he had fully explained himself, I said, " I am almost afraid to undertake such an enterprise. It will be no small matter to carry on such operations as you propose without detection. Don't you think you are trying to do too much?"

" I know that we will be operating on a rather large scale, but if we go about the matter in the right way there need be no serious danger. We can begin on a moderate basis, and extend our business as we go on, replacing the borrowed money in the treasury as it comes back to us. I and my two friends will be responsible for procuring the capital, if you will consent to be the bearer between here and Philadelphia and New York."

" O, sir, you must not let me be known to any third party in an affair of this kind. If you will deliver to me the money in person, or cause it to be placed where I can get it without danger of being detected, I will undertake the job."

" Well, that is all right. I will arrange everything for you, so that you will be in no danger. I want this to bring in something handsome, for I am anxious to get out of Washington, and so soon as I can make enough money I intend to go South. My feelings have always been with the Southern people; and I consider that they have been the victims of unnumbered outrages."

" Why, ain't you afraid to talk in that manner, you a government employee? Don't you know that I am for the Union?"

" So am I," said he; " but, for all I can make out, the Union is a great big hobby-horse for speculations, and as other people are making money out of it, I don't see why I might not."

An Electrotype Plate Bargained for.

I then returned to what had been my chief object in meeting him, by telling him that I wanted one of those electrotype plates. He seemed to be rather disinclined to accommodate me in this matter at first; but as I was persistent, he finally consented, and we parted, with the understanding that we were not to meet again until I was ready to report the result of our operations, and hand him his share of the profits.

The next day a plate was delivered to me at the Kirkwood House, which I immediately put under lock and key in my trunk. Subsequently I received a note, informing me that I would find a package under the cedar tree in the Smithsonian grounds, and that I had better go and get it as soon after dark as possible, for fear some of the workmen might pick it up.

The package, which, on examination, was found to contain fifty-five thousand dollars' worth of government paper, was waiting for me, covered with loose leaves to screen it from any casual passer-by, when I visited the designated spot.

Securing my booty, I returned to the hotel, rang the bell for my bill, and started for Philadelphia with all possible expedition.

The plate which I had in my trunk was for one hundred dollars' compound interest notes. Not very long after, I and my associates obtained another one for printing fractional currency.

On reaching Philadelphia, I commenced operations immediately in connection with certain brokers and others, and bought a large amount of bogus Confederate bonds. Having obtained these, I went to New York, where I took rooms in a private house on Greenwich Street, deeming a hotel rather too conspicuous; and communicating with my associates there, we went to work with energy to turn the money belonging to Uncle Sam, in our possession, over and over as rapidly as we could, making it pay us a handsome profit at each turn.

A LIVELY TRADE IN BOGUS SECURITIES.

Some of this cash was put into the bounty and substitute brokerage business, but a large part of it was invested in bogus Confederate and other securities, which were sold to brokers for the English market. One private banker took sixty-two thousand dollars' worth, and another twenty-one thousand dollars' worth, while smaller amounts were scattered about in various directions, we receiving English exchange and gold at market rates, which we turned into greenbacks.

This business finally grew to such an extent, that it was found to be convenient to communicate with London direct. Correspondence was therefore established with a banking-house on Regent Street, and until the close of the war a lively traffic in real and bogus Federal and Confederate securities was maintained.

After we had been operating six days with the money obtained from the treasury, I telegraphed to my confederate in Washington, stating how much had already been made, and asking whether I should keep on. The reply was, to give myself plenty of time, and to keep the thing going for ten days longer, and then close out, and return to Washington in time for the monthly reports to be made out. At the end of the ten days there was but five thousand dollars' worth of Confederate bonds remaining on our hands undisposed of.

I posted to Washington, and having notified my confederate there when he might expect me, he met me in the Capitol grounds, and I gave him a statement of the account between us as it then stood, turning over to him the borrowed money, and half of the profits of the speculations that had been carried on with it. He informed me that I was just in the nick of time, as the reports had not yet been made out, but they were about being, and he was beginning to get the least bit uneasy concerning me.

I continued to take an active part in such transactions as these for several months, travelling to and fro between Washington, Philadelphia, and New York, and often having about me immense sums of money. At length, however, I became afraid to risk it any longer, as Colonel Baker had commenced his investigations in the treasury department, and accordingly went out of the business of money-making for the time being. I did the fair thing by the treasury people in giving them a hint with regard to Baker, and then made haste to get out of the way until the storm should blow over.

As things turned out, it was not, by any means, as much of a storm as I expected it to be. Baker failed to strike the right trail, and the revelations which he made, while sufficiently scandalous, were with regard to matters of very secondary importance, and he dallied so much with these that the scamps were able to get ready for him.

This treasury investigation did not do very much credit to anybody concerned in it. Baker blundered badly, and failed to get the main facts, which he could and should have gotten. He, however, succeeded in proving in a most positive manner that the moral characters of certain prominent officials were about as bad as they could be, and that they were in every way improper persons to hold the important positions they did. Despite the disgraceful disclosures that were made

with regard to them, however, these men were able to secure
the support of those whose duty it was to have brought
them to punishment, and they were retained in office in spite
of Baker, and in defiance of public opinion.

WHAT MIGHT HAVE HAPPENED.

Now, suppose that Mr. Chase, and Mr. Jordan, and Mr.
Garfield, and the others who shielded the guilty parties, and
who endeavored to represent Baker as a conspirator, had, by
any means, found out who I was, and what I had been doing
in connection with the treasury? What a perfect godsend
a discovery of my transactions would have been! The whole
party would have turned upon the rebel secret-service agent
with a ferocity that would have been intensified by the fact of
her being a woman; and any amount of patriotic indignation
would have been poured upon my head. Hanging, in the
opinion of these honorable gentlemen, would have been too
good for me; and there is no knowing how many votes they
would have gained by denouncing me as a fiend in human
shape. The fact that I was a Confederate secret-service agent,
and was doing what I did to advance the interests of the
cause to which my allegiance was given, would only have
made matters ten times worse for me had my performances
been found out.

Luckily, however, I was smart enough to take proper precautions before putting myself in danger, and when I clearly
saw trouble ahead quietly got out of the way. It was not
the woman who was working for the Confederacy, and who
was under obligations to do those whom she regarded as her
enemies and the enemies of her cause all the injury in her
power, who fell into Baker's hands, but certain high Federal
officials, who were under oath, and who were intrusted with
some of the most responsible duties that could possibly be
intrusted to any men. These people were under obligations
of fidelity to the trusts confided to them, which they could not
thrust aside without making themselves morally and legally
liable to the severest condemnation. In spite of this, however, and in spite of the facts that they were guilty of transactions which deserved punishment, and that ample proofs
of their unfitness for the positions they held were produced,
they found ardent and efficient supporters in men of the highest stations, who, day after day were denouncing the rebel-

lion as the sum of all villanies, and who aimed at making the public believe that they were the most patriotic of citizens.

The why and wherefore of all this I do not pretend to understand, and can only congratulate myself on the fact that I was lucky enough to avoid being made a scapegoat of. I well knew the risks I incurred when I consented to become a party to the transactions I have recorded; but, had I been captured and made to suffer, while my confederates were enjoying the protection of some of the chief officers of the government, I would scarcely have thought that justice was being administered with exactly an even hand. As, however, I was not captured, I presume that I have no cause to complain because other people were not punished as they should have been; only, it seems to me to be a queer way of managing the treasury department of a great nation to permit such men as those I have referred to to hold the positions they did, in the face of such facts as were brought to light concerning them, and to treat the detective officers who expose their misdeeds as the really guilty party.

Counterfeiting Government Securities.

In the matter of notes and bonds printed from the duplicate plates obtained from the treasury, an immense business was done both in this country and in England. The person to whom I gave the first plate delivered to me printed eighty-five thousand dollars' worth of one hundred dollar compound interest notes from it. These were, so far as appearances were concerned, just as good as the genuine ones issued from the treasury department. Of this batch, twenty-five thousand dollars' worth were sent to England, and we received exchange for them. The rest were disposed of to the banks, and through various channels.

The bankers and brokers, both here and in England, took these bogus notes and bonds without any hesitation whatever, as indeed there was every reason they should; for there was nothing to distinguish them from the genuine ones that could avail for their detection by ordinary purchasers.

It is impossible for me to give any idea of the enormous amount of this kind of counterfeiting that was done without apparently any serious effort being made on the part of the Federal government to check it. I and my associates had the handling of bogus paper representing immense sums, which we disposed of advantageously ; but the amounts that passed through our hands only represented a very small proportion of what was issued during the war.

The headquarters of the dealers in bogus currency and securities were chiefly in Wall and Fulton Streets, although a number of these swindlers were located on Broadway. With each succeeding month, during the continuance of the war, the spirit of speculation seemed to increase, and men became more and more eager to make money, and less particular how they made it. It was not always obscure men and insignificant banking concerns that were wittingly engaged in this traffic in unlawful paper, but there were plenty who stood high in the esteem of the public, and whose reputations for probity were supposed to be unimpeachable.

As for myself and other Confederates, we took all the advantage we could of the general demoralization, and not only replenished our treasury, so as to be able to carry on many operations that otherwise would have been impossible, but worked in many ways to turn the criminal selfishness and unpatriotic greed of people, with whom we were brought in contact, to account, for the benefit of our cause.

CHAPTER XLII.

BOUNTY-JUMPING.

HE bounty-jumping and substitute-brokerage frauds arose out of a contest between the efforts of the Federal government to maintain the armies in the field at their maximum strength, and the determination of nearly the entire body of male citizens to escape military duty by any means in their power.

Under the terms of the conscription law, persons drafted were permitted to furnish substitutes, if they could get them, and consequently the purchasing of substitutes became an important branch of industry, in which many thousands of dollars capital were invested, and in which immense sums of money were made. This traffic in human flesh and blood would have been bad enough had it been honestly conducted, but, from its very nature, it held out inducements for fraudulent practices which were irresistible to a majority of those engaged in it.

Anything like volunteering, in a proper sense of the word, had ceased long before my arrival at the North, but each locality being anxious to avoid the conscription, made desperate efforts to fill its quota of men by offering bounties, greater or less in amount, to encourage enlistments. The payment of these bounties was a direct encouragement to desertion; and, as a very different class of men were tempted by them from those who had enlisted, out of patriotic motives, at the outbreak of the war, a vast number of those who pocketed these premiums were very willing to go through with the same operation again, and as often as it was practicable to do so.

Bounty-jumping, or escaping from the recruiting officers, and enlisting over again, was carried on, in a greater or less degree, all over the country, but the headquarters of the bounty-jumpers and substitute-brokers was in New York.

The Purchase of Enlistment Papers.

It was to New York that the agents of interior counties came for the purpose of filling their quotas, and they always found a horde of brokers ready to accommodate them with real and bogus enlistment papers, each one of which was supposed to represent an able-bodied man, fit for military duty, who had passed the mustering officers, been accepted, and was then ready for service. Whether the papers were bogus or genuine mattered very little to those who purchased, so long as they could obtain credit on them from the authorities at Washington. It would probably not be making too large an estimate to put down one half of the enlistment papers sold to country agents and others as forgeries, while not one half of the genuine ones, no, not one fourth, represented men actually ready for duty.

Of course such stupendous frauds as these could not have been carried on without the criminal connivance of the officials of various kinds, who were, in one way or another, connected with the enlistments. There may have been some honest officers, soldiers, and civilians connected with this service in New York during the last year of the war, but I was never lucky enough to meet any. So far as I could see, the whole of them, — commissioned officers, non-commissioned officers, surgeons, clerks, notaries public, and others, were intent only upon making all the money they could while the opportunity for making it lasted.

The bounty-jumping and substituting-frauds were perpetrated in such an open and barefaced manner that I could not help wondering why some efforts were not made by the authorities at Washington to check them. At length, however, the services of Colonel Baker were called in, and he succeeded in creating quite a panic among the swindlers by the investigations which he instituted, and the large number of the arrests he made. The war, however, came to an end before he succeeded in discovering a hundredth part of the rascalities that were going on, so that, practically, his investigations were of very little benefit to the government.

The rates which were paid for substitutes varied from five hundred to twenty-one hundred dollars. The parties with whom I was associated enlisted chiefly for the army, and did very little for the navy. The bulk of our profits, so fast as they were made, went to Canada or England, and some of the parties who received the money are to-day living in luxury on it.

How the Recruits Escaped.

The recruits, when they were enlisted, and when they did not escape from the recruiting stations, — as hundreds of them did every day, — were sent to Governor's Island. It might be supposed that once there, they would have been safe. They would have been, had the officers, commissioned and non-commissioned, been honest. The temptations for gain, however, were too great, and there was not a person in authority on the island who was not pocketing hundreds of dollars every week by conniving at the escape of recruits. I have known some of the regular professionals jump as high as sixteen bounties, walking away from Governor's Island every time they were sent there with as much ease as if there was no such thing as army regulations and martial law in existence.

The way this was managed was by the purchase of passes. In going through the boat-house, a slip of paper, with the number of passes on it, would be put in a book on the table, and on returning, the passes would be found in the same book. The money for these could either be folded in the slip, or an order on the broker's office be given to the sergeant.

One application for a substitute that was made at the office with which I was connected, was from a very prominent and very wealthy gentleman of New York, who was willing to pay as high as twenty-one hundred dollars for some one to take the place of his son, who had been drafted. This old gentleman was noted for his advocacy of the war, and for his bitterness in denouncing the South, and yet, when it came to letting his son go and do some of the fighting, his patriotism tapered down to a very fine point, and he was willing to send any number of substitutes if necessary, but not his son, if money could purchase his exemption. He was a very fair sample of the kind of patriots I was in the habit of meeting; and I could not help contrasting the whole-souled enthusiasm of the Southern people with the disposition shown by so many prominent adherents of the Federal cause, to let anybody and everybody who could be purchased or beguiled do their fighting for them, rather than to venture within smelling distance of gunpowder themselves.

As it was all in the way of business, however, I and my partners endeavored to accommodate this old gentleman.

I knew of a couple of barbers in Brooklyn, well built, and hearty young colored fellows, and I accordingly went to them, and finally induced one of them to enlist as a substitute for the old man's son. He came over to our office, and on being enrolled, received five hundred dollars, with a promise that the rest of his bounty would be handed to him by the officer on the island. Privately, however, he was told how he might make his escape by giving the sergeant at the gate fifty dollars, but was warned not to return to the city, or he would be arrested and tried for desertion. He acted according to instructions, and deserted so easily that he was tempted to try it over again several times, and I believe he managed to pocket several bounties without being caught.

ENLISTMENT OF EMIGRANTS.

The emigrant depot at Castle Garden, however, was the great resort of the bounty and substitute brokers, some of whom actually had agents in Europe, who deceived the poor people there with all kinds of promises, and then shipped them, to become the prey of scamps on this side of the Atlantic so soon as they set foot on our shores.

All manner of inducements to enlist were held out to the poor Irish and Germans at Castle Garden. They were surrounded by crowds of shouting and yelling brokers until they were fairly bewildered, and found themselves enlisted before they well knew what was the matter with them. To those who hesitated, the most lavish promises were made; their wives and children were to be cared for; they were to receive one hundred and sixty acres of land; money in larger sums than they had ever beheld before was flaunted in their faces. One fellow would shout, "Here you are, sir; come this

way; I'm your man; I have five hundred dollars for you."
Another would say, " Here is five hundred dollars and a land
warrant; " and another, " I have twenty-one hundred dollars
for you if you will come with me."

The poor devils, deafened by the clamor around them,
tempted by the magnificent inducements held out to them, and
believing that they really had at last reached the Eldorado of
which they had been dreaming, in the majority of cases surrendered at discretion, and were marched off to act as substitutes for able-bodied American citizens who had no fancy for
fighting the rebels. Every broker's office had its runners, just
the same as the hotels, who were posted at the emigrant station whenever a vessel load of human beings came into port;
and among them the poor foreigners, who came over here to
better their fortunes, had but little chance to become anything
but food for Confederate bullets.

On one occasion I saw a squad of Germans who had just
landed, and who seemed to be looking for some one. As a
runner approached them, their head man, who acted as interpreter, drew from his pocket a letter, and asked, " Are you
Captain P. ? "

" I am here in his place," replied the runner. " What can
I do for you ? "

The German hesitated a moment, and before the runner
could fairly commence work with him, Captain P. made his
appearance from the purser's office, where he had, doubtless,
just been receiving intelligence of the arrival of his human
cargo. The runner seeing P., and knowing that his opportunity was now gone, went off to seek for his prey elsewhere,
while the captain proceeded to take the party in charge with
small ceremony.

" Is your name P. ? " queried the leader.

" Yes, and you are —— ; " and without more ado, he hurried them off to a den in Greenwich Street, where they were
forthwith enlisted in the Federal service.

These people, like thousands of others, had been picked up
in Europe by agents, under all kinds of pretexts and promises,
and shipped for this side of the ocean just like so many cattle.
Captain P. considered himself as their owner, and he sold
them to the government exactly as he would have sold cattle,
if that sort of traffic had been as profitable as dealing in white
human beings.

On one occasion, when I was at the station, I heard a runner endeavoring to persuade a party of Irishmen to enlist, by representing that if they would do so, the Federal governmennt, after it had got through with putting down the rebellion, intended to declare war with England, and to undertake the liberation of Ireland. He said that the conduct of England in the Trent affair was an insult, for which redress would be demanded; but that the government, before declaring war, was anxious to have as many Irishmen as possible in the army, feeling assured that they would fight against their old enemy with even greater ferocity than the Americans.

The Irishmen, all of whom seemed to have more or less whiskey in them, became very much excited, and went off with the runner to attend a meeting, which he told them was being held for the purpose of taking measures for the liberation of Ireland. The place of meeting was a recruiting office, and the liberation of Ireland, or any other good work, was the last thing thought of by the people whom the unlucky foreigners found there.

The wives of these men — many of them poor, thinly-clad creatures — were eager for them to go, especially when they heard that such large sums were being paid, cash down, for bounties, and were beguiled by all sorts of promises with regard to being taken care of by the government, and given so many acres of ·land when the war was over.

The government was probably as little responsible for the frauds perpetrated upon these poor, ignorant foreigners, as it was for the many other rascalities that were going on. It is a fact, however, that the Federal armies, during the last eighteen months of the war, — and probably during a much longer time, for I am referring only to matters that came under my own observation, — were mainly recruited from these foreigners, who had nothing to do with the quarrel between the South and the North, and who were induced to become food for powder under all manner of false and fraudulent pretexts.

AN INEFFICIENT SYSTEM OF RECRUITING.

The amount of money that was squandered, through the system of recruiting adopted by the Federal government, cannot be estimated, while evils far worse than the waste of money were encouraged. Playing the part I was, I had every reason to be satisfied with the way things were being managed, but now that the war is over, I suppose I have the same right to express an opinion with regard to this as any other matter of public policy.

I thought at the time, and think still, that a most unstatesmanlike blunder was committed in permitting conscripts to furnish substitutes, and in paying bounties to encourage voluntary enlistments. The results were, that the government did not get the men it needed, while villanies, the demoralizing influences of which penetrated to nearly every class of society, were directly encouraged.

There should have been a rigid conscription law, under which all citizens, whether rich or poor, would have been treated exactly the same. The men who were drafted, if fit for service, should have been compelled to shoulder their muskets and go to the front.

If there was any justice in the war at all, it was a rich man's fight just as much as it was a poor man's; and when the time came for deciding who should and who should not take a turn on the battle-field, the chances ought to have been equal, between the rich men and the poor men, of drawing prizes or blanks in the lottery.

Had things been managed as I have suggested, not only would impartial justice have been done, but the proportions of the national debt would have been greatly curtailed, while the generals in the field would have kept their ranks full, and the downfall of the Confederacy would have occurred at a very much earlier day than it did.

Colonel Baker undertakes to Investigate the Frauds.

During the whole time that I was interested in this bounty-jumping and substitute-brokerage business, it was a matter of constant surprise to me that some effort was not being made by the government to put a stop to the outrageous frauds that were being committed in the most open manner every day.

The matter finally was taken in hand by Colonel Baker, who came on to New York, and located himself at the Astor House, for the purpose of instituting an investigation. He kept himself very quiet, and endeavored to prevent those against whom he was operating from knowing that he was in the city until he was ready to deal with them. It was necessary that he should have some assistance, however, in order to begin right; and, by that peculiar good fortune by which I was attended, during most of my career as a soldier and secret-service agent, something prompted him to send for me, to see whether I would not undertake to find out certain things for him which he was anxious to know, but which he was afraid to trust either himself, or any of the male members of his force to look into, lest they should be identified, and the alarm be given.

When I received a "strictly private and confidential" note from Colonel Baker, requesting me to call on him at seven o'clock, on a certain evening, at the Astor House, I scarcely knew what to make of it; and, fearful that something against me had been discovered, I was in considerable doubt as to whether to respond or not. My previous experience with Baker, however, had taught me that, in dealing with him, the bold way was much the best way; and so, after turning the subject over in my mind, I concluded to see him at the hour mentioned, for the purpose of finding out what it was he wanted of me.

BAKER ASKS ME TO HELP HIM.

I accordingly went to the Astor House, and sent up my name. The colonel met me in the parlor, and, as he seated himself beside me, he said, with a smile, "Now tell me, my good woman, what have you been doing with yourself?"

This might be a merely friendly greeting, and it might be just the opposite; but, although I almost feared that my time was come, I was determined not to give him a chance to suspect me by my words or manner. So I said, "O, I have been visiting my relations."

"I received your letter," continued the colonel, "but I have been a little surprised at not seeing you in Washington since your return from the West."

"I didn't go to Washington, because I really didn't care to see you. The fact is, I made such a bad failure in what I undertook to do on that trip, that I was ashamed of myself."

Baker, however, took a good-natured view of what he was pleased to call my bad luck, and went on to tell me what his errand in New York was, and to ask me to aid him in certain matters that he mentioned.

I professed to know little or nothing about the bounty and substitute frauds, but, after discussing the subject pretty thoroughly with him, consented to try and find out what he wanted, and to sound certain people for him, in order to ascertain whether they were willing to aid him in carrying on his investigations.

The first thing I did after parting with Baker was to warn my associates, so that they might close out before it was too late to do so on advantageous terms. What became of the others in the business I did not care, and was rather glad than otherwise to have an opportunity of putting Baker on their track.

In a couple of days I furnished the colonel with the information he wanted, and, before a great while, the whole bounty-jumping fraternity were thrown into consternation by his raid upon them.

Baker at first represented himself as the agent of an interior county, and in that capacity he bought up a large number of forged enlistment papers, and became acquainted with the men who had them for sale, and with the manner of preparing them. He also disguised himself in various ways, and jumped several bounties in the course of one day. One of his men was enlisted, sent over to Governor's Island, bought off, enlisted again, and bought off again, for the purpose of demonstrating how the thing could be done. Finally, when he understood the whole business, he laid his plans, and made an immense number of arrests; but before he had more than fairly gotten under way with his work the assassination of Mr. Lincoln occurred, and he was recalled to Washington, to take a part in the search that was being made for Booth and his companions.

During the time I was engaged in the bounty and substitute brokerage business, I was interested, in a greater or less degree, in several other enterprises, and went on several expeditions, the particulars of the most important of which will be related in subsequent chapters. My circle of acquaintance among the better class of people was large, and I took great pains to keep on the best terms with ladies and gentlemen of influence who were known. to be ardent supporters of the Federal cause.

In conjunction with some other ladies, I at one time started on a begging expedition, and after canvassing a large part of Brooklyn, I went up to Albany. I collected, in all, seventeen hundred dollars, half of which I gave to the Soldiers' Aid Society, and the other half to the Southern Relief Fund, in which I had a more particular interest.

Among the noted characters whose acquaintance I made at this period was Jim Fisk. I had heard a great deal about him, and had a strong desire to see him. Hearing that he was to dine with certain parties at Delmonico's, I hired a handsome turnout, and, dressing myself very elegantly, went there with a couple of friends.

On entering the dining-hall, I inquired of the waiter whether Mr. Fisk was in the room. He replied that he had just come in, and pointed him out to me. I went, with my friends, to the table next to his, for I was anxious to have a good look at him, and to hear him talk.

Fisk was one of the finest looking men I ever saw. He had a very handsome head, and a large, noble eye, and he was as pleasant and affable in his manners as he was attractive in his personal appearance. I was greatly taken with him at first sight, and became inspired with a very ardent desire to make his acquaintance.

He glanced over at my little party with a smile, as much as to say, " I wonder who you are ! " We were ready to leave before he was, but I said to my friends, " Let us wait a little ; I am expecting some one ; " my object being to find an opportunity to exchange words with Fisk. At length I saw that he was through his dinner, and so said, " I do not believe my friend is coming ; perhaps we had better not wait any longer." We then walked slowly towards the door, and I lingered as long as I could at the cashier's desk, paying for my dinner. Fisk passed by me, and as I and my companions went out, he was standing in the door-way, conversing with some one. When stepping into the carriage, I purposely dropped my handkerchief, and had the satisfaction of seeing him come forward and pick it up. He handed it to me with a smile, and made a very courteous bow in return for my rather profuse expressions of thanks.

Fisk afterwards recognized me a number of times when I met him driving in the Park, and twice, when I went to see him on business, he complied with my requests without the least hesitation. One of my interviews with him was when I was on a begging expedition for the Soldiers' Aid Society. He gave me three hundred dollars, of which I gave twenty-five dollars to the society, and the balance to the Southern Relief Fund. My second call was to ask for a pass for some poor soldiers. He granted it immediately, without asking any questions, and did not have any idea that the soldiers

32

were escaped Confederate prisoners, who were trying to get through to Canada.

Fisk may have been profligate in his life, and, from a certain standpoint, may have been a bad man. He had some truly noble qualities, however, and it is no wonder that he had so many warm personal friends.

Among the other incidents of this period, a little speculation in oil stock is worthy of a brief mention. While on a visit to Philadelphia I met an oil man, who, after a good deal of talk, finally induced me to take a small interest in his company. I learned, however, from one of my Confederate friends, very shortly after, that the thing was a fraud, and sold out, fortunately, at a profit.

BUSHROD R. JOHNSTON.

GIDEON J. PILLOW.

THOMAS C. HINDMAN

LEONIDAS POLK.

CHAPTER XLIII.

THE SURRENDER OF LEE.

MAKE no pretence of relating in detail my movements while acting as a Confederate secret-service agent at the North, as such a course would but increase the bulk of this volume without adding to its interest, and would be apt to weary, rather than entertain the reader. I was coming and going constantly, my principal line of travel being between New York and Washington, although I made a number of trips to Canada, and to various points in the States. While conducting the operations which have just been narrated, I was, also, as will readily be understood, transacting business of a varied nature on account of the Confederacy, and sometimes was kept very steadily on the road. A narration of my movements just previous to the close of the war will give a sufficient notion of the kind of work I was engaged in, and will serve to complete the story of this portion of my career.

Shortly after my interview with Colonel Baker at the Astor House, and my consequent withdrawal from all connection with the bounty and substitute brokerage business, I was requested to make a journey to the West, for the purpose of procuring some information which my associates deemed of importance.

A number of the Confederate agents were maturing another

499

grand scheme for the release of the prisoners, and, I think, had some idea of organizing them into an army, for the purpose of an attack in the Federal rear.

The Johnson's Island failure had so completely discouraged me, that I had no faith in any schemes of this kind, although my profound sympathy for the poor prisoners induced me to attempt anything in my power in their behalf. I thought that, even if I could not procure their release, I at least might do something to aid them, and to promote their comfort. I therefore accepted the mission confided to me without hesitation, and once more turned my face westward.

My first stopping-place was Dayton, Ohio. There, in accordance with my understanding with those who had sent me, I dressed myself as a poor girl, and began to look for a situation to do housework. I was rather a novice at this business, but thought that I was not too old to learn, and had the satisfaction of knowing that in case I and my employers did not get on agreeably together, there was no particular necessity for my remaining a moment longer than suited my own convenience.

One Way of getting Information.

I was not very long in obtaining a situation in a family of Union proclivities, and by a few well-directed inquiries, and by listening to the conversation that was going on in the family, I discovered that there were a number of "Copperheads" in the city, and learned the names of some of the most prominent of them. I also picked up much other useful information that might otherwise have been unattainable.

Before I had been in the house three days, the bad temper of its mistress got the better of me, and, concluding that it would be impossible for me to endure her insolence any longer without unpleasant consequences to both of us, I resolved to leave.

This woman had a vile temper, and it seemed to me that she did nothing but scold and find fault from morning till night. As her treatment of me was undoubtedly exactly what she accorded to every young woman she took into her employ, I wondered how she ever managed to keep a servant. I am sure that had I been under the necessity of earning my bread and butter by doing housework I never could have endured such a termagant, and I felt sentiments of sincerest pity for poor girls who are compelled to put up with the insolence and bad tempers of people of this kind.

Having made up my mind to leave, I commenced looking about me for another situation, and very speedily found one to my liking in a Copperhead family.

My arrangements being made, the next time the madam undertook to be saucy to me, I answered her in her own fashion, and in a few moments we were engaged in a furious quarrel, which I doubt not would have appeared amusing enough, and ridiculous enough, to any impartial looker-on. Finally I said, with all the dignity I could command, "Madam, I will leave your house this instant, for you shall never have the satisfaction of saying that you discharged a Cuban from your employ."

"Why, are you a Cuban?" she said, calming down somewhat.

I then began to speak Spanish to her, and at this unexpected development she put on the most puzzled expression imaginable.

Without paying any more attention to her I went out, and engaging a man to take my trunk, began to prepare for my departure. When my trunk, with the Cuban express card on it, came down stairs, I pointed it out to her, and she opened her eyes considerably. She now began to be a trifle more gracious in her manner, and making a rather awkward apology for her behavior, saying, that she did not mean anything, and that I must not mind her being a little hasty tempered, and requested me to reconsider my determination to leave.

I told her that there was no use saying anything on that point, as I had already made an engagement elsewhere. She inquired where; and I said, with so and so, around the corner, mentioning the names of the persons.

"Why," said she, opening her eyes, and throwing up her hands in horror, "you are not surely going with them! Don't you know that they are rebels?"

"Well, suppose they are; they are as good as other people, if they behave themselves. We have plenty of rebels in Cuba."

Seeing that it was impossible to restrain me from going, she offered to pay me for the time I had been in her employ; but, with a rather contemptuous wave of my hand, I told her she might keep it, or, if she wished, give it to some charitable object, as I was not in need of it; and without more words with her, walked out of the house, and betook myself to my new quarters.

AMONG FRIENDS.

In the evening, as I was going out of the room where the family were at supper, I heard the old gentleman, who sat at the head of the table, say to his wife, " Where did you come across that nice, tidy piece of furniture? "

The lady replied, " O, she was at Mrs. B.'s, and they were too much down on the rebels to suit her."

When I came into the room again, the old gentleman, turning towards me, inquired, "Are you a Yankee girl?"

" No, sir," I replied; " I am a Cuban, and am a true Southern sympathizer."

" Well, if that is the case, you have got into the right place at last. I am from old Virginia, and I would not have one of those d—d Yankee women about the house."

In the evening the lady of the house came to my room just as I was unpacking my trunk. She seemed to be surprised at the extent and style of my wardrobe, and exclaimed, " Dear me, what a lot of nice things you have there ! "

" Yes," I replied. " Where I came from we are accustomed to having nice things."

As I thought that some curiosity with regard to me would be excited, I resolved to try and overhear the conversation between the old lady and her husband; so, when she left me, I hastily slipped off my shoes, and, cautiously following her down stairs, stood at the door of the parlor and listened. She gave quite a glowing account of the elegant dresses and other matters she had seen in my trunk, and said, " I wonder who she is, for she has not always been a servant, that is certain."

" No ; she don't look like a servant," said the old gentleman.

" Suppose she should be a spy?"

" Well, she may be, and we will have to be cautious what we say before her. Is she in her room? "

" Yes."

" I will have a talk with her to-morrow, and try and get her to say something with regard to who she is, and where she comes from."

This was all very satisfactory, so far as it went, and I crept back to my room as softly as I could, and went to bed.

The next morning the old gentleman came into the room when I was arranging the breakfast-table, and said, without any preliminaries, " Were you ever married? "

" Yes, sir; I am a widow."

" And you were never married again? "

" No, sir."

" Wouldn't you like to be ? "

" Well, I wouldn't mind if the right kind of a man offered himself. I don't care to marry any of your Yankees, however, and the Southern boys are all in the field."

" Look here; ain't you from the South ? "

" I have been there."

" I thought so. Because you found yourself among strangers, and got out of money, is, I suppose, the reason why you have hired out."

" Yes, sir. It is rather hard, after having had plenty, and after being waited on by servants, to do this kind of work; but it is honorable."

" Put down those plates," said the old gentleman, with considerable emphasis; " you can't do any work for me; but my house is open to you, and you are welcome to stay as long as it suits you.

" Here, old woman," he cried to his wife, who just then came into the room, " she is not going to be a servant in our house; she is a genuine Southerner, and we must treat her as well as we know how."

OBTAINING INFORMATION ABOUT THE PRISONERS.

I was forthwith installed as a privileged guest, and in the course of a few days I was introduced to a number of Southern sympathizers. Among my new acquaintance was a Confederate soldier who had escaped from one of the prison camps, and who was endeavoring to make his way South. From him I learned that Cleveland was a general rendezvous for escaped prisoners, and I accordingly resolved to go there.

I had given my entertainers to understand that I was on some secret errand, but did not tell them what; while they appreciated the importance of saying no more than was necessary about such matters, and asked me no impertinent questions. When I made up my mind to leave, I went to the old gentleman, and told him that I desired to go South where I had friends, and where I could get money.

He asked me how much money I would require for my journey, and I told him that I thought about six hundred dollars would see me through.

" Well," said he, " I can get that for you ; " and going out, he soon returned with the amount, remarking, as he gave it to me, " We Copperheads can always raise some money for the cause, even if we have no men."

The old gentleman took me to the depot in his buggy, and bought me a ticket for Cincinnati. He also gave me a letter to the head of the Copperhead ring there. This document I had, however, no use for, although I accepted it, as I did the six hundred dollars. I had at the time the sum of ninety-three thousand dollars on my person, and had in deposit in several banks over fifty thousand dollars. The six hundred dollars I accepted as a contribution to the cause, and on the principle that every little helps.

Bidding my aged friend farewell, I took my seat in the train, and was soon on my way to Columbus — for I had no intention of going to Cincinnati. On reaching Columbus, I took rooms at a new hotel near the depot, and made some inquiries with regard to the prisoners; but before I could make any definite arrangement concerning them, I received a telegraphic despatch, directing me to go to Canada immediately.

A Contribution to the Relief of the Prisoners.

I, therefore, contributed three thousand dollars of the money which I had with me, and which I regarded as Southern property, for the relief of the prisoners, and for the purchase of necessary clothing. A Mrs. R. had charge of this prisoners' relief fund, and I had every confidence that the money in her hands would be properly bestowed.

Proceeding as rapidly as I could to Canada, I had a conference with the agent there, and then hastened to New York. In. that city I found a host of Confederates who were anxiously waiting to receive their instructions from me. One was to go to Nassau, as supercargo ; another was to sail by the next steamer for Paris, to receive opium and quinine ; a third was to proceed to Missouri ; a fourth to the north-western part of Texas, and so on. Giving each his proportion of cash for expenses, and telling them whom to draw on in case they were short, I bade them good by, and wished them success.

These matters being arranged, I went to see the broker

with whom I was in partnership, and found him considerably exercised. We had a long talk about the situation, and he expressed himself as very uneasy about the march Sherman was making through the Carolinas, and its effect upon the Confederate bonds we had on hand. I was not as easily frightened as he was; but I could not help acknowledging that if Sherman succeeded in accomplishing what he aimed at, it would be bad for the cause of the Confederacy, and that it would do much to kill the sale of the bonds. I therefore allowed myself to be persuaded into making a trip to London, for the purpose of a personal interview with our agent there, the idea being, without letting him or others see that we were uneasy, to persuade him to sell off the paper we held at almost any price.

A VISIT TO LONDON AND PARIS.

I accordingly proceeded to London by the next steamer, and on finding the agent, was soon plunged into business with him. Confederate bonds were not selling very well just at that time, but as ours cost us very little, we could afford to dispose of them at very moderate figures and still make a handsome profit. I put mine on the market as rapidly as I was able, but before I had cleared out the lot, intelligence was received that Sherman had established communication with Grant, and many persons jumped at the conclusion that this was a virtual end of the rebellion. When this news was received, I was on a flying visit to Paris. I did not think that the end was as near as many persons supposed, but saw very clearly that there was no market in London just then for Confederate bonds; and, congratulating myself that I had made out as well as I had, I posted to Liverpool, and arrived there just in time to catch a steamer.

As we were going into New York harbor we heard the news of Lee's surrender, which had taken place the day before, from the pilot. He was unable to give us any particulars, and every one on the steamer was consequently in a fever of anxiety to get ashore, and learn the full extent of the disaster to the Confederate arms. No one was more anxious than myself, as no one had reason to be, and the idea that the hitherto invincible army of Virginia — the conquerors in so many well-fought fields — should at last be compelled to yield to the enemy fairly stunned me.

Many of the passengers seemed to think that this was practically the winding up of the war. I could not bring myself to believe this, for I knew that the Confederacy had other armies in the field who were both able and willing to fight, and who were led by generals as skilful and as indomitable as Lee. My heart burned hot within me to continue the fight, and I resolved to stick by my colors to the last, and to labor with even more than my accustomed zeal for the Confederacy so long as a shadow of hope remained.

When the vessel reached the wharf I went ashore, and proceeded to the Lafarge House, from whence, as soon as I could get some of the sea rust from my person, I called a carriage, and ordered the driver to take me, as fast as he could, to the office of the broker in Wall Street with whom I was in partnership.

WALL STREET, NEW YORK, AFTER THE NEWS OF LEE'S SURRENDER.

Wall Street, especially in the vicinity of the Exchange, was fairly packed with a furious, excited mass of human beings, yelling, shouting, cursing, and not a few absolutely weeping. It was a spectacle to be remembered ; nothing that I had ever beheld — and I had certainly participated in many exciting scenes — at all resembled it. Some of the thousands of faces were surcharged with unspeakable horror; despair, overpowering despair, was written on others ; curses and blasphemies were heard on every side, and it might have been supposed that all the lunatics in the country had been turned loose in this narrow thoroughfare.

Any one familiar with this section of New York, however, could see at a glance that some momentous event had occurred which had seriously affected innumerable important financial operations, and that in a moment great fortunes had been lost and won.

At length we reached the office I was seeking, and my partner came out to meet me, and to assist me to alight from the carriage. His face wore a very sickly smile as he said, " I am glad to see you ; you have made a quick trip."

" Yes," I replied, as we hurried into the back office. " Regent Street has no charms for me in such times as these."

" Well," said he, as he turned the key in the lock of the door, fairly gasping for breath as he asked the question, and pale as a sheet, " have we lost ? "

"No, we have not exactly lost, but we have not made anything worth speaking of."

"Well, so long as we have not lost, we have done pretty well."

"What is the news?"

"Lee has surrendered, and the Confederacy has gone up; that is the whole sum and substance of it."

"But there are other armies in the field, and they will probably be able to hold out. It does not follow that the Confederacy is gone up because Lee has surrendered."

"People about here think differently; at any rate, the Confederate bond-business is killed."

I did not care to argue this point with him, as his only interest in the Confederacy was in what he could make out of it. So I asked, "Have you got in all the money?"

"Yes," he replied; "but the bonds have gone up higher than a kite."

"Well, you bring your books and make out your statement; we will have a settlement at once, for I intend to get out of the country as fast as I am able."

A Settlement of Accounts.

The next day I met him in accordance with our agreement, and presented my statement, with a proposition that he should take half the bonds in my hands, and we stand equal losses.

This he refused point blank to do, and professed to be highly indignant that I should make such a proposition.

I then refused to settle; at which he got very angry, and threatened to have me arrested, indulging in some strong language, which did not frighten me a bit; for, apart from the fact that I did not scare easily, I knew that I had the advantage of him, and that he would not dare, for his own sake, to carry his threat into execution. I had about sixty thousand dollars of his money, while he had only about eighteen thousand of mine, in consequence of which, although he indulged in a good deal of bluster, he finally consented to settle on equal terms — share and share alike, both in the profits and the losses. This matter being arranged, I bade him farewell, glad enough to get rid of him, and glad to get out of such a business. Such was the end of my secret banking and brokerage transactions.

CHAPTER XLIV.

THE ASSASSINATION OF PRESIDENT LINCOLN, AND END OF THE WAR.

Another Western Trip. — Delivering Despatches to Quantrell's Courier. — A Stoppage at Columbus, Ohio. — News of the Assassination of President Lincoln. — Return to New York. — Derangement of Plans caused by the Assassination. — I again go West. — Mr. Lincoln's Body lying in State at Columbus. — Return to Washington, and Interview with Baker. — I meet a Confederate Officer, and get him to take a Message for me to the South. — An aged Admirer. — Colonel Baker proposes that I shall start on an Expedition in search of Myself. — A Letter from my Brother, and a Request to meet him in New York. — A Determination to visit Europe. — I accept Baker's Commission, and start for New York.

S I did not know, and certainly did not appreciate the full extent, or full importance, of the great disaster that had befallen the Confederate cause, so soon as my business in Wall Street was brought to a conclusion I sought a conference with the agents with whom I had been co-operating. They were inclined to take the gloomiest possible view of the situation. With the fall of Richmond, and the surrender of Lee's army, the people of the North seemed to have concluded that the long contest with the South was over, to all intents and purposes. It was but natural, perhaps, in view of the intense excitement which prevailed, and the unanimity of public opinion, that the Confederate agents should have regarded the future of the contest in a great degree from a Northern standpoint, and should have been largely influenced by the opinions which they heard expressed on every side.

I, however, was not disposed to give up while a Southern soldier remained in the field, and, after a full discussion of the condition of affairs, I persuaded my companions to view matters as I did. Richmond was our capital, but it was not the whole South; and Lee's army, important as it was, was far from being the whole Confederate force. General Joe John-

508

ston had an army of veterans very nearly if not quite as large as that of Lee's, and was capable of prolonging the contest for an indefinite period; while, throughout the West, there were a number of detached commands, of more or less strength. If these could be united, and a junction effected with Johnston, or communication established with him, so that they could act in concert, it would be possible to keep the Federals at bay for a good while yet. If the fight was continued resolutely, there was no knowing what might happen to our advantage; for, as we all knew, the people of the North were heartily sick of the war, while England and France were impatient to have it come to an end, and would much prefer to have it end with a victory for the Confederates.

Having professed an eager desire to work for the cause so long as there was a cause to work for, my associates suggested that I should proceed immediately to Missouri with despatches for Quantrell, which it was important he should get at the earliest possible moment, and also for the purpose of consulting with the agents in the West with regard to the best methods of proceeding in the present perplexing emergency.

I accepted the mission without hesitation, and, always ready to attend to business of this kind at a moment's notice, with scarcely more than a change of clothing in my travelling satchel, I was soon speeding westward.

Meeting Quantrell's Courier.

I did not get as far as Quantrell's headquarters, as I was lucky enough to meet with one of his couriers, to whom I delivered the despatches. This man, to whom I was tolerably well known, was very eager to have me go with him to the general, saying that I could be of the greatest possible service in the present juncture by acting as his spy, and as bearer of despatches to the agents in the North. I, however, was compelled to decline, as I felt that I had more important work to do in my present field, which it would not do for me to drop.

Having discharged this errand, I went to Columbus, Ohio, where I found considerable confusion prevailing on account of the escape of some prisoners. I took rooms at the Neil House, and had conferences with several persons concerning the affairs at the South. At an unusually early hour I retired, being very weary on account of having travelled, almost without interruption, for several days, and having lost my sleep the night before, but feeling rather happy on account of a Confederate victory of which I had heard.

The Buzzing of the Telegraph Wires.

I was soon asleep, but could not have been so very long, before I was awakened by the continual buzzing of the telegraph wires, which were attached to the corner of the hotel. I paid but little attention to this singular noise, and dozed off again. A second time I was awakened by it, and began to conjecture what could be the matter. I knew that something very important must have happened, and thought that the Federals must either have achieved a great victory, or have met with a great defeat. I was too tired, however, to attempt any inquiry just then, and, with all sorts of fancies floating in my mind, as the constant buzzing of the wires, which never ceased for a moment, sounded in my ears, I dropped off into a sound sleep, and did not awaken until morning.

I arose quite early, and going to the window, saw that the whole front of the building was draped in mourning. Wondering what this demonstration could mean, and thinking that the death of some prominent general must have occurred, but never for a moment suspecting the terrible truth, I made my toilet, and descended to find out what was the matter.

The Assassination of Lincoln.

A great number of people, notwithstanding the early hour, were moving about the hotel, and a considerable crowd was already assembled in the hall. Still wondering what could have happened, I asked a gentleman whom I met hurrying down stairs what was the news, and he told me that President Lincoln had been assassinated by one J. Wilkes Booth the night before !

This intelligence startled me greatly, both on account of the terrible nature of the crime itself, and because I felt that it could work nothing but harm to the South. I also felt for Mr. Lincoln and his family ; for I liked him, and believed that he was an honest and kind-hearted man, who tried to do his duty, as he understood it, and who was in every way well disposed towards the South.

Descending to the drawing-room, I found a large number

of ladies there, many of whom were weeping, while, in the street, the crowd was increasing, and every one seemed to be in the greatest excitement. Across the street the State House was being draped in mourning, while a number of persons already wore mourning emblems. Before the day was over nearly every one had on some badge of mourning, and nearly every house was draped, in a greater or less degree, in black. I did not attempt to imitate my neighbors in this matter. I was sincerely sorry, both for personal and political reasons, that this dreadful event had occurred; but, nevertheless, Mr. Lincoln was the enemy of the cause I loved, and for which I labored, and it would have been intensely repugnant to my feelings to have made any outward manifestations of mourning. At the same time it is possible I may have mourned in my heart with more sincerity than some of those who were making a greater show of their grief.

This sad event rendered it necessary that I should have an immediate conference with my associates in the East, and I therefore returned as fast as I could to New York, and from thence went on to Washington.

The assassination of Mr. Lincoln had caused a derangement of the plans, and no one knew exactly what had best be done next. I was requested, however, to make a trip west again, for the purpose of communicating with certain parties, and accordingly departed on my last errand in behalf of the Confederacy.

LINCOLN'S BODY LYING IN STATE.

My business being transacted, I started to return, and again found it necessary to pass through Columbus. When I arrived there the body of Mr. Lincoln was lying in state. The town was crowded with people, and it was impossible to get a room at any of the hotels. I went to the Neil House, but was obliged to content myself with a bed on the drawing-room floor, my accommodations being, however, quite as sumptuous as those of hundreds of others.

I doubt if the little city ever had so many people in it before, and all day long a stream of men and women poured in at one door and out at the other of the apartment where the casket containing the remains of the president was lying in state. It was a sad sight, and it troubled me greatly — so greatly that I was scarcely able to eat or sleep; for, in addition to my natural grief, I could not prevent my mind from brooding on the possibly detrimental effects which the assassination would have on the fortunes of the South.

After an early breakfast the next morning, I took the eastward-bound train, and returned to Washington, and on reaching that city, called to see Colonel Baker. We exchanged but a few words, as Baker said that he had an engagement, which he would be compelled to attend to immediately, but he would see me at half past seven o'clock, at my hotel.

Meeting with a Confederate Officer in the Capitol.

Leaving him, I started off for the purpose of trying to find out something about Mrs. Surratt and the other prisoners, and their probable fate. In the Capitol I met a Confederate officer, whom I knew. I was astonished to see him, and going up, I said, —

"O, what could have induced you to come here at such a critical time as this?"

"To see and hear what is going on," he replied.

"This is an awful affair."

"Yes; and it is particularly unfortunate that it should have happened at this particular time."

"When will you return?"

"To-night, if somebody less amiable than you are does not recognize me and take me in charge."

I then asked him if he would carry a letter through for me to my brother, and on his promising me that he would, I made an engagement for him to go to my room in the hotel. He would find the door unlocked, and the key inside, and I would meet him at five o'clock, or shortly after. I then took leave of him, bidding him be careful of himself, as the people were excited and suspicious, and he might easily get himself into serious trouble.

Returning to the hotel, I noticed quite a number of ladies in the drawing-room as I passed by. I thought I would join them, for the sake of listening to the different conversations that were going on, thinking that perhaps I might hear something that it would be advantageous for me to know. On reaching my room, therefore, I dressed myself in a handsome black gros-grain silk dress, and putting a gilt band in my hair, descended, and took a seat at one of the drawing-room windows, facing on Pennsylvania Avenue.

Those around me all appeared to be discussing the tragedy,

and many absurd theories and speculations were indulged in with regard to it. I was indignant, as I had been a number of times before, to hear President Davis, and others of the Confederate leaders, accused of being the instigators of the crime. I well knew that they were incapable of anything of the kind; and Mr. Davis, in particular, I had reason to believe entertained a high respect for Mr. Lincoln, and most sincerely lamented his death, and especially the manner of it, feeling that he, and the whole people of the South, would be, to a greater or less degree, held censurable for something they had nothing to do with, and which they were powerless to prevent.

A Hotel Acquaintance.

After I had been gazing out of the window some little time, watching the crowds of people passing to and fro along the street, an elderly gentleman came up, and after addressing a few courteous words, asked if I was a resident of the city.

I replied that I had arrived only a few hours before from Columbus, Ohio, but that I was a Cuban.

"Ah, indeed," said he; and, taking a seat beside me, he commenced a conversation, by asking, "What do your people think of our war?"

"O, they think it is very bad; but it is to be hoped that it is about over now."

"What do you think of the assassination of the president?"

"That is much to be regretted; but you know we Spaniards do not take such things quite so much to heart as some people."

"It will be a bad thing for the South, and especially for some of the Southern leaders; they will be sure to hang Jeff Davis."

I thought that it was catching before hanging; but, concluding that, perhaps, it would be best not to put all my thoughts into words, I merely said, "I scarcely agree with you, sir. Why should one man die for the deeds of another?"

"O, those Southern leaders are all corrupt, and they sent Booth here with instructions to do this deed, for the purpose of enabling them to carry out some of their schemes; they are a set of fiends, thieves, and cutthroats, from beginning to end, and there is not an honest man among them."

This excited my anger greatly; but, considering that, under the circumstances, discretion was the better part of valor, I

33

stifled my feelings, and concluded to cultivate this old gentleman's acquaintance further, with the idea that perhaps I might
be able to make use of him in the execution of any plans I
might have for the future.

Taking out my watch, I found that it was half past three
o'clock; so, excusing myself, I went to my room, and put on
my hat to go out. On coming down stairs again, I found my
new acquaintance in the hall, near the ladies' entrance. He
asked me if I was going shopping; and on my replying that
I merely proposed to go as far as the executive mansion, for
the sake of a little exercise, he suggested that I ought to
have an escort, and volunteered to accompany me. I thought
this rather an impudent proceeding, considering our very
brief acquaintance; but not knowing what advantage he might
be to me, I accepted his attentions, with apparently the best
possible grace.

Getting into a street car, we rode as far as the Park, opposite to the War Department. Taking a seat together under
the trees, we entered into a conversation, which convinced me
that the old gentleman was a harmless eccentric, who had
become suddenly smitten with my charms. He had some
very odd notions about politics, finance, and the like, but
from such matters as these he ere long began to discourse
upon my personal attractions, and finally became quite tenderly
demonstrative towards me. I believe the old gentleman would
have asked me to marry him, had I given him the least encouragement, but I was beginning to find him a nuisance, and
resolved to return to the hotel.

He persisted in going with me, and when, on reaching the
hotel, I hastily and somewhat impatiently excused myself, for,
looking at my watch, I saw that it was ten minutes past five
o'clock, he asked whether he might escort me to supper. I
said that he was very kind, and to get rid of him, promised
that he might have the pleasure of my company to the evening meal if he desired it. I then bounded up stairs, anxious
to keep my appointment.

When I reached my room door it was locked, but in a
moment more the key was turned, and, on going in, I found
my Confederate officer waiting for me. He said that some
one, after he had been there a short time, had tried to get in;
he had put his foot against the door to prevent it from being
opened; whereupon the person outside had worked at the
lock for a while with a key. I replied, that he need not be

alarmed, as it was probably one of the chambermaids with clean towels, and that being unable to obtain admission, she had left them on the knob of the door.

He told me that he would be compelled to leave the city at eleven o'clock, and, as he had several things to attend to, if I wanted to send anything by him, it would be necessary for me to get it ready at once. I therefore seated myself to write, but, on a moment's reflection, came to the conclusion that the risk was too great, as he was not unlikely to be captured, and determined to give him a verbal message.

After discussing the situation with as much fulness as we were able, with the brief time at our disposal, I went to my trunk, and, getting an envelope, sealed twenty dollars in it, and handed it to him, as I knew that he must be short of money. He made some to do about taking it, but on my insisting, he put it in his pocket, with an effusion of thanks, and said farewell. I turned the gas in the hall down until I saw him out of sight, and then prepared myself for my interview with Colonel Baker.

On reaching the drawing-room, I found there the old gentleman who had been so attentive during the afternoon, and who was apparently waiting for me rather impatiently. We had scarcely started a conversation, however, before Baker came in, with a friend of his from Baltimore. I excused myself with my aged admirer with very little ceremony, and retired with Baker and his friend to the private parlor, where we could talk without being disturbed.

Baker has a Proposition to Make.

As we seated ourselves, Baker said to his friend, " This is one of the best little detectives in the country, but, unfortunately, she does not like the business."

" O, the business does well enough," I replied ; " but I don't like having bad luck in it."

" We can't always have good luck, you know," said Baker ; " but I have a job on hand now which I want you to undertake for me, and which I think you can manage if you will do your best. If you succeed, you shall be paid handsomely."

" O, colonel, you are not going to hold out the pay as an inducement for me to serve the country, are you ? " I could not say " my country."

" O, d—n the country ; you don't suppose we are going to

work for it for nothing, do you? I want you to find this woman who is travelling and figuring as a Confederate agent. Some of my people have been on her track for a long time, but she is a slippery customer, and they have never been able to lay hands on her."

I knew it was myself Baker meant, especially when he took out of his pocket a picture similar to the one the detective had shown me on the cars a number of months previous.

Baker continued. "Here is her picture; you can take it, for I am having some more struck off. I am going to capture her ladyship this time, dead certain, if she is in the country, as I believe she is."

My sensations on hearing Baker utter these words cannot be described. What could make him so eager to capture me just at this particular moment? Could he possibly suspect me of having anything to do with the assassination plot? The very idea of such a thing made me sick, for I felt that, excited as every one then was, an accusation of this kind was all but equivalent to a condemnation. I managed, however, to maintain my composure, but inwardly resolved that the best thing I could do would be to leave the country at the earliest possible moment.

After discussing the method of procedure with regard to the search I was to institute for myself, I asked Baker what he thought the result of the trial of the prisoners accused of being implicated in the assassination plot would be.

"O," said he, "they will all hang."

"Now, I think that will be too bad. Even if Mrs. Surratt is proven to be guilty, they might commute her sentence. It will be a terrible thing to hang a woman, especially as she was not actually one of the assassins. Do you really think she is guilty?"

"No; but the affair was planned in her house, and she is in a good part responsible for it. I am very much in hope that a full confession from her will be obtained by her priest."

"But, colonel, the evidence against her is all circumstantial, and surely it is not right or lawful to sentence her to death, unless it is absolutely proven that she is guilty."

"In times like this, it would never do to acquit her, or to send her to prison, for the mob would take the law into their own hands. Besides, it is necessary to make an example."

Baker's friend here said, "I am glad that they got Booth."

At this remark I scanned Baker's countenance closely. He

smiled, and said, "So am I. I intended to have his body, dead or alive, or a mighty good substitute for it, for no common criminal is worth the reward."

This was a very queer expression, and it set me to thinking, and to studying certain phases of Baker's character more closely than I had ever done before. The colonel and his friend then left. I was to have until nine o'clock the next morning to decide whether I would undertake the business he desired me to or not.

MY BROTHER SUGGESTS A TRIP TO EUROPE.

The next morning, before Baker came, I received my mail, and in it a letter from my brother, who expected to be in New York in a few days with his wife and child. He proposed that, as we were the sole remnants of our family, we should continue with each other in the future, and intimating that, considering the present distracted state of the country, it would, perhaps, be best for us to go to Europe for a time, until things quieted down somewhat.

This letter decided me upon what course to pursue, and I determined to accept the commission from Baker, thinking by so doing I would more effectually prevent any of his detectives discovering my identity, while so soon as my brother and his family arrived, we would proceed across the Atlantic without further delay, and remain there until the time should come when no one would have any object in troubling us.

The army of Joe Johnston, like that of Lee, had been surrendered, and it was evident to me that the war was practically at an end, although I thought it not impossible that it might be prolonged in a desultory manner for some time yet in the West and South-west. I could plainly see, however, that further fighting would do no good, and that the Confederate cause being lost, my mission in connection with it was at an end, and my sole duty now was to consider my own welfare and that of my family.

All the bright dreams of four years ago had vanished into nothingness, and yet I could not regret having played the part I did. I loved the South and its people with a greater intensity than ever, while at the same time many of my prejudices against the North had been beaten down by my intercourse with its people during the past eighteen months. There were good and bad in both sections, and I believed that if the good men and women, both North and South, would now earnestly and patriotically unite in an endeavor to carry out the ideas of the founders of the government, they would, ere many years, be able to raise the nation to a pitch of greatness such as had yet been scarcely imagined.

As for my own experiences, if not exactly what I had expected them to be, they were sufficiently rich and varied in incident to satisfy all my ambitions. I had participated in bloody battles and sieges, and in the thickest of the danger had borne myself so valorously as to win the commendation of men who did not know what fear was, while, in addition to the campaigning I had gone through, my adventures as a spy and secret-service agent, were not only of advantage to the cause I had espoused, but they had supplied me with exciting and absorbing work which had demanded the best exercise of all my faculties. I felt that I had reason to be proud of my war record, and was the better satisfied with myself, as I knew that I had won the approbation of noble-minded men whose esteem was well worth winning.

When Colonel Baker called, therefore, to hear my decision, I told him that I would undertake to do what he desired. He accordingly gave me my instructions, and I was astonished to find how much he knew of some of my movements. He and his men must have been on the point of capturing me many times, and they undoubtedly would have done so, had I not had the wit to take the course I did in cultivating his acquaintance. With many self-congratulations at having been successful in escaping thus far, and resolved that, if possible, Baker should not know me except as one of his own agents, I started for New York on a search for myself ostensibly, but in reality to wait anxiously for the coming of my brother, in whose company I proposed to get beyond the reach of the detective corps, with which I had been so long associated in such a singular manner, with all the expedition I could manage.

CHAPTER XLV.

A TOUR THROUGH EUROPE.

T was not many days before my brother arrived with his wife, two children, and nurse. It was a most joyful reunion, and I tried to be as affectionate as I knew how to my sister-in-law and the pretty little babes, one of whom was a namesake of my own. It was impossible for me, however, to feel towards her as I did towards my brother, and I fancied that she was not as well disposed towards me as she might have been.

Once together, our arrangements were soon made, and we left New York on board of one of the Cunard steamers. I wondered what my friend Colonel Baker would think of my disappearance, and could not help laughing at the neat trick I had played upon him.

Despite the reasons I had for being glad to find myself speeding towards a foreign shore, it was not without a pang of regret that I watched those of America fading in the distance. This, after all, was my country, where dwelt my friends; here was the scene of the great events in which I had taken a not altogether unimportant part; and it was like separating from a portion of myself to sail away from such a land, and to feel that, probably, I might never return.

Before we had been long at sea, however, I had something else to think of than sentimental regrets. Both my brother

519

and myself were compelled to succumb to seasickness, which, although it did not affect us as violently as it did some of the other passengers, was sufficiently unpleasant to absorb all our thoughts. My sister-in-law, being a hardened traveller, escaped, but the negro girl, who acted as nurse for the children, was taken very badly, and between her agony and her fright she was a most ludicrous object.

In a couple of days I was well enough to enjoy myself; and my brother, who had made the acquaintance of the doctor, introduced him to me. This gentleman was a fair-haired Anglo Saxon, and he appeared to think it incumbent upon him to pay me particular attention. I was quite willing to cultivate his acquaintaince, and he was so much encouraged by my amiable demeanor towards him, that he very speedily began to be even unpleasantly polite, and I was anxious to devise some means of getting rid of him. I did at length succeed in finding a rival to him in a somewhat odd fashion.

A COUPLE OF HANDSOME SPANIARDS.

Among the passengers were two quite handsome young Spaniards, who kept pretty much to themselves, apparently for the reason that no one was able to talk to them. I noticed that one of them followed me a good deal with his eyes, and resolved, if a favorable opportunity offered, to strike up an acquaintance with him.

One morning, after breakfast, I and my friends came up on deck, and the doctor, who had been acting as my escort, excused himself to go and make his sick calls. The two young Spaniards stood leaning on the guards, and from the way they looked at me I judged that I was the subject of their conversation.

Leaving my brother and his wife, I went and seated myself near them, but gave no indication that I was noticing them particularly. They had heard me speak English to my brother and sister, and the others with whom I had engaged in conversation, and had no reason to think that I understood any other language.

I had scarcely taken my seat, when they commenced to talk about me in Spanish, commenting upon my elegant dress, and the sparkling diamonds which adorned my person, and expressing a desire to know who I was. At length one of them said, " O, how I would like to speak the American language !

She is a handsome senorita, and evidently very rich; if I could converse with her I would soon have an introduction."

"Yes," said the other, "I should like to know who she is."

"O, there is something the matter with me," said the first, putting his hand to his breast.

"You are in love. You had better get somebody to act as interpreter for you."

Just then the doctor came up and interfered with my amusement. He said, as he seated himself beside me, "If it is not impertinent, may I ask how long you have been a widow?"

"About two years," I replied.

One of the young Spaniards, who could understand a little English, said to his companion, "She is a young widow."

"That makes no difference," said the other.

I said to the doctor, "I wonder if we can see any fish?" and walked to the side and looked overboard.

I stood quite close to Pablo, the young man whom I supposed to be falling in love with me, and as we turned away, after looking into the water for a few moments, I dropped my handkerchief on purpose.

The Spaniard picked it up, and, touching my arm, handed it to me, raising his sombrero politely as he did so.

I smiled, and thanked him in his native tongue. It was most amusing to see the expression of horror that overspread his countenance as he heard me, and thus discovered that I must have understood the conversation he had been holding with his friend.

So soon as the doctor left me, he advanced, and, taking off his hat, asked me if I was a Spaniard. I replied that I was of Spanish descent; whereupon he began the most profuse apologies, and hoped that my ladyship was not offended at the remarks that had passed between himself and friend. I said that so far from being offended, I felt highly complimented by the flattering opinions that had been expressed with regard to me; and thereupon the young gentleman and I started a flirtation that lasted for the balance of the voyage, and that, in addition to being agreeable enough in itself, had the effect of keeping the doctor somewhat at a distance. He was most solicitous for us to visit Spain, and was not satisfied until he extorted from my brother a promise to do so.

This young gentleman continued his attentions to myself after we got to London; and on account of some sight-seeing, in which he had planned to have my company, he and his

friend missed the steamer in which they expected to have
sailed for Spain, and were obliged to remain for a number of
days beyond their appointed time.   I do not think that either
of them regretted this very much.   I am sure one of them
did not.   My brother did not like my friend Pablo, thinking
him proud and haughty; but this was merely a Castilian reserve of manner, and I thought it rather an attractive characteristic than otherwise.

At length our young Spaniards left us, and we began to
plan our future movements.   My brother was very anxious to
go to the Continent immediately.   He did not like the English
climate or the English people, saying that they had always
been our enemies, and that during the late war they had acted
treacherously to both parties.   The French, he contended,
were the true friends of America, while their beautiful country
was far better worth visiting than this damp, foggy England.

I had no great preference, being willing to go almost anywhere, and consequently, although there was much in England
that I desired to see, acceded to my brother's wishes without
hesitation, and consented to try France first, and to keep
England in reserve, to be explored after we had visited the
Continent.

The Naval Depot at Cherbourg.

Crossing the Channel, we entered France at Cherbourg, the
great naval depot.   At this place were several vessels which
had been negotiated for by the Confederates, and which, if
they could have been obtained, would greatly have strengthened our little navy.   Without stopping, however, to examine
these, or other objects of interest, we speeded on to Paris,
where we took rooms at the Grand Hotel.

We were more fortunate than Mark Twain represents himself to have been, and were not bothered with guides.   My
brother had been educated in Paris, while I had seen a little
of it, and we both could speak French.   My brother was well
acquainted with the city, and he was anxious to show his wife
and myself all that was worth seeing in it.   We accordingly
hired a handsome private livery, and prepared to enjoy ourselves in the best style.

The magnificence with which I was surrounded was in great
contrast to what I had been accustomed to in America, and it
was difficult for me to appreciate the fact that I, the elegantly
attired woman, who was enjoying, or endeavoring to enjoy, the

BEAUTIFUL FRANCE.

manifold pleasures of Parisian life, had but a short time before been wearing a uniform of gray, and living the roughest kind of a life in camp and on the battle-field. I could not honestly say to myself, however, that I preferred the luxury and splendors of the great French capital to the woods and fields of my dear South ; and I have had as blissful sleep, wrapped in my soldier's blanket, out under the stars, as I could get in the most expensive apartments of the Grand Hotel.

Our days and nights in Paris were spent in sight-seeing, theatre-going, and in endeavoring to find all the enjoyment that money could buy. We did enjoy ourselves ; for there is no city in the world that is better worth seeing, or that presents greater attractions to the visitor, than Paris.

SIGHT-SEEING IN PARIS.

The Louvre, the Tuileries, the Arc de l'Etoile, the ancient Cathedral of Notre Dame, with its grand architecture and its many associations, with a visit to the Jardin de Mabille in the evening, employed our first day. It was all very interesting, but I could have had greater satisfaction in investigating into matters that represented more particularly the industries and resources of the country. As for the famous Mabille, it is nothing more than a beer-garden, while the doings that are permitted there and at the Cloiserie de Lilas, are such that they are not fit places for decent people to visit. I was heartily disgusted with both of these gardens — disgusted with what I saw, and more disgusted with people who looked like ladies and gentlemen, gazing with approval and applause at performances that had no attractions except their indecency.

A drive on the Bois de Boulogne, which was on our programme for the next day, I really enjoyed greatly, as I did also a visit to the Lyrique Theatre, where I saw finished acting and elegant stage setting, such as I had never been accustomed to in America. In the course of our stay in Paris we visited nearly all the principal theatres ; and although I never was much of a play-goer, everything was done in such finished style that it was a real gratification to attend these performances.

The College de France, where my brother had been educated, and the Medical School in which he had studied, interested him greatly, but I was satisfied with looking at them from the outside. I was not curious, either, to visit the

Catacombs. My brother persuaded me to go to this city of the dead ; but when about to descend into the dark caverns, filled with the mouldering remains of poor humanity, I shrunk back, and refused to enter. I had too much reverence for the sleepers to make their last resting-place a resort for the curious. I feared not the dead; but to have gone among these skeletons would have revived memories of the past that were anything but pleasant ones. It made me shudder to think how many poor souls I had seen launched into eternity without a moment's warning, some of them, perhaps, by my hand. The idea of such a thing was horrible, although in the excitement of a great battle the slaughter that is going on is as little thought of as are the dangers to one's self.

The Emperor and Empress.

At the Invalides we saw the magnificent Tomb of Napoleon I., the most imposing monument that has, perhaps, ever been erected to any monarch. As we were leaving, we were gratified with a sight of the emperor and empress, who were visiting the building. The empress was a very handsome woman, and looked as if she was a very amiable one. She was dressed in a silk robe, of a light lavender color, which was very elaborately trimmed with lace. Her bonnet was of the same lavender tint, and was trimmed with white. A pair of white kid gloves, and a point-lace scarf fastened with a brooch of emeralds and diamonds, completed the toilet. The emperor was in uniform. He was a rather diminutive man, with a keen eye, and he reminded me not a little of General Beauregard. Any one who could have seen the two, would have said, unhesitatingly, that they were relatives.

Sight-seeing in Paris was an agreeable enough employment, but I very soon had enough of it, and was not sorry to leave for Rheims, the great wine mart. This city is distant between three and four hours from Paris by the railroad, and is a very interesting place, as well because of its historical associations, as because it is a great industrial centre.

The Cathedral of Rheims.

The great cathedral is a magnificent building, which I took particular pleasure in visiting, for the reason that in it all the old kings of France were crowned. It was here that Joan of

Arc, clad in full armor, and with her consecrated banner in hand, witnessed the coronation of the king for whom she fought so well, and whose dominion she was mainly instrumental in securing. I almost imagined, as I stood in the cathedral, that I could behold the splendid scene that was presented on that occasion.

At the time of my visit to Rheims, however, I was of a more practical turn of mind than I had been a few years before. The romance had been pretty well knocked out of me by the rough experience of real life ; and although I was better able to appreciate the performances of Joan of Arc at their true value, somehow they did not interest me to the extent they once did. I took more pleasure in watching the processes of manufacturing the famous champagne wines, and in speculating as to whether such a profitable industry could not be introduced into the United States.

WINE MANUFACTURE.

I have every reason to believe that wines, as fine in flavor as any of the European brands, can be, and in time will be, made in America. They will not be the same, and will have a peculiar flavor of their own ; for the flavors of wines depend upon the soil where the grapes are grown to such an extent that very different kinds are manufactured from grapes growing but a short distance from each other. Our American wines, even if of a somewhat different flavor, ought, however, to be just as good, in their way, as are the European. The fact is, that some of our wines will already compare very favorably with those brought from abroad. We cannot as yet, however, produce anything equal to the very finest brands ; but we will do that in time, when we learn some of the delicate points about cultivation and manufacture which the Europeans have been for centuries acquiring. Vinticulture is a business that is particularly well suited for many portions of our Southern States, and it is to be hoped that the people may be induced to take it up much more largely than they have ever yet done.

In this part of France it is possible to travel for miles through a highly-cultivated country and not see the sign of a building of any kind. The people congregate in small villages, which is certainly more social than living in isolated farm-houses. The houses in these villages are mostly small, are built of stone, and reminded me not a little of some huts in the Kaw Indian reservation. They are made very attractive, however, by being surrounded by neat little gardens, filled with flowers, which are tended with great care.

There was one thing I saw in Rheims which pleased me very much. It was a troop of round, rosy-faced girls, who came running, laughing, and singing, out of a factory, at evening, as full of sport as if they had been playing all day, instead of earning their bread and butter. They were so fresh and wholesome-looking, and apparently enjoyed life so much, that I could not but admire them. Such people as these are the real wealth of a country, and it is no wonder France is rich and prosperous when she has such citizens.

FRANKFORT AND ITS SURROUNDINGS.

From Rheims, we passed on, and made a flying visit to Homburg, the famous watering-place, and from there went to Frankfort on the Main. On one side of the city are to be seen the mountains, while on the other extends a rich, fertile plain. I almost wished that I was the wife of one of those good-natured, honest, industrious German farmers we were constantly meeting, so that I might live and die in a snug, home-like little farm-house, half hidden by the grain, and surrounded by flowering shrubs and vines, such as were to be seen on all sides. Nowhere have I beheld more evidences of solid comfort and downright good living than in the vicinity of Frankfort, and there are no people on the earth happier than these hard-working but contented Germans, who know how to enjoy life in right honest fashion.

The small villages in this section of Europe are quite numerous, and the people are disposed to be most kind and hospitable, particularly to Americans. We met several persons who had been in America, who were apparently rejoiced to see us, and who overwhelmed us with invitations to visit them.

The costumes of the working classes are very odd. The women wear muslin caps, short blue or white skirts, and shoes with wooden soles. The men are attired in blue frocks, and sometimes in the queerest-looking swallow-tailed coats of white and buff linen.

Some of the parks surrounding the mansions of the nobility are very beautiful, being laid out with much taste, and filled with deer, swans, and other animals. The zoölogical garden in Frankfort is much the finest in Europe, being greatly superior in the number and variety of the animals to those of Paris and London.

THE DESOLATION OF POLAND.

Having exhausted the sights of Frankfort, we prepared to move on, and there was considerable debate as to whether we should next go to Italy or to Russia. I was most anxious to visit Poland; and so it was finally determined that we should go there. I was sorry for having taken this trip afterwards, for there was nothing in Cracow — a city ruined and desolated by war — that could give me pleasure. Indeed, the whole land looked as if it was under a blight. I took advantage, however, of the occasion to renew my acquaintance with M. Koskalosky, a young Pole, whom I had met in Paris just before the close of the war. He was a very pleasant, cultivated gentleman, and a sincere friend of the South. I hope that the time will come when the people of Poland will be able to regain their independence. They are cruelly oppressed now, and their beautiful country is a waste and desolation.

Instead of going to Italy, we now returned to Paris, having seen much to interest and delight us, but having, after all, found no country that was the equal of America, towards which my heart turned with increasing fondness the longer I was absent from it.

In Paris we met Mr. Dayton, the minister from the United States, and were quite cordially received by him. I had carefully avoided going near this gentleman on my former visit, because I was aware that he knew me, and thought that, perhaps, he might bear me some ill will. He was pleasant enough, however, and I sincerely regretted not having met him sooner.

At the Hotel de Louvre, where we stopped, there was quite a list of old Confederates, some of whom had been my army companions. I had the advantage of them, for they had only known me as Lieutenant Harry T. Buford, and they did not recognize me in female attire. Being extremely anxious to know what they thought of me, I obtained introductions to most of them, and began to try and get them to commit themselves.

Colonel M. was the first one I spoke to on this delicate subject. After inquiring about the condition of affairs in America, I asked him if he knew what had become of that female officer who figured so extensively during the greater part of the war.

"O," said the colonel, "I knew her very well. She was in my corps for a time, but afterwards she went West, and I do not know how she finished her career."

"What do you think of her?"

"She is a very fine woman, and made a good officer. She was very popular indeed."

"Do you think that it was proper for a woman to do as she did?"

"Well, no, not exactly; but she did so much good for the cause, that she can well be excused. If the men had all been as plucky, things would have turned out very different. She always bore an excellent name, and I would fight for her in a moment if I heard any one traducing her. I would like very much to see her again, and would be willing to travel all the way back to America to have that pleasure."

The reader may imagine the sensations of pleasure which this enthusiastic opinion of myself caused me. I was aching to tell him who I was, but there were others whom I desired to question, and so concluded to preserve my secret a little longer.

While I was talking with Colonel M., a servant in livery appeared, with a card on a silver waiter, from Colonel D. and Major C. I did not recognize the names, but said I would receive them, and so shook hands with Colonel M., giving him a hearty request to call on me again.

The two gentlemen appeared, and the colonel said, "You do not appear to remember me."

"No, sir," I replied. "I think I recollect your face, but I cannot recall where I have met you."

"Do you not recollect meeting me in Cuba, at So-and-so's house?"

"O, certainly, I do; I must ask that you will excuse my forgetfulness."

"I was looking over the list of arrivals, and seeing your name, thought that I would take the liberty of calling to inquire after your health."

I asked whether he had met my brother's family; and on his saying that he had not, I conducted him and his friend to their parlor. Leaving the major for my brother and his wife to entertain, I took the colonel to a remote part of the room, and after some preliminary conversation, asked him the same questions that I had Colonel M.

He expressed admiration of my valor, but was so bitter in denouncing me for assuming male attire, that I was thoroughly disgusted with him.

A few days after this, I returned with my brother and family to London, and immediately on my arrival in that city wrote two letters, one to Colonel M. and the other to Colonel D., telling them who I was. Colonel M. replied, expressing great gratification at having met me, and a wish that I had made known to him that I was the heroine of whom he had such a decided admiration. Colonel D. did not reply; but his friend Major C. wrote me a letter in French, in which he endeavored to apologize for him, and expressed a wish, for his own sake, that I would return to Paris, as he was anxious to be better acquainted with a lady who had performed so many valorous exploits.

A Brief Visit to London.

We remained about fifteen days in London, stopping at the house of a friend, Mr. T., a right jolly fellow, who had resided in England for many years. Shortly after our arrival we visited Hyde Park, a very beautiful pleasure-ground, but not to be compared with the Parisian parks. This event was a source of much gratification to me, as it gave me an opportunity to see her majesty Queen Victoria, who drove by in a carriage with six horses. For this lady I always had a great admiration, esteeming her a model queen and a model mother. She was dressed with great neatness and simplicity, and there was nothing showy or ostentatious about her.

From London we went to Manchester, and I was interested in the great mills and factories, and in a grand cattle show which was in progress. With the display of fine blooded animals I was especially delighted. Notwithstanding, however, that there was so much to see and to occupy my attention, I was by this time getting homesick, and my eyes were frequently cast longingly westward. I was impatient to return to America, and my brother was equally so; and consequently, ere long, we were once more standing on the deck of a vessel homeward bound, for, after all, it was impossible for us to think of America but as our home.

34

Our decision to return, however, was far from pleasing to
my sister-in-law, who desired to reside in Spain. She blamed
me for influencing my brother contrary to her wishes, and was
jealous of my affection for him. The result was, that a coolness sprang up between us that made our intercourse with
each other anything but a pleasure to either.

On our arrival in New York, my brother was persuaded
by his wife to go to Mexico, where her sister resided. I
was not willing to go with them; and the result was, that
we parted company, with many regrets on my side, at the
prospect of a long separation from a brother whom I loved
dearer than myself, and with whom I had only recently been
reunited, after having scarcely seen each other during many
years.

It could not be helped, however, and I felt that it was best
he should go with his wife and children, leaving me to make
my own way in the world, as I had been doing for so long a
time. When they were once off, I turned my attention to my
own affairs, and began to make plans for the future. Before
determining, however, on any particular course, I concluded
that I would make a trip through the South, for the purpose
of observing the condition of the country, and of finding out
whether there was anything I could do to advance the interest
of the people among whom my lot had been cast for so many
years, and who were endeared to me by so many of the strongest ties.

CHAPTER XLVI.

SOUTH AMERICAN EXPEDITION.

A Southern Tour. — Visit to Baltimore and Washington. — The Desolations of War as Visible in Richmond, Columbia, and Charlotte. — A Race with a Federal Officer at Charleston. — Meeting with old Friends at Atlanta. — A Surprise for one of them. — Travelling over my old Campaigning Ground. — The forlorn Appearance of Things in New Orleans. — Emigration Projects. — I make some Investigation into them, and decide to go to South America for the Purpose of looking at the Country, and reporting to my Friends. — The Venezuelan Expedition and its Projector. — I suspect that it is a mere Speculation, but conclude to accompany it. — My third Marriage. — I endeavor to persuade my Husband to seek a Home in the Far-West, but on his Refusal, sail with him for Venezuela. — Forty-nine Persons packed in a small Schooner, with no Conveniences, and with scanty Provisions. — A horrible Voyage. — Sighting the Mouth of the River Orinoco.

FTER the departure of my brother and his family, I started for the South. My first stopping-place was Baltimore, where I met many old friends, who expressed themselves as very glad to see me again, but who represented the condition of things at the South as most deplorable. What I learned from them made me more than ever resolved to continue my journey; for, although the war was over, I was still anxious to do something, so far as my power extended, for the Southern people. I accordingly announced my intention of making a tour through the late Confederacy, for the purpose of seeing for myself exactly what the situation really was; but preferred first to go to Washington, with a view of consulting certain persons there.

I was advised, in the strongest manner, not to visit Washington at this time, and was assured that it would be a very perilous thing to do. Naturally a little obstinate and self-willed, the opposition of my friends only made me the more desirous of carrying out my original intention, no matter what the hazard might be. To Washington, accordingly, I proceeded, and called on some acquaintances, who received me with the utmost cordiality.

The person whom I particularly wished to see — an official in the war department — had, however, gone South. My friend Colonel Baker was also out of the city. I did not know whether to congratulate myself or not at missing a meeting with him. I was resolved, on going to Washington, not to fight shy of him, and to give him an opportunity to pay off old scores if he wished. Baker was certainly the person of all others who had a right to have a grudge against me, and yet I had an ardent desire to meet him again, just to hear what he would have to say about the tricks I so successfully played upon him. As the colonel was out of the city, however, I did not have the pleasure of exchanging notes with him, and I do not know to this day whether he ever discovered that I was a Confederate secret-service agent.

Finding that there was nothing to be done in Washington, I went on to Richmond, where I took up my quarters at the Exchange Hotel. The news of my arrival soon spread around, and I received ample attentions from many old Confederate friends, who seemed disposed to treat me with all possible kindness.

RICHMOND AFTER THE WAR.

The Richmond I beheld, however, was a very different place from the beautiful city I had visited for the first time in the summer of 1861, just before the batte of Bull Run. A four years' siege, ending in a fire which had consumed a large portion of the city, had destroyed its beauty as well as its prosperity, while the inhabitants wore such forlorn faces that I felt sick at heart at beholding them.

I hastened away, therefore, and passed through Charlotte, North Carolina, and Columbia, South Carolina, where the same dismal changes were visible. Charleston was badly battered and burned, but was not in quite as bad a plight as the other places named. The finest portion of the city was destroyed, however, and it looked very desolate.

I went to the Charleston Hotel, where I met an old friend from Columbia, who invited me to accompany him and some others on an excursion. His married daughter, and several intimate acquaintances, who were of the party, were introduced to me, among them a Yankee captain, who had married a fair daughter of South Carolina, who, with all her relatives, were strong secessionists.

This officer attached himself particularly to me, and urged me to give my views about the war, and the present condition of affairs, in the way of an argument with him. We accordingly had a very animated conversation for some time, and he was obliged, finally, to retire from the contest, saying, that he could not quarrel with me as I was a lady, and, moreover, had everybody on my side. I did not think him a very brilliant genius, but he was quite a good fellow in his way, and to show that there were no hard feelings between us, we shook hands, and declared ourselves friends.

The next day one of the officers had the audacity to call on me simply out of curiosity. He had heard about my serving in the Confederate army in male attire, and he wished to see what kind of a looking woman I was. I thought it a rather impudent proceeding, but concluded to gratify him. I accordingly walked into the drawing-room where he was, and after some little conversation, which was conducted with considerable coolness on my side, he invited me to take a ride with him.

I was astounded that he should make such a proposition, knowing who I was, and I being where I was, surrounded by the friends of the cause I had served, while he, of course, expected to figure in his Federal uniform by my side.

I scarcely knew what to say; but finally told him that I could not go, as I had an engagement. This, however, was a mere pretence, and was intended to gain time for consultation with my friends. Some of these, however, suggested that I should accept the invitation, and give him a genuine specimen of my abilities as a horsewoman.

A Trial of Equestrian Skill.

I accordingly went to every livery stable in the city, until I at length found a very swift horse, that I thought would suit my purpose. This being secured, I wrote a challenge for him to ride a race with me. We were to ride down the main street. He, without being aware of what was on foot, accepted; and the next afternoon, therefore, we mounted our steeds and started. When we arrived at the appointed place, I said, " Let us show these people what good equestrians we are."

He gave his horse a lash, but I reined mine in, telling him that I would give him twenty feet. When he had this distance, I gave my steed a cut with the whip, and flew past my cavalier like the wind, saying, loud enough for every one to hear me, " This is the way we caught you at Blackburn's Ford and Bull Run."

This was enough for him; and turning his horse, he rode back to the hotel, to find that a large party there were interested in the race, and that there were some heavy bets on the result, the odds being all against him. This gentleman, apparently, did not desire to continue his acquaintance with me, for I saw no more of him.

A few days after this occurrence I said farewell to my Charleston friends, and went to Atlanta, were I was very warmly received. The surgeons who had been attached to the hospital, and many others, called, and a disposition to show me every attention was manifested on all sides.

The Federal General Wallace and his staff were stopping at the same hotel as myself, as was also Captain B., one of the officers whom I had met in Washington, and whom I had used for the purpose of getting acquainted, and of furthering my plans in that city. I met this gentleman in the hall, and passed friendly greetings with him, and shortly after he came into the parlor for the purpose of having a friendly chat. The captain, up to this time, had never suspected in the least that I was not, and had not been, an adherent of the Federal cause ; and not supposing that I had any special interest in the war, our conversation turned chiefly upon other topics. I knew that he must shortly be undeceived, but I did not care to tell him about the part I had taken in the contest, or the advantages I had taken of his acquaintance with me.

UNDECEIVED.

While we were talking, Confederate General G. T. Anderson came in, and called me " Lieutenant." The astonishment of the captain was ludicrous. He could not understand what the general meant at first, and thought it was a joke. The truth, however, came out at last, and he learned not only that I was a rebel, but that when I met him in Washington I was endeavoring to gain information for the Confederates.

The captain, being somewhat bewildered, took his departure soon after, and at the invitation of General Anderson, I went out to visit the intrenchments. When we got back, I found that General Wallace had been informed as to who I was, and that he was anxious to see me. I said that I would be very glad to meet him; and the general, and a number of his officers, accordingly came into the parlor to see me. General Wallace was very pleasant; and, as we shook hands, he complimented me, with much heartiness, upon having played a difficult part so long and so well, and with having distinguished myself by my valor. I thanked him very sincerely for his good opinion of me, and then fell into a lively conversation with him and his officers.

One of the officers asked me to ride with him; but I begged to be excused, as I did not think it would look well, especially in Atlanta, where everybody knew me, to be seen riding out with an escort wearing a Federal uniform. He understood and appreciated my feelings on the subject, and said no more about it.

The next evening I started for New Orleans, and passed over a good deal of my old campaigning ground before I reached my destination.

My journey through the South had disclosed a pitiable state of things. The men of intellect, and the true representatives of Southern interests, were disfranchised and impoverished, while the management of affairs was in the hands of ignorant negroes, just relieved from slavery, and white "carpet-baggers," who had come to prey upon the desolation of the country. On every side were ruin and poverty; on every side disgust of the present, and despair of the future. The people, many of them, absolutely did not know what to do; and it is no wonder, that at this dismal time, certain ill-advised emigration schemes found countenance with those who saw no hope for themselves or their children but either to go out of the country, or to remove so far away from their old homes that they would be able to start life anew under better auspices than were then possible within the limits of the late Confederacy.

THE DESOLATION OF NEW ORLEANS.

New Orleans, once a great, wealthy, and populous city, was in a pitiful plight. The pedestal of Jackson's statue, in the public square, was disfigured by inscriptions such as those who erected it never intended should go there, which were cut during the occupancy of the Federal army, while the once pretty flower-beds were now nothing but masses of weeds and dead stalks.

Along the levee matters were even worse. Instead of forests of masts, or the innumerable chimneys of the steamboats, belching forth volumes of smoke, or huge barricades of cotton, sugar, and other produce, or thousands of drays, carts, and other vehicles, such as thronged the levee in olden times, the wharves were now silent, and served merely as promenades for motley groups of poor men, women, and children, who looked as if they did not know where the next meal was to come from.

The desolation of the great city sickened me, and I was the more indignant at what I saw, for I knew that this general prostration of business, and impoverishment of all classes, was not one of the legitimate results of warfare, but that ambitious and unscrupulous politicians were making use of the forlorn condition of the South for the furtherance of their own bad ends.

I longed to quit the scene of so much misery, and fully sympathized with those who preferred to fly from the country of their birth, and to seek homes in other lands, rather than to remain and be victimized, as they were being, by the wretches who had usurped all control of the affairs of the late rebel states.

FLYING FROM THE COUNTRY.

Taking advantage of the condition of mind and pocket which a great many people were in, a number of emigration schemes were started, most of them, I am confident, by swindlers. Many persons were so anxious to get away, that they did not exercise even common prudence in investigating the facilities that were offered them, and the result was, that they did much worse than if they had remained. The sufferings endured by some of these emigrants cannot be estimated, and the story of their attempts to find homes for themselves and their children in some land where they could live in peace and quietness, and enjoy the fruits of their labor without fear of being plundered, is one of the saddest and dreariest pages in the history of the country.

I was much interested in these emigration schemes when I first heard of them, and was extremely anxious to investigate them, for my own sake as well as for that of my suffering fellow-country people of the South. Venezuela was one of the countries which it was proposed to colonize, and representations were made, to the effect that the Venezuelan government would extend a cordial welcome to emigrants, and would aid them in establishing themselves.

I consulted with a number of wise and prudent men with regard to this Venezuelan project, but did not get much encouragement from them. They said that they would prefer to see the country for themselves, and to find out exactly what the government was willing to do, before they would care to invest any money. They thought that the country was rich and fertile, but that many of the reports about it were palpably exaggerations, having been gotten up in the interests of speculators. It would consequently not be a prudent thing for any one to emigrate there, unless some trustworthy person should undertake to go and see what was to be seen, for the purpose of making a strictly truthful report.

I Propose to Visit Venezuela.

I accordingly informed my friends that I would go and see for myself, and would certainly bring back such an account as could be relied upon.

It having been announced that I intended to go to Venezuela, I was called upon at the City Hotel, where I had my quarters, by Captain Fred. A. Johnston, who was fitting out an expedition. He gave me a most glowing account of the country, describing it as a perfect paradise, although I speedily judged, from his conversation, that he knew nothing about it, except from hearsay.

I had no difficulty in reading Captain Johnston's character, and what I saw of him subsequently only confirmed my first impressions. He was a nervous, excitable man, with more bombast than true enterprise. He was anxious to make money, and to make it very quick, and was consequently not particularly scrupulous about the means. He had a tolerably good education, but was not smart enough to put it to good use, and he was always engaged in some wild speculation or other, but never could accomplish anything. He was a plausible man, however, and a good talker, and, considering how many people felt at the time, it was no wonder a number were deceived by him.

After a long conversation with Johnston, I made up my mind to go with him, and in the mean time secretly advised my friends not to put any money in his or any other expedition until they heard from me. I was visited by a number of persons, who, on being informed that I proposed to go with Johnston's expedition, said, in effect, " We will depend upon the report you make as to the climate and the country, for we have families to support, and we do not want to run the risk of going to a foreign land, about which we know absolutely nothing." I promised to make a faithful report, and took care to say nothing to Johnston, or others interested in the manner he was, about what my intentions were, or about my discouraging other people from emigrating.

PREPARATIONS FOR THE VOYAGE.

I commenced making my preparations, and Johnston, who was apparently beginning to consider me a valuable ally, came and invited me to go over to Algiers, across the river from New Orleans, with him, for the purpose of meeting the others who were going. I found a number of proposed emigrants at Algiers, who were waiting for the vessel which was to convey them to their new homes. They all seemed to be in a cheerful mood, and well satisfied at the prospect of speedily getting away from a land where there was so much suffering.

A meeting was called for the purpose of consultation with regard to chartering a vessel and arranging for supplies, and Johnston greatly desired me to deliver an address. This I declined to do ; but I took occasion to say, that while it might be well enough for single men to engage in an enterprise of this kind, it was, in my opinion, rather too risky a thing for those who had families dependent upon them.

After my return to the city I reviewed the situation in my mind more clearly than I had hitherto done. I was becoming less and less satisfied with the way things looked, and could not help asking myself, Why should I make any attempt to leave the country I had fought for, and give it up to the carpet-baggers and negroes? or why should I interest myself in such an enterprise as this one of Johnston's, merely for the purpose of gaining information for people whose duty it was to look out for themselves? I called, in my perplexity, on an old gentleman who had been a good deal in California, and asked his opinion of the Pacific slope, and of the advisability of those who wished to emigrate from the South going there.

He said that there was not a country in the world equal to California, and it would be vastly better for those who wanted to find new homes to find them there, or in some other portion of the far west, rather than to go to South America. As for Johnston, he said that he would not take his own family to Venezuela until he had looked at the country himself, and it was doubtful whether he would then.

The poor people whom Johnston had enlisted in his scheme, however, had their hearts set upon going to Venezuela, and nowhere else; and though my heart ached at the disappointment, and perhaps severe suffering that was in store for them, I saw that it was useless to attempt to turn them from their purpose. They had their new homes all pictured in their imaginations, and Venezuela appeared to them like a second Garden of Eden, where all was peace, happiness, and prosperity, with no free negroes or carpet-baggers to intrude upon them.

Many of this band of emigrants were most estimable people; but, as I speedily discovered, there were some worthless ones among them, and I dreaded, more and more, the execution of the task I had set myself to do. Having, however, announced my intention of going, and having excited the expectations of my friends, I concluded that it would not do to back out, and so determined to go through with the thing, no matter what the consequences might be.

Among the emigrants who had enlisted in Johnston's band was a young Confederate officer, Major Wasson. He was a remarkably fine-looking man, with long, wavy, flaxen hair, which he wore brushed off his forehead, blue eyes, and fair complexion. The day before going over to Algiers with Johnston I had seen him on one of the street cars, and was very much struck with him. At Algiers I had some conversation with him, and invited him to call on me at the hotel. This he did; and I discovered that he was a stranger to all the rest of the band of emigrants, that he was anxious to get out of the country, and that, attracted by Johnston's representations, he had resolved to go to Venezuela with his expedition.

After that I saw a great deal of Major Wasson, and a strong attachment sprang up between us. A few days before we were to sail, he asked me to accept his hand, and I did so willingly; for not only did I admire him greatly, but I felt that it would be better in every way that I should accompany the expedition as a married woman.

We were accordingly married, and for some days kept the matter secret, it being our original intention not to say anything about it until after we were out at sea. As I was, however, pursued by the attentions of several other gentlemen, we finally concluded that the fact of our being husband and wife had best be announced.

A small schooner was finally procured, and preparations for our departure were pushed rapidly forward. Just as we were on the point of sailing, however, the owners of the vessel, who had not received their money for her, attempted to regain possession. We were all arrested, therefore, but after a long investigation of the case, were released, and the schooner delivered into our hands. This was a disagreeable and discouraging commencement, but it would have been well for the entire party had it been the worst misadventure that befell us.

As the time for departure drew near, I lost confidence in Johnston more and more, and almost at the last moment endeavored to persuade my husband to refrain from embarking, suggesting that we should seek a home somewhere in the West. He, however, was resolved to go, and I yielded my better judgment to his wishes, and went aboard, very much against my inclination.

Sailing of the Expedition.

The expedition consisted of forty-nine persons, including children, all of whom were stowed away in the hull of a small schooner, without regard to decency, and without many of the necessities of life. I did not find out how badly provided we were for a voyage until after we were at sea; but when I did discover what treatment was in store for us, I was boiling with indignation. There were no conveniences of any kind; scarcely provisions enough to sustain life; the water was foul, from the impure barrels in which it had been placed; while the conduct of some of the persons on board was an outrage on the very name of decency. Our diet was beans and hard tack for breakfast, the same for dinner, with the addition of duff for dessert; and this bill of fare was repeated, day after day, until we entered the River Orinoco.

It was a terrible voyage; and, although I had passed through some rather rough experiences in my time, and was accustomed to hardships, it will always live in my memory as one of my most painful experiences. My sufferings, however, were nothing in comparison with those of some of the poor women and children who were with us, and I was indignant, beyond expression, at the idea of their being victimized in the manner they were.

At length, after a cruise that, brief as it was, was fast becoming intolerable, we entered the mouth of the Orinoco, and the despairing band of emigrants began to pluck up their spirits, for now they were fairly in sight of the paradise which had been promised them.

CHAPTER XLVII.

VENEZUELA.

Taking a Pilot on Board. — A perplexing Predicament. — Beautiful Scenery along the Orinoco. — Negro Officials. — Disgust of some of the Emigrants. — Frightened Natives. — Arrival at the City of Bolivar. — The United States Consul ashamed of the Expedition. — Death of my Husband. — Another Expedition makes its Appearance. — Sufferings of the Emigrants. — I write a Letter to my Friends in New Orleans warning them not to come to Venezuela. — Rival Lovers. — I conclude that I have had enough of Matrimony, and encourage neither of them. — A Trip by Sea to La Guayra and Caraccas. — I prepare to leave. — What I learned in Venezuela. — The Resources of the Country.

HE sight of the promised land, of which such glowing accounts had been given them, filled our company with extravagant joy. Alas, they little knew what was yet in store for them ; but the prospect of being able to leave the wretched little schooner was such a pleasant one, that they scarcely thought of the future, and almost any fate seemed preferable to remaining on board of her.

We had not been in the neighborhood of the mouth of the river long before a small, light canoe put out towards us, and its occupant, hailing us in Spanish, asked whether we did not want a pilot.

I was the only person on board who understood him, and as he came alongside the captain refused to let him come on board. Some of the men, thinking that he had hostile intentions, produced their pistols, and for a time there was a prospect of trouble.

I accordingly went to Johnston, and said, " Now, Captain Johnston, you are in a nice fix. This man is a pilot, and you cannot go up the river without his assistance. If you attempt anything of the kind you will be considered a pirate."

This frightened Johnston, and I laughed in my sleeve to see the perplexity he was in. After leaving him to his reflections for a few moments, I said, in a whisper, " This man is a government pilot, and your vessel and crew are in imminent danger. It won't do to trifle with these Spaniards, I can tell you, for if you do, they will make short work of the whole party."

Johnston saw the point, and telling the captain of the schooner who the man was, he was permitted to come on board. The arrival of the pilot created quite a commotion, and no little surprise was expressed at the fact of his being a negro. The man, however, understood his business, and managed the vessel very skilfully. Without his assistance we would never have been able to have ascended the beautiful Orinoco, or have steered the schooner among the numerous islands.

GOING UP THE ORINOCO RIVER.

The scenery along the river was truly beautiful, and all admitted that, whatever else the country might be, it was certainly fair to look upon. I had not much confidence, however, that, on closer inspection, it would prove to be the earthly paradise we were searching for, but kept my thoughts to myself, for I knew that there would not be much use in expressing them.

The first village we came to was Coraeppa, where we took on board another pilot, Antonio Silva by name. He was a bright colored half-breed, and, like the negro, was skilful in his business. When he boarded us, the captain exclaimed in disgust, " Good Lord, are all the officials in this country niggers? " A good many of the emigrants were quite as much disgusted as the captain, and seemed to think that if the negroes were of as much importance as they seemed to be in Venezuela, it would have been just as well to have remained at home and fought the battle for supremacy with the free negroes and carpet-baggers on familiar ground.

That night we anchored at Baranco, with a great uncertainty before us as to whether we would be permitted to proceed any farther or not. At this place I caught the first fish, which was a grateful addition to our bill of fare. Some of our people went in bathing, — a performance which astonished the natives, who were afraid to venture into the water on account of the alligators, which abounded in rather startling profusion. Others obtained permission to go on shore, and created a sensation by doing so. The ignorant natives, who had no idea who we were, promptly abandoned their houses, and, leaving everything behind them, fled to the forests.

They imagined that we were a band of pirates, who were coming to take possession of the country.

A messenger was now despatched to the city of Bolivar to notify the governor of our coming, and, with considerable uncertainty as to the reception we were likely to meet with, the next morning we resumed our slow progress up the river.

At Los Tablos we were commanded to stop, and a most primitive piece of artillery was pointed at us, which excited some derision in my breast, but which appeared to inspire terror in that of Captain Johnston, for he was in much agitation lest the authorities on shore should take a notion to fire on us.

We reach the City of Bolivar.

After some parley, however, we were permitted to pass on to the city of Bolivar unmolested. On arriving off that place, the order was given that nobody should go ashore, much to the dissatisfaction of every one, for there was not a man, woman, or child on the steamer but was anxious to leave her at the earliest practicable moment.

After a time, the United States consul, Mr. Dalton, boarded us. He denied being the consul when my husband spoke to him, and said that he was heartily ashamed of such a shabby expedition. In spite of his denial, however, I knew that he was the consul, and determined to demand his assistance in case it should be necessary.

I now resolved to land and look out for myself, and appealed to my husband to come with me, saying that I had money enough about me for all our present needs, although the other members of the expedition were not aware of the fact, and that I could draw more, if it should be wanted, through the consul.

My husband, however, refused to go, and said that he would stick by the expedition to the last. I suggested that they would be far from sticking to him in case he was left destitute, and, thoroughly disgusted with the whole business, I left the schooner and went to the hotel.

At the hotel I met several very nice people, with whom I was soon on friendly terms, and was rejoiced to find myself once more in reasonably comfortable quarters, after what I had gone through with. The hotel was kept by a German, who had married a Venezuelan woman, and it was very well managed.

Once on shore, and free to do as I pleased, I proceeded to carry out the purpose I had in view when I started. I called on the consul, and explained matters to him, and through him obtained an introduction to the governor and his family. By all the persons I met I was well received, and a general desire was shown to give me such information as I needed with regard to the country, and the inducements which it might hold out for emigrants from the United States.

While I was thus employing myself on shore my husband stuck to the schooner. Finally, however, he too became so much disgusted that he concluded to take my advice, and abandon Johnston and his whole enterprise. In a day or two he left, and started for the gold mines, to find that the black fever was raging there to such an extent that it was dangerous for him to remain. He therefore returned, and went to Caraccas, where, shortly after his arrival, he was taken ill with the black vomit and died.

Inspecting the Country.

I remained in the city of Bolivar for several months, making occasional excursions into the country in the neighborhood, and going up the River Orinoco as far as San Fernando. My object was to find out all I could about the natural resources and climate of Venezuela, for the purpose of advising my friends in New Orleans; and through the kind assistance of my Venezuelan acquaintances, who interested themselves greatly in my labors, and aided me by every means in their power, I was, ere long, in possession of ample information to enable me to form an opinion as to the desirability of people from the United States seeking new homes in this part of the world.

The expedition, of which I was a member, was followed, not a great while after, by another one of equally shabby character, under the charge of a Dr. Price. This was made up of poor families, who had scarcely anything with them which would have enabled them to start farming, or business of any kind, in a strange land. These people were sent on shore by Price, who immediately slipped away, and left them to their fate, not caring what became of them.

It was an outrage, which cannot be denounced in too strong terms, to take these poor people out to Venezuela without capital, and without any means of support; and no punishment

35

I can think of would have been too severe for the men who
did the deed.

As for the emigrants, they were indignant at the treatment
they had received, and having nobody else at hand to vent their
grievances upon, fell to blaming the United States consul and
the Venezuelan authorities. They would not acknowledge
the consul, and some of them abused him in the grossest manner. This made him powerless to act for them. I interested
myself as much as I could in behalf of such as were disposed
to be tractable, and succeeded, through the consul's influence,
in procuring passage back to the United States for several of
the unfortunates. The rest scattered over the country ; some
of them died, some found precarious employment of one kind
or another, and some tried to make their way home again.

I ADVISE MY FRIENDS IN THE UNITED STATES TO REMAIN AT HOME.

After the arrival of Price's expedition, I considered it my
duty to communicate with my friends in New Orleans, without
more delay, for the purpose of warning them, and all others who
were disposed to emigrate, not to think of doing anything of
the kind. I accordingly wrote a letter advising those who
thought of emigrating to Venezuela, to let it alone, and denouncing Johnston and Price for holding out inducements to
poor and ignorant people which they had no assurance whatever would be realized. I said that it would be useless for
any persons from the States to come to Venezuela without
plenty of capital to carry on any such operations as they
might engage in, and that if they did come they would have
to submit to the laws of the country, and take their chances
with its citizens. One great objection to any emigration
schemes, however, was the instability of the government, and
the fact that Venezuela had no national credit. The Governor
of Bolivar said that Venezuela would be glad to have industrious people come to it from the United States, or any other
country, and that facilities would be afforded for them to take
up lands at low rates, but he had no supplies to give half-
starved men and women who might be landed within his jurisdiction, and was anxious that no one should come under any
misapprehensions as to what reception they would be likely
to have on their arrival.

I stated the facts within my knowledge plainly, and reviewed the situation in such terms that there could be no misunderstanding of my meaning, and before sending my letter, had it countersigned by the governor, his brother, the consul, and a number of Americans who were in the city.

SOCIAL PLEASURES OF BOLIVAR.

This duty having been performed, I felt free to enjoy myself, and having by this time quite a large circle of acquaintances, I found very little difficulty in the way of having a good time.

Two young gentlemen, Señor Sayal and Señor Rodriguez, both became very attentive to me, and very jealous of each other, and very jealous also of Major G., a gentleman whom I esteemed very highly. I was afraid at one time that Sayal and Rodriguez would have a serious difficulty, and perhaps kill each other; the last named, especially, was very violent, and declared that any man who stood in his way should die. As for myself, the party chiefly interested, I cared nothing for either of them, except in the way of friendship, and had no intentions of marrying again. My matrimonial experiences hitherto had been so unfortunate, that I came to the conclusion I had better live single, and travel about to see the world, relying upon myself for protection.

While residing in Bolivar I conformed to all the customs of the place, and endeavored to see all that was worth seeing. A number of families welcomed me most cordially to their homes, and in company with my friends of both sexes, I went on several pleasant excursions. It was quite a popular custom to go up the river, on a Sunday morning, to Marichal or San Rafael, to bathe. At these places there were regular bathing grounds, resorted to by the people of Bolivar, and the washer-women also went there to do their work. The method of washing clothes was peculiar; they would be thrown over smooth stones, and beaten with sticks while drenched with water. This process, it is scarcely necessary to say, is terribly destructive to the clothing.

The city of Bolivar is a very beautiful place. It is built on the brow of a hill, overlooking the River Orinoco, on one side, and a lagoon on the other. Behind the city are the Marichal Mountains, in which gold is to be found, but scarcely in paying quantities.

The people of Bolivar are hospitable and agreeable in their manners, and those with whom I became acquainted did all they could to make my time pass pleasantly. I attended several fandangos with Señor Sayal and Señor Rodriguez, as as well as other entertainments.

After having resided in Bolivar for several months, I concluded to visit other portions of the country, and accordingly made a trip around by sea to La Guyra, and from thence to. Caraccas. To my great surprise Rodriguez came after me by the next steamer, and began to be more attentive than ever. He introduced me to his relatives who resided in the neighborhood of Caraccas, and appeared to be resolved to make sure of me, now that he had his rivals at a distance. I, however, gave him very little encouragement, although, had I felt anxious to marry again, I perhaps would have done well to have been more gracious to him. He was one of twelve sons, and his parents were very wealthy, owning immense estates and large herds of cattle, which must have yielded them a great income.

Farewell to Venezuela.

With this visit to Caraccas concluded my Venezuelan experiences, for, notwithstanding the assiduous attentions of Señor Rodriguez, I could not be persuaded to remain, and made my preparations to return to the United States. Taking passage on a schooner bound for Demerara, in British Guiana, I said adieu to my Venezuelan friends, having made up my mind that my own country was the best to live in after all, and that in it thereafter I would seek my fortune. My Venezuelan trip, however, was, notwithstanding the ungracious auspicies under which it was commenced, a source of gratification to me. It made me acquainted with a portion of the world that was well worth looking at, and it was the means of bringing me in friendly relations with a number of excellent people, for whom I shall always have a warm regard, and to whom I shall always feel indebted for many unsolicited kindnesses.

The personal gratifications which the trip afforded me amply repaid me for all the expense and trouble I was put to in making it; but, beyond this, I have the satisfaction of knowing, that by accompanying Captain Johnston's expedition as I did, and under the peculiar circumstances I did, I was the means of preventing a great number of persons in the Southern states from being swindled by speculators who, taking advantage of the unsettled condition of the South after the war, and the discontent of a large portion of the people, were endeavoring, without proper means or facilities for carrying out their proposed objects, to organize colonization parties to go to various places in South America.

My experiences in Venezuela convinced me that it was no place for poor Americans to go to. For people who had capital, and the skill and energy to use it properly, it held out many inducements, but no more and no greater than were held out by the Western portions of our own country.

VENEZUELA AND ITS PRODUCTS.

Portions of Venezuela are very beautiful, and the scenery along the banks of the Orinoco, especially, is lovely in the extreme. The country is, much of it, fertile, and its mineral wealth is very great, but it is undeveloped, and those who attempt its development will be tolerably certain to have a hard time of it, and to expend a great deal of money before they get much return, either for their cash or labor. Apart from everything else, the climate is very trying, especially to strangers; and this of itself is a good and sufficient reason why residents of the United States would do well to tempt fortune elsewhere.

Along the banks of the Orinoco and its tributaries the vegetation is most luxuriant, and all kinds of tropical fruits abound in the greatest profusion. The forests contain mahogany, lignum-vitæ, and the chinchona tree, from which quinine is made. In the interior are to be found the Caoutchouc or India-rubber tree, and half a dozen varieties of the cotton tree. Some of the latter are, I think, especially worthy of the attention of those who are interested in cotton-growing, and with proper cultivation they might be made to yield far more valuable results than they do. Tobacco grows wild, and is cultivated to some extent, but the natives, although they are inveterate consumers of the weed, do not understand how to cure it properly

The diet of the Venezuelans is largely made up of fruits, of which they have a great variety, such as the banana, of which there are half a dozen different kinds, cocoanuts, figs, mangoes, manzanas de oro, or golden apples, marma apples, guavas, oranges, grapes, and pomegranates. The melons are very plentiful, and, although small, are sweet and well flavored.

Sugar is made to some extent from the cane, which bears a strong resemblance to the maple sugar of the United States. Yams and sweet potatoes are very abundant, and there is a hardy species of cabbage which grows on the edges of marshes, and which sometimes attains a height of eighteen or twenty feet. The calabashes grow to an enormous size, and are used for carrying water. The onions are numerous, but small.

The flowers grow in great profusion, and are very beautiful. The mariposa attains to the height of the oleander, and has gorgeous white and scarlet blossoms. The zueco is a bright little plant, and is very fragrant. The people of Venezuela are exceedingly fond of flowers, and always have a great number of them about their dwellings.

The birds of Venezuela, for the most part, are of very rich plumage. There are several varieties of parrots, of which the macaw, and the green and gray parrots, are the talkers. The paroquets are very diminutive, and are beautiful little birds. The cock of the rocks, which is the color of the redbird of the United States, is easily domesticated; it has a ruffle of feathers about an inch in length, which encircles its neck from the wings to the beak. The ayax is a bird that is heard last in the evening and first in the morning; it has a very peculiar cry, and the natives are exceedingly superstitious about it, thinking that should they kill it some misfortune is certain to happen to them.

The lizards and other reptiles are too numerous for description. In the huts of the poorer classes, lizards, scorpions, roaches, and other live stock live on the most intimate terms with the human inhabitants, and do not appear to interfere very materially with their comfort.

The forests and jungles are filled with panthers, jaguars, and South American tigers. The last named are very ferocious, and the natives stand in great fear of them.

The People and Government of Venezuela.

The people of Venezuela are very superstitious, and are exceedingly particular about their religious observances. In their manners they are courteous and unaffected, and some of their household ways are very primitive. Their meat is cured in strips, and their corn is ground between two stones, the under one of which is hollowed out to some extent. This kind of work is chiefly done by the women. The men make hammocks out of grass, bark, and cotton, and employ themselves in the cultivation of the ground, and in the care of live stock and the pursuit of game. In the summer time the hammocks are swung out in the open air between two trees, or in rude huts with no sides to them. The milk of the ass is preferred to that of the cow or goat. Most of the cooking is done in earthenware jars or pipkins. Earthenware jars, of a peculiar make, are also used for keeping water for drinking purposes in.

The principal exports of Venezuela are cattle, hides, tallow, and coffee from the La Guayra and Maracaybo districts. The United States consul at Bolivar, while I was there, was interested to some extent in gold mining. The quartz was brought from the Caratol mountains, nearly two hundred miles distant, on the backs of donkeys, and was purchased by the consul from the natives with merchandise. Having obtained the quartz, he crushed it, and extracted the metal, which was forwarded to the mint in Philadelphia. The mineral wealth of Venezuela is very great; gold, silver, copper, and tin abounding in large quantities. The mines, however, are, for the most part, far distant from the commercial centres, and are very inefficiently worked. It would pay capitalists to go into the mining business in Venezuela if they could get some railroads built, or even if they could get some good common roads made.

The country away from the seaboard or the watercourses is thinly settled, and there is not likely to be any great increase in the population until the facilities for easy travelling are much greater than they are, or were at the time of my visit. The roads to the mines are mere paths, not larger than cattle trails.

The natives in the interior suffer many hardships and privations, and any one going to Venezuela without ample capital, must expect to do the same. One great source of annoyance to the country people is the jigger, — a species of worm which buries itself in the feet, generally under the skin near the toe-nails. It is very painful under any circumstances, and it not infrequently causes the loss of the toes.

As in nearly all of the South American states, the government of Venezuela is very unsettled ; and the schemings of ambitious politicians, who are ready at any moment to resort to arms for the accomplishment of their ends, render both life and property to some extent insecure. To be sure, the revolutions which occur there from time to time do not, as a rule, cause any great amount of bloodshed, notwithstanding the commotions they make, but they have the effect of leaving a sense of insecurity on the public mind, and of preventing improvement which otherwise might be made. The white people are, for the most part, well educated and intelligent, but they do not appear to understand the art of self-government; while the negroes, Indians, and half-breeds seem to be incapable of doing anything to advance their own condition, or to promote the interests of the country. With such a heterogeneous population as resides within its borders, and with the educated whites so greatly in the minority as they are, there is not much prospect of Venezuela speedily attaining the position her agricultural and mineral resources would seem to entitle her to.

CHAPTER XLVIII.

DEMERARA, TRINIDAD, BARBADOES, AND ST. LUCIA.

From Venezuela to Demerara. — The Hotels of Georgetown, Demerara. — The United States Consul at Georgetown. — A Visit to a Coffee Plantation. — A Cooly murders his Wife. — Excitement in the Streets of Georgetown. — The Products of Demerara. — Fort Spain, Trinidad. — A very dirty Town. — Bridgetown, Barbadoes. — Having a good Time among old Friends. — A Drive to Speightstown. — St. Lucia. — The old Homestead. — Reminiscences of Childhood. — The Past, the Present, and the Future. — The Family Burying-ground.

HE schooner Isabel, in which I sailed for Demerara, had a rather unsavory cargo in the shape of cattle; but being an experienced traveller, and accustomed to roughing it, I did not permit myself to be annoyed by my surroundings; and as the weather was fine, I greatly enjoyed this brief cruise along the tropical South American coast.

There were two lady passengers besides myself, whose companionship I found very agreeable; and I had with me a number of pets, whose capers and gambols afforded all on board much amusement. These pets were two monkeys, a young South American tiger, two parrots, and a dozen paroquets. One of the monkeys was named Bob Lee, while the tiger was called Joe Johnston. One of our chief diversions was to get up contests between these animals over their meals. The monkey, being of more mature age and of superior cunning, almost invariably got the better of his antagonist, although the tiger would make a good fight. This tiger was very tame and very gentle, and he liked nothing better than to be taken in my lap and petted.

On landing at Georgetown, we were beset by negroes, offering us sapadillos for sale; but, disregarding them, I bade adieu to my travelling companions, and went to the Prince of Wales Hotel, and asked for accommodation. The sapadillo, I may remark here, is a small fruit, shaped something like a pear;

553

the skin is roughish, and the flesh inside is of a maroon color, and rather tart to the taste. The Prince of Wales Hotel was kept by a negro; on discovering which, I was rather dubious about stopping there. The captain of the schooner told me that there was another hotel kept by white people; but, on inspecting it, I concluded that it would be wise for me to take up my quarters at the African establishment.

The hostess of the Prince of Wales Hotel was a mulatto woman, of about forty-five years of age. She was quite good-looking, and had been the wife of an English sea captain, by whom she had two daughters. Her husband was dead, and one of her daughters was married to a white man, who was extensively engaged in coffee-growing. This woman was very intelligent herself, and she had taken pains to have her children carefully educated. As a hotel keeper, she was much above the average; and during my stay in her house, she did every thing possible to make me comfortable.

The captain of the schooner introduced me to a number of prominent people in Georgetown, and I went of my own accord to call on the United States consul. This official was a German by birth, and he was engaged in making a collection of animals for the Zoölogical Garden of Frankfort-on-the-Main. His wife, a very pleasant woman, took a great deal of interest in his pursuits, and devoted a large portion of her time to the care of the numerous pets, in the way of monkeys, dogs, cats, and squirrels, with which the house abounded.

A Contribution for my Relief.

Among the persons with whom I became acquainted was an officer belonging to a United States man-of-war which was lying in the harbor. This gentleman, hearing that I was one of a party of emigrants from the States, and was on my way back, supposed that I must be in destitute circumstances. He accordingly represented my case in such a way, on board his ship, that a considerable sum of money was raised for me, and the commander of the vessel called at the hotel to give it to me, and to offer me such other aid as he was able to bestow. The consul, when he heard of this occurrence, was much annoyed that I had not informed him that I was in want of money, in order that he might have assisted me. I had some trouble in making these good gentlemen understand my real position. They were very indignant over the story I told with regard to the manner in which people in the Southern States had been deluded into emigrating to Venezuela, and other portions of South America, and promised to use their influence to check the schemes of such men as Johnston and Price.

Having expressed a desire to proceed on my journey northward, the consul introduced me to the captain of a vessel which was shortly to sail for Barbadoes, and I arranged with him for a passage.

While waiting for the vessel to sail, I made a trip into the country, to visit the coffee plantation of Mr. Waite, the husband of my landlady's daughter. When we reached the plantation, we found everybody there in considerable excitement over a murder that had just been committed. A cooly who was jealous, had, it appeared, cut the throat of his wife, her crime being that she had looked at another man. Mr. Waite assured me that there was nothing strange about such an occurrence a this, and that such outrages were happening constantly.

Much Ado about Nothing.

On our return to Georgetown, we found that place in a commotion. The people were rushing about the streets, yelling at the tops of their voices, and making a terrible to do. I supposed, of course, that it was another murder, but was informed that the excitement was caused by the pound-master making a raid on the goats, which were permitted to roam about the streets contrary to law. These goats being the chief means of support of many of the poor people, their arrest by the pound-master was, from a South American point of view, a very much more serious matter than the murder of a cooly woman.

Another sensation was shortly after caused by a fellow from New Jersey absconding with a large sum of money. He had started some kind of speculation, and had induced a number of people to invest their means. Having secured a good round sum, he quietly slipped away, carrying the cash with him. There was, of course, an immense amount of indignation among the sufferers. One of the victims, an old Scotchman, gave me a most pitiful recital of the manner in which he had been swindled. I, however, gave him but little comfort, and told him I thought he deserved to lose his money, for not having more wit than to trust it in the hands of such a transparent rogue as this fellow appeared to be.

During my visit to Mr. Waite's coffee plantation, and during other excursions I made to the interior, I had excellent opportunities afforded me for seeing the country in the vicinity of Georgetown, and of obtaining information concerning it.

The Vegetables and Animals of Demerara.

Like Venezuela, this portion of Demerara is very beautiful to the eye, and is very rich in products of the soil. The palm trees grow to a great size, and are useful in innumerable ways. The adobe, or mud huts of the poorer classes, are invariably thatched with palm leaves, interwoven with cane, and plastered with mud. This kind of a roof has merits, but it also has some disadvantages, not the least of which is, that it affords an admirable habitation for ants, lizards, snakes, roaches, scorpions, and spiders, of all colors and sizes. The people, however, do not appear to mind this vermin, and it has seemed to me that they rather enjoyed sharing their habitations with the venomous reptiles and insects. Of the fibres of the palm are made various kinds of cordage, nets, hammocks, lassos, mats, and many household conveniences.

There are a number of different kinds of cactus, some of which grow to a great height. The fruit of the scarlet variety is made into a kind of preserve, which is pleasant eating, resembling in flavor that made from the crab-apple. From this fruit, also, an agreeable drink is prepared, which is very refreshing.

From the candle tree, the natives, at certain seasons, extract the sap by making incisions in the bark. This sap, which is oily in its nature, is caught in earthen bowls, and after it solidifies, — which it does very rapidly on being exposed to the air, — is made into candles.

The milk tree is treated in the same manner. The juice, when it is first extracted, is thin and watery, like that of the grape vine. After standing for a short time it thickens, and becomes of the color of goat's milk. When it is in this condition the natives drink it, and are exceedingly fond of it. If permitted to stand a sufficient time, the milk solidifies to the consistency of thick jelly, and then twists of cotton are dipped in it, and are used for candles.

The guaca is a powerful antidote for poisons, and is used

WILD HUNT IN VENEZUELA.

to cure the wounds caused by the bite of snakes and insects. It is also said to be an antidote for the virus of a mad dog. The odor is very peculiar, but not unpleasant.

The tamarind trees grow to a large size ; their fruit greatly resembles the bean of the honey locust of the United States. The tamarind beans, when preserved, make a cooling beverage, by being soaked in water, which is useful in the sick-chamber, especially in fever cases.

The pili is used for the manufacture of ropes, cordage, and sacks, and I think would make good paper. Of the divi, cart wheels are made. The nutmeg trees grow luxuriantly without cultivation. These are only a few of the vegetable products of Demerara, but they will suffice to give the reader a general idea with regard to the products of the soil.

The snakes of Demerara are of all sizes, kinds, and colors. One of the most curious is a small snake, which is spotted with twelve different colors ; these are chiefly found lodged in the branches of the bamboo. They are said to be harmless; other varieties, however, are exceedingly venomous.

There is a species of red ant, which builds its habitations up in the forks of the trees, where they look almost like the prairie dog villages of our western country. The houses are made of mud, which is collected into a ball, and then pushed up the tree by the insect, with infinite labor.

The birds of Demerara are as numerous and as gorgeous in their plumage as those of Venezuela. The parrots of all kinds, especially, abound in immense numbers. While I was at Georgetown, my friend, Captain M., shot at some parrots who were in a mango tree feeding on the fruit, and wounded one, which fell and lodged in the fork of two limbs, making such a pitiful cry that he had not the heart to shoot again. The mate of this wounded bird attended to its wants with infinite care, bringing it food and water for several days, until it died. The last day water was brought every hour; and when at length the sick bird died, the mate uttered a most human-like cry of sorrow and despair. The parrots of all kinds go in couples, and like the pigeons, they migrate in the rainy season.

The humming-birds appear to be quite as numerous, while there are even more varieties of them than there are of the parrots. They are beautiful little creatures, and I never became tired of watching their motions. Like the parrots, these tiny birds seemed to be gifted with extraordinary intelligence.

My vessel being at length ready, I sailed for Barbadoes, by way of Trinidad. The weather was very rough for a couple of days, and as a consequence I was terribly sea-sick. I however recovered before we reached Port Spain, and having a tremendous appetite, I made sad havoc between meals with the captain's sweetmeats, sardines, and crackers. He was a whole-souled, jolly sort of a man, who, in consideration of my being his only lady passenger, paid me particular attention, and placed his private larder at my disposal.

When we reached Port Spain, the chief town of the Island of Trinidad, the captain said that we would have to remain there about eight hours, and that I and the other passengers had better step ashore and see the place. We accordingly strolled about the town until it was time for the vessel to leave, but were not impressed with its beauty. It was a very dingy-looking settlement, with a very ragged and dirty native population. There were a few Englishmen, but the majority of the people were negroes or half-breeds, whose habitations were disgustingly dirty and squalid.

I was not sorry to get away from Port Spain, although if there had been time I would have taken pleasure in exploring the interior of Trinidad, and especially in visiting the famous pitch lake, in the south-western portion of the island.

A quick run brought us to Bridgetown, Barbadoes, where I felt at home, having visited the place on blockade-running business during the war, and having a number of acquaintances residing there, who, I anticipated, would be glad to see me for the sake of old times. I was not disappointed, for, on taking up my quarters at the Prince Albert Hotel, I soon fell in with friends, who welcomed me as heartily as I could have desired, and who exerted themselves to make my visit in all respects a most enjoyable one.

HOSPITALITIES OF BARBADOES.

The day after my arrival, Captain F., of Liverpool, came with a handsome carriage and pair, and invited me to drive out with him and some other friends, on a tour of inspection of the points of interest on the island. We went first to the barracks, to see a drill of the British troops stationed there, and afterwards drove to Speightstown, over a broad road lined with cocoanut trees, which presented a truly magnificent appearance. These graceful trees are extensively used in Barbadoes for dividing the farms instead of fences or hedges, and the use which is made of them adds greatly to the attractiveness of the landscape. On our way, we stopped at two dairy farms, and I obtained some good buttermilk, a beverage of which I am very fond. My companions, however, did not take kindly to it, and in true British fashion quenched their thirst with ale and beer. This trip to the interior was a delightful one in every respect, the country being very beautiful, and I enjoyed it greatly; more, perhaps, than I otherwise would, on account of having just made a sea voyage.

On returning to Bridgetown, the whole party of us were invited to dine with a wealthy American gentleman, who had just arrived by the steamer, and who was on a visit to a number of the West India Islands. He was very much interested in my account of South America, and of my experience there, and agreed most heartily with me that it was the worst kind of folly for people to emigrate to Venezuela, or any other of the South American states, unless they had ample capital; even with ample capital, he thought that they could do better at home, despite the unsettled condition of affairs incident to the late war.

Captain F., having been informed of my intention of sailing by the next steamer, and of stopping at St. Lucia, for the purpose of visiting the home of my early childhood, regretted that he would see so little of me, as his vessel was to leave the next day. I was sorry too, for he was a very agreeable man, and professed to have a very high opinion of me on account of my services in behalf of the Confederacy. Being unable to show me more attention himself, the captain brought a number of his Barbadoes lady friends to see me, and kindly commended me to their consideration. He then said that as he would pass St. Lucia before the mail steamer in which I intended to take passage would reach there, he would scarcely be likely to see me again, and so wished me a safe journey back to the States, and all manner of good luck in the future.

Three days after his departure my steamer was ready to start, and I said good by to my Barbadoes friends with real regret, for they had been most kind to me, and had fairly overwhelmed me with their attentions. Being bent upon visiting my relatives and my early home, I purchased a ticket permitting me to stop at St. Lucia until the next steamer, and after a short and pleasant cruise, which was not marked by any incident of note, we reached the island which was endeared to me as being my mother's birth-place, and on account of my residence on it, being among the most fascinating recollections of my childhood.

As I was preparing to leave the steamer, I was surprised by the steward bringing me a beautiful basket filled with different kinds of fruit. A card which accompanied it told me that it was from Captain F., who had been obliged to stop at St. Lucia for repairs, having broken a mast. On going on shore, I sent the captain a note, requesting him to call on me at the residence of my cousin, the old family homestead. This he did, and I introduced him to my relatives. His visit was a short one, however, as his vessel was almost ready for sea, and so he said good by again, and for the last time. I have never seen him since.

MY CHILDHOOD'S HOME.

It was not without a certain feeling of sadness and strangeness that I found myself once more domiciled in the old-fashioned stone house where I had lived with my father and mother, and brothers, and sisters, when a little girl. The house and its surroundings were much the same as they were many years before, and yet there was something oddly unfamiliar about them, and it took me some time to reconcile my recollections with the realities. The stone house, built in the English fashion, the marble floor, the ancient furniture of Spanish make, the stone water-pool and stone filter, and the banana and prune bushes which grew at my mother's window, were, however, all as they had been, and as if I had left them but yesterday.

In gazing on these familiar objects, I was forced, in spite of myself, to think of the many years that had passed since I had last seen them, and of the many things that had happened. The happy family that had gathered under this roof had been scattered, and most of its members were dead; while I, the darling of my father and of my gentle mother, what a strange career I had gone through — stranger far than that of many a heroine of romance whose adventures had fascinated my girlish fancy! I was yet, too, a young woman, and what strange things might not the future have in store for me? It was enough, however, just then to think of the past and of the present, without perplexing myself with speculations as to the future; and I gave myself up to such enjoyment as a visit of this kind to a fondly remmembered home of childhood was able to afford.

After viewing the old house and its immediate surroundings, I went to the family burying-ground in search of the weather-stained vault, which contained the earthly remains of near and dear relatives, among others, of a sister and a brother, whose faces I never beheld after I left Cuba to go to New Orleans to school. The ivy and the myrtle grew so thick about it as almost to hide the inscription; and yet there was something beautiful in the appearance of the spot, which marked it as the fitting resting-place for the beloved dead. As I stood by this vault, and thought how lonely I was in the world, and how unpropitious the future seemed, I thought that if it could be the will of God that my spirit should be taken to himself, I would gladly have my body rest here beside those of my brother and sister. I was reluctant to leave the place, but felt impelled to go on and seek the destiny that awaited me in another land, and resolved to be as courageous as ever in meeting whatever fate or position the future might have in store for me. Before leaving the tomb I knelt down to pluck some ivy leaves, to carry away as remembrances, but as I stretched out my hand to gather them, something restrained me, and I went away empty-handed as I had come.

I remained in the old homestead, enjoying the hospitality of my cousins, until the arrival of the steamer, and then said farewell to St. Lucia—my visit to it having been the happiest episode of my journey.

36

CHAPTER XLIX.

ST. THOMAS AND CUBA.

FROM St. Lucia I went to the Danish Island of St. Thomas, where one of my friends of the war time, to whom I had written announcing my intention of revisiting the place, was expecting my arrival. When we entered the harbor, the passenger boat, which was to take us ashore, came off to the steamer, and as she neared, I recognized my friend. I waved my handkerchief to him, and he took off his hat, and when the boat came alongside he sprang on board, and shook me most cordially by the hand, expressing, as he did so, the greatest gratification at seeing me again.

When we reached the wharf I met another of my old war acquaintances, the Italian consul. He, also, was glad to see me, and asked me all manner of questions about where I had been, and what I had been doing since the blockade-running business had come to a stand-still. I walked between my two friends up to the hotel, where I found that a fine large room had been engaged for me, and, once fairly installed in it, the visitors came pouring in, one after the other; first, the proprietor and his wife, then the Danish commandant's wife, then half a dozen others, until I was obliged to go into the drawing-room and hold a regular reception.

Nowhere during my trip had I been welcomed with a more hearty and sincere courtesy, or with a more evident disposi-

562

tion to make a heroine of me. All through the evening people were coming in, some of them acquaintances, who, having heard of my arrival, were anxious to extend a welcome ; and others, strangers, who had learned something of my adventurous career, were desirous of being introduced to me. One of the most agreeable of my visitors was Mr. English, the correspondent of a newspaper in Manchester, England. He was a fine, dashing young fellow, overflowing with wit and humor, and his lively conversation created a great deal of entertainment.

During the evening some of the company amused themselves with dominos, others with cards, while I was surrounded constantly by quite a little crowd of persons who persisted in having me relate to them some of my adventures. After a time wine, ale, and cakes were brought in, and the gentlemen, and some of the ladies, too, regaled themselves with cigars and cigarettes. It was nearly twelve o'clock when the Italian consul, a white haired old gentleman, arose, and asking to be excused, wished us good night. As I was tired I followed him, asking my kind friends to excuse me, and so the party broke up.

I slept late the next morning, and was awakened by a tap at my door. It was Mrs. Captain B., who wished to know if I was sick. I said that I was quite well ; whereat she smiled, and said she would send me a cup of chocolate. The girl soon came with the chocolate, and after drinking it, I dressed myself and went down to the drawing-room. As I passed the consul's office, he came out and gave me a " good morning," and offered me his arm to take me in to breakfast.

After breakfast, I was joined in the drawing-room by quite a large party of ladies and gentlemen, who proposed that I should go with them through the fort, and up to the top of the hill to see the scenery.

THINGS TO BE SEEN AT ST. THOMAS.

The town of Charlotte is built on three hills, from the summits of which beautiful views of the harbor and the island are obtained. One of the features of the scene is a rock, called Frenchman's Cap. It is almost perpendicular, and is, I believe, considered dangerous to shipping. Scorpion Rock is inhabited only by the horrid reptiles from which it takes its name. They are unusually abundant there, and for that reason it is generally given a wide berth, as no one cares to make its intimate acquaintance.

The principal fortifications of St. Thomas are Fort Christiana, and Prince Federick's and Mohlenfel's batteries. These are occupied by a small force of Danish soldiers, who are clean and tidy looking, but otherwise are not remarkable in appearance.

It was under the guns of Fort Christiana that the blockade-runners were accustomed to receive their cargoes; and, notwithstanding the supposed vigilance of the United States fleet, most of them managed to get off in safety. On my former visit to St. Thomas, one of the Federal officers was pointed out to me as being in the trade himself. On one occasion, at least, where the consul notified him, he permitted a vessel, with a contraband cargo, to put to sea, and did not pretend to give chase until she was so far away that there was no hope of overtaking her.

As the reader will, perhaps, remember, on the occasion of my previous visit to St. Thomas, I had the satisfaction of seeing the Confederate cruiser Florida come in, and coal, and get away again in safety, through a clever trick played upon the Federals. The Florida took in her coal and supplies at the King's wharf, and when she was ready for sea, one of the sailors, pretending to be an Englishman, went to the consul, Mr. Smith, and told him, that as they were coming in they saw the Florida off to the westward of the island. Mr. Smith, accordingly, gave orders to the Federal man-of-war to go out and look for her, and so soon as the Federal cruiser was out of the harbor, and heading westward, Captain Maffitt, having steam up, put on all speed and went out after her. Before the Federal commander discovered that he had been duped, the Florida was out of sight and out of danger.

The Danish commandant told me that he was heartily sorry the war closed so soon, for the people of St. Thomas profited greatly by it. He was of the opinion that could the South have held out for another year, the great powers of Europe would have interfered in her behalf, and she would have. secured her independence.

Through the exertions of my friends to make my visit to St. Thomas a pleasant one, the time passed rapidly, and when the arrival of the steamer Pelyo gave me warning that I must prepare for my departure, I would gladly have prolonged my stay for a number of days more, had it been possible to do so.

The time of leave-taking was come, however, and I was escorted on board the steamer by quite a large party, many of whom, as I said good by, eagerly requested me to correspond with them, and to keep them posted about my movements ; as they expected that I would scarcely be satisfied unless I undertook some strange adventures.

The steamer stopped at Porto Rico, but I did not go on shore, not liking the looks of the place. We only remained for a few hours to take in some freight and passengers, and then were off to sea again. Among the passengers was a young Spanish officer, Captain F. Martinez, whom I had met before, and who knew that I had served in the Confederate army. He came up to me, and gave an officer's salute, at which I laughed, and held out my hand to him, saying that the time for that sort of thing had passed. We then fell into an animated conversation about the war, and other matters ; and during the rest of the trip he paid me every attention in his power.

As we were promenading the deck together in the evening, he informed me that he was engaged to a young lady in Santiago de Cuba, and he was very solicitous that I should stop there and see her. I was not unwilling, as I had relations residing near the city whom I was anxious to visit ; and so I made arrangements for a return to another of the homes of my childhood.

A Visit to Santiago de Cuba.

When we reached Santiago, I called with Captain Martinez upon his betrothed, and was much pleased to see that he had made so excellent a choice. The young lady was very pretty and amiable, and belonged to a wealthy family.

Having notified my cousin, who was married to a Prussian gentleman, of my arrival, I went out to her home, about ten miles in the country, and remained a day or two with her.

In the city I was waited upon by many distinguished people, and was invited to dine at the mansion of the general in command of the Spanish forces. At this dinner my health was proposed, with some complimentary remarks, at which honor I was immensely flattered ; and after it was over, the company adjourned to the grand plaza, to listen to the military band, and to see the beauty and fashion of Santiago.

Santiago de Cuba is a very old town, and it has an extensive commerce. The chief exports are coffee, sugar, cigars, and fruit. The harbor is a fine one, and during the war it was a favorite resort for blockade-runners.

The day after the dinner at the general's mansion, I went on board the steamer and started for Havana. That city was reached in due time, and once more I found myself on familiar ground, and among friends who were ready to extend me a hearty welcome for the sake of old times.

My brother's family and other relatives resided outside of the walls. I sent them word of my arrival, but did not go to the house, on account of differences with my sister-in-law. During my stay in Havana my brother visited me frequently, as did also my niece, — my sister's daughter, — and my nephew, who acted as my escort to the theatre and other places.

In addition to my relatives, I had many acquaintances in Havana who were glad to extend the hospitalities of the place to me. Among others, General Juaquin Mansana, and the officers of his staff, were all warm friends of mine, and they seemed never to tire of paying me attentions. I was also acquainted with a great number of people with whom I had had confidential business relations during the war; and they, too, did what they could to make the time pass pleasantly.

Once more in Male Attire.

Shortly after I reached Havana, there was a grand religious festival, and, at the suggestion of General Mansana, I consented to appear in the procession in uniform. The general, enjoining me to keep the matter a secret, presented me with a handsome Spanish military suit. I attired myself in this, and arranging my disguise so that my most intimate friends would not know me, I took my place in the procession in a carriage beside Colonel Montero, which drove just behind that of the general.

The colonel especially requested me not to let the other officers and soldiers know who I was, as there might be some excitement created if any one suspected that a woman, disguised as an officer, was in the procession. I accordingly kept my secret, and was not recognized. During the day I several times passed quite close to Mr. Savage, the United States consul, and the members of his staff, and it amused the general greatly to see that they had not the slightest suspicion as to who I was. I was also introduced to a number of ladies as a young Spanish officer, who had been educated in England.

MATANZAS.

This plea was put in on my behalf, because my Spanish accent was none of the best, my long non-use of the language having caused me to lose the faculty of speaking it in such a manner as to do entire credit to my ancestry.

This procession took place on Friday, and General Mansana, as we were about starting out, told me that there was a steamer in the harbor with some emigrants on board, who were going to South America. He asked me if I would not see them, and, by relating my experiences, try and persuade them to return home again. This I promised to do.

In the evening, after the ceremonies were over, we went to the theatre, where we found quite a brilliant audience assembled. Before the performance was over, General Mansana said that he was hungry, and retired. The rest of the party remained until the curtain fell, when we went to a restaurant and had supper. After supper we drove to the Plaza de Armas, where a room had been assigned me in the palace, and I changed my costume as rapidly as I could, appearing once more in female attire.

ILLNESS OF GENERAL MANSANA.

As I was coming out, Colonel Montero met me in the hall, and said that the general had been taken quite sick. I asked if I could see him; and on a messenger being sent, word was conveyed to the colonel that the general wished to speak with him. He soon returned, and invited me to go into the sick chamber. The general was in bed, and the doctor was in attendance on him. He complained of severe cramps, but did not think that anything serious was the matter, and invited me to call on him the next morning, when he expected to be better.

After breakfast, the next morning, I went to the general's quarters; but the guard had orders not to admit any one. I sent in my card, however, and in a few moments the chief of staff came down and asked me to walk up to the reception-room. The surgeon in attendance made his appearance, and said that the general was worse instead of better; but that I could see him if I would promise not to speak. I accordingly went into the sick-room, and found the general looking very bad indeed. He smiled at me, and seemed to be glad that I had called. I then retired, as I found that I could be of no assistance, and went to see the emigrants.

I gave them an account of my experiences and observations in South America, and advised them, in the strongest possible terms, not to pursue their journey any farther, but to return home ; and, if they wanted to get away from the South, to go West. Some of them were much impressed with what I said, and came on shore to see me. I invited them to the hotel to take dinner, and went into the matter more particularly, showing them the great risks they would run, and the small chance they would have of establishing themselves in a satisfactory manner.

This interference on my part was bitterly resented by some of the leaders of the expedition, who expressed a desire that I should not come on board the steamer again. I had no wish to do this, having performed my duty, and I was willing now that they should take their own course and abide the consequences ; although I was sorry for some of the poor women, who I knew would regret not having followed my advice.

My expostulations proved of no avail, and the steamer sailed for South America, after her old, worn-out and worthless boiler had been patched. The vessel itself, like the boiler, was worn out, and they were obliged to put in at St. Thomas with her, and charter another boat. Some of the people, I believe, returned to the United States from St. Thomas, while the rest were glad to get back the best way they could, after a very brief experience of Para, the port for which they were bound. After reaching their destination, and endeavoring to effect a settlement, they very soon came to the conclusion that my advice was good.

On Sunday morning I learned, to my infinite sorrow, that General Mansana was dead ! The funeral took place the next day, and the body, having been embalmed, was carried through the streets, followed by his carriage, dressed in crape, and his favorite horse. The funeral was an imposing but sorrowful spectacle, for the general was a good man ; and although, like other public men, he had his enemies, he deserved and enjoyed a great popularity.

With this visit to Havana concluded my trip to South America and the West Indies. In some of its aspects it was far from being enjoyable ; and yet, on the whole, I managed to have a pretty good time, and I did not regret the journey. I had learned a great deal about a part of the world that it was worth while to know something about, and I had met a great many good friends whom I was exceedingly glad to

GOING INTO THE MOUNTAINS.

meet. Taking it all in all, the pleasures of the trip far more than counterbalanced its disagreeable features, and the main thing I had to complain of was, that I returned to the United States with a much lighter pocket-book than when I set out.

Shortly after Géneral Mansana's death I took the steamer for the United States, and was soon in New York. making but one brief stoppage at Matanzas on the way.

CHAPTER L.

ACROSS THE CONTINENT.

Across the Continent in search of a Fortune. — Omaha. — A Meeting with the veteran General Harney. — Governor C. asks me to introduce him to the General. — The Backwoodsman and the veteran Soldier. — The General induces me to tell the Story of my Career, and gives me some good Advice. — Off for a long Stage-coach Ride. — Rough Fellow-Travellers. — An unmannerly Army Officer taught Politeness. — Julesburg. — An undesirable Place for a permanent Residence. — An atrocious Murder. — More unpleasant travelling Companions. — Cheyenne. — A frontier Hotel. — Lack of even decent Accommodations. — An undesirable Bedfellow. — A Visit to Laporte. — Again on the Road. — A Water-Spout in Echo Canon. — The Coach caught in a Quicksand. — Mormon Hospitalities. — Salt Lake City. — Arrival at the City of Austin, Nevada.

N my return to the United States, I found the financial and political situations, especially at the South, more deplorable than ever. The era of true reconstruction seemed to be even farther off than it did when Lee surrendered, and the freedmen and carpet-baggers were having things completely their own way throughout the length and breadth of the late Confederacy. The people were oppressed and harried without mercy and without hope of redress by the black and white adventurers whom the fortunes of war had given the control of their affairs, and it was very apparent that there could be no revival of business worth speaking of while such a state of affairs existed. I greatly desired to settle in the South, but my own fortunes were at a low ebb, and I saw very plainly that if I expected to improve them it would be necessary to go elsewhere.

After giving the matter mature consideration, and making inquiries in a number of quarters, I determined to try my luck in the mining regions of the Pacific slope, as they seemed to hold out inducements that no other part of the country did. Apart, however, from all questions of pecuniary profit, I was animated by a strong desire to explore for myself a territory concerning which I had heard so much.

Having once resolved to cross the continent in search of a home, I did not stop to make many or very elaborate preparations, being too old a traveller to encumber myself with an excess of baggage. Purchasing a ticket for Omaha, I was soon on my way to that place by the Niagara, Fort Wayne, and Chicago route.

At Omaha I found snow on the ground, and the weather quite cold, too cold for one who had just come from a tropical climate to venture on a stage journey of many hundred miles, through the wilderness with no thicker or warmer clothing than that which I had with me. I was now in somewhat of a predicament, and began to regret that I had trusted quite so much to my travellers luck, and had not furnished myself with a more comfortable outfit.

I went to a dry goods store to purchase some woollen underclothing, but was unable to procure any. Fortunately, at the International Hotel, where I was stopping, there was a lady who intended to remain at Omaha for some time, and when she learned of my difficulties, offered to sell me hers. This offer I accepted without hesitation, and thus, by the merest chance, found myself equipped in proper style for my long and tedious journey and its necessary exposures to the weather.

RENEWING MY ACQUAINTANCE WITH GENERAL HARNEY.

At the International I had the good fortune to meet an old friend whom I had not seen for a number of years, and with whom it was a pleasure of the most genuine kind to renew my acquaintance. This was the veteran soldier, General W. S. Harney. He was, apparently, as glad to see me as I was to see him, and insisted on escorting me in to dinner, rather, I think, to the astonishment of some of the guests.

The general had a special table for himself and friends, and as we took our seats the eyes of everybody in the room were fixed on us. The dinner was a good one in its way, the bill of fare being largely made up of buffalo and antelope meat, and various kinds of game, and, as I was desperately hungry, I enjoyed it greatly. While we were dining the general chatted very freely, and narrated many curious incidents of his career in the army, and expressed his views on the late

war with the utmost freedom. He said that he was a true
Southerner in his sympathies, and that his extreme age alone
had prevented him from offering his services to the Confederacy. He, however, had helped the cause as much as
he could with his means and influence, and his only regret
was that he had not been able to take an active part in the
great conflict.

General Harney, it appears, had heard some mention of my
adventures, and was very anxious to ask me about them. He
did not, however, think that the dinner-table of the International Hotel of Omaha was exactly the suitable place to bring
up a subject about which I might have some hesitation in
speaking, and so deferred asking me any questions until a
better opportunity offered.

When we returned to the drawing-room I met some St. Louis
people whom I knew, and, engaging in conversation with them,
the general politely asked to be excused, and said that he
would like very much to have a conversation with me in his
private parlor after four o'clock.

When he was gone, Governor C., a tall, lank, shambling
backwoodsman, stalked up to me, and, in an awkward sort of a
way, introduced himself. He desired to make the acquaintance
of General Harney, and wished to know if I would not do the
" polite thing " for him, that is, give him an introduction to
the general. It struck me that, considering his official position, he might as well have introduced himself; but, as he
apparently did not know how to do this gracefully, I told him
that if the general was willing, he and the governor should
become acquainted after four o'clock, if he would meet me in
the drawing-room.

At the appointed hour I descended from my room, where I
had been arranging my toilet, and found this model specimen
of a statesman pacing uneasily backwards and forwards in
the hall, waiting for me. For a wonder, his hat was in his
hand instead of on his head, which I took to be an indication
that his mother had taught him one or two points of etiquette
in his youth, which he had managed to retain in his memory.

When he saw me, he came shambling up with that queer
gait of his, and said, with a grin, " I am on hand, you see ; we
western men are generally prompt when we have engagements with the fair sex."

" Yes, I see you are punctual; it is a good habit. I once
knew a man who made a large fortune by punctuality."

"Haw, haw, haw!" roared the governor, stretching his mouth nearly from ear to ear. "That's pretty good. All of us people out here are trying to make fortunes, and to make 'em quick; so I guess we'd better make a point of being punctual. Haw, haw, haw!"

I then led him to the general's private parlor without more ado, and gave the desired introduction.

This ceremony performed, the governor evidently did not know what to say or do, but after a moment's hesitation he extended his hand, and seizing that of the general, shook it as if he were working a pump-handle. The general, who understood what kind of a customer he. had to deal with, stood up and saluted his new friend with a characteristic gesture, and passed a few formal words with him. After a very brief conversation, the governor, impressed by the general's peculiar manner, and appreciating the force of the maxim that "two are company and three a crowd," said that he would give himself the pleasure of calling again, and bowed himself out.

When we were alone, in compliance with the general's request, I gave him an account of my adventures while acting as an officer in the Confederate army and as a secret-service agent. He appeared to be intensely interested, and frequently interrupted me to ask questions, or to express commendation. We conversed for two hours, when the announcement was made that supper was ready.

After supper we returned to the private parlor again, and I explained my plans for the future, and asked his advice. This he gave in the kindest manner; and, as his experience of affairs in the West, and his knowledge of the western country and people was most extensive, it was extremely valuable to me.

He said that I was a young woman yet, and that I would, undoubtedly, have offers of marriage; but, for my own sake, he hoped that if I did marry again, I would choose the right kind of a man, and not permit myself to fall into the hands of some adventurer. He thought that I was taking a great risk in going out to the mining region, and believed that it would be much better for me to settle in my native island, or else somewhere in the South. After all that I had done for the South, he said that I ought to be able to live there like a princess.

I told him, however, that the idea of receiving any assistance from the Southern people, situated as they were, was most abhorrent to me, and that, as I was young and in good health, I preferred to seek my own fortune and in my own way.

"Have you any arms?" he inquired.

"Yes, two strong ones," I replied, holding them out.

The general laughed, and said, "Yes, those will be of service to you if you are going to seek your fortune, but out among the mines you will need arms of another kind."

He then gave me a revolver, saying that I might have need for it, and also a buffalo robe and a pair of blankets, which he was certain I would find useful.

That night I slept but little, thinking of the general's advice, and of the unknown future before me. Towards morning I fell into something like a doze, but before I was fairly asleep I was called, and told that it was time to get ready for the stage.

I found General Harney up and waiting for me. We took breakfast together; and as I got up to go to the stage, he said, "Remember the advice of your best friend. I only wish that I was thirty-five years younger; you should not make this journey alone."

This was so flattering that I could not help permitting my wishes to run in the same channel.

Off for a Ride across the Plains.

After I was seated in the back of the coach, snugly wrapped up in my blankets and buffalo robe, a basket of eatables was handed in to me, and just as we were about to start the general leaned in, and, kissing me on the forehead, said, "Farewell, my child; if we should never meet again, God will take care of you;" and then turning to the driver, he told him to take good care of me, as I was a particular friend of his.

The driver said, "All right, sir; I will look after her;" and, cracking his whip, off we went, with nearly half the continent yet before me to be travelled before my journey should be ended.

My travelling companions were a rather rough set. The men on the front seat — who proved to be, what I took them for, mountaineers — had some whiskey, of which they partook rather more freely than was good for them, and they were a little inclined to be boisterous. They did not make themseives disagreeable to me, however, and were evidently inclined to be on their good behavior on account of a lady being present. In spite of their rough manners they were better gentlemen than the fellow who sat next to me, and who wore more stylish clothes than they did. They used no blackguard language or profanity, and showed a disposition to be attentive to me whenever they had an opportunity.

This other man, however, swore fearfully, and, in spite of my being on the seat with him, made use of language such as no true gentleman would degrade himself by using under any circumstances. At length, noticing the expression of disgust on my face, one of the mountaineers on the front seat, said, " See here, old chap, just remember there is a female aboard this stage-coach, will you ? "

The other replied, " I am a captain in the United States army, sir, and I wish you to respect my commission."

SIMMERING DOWN.

" I don't care a d—n who you are," said one of them, called Bill by his companions. " You simmer down mighty quick ; " and with that he took him by the throat and choked him till he was nearly black in the face.

This treatment was effectual, and he did simmer down ; and I was annoyed no more by him during the balance of the trip, while Bill and his friends earned my hearty respect despite their rough ways, and their over-fondness for whiskey-drinking.

I shall not attempt to describe the rough and toilsome ride over the plains. It was scarcely such a journey as one would make for a mere pleasure trip, and yet it was one worth making, if only for the reason that it afforded an opportunity to study, with some minuteness, a country that ere many years will probably be the seat of empire on this continent. Much of this land between Omaha and the Rocky Mountains is, undoubtedly, capable of great improvement under a proper system of cultivation, and that it ultimately will be settled and improved there can be no doubt. Just at present, however, there are more inviting regions to which settlers may be expected to flock in preference.

In course of time we arrived at one of the most remarkable products of Western civilization, — the town of tents, called Julesburg. I had seen a great deal of life, and a great deal of rough life; but when I beheld this place, I thought that I would prefer to be excused from choosing it as a permanent residence. In fact, a very brief stay in Julesburg was eminently satisfying, and I was quite content to leave it, with a hope in my heart that I would never be compelled to find myself within sight of it again.

The Delights of Julesburg.

Card-playing and whiskey-drinking, embellished with blasphemy, seemed to be the chief occupations of the Julesburg citizens, while murder was their commonest amusement. Many of these men had been brought up and educated in civilized communities, and knew what decent living was; and yet, so soon as they would get out here, they would throw off all restraint, and develop into worse savages than the red men. Such a collection of fiends in human shape as Julesburg was at the time I visited the place, I hope never to see again. The women were, if anything, worse than the men, and I did not meet more than two of my own sex while I was there who made the most distant claims to even common decency or self-respect.

The reckless bloodthirstiness of most of the men baffles description. Pistols and knives were produced on the slightest provocation, and often on no provocation at all, and no ties of friendship appeared to be strong enough to check the murderous propensities of some of the ruffians.

While standing in the board shanty, which was dignified by the name of a station, waiting for the stage to come up, I saw a fiend, in human shape, deliberately shoot down a young man of about twenty years of age. While his victim was writhing on the ground, he stepped up and fired two more shots into his prostrate body, and then, pulling out a huge knife, was about to cut his throat. Two of the murderer's comrades, who seemed to have a little humanity in them, now interfered, but only to have him turn upon them, with his eyes flashing with fury and his mouth full of oaths. I expected to see a general free fight, but the fellow, apparently satisfied with his bloody work, permitted himself finally to be persuaded to leave his victim and go away. I had witnessed many shocking scenes, but nothing so atrocious as this, and I was heartily glad when the stage shortly after drove up, and I was able to say farewell to Julesburg.

THE TRAPPER'S LAST SHOT.

It is due to these desperadoes, however, to say that they are not entirely without some good qualities. When they have any reason to think that a woman is really respectable they will protect her, and they are always free with their money, and ready to help any one who may be in distress. Their vices, however, so far outnumber their virtues, that their good deeds will scarcely count for much when they are called upon to settle their final accounts.

A HARD SET OF TRAVELLING COMPANIONS.

My companions of the stage coach, as we rolled out of Julesburg, were a rougher and more unpleasant set than the first party, and one of the most disagreeable among them was, I am ashamed to say, a woman. The men were tolerably full when we started, and we were scarcely off before they produced a bottle, and, after taking some of the fearful smelling whiskey which it contained, passed it around. I begged to be excused from partaking, but the other female passenger was not so fastidious, and she took a good drink every time it was handed to her. Her whiskey-drinking capacity was great, equal to that of any of the men.

The language this woman used was frightful, and she seemed to be unable to open her lips without uttering some blasphemous or obscene expression. Finally, having taken eight or nine big drinks from the bottle, she became stupidly drunk; and then, to vary the monotony of her proceedings, she produced a filthy pipe, which she filled with the blackest plug tobacco, and commenced to smoke. The fumes from this pipe were sickening to me, but I was willing to let her smoke in peace, for it at least kept her quiet, and soothed her until she fell into a deep and drunken sleep.

In this fashion we rolled along until we came to Cheyenne, which appeared to be quite a town, and a decided improvement on Julesburg. A number of moderately good-looking houses were already occupied, while others were in process of erection, and everything seemed to indicate that this, in a short time, was likely to be a really thriving place. The driver pulled up his horses, shouting, "Cheyenne House!" and out the occupants of the stage coach tumbled, the drunken woman and all, although she was so far gone that one of the men was forced to almost lift her out, to prevent her from falling flat on the ground.

37

The Cheyenne House, in spite of its rather imposing name, was, taking it all in all, the worst apology for a hotel I had ever met with in the course of my rather extensive travels. It was a frame building, of the rudest construction, while the lodging rooms — about eight by ten feet in size — were merely separated from each other by canvas partitions, which rendered any real privacy an absolute impossibility. The beds, or rather the bunks, in these rooms were large enough for two persons, and it was expected that two persons would occupy each of them, the luxury of a single bed being something unheard of in that locality. The mattresses and pillows were made of flour bags, — the miller's brands still on them, — stuffed with straw, and the coverlets were a pair of gray army blankets, with " U. S. A." plainly marked — undoubtedly the plunder of some rascally quartermaster who was bent on making his residence on the frontier pay him handsomely, even if he had to cheat the government.

On entering the hotel, we were ushered into a good-sized room, the floor being made of the roughest pine boards, from which the tar exuded in thick and sticky lumps. A large railroad stove, heated red hot, was in the centre of the room, and was surrounded by a motley crowd of men, who were sitting in every describable posture, smoking, chewing, spitting, and blaspheming in a style that indicated a total ignorance on their part of the fact that they had souls to be saved. It was impossible to get near the stove, although it was quite cold, for none of these men offered to move, and seemed to consider a poor little woman, like myself, as something entirely beneath their notice.

To my great satisfaction I did not have to remain long in this choice company, for supper was announced as ready within a few moments of our arrival. I requested to be shown the wash-room, and, on reaching it, found there a few old tin wash-basins, all of which were vilely dirty, a sardine box with a lump of home-made soap in it, and a vile-looking tow towel on a roller, which, in addition to being utterly filthy, did not have a dry place on it as big as half a dollar. Fortunately I had my own soap and towels in my satchel, and managed to perform my ablutions in a moderately satisfactory fashion. As for the basins and towels belonging to the place, I should not have hesitated to have used them, rough as they were, had they been moderately clean, for, on the frontier, we have no right to expect the accommodations of the Grand

Central Hotel of New York, or the Hotel de Louvre of Paris, and must expect to rough it. Still, even on the frontier, soap and water are cheap, and people who profess to keep hotels, and who take the money of the public, ought to make some effort to have things reasonably neat and tidy.

The dining-room was like the rest of the building, of the roughest possible construction. The table was covered with a dark colored oil-cloth, full of grease and dirt, and the supper, although it was such as a hungry traveller could have relished had it been properly prepared, was so uninviting in appearance that I could eat but little of it.

Being much fatigued, so soon as I had swallowed a few mouthfuls I sought my room, but, on arriving there, found, to my utter astonishment, that the woman who had come with me in the stage was occupying the bed. When I remonstrated, I was told that it was impossible for me to have a room to myself, and speedily found that I either had to submit or else pass the night in the parlor among the roughs congregated there. The alternative of sharing the bed with my fellow-traveller was preferable, for there at least I should be safe, as the room was over the landlord's private apartments, while the parlor being over the bar-room, was liable to have a bullet coming through the floor before morning.

I accordingly submitted to circumstances, but did not obtain much satisfaction from my couch, for, independently of its unpleasant human occupant, it was fairly alive with vermin. My companion, however, snored away in happy unconsciousness of any such disturbances, being stupefied with whiskey, and overcome by the fatigues of travel. She was evidently accustomed to this sort of thing, and was not disposed to be fastidious.

The next morning she was called to go in the stage. I having determined to remain for a day or two, was therefore to part company with her. She got up, and I was surprised to see that she had been in bed all night without removing any of her clothing. From under her pillow she took a belt containing a formidable-looking knife and a six-shooter, which she buckled around her waist, and as she did so, seeing that I was awake, asked, in a sarcastic sort of way, "How did you sleep?"

"Not much," I replied. "This kind of a bed don't suit me."

"Well, I've slept too d—d much," she said. "I am tired

yet; I'd as lives sleep on a board or a rock as on one of these d—d old straw beds!"

This was nice language for a woman to utter, but it was nothing in comparison to some that I had heard her use the day before. Soon, to my infinite relief, this delectable creature was gone, and I was left to myself.

After breakfast that morning, I inquired for the superintendent and road agent, Mr. Rube Thomas, but learned that he was not in the town. I then asked for Mr. J. Stewart, another road agent, and a very affable, obliging gentleman. This gentleman was, fortunately for me, in Cheyenne, and he waited on me very promptly when he received my message, and expressed himself as willing to do anything in his power to assist me.

I desired to go to Camp Davy Russell, and Mr. Stewart, in the kindest manner, said that he would procure a conveyance, and drive me there himself. He did so; and during our drive he took a great deal of pains to point out the features of interest, and to explain a number of useful points about the country, its people, and its prospects. On reaching the camp, I presented to General Stephenson a letter of introduction from General Harney, and was very kindly received by him. After a conference with General Stephenson, I returned to Cheyenne with Mr. Stewart, but found that, in consequence of the crowded condition of the stage, I would have to remain till the next day.

Mr. Stewart, knowing how uncomfortable I was at the hotel, then offered to take me to Laporte, and place me in rather better quarters. This kind offer I eagerly accepted, and soon found myself under the excellent care of Mrs. Taylor, the station-keeper's wife, and her sister, who did all that was in their power to make me comfortable, and to make the time pass agreeably. I passed several pleasant days with these hospitable ladies, employing my time in horseback riding, rambling over the mountains, gathering moss-agates, and visiting the wigwams of the Indians.

AMONG THE INDIANS.

The red men smiled on me in a rather disdainful sort of way, and evidently regarded me as an enemy. I wished most sincerely that I understood their language, if only for the purpose of explaining my friendly feelings towards them. I had

THE SOUTH PASS.

SHURTLEFF Del.

much more respect for these savages than I had for the ruffianly white men who were dispossessing them of their country. In one camp I did find an old woman who spoke English
quite well, and had a long conversation with her. She said
that vice was almost unknown among her people before the
white men came, but that they corrupted the young girls, and
supplied the men with whiskey, until now there was getting
to be fewer and fewer good Indians every day.

The coaches, at each trip, continued to be so crowded that
it was impossible for me to get a place in one, and, as I was
anxious to proceed, the agent at length arranged to put on an
extra for the accommodation of myself and several other travellers who also were waiting somewhat impatiently. When I
was about starting, Mr. Stewart gave me a letter of introduction to the Mormon proprietor of the Kimble House, in Salt
Lake City.

After a few days' travel we came to Echo City, at the
entrance of Echo Canon, where we met with an accident,
which might have had unpleasant consequences, but, as no
lives were lost, we regarded it as rather an agreeable variation of the monotony of our journey.

A water-spout in the mountains had flooded the road, and
the driver, in attempting to force his way through a rather
bad-looking place, managed to get the coach and the horses
stuck fast in a quicksand. The passengers were obliged to
swim out on the backs of the horses, and escaped with no
other damage than wet clothing. Fortunately, we were near
the house of a Mormon, who received us very hospitably, and
who, while his three wives were endeavoring to make us as
comfortable as circumstances would permit, went and got two
yoke of oxen and pulled the coach out.

First Acquaintance with the Mormons.

I had heard so much against the Mormons that I was under
the impression they were all thieves and cutthroats. I confess
that I was most agreeably disappointed in them from this, my
first acquaintance, to the time of my taking a final leave of
Utah. The homes, farms, dress, and behavior all indicated
that they were a hard-working, industrious people, while they
appeared to be entirely free from many of the worst vices of
the Gentiles.

While stopping at this house in Echo Canon, I ventured to

make a few inquiries about their customs and belief, which were very politely answered; and I was in the midst of a very interesting conversation with one of the wives, a woman of about fifty-five, when I was interrupted by the driver calling upon me to get into the coach.

The rain having freshened the air somewhat, I asked the driver to permit me to sit with him outside as we went through the canon, in order that I might see the scenery. He consented, and assisted me to a seat on the box, and as we passed through the canon, he explained the points of interest to me. He was quite a handsome young fellow, and very intelligent.

On entering the Bear River Valley, my eye met, on all sides, little white cottages or neat log houses, surrounded by well-cultivated and well-watered farms and orchards, where not many years before was but a burning plain, covered with sage bushes, and the home of the Ute Indian, the buffalo, the elk, the antelope, the coyote, and the silver gray fox. Through the untiring industry and good management of people who had been driven from their homes in Ohio, Illinois, and Missouri, this desert had been transformed into the paradise I beheld. The Mormons fled here to escape persecution, desiring only to get as far away from their enemies as possible, and after many years of toil and hardship they achieved results of which they had a right to be proud, and which entitled them to a more kindly consideration than had been accorded them when residing in the States.

Having passed the Bear River Valley, we were soon in the great metropolis of Mormondom, and driving through wide streets and avenues, past houses that were evidently the abodes of thrifty well-to-do people, the coach at length drew up before the door of the Kimble House.

The proprietor came out, and ushered us up stairs to the parlor, a large, airy room, plainly but comfortably furnished, and soon a little girl came and said that she would show me my room. The furniture in this was somewhat primitive in its style, but everything was neat and clean, and the accommodations, if not exactly such as the Fifth Avenue Hotel offers, were all that any reasonable person had a right to expect.

So soon as I was fairly settled in the hotel, I presented the proprietor the letter of introduction from the road agent at Cheyenne, and had quite a long conversation with him. He gave me much good advice about my future movements, and seemed disposed, in every way, to be as kind and obliging as he could. From him I learned that there were a number of old Confederate soldiers in the city and vicinity ; but as I was anxious to get to the Eldorado, where I expected to make my fortune, with as little delay as possible, I made no attempt to find any of them.

After taking a rest for a day or two in Salt Lake City, I again started on my journey westward. At Ruby Valley, in Nevada, I met a gentleman who was engaged in mining operations, and he advised me strongly to go to the Reese River gold regions. I was not greatly prepossessed with him, and yet he was certainly a man of intelligence and cultivation, and, as what he told me only served to confirm what I had heard from other persons, I concluded to take his advice. On arriving at Austin, a new city in the mountains, near the Reese River, I accordingly left the stage and took lodgings at the Exchange Hotel, which was kept by a Slavonian by the name of Mollinely.

CHAPTER LI.

MINING IN UTAH AND NEVADA. — THE MORMONS AND THEIR COUNTRY.

HE sleeping apartment assigned me at Austin was not the most agreeable, being next to a room occupied by some drunken fellows, who kept up a terrible noise nearly all night; and, as I thought that most likely I would have to put up with this sort of thing nearly all the time if I remained in the hotel, I determined to look for lodgings elsewhere. A gentleman to whom I spoke about the matter said, that he knew of a private house where rooms were sometimes to be had, and offered to go and see if I could obtain accommodation there.

While he was gone, the chambermaid brought from the room next to mine two pairs of pistols, two large knives, and a razor, and informed me that their owner was a noted desperado, called Irish Tom, and that he had killed two men.

I had some curiosity to see this individual, but did not care particularly to make his acquaintance. My curiosity was soon gratified, for he came to the parlor inquiring for his weapons. Instead of being angry with the chambermaid for having taken them from his room to show them to me, he seemed to feel rather complimented that I should feel an interest in them and him. He was a tall, good-looking Irishman, with a very pleasant face, and had as little of the ruffian in his appearance

584

as any man I had met on the frontier. I was informed that he never attempted to hurt well-behaved people, and that he often submitted to the grossest kind of insults from some of his intimates. Men of his acquaintance had been known to slap him in the face, and he would take no notice, but walk away as if nothing had happened. With others, however, he would have no mercy, but would produce a pistol or knife at the slightest provocation. Tom was rather noted for his polite bearing towards the ladies, which I considered as an evidence that he was not as bad, by any means, as he might have been.

My friend, who had gone to look for lodgings for me, returned, and said that he had secured me a very good room. I accordingly left the hotel, and had reason to congratulate myself in my change of quarters. My landlady was a Pennsylvanian, and was disposed to do all in her power to make me comfortable, and to assist me in carrying out the object I had in view in taking up my residence in Austin. She introduced me to a restaurant-keeper, who agreed to supply me with my meals, and also to a number of the prominent people of the place —. the judge, the doctor, the Methodist minister, and others.

QUEER PEOPLE.

The aristocracy of Austin was made up of an odd lot of people, who, however, had the best possible opinion of themselves, even if they did use bad grammar, swear hard, and drink unlimited quantities of whiskey. I, however, always had a happy faculty of adapting myself to circumstances, and I was soon on excellent terms with most of my new acquaintances.

Among my friends was an individual of about sixty years of age, who, from his conversation, seemed to have been at one time accustomed to mingle in really good society. He was a widower, and was extensively engaged in mining operations. I had not known him more than a couple of days before he asked me to marry him, and offered to give me an interest in his mines if I would accept him. I thought that this was a rather abrupt style of courtship, and felt constrained to decline. He took my refusal good-naturedly enough, and was evidently not sufficiently in love with me to break his heart because he could not get me.

Subsequently I met a gentleman who paid me attention, and to whom I became sincerely attached. We were married in a very quiet manner; for neither of us desired, any more than we could help, to be made the subjects of the gossip of a mining town.

Shortly after my marriage I made a flying trip to New Orleans, for the purpose of seeing my brother, and some of my relatives. Immediately a rumor was started that I had run away; and when I returned I found that all kinds of stories had been set afloat about me. My re-appearance, however, set them all at rest; and, as my husband and myself zealously attended to our own business, and let that of other people alone, we were permitted to dwell together in peace.

When I got back from New Orleans, we purchased a snug little stone house, and I devoted myself to advancing my husband's interests as much as possible, and to making our home comfortable and attractive.

My husband, for a time, prospered in his mining operations; and, although there were some envious people who spoke ill of him and of me, we succeeded in gaining the esteem of such of our neighbors as were worth knowing, and did not disturb ourselves about what might be said of us by those who were disposed to speak evil.

The city of Austin, which is near the centre of Nevada, at this time (1868) contained from fifteen hundred to two thousand inhabitants, most of whom were in some way connected with the mines. There were about a dozen stores, one hotel, four or five lodging-houses, half a dozen restaurants, more drinking-saloons than I ever undertook to count, Catholic and Methodist churches, a Masonic hall, and five quartz crushing-mills, only one, however, of which was in operation.

Mining Speculations and Swindles.

There was any amount of speculation in mines and mining stocks, and any amount of the worst kind of swindling going on all the time. Some of the mines were good ones; but others were mere pretences, and were worth nothing at all. Many of these bogus mines were sold to eastern capitalists by experts, who made a specialty of working frauds of this description.

It was while residing in Austin that I first heard the expression "salting" applied to mines, and learned what it meant. Salting, however, was only one of a number of frauds that were practised every day.

SCENES AT EL DORADO.

It grieved me greatly that my husband should be compelled to associate, and to transact business with such scoundrels as the men about him. His partner, especially, was as worthless a scamp as there was in the district; and, as I felt certain that he would in time be held responsible for some of the doings of this fellow, I persuaded him to give up mining, and to seek a home in some locality that offered greater advantages for living, as decent people ought to live, than Austin did.

My husband accordingly sold out his interest in the mines, and we removed to California, where we purchased a lovely place in the Sacramento valley. This was just such a home as I had always sighed for, and I was perfectly happy in the idea of settling down, and living a quiet contented life for the rest of my days.

It was not to be, however. My husband had the gold fever, and he found it impossible to be satisfied with what would have satisfied most reasonable people. He was restless and irritable, and was all the time anxious to be off to the mines again.

We had not been settled in our new home more than a few months, when, to my infinite regret, he insisted on starting off for the new Eldorado in Utah. He then passed a year prospecting in Bingham Canon, Camp Floyd, Eureka, and Tintic, and expended all his money without achieving anything. He was then compelled to accept the foremanship of a mine in the Lucine district, and after he had been working in that capacity for some time, was promoted to superintendent.

One of the members of the firm by whom my husband was employed was a gentleman, and was honest, as honesty went in that region. The other was a drunkard, and a fraud of the worst kind. This man, some time before this, had started a settlement, which he named after himself, and had built a smelting furnace, all for the purpose of selling some bogus mines. He also perpetrated an infamous swindle on some English capitalists, in relation to a mine in Nevada.

A "SALTED" MINE.

The way the thing was done was this, and it will serve as an illustration of the kind of swindles that were constantly being perpetrated in connection with mines.

He sent to Virginia and purchased some rich ore from the Comstock mine, for the purpose of salting the mine which he wished to sell. This was a silver-bearing lead, but there was not enough metal in the ore to pay for getting it out. It was necessary, however, in order to effect a sale, to give the impression that it was very rich. The smelter, therefore, run out about three thousand bars, which were supposed to be silver, but which were in reality half lead.

These were hauled to the depot, where the persons who proposed to purchase could see them; but after dark they were taken back to the mine, and the next day the teams took them to the depot again. This was done for three successive days, and the Englishmen, seeing such enormous amounts of metal, became greatly excited, and offered a million dollars for the mine. The speculator refused, and then they offered a million and a half. This offer he closed with, and a day was set for the inspection of the mine.

The "dumps" were thoroughly salted, and arrangements were made for the assayer and mining expert to be in attendance. The proposed purchasers had their expert with them, a German professor from Freiburg. This professor had a large sack with him in which to put samples of ore, and when going down into the mine he gave it to one of the men to carry for him.

The speculator had on a large blanket-coat, with immense pockets in it, which were filled with rich ore. The man with the sack was also provided with a small quantity, to be used in case of emergency. Every time the professor put a piece of ore in the sack, so soon as his back was turned the speculator or his man would drop in some of the rich ore. The result was, that when the assays were made, they rose from three thousand to fifteen thousand dollars to the ton.

The Englishmen were in ecstasies, and insisted on the contract being drawn up immediately. Part of the purchase money was then paid down, and the rest was to be forthcoming in thirty days. When the thirty days expired the purchasers took possession, only to find that they had been duped in a most outrageous manner. By the time the discovery of the fraud was made, however, the swindlers had fled, and the Englishmen had nothing to do but to return to London with empty pockets.

One of them, however, tried his luck again in Little Cottonwood, in the Wellington district, but with no better success.

My husband was at this time superintendent of one of the Wellington mines, and I consequently had ample opportu-

DOWN THE SIERRA NEVADAS.

nities to study mining life, and to become acquainted with the numerous frauds that were going on. I was also thrown in a good deal with the Mormons, and was able to study their characters and manners.

Little Cottonwood canon is about twelve miles long, is very narrow, and very deep. A stream runs down the middle of it, which is very swift in the months of June and July, when it is full, on account of the melting of immense quantities of snow on the mountains.

THE GOLD REGION OF NEVADA.

Tannersville is a town, or settlement, named in honor of a woman who kept a hotel or stage-station there. There was a mill and smelter at that place at the time of which I am writing.

Alta City, at the foot of the two canons, — Big and Little Cottonwood, — is a town of rather more importance. When I was there it had three stores, a hotel, a couple of lodging-houses, a livery stable, and a large number of drinking-saloons. The dwelling-houses were mostly very small, and were entirely invisible in winter, being covered by the snow. The snow usually commences to fall about the middle of September, but I have seen it in August. During the winter many parts of the canon are impassable, except by the use of sledges and snow-shoes, and there is constant danger from avalanches, which carry everything before them.

The Wellington mine lost its foreman and a miner through an avalanche while I was there, and many men have lost their lives in this canon, their bodies remaining buried beneath the snow until spring.

I doubt whether many of the mines in this district will ever be successfully worked. The Emma is one of the best, and I think could be made to pay, if judiciously operated. This mine is situated in the side of the mountain, and is almost perpendicular. On looking at it, it is impossible not to wonder how the owners ever reached it, or are able to work it. I believe that there is an immense lead of silver here which will yet be unearthed.

This part of the country offers a rich field for the botanist and naturalist. The flowers are in the greatest profusion, and are of every imaginable hue. They grow from the mouth of the canon to some of the highest points on the mountains.

The wild cherry, the whortleberry, the serviceberry, the thimbleberry, and the dewberry are very abundant.

On the very summits of this immense range will be found clear blue lakes, filled with spotted trout. How they have managed to get there is more than I can tell.

When the highest points are reached, if one looks aloft the broad-winged eagle may be seen wheeling in the air; while upon the ground are the beautiful mountain squirrels, busily engaged in gathering their winter stores. I have often sat for hours and watched these nimble little animals. There are as many as six different varieties of squirrels, some of which are not larger than mice, while others, the size of the common gray squirrels of the Eastern States, are beautifully striped, and vary in color from light gray to dark brown. The greatest enemies of these harmless animals are the eagle and the mink.

Large rats abound in the woods, as do also the brown weasels. These last-named animals are about eighteen inches in length from the nose to the tip of the tail. The head is small, and the eyes, which are very prominent, are of a soft, lustrous black. The weasels are very cunning, and are especially destructive to the mice and squirrels. I have seen two old ones kill as many as six or eight mice in a day, in my home, and carry them, one at a time, across the ravine to their young in the woods. While carrying a mouse, however, should a squirrel appear, the weasel will throw down the mouse, and go after this fresh game, and then come back and get the mouse.

To my great satisfaction, my husband at length got tired of working in this region, and under so many disadvantages, and concluded to try his fortune elsewhere. He had quite a notion of New Mexico, which he thought held out inducements for fortune-seekers; but I was beginning to be out of the notion of the whole business, and was anxious to be among a different class of people from those who, for the most part, make up the population of the mining districts. There was so much outrageous swindling going on when we were there residing, that I was disposed to regard almost any move as a good one, and very willingly turned my face eastward again.

We went first to Salt Lake City, where we remained for some time, and I consequently had excellent opportunities afforded me for becoming intimately acquainted with a number of Mormons, and of learning a great deal about their religion, and their manners and customs.

AMONG THE MORMONS.

The lady with whom I boarded had been an early convert to Mormonism, had resided at Nauvoo at the time the exodus was determined upon, and had been one of the band of emigrants, who, fleeing from persecution, had sought a home among the mountains of Utah. She had been one of twelve wives, and was a strong advocate of polygamy. When she saw that I really desired to know something about Mormonism, not from mere curiosity, but from a genuine wish to gain information that would enable me to form an impartial judgment, she took great pleasure in answering all my questions, and in providing me with facilities for pursuing my inquiries.

She was a very intelligent woman, and her account of the persecutions to which the Mormons were subjected at Nauvoo, and the suffering and hardships they endured during the long and toilsome journey to a place where they hoped to be forever undisturbed, was most interesting. She had quite an extensive library, to which I had free access, and she took a great deal of pains in directing my reading, and in explaining points which I found to be obscurely stated in the books.

As I was the only boarder in the house, my husband being away in the canon most of the time, we were naturally thrown much together, and after we became intimate she took me into her confidence to an extent that she would not have done had we been comparative strangers.

Among other things, she showed me her Endowment robes, which she wore when she became a member of the Mormon church. This dress consisted of a linen garment, something like a pair of drawers. It was very full, and had a body and sleeves attached. Over one side a heart-shaped piece was cut out, and the edges worked with a button-hole stitch. Curious figures were also worked on the sleeves and on the left hip. The robe proper was something like a priest's surplice. The slippers, which, like the rest of the dress, were of linen, resembled moccasons. A tall pointed cap, with holes for the eyes, which is drawn down over the face during the ceremonies, completed this singular attire.

The decorations worn by the men while taking the oath were also shown to me. They consisted of a regalia of Mazarine blue silk, with a representation of the Temple of Solomon in the centre, and a heart, surrounded by a number of emblems similar to those in use by the Masons. She told me that the oath was very similar to that which the Masons used, and that it was administered to both men and women.

POLYGAMY.

During my residence in Salt Lake City, I became acquainted with Brigham Young, and a number of the bishops, and other prominent Mormons, and I formed a very high opinion of them. There certainly has seldom or never been so well-governed a people as the Mormons were before the Gentiles found them out, and insisted on intruding on their domain. As for polygamy, it is a part and parcel of their religion, and has the sanction of the same Bible that the Christians, both Catholic and Protestant, acknowledge; and I cannot see why the Mormons should not be permitted to hold their religious beliefs the same as other sects. I do not believe in polygamy myself, but if other people think it is right, and choose to practise it, that is their business and not mine.

Whether polygamy, however, be right or wrong, there is this to be said in favor of the Mormons. The men marry according to the custom of their church, and they acknowledge and provide for the women who bear them children,— which is a good deal more than a great many people who denounce polygamy and Mormonism do. The Mormon religion professes to be based upon the Bible, what they call " The Book of Mormon " being merely a later revelation; and I have heard as good, sound, practical sermons preached in Salt Lake City by Mormons who worked hard all the week earning bread for their families, as I ever heard anywhere.

I have listened to the preaching of nearly all the principal bishops, and I never heard any of them utter a word that was not good doctrine, calculated to make men and women better and more honorable in all their dealings with their neighbors. Most of these sermons were in a much more practical vein than some I have heard in fashionable churches a good many hundred miles eastward of Salt Lake City; but I liked them none the less for' that; and I respected the preachers, for, so far as I was able to see, they practised exactly what they preached, and did not have one religion for the Sabbath and another for working days.

SALT LAKE CITY.

I never saw or heard of a gambling den or a drinking saloon being kept by a Mormon; and many of the degrading vices which flourish in Gentile communities, were absolutely unknown in Salt Lake City when the Mormons were its only residents. Even now, the standard of morality is higher in this and other Mormon towns than it is in any place that I know anything about between Omaha and the Pacific coast; while in real thrift and industry the Mormons are out of all comparison superior to their Gentile neighbors.

These people went to Utah, hoping and expecting to separate themselves from the rest of the world, in order that they might worship God in their own way without molestation, and they ought to be permitted to do it. Through many years of toil and indefatigable industry they transformed the barren wilderness into a blooming Paradise. Conducting the water down from the mountains, they succeeded in bringing the sandy plains, covered with sage bushes, under cultivation, and what was once a dreary desert, is now fertile fields, yielding luxuriant harvests, or orchards bearing the most delicious fruits.

A MORMON HOUSEHOLD.

During my stay in Salt Lake Valley, I boarded for several months in the house of Bishop Nilo Andrews, at Sandy Station, and was on very intimate terms with five of his six wives. They were all smart women, and their children were, without exception, fine looking, strong, hearty, and intelligent. The bishop was passionately fond of his children, and took the greatest pains to have them well educated. His daughters he escorted to all public gatherings and entertainments that it was proper for them to attend, and did all in his power to make life enjoyable for them.

The bishop was about sixty years of age, and was as hale and hearty as a man of thirty. He was not a bit afraid of work, and could get through an amount of it that would have shamed many a younger man. I never want to receive better hospitality than I did from him; and when he found that ·I was desirous of obtaining correct information about the Mormons, he expressed himself as willing to tell me anything I wished to know.

He was quite a learned man, and like all the Mormons I ever met, was thoroughly posted in the Bible and in biblical his-
38

tory, and was able to explain, in a satisfactory manner, the points of coincidence and differences between Mormonism and other religious systems. The bishop told me that the greatest pains was taken in the matter of religious instruction, and that men and women who could not read, and even quite young children, often knew most of the Bible by heart.

THE MORMON SECTS.

There are a number of sects among the Mormons, between which some jealousy seems to exist. Of these, the Brighamites, the Gadites, and the Josephites are the principal. What the differences between them are I never could exactly make out. Another matter I never clearly understood, was the status of sealed wives. I could not comprehend by what theory a Mormon could marry a widow for her lifetime, while all her children born of the second marriage would belong to the first husband in the next world.

The City of Salt Lake is located on the banks of the River Jordan, a stream which connects Great Salt Lake and Utah Lake. It is about three miles distant from the mountains, which lie to the eastward. The streets are very wide, and are, many of them, very handsome in appearance, being lined with cotton-wood and sycamore trees, and having streams of water running through them. This last is a specially attractive feature.

Most of the houses are well built, and are very neat and pretty, being supplied with all the conveniences and comforts reasonable people can desire. Each house has a small garden and orchard attached, which are invariably kept in the best possible order.

Brigham Young's residence is of stone, and is surrounded by a wall. Over the entrace is a bee-hive, emblematic of industry, and over the large gate is a spread eagle. The house is plain, and not at all pretentious, but it is neat and substantial looking. The walls of the office are ornamented with some fine portraits of Joseph Smith and other Mormon celebrities.

Brigham Young is a light-complexioned man, rather inclined to corpulency, but strong and hearty in spite of his years and the labors he has undergone. He has a large, full head, a keen blue eye, and an easy, affable manner that is very engaging. I found him to be a pleasant, genial gentleman, with an excellent fund of humor, and a captivating style of conversation.

The great Tabernacle, which will be used for the purpose of worship until the Temple is completed, is an immense building, which will seat fifteen thousand people. The pews are built in tiers, so that each person in the building can have a view of the altar. The altar is a large and imposing structure. In its rear is the organ and a space for the choir. This organ is the second largest in the world. It was built entire in Salt Lake City. The work on the Temple is going on all the time, slowly but surely, and the expectation is to have it finished by the time of Christ's second coming. He will then dedicate it, and it will be the great religious centre of the world, where all true Christians will come and worship.

Every ward of Salt Lake City has its public school, and efforts are made to give every child a good practical education. There are four large hotels, three banks, three printing offices, a large, well-regulated hospital, numerous manufactories of various kinds, and several flouring and other mills.

There are several large towns in the neighborhood of the city, and new settlements are continually springing up. Springville, about fifty miles to the south-east, is a very beautiful place. At the time of which I am writing a railroad down the centre of the valley was in operation, and two others were in contemplation.

The mineral wealth of Utah is practically inexhaustible. Iron, gold, silver, copper; lead, salt, alum, gypsum, soda, arsenic, and slate abound in immense quantities.

Salt Lake is a very large body of water, of a much greater specific gravity than that of the ocean. No living thing can exist in it, and in its deepest parts no soundings have ever been able to find a bottom. There are three islands near the middle of the lake, which are said to be rich in metals.

In the southern part of Utah, called Dixie, cotton and cattle are raised. On the banks of the Sevier River are very fine grazing lands. The Mormons claim that there have been some discoveries of gold and silver made in this section.

Taking it all in all, my residence in Salt Lake city was both pleasant and profitable to me; and when the time came for me to say farewell to my Mormon friends, I did so with many regrets, and with many wishes that they might escape persecution from their enemies. I could not agree with all of their religious doctrines, but I learned to regard them as an industrious, hard-working, and honest people, and as, consequently, deserving of respect and sympathy.

After a sojourn of a number of months in Utah, I prepared to journey eastward again, having scarcely bettered my fortunes, but having seen some varieties of life worth seeing, and having gained some valuable experiences, not the least valuable of which was, that mining speculations are things that people who have consciences should have as little as possible to do with.

A BUFFALO HUNT.

CHAPTER LII.

COLORADO, NEW MEXICO, AND TEXAS. — CONCLUSION.

Denver. — Pueblo. — Trinidad. — Stockton's Ranche. — A Headquarters for Desperadoes. — Cattle Stealing. — A private Graveyard. — Maxwell's Ranche. — Dry Cimmaron. — Fort Union. — Sante Fe. — The oldest City in New Mexico. — A wagon Journey down the Valley of the Rio Grande. — Evidences of Ancient Civilization. — Fort McRae and the Hot Spring. — Mowry City. — The Gold Mining region of New Mexico and Arizona. — El Paso. — A thriving Town. — A stage Ride through Western Texas. — Fort Bliss. — Fort Quitman and Eagle Spring. — The Leon Holes. — Fort Stockton. — The Rio Pecos. — A fine Country. — Approaching Civilization. — The End of the Story.

ITH my little baby boy — born during my sojourn in Salt Lake City — in my arms, I started on a long journey through Colorado, New Mexico, and Texas, hoping, perhaps, but scarcely expecting, to find the opportunities, which I had failed to find in Utah, Nevada, and California, for advancing my pecuniary interests. Apart, however, from profits that might result from it, the journey would be worth making for its own sake, for, from what I had heard of this section of the Western country, great things were to be expected of it in the near future ; and the satisfaction of seeing and judging of the nature and extent of its resources would amply repay me for the trouble of making a trip through it.

After leaving Salt Lake City, the first place of importance reached was Denver, Colorado, on the Platte River. This I found to be a well built and very thriving town, of about eight or ten thousand inhabitants. Among its public institutions were a branch of the United States Mint, and several hotels, churches, and banks. Denver was, until the completion of the Pacific Railroad, the chief trading centre in this region. Since the completion of the railroad, however, its importance in comparison with other places has, in some degree diminished; but as the country becomes settled, it may be expected to increase in wealth and population, and it will probably, ere a great many years, be one of the finest cities in the whole West.

Among the new towns which have recently sprung up in Colorado is Pueblo, nearly two hundred miles south of Denver, and the terminus of the narrow gauge railroad which taps the Pacific Railroad at Cheyenne. This town takes its name from the Pueblo Indians, who are much farther advanced in civilization than most of the aborigines, and who deserve much credit for their industrious habits and their efforts to prosper.

Trinidad, still farther to the south, is an old Mexican town, and is the centre of an extensive cattle and sheep raising country. There is a constant war going on in this region on the subject of stock between Americans, Mexicans, and Indians. Cattle thieves, who steal stock from Texas and Mexico, rendezvous near Trinidad, and, as they are not particular whom they plunder, so long as they are able to do it with impunity, their presence is anything but agreeable to people who desire to live reasonably peaceable lives, and to get along by minding their own business.

A Colorado Ranche.

Some distance from Trinidad is Stockton's Ranche, in the midst of a wild, unsettled country, and the only house within a circuit of many miles' ride. This is a noted headquarters of the desperadoes who infest New Mexico and Lower Colorado. The building is two stories in height, is quite large, and contains a store and drinking-saloon. On a mound above the house is a graveyard, in which twenty-one people have been buried. Only three out of this number had died natural deaths, the others having been shot down like dogs, for some real or fancied offences. Stockton has killed several men himself, while many more have fallen by the hands of his confederates.

Stockton was a small man, restless in his movements, and with a fierce black eye. He had a wife and a very interesting family, for whom I felt much sympathy when I learned what a desperate character he was. His wife, who seemed to be a very nice, clever woman, was much troubled with regard to him. She told me that she was always uneasy about him when he was away from home, and that, at times, even when he was sleeping in his bed, she was harassed with fears lest some one should come and take him for the purpose of shooting him.

While I was at the Ranche, Stockton sent out some of his men to get some cattle at Maxwell's Ranche, which he claimed as his. His instructions were to take the cattle at all hazards, and to capture the men who were supposed to have stolen them, dead or alive. The herders were generally selected for their utter recklessness, and as a rule they cared neither for God nor man, but would shoot down any one who offended them, without pity or remorse. Most of these herders are very young men, and are generally athletic and handsome. Some of them, from their appearance and conversation, appear to have been well reared ; and if asked why they have come to the frontiers to lead such a wild life as this, they will frankly say, that they are trying to make their fortunes, and that they expect to do it in a couple of years. They are usually disappointed in these expectations ; and those who do not give up in disgust, and return to civilization, fall into the habits of the country, and soon become as finished desperadoes as those who have been born and brought up there. Some of them, however, engaged in this kind of life because they really like it, and because they feel a certain freedom and unrestraint in roaming about in the open air.

LAWLESSNESS.

Whenever a freight train, either American or Mexican, passed, Stockton would buckle on his belt of six-shooters, and, with a big negro, armed in a similar manner, as his body-guard, step out into the road with a roll of brands in one hand and a pistol in the other, and inspect the brands on each head of cattle. Should the brands compare with his, he would take them from the train, and let the freighters make out the best way they could. He has many times stopped and broken up freight trains bound for Sante Fe and the interior, to the infinite injury of the merchants who depend upon the freighters for their goods. The traders, however, appear to be powerless before this and other desperadoes, and the government which takes their taxes, under the plea of affording them protection, ought certainly to do something to prevent them from being at the mercy of men who recognize no laws but their own fierce wills.

On one occasion Stockton, through some of his employees, duped two men from Maxwell's Ranche, who, he asserted, had stolen cattle from him. When he had them in his power he started off, leaving the impression on the minds of their friends that he intended to take them to Trinidad, for the purpose of delivering them up to the sheriff. Instead of doing this, however, he carried them into a side road and there shot them, leaving their bodies to be devoured by the coyotes, or, perhaps, buried by some casual passer-by. For this deed he was arrested and lodged in jail. He was liberated, however, almost immediately, without even the form of a trial, the officers being too much afraid of him and of his confederates to detain him.

The occurrences which I have related will illustrate the kind of life that is led in the cattle raising country of Colorado, New Mexico, South-western Kansas, and Texas. I named this place Bandit House, and the ford in the stream near by, Dead Man's Crossing, — which are expressive and appropriate, if not poetical.

A Wealthy Ranchero.

Beyond Stockton's is General Maxwell's Ranche. Maxwell is the wealthiest American in Southern Colorado. I believe he got his start in life by marrying a Mexican woman, who inherited an extensive Spanish grant. Maxwell has quite a large family, and he bears a better reputation than do most of the old settlers. He is a great gambler, and is much interested in horse-racing, but is disposed to be kind and hospitable to strangers.

Crossing quite an extensive piece of country, the Dry Cimmaron is reached. Here some enterprising Englishmen, headed by a Mr. Read, have taken up a large tract of land, and have established a colony. They have built a very neat little town, and when I passed through there, their affairs seemed to be in a thriving condition. The town is located on a rather high and dry elevation, which takes its name from the scarcity of water in the branch of the Cimmaron River, which runs by it.

Dry Cimmaron was for a time a stopping-place for the stages from the Elizabethtown mines, which connected with the Southern lines. It is on a more direct route for the cattlemen and freighters; but, although it has plenty of wood, it is

BRANDING CATTLE, STOCKTON RANCH.

open to objection as a cattle and freight station, on account of the insufficiency of the water supply.

A FRONTIER FORT.

The next point of interest is Fort Union, in New Mexico, about sixty miles south of Dry Cimmaron. This fort, which, at a distance, looks like a small city, is built of adobe, or white bricks, and is plastered inside and out with gypsum, which gives it a rather dazzling-white appearance. The garrison consists of five companies of infantry and one of cavalry. Fort Union is the central supply depot for the frontiers, and is a very important position. Some distance off, in the mountain, is a steam saw-mill, which supplies all the lumber used in and about the fort. This saw-mill is protected by an armed guard of soldiers. There is also a blacksmith shop, a wagon shop, a carpenter shop, and a post office. Each company has a garden and several cows, and the men seem to take a great deal of pride in keeping everything in the best possible order. This fort and its surroundings do much credit to the officers who planned them, and who have succeeded in making such a nice-looking place out of a frontier military post.

From Fort Union to Santa Fe the traveller passes over some rough country. Santa Fe is the oldest city in New Mexico, and one of the oldest in the country. It has been, and undoubtedly for a long time will be, an important centre of trade between the United States and Mexico. The ground in and about the city is all owned by Mexicans, or people of Mexican descent, who refuse to sell on any terms, but who will lease to Americans. The houses are chiefly one and two story structures, built of adobe, and covered with tile or thatch. They are cool, pleasant, and comfortable in summer. The hotel, which is kept by an American, but which is owned by a Mexican, who has refused to permit any alterations or improvements to be made, stands on the corner of the plaza, or great public square, which was laid out by the founders of the city. During the war, the Union soldiers insisted on erecting a monument on the plaza to the memory of their fallen comrades. This gave great offence to the old residents, who regarded the structure as an injury to the appearance of their public square; but as they were powerless to prevent its erection, they were compelled to submit with the best grace they could. As the monument is not a very elegant-looking affair, it is not surprising that those who were not interested in it could not bring themselves to admire it.

So old a city as Santa Fe, of course, has an interesting history, but a recital of the events which have made it famous is scarcely called for in such a narrative as this. It is, in its peculiar way, a handsome place, and has a venerable appearance, which is quite imposing. Santa Fe contains about twenty thousand inhabitants.

It was in the month of November that our little party started down the fertile valley of the Rio Grande from Santa Fe, but the weather was warm and pleasant, the great elevation giving this region a deliciously dry and healthful climate. There were seven of us in all, and for the sake of companionship and mutual protection we engaged a large wagon drawn by six mules.

Central New Mexico.

It was about ten o'clock in the morning when we rolled out of Santa Fe, and our first camping-place was an Indian village, where we found a neat little adobe house, of which we took possession while resting ourselves and preparing our supper. One of the gentlemen made the coffee, while the others employed themselves in cooking the provisions, or in roaming about, looking at, and trying to converse with the Indians, or viewing the scenery. My travelling companions were all pleasant people, and we enjoyed ourselves hugely. Mr. McKnight, the owner of the wagon and mules, was an exceedingly gentlemanly man, and I shall always bear him in kindly remembrance for his attentions to me and to my little boy during this journey.

Once on the road again, we followed the valley southward, stopping the next day for our dinner at an Indian village, which was situated at the foot of a lofty mountain, and which overlooked the Rio Grande. After having dined, we struck across a stretch of high, dry table land, covered with sage-bushes, of which we gathered a quantity as we went along, to be used as fuel in cooking our supper. We reached the Rio Grande again about nightfall, and had a grand supper, some of the gentlemen having succeeded in killing half a dozen wild ducks and one rabbit, and in catching one fish.

From this point we pursued our way down the valley, passing a number of old Mexican towns, and plantations of cotton and sycamore, which indicated that the land had once been thickly settled with people of no mean civilization, until we reached Fort McRae.

This valley of the Rio Grande is a magnificent route for a railroad, and I doubt not that in a few years it will be found worth while to build one. There is plenty of water and timber, and the country offers many inducements to industrious settlers. The principal towns are Albuquerque, Valencia, Socarro, Dona Ana, and Mesilla. The Pueblo Indians have a number of settlements, and the portions of country inhabited by them are generally in a high state of cultivation. These Indians own a great many cattle, sheep, and horses, and they support a number of churches and schools.

Near Fort McRae is the famous hot spring. It is situated on a high mound, and its depth has never been sounded. This spring is in a state of constant ebullition, is very clear, very hot, and is possessed of valuable medicinal properties. Consumptives are especially benefited by the use of its waters. Around the edge is a rough crust of lime, which takes all imaginable shapes. The water of the spring will cook eggs quicker than ordinary boiling water, and when cool it is very pleasant to the taste. A short distance off is a cold spring, near which is a famous Indian camping-ground.

Striking south-westward from Fort McRae, we came to Rio de los Mimtres, near the head of which is Mowry City, founded by Lieutenant Mowry, who could not have had any very clear ideas as to what he was about when he attempted to make a settlement in such a place. Mowry City has a hotel, one or two stores, and more drinking-saloons than do it any good. That it will ever be much of a place I do not believe. There is not water enough in the river the greater part of the time to float two logs together, and in very dry weather one can step across it without wetting the feet. A sudden shower will, however, convert this puny creek in a short time into a raging river, which carries everything before it, and then it will subside as suddenly as it arose.

From Mowry City, which I regarded as a fraud of the worst kind, we went to Pachalalo, where we found a very beautiful ranche, owned by a Canadian, who had taken a great deal of pains in improving and beautifying his place. He had made a pretty artificial lake, which, like the rest of the ranche, was supplied with water brought down from the mountains.

A visit was now made to Silver City, a new settlement in the mountains, containing, probably, about fifteen hundred inhabitants. There were three quartz mills, but nothing worth talking about appeared to be doing in the way of getting out metal. None of the mines were paying expenses, chiefly, I thought, through a lack of competent persons to treat the ore, which seemed to be rich enough. Another and very great difficulty in working these mines, however, was the absence of transportation facilities, and the presence of hostile Indians. A railroad will aid immensely in developing this country, which is one of the richest in the world in minerals. On the San Domingo, San Francisco, and Gila Rivers are admirable grazing lands, which will be very valuable to somebody in the course of time. The attractions of this country are very great, and it will doubtless be rapidly settled in a few years.

This country, however, did not hold out any great inducement for me at the time of my visit, and, after taking a look at it, I turned back, and passing through Mesilla, went to El Paso, in Texas, where I remained two days, preparatory to taking the overland stage for a journey across the Lone Star State.

El Paso is the terminus of the overland stage route, the mails being conveyed from there to the interior on horseback. This town is one of the prettiest on the Rio Grande, and there is more business done there than in any place in that whole region outside of Santa Fe. El Paso contains a number of really fine buildings, which would do credit to some Eastern cities. The country in the vicinity produces corn, wheat, and all kinds of vegetables in great abundance. Excellent grapes grow without cultivation, from which the best wine I ever drank, outside of France, is made. The climate is very healthy, the soil fertile, being capable of producing anything that will grow in Louisiana, and the water abundant for all purposes.

THE STAGE ROUTE ACROSS TEXAS.

The overland stage from El Paso passes through a number of small villages, along the banks of the Rio Grande, until Fort Bliss is reached. This country contains some of the finest grazing lands for sheep in the world. The next place is Fort Quitman, where a large garrison is stationed, and leaving this, the road passes through a well-timbered country, abounding in live-oak, cedar, and taskata — a species of pine,

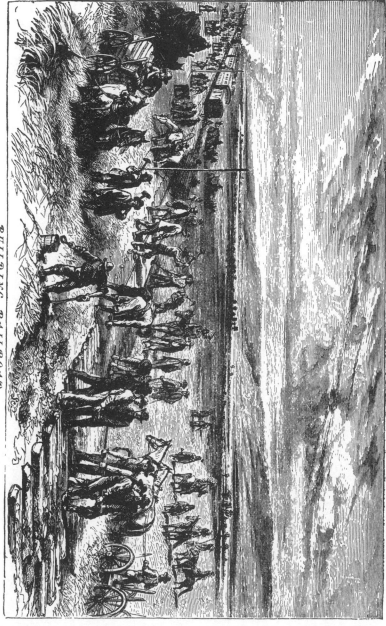

BUILDING RAILROAD.

which makes a very intense heat when used for fuel. Eagle Spring, a short distance from Fort Quitman, takes its name from the immense number of eagles that build their nests and rear their young in the rocky cliffs. The scenery here is very beautiful, but it is considered one of the most dangerous spots on the route, on account of the opportunities which it offers to the Indians for an effective attack.

Leaving the river, and making the interior, we were not long in arriving at about as rough and unpleasant a piece of ground as I ever travelled over. In this strip of territory, of about thirty miles in width, rattlesnakes and horned toads are more abundant than the scorpions on Scorpion Rock, at St. Thomas.

The Leon Holes, which our stage next reached, are three in number, and the water is very brackish. No bottom has ever been found to them. They say that a freighter, who wished to tighten the tire of a wheel, threw it into one of these holes, but when he was ready to start it was not to be seen, having passed completely out of sight.

About seven miles from the Leon Holes is Fort Stockton, and beyond that is a station-house, kept by a man who had the reputation of dishing up for his guest pretty near everything and anything that could be eaten. The place, however, was neat and clean, and as the cooking looked inviting, I, being too hungry to be over-fastidious, ate what was before me, and asked no questions.

We next travelled through a number of beautiful valleys and over rolling prairies, abounding in buffaloes, antelopes, and deer, until the Rio Pecos was reached. This is a bold and muddy stream, and when, as the stagemen say, it gets on a rampage, it rushes on in a perfect torrent. The station-keeper at this point was a small man, who blasphemed enough for six large ones. In spite of his foul language, however, he was a good housekeeper, and everything about his place looked nice and in good order.

Our stage now rolled through one of the richest stock-raising countries in America — a country which, when the Texas and Pacific Railroad is built, will certainly be rapidly settled.

The farther we now proceeded the more frequent became the signs of civilization, and, as with this journey, through a most interesting but little-known section of the country, was the last of my adventures that is likely to be of interest to the majority of readers, this seems to be a proper place to bring this narrative to a close. Perhaps my story was worth the telling, perhaps not — the great public, to whom I have ventured to confide a plain and unpretentious account of my adventuresome career, will be a better judge of that than I am. All I claim is, that my conduct, under the many trying and peculiar circumstances in which I have been placed, shall be judged with impartiality and candor, and that due credit shall be given me for integrity of purpose, and a desire to do my whole duty as I understand it. For the part I took in the great contest between the South and the North I have no apologies to offer. I did what I thought to be right; and, while anxious for the good opinion of all honorable and right-thinking people, a consciousness of the purity of my motives will be an ample protection against the censure of those who may be disposed to be censorious.

THE END.

Wisconsin Studies in Autobiography

William L. Andrews
General Editor

Robert F. Sayre
The Examined Self: Benjamin Franklin, Henry Adams, Henry James

Daniel B. Shea
Spiritual Autobiography in Early America

Lois Mark Stalvey
The Education of a WASP

Margaret Sams
*Forbidden Family: A Wartime Memoir of the Philippines,
1941–1945*
Edited, with an introduction, by Lynn Z. Bloom

Charlotte Perkins Gilman
The Living of Charlotte Perkins Gilman: An Autobiography
Introduction by Ann J. Lane

Mark Twain
*Mark Twain's Own Autobiography: The Chapters from the North
American Review*
Edited, with an introduction, by Michael Kiskik

Journeys in New Worlds: Early American Women's Narratives
Edited by William L. Andrews

American Autobiography: Retrospect and Prospect
Edited by Paul John Eakin

Caroline Seabury
The Diary of Caroline Seabury, 1854–1863
Edited, with an introduction, by Suzanne L. Bunkers

Marian Anderson
My Lord, What a Morning
Introduction by Nellie Y. McKay

American Women's Autobiography: Fea(s)ts of Memory
Edited, with an introduction, by Margo Culley

Frank Marshall Davis
Livin' the Blues: Memoirs of a Black Journalist and Poet
Edited, with an introduction, by John Edgar Tidwell

Joanne Jacobson
Authority and Alliance in the Letters of Henry Adams

Cornelia Peake McDonald
A Woman's Civil War: A Diary with Reminiscences of the War, from March 1862
Edited, with an introduction, by Minrose C. Gwin

Kamau Brathwaite
The Zea Mexican Diary: 7 Sept. 1926–7 Sept. 1986
Foreword by Sandra Pouchet Paquet

Genaro M. Padilla
My History, Not Yours: The Formation of Mexican American Autobiography

Frances Smith Foster
Witnessing Slavery: The Development of Ante-bellum Slave Narratives

Native American Autobiography: An Anthology
Edited, with an introduction, by Arnold Krupat

American Lives: An Anthology of Autobiographical Writing
Edited, with an introduction, by Robert F. Sayre

Suzanne L. Bunkers
Diaries of Girls and Women: A Midwestern American Sampler

Jim Lane
The Autobiographical Documentary in America

Sandra Pouchet Paquet
Caribbean Autobiography: Cultural Identity and Self-Representation

Mark O'Brien, with Gillian Kendall
How I Became a Human Being: A Disabled Man's Quest for Independence

Elizabeth L. Banks
Campaigns of Curiosity: Journalistic Adventures of an American Girl in Late Victorian London
With a new introduction by Mary Suzanne Schriber and Abbey L. Zink

Miriam Fuchs
The Text Is Myself: Women's Life Writing and Catastrophe

Jean M. Humez
Harriet Tubman: The Life and the Life Stories

Voices Made Flesh: Performing Women's Autobiography
Edited by Lynn C. Miller, Jacqueline Taylor, and M. Heather Carver

Loreta Janeta Velazquez
The Woman in Battle: The Civil War Narrative of Loreta Janeta Velazquez, Cuban Woman and Confederate Soldier
With a new introduction by Jesse Alemán